Philip

LOIRE

'...the charming stone fronts of the châteaux conceal tales of obscene extravagance, political intrigue, courtly corruption, murders even.'

DOGANguides

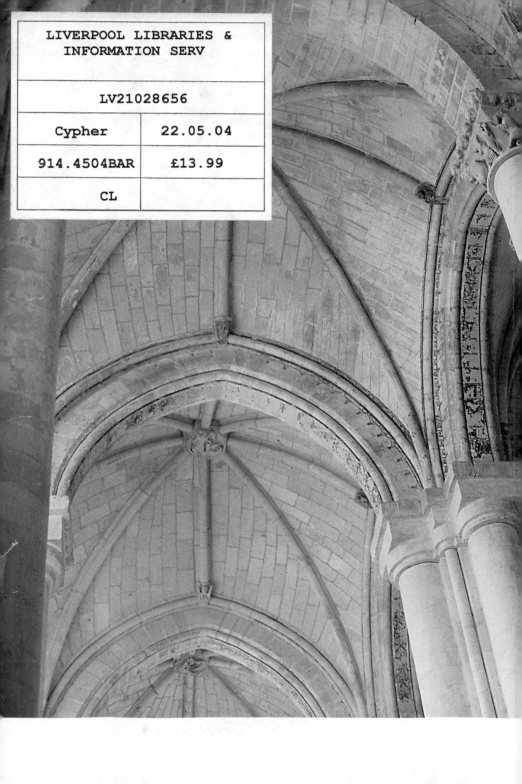

1 Church of Notre-Dame, Cunault

2 Shop window, Amboise
3 Lutes, Fontevraud
4 Fontevraud Abbey
5 Château de Chenonceau

6

6 Château de Langeais
7 Château de Montreuil-Bellay

8 Château d'Ussé

9 Orléans Cathedral
10 Half-timbered building, Tours

11

12

11 Mosaic menu, Saumur
12 Vineyard in the Chinonais region
13 Baker's sign, Montreuil-Bellay

14

14 The Loire at Champtoceaux

15 Cathédrale St-Maurice, Angers

About the author

Philippe Barbour once spent a wonderful year as an English assistant teaching in Tours, and lived literally a stone's throw away from the Loire. He would go every day to pay his respects to the majestic river, seeing its character change with the seasons. While in Tours, Philippe went to visit many of the great sights around the Loire Valley, but also started discovering a wealth of equally fascinating smaller sights, both over-ground and underground, scattered all round the region. Since his time in Tours, he has returned to the Loire practically every year.

Author's acknowledgements

I owe a huge debt of gratitude to Anselm Eustace for the dedication and accuracy with which he updated most of the practical information in this edition. Thanks yet again to the press officers in the Loire Valley, who have greatly helped me in my research, and have contributed to making it such a pleasure. Special thanks to Lygie Rothon in the Loir-et-Cher, Pierre Sabouraud, Frank Artiges and Samuel in Touraine, Hélène Ramsamy in Anjou and, for organizing a fantastic time in Chartres country, Christophe Gavet and Fabienne Talbot. I also bow to my fine friends John Lotherington, Jean-Louis Sureau and Tristan Magineau. Lastly, thank you to Matthew Teller for his diplomatic editing.

Contents

Cadogan Guides
Highlands House, 165 The Broadway, London
SW19 1NE
info@cadoganguides.co.uk
www.cadoganguides.com

The Globe Pequot Press
246 Goose Lane, PO Box 480, Guilford,
Connecticut 06437–0480

Copyright © Philippe Barbour 1997, 2001, 2004

Cover photographs ©Château du Rivau and John
    Ferro Sims
Additional photography © John Ferro Sims, p. 10
    ©Philippe Barbour
Maps © Cadogan Guides,
    drawn by Map Creation Ltd
Managing Editor: Antonia Cunningham
Editor: Matthew Teller
Design: Sarah Rianhard-Gardner
Proofreading: Rhonda Carrier
Indexing: Isobel McLean
Production: Navigator Guides

Printed in Italy by Legoprint
A catalogue record for this book is available
    from the British Library
ISBN 1-86011-141-6

The author and publishers have made every effort to ensure the accuracy of the information in this book at the time of going to press. However, they cannot accept any responsibility for any loss, injury or inconvenience resulting from the use of information contained in this guide.

Please help us to keep this guide up to date. We have done our best to ensure that the information in this guide is correct at the time of going to press, but places and facilities are constantly changing, and standards and prices in hotels and restaurants fluctuate. We would be delighted to receive any comments concerning existing entries or omissions. Authors of the best letters will receive a copy of the Cadogan Guide of their choice.

Introduction

The Loire inspires romantic images of pure white fairytale palaces along this, France's longest and most famous river. One of the region's châteaux, Ussé, supposedly even inspired Charles Perrault's fabled story of Sleeping Beauty. In this guide we aim to show the glory of the châteaux of the Loire Valley, but also that they and the region aren't as spotless, innocent or limited as their popular image may have you believe. Here, we peer behind the charming stone fronts of the Loire castles, which conceal tales of extravagance, political intrigue, courtly corruption, murders even.

It is often thought that the Loire's châteaux date almost exclusively from the late 15th and early 16th centuries, when late-Gothic exuberance was fused with new Renaissance fashions rushed back from French military campaigns in Italy. However, dramatic Loire castles in the form of formidable fortifications remain in great number from well before this time. Some of these donjons date back a thousand years, as do the other fine buildings that make another significant contribution to the Loire Valley's outstanding cultural and architectural legacy – its great religious foundations. These mushroomed up along the Loire and its tributaries in vast numbers and were embellished with fine works of art, the enriching manure of money once again provided by royals and aristocrats. The Loire-side cathedrals and churches at Fontevraud, St-Benoît, Cunault and Candes-St-Martin offer fine examples. This third edition of Cadogan's guide to the Loire also features the two most phenomenal medieval cathedrals of northwestern France, Chartres and Bourges, rivals in Gothic brilliance, which spectacularly show the might of the Church in the medieval towns.

Successive royal dynasties – the Capetians, the Plantagenets and the Valois – all left their mark along the Loire Valley through the medieval period; the section of the Loire covered in our guide is in fact commonly known as France's Valley of the Kings. But you might equally talk, if not of the Valley of the Queens, at least of the Vallée des Dames. Joan of Arc triumphs as the heroine of Loire history. Catherine de' Medici has been portrayed too easily as its greatest villain. Diane de Poitiers was the rival who beat Catherine in King Henri II's affections. Agnès Sorel, a famed and infamous earlier royal mistress, didn't manage to win the country's affections with her extravagant ways and fashions, but Charles VII appears to have found her much more appealing than moralizing Joan. Then there were the wives of the lords who commissioned the châteaux; their husbands were so often away with the peripatetic court that these *châtelaines* were frequently left to help oversee the building plans.

However, the Loire isn't all about royalty and aristocracy, you may be relieved to hear. Down on the now quiet cobbled riverside quays, where so much of the commerce in the region was carried out over so many centuries, you can try to re-create in your mind the sound and bustle of carts loading and unloading all manner of goods that travelled along the river, barrels of wine in particular. Sancerre, Touraine and Anjou remain important French wine-producing areas, while the Orléanais, Blésois and Loir (without an 'e') yield lesser-known wines. Touraine is popularly known as the Jardin de la France, the Garden of France, in recognition of its

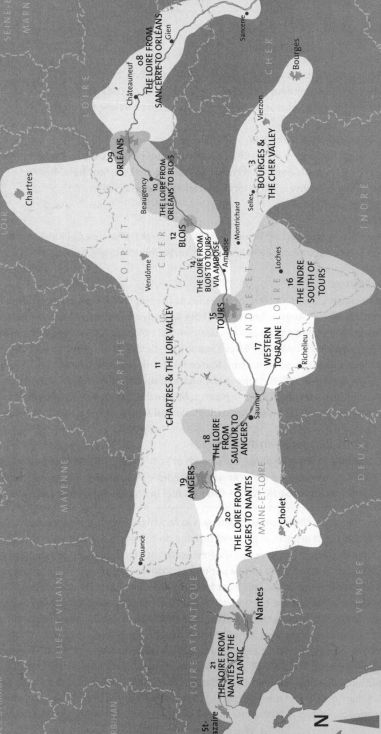

PARIS

SEINE-ET-MARNE

MARNE

LOIRE

Chartres

Châteauneuf

o8 **THE LOIRE FROM SANCERRE TO ORLÉANS**

Gien

Sancerre

EURE-ET-LOIR

o9
ORLÉANS

Beaugency

10
THE LOIRE FROM ORLÉANS TO BLOIS

Vierzon

Bourges

CHER

3
BOURGES & THE CHER VALLEY

Selles

LOIR-ET-CHER

Vendôme

12
BLOIS

14
THE LOIRE FROM BLOIS TO TOURS VIA AMBOISE

Montrichard

Amboise

INDRE

11
CHARTRES & THE LOIR VALLEY

SARTHE

ORNE

15
TOURS

INDRE-ET-LOIRE

Loches

16
THE INDRE SOUTH OF TOURS

17
WESTERN TOURAINE

Richelieu

Saumur

18
THE LOIRE FROM SAUMUR TO ANGERS

MAYENNE

19
ANGERS

20
THE LOIRE FROM ANGERS TO NANTES

Pouancé

MAINE-ET-LOIRE

Cholet

VIENNE

DEUX-SÈVRES

VENDÉE

ILLE-ET-VILAINE

Nantes

LOIRE-ATLANTIQUE

21
THE LOIRE FROM NANTES TO THE ATLANTIC

St-Nazaire

MORBIHAN

CÔTES-D'ARMOR

MANCHE

ALLIER

N

20 km
10 miles

The Best of the Loire

Major Châteaux

Amboise; Angers; Azay-le-Rideau; Blois; Brissac; Chambord; Châteaudun; Chaumont; Chenonceau; Cheverny; Chinon; Loches; du Lude; Montgeoffroy; Le Plessis-Bourré; Saumur; Serrant; Sully-sur-Loire; Ussé, Valençay, Villandry.

Lesser-known Châteaux

Beauregard; Bouges; Brézé; Chamerolles; du Moulin; Gizeux; Le Grand-Pressigny; Gué-Péan; Langeais (for the interiors); Luynes; Montrésor; Montreuil-Bellay; Le Plessis-Macé; du Rivau; Talcy (for the interiors); Troussay; Villesavin.

Towns

Amboise; Angers; Briare; Beaugency; Blois; Bourges; Chartres; Chinon; Clisson; Loches; Nantes; Orléans; Richelieu; Sancerre; Saumur; Tours; Vendôme.

Museums

Jean Lurçat's *Chant du Monde* tapestries at the Hôpital St-Jean in Angers; Musée David d'Angers in Angers; Tapestries of the Apocalypse in the Château d'Angers; Maison de la Magie and Musée des Beaux-Arts in Blois; Palais Jacques Cœur, Musée du Berry and Musée Maurice Estève in Bourges; Centre International du Vitrail and Musée des Beaux-Arts in Chartres; Musée International de la Chasse in the Château de Gien; Musée de la Préhistoire in the Château du Grand-Pressigny; Musée des Beaux-Arts and Musée Dobrée in Nantes; Musée des Beaux-Arts in Orléans; Escal' Atlantic in St-Nazaire; Musée Archéologique and Musée des Beaux-Arts in Tours.

Religious Buildings and Art

Cathédrale St-Maurice in Angers; Church of St-Nicolas in Blois; Cathédrale St-Louis in Blois; Church of St-Aignan in Brinay; Cathédrale St-Etienne in Bourges; Church of St-Martin in Candes-St-Martin; St-Louis Chapel in Champigny-sur-Veude; Cathédrale

general fertility. The whole Loire Valley is in fact highly productive, fruit orchards densely planted in parts, vegetables thriving on the river sands. As well as the game that proliferates in the Loire forests, freshwater fish land on many a restaurant plate.

Thoughts of water bring us to a popular misconception about the Loire Valley: that it's all about the one river. This is far from the case. Several major tributaries add not just to the weight of the Loire's waters, but also to the greater Loire Valley's cultural importance, particularly the splendid trio of the Cher, the Indre and the Vienne joining the Loire from the south. The main river to merge with the Loire from the north is the mighty Maine, a combination of the delectable Loir, the Sarthe and the Mayenne. Lesser-known little rivers steal up more surreptitiously from both north and south, like the meadowy Cisse, the sun-drenched Authion and the vinous Layon.

Still better hidden is a whole underground Loire Valley of limestone caves and quarries converted to all manner of new uses. The finest limestone of Bourré on the

Notre-Dame in Chartres; Basilique de Cléry-St-André; Church of Cunault; Abbey of Fontevraud; Carolingian Oratory in Germigny-des-Prés; Church of St-Ours in Loches; religious legacy east of Loches; Romanesque churches in the Loir valley; Cathédrale St-Pierre in Nantes; Cathédrale Ste-Croix in Orléans; Crypt of St-Aignan in Orléans; Abbaye de Pontlevoy; Church of Le Puy-Notre-Dame; Church of St-Aignan in St-Aignan-sur-Cher; Abbey of St-Benoît-sur-Loire; Abbey Church of St-Florent-le-Vieil; Church of St-Pierre in Saumur; Church of Notre-Dame de Nantilly in Saumur; Notre-Dame-des-Ardilliers in Saumur; Church of St-Nicolas in Tavant (for its Romanesque frescoes); Cathédrale St-Gatien in Tours; churches along the Vienne.

River Stretches

The Loire by Sancerre; the Loire south bank from Gien to Châteauneuf-sur-Loire; the Loire south bank from Muides-sur-Loire to Blois; the Loir from Chartres to Angers; the Loire from Blois through to Nantes; the Loire estuary; the Cher valley; the Cisse valley; the Indre and Indrois valleys; the Creuse and Claise valleys; the Vienne and Manse valleys; the Aubance and Layon valleys; the Sèvre Nantaise in Muscadet country.

Gardens

Château de Chamerolles gardens; Festival International des Jardins at the Château de Chaumont; Maulévrier Parc Oriental; Château du Rivau garden; Prieuré de St-Cosme garden; Château de Villandry gardens.

Curiosities

Pagode de Chanteloup near Amboise; Beaugency Town Hall embroideries; Briare's Pont-Canal; Chartres' Maison Picassiette; Musée du Vieux Chinon et de la Batellerie in Chinon; Zoo de Doué-la-Fontaine; Aquarium de Touraine in Lussault; Celtic animal statues in Orléans' Musée Archéologique; Ecole Nationale d'Equitation/Cadre Noir outside Saumur; troglodyte sites south of Saumur; Zooparc de Beauval near St-Aignan-sur-Cher; Espadon submarine in St-Nazaire; Musée du Compagnonnage in Tours; Musée du Gemmail in Tours.

Cher, from which some of the greatest Loire châteaux were built, is especially praised for its whiteness – it's said to grow even whiter with age. You might draw a comparison with the way that these modern tourist times have embellished the reputation of the Loire châteaux and the Loire Valley. Look more closely, however, at the tints of the limestone blocks so characteristic of the region's buildings and you'll realize they're much more complex than you may have thought at first sight. You'll see that the stones aren't a uniform colour at all; some of the blocks may be white still, but some are grey, some yellowing, some positively brown with age – and many have been replaced altogether.

Here we've tried to take a slightly closer, slightly more realistic look at the Loire's history and cultural heritage than is generally the case in tourist guides. But we have to admit at the same time that the region is so utterly beautiful and fascinating that it's impossible not to be beguiled by its exceptional qualities.

A Guide to the Guide

The first stretch of river on the planet to have been declared a World Heritage Site by UNESCO, the Loire covered by this guidebook has long been a world-famous tourist destination, with very good reason. Our guide also covers in detail the river valleys that help make up the greater Loire Valley region, and that share many characteristics with the mighty Loire: majestic meanders, splendid châteaux, courtly towns, vine-covered slopes, and a plethora of dramatic underground caverns.

The guide starts, in the east, with the favoured land of the Capetians, the **Orléanais**, so close to Paris and at the Loire's crowning point, and the **eastern Berry** (including the Sancerrois), early acquired by the first French medieval dynasty. Next come the **Blésois** and **Touraine**, haunts and great hunting grounds of the Valois kings – Charles VII came here after running away from Paris at the start of the 1420s, and his successors stayed on for a century and more. Then comes **Anjou**, most famously connected with an English, not a French, royal dynasty, as the birthplace of the Plantagenets. Approaching the Atlantic coast we arrive at **Nantes**, once capital of the independent duchy of Brittany but swallowed up by the Valois in the late medieval period.

For this third edition, we have added pieces on **Chartres** – a magnificent city not just because of its world-famous cathedral – and on **the Loir** (without an 'e') **valley**, which flows so very prettily down from Chartres to Angers, offering typical regional delights in exceptionally peaceful surrounds.

History

02

Prehistory

How Gregory of Tours, misled by the Bible, underestimates the age of the world and completely ignores the roots of civilization along the Loire

Gregory of Tours, that unique and splendidly inaccurate recorder of the history of the world as seen from the end of the 6th century, told a particularly mean tale about the dog-eat-dog world of the early Merovingians. He wasn't so hot, though, when it came to recounting earlier Loire history in his extraordinary book, *The History of the Franks*. His aim was more grandiose than the title suggests: he wished in fact to relate the history of the world from its beginnings up to his day. Unfortunately, he relied much too heavily on the very limited, very irrelevant stories contained in the Bible as a source for the millennia before the Franks or, to be more imprecise, the 5,792 years he calculated had passed between the beginning of the world to the time he finished his work.

The Bible has little to say on men and civilizations along the Loire. So the well-intentioned bishop, who lived by the great river, failed to mention the neolithic dolmens and menhirs (standing stones) scattered around the region, most densely in the Saumurois. Mind you, even specialist archaeologists today have trouble telling us much about the civilization behind these megaliths, beyond vaguely dating their construction to between 5000 and 2000 BC. Nor is there any explanation by Gregory of the commercial activities of prehistoric man along the valleys in this region, and at Le Grand Pressigny in southern Touraine in particular. Their tool-making business here became thoroughly European from 2800 to 2400 BC at least, the high-quality flints being exported across the continent.

c.500 BC–AD 260
Celtic Druids gather along the Loire before Caesar has the Gauls' guts for garters

Gregory also omitted to mention the arrival of the Celts. An influx from the east into what became known as Gaul is rather vaguely thought to have occurred from around 500 BC or earlier. The main Celtic (or Gaulish) groups to settle along the Loire Valley were the Carnutes in the Orléans region, the Turones in the vicinity of Tours, the Andes in the Angers area, and the Namnetes around Nantes. The Bituriges were the powerful group that settled around Bourges, down the Cher. The Loire river constituted, for a good many centuries before the Roman and Christian eras, a trade route with the Greeks, who had founded Marseille on the Mediterranean as early as 600 BC.

Gregory even failed to give any account of Julius Caesar conquering Gaul! The Roman megalomaniac did the job himself, of course, in his *Conquest of Gaul*, subtly distancing himself from the glorifying accounts of his campaigns by writing in the third person. Caesar relates some interesting details about the Celtic way of life, including a reference to the great annual gathering of druids from the various tribes across Gaul, supposed to have taken place around St-Benoît-sur-Loire, east of Orléans (*see* p.98). Caesar's subjugation of Gaul in 56 BC caused the rival Celtic tribes to unite, and in 52 BC a unified Gaulish uprising took place. The Carnutes were the first to show their defiance. Caesar returned to wreak revenge for the widespread insubordination. The terrible devastation of Cenabum, as the Romans called the Carnutes' capital on the site of present-day Orléans, is dispassionately retold by Caesar. His legacy was several hundred years of supposed Pax Romana – with occasional abortive uprisings – in the Gallo-Roman society created in his wake. Under Roman and Roman-style administration, Italian customs became mixed with Celtic ones, religious practices included. Big Gallo-Roman towns grew up in the region, Autura (Chartres) Aurelianis (Orléans), Caesarodunum (Tours), Juliomagus (Angers), Portus Namnetum (Nantes) and Avaricum (Bourges) the most important. Gallo-Roman roads connected the towns, while villas sprang up in the countryside and, after a long period of Roman protectionism, it was permitted to cultivate vines in the Empire's provinces.

260–732
Barbarian leaders and brave bishops

As the Roman Empire gradually weakened, pagan hordes began flowing into Gaul from the east, as did Christianity, which slowly but steadily established itself. The first Frankish incursions took place in the mid-3rd century, mainly in the east of Gaul. Under threat of these invaders, the Gallo-Roman towns erected defensive walls, fragments of which can still be seen in some of the big Loire cities.

Certainly as early as the 3rd century, preachers and bishops were spreading the Christian message in the Loire. St Gatien, for example, is reckoned to have been established in Tours in the second half of the 3rd century, at a time when the Roman Empire was still persecuting Christians. The big cities all had a bishop comparatively early. A converted Roman soldier who became bishop of Tours in the 4th century became one of the most important figures in French and European Church history: St Martin. Some of his deeds, his work in converting France to Christianity and as bishop (*see* Tours, p.259), as well as the unseemly dispute at Candes over his dead body in 397, are memorably recounted by Gregory of Tours. In fact, such is the importance Gregory ascribes to the saint that for the first section of *The History of the Franks* he takes as his parameters the beginning of the world down to the death of St Martin. Martin helped establish the first monastic community in France, near Poitiers, some way south of the Loire Valley, and took it upon himself to set up the second, in 372, at Marmoutier, on the north bank of the Loire outside Tours. In Chartres, a long-venerated shrine dedicated to an earth goddess was, as was so often the way, handily converted into a shrine to the Virgin Mary.

Another particularly celebrated early Loire saint was Aignan, bishop of Orléans, a man who helped save his city from barbaric invaders long before Joan of Arc. The enemy, one in a line of the great 5th-century waves of invaders, was the dreaded

Attila the Hun. St Aignan raised the alarm early enough for Roman legions under Aetius to come to Orléans' rescue, and the Hun was repulsed in 451.

The Frankish Merovingian dynasty had recently been founded, and it is on the bloody history of the beginnings of this dynasty that Gregory of Tours concentrates his writings. The tales are of rivalry in high places, the factions resorting to the lowest of methods to gain power. Clovis was the most important figure in the dynasty, ruling from just after the Western Roman Empire officially disappeared in 476. Clovis' wife, Clotilde, crucially converted him to Christianity, with a little help from St Martin. Hard pressed by the Alamanni, Clovis paused at St Martin's tomb in Tours in 496 and promised to adopt the new religion if he was granted victory. He won and converted. In 511 the Council of Orléans importantly enshrined the alliance between the royal family and the Church in the Frankish territories. Gregory of Tours believed St Martin helped him too, curing him of a bad illness when he visited his shrine. The grateful Auvergnat stayed to become bishop of the place and write his fabulous history.

Around and after Gregory's time, important new religious institutions sprang up along the Loire. The one that acquired the most fame, due to a highly prized relic, was the abbey of Fleury, which later became known as the abbey of St Benoît (Benedict in English). In the 670s a party of monks from the abbey travelled over to the southern Italian mountain where the deeply venerated and influential saint had died and claimed that they had gathered his bones and brought them back to their abbey – a great pilgrimage draw for the future.

732–987
A brief Carolingian Renaissance before the violent Vikings

Virtually nothing remains of the Merovingian civilization along the Loire. Nor does much from the Carolingian dynasty that followed. At the start of the Carolingian times, Charles Martel halted the Arab surge northwards, beating the Moors in an important battle somewhere between Poitiers and Tours in 732 – some reckon it may have taken place on the southern Touraine plain of Sainte-Maure. Charlemagne, Martel's grandson, became the great conquering, Christianizing, first Holy Roman Emperor. In the Carolingian renaissance of learning during his reign, both Tours and the abbey of Fleury became enormously influential centres of intellectual life in Europe. The scholar Alcuin of York, based at St-Martin's in Tours from 796, made this the centre of a renowned school. Théodulfe became the powerful Spanish head of Fleury at the start of the 9th century, appointed by Charlemagne. Among incredible gifts the emperor received was the Sancta Camisia, supposed blouse of the Virgin Mary, donated to him by Empress Irene of Constantinople, mistakenly hoping that her daughter might be married to Charlemagne, thus reuniting the Western and Eastern Christian empires.

The mid-9th century saw the rapid collapse of the Carolingian empire. The Vikings raided, Norse (or Norman) long boats penetrating far up the Loire. Nantes was taken in 842, Angers was sacked in 853–4, and the Vikings continued upriver to Orléans. No respecters of religion, by way of example of their brutality, they slashed the bishop of Nantes' throat at his cathedral altar. Loire monks fled east, taking their relics with them. Much was pillaged or destroyed. On a brighter note, in 876, one of Charlemagne's grandsons, King Charles the Bald, donated the Sancta Camisia to the cathedral of Chartres. This enormously precious relic is even supposed to have repulsed a Viking attack in 911; the Norse leader Rollo converted to Christianity and settled down as first ruler of the duchy of Normandy. A Breton chief, Barbetorte (Twisted Beard), finally managed in 937 to dislodge the Normans from Brittany.

987–1101
Capetian kings, powerful counts, and a crusading church

In the chaos caused by the Norman invasions, the regional counts set up under the system of the Carolingian empire asserted their independence from the small-scale kings of France of the time. The Robertian or Capetian family started to assert its authority in the 9th century as the Carolingian line faded, ready to provide a new line of kings of France or, more truthfully, kings of the Ile de France (the area around Paris), as the extent of royal authority had been severely reduced. Orléans and the Orléanais had, however, remained part of the royal territories and the little kings of the period were divided between their liking for their cities on the Loire and the Seine. Several late Carolingians were crowned in Orléans, and Hugues Capet had his son Robert sworn in as king by sacred ceremony in the city's cathedral of Sainte-Croix on Christmas Day 987. Most significantly, the monarchy was proclaimed hereditary and indivisible on that day. The early Capetians remained particularly attached to the Orléanais, Henri I dying at a home of his in Vitry-aux-Loges, Philippe I buried at St-Benoît.

West along the Loire, the independent counts of Blois and Anjou exerted their own authority, or at least fought for it among each other. Thibaud le Tricheur (the Cheat) asserted himself as count of both Blois and Touraine in the mid-10th century. Foulques Nerra, the Black Falcon, one in a line of family Foulques to rule Anjou, emerged as a formidable predator from the west. He ousted the count of Blois from the lands of Touraine at the start of the 11th century, and to protect his newly acquired territories he built a ring of massive keeps, stamping his authority on his expanded possessions. Touraine was officially joined to Anjou by Foulques Nerra's successor, Geoffrey Martel of Anjou, in 1044.

The Church was also busily asserting its power in this period. By the start of the 11th century, Fulbert, Bishop of Chartres, had turned the cathedral school there into one of the most important centres of Christian learning and pilgrimage in Western Europe. At the end of the 11th century, Pope Urban II travelled as far west as as Angers in his quest to unite European nobility to go on the first Crusade to deliver the Holy Land from the so-called infidel. Several nobles would bring back precious relics from the long-running campaigns, firing their own and the populace's credulous imaginations. Staying at home in France, one of the most charismatic religious figures of the times, the preacher Robert d'Arbrissel, founded the great abbey of Fontevraud in 1101.

1101–1328

The Plantagenêts of Anjou win England and an empire after accusations of adultery in Antioch

After the Black Falcon, the later Foulques V of Anjou (also King of Jerusalem), had a son Geoffroy, who showed a predilection for placing a piece of broom in his helmet. From this came his famous nickname, Plantagenêt (*genêt* being French for broom). Foulques V having already got his hands on Maine (the province between the Loire Valley and Normandy) through marriage in 1109, arranged for Geoffroy to wed Matilda, daughter of Henry I of England and Normandy. Geoffroy, impatient for his inheritance, took control of Normandy in 1144. His heir was Henri Plantagenet.

The French king in the middle of the 12th century, Louis VII, had married Eleanor of Aquitaine, heiress to a vast swathe of southwest France. The two proved incompatible and there were even rumours that Eleanor had committed adultery in Antioch during the second Crusade. The royal couple was granted a divorce in 1152, at Beaugency on the Loire, and Eleanor took back her dowry. Two years later it was presented to Henri Plantagenet in one of the most significant marriages in western European medieval history. After his marriage, Henri exerted pressure on the embattled English king, another figure stemming from the Loire and a grandson of William the Conqueror, Etienne de Blois (alias King Stephen I). The latter recognized Henri as the rightful heir to the English throne. When Stephen died in 1154, Henri became King Henry II of England, first in the Plantagenet dynasty that was to rule briefly, but memorably, on both sides of the Channel.

Thanks to Eleanor of Aquitaine's dowry, Henry II controlled an empire stretching from the Pyrenees to the border with Scotland. Chinon in Touraine became a favoured seat of power, reasonably close to the centre of his territories. Henri appointed an able administration and ruled firmly, imposing a good measure of centralized control. He also tried to take away some of the Church's independent powers, especially its right to try its own members, quarrelling bitterly and disastrously with his former friend, appointed Archbishop of Canterbury, Thomas à Becket. The latter's murder by knights of the king in Canterbury Cathedral in 1170 led Henry to perform acts of expiation, which included commissioning the building of religious foundations, some in the Loire Valley.

It was hard for Henry II to keep his diverse regions together, especially with his wife and eldest son Richard (the Lionheart) plotting against him. Richard pledged his allegiance to the new French king from 1180, Philippe II Auguste. This Capetian was a formidable fighter. His close friendship with Richard the Lionheart came to an end when the two fell out on the third Crusade. Returning to France, they fought bitterly. Richard was mortally injured in fighting in 1199, dying in Chinon. His body was taken to nearby Fontevraud abbey to be buried alongside those of his parents. Richard's brother and successor, John, proved no match for the capable Capetian. John famously lost practically all his French territories and is known in France as Jean sans Terre (Lackland). Anjou and Touraine quickly came into Philippe Auguste's possession, in 1202 and 1205 respectively. The Blésois, too, entered the royal domains.

The Capetians were now really beginning to assert their authority as kings of France. Blanche de Castille was queen regent for another of the important unifying Capetian kings after Philippe Auguste, the pious Louis IX, or Saint Louis. She ordered work on the massive new defences of Angers castle, begun in 1230. Brittany, that thorn in the side for the acquisitive French royal family for a couple of centuries to come, lay all too close.

Over the 13th and 14th centuries the Capetian kings granted royal appanages to brothers or sons, territories for them to look after for their lifetime – a useful way of maintaining royal family control of the provinces. Louis IX gave the duchy of Anjou to his brother Charles. The latter, as Charles I of Anjou and also count of Provence, was actually more interested in warring for the papacy and in self-aggrandizement abroad than staying put; in fact, he became the head of another extraordinary Angevin empire, being declared king of Naples and Sicily by the pope in 1266. Charles' descendants ruled over Naples for some time, and held on to Provence. France during this period was by no means a unified entity, but was split into semi-autonomous regions where all sorts of different powers, royal, noble and religious, flexed their muscles and tested each other's strength.

The Church had some particularly powerful branches. At the start of the 14th century, King Philippe IV le Bel suppressed the Knights Templars, a Church-backed military religious order that had amassed extraordinary powers and riches from its role in administering the finances of the Crusades. They were imprisoned in Chinon castle, then tortured and executed on the most infamous of trumped-up charges.

1328–80
The Valois succession sparks off the Hundred Years' War between France and England

Philippe le Bel's heirs were cursed. By 1328 his three sons had ruled and died, leaving behind only girls. His daughter Isabelle had married the English king, Edward II. Who was to inherit the French throne when females had been declared ineligible? Philippe, a grandson of the Capetian King Philippe III, represented the Valois claim. Edward III, son of Isabelle and Edward II, argued that even if women could not succeed, the inheritance could be passed down via a female line. The French barons, however, elected the Valois candidate, who became King Philippe VI of France, and thus set in motion the terrible Hundred Years' War between England and France.

King Jean le Bon, Philippe VI's son and successor, was captured by the English in Poitou in 1356, and taken over to England as a prisoner for a time. He had created appanages for his sons (apart from the eldest, who would succeed him as Charles V). One had become Louis Duc d'Anjou, another Jean Duc de Berry and a third the Duc de Bourgogne (Burgundy). These powerful provincial princes were all wilful and cruel rulers, vying to outdo each other as patrons of the arts (the fabulous works they commissioned survive to this day), while outbreaks of plague and famine and widespread poverty drove common people to the desperate uprisings known as the

Jacquerie. The Loire mariners and merchants, however, managed to form a strong body to defend their common interests in the 14th century.

1380–1431
King Charles VII flees to the Loire in the second phase of the Hundred Years' War, and Joan of Arc brings timely relief

While Charles V consolidated French royal power, this crumbled under his son and successor Charles VI, who was prone to increasing fits of madness through the first two decades of the 15th century. His weakness precipitated the second bout of the Hundred Years' War, as rival provincial royal factions, the princes of Orléans and Burgundy, started a civil war. The parties each called on the English to support their cause, not realizing the danger of such an appeal until it was too late. The English Crown had decided to exercise its own rights in France. The first great English victory was at Agincourt in northern France in 1415. Charles Duc d'Orléans was the most important French figure of royal lineage taken prisoner. In 1418 the French dauphin Charles, heir to the French Crown and Duke of Touraine and Berry through his great-uncle Jean, fled Paris. Forced south of the Loire, he headed first for the Berry and then for Chinon and Loches in Touraine.

This enforced move would give rise to the great royal period in the Loire Valley. The line of French kings who followed Charles VII – Louis XI, Charles VIII, Louis XII and, for a time, François I – would stay based in the valley even after the English had been ousted from most of France. With their courtiers, the last three would see in the French Renaissance and other massive changes in lifestyle from around the start of the 16th century. As the court shifted centre according to the preference of the particular reigning monarch, a handful of Loire Valley cities became royal, prosperous and beautiful in their turn – Bourges, Chinon, Loches, Tours, Amboise, Blois. The kings and courtiers encouraged merchants, particularly of luxury goods, who in turn were made wealthy and enriched the Loire's cultural legacy.

However, first the dauphin Charles had to extricate himself from dire straits. The second half of the Hundred Years War had started with King Henry V of England's victory at Agincourt in 1415. Henry then had himself declared heir to the French throne by the 1420 Treaty of Troyes. Charles proclaimed himself king of France at the Duc de Berry's château of Mehun-sur-Yièvre in 1422. But a man of action was needed to help him out with the English enemy. Joan of Arc proved herself to be that man. She arrived in Chinon from Lorraine in 1429, instructed, she said, by heavenly voices to help the French forces free Orléans and boot the English out of France. With her extraordinary powers of persuasion she convinced people in authority. The French powers were desperate for a miracle; most importantly, Orléans was being besieged by English troops.

Joan picked out the king in the Chinon court crowd and in a private hearing with him persuaded him to back her. After undergoing tests of her beliefs and her virginity, she joined the French troops marching to the beleaguered Loire city. Her dogged part in the subsequent fight led to the release of Orléans, which adopted her as its Maid. She then participated in a string of French victories in the Orléanais that summer, at Jargeau, Meung, Beaugency and Patay. The French fortunes seemed to be changing. Historically speaking, however, it should be noted that before Joan there had already been French victories at Baugé in 1421, beating the English in Anjou, and at Montargis, in the northern Loiret, in 1426. The independently minded Joan continued in her campaigns, despite frictions with Charles VII's favourite La Trémoille, who stopped her briefly at the Château de Sully. She was soon captured by the enemy, and we know the fate that awaited her at Rouen in Normandy in 1431. The ungrateful French king didn't lift a finger to rescue her from the flames.

1431–61
The late Gothic chivalric courts of the Loire Valley

Charles VII had been married to Marie d'Anjou when they were both children, as was the custom. Marie's was the more typical lot of the contemporary female, stuck in a perpetual cycle of childbirth. Most of the 14 children she bore didn't survive long. Charles VII, his family and court spent a time exiled from Paris in the beautiful city of Bourges, and in fact the king was mockingly called Le Petit Roi de Bourges. In the second part of his reign, Charles installed his influential and beautiful mistress, Agnès Sorel, at Loches. She was feted as a great beauty and fashion-setter of her times, and the king splashed out a fortune from the public purse on her exotic furs and silks. Vast sums would equally be poured into increasingly sumptuous châteaux.

In these chivalric times, hunting, falconry, jousting and real tennis were favourite pastimes of many of the Loire kings. One courtly companion of Charles VII, René d'Anjou, or Le Bon Roi René as he is popularly known in French history, was the grandson of Louis I d'Anjou, count of Provence and legitimate heir to the kingdom of Naples, for which he unsuccessfully fought. René was renowned for his love of chivalric culture, in particular jousting, poetry and roses. Moving from little castle to little castle in Anjou, he and Charles VII enjoyed their refined pleasures together while Charles neglected his wife.

Charles d'Orléans, a relative of Charles VII captured at Agincourt, and a hero of Joan of Arc's, was finally released from captivity in England in 1440 and went back to his home in Blois to establish another artistic chivalric court there. Late in life, Charles d'Orléans was blessed with a son, Louis d'Orléans, who would eventually inherit the throne in extraordinary circumstances. As for Joan, her part in freeing France from the English was recognized in a rehabilitation trial in Orléans. This was in 1456, three years after the end of the Hundred Years' War.

It was the ordinary people in France who suffered most terribly in the Hundred Years' War. One tax census in the Orléanais, dating from 1450, close to the end of the conflict, records that there was no tax to be paid in one walled town: '*Néant, parce que tout est en désert. Il n'y a que petits enfants mendiant* (Nothing, because all is deserted. There are only little beggar children there).'

1461–83
King Louis XI, paranoid but well prepared

Louis XI, Charles VII's son and successor, has suffered particularly badly from adverse fictionalization of his character by Walter Scott in *Quentin Durward*. Recent history has tried to redress the balance with serious studies of this difficult man's actions. He was brought up in Touraine, hated Agnès Sorel, and twice tried to rise up against his father, running off to live in Flanders for a time. Louis was first married to Margaret of Scotland (daughter of King James I) at the Château de Tours in 1436, but detested her – the young couple had no children before Margaret died. His second wife was Charlotte de Savoie. Crowned king in 1461 after his father's death, Louis effectively chose Tours as the capital of France. He lavished favours on Touraine, encouraging all sorts of business enterprises. Most notorious for his *fillettes* (not little girls, but dreadful iron prison cages) at his châteaux at Plessis-lès-Tours and Loches, he is now more roundly depicted as a king who successfully advanced the unification of the provinces for the French Crown, helping bind the nobles to the royal cause by creating the exclusive Order of St Michael (*see* p.232). His administration was pragmatically business-minded, developing such important industries as the French postal service and a silk trade based in Touraine, where mulberries were planted in large numbers.

Louis XI was also extremely vigilant about the provisions he made for his children. While his heir, Charles, was meticulously groomed for kingship at the Château d'Amboise, he arranged for the marriage of his intelligent, crippled daughter Jeanne de France to another Louis, the son of Charles Duc d'Orléans, in 1476. The idea was apparently in part to put a halt to the ambitions of that branch of the royal family.

Louis XI was a deeply superstitious man in a deeply superstitious age. His belief in divine intervention, especially by the Virgin Mary, was extremely powerful, but his paranoia seems to have grown with age. He asked for the Italian Christian mystic, François de Paule, to come to his bedside as death approached, and this influential religious figure would remain close to the monarchy for some time to come.

1483–98
King Charles VIII discovers Italy and deals Brittany a marriage blow

Under Charles VIII, the Château d'Amboise would become the French royal head-quarters. But at the start of his reign his sister, Anne de Beujeu, with her new brick-patterned castle at Gien, east of Orléans, acted as regent for a brief period until her little brother came of age. Louis d'Orléans became rebellious, forming an alliance with the independent Duc François II de Bretagne, based at his castle in Nantes, to revolt against the regency in what is known in French as the Guerre Folle (the Mad War). Brittany's independence was drawing to an unhappy end, however. At the Traité du Verger in 1488, François II de Bretagne was forced to accept – among other constraints – not to marry his daughters without French royal consent. The Breton leader died the same year, leaving the 11-year-old Anne as his successor. Two years later, in a bid to ensure the duchy's independence, she was betrothed by proxy to Maximilian of Austria. Charles VIII's troops marched into Brittany, and Anne de Bretagne, in surely one of the least romantic proposals in French royal history, was forced to marry the young French king in 1491. The ceremony took place in the Château de Langeais along the Loire.

Charles soon went galloping off to Italy to assert inheritance rights there. He was unsuccessful, but fell for Naples and gathered together cartloads of art as booty. He also bought the services of a whole bunch of specialist Italian artists, from architects to a parrot trainer. Charles and his army only just made it back to France, almost being wiped out when trapped by enemies at Fornovo in 1495. Philippe de Comines, servant to both Louis XI and Charles VIII, recorded events in his unreliable *Mémoire*.

Just a few years after his lucky escape in Italy, Charles VIII met his maker in the most banal of household accidents in 1498; he banged his head on a door in the Château d'Amboise and promptly died. Anne's marriage contract forced her to marry his successor, his cousin Louis d'Orléans, who became Louis XII. The latter was pleased to find an excuse to spurn the crippled Jeanne, daughter of Louis XI, for a better prize.

1498–1515
King Louis XII sees in the French Renaissance

Louis XII moved the court to his home town of Blois, while continuing to pursue French royal claims and ambitions in Italy, again unsuccessfully. But the defeated nobles came back with their heads crammed full of ideas on Italian decoration, and these were adopted in new Loire architecture in particular. Declared the Père du Peuple (Father of the People), Louis XII was relatively popular at home. Many of the acts of his reign took place at the Château de Blois. By Anne de Bretagne, Louis had a daughter, Claude, who would become the wife of the next French king, as Louis and Anne had no son. A short time before he died, Louis was briefly married to the young beauty Mary Tudor, sister of King Henry VIII of England.

1515–47
King François I, the French answer to Henry VIII

The monumental French king of the 16th century was Louis XII's successor in 1515, his nephew and son-in-law François d'Angoulême, who became François I on his accession. François had been brought up at Amboise by his mother, Louise de Savoie. His sister, the bright and well-educated Marguerite d'Angoulême, was taught with him. François I proved more than a match for Henry VIII of England, ordering sumptuous new palaces such as the Château de Chambord, but not for Habsburg Charles who, with the backing of the massively wealthy Fugger family bankers, won the fight between them for the post of Holy Roman Emperor, as well as becoming king of Spain.

François continued the violent French royal love affair with Italy. The first foray was successful, the Battle of Marignano securing Milan. Leonardo da Vinci was among the treasures brought back. François got himself into terrible difficulties in another Italian campaign, and was captured at the Battle of Pavia in 1525, the year after his first wife had died. While in captivity in Spain, his marriage to his captor's sister, Eleanor of Austria, was agreed.

In 1532, Brittany was officially signed over to France at the Château de Nantes. But conflict was spreading across the country as the debate on religious reform started by Luther in Germany caught on. The radical reformer Calvin studied in the Loire region in the 1530s before heading for the safety of Geneva. François I became interested and then embroiled in the grave matter of Church reform. Then someone had the audacity, in the so-called Affaire des Placards (not cupboards here, but pamphlets), to pin up a piece attacking the Catholic Mass on the king's very bedroom door, and François I suddenly decided to suppress the would-be reformers, who became known as Huguenots, or Protestants. The seeds were being sown for the terrible French Wars of Religion later in the century. Meanwhile François I moved his attentions more and more towards Paris and away from the Loire.

1547–89
Henri II, Catherine de' Medici, their three kingly sons and the French Wars of Religion

The religious situation got worse under François' son, Henri II, who married Catherine de' Medici, notorious in history. She wasn't the only forceful woman in his life; his mistress, Diane de Poitiers, was also a strong influence. While the extravagance of the court was somewhat curbed in Henri's time, Protestantism was spreading like wild fire and Henri ordered the Huguenots' persecution. Although the royal children were brought up at Amboise, the Loire became less and less the centre of royal and court life. Henri II died from an accident in a tournament in 1559, leaving only young sons. Religious factions and powerful families on both sides had become more entrenched in their positions during his reign.

The sickly King François II, married young to Mary Queen of Scots, was a puppet ruler who wouldn't last long. Mary's uncles, the ultra-Catholic de Guise duke and Cardinal de Lorraine, had acquired considerable control. Catherine de' Medici tried at first to pacify the feuding parties. But the Conjuration d'Amboise, a plot by leading Protestant nobles to kidnap François II and assassinate the de Guises, was uncovered in 1560. Those caught were treated ruthlessly; many drowned in the Loire. François II died of illness at the Hôtel Groslot in Orléans the same year. Catherine de' Medici struggled on for several years as regent for the new French king, Charles IX.

The bloody Wars of Religion really got under way in 1562 and would last until the end of the century. These wars weren't only about the bitter struggle between Catholics and Protestants, but also about the battle for power between the great families of France, the de Guises, the Chastillons/Colignys and the Bourbons/Condés;

even the royal family itself was threatened. Orléans became one of the strongholds of the Protestants in the first war. The de Guise troops were massed against them, but François de Guise was killed in the battle. The first bout of fighting ended with the peace of Amboise in 1563. The infamously cowardly St Bartholomew's Day massacres of Protestants took place in a later outburst in 1572, and were particularly bloody in some of the major Loire towns.

King Henri III took over the reins from 1574, after his brother Charles IX died. The ultra-Catholic Ligue was founded in 1576 by the mighty Henri de Guise le Balafré (Scarface), that family's faction threatening royal authority still further. Such was Henri III's fear that he snapped, ordering Henri de Guise's execution in his own royal château of Blois at the meeting of the Estates General in 1588. Henri was assassinated in his turn in 1589, dying without heirs. His pious wife was left to mourn in royal white at Chenonceau. The Valois line was at an end.

1589–1789
Bourbon kings begin with Henri IV and move away from the Loire

The Protestant Henri de Navarre became King Henri IV, as Henri III had agreed. But the religious wars were still raging. Henri IV was much aided in the task of reviving French fortunes by his trusted companion in arms and minister Maximilien de Béthune, who became Duc de Sully and was given the splendid château of that name on the Loire. The Edict of Nantes of 1598 allowed for limited toleration of religion for the Huguenots – a new official tolerance had been proclaimed. In Saumur, the reforming Duplessis-Mornay was even able to set up the Protestant Academy, which became for a short time a great centre of new learning.

Political power had moved firmly to Paris, however. The Loire was a place of retreat. Blois even became something of a town for exiles, Henri IV's wife, Marie de' Medici, being sent there as an awkward queen mother under Louis XIII. This king's rebellious brother, and for a long time heir presumptive, Gaston d'Orléans, would follow later. He took part in all attempts to oust Cardinal Richelieu, Louis XIII's extraordinary counsellor, who amassed phenomenal power and wealth, including enough to create a whole new town and massive new château on the Touraine border, named – surprise, surprise – Richelieu. Before Cardinal Richelieu, it was the Duc de Luynes, his country château also in Touraine, who had held the strings of power.

The mid-17th century saw a revolt of princes and nobility, the Fronde, as little Louis XIV came to the throne. Inheriting her obstreperous nature from her father, Gaston d'Orléans, La Grande Mademoiselle caused havoc, even marching on Orléans. As absolutist monarchy took a firm hold on the country, and centralized control, the Loire became still further distanced from political action. Royal representatives, the *intendants* appointed by the king, were sent out to rule the new regions, or *généralités*, the important administrative towns of the time in the Loire Valley being Orléans and Tours. Louis XIV did enjoy the odd jaunt to Chambord, built to his scale of pomp. His Revocation of the Edict of Nantes in 1685 was the culmination of the French

Counter-Reformation, stamping the authority of Catholicism on the country. The previously Protestant Saumur, for example, was swamped by Catholic foundations. The persecution of Protestants that ensued led a large number of them, in particular merchants, to leave France.

The western end of the Loire, however, found itself with several sources of wealth in the 17th century. Anjou wine and fruit were successfully exported. Slate mining also became important there. And from the mid-17th century the French colonies began to bring vast riches to some of the Loire towns, most especially Nantes. This town's top merchants grew fabulously wealthy on the triangular slave trade in the 18th century. Louis XV paid little attention to the Loire, except to send his many daughters packing to religious school at the abbey of Fontevraud – the place had maintained connections with royal blood through a long line of well-connected abbesses. The foolish king, swayed by his favourite women, also sent his most able minister, the Duc de Choiseul, into exile in the Loire.

And what of the more ordinary people through these centuries of tales of kings, counts and nobility? Many lived in abject misery. An aristocratic young Briton staying at the Château de Chanteloup before the Revolution noted the poverty of the masses succinctly:

A fat goose was 15p English, and a fat fowl 4p, yet in spite of fat geese and fat fowls, the poor live on bread and water from Monday to Sunday.

1789–1800
Revolution and the Guerre de Vendée

The Loire was meek and marginalized by the end of the Ancien Régime, and wasn't rocked particularly violently by the Revolution, although in towns such as Blois many churches were brought down. Orléans briefly became the seat of a high court investigating so-called crimes against the nation. Slave-trading was banned, and the new geographical administrative units of France, the *départements*, were created during this period. Many châteaux and religious buildings, rather than being destroyed through hatred, were pragmatically turned into barracks or prisons (most notoriously Fontevraud abbey) or, temporarily, 'temples of reason'.

The anti-Republican Guerre de Vendée (Vendée War), however, deeply affected the west of Anjou and Nantes, as well as the Vendée just to the south, and belies the general impression that the French Revolution wasn't challenged by Frenchmen on their own soil. An uprising by staunchly Catholic peasants supporting their clergy gained momentum when pro-royalist nobles joined their cause. They swept northwards, passing through southwestern Anjou up into Maine, before being savagely halted by Revolutionary troops. The bitter memories of these events remain vivid in western Anjou, an area where the bicentenary of the Revolution was certainly not seen as a cause for celebration. The anti-Republican fighters of the Guerre de Vendée are regarded as heroic figures there.

1800–1900
Nineteenth-century upheaval

The 19th century was characterized by radically shifting regimes and bouts of social upheaval. After the end of Napoleon's follies, the Prussians briefly marched as far as Tours and then the French monarchy was restored. Republicanism, though, continued to fight its patch, the second and third French republics divided by the mid-century Second Empire, which ended with a disastrous but brief war with Prussia. The Prussians under Bismarck provoked the French into attacking them in 1870. Very quickly the French troops had to retreat and a new emergency government was forced to flee Paris as the Germans advanced, Léon Gambetta memorably escaping by hot air balloon to Tours. Two armies along the Loire, led by d'Aurelle and Chanzy, were put out of action by the Prussians, who came as far as Tours once again. France was forced to give in to terms very favourable to the enemy. The cantankerous Comte de Chambord failed to take his chance to restore the monarchy immediately afterwards. Instead came the Third Republic, which expelled the would-be French royals and lasted until the outbreak of the Second World War.

Loire trade was profoundly altered in the 19th century, in particular by the arrival of the railway mid-century. The great river itself and its network of tributaries had served as extremely important trade routes from ancient times. But ships had been growing larger and larger through the Ancien Régime, which meant that full-scale Loire navigation had become more awkward before the Revolution; even Nantes was no longer easily accessible to large seafaring vessels, and river activity moved out towards the estuary. Suddenly, with the railways, the waterways were abandoned. Many riverside towns along the Loire Valley have retained their picturesque cobbled quays, which went quiet practically overnight. Urban expansion further altered the towns, as did industrialization, although this was limited along the Loire. Phylloxera blighted its vines at the end of the century, as elsewhere across France.

1900–
The 20th century and into the 21st – from world wars to a nuclear Loire

German aggression dominated the history of France for the first half of the 20th century. The First World War emptied the French countryside of its young men, remembered in monuments and plaques in every village. Soviet-style communism was somewhat surprisingly the subject of debate at the Congrès de Tours of 1920. At this meeting the French Left split into two, with the formation of the Socialist and Communist parties that went on to dominate that half of politics almost to the end of the century.

Tours became the fleeting capital of the French government on the run at the beginning of the Second World War, Winston Churchill flying over for a last desperate meeting before the Germans overran the country. The few attempts to halt the advance, such as that by 300 North African snipers in Tours, were doomed. The shipbuilding stretch of the Loire by St-Nazaire, where many of the great French transatlantic liners were built, was taken over for German uses and U-boats. During the war, most of the river crossings were bombed. The scars of this new aerial warfare, inflicted by Germans and Allies alike, are obvious to this day in several Loire-side towns, notably along Tours' riverbanks, or in the centre of historic Orléans, while smaller riverside towns, such as Gien and Sully to the east, had to be almost entirely rebuilt. The Cher river running through Touraine served as part of the dividing line between German-occupied and Vichy France until the close of 1942, the château of Chenonceau even acting as a bridge by which Resistance workers passed from one territory to the other.

It hasn't all been plain sailing for the Loire since the war. Despite the general growing prosperity, major industries, such as shipbuilding close to the estuary, have dwindled. The new French regions were created in the 1960s, when some bizarre divisions were made along the Loire; the stretch covered in this book is split between the Région Centre and the Région Pays de la Loire – all a bit of a mess and going against historical affiliations. On the Loire itself, the installation of a string of nuclear plants went ahead relatively unchallenged, until the authorities tried to build one near Nantes, in a more combative area that was once a part of independent Brittany.

The image of the Loire Valley held by other French people is of a deeply bourgeois part of the country still, and a strongly Catholic one. Church attendance remains relatively high on Sundays. The towns, though, have been swinging between the Right and the Left recently. In the 2001 local elections, to the whole country's surprise, the flamboyant socialist minister Jack Lang lost control of Blois, while traditionally deeply conservative Saumur amazed everyone even more, electing an ecologist as mayor. Economically, unemployment as everywhere in France became an increasing problem in the 1990s.

But the Loire Valley has some solid business strengths. The Orléanais benefits from its proximity to Paris, taking the overspill from the capital and offering space for green-field sites. The cosmetics industry flourishes here, to such an extent that one area next to Orléans has been comically nicknamed Cosmetics Valley. At the same time, the high-speed French trains, the TGVs, have brought the major Loire towns much closer to the capital, encouraging people to move around more easily; some even commute daily from Tours to Paris, for instance, able to return to the peace of the Loire every evening. Selling the Loire's history has, of course, become a major part of the valley's economy since the war, the region profiting enormously from the tourist boom. And in 1996, Pope John-Paul II came to Tours, along with his special "popemobile" car; he came to celebrate the past, and the 16th centenary of the death of Gregory's hero, St Martin.

Art and Architecture

Introduction: Architecture that's Not Quite as Empty as You May Think

Architecture stands head and shoulders above the other arts in the Loire. But can we just forget for a while the gracious and turreted 16th-century châteaux, their ever-so-pretty heads vainly reflected in rivers, and hold off fantasizing about Chenonceau, Chambord and Azay-le-Rideau just for a few moments? Loire architecture isn't simply about the so-called French Renaissance châteaux. The region has a rich legacy of 500 years of well-preserved remains from before their time, with one of the densest concentrations in France of fine medieval architecture.

In fact, the Loire experienced three great periods of architecture; very roughly, time-wise, these are: the Romanesque, in the 11th and 12th centuries; the Gothic, emerging from around the mid- to late 12th and lasting to the very end of the 15th century; and the French Renaissance, through the 16th century, after which grandiose building projects grew less common, although there are some notable exceptions. As well as the secular architecture – the fortified castles, the more delicate châteaux and the boastfully ornate town houses – religious architecture was prominent in each period. The Church, after all, was a massively powerful multinational in those times, commissioning a wealth of new building. Along the Loire Valley you'll find a few fine cathedrals, the remains of extensive abbeys, great churches, and splendid little chapels. Crude capital carvings, delicate rib-vaulting, more or less naive statues of saints, the odd more sophisticated tomb or reliquary, even some rich tapestries, all add visual interest to these spiritual houses. Stained-glass windows contribute further to the religious and decorative effects, although many of the original works in this art were lost through time and periods of violence; the Hundred Years' War, the French Wars of Religion, the Revolution and Second World War bombings destroyed substantial amounts of Loire art and architecture.

What happened to all the original art that adorned the château interiors? Time and again you'll be reminded by guides on visits that up until the Bourbons, the courts and courtiers rushed from one property to another, taking their prized possessions with them in chests. Then there is the recurring problem of the French Revolution; some castles were ransacked, others were sold, and thus many were emptied as aristocrats fled into exile abroad. Some châteaux lost their lives, dismembered, in many cases, a fair few years after the Revolution. A good number of others suffered the ignominy of becoming barracks or prisons. However, people tend to underestimate the number that actually remained relatively unscathed, or that reverted to aristocratic proprietors; and in recent times, regional authorities that have acquired others have worked hard to promote their châteaux in the battle for tourist numbers, revamping the interiors with important acquisitions. Artefacts from châteaux were also saved and pooled in certain cases, and the fine arts museums in both Orléans and Tours, for example, contain extravagant works plucked from many castles.

A brief word of warning about that broad term 'château' in French – this can refer just as well to a massive medieval fort as to a dainty morceau of Ancien Régime masonry. And be on the lookout for the occasional towering donjon, the word for a keep, not a dungeon, the centrepiece of the *château-fort*, or fortress. As to the building materials used for châteaux and noble houses, in the east of the area covered in this guide, brick was used as readily as stone, and the masons became quite playful with it, incorporating patterned motifs. Moving westwards, limestone, the Loire stone *par excellence*, soon comes to dominate the architectural scene, the buildings generally topped by slate roofs. Only around Angers, where the slate was quarried, does limestone give way to a darker, ugly-named stone, schist, often used in grand Anjou buildings, with a mixture of limestone.

Prehistory–AD 1000

Very little remains of Loire architecture or art from before the year 1000, but the legacy of neolithic civilization in the region, in the form of dolmens, can be found scattered around, notably in the Saumurois, southern Touraine and southwestern Anjou. One of the most impressive, and the largest, of the so-called Angevin dolmens is now captured within a café's confines, the **dolmen de Bagneux** on the southern outskirts of Saumur. The **Château du Grand-Pressigny** in southern Touraine has an interesting museum on prehistory.

Although the major Loire cities grew out of the most important settlements formed by the Gauls, developing considerably after the Roman invasion, virtually nothing from Celtic times has survived, and few vestiges of Gallo-Roman civilization along the Loire remain. Sections of ancient walls remain in many of the cities. **Gennes** has an overgrown amphitheatre, the **Château de Pont-Chevron** a couple of period mosaics, **Luynes** the arches of a relatively low aqueduct, **Cinq-Mars-la-Pile** a funerary tower, and **Thésée-la-Romaine** remnants of a market as well as a little museum, but these are pretty small affairs. Hardly anything made it through the pillaging and devastation wrought by the hordes of invaders in the late Gallo-Roman period and the much later raids of the Vikings. One superb cache, though, unearthed at Neuvy-en-Sullias, contained splendid animal-deities sculpted in bronze, probably from the 2nd century, now displayed in the Musée Archéologique in **Orléans**.

The great religious buildings of the first millennium have also disappeared, leaving us with the aptly named Dark Ages. One colourful exception survives at **Germigny-des-Prés**, its rare early 9th-century Carolingian church containing an apse still decorated with a blue and gold mosaic showing angels surrounding the Ark of the Covenant, God's hand reaching down from the sky.

Military Architecture at the Start of the Second Millennium

Suddenly, from the start of the second Christian millennium solid stone structures went up in large numbers and many have survived. The Angevin count, Foulques Nerra, at the end of the 10th century and the start of the 11th, left his mark on the region in the form of a ring of towering donjons, square stone defensive keeps. This type of architecture superseded the earth-mound, wood-fenced forts of the previous period, the latter inevitably more temporary constructions. Many of the stone keeps in this new military fashion have crumbled, but important ones dating back to the 11th and 12th centuries can be seen along the Loire west from Orléans, with **Loches** (the most interesting), **Beaugency** and **Montrichard** counting among the finest examples. These are impressive, severe-looking pieces of architecture, with sheer, cliff-like walls, particularly dramatic when jackdaws circle round them. There's some debate as to whether the oldest stone keep in France is the impressive one being restored at **Montbazon**, or the more dilapidated one at **Langeais**, dated by some to the very end of the 10th century. The skeletal keep at **Le Grand-Pressigny**, another fine example, again within a later château's walls, dates from the 12th century.

Romanesque Architecture and Art

Generally, the image of Romanesque architecture is of squat little churches lost in the countryside, with rounded arches and rounded apses. In this part of France, these charming rural churches are often crowned by a slate-covered tower which looks like a tough, pointed helmet, giving them a slightly defensive look. Dark inside, with few window openings and fat arches supporting barrel vaults, their walls and pillars would originally have been decorated, the sides with two-dimensional paintings in shades of ochre, depicting mainly New Testament Biblical scenes, the pillar capitals carved with a weirder, warring medieval menagerie, including stylized depictions of mythical creatures and frequent references to that ever-so-influential book in the early medieval period, *The Revelation to John*, alias *The Apocalypse*.

The best example of surviving Romanesque wall paintings can be found in the church of St-Nicolas at **Tavant**, the curves of the tiny room serving to impart a rare degree of movement to the figures. In fact, the Vienne valley region near Chinon, where you'll find St-Nicolas, has the distinction of a number of more or less restored Romanesque churches with murals. Other significant, if sometimes small, remnants of busy, gauche, yet powerful Romanesque art can be seen at the crypt of St-Aignan in **Orléans**, that of St-Aignan in **St-Aignan-sur-Cher**, St-Jean-du-Liget near **Loches**, and the Préfecture of **Angers**. The **Loir** (without an 'e') valley also offers a fine array.

But while the widespread image of Romanesque church architecture may be of small-scale buildings, across the Loire Valley the period saw some truly remarkable and substantial religious architecture go up. You just have to look at the height and bulk of the Tour Charlemagne in **Tours** to picture the vastness of the edifice to St Martin of which it once formed a part. Or most famously, admire the entrance tower to the abbey church of **St-Benoît-sur-Loire**. This influential building is propped up by superbly decorated capitals from the end of the 11th century.

At this time and from the beginning of the next century (when the Crusades began) other vast edifices were being erected to reinforce the power of the Church at home: **Fontevraud**'s abbey church, Le Ronceray in **Angers**, the church of Notre-Dame in

Cunault, St-Laumer (now St-Nicolas) in **Blois**, St-Mexme in **Chinon**, Notre-Dame-de-Nantilly in **Saumur**... these were impressive works, reflecting the might of the Church. Although on the whole sombre, architecturally they brought in innovations, generally from southwest France, developing the height and space of church building and, in particular, the expansion of the choir end. Fontevraud's abbey church interior is spanned by a row of cupolas. Several other churches, such as Le Ronceray and Notre-Dame in Cunault, adopted a new, hall style, with aisles reaching to the same height as the nave. Notre-Dame-de-Nantilly used the altogether simpler plan of an aisle-less nave. St-Ours in **Loches** adopted a unique feature, its nave bays topped by a roof with pyramidal towers, dubbed *dubes*.

Some of these grandiose churches were more highly decorated than others; the church of Cunault had hundreds of carvings on its capitals. St-Nicolas was given some fine decoration, as were two further churches not so far mentioned, that of Notre-Dame of **Beaugency**, with its delightful choir ambulatory, and that of **Candes-St-Martin**. This last was built on the spot where the great saint Martin had died in the 4th century. Pilgrimage, and relics in particular, motivated large numbers to travel to spots like this in the Middle Ages, and you can see at the church of Candes how the splendidly ornate porch, miraculously held up in the middle by just one slender finger of a column, faces the Loire, as though to greet and amaze the pilgrims, many of whom would have arrived by boat and walked up from the quays. One of the major routes to Santiago de Compostela passed this way, the Route d'Or.

Architecture could be highly practical in Romanesque times too. The kitchen of the abbey of Fontevraud, although its mushrooming silhouette and scaly roof may not be entirely true to the original, shows how the builders of the period could mix invention with practicality.

Chartres, Bourges and Anjou Vault into the Gothic

The most extraordinary development in religious architecture in the region in the 12th century occurred at three **cathedrals**. The cathedral of **St-Maurice in Angers** was where the Angevin vault was born in the mid-12th century. This splendidly elegant vaulting, with its particularly light look, spread far and wide as a model, but the finest examples are to be found in Anjou in particular. The church of St-Serge in Angers, the remnant of the abbey of Asnières and the church of **Le Puy-Notre-Dame** (built to honour a relic of the girdle of the Virgin Mary, a typical object of veneration in the medieval period) all show off the style. As well as its novel vaulting, Angers' cathedral contains some of the oldest stained-glass windows along the Loire. The tombs of Henri Plantagenêt, his wife Eleanor of Aquitaine and their son Richard the Lionheart lie serenely not in Angers, but in the abbey church of **Fontevraud** near Saumur.

Chartres boasted a massive Romanesque cathedral which was almost entirely destroyed by fire in 1194. Only its west front and the crypt containing the Virgin Mary's purported blouse survived – in its joy at this miracle, the whole community joined together to embark upon a phenomenal rebuilding enterprise, only in the elevating new, Gothic style. The cathedral's towering clumps of columns, its ranks of flying buttresses, and its wealth of stone carvings made it one of the marvels of Christendom. But it is best-known for its acres of Gothic stained glass, paid for not just by rich royals and nobles, but also by the town's merchant guilds who had become rich on the back of pilgrimage. Exactly at the same time as Chartres was going up, work began on an equally staggering cathedral south of the Loire, St-Etienne in **Bourges**. With its unique five statue-filled portals on the front and its buttresses, this cathedral is a true rival to Chartres.

Early Gothic Secular Architecture and Art

Interestingly, the greatest example of Angevin vaulting is in a secular building, one of the oldest hospitals to survive in France, the Hôpital St-Jean in **Angers**, ordered by Henri Plantagenêt to be run by lay authorities. The vaulting and slender columns combine to create surely one of the lightest pieces of architecture of medieval times. In stark, heavy contrast, one of Henri Plantagenêt's greatest power bases was the **Château de Chinon**. Although the buildings have mostly disappeared, the series of fortified walls and ditches remain extraordinarily impressive, reckoned to have formed the largest fortress in Europe for its time.

The early medieval châteaux were in fact formidable *châteaux forts*. None of these fortresses along the Loire looks more impenetrable than the **Château d'Angers**, with its heavy schist walls and elephantine towers, constructed to help guard the border of the royal territories against Brittany. Sharing its mix of schist and tufa constructions, the **Château du Plessis-Macé** in Anjou acted as a further regional outpost. To the east, the knobbly towered exterior of the **Château de Luynes** in Touraine also dates back to the 13th century.

For the next couple of centuries, châteaux would remain defensive military strong-holds, with sturdy corner towers, drawbridge-protected entrances, arrow slits for windows, and high guards' walkways (*chemins de ronde*) with machicolations through which to throw down projectiles. But gradually they would be constructed with a little more consideration to comfort and refinement, using neater blocks of stone, letting in a bit more light, and allowing a bit more room for good living.

Exquisite pieces of decorative art started being made for the lords who lived within the region's strongholds. The second half of the 14th century saw the making of some of the finest of all medieval French art, thanks to the brotherly rivalry and extrava-gance of the sons of King Jean le Bon. This was while the first part of the Hundred Years' War was raging and the Black Plague was striking regular terror into the popu-lace. Louis, who became Duc d'Anjou, concerns us most here. But his brother, Jean Duc de Berry, would have some of the greatest châteaux of the times portrayed in one of the most famous and fabulous of all medieval manuscripts, the *Très Riches Heures du Duc de Berry*. Among the depictions, the magical silhouette of the **Château de Saumur** stands out, built for Louis d'Anjou after 1360. Another monumental work Louis commissioned, in the 1370s, was a **tapestry cycle of the Apocalypse**, made in Paris in Nicolas Bataille's studios after the cartoons of Jean Bondol, court painter to King

Charles V (Louis and Jean's monarch of a brother). The tapestry, most often housed in Angers when it wasn't on tour, now hangs imprisoned in the château there. Tapestry had become popular in the medieval period, the methods of weaving brought over from the East. This art form would be commonly adopted in châteaux through to the Revolution to help adorn, embellish and even warm chambers. The attention to detail and the colours of the tapestry of the Apocalypse reflect some of the qualities of illuminated manuscript, the major painting form of the period (panel painting would only become popular a little later). The other great piece of art we owe to Louis d'Anjou's massive wealth is relatively miniature – he had a piece of Christ's **True Cross**, which had been brought back to the region in the mid-13th-century by an Angevin Crusader, wholly inappropriately smothered in precious jewels (*see* **Baugé**).

Another outstanding castle of this period, the **Château de Sully**, reflected in the very waters of the Loire, is thought to have been planned by Raymond du Temple, the architect to King Charles VI whose name is most commonly associated with the early Louvre in Paris. But as with so many Loire châteaux, this plan would be greatly added to with quirky, charming accretions down the centuries.

The Royal Family Moves to the Loire in the 15th Century

After the would-be Charles VII ran off to the Loire, court in tow, to escape the English army's arrival to fight the second half of the Hundred Years' War, the Loire Valley became the main base of the French royals until the 1520s. This led to an extraordinary flowering of architecture and art along the Loire. While most of the buildings of this period have had their interiors emptied, many of the exteriors, although often tampered with or substantially altered or amputated, still remain standing. During this time of the Loire Valley kings, a massively important new artistic influence would arrive from Italy at the very end of the 15th century, spelling the slow end of Gothic and the transformation to the so-called Renaissance style, reviving and developing models found in the ancient Greek and Roman worlds.

Each king wanted to stamp his mark on his own palatial homes. Charles VII, having spent a stint in his great-uncle's city of Bourges, developed the châteaux of **Chinon** and **Loches**, both rather vacant now, but still full of atmosphere. Louis XI favoured the **Château du Plessis-lès-Tours** and the **Château de Langeais**, the first reduced to a sad stump, the second grimly grey on the outside, but containing perhaps the finest and most colourful collection of tapestries of any Loire château, albeit not from the period, but gathered together at much later date. Charles VIII transferred royal attentions to the **Château d'Amboise**, where he had been brought up and which the previous two kings had been slowly expanding. He also added a wing to the **Château de Loches**. Louis XII, from a different branch of the royal lineage, transported the builders of Amboise to the **Château de Blois**. François I was such an oversized character that not surprisingly he's associated with countless châteaux, including the expansion of the Château de Blois and the Château d'Amboise (although it was his mother, Louise de Savoie, who really saw to the development of the latter), and of course the construction of the totally new, awe-inspiring and absurd **Château de Chambord**. But before considering the transitional architecture of places like Chambord, we focus on the beautiful elaboration of late Gothic.

15th-century Religious Architecture and Art

In terms of royal-sponsored religious architecture in this period along the Loire, Louis XI's deep anxieties left the greatest marks, most notably encouraging the completion of the **Basilique Notre-Dame-de-Cléry**, where he was buried, but also helping to pay for the expansion of such churches as Notre-Dame-de-Nantheuil in **Montrichard** and Notre-Dame-de-Nantilly in **Saumur**. The late Gothic jewel of a chapel at the **Château d'Amboise** also stands out among royal commissions. Other aristocrats had chapels built or embellished for themselves and sometimes the community. Death encouraged fine art; artistic attention was lavished on the tombs of the ultra-wealthy royals and aristocrats. In many cases they were badly damaged during the Wars of Religion or the Revolution, as for example the tomb of Jean de Berry in **Bourges** or that of Agnès Sorel at **Loches**. Sadly, little religious art in the form of panel painting from this period has remained in the Loire. A couple of exceptions do stand out. Nondescript **Nouans-les-Fontaines** in eastern Touraine mysteriously boasts a rare painting by Jean Fouquet, Charles VII's court painter, often considered the first known great French painter. His *Deposition of Christ* is a vast and harrowing work. The **Château de Loches** contains a triptych attributed to another outstanding period painter, Jean Bourdichon. The great court composer of the late 15th century, who wrote for three French kings, was Johannes Ockeghem, an example of the Flemish influence of the times, the intertwining voices in his music comparable to the intriguing tracery of late Gothic church windows.

15th-century Secular Architecture

While grand Gothic religious architecture seemed very carefully and geometrically planned, secular architecture was much less meticulously and mathematically conceived in the late-Gothic period. Certainly symmetry of façades and windows wasn't a major concern, unlike in important Gothic churches and the later Renaissance style. But the style was often wonderfully exuberant.

The Loire châteaux of the period were particularly distinguished by their prettifying towers and *lucarnes*, the latter the pointed dormer windows reaching increasingly extravagantly skywards from slate roofs. Many courtiers would build country seats to suit their rank. The **Château de Baugé** offers a typical example of early 15th-century architecture, built for the dukes of Anjou. The **Château du Plessis-Bourré** is the image of an ordered late medieval castle, constructed between 1468 and 1473 for Louis XI's most trusted minister. On a square plan, marked with round towers on each corner, encircled by the protective belt of a moat, its flat walls dotted with mullion windows, it is one of finest examples of the well-planned late-Gothic castle. From a little earlier, the remnant of the **Château de Montsoreau** is another deeply appealing example of the period, with typical *lucarnes* breaking through the roofs, reflected in the Loire. The **Château de Chaumont**, majestically situated in woods above the great river, bears typical late-Gothic punning symbols on its massive entrance towers, reached by a drawbridge.

Most interior decoration inside these late-Gothic châteaux has been lost, except for travelling chests. **Le Plessis-Bourré** is one castle to have retained some original wall paintings, with its shocking painted ceiling. Often the private chapels or oratories attached to the castles constitute their most ornate and best-preserved rooms. The **Château de Montreuil-Bellay**, for example, has a ceiling on which angels still sing – apparently to a tune by a Scottish composer! At the dilapidated **Château de Pimpéan**, the chapel has retained its murals. It's not usual to think of brick châteaux in association with the Loire Valley, but there are quite a number to the east, the **Château de Gien**, with its mysterious brick patterns, and the **Château du Moulin**, one of the most romantically moated of all Loire châteaux, among the finest.

Courtly towns would grow up around the Loire valley's royal centres, becoming wealthy from the demand for luxury goods. You can admire a particularly important, dense and picturesque set of late medieval houses in **Bourges**, most magnificent of which is the Palais Jacques Coeur, with a sensational array of highly decorated fireplaces (a feature which would add grace and warmth to so many château interiors). In **Chinon**, as in the old courtly and mercantile quarters of important towns like **Tours** and **Blois**, the Gothic staircases attached to the exterior in the form of towers make the urban architecture particularly appealing. Playful, often lewd, Gothic carved figures clamber up the outer beams of some of the grandest town houses. Jesters play their tricks on the Maison des Acrobates in **Blois**, while a riot of figures and carvings attack the façade of the Maison d'Adam in **Angers**, both amazing examples of this kind of house. **Chartres** too contains a mass of fine timberframe houses.

Transitional Architecture from Late Gothic to French Renaissance

The late-Gothic style was often extremely exuberant, imaginative, playful. The châteaux which began to fuse traditional French forms with newer Italian-inspired features at the start of the 16th century would cling on to certain cherished forms, although the Renaissance would, in general, reduce the imaginative play – and the potential for utterly charming chaos – of the great architecture of 15th century France.

With some of the transitional châteaux, the kind of decorative but indecorous carving seen on the outside of some late-Gothic town houses can still be viewed inside, particularly in carved *culs-de-lampe* at the bottom of vaults or ribs. Even the **Château d'Azay-le-Rideau**'s kitchen shows a stone dog chewing on a bone, and a bare bottom sticking out prominently into the air, while the **Château d'Amboise** conceals a wealth of comic grotesques. 'Filthy' Gothic forms did live on, even in the clean-up act of the Renaissance.

Family heraldic devices, symbols (the most famous and repeated royal ones being the fleur-de-lys for all, the ermine's tail and Franciscan cords for Anne de Bretagne, the porcupine for Louis XII, the salamander for François I, the arrow-pierced swan for his mother, Louise de Savoie, and the full ermine for his wife, Claude de France) and inter-twined initials, particularly over door entrances or on monumental fireplaces, also survived for some time in the shift from one style to another. The Loire *lucarnes* not only stayed a while, but also became increasingly ornate as late-Gothic gave way to Renaissance. Sometimes they bore coats of arms or allegorical symbols.

Perhaps the greatest distinguishing feature of French Gothic secular architecture, the tower – either in the form of the solid round towers of defence or of spiral stair-cases set out from the building – survived for a time as well. The apogee of the Gothic tower is to be seen at the **Château d'Amboise**, the massive Tour des Minimes and Tour Heurtault, 20m in diameter, built at the very end of the 15th century and large enough to allow carriages to ascend the 150m of ramps within.

Even several of the greatest so-called French Renaissance châteaux of the Loire, **Chenonceau**, **Azay-le-Rideau** and **Villandry**, retained pieces of Gothic towers, in the case of the first two separated from the main building. The **Château du Lude** on the Loir has mighty barrels of masonry on its ends, even if decorated with Renaissance medallions, while the **Château de Valençay** and the **Château du Gué-Péan** closer to the Cher boast the most eccentric tower roofs. **Chambord**'s corners were marked by the largest towers of all. Many other châteaux juxtaposed late-Gothic forms with the Renaissance, such as the **Château d'Ussé** and the **Château de Blois**. The last, along with Chambord, contains the most extravagant stair tower on the Loire – both feats of architecture in their own right.

These buildings also reflect a set of new influences. Built (or started in Chenonceau's case) in the first half of the 16th century, they actually combine French Gothic and Italian Renaissance forms. In the last decade of the 15th century Charles VIII had rushed hot-headedly off to Italy with his army to lay claim to certain inheri-tances there. Seduced by the Italian way of living, he tried to bring some of it back with him, not only in the form of booty, but also in the form of artists. Among the first wave of Italians imported into the Loire to put an Italian stamp on French architec-ture were Domenico da Cortona and Fra Giocondo, not to mention the landscape gardener Dom Pacello da Mercoliagno. Charles VIII's successor, Louis XII, added further French royal claims on Italy, and further Italian influences were carried back after his failed invasion. François I continued the trend. Courtiers started to change the styles of their houses.

One of the clearest examples of the way Italianate features were absorbed into Loire architecture is provided by the François I wing at the **Château de Blois**, built by the 1520s. You can see how several ultramontane details have encroached. On the inner side, there are the network of horizontal bands dividing up the façade and dimin-ishing the vertical lines, the heavily decorated cornice, the putti in niches and the openwork of the staircase. On the outer side, the rows of loggias imitate what was going on in Rome. These elements are grafted onto French Gothic. The façades are stamped with salamander symbols, the putti are placed in the typical Loire *lucarnes*, and, most outstanding of all, the great stair tower protrudes proudly from the building.

Like a nanny tidying up the mess after children have been playing, or as in **Rabelais'** *Gargantua* (written around this time) when the humanist teacher comes to impose order on the chaotic studies of the initially unruly giants, the Renaissance would quickly tame the exuberant, show-off delight of late Gothic. Of course, behind the Italian forms lay higher ideals of harmony and order. The most famous Italian import of them all had the most advanced mind of his time. **Leonardo da Vinci** was enticed over by François I to Amboise, where the Tuscan genius died in 1519. He may have been involved in the planning of the **Château de Chambord**, which had just got underway, with its ingenious stair tower, its extravagant roofscape and its stamp of massive royal power. Its great Greek cross form (normally reserved for churches) combined with that of the typical square fortress was deliberately built in the middle of a forest teeming with game. Sadly, of the many great works of art that François I collected to decorate his palaces, none are left in the Loire.

Many smaller Gothic-to-Renaissance buildings lie scattered around the countryside, a few lesser-known ones open to visitors, like the charming **Château de Villesavin**, hidden in woods. Also near Chambord, **Troussay**, a *gentilhommière* rather than a château, offers a good example of the kind of home that noblemen a step down the social ladder had built for themselves in this transitional period. (Inside, Troussay lovingly preserves a collection of wonderful Renaissance scraps.)

The **Château de Villandry**, back among the most famous châteaux of the period, is now particularly celebrated for its formal gardens (actually an early 20th-century re-creation of a Renaissance garden). The **Château de Chamerolles** and the **Château de Beauregard** count among other châteaux to have recreated Renaissance-style *jardins*. The carefully planned garden had developed in medieval monasteries in France, but Italian finesse imposed further influences which came to dominate in the châteaux. Many aristocratic Loire homes were surrounded by ultra-neat *parterres* laid out in carefully controlled geometric patterns, such as those also to be seen at the **Château de Chenonceau**. Delightful château chapels are another place where you can often admire Italianate touches. The chapel of the **Château d'Ussé** offers a fine example of the Renaissance in the Loire. Greatest of all in this sphere is the chapel of the **Château de Champigny-sur-Veude**. As to the **Château du Rivau**, it boasts the most magnificent Renaissance stables, as well as playful new gardens paying homage to Rabelais.

The Renaissance stamped its mark on religious architecture in towns and villages as well, for example in the tops of **Tours** cathedral's towers, or with the work of Jean de l'Espine in **Angers**. The **abbey of Fontevraud** was substantially altered to reflect the new fashion and given the largest Renaissance cloister in France, with a painted chapterhouse to boot. Rich tombs continued to be commissioned. Anne de Bretagne ordered particularly moving ones, for her children in **Tours cathedral**, for her father in **Nantes** cathedral, both joint works by the much-respected Tours sculptor Michel

Colombe and an Italian artist. Other examples of funerary art for aristocrats can be seen in chapels close to châteaux, for example at **Montrésor** and **Gizeux**.

This early 16th-century period of transition left many delightful and particularly memorable buildings. But was the French Renaissance a good thing for Loire architecture? It depends on your taste, of course, but the exuberance, eccentricity and individuality that the late Gothic exhibited is hard to surpass even if, intellectually and mathematically, the Renaissance appears more robust. On reflection, the majority of great Loire châteaux date from the time just before rigid Renaissance discipline had imposed itself on the French imagination, the fusion of Gallic late-Gothic and Italian Renaissance producing marvellous results.

In literature, the beautiful mixing of classical forms and the French language counted among the aims of the so-called Pléiade poets, which included two great writers hailing from the Loire region, **Joachim du Bellay** and **Pierre de Ronsard**, the latter arguably the greatest lyric poet in French, a marvel to read, his verse flowing like a majestic river.

The Second French Renaissance

The châteaux of what the French sometimes refer to as the *seconde Renaissance*, roughly speaking the second half of the 16th century, are more sober than those of the first French Renaissance. Examples in the Loire Valley include the **Château de Beauregard** and the central section of the **Château du Grand-Pressigny**. This architecture looks much more restrained, and rather duller. However, the most exciting addition to Loire Valley castles in this period produced the most enticing of all French châteaux – the **Château de Chenonceau**, whose wing spanning the river Cher was commissioned by the Queen Mother of the time, Catherine de' Medici, in the 1570s. The controlled elegance of its bays contrasts with the unpredictable shimmering light thrown onto it from the water below. Jacques Androuet du Cerceau, both architect in Orléans and recorder of royal châteaux, executed splendid black-and-white bird's-eye drawings of this and other French royal châteaux at the end of the 16th century, giving an excellent idea of their forms in that time, and of their gardens. Some fine Renaissance town façades survive too, notably in **Bourges**, **Blois**, **Chartres** and **Tours**.

A much less well-known and less refined piece of art thought to date from the mid- to late 16th century survived underground in the **Caves Sculptées de Dénezé**, the carvings seemingly crammed with satirical or critical references to contemporary politics. The limestone in many parts of the Loire Valley had long been exploited for building; the quarries were then used for storage and, in the coming centuries, increasingly for housing. Some of the oldest, most diverse **troglodyte houses** in the Loire Valley can be seen along the Loire east of Saumur, below Saumur around Doué-la-Fontaine, and along the Cher around Bourré. As for the extraordinary **Château de Brézé**, it combines 16th-century architecture with some of the most impressive underground chambers of the lot.

The Classical Period of the 17th and 18th Centuries

Great architecture didn't simply fizzle out in the Loire after the Renaissance. Several splendid Loire châteaux date from the 17th century, reflecting developments in classical forms. The Mannerist **Château de Brissac**, breaking out of medieval chains, the supremely ordered Gaston d'Orléans wing of the **Château de Blois** by the illustrious François Mansart, and the **Château de Cheverny**, the last and perhaps most elegant of the Loire châteaux, all date from the first half of the 17th century. Cheverny has retained outrageously rich interiors (Jean Mosnier the main painter-cum-interior decorator associated with it), as well as one of the finest art collections in a Loire château. Some of Brissac's beams are also smothered with a mass of miniature landscapes.

A much grander Loire château than Cheverny once held a far more extraordinary art collection still, one of the most important ever gathered in Europe by an individual. That man was Armand du Plessis, Cardinal de Richelieu. Only one measly pavilion of his vast 1630s home remains, but the model new town of **Richelieu**, a utopian geometric plan with a staggering covered market place and a noble church, stands almost intact, if a little desolate, in southern Touraine. The innumerable works of art collected in the château were dispersed. Some of the finest, such as Michelangelo's *Dying Slaves*, were packed off to the Louvre, while a fair number, including the paintings of the elements seen through aristocratic fantasies by Deruet, ended up in the excellent **Orléans** fine arts museum, which also houses a rich collection of 18th-century religious paintings seized from local religious establishments during the Revolution.

An interesting development down the centuries was the popularity of the portrait. It became a trend in certain swanky homes to commission a whole room full of depictions of famous men. The **Château de Beauregard** contains one of these portrait galleries, offering a visual history of great men (and their fashions) over several centuries. The Château de Blois displays works from other such portrait galleries. More harrowingly, the chapel within the elegant mix of tufa and schist of the **Château de Serrant** displays a family tomb by the sculptor Coysevox. Serrant also has the rare distinction of a park landscaped in the English style. Still more exaggerated in emotion than Serrant's tomb, one of the most compellingly hideous mixes of sickly-sweet funerary art you're likely to have the shock of encountering hangs out in the church of **Châteauneuf-sur-Loire**.

Little art exists around the Loire Valley from the Ancien Régime except that produced for or portraying aristocrats. One exception meriting attention is the 17th-century engravings by Abraham Bosse, displayed in the museum of fine art in his home town of **Tours**. Bosse's works not only show prissy people at art and play in a renowned allegorical series on the senses; they also depict a wide variety of professions and backgrounds.

Many Loire châteaux have undergone facelifts and aesthetic cuts in their time. In the 17th and 18th centuries several were altered in the same manner – one wing demolished to open up their views – two of the most obvious examples being the

Château d'Ussé (also given a whole extra 17th-century wing out of keeping with the rest), and the Château de Chaumont. With the delightful Château du Gué-Péan, the mid-16th-century form encloses a 17th-century hunting lodge. At the start of the 18th century, Roger de Gaignières charmingly illustrated many Loire châteaux and religious edifices as they looked in his day.

Town and village houses of both the 17th and 18th centuries survive, but you'll find very few grand buildings from the 18th century in the Loire Valley. Worthy of mention is the elongated Loire-side Château de Ménars (not open to the public) near Blois, while all that remains of the even longer Château de Chanteloup is its adorable, clownish pagoda. One rare castle from this period does survive almost intact inside as well as out, though: the Château de Montgeoffroy dates from just before the French Revolution, built for the Marquis de Contade, the table still set as though it has just been left. Another château which displays the finery and new refinements of the century inside is the Château de Talcy, but its outer forms are much older.

Jacques V Gabriel left his mark on the cityscape of Blois in the 18th century, designing, among other things, the most elegant bridge over the Loire. Nantes, with all the wealth pouring in from the slave trade, became grander and grander through the 18th century. To see more of 17th- and 18th-century painting and sculpture, the fine arts museums of Nantes, Orléans, Blois, Tours and Angers merit a visit. And go to the Château de Gien to admire a collection of hunting paintings by royal-commissioned Desportes and Oudry among the many topical precious objects on display.

Catholicism Triumphant

In the period between the Wars of Religion and the Revolution, combative Catholic architecture was used as another instrument to crush Protestantism. Henri IV, the king at the end of the Wars of Religion, did however try to patch up differences and supported the rebuilding of the Protestant-bombed cathedral of Orléans in the outdated but original Gothic style.

After Henri IV, the centralizing powers used church construction and the foundation of new religious orders as important means of reinforcing Catholicism. The one-time Loire Protestant capital Saumur was swamped with Catholic architectural propaganda, including a Catholic pilgrimage church with an enormous and spectacular breast of a dome, Notre-Dame des Ardilliers. Blois' church of St-Vincent-de-Paul is a typically overdone piece of Jesuit Counter-Reformation grandeur, and the town's Cathédrale St-Louis offers the curious sight of a late 17th-century building in Gothic form. Dating from the early 18th-century, the abbey of Pontlevoy looks as much like a military school as a religious establishment. Still more surprising are the Ancien Régime parts of the Chartreuse du Liget, a foundation lost in the forests east of Loches with ruins dating back to Henri Plantagenêt's time.

19th-century Nostalgia

The 18th century ended, of course, with the French Revolution, châteaux and churches attacked as part of the political action. Many major castles and religious buildings went through a terrible period during the Revolution and the Napoleonic era which followed so fast on its heels. Some châteaux were destroyed. Several were turned into prisons or barracks, their fabric scarcely respected by their new inhabitants. Some were sold off, only to be dismantled by entrepreneurs who would sell the stone.

On a more edifying note, many of the leading men of the first half of the 19th century were recalled in **David d'Angers'** medallions. He also sculpted many historic heroes for various French towns, including Le Bon Roi René for Angers. But his most famous work is the sculpture on the tomb of Bonchamps at **St-Florent-le-Vieil**, one of the most powerful and moving of images of the century, recalling one rare charitable moment in the terribly violent and divisive anti-Republican Guerre de Vendée. A vast range of more diverse types is brought to life in **Balzac**'s fictional *Comédie Humaine*, a huge interconnecting series of novels set in this period, several of them taking place in the Loire Valley.

Another writer, Prosper Mérimée, as minister of culture, went around the country in the middle of the century frantically making lists of the great mass of France's architectural heritage that needed to be saved. The French looked back nostalgically to the past after periods of such dreadful upheaval. Commemorative work came into its own, especially recalling the unifying, strong heroine Joan of Arc. Romanticization of the past included building neo-Gothic and neo-Renaissance châteaux and restoring the real things more or less successfully. René Hodé was particularly prolific in Anjou, creating new castles in the countryside. Joly-Leterme was a rather less successful restorer in most cases. Rather better than him were de la Morandière and Sanson, both of whom did their neo-Gothic best, for example, on the **Château de Chaumont**, Sanson adding the monumental stables. The most famous name in Loire restoration work is Félix Duban, who led the restoration of the **Château de Blois**, both inside and out. Of course, it's understandable that the period's proprietors wished to install some modern comforts, so don't be surprised to bump into the odd heating system, even a lift in the Château de Serrant, while at the very spacious **Château de Brissac** one *châtelaine* removed one floor to install a theatre!

New civic projects were instigated in the cities, especially the opening up of major arteries or boulevards, following the example of Haussman in Paris, while the railways also demanded new provisions from mid-century. **Tours**, for example, boasts the most splendid station, by Victor Laloux. Laloux also designed the shiny new basilica of St-Martin in the city and the showy Hôtel de Ville (not forgetting, more famously, the Gare d'Orsay in Paris). The Tours town hall entrance is held up by vast telamons, the work of the Tourangeau sculptor François Sicard, quite well represented in the region, who worked into the early 20th century. One notable project which combined engineering with art and which is associated with the name of the great Gustave Eiffel is the supremely elegant Pont-Canal de **Briare**.

Stained glass revived as an art, with the likes of Lobin decorating **Blois cathedral**, and the churches of Les Mauges commissioning much work to commemorate the pro-Catholic uprising of the Guerre de Vendée, most notably at the church of **Le Pin-en-Mauges**. At **Blois** and **Gien**, pottery thrived, Gien's production still well known, while in **Briare** tiles for mosaics and more prosaic uses became an important local industry.

20th Century

In postwar times, the distinguishing feature, rather than innovation, has perhaps been the demonstration of greater respect for the Loire's rich legacy. There have been mistakes too, such as the 1950s concrete bunker in which **Angers'** Apocalypse tapestry was placed, but the city can be proud of having attracted **Jean Lurçat**'s modern Chant du Monde tapestry cycle and displaying one of the most successful transformations of a partly ruined church building in Pierre Prunet's conversion of the Eglise Toussaint into the David d'Angers museum.

In the Loire-side cities many of the stained-glass windows were blown out during war bombing. The name of Max Ingrand crops up time and again in the work to replace them. For example, he did many of the windows for **Gien**'s church of Ste-Jeanne d'Arc, an interesting brick-patterned reconstruction. But mercifully, the medieval stained-glass windows at **Chartres** survived intact. And the art form still thrives in the city, both at the Centre International du Vitrail and in smaller ateliers. On a more eccentric note, the Maison Picassiette in the Chartres outskirts reveals a local cemetery sweeper's obsession with naive art depictions in mosaics.

Two places focus on novel 20th-century art forms: the Musée du Gemmail in **Tours**, where paintings, often by famous artists such as Picasso, are interpreted in a new light in shards of stained glass; and the Musée de l'Objet in **Blois**, with challenging presentations of – yes – objects. There are artists' studios dotted all around the Loire and exhibition spaces such as the Centre de Création Contemporaine in Tours and the Bouvet-Ladubay gallery in **St-Hilaire-St-Florent** near Saumur. Few are more curious than the troglodyte homes of Richard Rak and Jacques Warminski in **Anjou**, the latter referred to as l'*Hélice terrestre*, a more-or-less successful work of art outside and in. A few pieces of modern architecture stand out in Orléans and Tours, notably the baseball-hatted conference centre by Jean Nouvel (who designed the extraordinary Institut du Monde Arabe in Paris) in **Tours**. The art of modern and futuristic gardening is celebrated at the annual international garden festival of the **Château de Chaumont**, with some designs that look like prototypes not simply for our 21st century, but for a different planet.

Topics

04

The Loire River

...often my eyes were attracted to the horizon by the beautiful gold strip of the Loire where, among the waves, the sails drew fantastic figures that then fled, carried off by the wind.

Balzac, *Le Lys dans la vallée*

Green to Baudelaire's eyes, silvery for Flaubert, blonde to Péguy, blue to Lemaître, of crystal for La Fontaine, the Loire could seem golden to Balzac. All these great writers would have witnessed a quite different Loire from the one you see today, a river teeming with boats going about their business. While today it's the busy roads hemming in the Loire along great stretches that carry the traffic, it was the river itself that was the major trade route for so many centuries. Museums at Châteauneuf-sur-Loire, Chinon and Montjean-sur-Loire recall the importance of commerce along the *fleuve* (the French word for a great river) and its tributaries. They show the variety of boats that plied the region's rivers, from primitive dugouts to the improbable paddle steamers of the early 19th century. But the days of Loire shipping were numbered anyway by the time of the steamers, as the railways arrived in the mid-19th century. Today the enormous quays in the major towns and the surprisingly substantial ones in little riverside villages along the Loire (often with a cluster of mariners' cottages left standing nearby) still bear witness to the former importance of the river trade.

The Loire is an enormously long river, just over 1,000km in length. We cover a good section of it in this guide book, going from Sancerre in central France to the Atlantic at St-Nazaire. But it actually starts not far from the Mediterranean, a mere 160km north as the crow flies from where the Rhône spews out into that sea via its marshy Camargue estuary. For a surprising distance the Loire and the Rhône roughly parallel each other – only flowing in opposite directions. At their closest, the two rivers lie just 30km apart. Goods could be transported from one to the other, making possible a river trading link between the Mediterranean and the Atlantic. The Loire is thought to have been a route that connected the Celtic and Greek trading worlds, Cornish tin apparently among the products making its way from one to the other in this manner.

The banks of the Loire have long been open to civilization then. Celtic settlements sprang up early along the river, foundations for the later Gallo-Roman cities. The Romans knew the Loire well, but as the Liger (the people who live along the Loire are still known in French as Ligériens). St Martin founded the second Christian monastery in France along its banks in the 4th century. The Viking invaders came up it to create havoc and devastation in the 9th century, providing a suitably gory ending to the Dark Ages. In the 13th century Loire mariners set up an association to protect their rights along the length of the trading river and to ensure its good maintenance. Created in 1215 and lasting until 1773, the Communauté des Marchands Fréquentant la Rivière de Loyre et Fleuves Descendant en Icelle defended its members' joint interests in the face of the tolls imposed by different proprietors along the river network. The association also tried to make sure that dredging and the marking of navigation channels were carried out.

Memorable images of the Loire and its vessels stand out through history: St Martin's body carried by boat up to Tours, the November trees so surprisingly springing into flower; pilgrims arriving on the quays of Candes-St-Martin to visit the place where the great evangelizer died; Viking longships sowing heathen terror; Anne de Bretagne coming from Nantes to Langeais by boat for her enforced marriage to King Charles VIII, her extravagant belongings in tow; the plotters of the Conjuration d'Amboise in the 16th century being drowned in bags; tens of thousands of anti-Republicans crossing the river at St-Florent-le-Vieil in the Guerre de Vendée, others being drowned by the Revolutionary leaders of Nantes in dreadful couplings; the Second World War bombings...

As the late Loire artist Jacques Warminski described it to me once, the Loire is a capricious creature whose course resembles that of an Anjou *boule de fort*, the unevenly weighted bowl that makes its unpredictable, drunkenly swerving way towards its destination. Actually, the Loire's extreme natural waywardness was curbed from medieval times on with the building of levees, the riverside banks that generally stop it from spilling over. These levees were begun under Henri Plantagenêt in the 12th century. Many of the Loire roads were built on top of them, affording good views of the river and countryside around, as you'll see. These days the Loire only rarely tries to act in unruly manner. Although the French often refer to the Loire as the last great wild river in France, it is relatively well behaved most of the time – to the extent that nuclear power stations have been ever-so-reassuringly placed along its length. The Loire Valley has become the Nuclear Loire Valley. If you followed the journey right through this book you'd see four such power stations spewing their cloud-sized plumes into the air.

While nuclear power has flourished in the postwar period, fish numbers have dwindled. Pollution has been a problem, but seems to be easing slightly. The Loire salmon, despite a number of obstacles conspiring against them along the way, are starting to reappear slowly, and in very small numbers make their laborious journey upstream. You're much more likely to be able to eat shad fished from the Loire, or eel, although *sandre*, considered the Loire Valley fish *par excellence*, will most times probably come from way out east in Europe. Aquariums at Lussault and near Romorantin-Lanthenay allow you to see some of the types of fish that may land up on your holiday plate while they're still happily swimming around. On the river itself you may see *carrelets*, the square nets lowered into the water, or, in summer, men out in their little *barques* (the punt-like Loire Valley boats) fishing with rods. In Anjou, large numbers of fishermen take to the jetties that emerge as the water level drops in the heat, and in season a few privileged hunters erect floating camouflaged cabins on the water for duck shooting.

The gravelly and sandy shores and numerous islands of the Loire provide good havens for birds, particularly when they're migrating. Species you may see along the Loire include terns (like refined, petite gulls), sandpipers and ringed plovers. You may spot the odd kingfisher shooting past, or sand martins flitting to and from their nests dug into the sandy banks. Mallards, teal, coots and moorhens swim around the quieter waters. Ospreys, hovering on the spot before diving, put in an appearance, as do grebes and large cormorants, which can be seen fishing from August to April. The grey heron stands out as the most majestic bird you can spot on the Loire. You'd be lucky to catch sight of the European beaver, though, which doesn't build dams here, but digs a home only accessible by water. Weasels and polecats count among the less popular inhabitants, but the little metallic-blue Hoplia beetles peculiar to the Loire were once prized as jewels. Of the trees that give the Loire banks their particularly lovely appearance, the willows are the most distinctive, the purple variety a Loire speciality. Ash and elm also often line the river bank.

In summer and the major tourist season, you'll see a very different Loire from that of the rainier months. In winter the Loire can become massively bloated. I've witnessed the rare sight of it clogged with huge chunks of ice cracking painfully apart – this exceptional occurrence in the mid-1980s destroyed the bridge at Sully. In summer the river looks much less formidable. The waters dwindle and split into branches, following much narrower courses and sometimes abandoning whole portions of the river bed, leaving *boires*, isolated pools of trapped water, and great sandy expanses. Avoid the temptation of walking on these unless you see the locals doing so – they can hide quicksands (*sables mouvants*). The advice for you should you come across such dangers is to turn round immediately and follow your tracks back to where you started from. Swimming is forbidden in the Loire as even in summer its currents can be treacherous. The river bed also goes down in deceptive shelves. But you can go canoeing on the Loire in places and a few of the old-fashioned boats have been revived for little tourist outings, as we indicate in the touring chapters.

Despite busy roads rushing along large stretches of the Loire, this remains a magnificent and majestic river. Recognizing this, in the year 2000 UNESCO declared most of the section covered in this guide book a World Heritage Site, just barring those parishes containing nuclear power stations. The Loire is the first river to have received this UNESCO distinction. But although such official admiration and tourist attention is focused on the Loire river, in fact the majority of the so-called Loire châteaux, Loire churches and Loire courtly towns were built beside tributaries of the great river, in the so-called Loire Valley, a region which needs some clarification.

The Loire Valley – Purest of French Regions?

Le fleuve le plus national pour nous est la Loire. (Our most national river is the Loire.)
Balzac

The Loire Valley is the most French of regions and yet not a region at all, administratively speaking. It's traditionally considered to stretch from somewhere east of Orléans to the western end of Anjou, and thus is split between two official administrative French regions, Centre and Pays de la Loire. (To confuse you just a little further, there's a *département* called quite simply the Loire, but this isn't in the tourist region of the Loire Valley at all; it's far away in the Rhône-Alpes region, with St-Etienne its capital!)

Foreign students flock to the Loire Valley, as the purest of French is supposed to be spoken here – there's said to be no regional accent. So the Loire Valley is a region that isn't a region with an accent that is without accent (the educated urban Loire Valley accent could perhaps be compared to BBC or Oxford English). If the Loire region covered here has an overall, clichéd identity, though, it is of purity: purity of accent, purity of typically French countryside, purity of traditional French food and wine, purity of archetypal French châteaux.

Many tourist guides define the Loire Valley as the region of the Châteaux de la Loire. But where do the châteaux of the Loire begin and end? More of the Loire Valley châteaux lie along tributaries of the Loire rather than along the great river itself. There is, however, a typical look to the Loire Valley region which might help to define it: the gentle slopes and meanders of the rivers, the limestone banks and caves, the Romanesque churches and blonde châteaux, the vineyards and orchards, the soft, white light. And looking at the buildings of the region, you can't help but notice the importance of limestone and slate, devoted their own topic below.

One aspect that makes the Loire Valley such a very French region is suggested in Balzac's line quoted above. Historically, it is indissociable from certain vital moments and movements of national pride. Joan of Arc's leading role in this is indisputable. And whatever the shortcomings of the Valois kings who settled in the Loire Valley for a while, during their stint here, defining events took place. Despite King Charles VII's weakness, in his time the English were sent packing, losing most of their continental baggage; during Louis XI's reign from Touraine, the notion of the French nation was cemented by the acquisition of new provinces and by important new economic measures; wild Brittany was tamed and brought into the fold by the actions of Charles VIII and François I. These kings all encouraged and sponsored a vibrant culture in the Loire Valley that has become a source of great pride for the whole country, and instantly recognized abroad. They and their entourage commissioned their sump-tuous and unforgettable châteaux and caused many beautiful courtly towns to thrive. The Loire Valley does represent something of a psychological divide in the French mind, though: this is where western France divides between north and south.

A few hugely influential French writers came from the Loire Valley and have been adopted as national icons. If Balzac was right in saying that the Loire is the most national of France's rivers, then it's probably fair to say that Balzac, from Touraine, is now considered the most national of French writers. Rabelais, a local boy too, is a figure who, however little read or understood, has become a French hero. Ronsard and du Bellay, a couple of the most influential poets from the group of 16th-century versi-fiers referred to as the Pléiade, and seen as early champions of the French language, are strongly associated with the Loire Valley. Ronsard even embarked on what he vainly hoped would be an epic for the French nation and language, the *Franciade*.

All told, many consider that the seeds of modern France sprang up in the Loire Valley. It's hard to pin down specifically Loire Valley traditions, Loire Valley cuisine doesn't really exist as such and it's impossible to imagine a Loire Valley separatist movement! Even if the Loire Valley is hard to define precisely, it just feels quintessen-tially French.

Black and White Loire

Going underground in the Loire Valley, you'll find the sources for the main materials from which not just the Loire Valley châteaux but also most of the Loire Valley towns and villages were built – limestone and slate. Tufa, or *tuffeau* in French, is the special type of limestone that dominates. But before digging deeper into the subject, first let's dismiss the distracting side issues here, brick and schist.

In the east of the region covered in the guide, in the Orléanais and Blésois in particular, you will find brick in a good number of castles, often put to decorative effect. The Château de Gien offers a fine example, with its mysterious patternings; the Louis XII wing of the Château de Blois another. One of the most romantic of all the châteaux covered here, the Château du Moulin, reflects its ruddy complexion in its moat. Many grand town houses in Orléans and Blois were also built of brick.

In the west of the Loire Valley, around Angers, the limestone hits schist. The contrast between the typical pale, soft Loire Valley stone and the much grittier, darker rock could scarcely be stronger. The local architecture immediately reflects the change to schist, although many of the châteaux west of the geological dividing line did insist on adding a little limestone to lighten their looks, for example at Angers, Serrant, Brissac and Le Plessis-Macé. Schist isn't actually as ugly as it sounds, containing tinges of oranges and browns, but it does come as a bit of a shock after all that lovely light limestone.

The tufa was quite easily extracted from the Loire Valley riverside cliffs. You can visit numerous natural limestone grottoes and former quarries in the region. Hermits and religious communities apparently discovered the advantages of the limestone caves in these parts in the Dark Ages. The monastery of Marmoutier, founded by St Martin outside Tours, was built in part into the Loire cliff. At Chinon by the Vienne you can still visit the wonderful cave with its magical well where Jean le Reclus settled. Loire Valley tufa became increasingly excavated for construction through the medieval centuries. Some in the region say it was used to build Westminster Abbey in London; certainly vast numbers of fine churches as well as châteaux were built in limestone along the Loire and its tributaries, a tradition which continued through the Ancien Régime.

The careful quarrying of neat blocks left a whole mass of man-made caves in the region. These have been put to an ever-growing variety of uses. In wine-producing areas like Vouvray and Montlouis, the Saumurois or along the Cher, Vienne and Loir, they've been adapted to store wine, even to serve as wineries. More extraordinarily, many were transformed into troglodyte homes, particularly in the Saumurois. While the more common type of quarry was dug into cliffsides, around Doué-la-Fontaine they were dug straight down into the ground, galleries leading off central craters. The Doué caves have also been turned to a multitude of uses: for homes, for farms, for silk production, for a zoo even. As to Les Perrières' huge interconnecting chambers, their weird forms resemble an Art Nouveau cathedral. Close to Saumur, horse town *extraordinaire*, the manure the beasts produce is put to good use by the mushroom growers who have taken over many of the cliffside caves. (Conditions are ideal for growing the fungi.) More fragrantly, squashed apples (*pommes tapées*) are smoked and bashed in a cave at Le Val Hulin, on the other side of Saumur. After the Saumurois, the Cher valley is the second most important troglodyte area. Bourré along the Cher is reputed to produce the purest white Loire Valley stone. Several of its former quarries have been turned into tourist attractions similar to those in the Saumurois.

Some have turned their caves to very artistic use. The eccentric late Jacques Warminski dug out a disorientating set of chambers, including one intriguing circular one that emits a musical note as you stamp around inside it. Richard Rak exhibits his paintings in a cave at Coutures, southeast of Angers, while extraordinary centuries-old silos in the grounds of the posh Le Choiseul hotel in Amboise are converted into an art gallery in high season. The most mysterious Loire troglodyte art is to be found in a scruffy cave at Dénezé-sous-Doué, where a panoply of messily carved figures appear to present an irreverent, possibly masonic view of 16th-century life. More recently, more accomplished sculptors have specifically created new tourist sights by carving quarry walls in Bourré, St-Hilaire-St-Florent and Loches.

In the caves east of Tours and in the Saumurois you can even seek out the odd former quarry or cave converted into a superbly atmospheric restaurant or hotel where you can briefly sample the troglodyte life for yourself. You probably wouldn't be so excited about staying down a Loire slate mine. While virtually all the limestone quarries of the Loire Valley have shut, some slate mines in Anjou are still producing the material which adds the black to the typical black-and-white Loire Valley buildings. Although limestone extraction can never have been a piece of cake, somehow the multitude of diverting uses to which the former stone quarries have been transformed romanticizes them. The memories of slate mining in the Anjou pits remain working class and miserable, serving as a reminder of all the sweat, toil and suffering that went into the production of the Loire Valley's great architectural legacy.

Joan of Arc in the Arts

One of the other great heroes of the Loire Valley beyond its limestone and slate, its builders and their works, rather less anonymous and much more frequently sung, is Joan of Arc. The Loire is where she knew her great triumphs. It was at Chinon in Touraine that she persuaded the Dauphin, the future King Charles VII, to trust in her, while it was in the Orléanais that she inspired a string of victories that helped in the long process of booting the English out of France to end the Hundred Years' War.

Sensible Orléans gets slightly carried away over its favourite Maid in the annual celebrations to mark the liberation of the town from the English siege of 1429. But beyond a little museum devoted to Joan in the town and one in the Château de Chinon, plus the commemorative statues and plaques to her that litter the Loire Valley, there's no serious and profound tribute paid to Joan in the region. If this stretch of the Loire along which she knew her finest hours of glory fails to do her justice as one of the most extraordinary figures in French history, then literature at least has played its part in devoting her the attention she deserves.

Some fine fiction, and some very silly stuff, has been written using her as the source of inspiration. George Bernard Shaw entertainingly dismissed, in the preface to his play *Saint Joan*, some of the mounds of more famous writings in which she's been reinvented. According to Shaw, Shakespeare's portrayal of Joan in *Henry VI* 'ends in mere scurrility'. In Schiller's *Die Jungfrau von Orleans* she's 'drowned in a witch's cauldron of raging romance... it is not about Joan at all, and can hardly be said to pretend to be, for he makes her die on the battlefield, finding her burning unbearable'. On Voltaire's outrageous *La Pucelle d'Orléans*, he writes: 'I certainly cannot defend it against the charge of extravagant indecorum. But its purpose was not to depict Joan, but to kill with ridicule everything that Voltaire righteously hated in the institutions and fashions of his own day.' To give you a taste of this work, in one of Voltaire's scenes Joan is courted by, and narrowly avoids giving up her virginity, to an ass!

Shaw rubbishes Mark Twain's interpretation of Joan of Arc: 'Twain's Joan, skirted to the ground, and with as many petticoats as Noah's wife in a toy ark, is an attempt to combine Bayard with Esther Summerson from [Dickens'] *Bleak House* into an unimpeachable American school teacher in armor.' Twain was inspired by the highly influential republication by Quicherat in 1841 of the reports of Joan's trial and rehabilitation. 'Later on,' continues Shaw, 'another man of genius, Anatole France, reacted against the Quicheratic wave of enthusiasm, and wrote a *Life of Joan* in which he attributed Joan's ideas to clerical prompting and her military success to an adroit use of her by Dunois as a *mascotte*: in short, he denied that she had any serious military or political ability. At this Andrew saw red, and went for Anatole's scalp in a rival *Life* of her which should be read as a corrective to the other.' That still leaves, among numerous other writers to have been inspired by Joan, such notable worthies as Paul Claudel, Charles Péguy and Maurice Maeterlinck to plough through. Shaw's own depiction of Joan hasn't been without its critics, although the confused conviction of his character comes across with great force.

It's ironic to observe that while the pens of so many notable literary figures have got carried away by her stirring life and legend, Joan herself was illiterate, or as a contemporary put it more quaintly, knew not A from B. But there's no doubt that Joan knew the power of the word when it came to winning people over. For an in-depth present-day interpretation of Joan, which places her brilliantly in her historical context and in the context of the subsequent interpretations of her by a very wide variety of causes, Marina Warner's *Joan of Arc: The Image of Female Heroism* proves engrossing. The author adds her own feminist reading of the Maid: 'She has extended the taxonomy of female types; she makes evident the dimension of women's dynamism. It is urgent that this taxonomy be expanded further...we must develop a richer vocabulary for female activity than we use at present, with our restrictions of wife, mother, mistress, muse.' Such is the profusion of readings of Joan's character that she remains a totally fascinating figure, extremely difficult to grasp – Bernard Shaw once described her as 'the queerest fish among the eccentric worthies of the Middle Ages'.

The 'queerer' side of Joan's wearing of men's clothing and armour was suppressed in the plethora of paintings of her executed in the 19th century, which tried to improve her wholesomeness and re-establish her femininity, putting her back in a dress, sometimes giving her an ostentatiously plumed hat. The numerous civic statues of Joan, in stark contrast, tend to show her triumphant in armour, a bellicose leader, often on horseback, full of heroic action, ready to mow down a whole army of Englishmen – although she claimed at her trial never to have killed a man. You may spot many further conflicting renderings of Joan in stained glass and tapestry along the Loire Valley. The depictions of Joan most people recall are those from films. In this medium she has inspired a handful of 20th-century classics, including Carl Théodor Dreyer's *La Passion de Jeanne d'Arc*, Marco de Gastyne's *La Merveilleuse Vie de Jeanne d'Arc*, Robert Bresson's *Procès de Jeanne d'Arc* and Cecil B. De Mille's *Joan the Woman*.

It may surprise you to learn that it was only in the early 20th century that Joan was canonized by the Catholic Church. But she has always been a difficult figure for that church to deal with; after all, it condemned her to death, helping her to become such an emblematic figure.

Dogs' Paws in Wine

Among the recipes cooked up by King Louis XI's talented cook Jean Pastourel, such as pomegranate soup, white pudding, rock partridge, royal bread soup, stork and hedgehog, is a dish of '*branches de bois de jeunes cerfs coupés menus et frits dans du saindoux avec des sauces au citron, au vin vieux, à la dodine – incorporant le jus de volailles rôties*' – basically, young stags' antlers served in a complex and exotic sauce. Hunting was one of the great courtly pursuits and excesses to excite the kings of France and there were always culinary joys to follow the thrill of the kill.

Louis XI was one of the Loire Valley kings particularly, perhaps pathologically, impassioned by hunting. It was a heady hobby when there was no warring. Royal activities, both at work and at play, were often basically barbaric it seems in the Middle Ages. Louis XI wrote in one telling letter: 'I have been informed from Normandy that the English army has disbanded for this year. I am returning to take and kill wild boar, not wishing to miss the end of the season while awaiting the other one to take and kill Englishmen.' Louis' hunting dogs were treated to obscene luxury, their collars decorated with gold studs, their food prepared by apothecaries, their paws sometimes bathed in hot wine, poor darlings – they could be utterly exhausted by a hard day's work romping through the forests. Louis' favourite, Mistodin, was dressed in robes and slept in a bed. Offerings and prayers for the hounds were made to St Hubert. When Louis was ageing and ill, he even organized a miniature hunt in his room to distract him from his neurotic superstitions – rats were released as he gave instructions to his dogs to catch them. Hunting was something of a religion for the Loire kings. Louis had his original tomb effigy portray him kneeling in huntsman's gear in front of the Virgin, a greyhound with gold-studded collar by his side.

Some of the greatest Loire châteaux have been described as glorified hunting lodges, not least Chambord. Chambord's park, on the edge of the Sologne, the hunting region *par excellence* in France, became the official hunting reserve of the French presidents. Former president Giscard d'Estaing even set an embarrassingly tacky novel against the hunting background of the Sologne, with adultery as a main theme. It's possible to imagine adulterous François Mitterrand, a French politician who liked to have it both ways if ever there was one, selling his principles again here. Several other châteaux have taken up the hunting theme as a tourist attraction. They're certainly not critical of the sport, but what they show is revealing. Gien's Musée de la Chasse particularly so, presenting a vast collection of works of art inspired by hunting, from guns encrusted with delicate figures and huge polished brass horns to pieces of fine art including canvases by official hunt painters to Louis XIV. The Château de Montpoupon's feisty old owner, Mlle de la Motte St-Pierre, recently opened a hunt museum in her château's outhouses with the help of her nephew, an art dealer, and from a more personal collection – several faded photos show her standing triumphantly over dead stags. The Château de Cheverny's pack, a formidable bunch of long-legged hounds who run across virtually every postcard of the château, can often be seen languishing in their kennels. Champchevrier and du Rivau are further châteaux which pursue the theme. Antlers, tusks and various hunting trophies are used to decorate rooms in innumerable Loire Valley castles. A living reminder of hunting in the region is the displays of falconry – another great passion among many of the Loire Valley kings – at the Zoo de Beauval near St-Aignan.

When there's a formal hunt in the Loire Valley, local people turn out not to protest but to cheer. While in the British countryside pro-hunt and anti-hunt campaigners seem savagely ready to tear each other apart, in the French provinces there seems to be little awareness that this might be an issue at all. Although France is often considered a relatively liberal country, the debate on such issues can seem to lag well behind much of the rest of northern Europe. The passions of your average Frenchman come into play here. You'd have thought hunting was in the blood, it's such a strong pull. It may be understandable to consider that the hunting of animals was an instinct in prehistoric men, some of whose hunting implements you can see well displayed at the Château du Grand-Pressigny's museum on prehistory. And explaining the niceties of animal rights might have been a problem for Gauls, who worshipped the creatures they hunted – the fabulous find of Celtic bronze animals, including stags and wild boar, displayed in Orléans' archaeological museum is well worth going to see. But your average contemporary French provincial man would no doubt argue that hunting down animals is still in the genes today, an irresistible urge.

While the cliché may be that half of Frenchmen are out fornicating at weekends (an image which French presidents have hardly helped dispel), in autumn and winter a huge proportion of them will genuinely be out roaming the countryside with their guns and their dogs, looking for any game they can have a go at; as a tourist you may find that the noise of gunfire can quite spoil a trip out into the countryside at this time of year. The nearest you may come to the kill on a summer visit to the Loire Valley, though, is eating in a restaurant where a stuffed doe's head looks irritatingly innocently out from the wall above you. And, glancing up at the ceiling, you may be delighted to see one of those tasteful wagonwheel candelabras, the bulbs fixed in place in upturned does' hooves.

Food and Drink

Were you to go by the giants' diet in Rabelais' books, you'd expect to be served cartloads of tripe at every meal in the Loire Valley, washed down with your personal barrel or two of wine. And you wouldn't be surprised to eat the odd stray pilgrim in a salad. The one Rabelaisian food you may still taste in the Loire Valley today is *fouaces* or *foués*, dough balls that puff up when cooked in a baker's oven. In reality, the common features of Loire cuisine include freshwater river and lake fish, goat's cheese in a variety of shapes resembling children's building blocks, orchard fruits, a plethora of vegetables (such as the asparagus grown on the alluvial valley river sands), game in autumn, and Loire wine sauces at any time of year. There isn't a particularly typical Loire cuisine. The region, with its great trade route of the Loire river, was open to all sorts of culinary influences across the centuries. Standards of cuisine are pretty high across the board.

Regional Specialities

Food

Meats: With its fair number of forests, you'll find plenty of game around the Loire Valley in autumn, with the likes of duck and venison on most menus and, increasingly, given their explosion in numbers, wild boar (*sanglier* in French) or the baby *marcassin*. *Rillons* are a pork speciality in Touraine, cooked in their fat, and to be distinguished from *rillettes*, which is a kind of coarse pâté. *Géline de Touraine*, the black hen of that region, is reckoned to be particularly tasty. *Andouillettes*, tripe sausages, are the food of Rabelais, while *cul de veau* from Montsoreau is veal rump. The Maine-Anjou cow is a special breed that was developed across those two provinces. You may find meat dishes incorporating some of the fruits of the region (for example pork with apples or prunes) as well as local mushrooms and wines, even honey sometimes.

Freshwater fish: *The* Loire fish dish is *sandre*, or zander, often translated as pikeperch. *The* fish sauce along the Loire is *beurre blanc*, made with shallots, butter, dry white wine and vinegar. (Orléans, by the way, used to be very well known in France for its vinegar.) Other fleshy freshwater fish you'll come across include pike (*brochet*), bream (*brème*) and shad (*alose*). Eels (*anguilles*) are quite a speciality along the rivers. *Matelote d'anguilles* is a stew incorporating both eels and red wine, and possibly prunes. You may also find lamprey (*lamproie*) around the place. *Friture*, little fried fish, is popular. Salmon, which used to swim upriver in large numbers, have had an increasingly tough time in the last century, but some still manage to return to their breeding grounds. In traditional manner, a Loire salmon might be poached in a *court-bouillon* of Vouvray wine. Sea fish and seafood feature on most menus nowadays, rapidly transported from the Atlantic, so the choice should be good.

Vegetables tend to be especially fine in the Loire Valley. Asparagus grows particularly well on the alluvial sands. So, too, does a large variety of other vegetables. Those grown locally in large numbers include onions, leeks, beans, cabbage and artichokes.

Cardon is a rare relative of the last, its stem served in white sauce. Fresh lettuces of all sorts also flourish. *Champignons de Paris*, button mushrooms, are grown in vast profusion in the darkness of the caves of the Saumurois. Apparently, over three-quarters of the production for the whole of France is here. Now the producers are branching out, supplying other mushrooms such as *pleurotes* and *pieds bleu*. Much rarer, the occasional truffle can be found in southern Touraine.

Cheese in the Loire means goat's cheeses essentially. The most reputed come from the Sancerrois (with its temptingly named *crottins*, or 'droppings', of Chavignol), from Olivet in the Orléanais, from Selles-sur-Cher in the Blésois, and from Ste-Maure in Touraine. Olivet also produces some cow's milk cheese, as do other little locations.

Fruit: From the orchards of the Loire Valley, pears and apples are made into some lovely desserts. Pears are a speciality of both the Orléanais and of Anjou. *Tarte Tatin*, a native dish of the Sologne in the Loir-et-Cher, invented by accident by an absent-minded woman, is an apple tart with a caramelized top which you'll find on menus everywhere. *Pommes tapées* and *poires tapées* are apples and pears dried using old techniques. Excellent strawberries, raspberries, blackberries and even kiwis grow along the Loire Valley. Quinces from Ay in the Orléanais are made into a jelly known as *cotignac*. Plums and prunes were once found in profusion, but are rarer now.

Among pastries and puddings, other than *tarte Tatin*, almond pastries are popular, such as the Pithiviers, an almond-based *pâtisserie* named after a town north of Orléans. Cormery is known for its macaroons. *Crémets d'Anjou*, a fresh cream cheese concoction, with cream and sugar added, makes for a deliciously light dessert. Some of the liqueurs of the region, such as Cointreau (made in Angers) or Combier (made in Saumur), or local wines can add delicate flavours to fine desserts. You'll find local chocolate specialities across the region. Among the most amusing are *crottins de cheval*, 'horse-dropping' chocolates from Saumur, and chocolate 'slates' in Anjou, covered with a blue-dyed coating.

Wine

The map in the colour map section at the back of the book shows the different Loire wine regions, and the following wine areas are devoted more detailed descriptions in the text: in the Cher *département*, Sancerre; in the Blésois, Cheverny and Cour-Cheverny, Cher valley wines and Touraine-Mesland; in Touraine, Vouvray, Montlouis, Chinon, and Bourgueil and St-Nicolas-de-Bourgueil; in Anjou, Saumur-Champigny, Saumur sparkling, the Coteaux du Layon and the Coteaux de l'Aubance. The Loir (without an 'e') valley also produces some vinous surprises.

You'll realize from the map and if you travel along the Loire that the region produces a wide variety of wines from vineyards dotted along hundreds of miles. Many of the wine areas produce red, white and rosé wines. Some produce sparkling. The Loire Valley region is probably best known abroad for its distinctive white wines, such as Sancerre, Pouilly-Fumé, Vouvray and Muscadet; for the rosé of Anjou; and for the reds of Chinon, Bourgueil and Saumur. The last also produces a sparkling wine that you may well be familiar with, Saumur *mousseux*.

But Loire wines have a misleadingly limited reputation abroad. Anjou, in reality the most diverse of all the Loire wine regions, has been particularly badly served by its popular image outside France of producing rosé wines overwhelmingly. And it's rather disappointing that, outside the country, it's difficult to find a wide selection of Loire wines in most wine merchants' shops – the choice is often poor. There are of course many discoveries to be made. The advantage of few wines being available abroad is that you wine buffs out there can have the pleasure of bringing back your own exclusives if you buy on the spot.

The wines of the Loire can seem very complex at first, but almost all the white wines are made from either Sauvignon Blanc or Chenin Blanc grapes, while Cabernet Franc largely dominates in the reds. The Loire's vine-growing areas are far north in terms of French viticulture, and this means that they're particularly susceptible to the variations in weather from year to year; as a consequence, quality tends to vary more than in regions where the climate is slightly more reliably warm. Spring frosts and cooler summers can clearly affect a vintage. The lie of the land counts for a good deal at such times, although better winemaking techniques have made Loire wines more reliable in recent years. Considering recent vintages along the Loire, 1996 was a good year, producing quality wines across the board, while 1997 has proved a great vintage, with superb results, particularly in the reds and the finest sweet white wines. 1998 was a good year once again, with some very good reds. The wines of 1999 turned out to be more average, and those of 2000 won't be remembered long. In 2001, the summer was disappointingly cool and wet. Things looked up in 2002, while 2003 proved to be spectacularly warm and sunny; but that and other factors meant that yields were much lower than in average years, even if the results should be intense.

Under the national classification system for French wines, the best vine-growing parts of France are controlled and tightly restricted by the designation of particularly suitable areas as distinct *appellations d'origine contrôlée*, abbreviated to AOCs. These *appellations* vary greatly in size – what counts is the suitability of the particular terrain chosen, the distinctiveness of the grapes it produces and the quality of the wines these give. Anjou alone has almost 30 different *appellations*, Touraine some 10. The title of *appellation d'origine contrôlée* is generally a guarantee of a good-quality wine. AOC wine labels on the whole state the vintage, or year the grapes were harvested, and will often bear the name of an individual property and vine-grower, showing that the wine is made on the estate (*domaine*, *clos* and château are the most common terms for a wine estate). There are also generic AOC wines, in France almost always regarded as being of a lesser quality than the estate-produced AOC wines. Beneath the AOCs come wines called *vin délimité de qualité supérieure*, abbreviated to VDQS, and below them simple *vin de pays*.

Sections of the official French wine authorities have laid out wine routes through the region and can send you useful brochures on them. For information on the wine routes and *appellations* of Sancerre, the Berry and the Giennois, contact the Bureau Interprofessionnel des Vins du Centre, 9 Route de Chavignol, F-18300 Sancerre,

t 02 48 78 51 07, **f** 02 48 78 51 08, *contact@vins-centre-loire.com*, *www.vins-centre.com*. For information about the wine routes of Touraine and the Blésois, contact Interprofessionnel des Vins du Val de Loire, Bureau des Vins de la Touraine, 19 Saure Prosper Mérimée, BP 1921, F-37019 Tours Cedex 1, **t** 02 47 05 40 01, **f** 02 47 66 57 32, *touraine@interloire.com*. The many wine *appellations* and routes in Anjou are covered by the Comité Interprofessionnel des Vins d'Anjou-Saumur, Hôtel Godeline, 73 Rue Planagenêt, F-49000 Angers, **t** 02 41 87 62 57, **f** 02 41 86 71 84. Finally, the vineyards of the west around Nantes are dealt with by the Comité Interprofessionnel des Vins du Pays Nantais, Maison des Vins, Bellevue, F-44690 La Haye Fouassière, **t** 02 40 36 90 10, **f** 02 40 36 95 87.

Other Drinks

French coffee is strong and black but lacklustre compared with the aromatic brews of Italy or Spain. If you order *un café* you'll get a very small *express*. If you want more than these few drops of caffeine, ask for *un grand café*. If you like milk in your coffee, order *un café crème*. At breakfast, the French tend to order *café au lait*, which contains only a small amount of coffee topped up with a large quantity of hot milk. The word for decaffeinated is *déca*. If you order *un thé* you'll most likely get a tea bag in a cup of hot water. You'll probably have to specify *au lait* (with milk) or *au citron* (with lemon) if that's what you're after. *Chocolat chaud*, hot chocolate, is also available. An *infusion* or *tisane* is a herbal tea; *camomille*, *menthe* (mint), *tilleul* (lime or linden blossom) and *verveine* (verbena) count among the most popular types.

Mineral water (*eau minérale*) comes either sparkling (*gazeuse* or *pétillante*) or still (*non-gazeuse* or *plate*). The usual international corporate soft drinks are easy to find, as well as a variety of bottled fruit juices (*jus de fruit*). Some bars also do refreshing freshly squeezed lemon and orange juices (*citron pressé* or *orange pressée*), served with plenty of chilled water. The French are fond of sweet fruit syrups, for example red *grenadine*, *sirop d'orgeat* (barley-water) or ghastly green *diabolo menthe*.

Beer (*bière*) in most bars and cafés is run-of-the-mill big brands from Alsace, Belgium or Germany, but Chartres produces small quantities of its own brew. Draft beer (*pression*) is cheaper than bottled beer. Pastis and red wine flavoured with spices make popular apéritifs. The French, by the way, offer *porto* (port) before a meal, not as a *digestif*. Cognac is drunk across France, while Cointreau and Combier are two orange liqueurs actually made in Anjou.

Restaurant Generalities

Most restaurants, unless they're very small, will normally offer a choice of set-price menus with two to five (or even more) courses. The menus are usually posted by the entrance, so that you can peruse the options and check the prices. Many restaurants offer a lunch menu at a good price, a fine way of trying out the more exclusive gourmet addresses. Opening hours tend to be from 12 or 12.30 to 2pm for lunch, while dinner can be served from as early as 7.30pm, with last sittings in many places around 9pm, though some places serve until later on summer evenings.

A proper full French restaurant meal normally begins with an apéritif served with little savoury snacks known as *amuses-bouches* or *amuses-gueules* (a *gueule* is a rather vulgar word for a mouth). The hors-d'oeuvre are the starters. The entrées or *plats principaux* are the main courses. (If you order a side salad it will normally come before or after the main course, so if you want it with the main course, explain this.) *Les fromages*, cheeses, are served before the *desserts*, the puddings. You could finish a meal with a *digestif* or a coffee, tea or an *infusion* or *tisane*, the last two herbal teas. Drinks to end a meal are often accompanied by *petits fours*, or chocolates. More ordinary meals consist of a starter, a main course and either cheese or pudding. A *plat du jour*, sometimes also referred to as the *plat du marché*, is the day's special, which could be eaten by itself. A *menu dégustation* is a selection of the chef's or the region's specialities. Eating à la carte will always be much more expensive than opting for a set menu, so avoid that extravagance if you're worried about your budget. A fair number of restaurants don't accept credit cards, so check if you're unsure.

Menus in cheaper restaurants sometimes include a bottle or a carafe of house wine in the price (signalled by the phrase *vin compris*). With the exception of some house wines, generally speaking wine in French restaurants isn't good value – it normally carries a very substantial mark-up. But French families would expect to splash out on a reasonable bottle when eating out. With the increasingly severe action to stop drink-driving some places now serve *le vin au verre*, wine by the glass. By contrast, with certain very sumptuous menus you may get a glass of a different type of wine with each course! For choosing your type of wine, see the wine section.

Service should be automatically included in the price of set menus nowadays, indicated by *service compris* (service included), sometimes abbreviated to s.c. If eating à la carte, consider adding a 10 per cent tip.

The restaurants recommended in this guide almost exclusively serve French food. Where prices are quoted for menus they're only there to give you a rough guide and will inevitably change in time. In towns especially, you'll find a growing number of fast-food chains and ethnic restaurants. North African restaurants (i.e. Moroccan, Tunisian or Algerian – the generic term is *maghrébin*) serving couscous (steamed semolina topped with spicy meat and vegetables) as the stock speciality are the most popular and numerous, along with Vietnamese and Italian restaurants. Crêperies are rarely noted in this book, but are easy to find.

To avoid disappointment with restaurants which have a well-established reputation or which are well located, call at least a day in advance to book a table. With *fermes-auberges* (farms-turned-inns) and a few other special types of restaurant, you *have* to call in advance to be served.

Vegetarians may have a tough time in France. Generally speaking, the French seem extraordinarily unaware about some people's wish not to eat meat. Normally you can find a choice among the starters, and ordering two or more of these à la carte may allow you to make up your own vegetarian menu. However, it can be difficult to know exactly what ingredients have gone into the preparation. You should be warned that

French Menu Vocabulary

Starters and Soups
(*Hors-d'œuvre et Soupes*)
amuse-gueule appetizer
assiette assortie plate of mixed cold hors
   d'oeuvre
bisque shellfish soup
bouchée mini vol-au-vent
bouillon broth
charcuterie mixed cold meats, salami,
   ham, etc.
consommé clear soup
potage thick vegetable soup
velouté thick smooth soup, often fish
   or chicken

Fish and Shellfish
(*Poissons et Coquillages*)
aiglefin little haddock
alose shad
anchois anchovies
anguille eel
bar sea bass
barbue brill
baudroie anglerfish
belon flat oyster
beurre blanc sauce of shallots and wine
   vinegar whisked with butter
bigorneau winkle
blanchailles whitebait
brème bream
brochet pike
bulot whelk
cabillaud cod
calmar squid
carrelet plaice
colin hake
congre conger eel
coque cockle
coquillages shellfish
coquille St-Jacques scallop
crabe crab
crevette grise shrimp
crevette rose prawn
cuisses de grenouilles frogs' legs
darne slice or steak of fish
daurade sea bream
ecrevisse freshwater crayfish
eperlan smelt
escabèche fish fried, marinated and
   served cold

escargot snail
espadon swordfish
esturgeon sturgeon
flétan halibut
friture deep-fried fish
fruits de mer seafood
gambas giant prawn
gigot de mer a large fish cooked whole
grondin red gurnard
hareng herring
homard Atlantic (Norway) lobster
huître oyster
lamproie lamprey
langouste spiny Mediterranean lobster
langoustines Norway lobster (often called
   Dublin Bay prawns or scampi)
limande lemon sole
lotte monkfish
loup (de mer) sea bass
maquereau mackerel
matelote d'anguilles eels in a wine sauce
merlan whiting
morue salt cod
moules mussels
omble chevalier char
oursin sea urchin
pagel sea bream
palourde clam
petit gris little grey snail
piballe elver
poulpe octopus
praire small clam
raie skate
rouget red mullet
St-Pierre John Dory
sandre zander or pikeperch
saumon salmon
sole (meunière) sole (with butter, lemon
   and parsley)
telline tiny clam
thon tuna
truite trout
truite saumonée salmon trout

Meat and Poultry
(*Viandes et Volailles*)
agneau (de pré-salé) lamb (grazed in fields
   by the sea)
andouillette chitterling (tripe) sausage
autruche ostrich
biftek beefsteak
blanc breast or white meat

blanquette stew of white meat, thickened with egg yolk

bœuf beef

boudin blanc sausage of white meat

boudin noir black pudding

brochette meat (or fish) on a skewer

caille quail

canard, caneton duck, duckling

carré the best end of a cutlet or chop

cassoulet haricot bean stew with sausage, duck, goose, etc.

cervelle brains

chapon capon

chateaubriand porterhouse steak

cheval horsemeat

chevreau kid

chevreuil venison

chorizo spicy Spanish sausage

civet meat (usually game) stew, in wine and blood sauce

cœur heart

confit meat cooked and preserved in its own fat

contre-filet sirloin steak

côte, côtelette chop, cutlet

cou d'oie farci goose neck stuffed with pork, foie gras, truffles

crépinette small sausage

cuisse thigh or leg

dinde, dindon turkey

entrecôte ribsteak

epaule shoulder

estouffade a meat stew marinated, fried and then braised

faisan pheasant

faux-filet sirloin

foie liver

foie gras goose liver

frais de veau veal testicles

fricadelle meatball

géline de touraine rare black hen of the region

gésier gizzard

gibier game

gigot leg of lamb

graisse, gras fat

grillade grilled meat, often a mixed grill

grive thrush

jambon ham

jarret knuckle

langue tongue

lapereau young rabbit

lapin rabbit

lard (lardons) bacon (diced bacon)

lièvre hare

maigret/magret (de canard) breast (of duck)

manchon duck or goose wing

marcassin young wild boar

merguez spicy red sausage

mouton mutton

museau muzzle

navarin lamb stew with root vegetables

noix de veau (agneau) topside of veal (lamb)

oie goose

os bone

perdreau, perdrix partridge

petit salé salt pork

pieds trotters

pintade guinea fowl

plat-de-côtes short ribs or rib chops

porc pork

pot au feu meat and vegetables cooked in stock

poulet chicken

poussin baby chicken

quenelle poached dumplings made of fish, fowl or meat

queue de bœuf oxtail

rillons pork pieces cooked in their fat; a speciality from Touraine

ris (de veau) sweetbreads (veal)

rognon kidney

rosbif roast beef

rôti roast

sanglier wild boar

saucisse sausage

saucisson salami-like sausage

selle (d'agneau) saddle (of lamb)

steak tartare raw minced beef, often topped with a raw egg yolk

suprême de volaille fillet of chicken breast and wing

taureau bull's meat

tournedos thick round slices of beef fillet

travers de porc spare ribs

tripes tripe

veau veal

venaison venison

Vegetables, Herbs, etc. (Légumes, Herbes, etc.)

ail garlic

aneth dill

anis anis

artichaut artichoke

asperge asparagus
aubergine aubergine (eggplant)
avocat avocado
basilic basil
betterave beetroot
blette Swiss chard
cannelle cinnamon
céleri (-rave) celery (celeriac)
cèpe ceps, wild boletus mushroom
champignon mushroom
chanterelle wild yellow mushroom
chicorée curly endive
chou cabbage
chou-fleur cauliflower
choucroute sauerkraut
choux de bruxelles Brussels sprouts
ciboulette chives
citrouille pumpkin
clou de girofle clove
cœur de palmier heart of palm
concombre cucumber
cornichon gherkin
courgette courgette (zucchini)
cresson watercress
échalote shallot
endive chicory (endive)
epinards spinach
estragon tarragon
fenouil fennel
fève broad (fava) bean
flageolet white bean
fleur de courgette courgette blossom
frites chips (French fries)
galipette large round mushroom
genièvre juniper
gingembre ginger
haricot bean
  (rouge, blanc) (kidney, white)
haricot vert green (French) bean
jardinière mixed vegetables
laitue lettuce
laurier bay leaf
lentilles lentils
macédoine diced vegetables
maïs (épis de) sweetcorn (on the cob)
marjolaine marjoram
menthe mint
mesclun salad of various leaves
morille morel mushroom
navet turnip
oignon onion
oseille sorrel

panais parsnip
persil parsley
petits pois small peas
pied bleu wood blewit (type of mushroom)
piment pimento
pissenlits dandelion greens
pleurote type of mushroom
poireaus leeks
pois chiches chickpeas
pois mange-tout sugar pea, mangetout
poivron sweet pepper (capsicum)
pomme de terre potato
potiron pumpkin
primeurs young vegetables
radis radish
riz rice
romarin rosemary
roquette rocket
safran saffron
salade verte green salad
salsifis salsify
sarriette savory
sarrasin buckwheat
sauge sage
seigle rye
serpolet wild thyme
thym thyme
truffe truffle

Fruit and Nuts (*Fruits et Noix*)

abricot apricot
amande almond
ananas pineapple
banane banana
bigarreau black cherries
brugnon nectarine
cacahouète peanut
cassis blackcurrant
cerise cherry
citron lemon
citron vert lime
coco (noix de) coconut
coing quince
dattes dates
figue (de Barbarie) fig (prickly pear)
fraise (des bois) strawberry (wild)
framboise raspberry
fruit de la passion passion fruit
grenade pomegranate
griotte morello cherry
groseille redcurrant

lavande lavender
mandarine tangerine
mangue mango
marron chestnut
merise black cherry
mirabelle mirabelle plum
mûre (sauvage) mulberry, blackberry
myrtille bilberry
noisette hazelnut
noix walnut
noix de cajou cashew
pamplemousse grapefruit
pastèque watermelon
pêche (blanche) peach (white)
pignon pinenut
pistache pistachio
poire pear
pomme apple
prune plum
pruneau prune
raisin (sec) grape (raisin)
reine-claude greengage plum

Desserts
Bavarois mousse or custard in a mould
biscuit biscuit, cracker, cake
bombe ice-cream dessert in a round mould
bonbon sweet, candy
brioche light sweet yeast bread
charlotte sponge fingers and custard
  cream dessert
chausson turnover
clafoutis batter fruit cake
compote stewed fruit
corbeille de fruits basket of fruit
coulis thick fruit sauce
coupe ice cream: a scoop or in cup
crème anglaise egg custard
crème caramel vanilla custard with
  caramel sauce
crème Chantilly sweet whipped cream
crème fraîche slightly sour cream
crème pâtissière thick pastry cream filling
  made with eggs
crémets fresh cream cheese, normally
  from Anjou and mixed with fresh cream
  and sugar
gâteau cake
gaufre waffle
génoise rich sponge cake
glace ice cream
macaron macaroon

madeleine small sponge cake
miel honey
mignardise same as petits fours
œufs à la neige floating island/meringue
  on a bed of custard
pain d'épice gingerbread
parfait frozen mousse
petits fours sweetmeats; tiny cakes
  and pastries
profiteroles choux pastry balls, often filled
  with crème pâtissière or ice cream, and
  covered with chocolate
sablé shortbread
savarin a filled cake, shaped like a ring
tarte, tartelette tart, little tart
truffe chocolate truffle
yaourt yoghurt

Cheese
(Fromage)
brebis (fromage de) ewe's milk cheese
chèvre goat's cheese
doux mild
fromage (plateau de) cheese (board)
fromage blanc yoghurty cream cheese
fromage frais a bit like sour cream
fromage sec general name for solid cheeses
fort strong

Cooking Terms and Sauces
à point medium steak
aigre-doux sweet and sour
aiguillette thin slice
à l'anglaise boiled
au feu de bois cooked over a wood fire
au four baked
barquette pastry boat
beignet fritter
béarnaise sauce of egg yolks, shallots and
  white wine
bien cuit well-done steak
bleu very rare steak
bordelaise red wine, bone marrow and
  shallot sauce
broche roasted on a spit
chaud hot
cru raw
cuit cooked
émincé thinly sliced
en croûte cooked in a pastry crust
en papillote baked in buttered paper
épice spice

farci stuffed
feuilleté flaky pastry
flambé set aflame with alcohol
fourré stuffed
frais, fraîche fresh
frappé with crushed ice
frit fried
froid cold
fumé smoked
galantine cooked food served in
  cold jelly
galette savoury pancake
garni with vegetables
(au) gratin topped with melted cheese
  and breadcrumbs
grillé grilled
haché minced
marmite casserole
médaillon round piece
mijoté simmered
pané breaded
pâte pastry, pasta
pâte brisée shortcrust pastry
pâte à chou choux pastry
pâte feuilletée flaky or puff pastry
paupiette rolled and filled thin slices of
  fish or meat
pavé slab
piquant spicy hot
poché poached
salé salted, spicy
sanglant rare steak
sucré sweet
timbale pie cooked in a dome-shaped mould
tranche slice
vapeur steamed
vinaigrette oil and vinegar dressing

Miscellaneous
addition bill (check)
baguette long loaf of bread
beurre butter
carte menu
confiture jam
couteau knife
crème cream
cuillère spoon
formule/menu set menu
fouace (or fouée) doughball which puffs up
  when cooked
fourchette fork
huile (d'olive) oil (olive)

lait milk
menu set menu
moutarde mustard
nouilles noodles
pain bread
œuf egg
poivre pepper
sel salt
service compris/non compris service included/
  not included
sucre sugar
vinaigre vinegar

Drinks
(Boissons)
bière (pression) beer (draught)
bouteille (demi) bottle (half)
brut very dry
café coffee
café au lait white coffee
café express espresso coffee
café filtre filter coffee
chocolat chaud hot chocolate
citron pressé fresh lemon juice
demi a third of a litre
doux sweet (wine)
eau water
  gazeuse/pétillante sparkling
  minérale mineral
  plate/non gazeuse still
eau-de-vie brandy
eau potable drinking water
glaçon ice cube
infusion/tisane herbal tea
  menthe mint
  tilleul lime flower
  verveine verbena
jus juice
lait milk
moelleux semi-dry
mousseux sparkling (wine)
orange pressée fresh orange juice
pichet pitcher
pression draught
sec dry
thé tea
verre glass
vin wine
  blanc white
  mousseux sparkling
  rosé rosé
  rouge red

while many people will be helpful, others may be uncomprehending ('well, you can eat the chicken then, or there's plenty of fish and seafood') or, worse still, not eating meat may be taken as a personal insult – in provincial France, vegetarianism can, like other perceived newfangled choices in ways of living, be seen by some as an attack on French tradition.

Markets and Picnic Food

In most villages, the market day is the event of the week, a social occasion for the locals. Celebrated for their fresh farm produce, French markets are fun to visit in their own right, but become even more enticing if you're cooking for yourself or gathering the ingredients for a picnic. In the larger towns you may find a market every day. Most markets finish around noon, when, in villages, the lunch siren goes off at the *mairie* (an old custom, designed to reach farm workers out in the field). In cities you can also find more established covered markets, *les halles*. Other good sources for picnic food are *boulangeries* (selling bread, but also tarts and pastries often), *charcuteries* (selling meat specialities, especially pork), *traiteurs* (delicatessens, selling a diversity of elaborate prepared dishes) and *pâtisseries*.

Cafés

That venerable French institution, the café, isn't only a place for a drink, but for many people also a home away from home, somewhere to read the papers, play cards, write letters, read a book, meet friends, or just unwind and watch the world go by. You can sit for hours over one coffee and shouldn't feel hurried by the staff. Prices for drinks are listed on the *tarif des consommations*; they go up according to whether you're served at the bar (*le comptoir*), at a table inside (in the *salle*) or outside (*en terrasse*).

Travel

Getting There

By Air

Arriving from overseas, **Paris-Orly** airport (code ORY), south of the French capital, is the most convenient international airport to fly in to for the eastern Loire: the town of Orléans lies around 100km southwest of Orly. **Paris Charles-de-Gaulle** airport (code CDG; also known as Roissy), north of the capital, does have very good train links with the major railway stations along the Loire Valley.

The cities of **Tours** and **Nantes** along the Loire itself have airports offering international flights to and from Britain. Nantes has the more significant airport of the two. Flights from Britain to **Angers** go via the hub of Clermont-Ferrand, which is slightly awkward, but the service is still quite swift. The other airport to consider if flying from Britain is **Poitiers**, just south of the Loire Valley, to which you can get flights on no-frills Ryanair.

Although the likes of Ryanair are slightly cheaper, **charter flights** can be good value, and offer the added advantage of departing from a wider range of regional UK airports.

Airlines

UK

Air France, t 0845 359 1000, *www.airfrance.co.uk*. Offers flights from London Gatwick to Nantes as well as to the major Paris airports. The flight time is around one hour. The Gatwick Express rail link departs every 15mins from London Victoria station during the day, the journey taking 30mins. Air France also flies from London Heathrow to Nantes and Angers via Paris, Bordeaux or Lyon, the whole journey to and from either of these well positioned Loire Valley airports lasting anything between 3 and 8 hours.

bmi, t 0870 607 0555, *www.flybmi.com*. Large range of flights from various British airports to Paris.

British Airways, t 0870 850 9850, *www.ba.com*. As well as flights to the major Paris airports of Orly and Charles-de-Gaulle, British Airways also operates one flight a day direct from London's Gatwick airport to Nantes.

easyJet, t 0871 750 0100, *www.easyjet.com*. Good choice of flights from London Luton, Liverpool and Newcastle-upon-Tyne to Paris CDG.

Ryanair, t 0871 246 0000, *www.ryanair.com*. Regular flights from London Stansted to Tours, Poitiers and Clermont-Ferrand; and others from Glasgow Prestwick, Dublin and Shannon to Paris Beauvais airport – awkwardly located 56km northwest of the city.

USA and Canada

Air France, 125 West 55th St, New York, NY 10019, **t** 800 237 2747, Canada **t** 800 667 2747, *www.airfrance.com*. Regular services to Paris Charles-de-Gaulle from Atlanta, Boston, Chicago, Cincinnati, Houston, Los Angeles, Miami, New York, Philadelphia, San Francisco and Washington. In Canada, from Montreal (3 daily flights), Toronto (1 daily flight) and Ottawa.

American Airlines, t 800 433 7300, *www.aa.com*. Flights from Boston, Chicago, Dallas, JFK, Miami, San Diego and San Francisco.

British Airways, t 800 AIRWAYS or 800 403 0882, *www.ba.com*. Wide selection of flights from many hubs in the United States and Canada to London, with onward connections to Paris and Nantes.

Continental, t 800 231 0856, **t** 800 343 9195 (hearing impaired), *www.continental.com*. Flights from Houston and Newark.

Delta, t 800 221 1212, **t** 800 831 4488 (hearing impaired), *www.delta.com*. Frequent flights from Atlanta, Boston, Chicago, Cincinnati, Houston, Los Angeles, New York, Philadelphia and San Francisco direct to Paris.

Northwest Airlines, t 800 225 2525, **t** 800 328 2298 (hearing impaired), *www.nwa.com*. Flights from Detroit to Paris.

United Airlines, t 800 864 8331, **t** 800 323 0170 (hearing impaired), *www.united.com*. Direct flights to Paris from Chicago, Denver, Los Angeles, Miami, Philadelphia, San Francisco and Washington.

Companies such as Thomson, Airtours and Unijet can offer return flights from as little as £80. Check out your local travel agency, the Sunday papers, Teletext and web sites such as *www.flightmapping.com*, *www.lastminute.com* *www.cheapflights.co.uk*, and *www.travelocity. co.uk*. In London, look in the *Evening Standard* and *Time Out*. Remember, there are no refunds for missed flights – most travel agencies sell insurance so that you don't lose all your money if you fall ill.

If you are flying from North America, it may be cheaper to fly to London and pick up an onward flight from there.

By Train

Travelling by high-speed train is an attractive alternative to flying from the UK. There are very good train links between London and the Loire Valley, but you need to book more than a fortnight in advance (and much longer in advance if possible) to get tickets at a decent price; otherwise rail travel can be uncomfortably expensive.

If you use the Eurostar service (t 08705 186 186 , *www.eurostar.com*), the best way of getting to the Loire Valley may be by going from either London Waterloo or Ashford in

Students, Discounts and Special Deals

UK

Besides saving 25% on regular flights, people under 26 have the choice of flying on special discount charters.

Students with the relevant ID cards are eligible for considerable reductions, not only on flights but also on trains and admission fees to museums, concerts and more. Agencies specializing in student and youth travel can supply ISIC cards.

Try:

Europe Student Travel, 6 Campden St, London W8, t (020) 7727 7647. Caters to non-students as well.

STA, Priory House, 6 Wright's Lane, London W8 6TA, *www.statravel.com*, t (020) 7361 6100; Bristol, t 08701 676 777; Leeds, t 0870 168 6878; Manchester, t (0161) 839 3253; Oxford, t 08701 636 373; Cambridge, t (01223) 366 966; and many other branches in the UK.

Trailfinders, 215 Kensington High St, London W8 6BD, t (020) 7937 1234, *www. trailfinders.com*. Tailormade itineraries and discounted flights.

USIT, Fountain Centre, College Street, Belfast BT1 6ET, t (028) 9032 7111, *www.usitnow.com*. Good student deals; branches across Northern Ireland and the Republic.

USA and Canada

If you're resilient, flexible and/or youthful and prepared to shop around for budget deals on stand-bys or even courier flights (you can usually only take hand luggage on the latter), you should be able to get yourself some rock-bottom prices.

Check out Airhitch for last-minute deals on stand-by tickets, and STA Travel for student discounts.

For discounted flights, try the small ads in newspaper travel pages (for example, *New York Times*, *Chicago Tribune*, and *Toronto Globe and Mail*).

Numerous travel clubs and agencies also specialize in discount fares, but may require you to pay an annual membership fee.

For more ideas and low-priced deals see the web sites at *www.xfares.com* (carry-on luggage only) and *www.smarterliving.com*.

Airhitch, 481 Eighth Avenue, Suite 1771, New York, NY 10001-1820, t 877 247 4482, *www. airhitch.org*. Last-minute tickets to Europe from around $195.

STA, t 800 781 4040, *www.statravel.com*, with branches at most universities and also at 10 Downing St, New York, NY 10014, t (212) 627 3111, and ASUC Building, Telegraph at Bancroft Way, 1st Floor, University of California, Berkeley, CA 94720, t (510) 642 3000.

TFI, 34 West 32nd St, New York, NY 10001, t 800 745 8000, t (212) 736 1140, *www.lowestair-price.com*.

Travel Cuts, 187 College St, Toronto, Ontario M5T 1P7, t (416) 979 2406, *www. travelcuts.com*. Canada's largest student travel specialists; branches in most provinces.

Kent to Lille; London–Lille takes a mere 1 hour and 40 minutes. Then simply change platform at Lille for a fast service to the main Loire Valley cities, thereby avoiding Paris completely. This means, for example, that Tours can be only some 5½ hours away from London Waterloo, Angers 6½ hours.

Alternatively, you can take the Eurostar service from London Waterloo or Ashford to Paris Gare du Nord; London–Paris takes just over 2½ hours. But then you'll need to cross central Paris to reach Montparnasse, the station from which trains leave for the Loire Valley. For more information on services on SNCF (the French national rail company), see 'Getting Around' below, or start by looking at its website, www.sncf.com.

If you plan to take some long train journeys, it may be worth investing in a rail pass. The excellent-value **Euro Domino** pass entitles EU citizens to unlimited rail travel through France for three to eight days in a month for £122–£306, or £88–£173 for 12–25-year-olds.

There's also the **Inter-Rail** pass (for European residents of at least six months), which offers 22 days' unlimited travel in Europe (countries are grouped into zones; you pay £149/219 for one zone for under/over the age of 26), plus discounts on trains to cross-Channel ferry terminals and returns on Eurostar from £60. Inter-Rail cards are not valid on trains in the UK.

Visitors from North America have a wide choice of passes, including **Eurailpass** and **France Railpass**, which can all be purchased in the USA. A one-month Eurailpass costs around $664/946 for those aged under/over 26 years.

Rail Europe handles bookings for all services, including Eurostar and Motorail, and sells rail passes:

UK, Rail Europe, 179 Piccadilly, London W1, t 08705 848 848, www.raileurope.co.uk.
USA, Rail Europe, t 877 257 2887, www.raileurope.com.

By Bus

Eurolines offers services from London to Tours (11½hrs), Angers (14hrs) and Nantes (13½–15¼hrs), There are daily services and prices are £77–85 return. Discounts are also offered for senior citizens, people under 26, and children under 12.
Information and booking: t 08705 808080 or t (0121) 455 0086 (hearing impaired), www.eurolines.co.uk.

By Boat

The Channel ports of Dieppe, Le Havre, Caen-Ouistreham and Cherbourg are all within reasonable driving distance of various sections of the Loire Valley, although you'll have to take quite tricky cross-country routes rather than motorways to reach the region. St-Malo is good for the western end of the Loire Valley, although the ferry crossings from the UK take a lot longer. If you take the short crossings to Calais, Boulogne or Dunkerque, then the drive to the Loire Valley will be a fair bit longer, but you can make good use of fast, if expensive, French motorways.

Brittany Ferries, Millbay, Plymouth PL1 3EW, t 08703 665 333 , www. brittany-ferries.com. Sailings from Portsmouth to Caen (6hrs), Cherbourg (4½–7hrs) and St-Malo (8¾hrs), from Poole to Cherbourg (2¼–4¼hrs), from Plymouth to Roscoff (6hrs), Cherbourg and St Malo; and from Cork to Roscoff (14hrs).

Condor Ferries, Ferry Terminal Building, Weymouth, Dorset DT4 8DX, t (01305) 761551, www.condorferries.co.uk. Sailings from Weymouth and Poole to St-Malo, and Portsmouth and Poole to Cherbourg in season.

Hoverspeed Ferries, International Hoverport, Dover CT17 9TG, t 0870 240 8070 , www. hoverspeed.co.uk. Seacats Dover–Calais (35mins) and Newhaven–Dieppe (2hrs).

Norfolkline, Export Freight Plaza, Eastern Dock, Dover CT16 1JA, t (01304) 218 400, www.norfolkline.com. An alternative option to consider from Dover to Dunkerque, for cars only, not foot passengers.

P&O Portsmouth, Peninsular House, Wharf Rd, Portsmouth PO2 8TA, t 08705 202020, www.poportsmouth.com. Day and night sailings from Portsmouth to Le Havre (5½–8hrs) and Cherbourg (2¾–9½hrs).

P&O Ferries, Channel House, Channel View Rd, Dover CT17 9TJ, t 08705 20 20 20, *www.poferries.com*. Ferry and superferry from Dover to Calais (1¼–1½hrs).

SeaFrance, Eastern Docks, Dover, Kent CT16 1JA, **t** 08705 711 711, *www.seafrance.com*. Sailings from Dover to Calais (1¼–1½hrs).

Prices vary considerably according to season and demand, and, as always, it pays to shop around for the best deal.

By Car

Taking your car on a **Eurotunnel** train is the most convenient way of crossing the Channel between the UK and France. It takes only 35mins to get through the tunnel from Folkestone to Calais, and there are up to four departures an hour every day. Peak time tickets for a car and passengers should cost around £170 return in the low season, rising to £300 return in the high season. If you travel at night (10pm–6am), it is slightly cheaper. Special-offer day returns (look for them on the website) range from £15 to £50. The price for all tickets is per car less than 6½m in length, plus the driver and all passengers.

If you prefer a more romantic arrival in France, with a dose of bracing sea air, you've plenty of choice; *see* 'By Boat', above.

For information on rules and regulations when driving in France, *see* 'Getting Around', below.

Eurotunnel: Information and bookings **t** 08705 35 35 35, *www.eurotunnel.com*.

Entry Formalities

Passports and Visas

Holders of EU, US, Canadian, Australian and New Zealand passports do not need a visa to enter France for stays of up to three months; most other nationals do. If you intend to stay longer, the law says you need a *carte de séjour* (from the *mairie*, or town hall), a requirement EU citizens can easily get around as passports are rarely stamped. Non-EU citizens had best apply for an extended visa before leaving home, a complicated procedure requiring proof of income, etc. You can't get a *carte de séjour* without this visa.

For further information contact your nearest French consulate.

Customs

Duty-free allowances have been abolished within the EU. Travellers from the US are allowed to bring home, duty-free, goods to the value of $800, including 200 cigarettes or 100 cigars; plus 1 litre of alcohol.

Much larger quantities – up to 10 litres of spirits, 90 litres of wine (only 60 litres of which can be sparkling wine), 110 litres of beer and 800 cigarettes, 200 cigars – bought locally and provided you are travelling between EU countries, can be taken through customs if you can prove that they are for private consumption only.

For more information, US citizens can telephone the US Customs Service, **t** (202) 354 1000, or see the pamphlet *Know Before You Go* available from *www.customs.gov*. You're not allowed to bring back absinthe or Cuban cigars.

Getting Around

By Train

The SNCF runs an efficient network of trains through all the major cities. Prices have recently gone up but are still reasonable. If you plan on making only a few long hauls the Euro Domino (*see* above) or France Railpass will save you money. Other possible discounts hinge on the exact time of your departure.

For ordinary trains (excluding TGVs and *couchettes*), the SNCF has divided the year into *bleue* (blue, off-peak) and *blanche* (white, peak) periods, based on demand: white periods generally cover Friday noon to midnight, Sunday 3pm to Monday 10am, and holiday periods (all stations give out little calendars).

If you are making a round trip of at least 200km and are making a stopover on Saturday night, you'll get a 25% discount (**Découverte Séjour**) on TGV travel, or on standard trains in off-peak periods. The **Découverte à Deux** tariff gives a discount of 25% if you are making a round trip as a group of between two and nine persons (no need for family relationship). Neither discount applies to tickets bought on the train itself.

Anyone over 60 can purchase a **Carte Sénior** (€45) valid for a year and giving 25–50% off individual journeys according to availability. There is also a **12–25 Carte** (€43) which offers 50% reductions in blue periods and a 25% reduction in white periods; both cards offer 25% off train journeys from France to 27 countries in Europe, plus other perks.

Anyone can save money by buying a second-class ticket at least a week to a month in advance (**Découverte J8 or J30**), the only condition being that you must use it at the designated time on the designated train, with no chance for reimbursement if you miss it.

Note that all **tickets** must be stamped in the little orange machines by the entrance to the platforms that say *Compostez votre billet* (this puts the date on the ticket, to keep you from using the same one over and over again). Any time you interrupt a journey until another day, you have to re-"compost" your ticket. Long-distance trains (Trains Corail) have snack trolleys and bar-cafeteria cars; some have play areas for small children.

Nearly every station has large computerized left-luggage lockers (*consignes automatiques*) that spit out a slip with the lock combination when you use them. They take about half-an-hour to puzzle out the first time you use them, so plan accordingly; also note that any recent terrorist activity in France tends to close them down across the board. **SNCF general information**: t 08 92 35 35 35 (€0.23/min), *www.sncf.com*. You can book advance tickets from the USA or UK prior to departure on this web site, and pay by credit card at an SNCF machine in France.

By Bus

The bus network and extent of services varies from *département* to *département*. The timetable options for anything but travel between the major towns will not be extensive, so check carefully on times of departure and return when heading out to smaller places. Major towns normally call their bus station the *gare routière* – they're most often, but not always, by the railway station. In smaller places, stops can be in slightly surprising spots. They may not be obvious, so check at tourist offices if you're in any doubt.

The timetable schedules aren't always to be trusted; the tourist office or shopkeepers near the bus stop may have a more accurate instinct for when a bus is likely to appear.

By Car

First, the requirements. A car entering France must have its registration and insurance papers. Drivers with a valid licence from an EU country, the US, Canada or Australia don't need an international licence. If you're coming from the UK or Ireland, the dip of the headlights must be adjusted to the right, so as not to dazzle oncoming traffic. All cars in France are required to have rear seat belts and these must be worn by rear-seat passengers. Carrying a warning triangle is mandatory; if you have a breakdown the triangle should be placed 50m behind the car.

Regarding roads and driving in France, there are three particularly important points to note. First, drive on the right-hand side of the road. Second, watch out for *priorité à droite*. France used to have a rule of giving priority to the right at every intersection. This has largely disappeared, although there may still be intersections, usually in towns, where it still applies – these should be marked, but are not always clear. Third, French motorists rarely if ever respect pedestrians, even at pedestrian crossings. It's a sad fact that something like twice as many people are killed on French roads every year as are killed in Britain (and a much higher percentage of the population than in the USA).

If you're involved in an **accident**, the procedure is to fill out and sign a *constat aimable*. If your French isn't sufficient to deal with this, try to find someone to translate for you so you don't accidentally incriminate yourself. The word for accident is the same in French.

Drink-driving is now being strongly campaigned against in France. From time to time you may see French police virtually blocking a road to make suspects blow into a breathalyser (the limit is 0.05% alcohol), particularly after Sunday lunch. Drivers can avoid worrying about this by not drinking alcohol at all. You have been warned. Fines for speeding, payable on the spot, begin at €135 and can reach an astronomical €4,500 if you fail the breathalyser. Often French drivers warn others about the presence of police traps by flashing their lights.

Petrol (*essence*) stations can be few and far between in rural areas, shutting for the night and on Sunday afternoons. Don't get caught out. Unleaded is called *sans plomb*; diesel is often referred to as *gazole* or *gasoil*. If an attendant helps you with oil, windscreen-

Car Hire

Car hire in France can be an expensive proposition. To save money, look into air and holiday package deals. Prices vary widely from firm to firm: beware the small print about service charges and taxes. It's often cheaper to book through car hire companies in your own country before you go. The minimum age for hiring a car in France is around 21 to 25, and the maximum around 70. If you decide to hire a car once there, local tourist offices can provide information on car hire agencies. Car hire firms are also listed for the larger towns in this book (*see* 'Getting There and Around' sections).

UK and Ireland
Avis, t 08700 100 287, *www.avis.co.uk*.
Budget, t 08701 56 56 56, *www.budget.com*.
Europcar, t 0870 607 5000,
  www.europcar.com.
Hertz, t 08708 44 88 44, *www.hertz.co.uk*.
Thrifty, t (01494) 751600, *www.thrifty.co.uk*.

USA and Canada
Auto Europe, 39 Commercial St, P.O. Box 7006, Portland, ME 04112, t 1 888 223 5555 , t (207) 842 2000, *www.autoeurope.com*.
Auto France, P.O. Box 760, 211 Shadyside Rd, Ramsey, NJ 07446, t 800 572 9655, *www.auto-france.com*.
Avis Rent a Car, t 800 230 4898 (USA), t 800 272 5871 (Canada), t 800 331 2323 (hearing impaired), *www.avis.com*.
Europe by Car, t 800 223 1516 (nationwide), t (212) 581 3040 (NY), *www.europebycar.com*.
Europcar, t 877 940 69 00, *www.europcar.com*.
Hertz, t 800 654 3131, t 800 654 3001 (international), t 800 654 2280 (hearing impaired), t 800 263 0600 (Canada), t 800 654 2260 (Canadian hearing impaired), *www.hertz.com*.

cleaning or checking tyre pressure they will expect a tip.

On *autoroutes*, or motorways, tolls are quite high. The network is excellent and greatly time-saving, but there are always more gentle, picturesque routes available. The toll-free N (or RN) roads form part of the national network and when there isn't a motorway paralleling them can be very busy, for example along stretches of the Loire. D roads (*départ-mentales*) are generally well maintained. Smaller C (or *communal*) roads can be pretty narrow at times. The speed limits are as follows: 130km/80mph on *autoroutes*; 110km/69mph on dual carriageways (divided highways); 90km/55mph on other roads; 50km/30mph in urban areas (coming into force as soon as you pass a white sign with a town's name on it and lasting until you pass another sign with the town's name crossed out).

The word for a **breakdown** is *une panne*; to break down is *tomber en panne*. If you break down on major roads or motorways, you can use the orange-coloured emergency telephones to contact rescue services or the police. Otherwise, if you're a member of a motoring club affiliated to the **Touring Club de France** (*www.touringclub.org*), ring them. If not, ring the police, t 17.

By Bicycle

Getting your own bike to France is fairly easy: Air France and British Airways carry them free from Britain, for example. From the USA or Australia, most airlines will carry them as long as they're boxed and are included in your total baggage weight. In all cases, telephone ahead to the relevant airline to check on terms and conditions.

On **Eurostar**, you need to pack your bike in a bicycle bag and check it in at least 24 hours before you travel, or wait 24 hours at the other end. Alternatively, Esprit Europe, t 08705 850 850, *www.espriteurope.co.uk*, can arrange for your bike to be transported on Eurostar.

The French are keen cyclists and if you haven't brought your own bike the main towns and holiday centres always seem to have at least one shop that hires out bikes – local tourist offices have lists. *Vélo* is the

Special-interest Holidays

For a complete list of tour operators, *see* the Maison de France web site at *www.france guide.com*, or get in touch with a French government tourist office in your country. Other sources of information include The French Centre, 164–168 Westminster Bridge Rd, London SE1 7RW, **t** (020) 7960 26 00, **w** *www.cei-frenchcentre.com*, and the Cultural Services of the French Embassy, 23 Cromwell Rd, London SW7 2EL, **t** (020) 7073 1300, **w** *www.ambafrance-uk.org*, or at 972 Fifth Avenue, New York, NY 10021, **t** (212) 439 1400, **w** *www.info-france-usa.org*. Alternatively, check out the information at *www.fr-holidaystore.co.uk, www.aito.co.uk* or *www.holidayfrance.org.uk*.

For information on firms offering self-catering accommodation, *see* p.82.

France

Ballooning
Champagne Air Show, 9 rue Thiers, 51100 Reims, **t** 03 26 87 89 19, **w** *www.champagne-connection.com*. Deluxe ballooning trips in the Loire.

Language
Tours is well-known for its language schools. Choices include:
L'Institut de Touraine, Place du 14 Juillet, **t** 02 47 05 76 83, **w** *www.institut-touraine.asso.fr*.
Centre Linguistique pour Etrangers, 7 Place Châteauneuf, **t** 02 47 64 06 19.
Tours Langues, 37 Rue Briçonnet, **t** 02 47 66 01 00, **w** *www.langues.com*.
Eurocentres Foundation, 56 Eccleston Square , London SW1V 1PQ, **t** (020) 7834 41 55; in the US **t** (703) 684 1494, **w** *www.eurocentres.com*. Non-profit organization, offering intensive general and business French in a professionally equipped centre in Amboise.

Wine
Classic Wine Tours, 65 ter, Av du Truc 33700 Merignac, **t** 05 57 00 02 10, **w** *www.classic-wine-tours.com*. Short wine-themed tours of the Loire and other regions.

Limousine
Leisure Tours, 36 rue Madeleine Vernet, 37270 Montlouis-sur-Loire, **t** 02 47 45 00 25, **w** *www.leisure-tours.com*. Tailor-made tours with multilingual drivers.

UK and Ireland

General Interest
Abercrombie & Kent, St George's House, Ambrose Street, Cheltenham, Glos GL50 3LG, **t** 0845 0700610, **w** *www.abercrombiekent.co.uk*. Quality city breaks to a variety of destinations.
American Express Travel, 89 Mount Street, Mayfair, W1K 2AW, **t** (020) 7659 0705, **w** *www.americanexpress.co.uk/travel*. City breaks and fly-drives.

Canal Tours and River Cruises
Abercrombie & Kent (*see* above for details). Barges and houseboats.
French Country Cruises, 29a Main Street, Lyddington, Oakham, Rutland LE15 9LR, **t** (01572) 821330, **w** *www.andrewbrocktravel.co.uk*. Canal and river cruises.
Hoseasons Holidays, Sunway House, Lowestoft NR32 2LW, **t** (01502) 502 588, **w** *www.hoseasons.co.uk*. Canal tours and river cruises.

Cooking and Wine
Arblaster & Clarke, Clarke House, Farnham Rd, West Liss GU33 6JQ, **t** (01730) 893344 , **w** *www.arblasterandclarke.com*. Organizes wine and gourmet trips to France, some of which take in the Loire.
InnTravel, Hovingham, York YO62 4JZ, **t** (01653) 629000, **w** *www.inntravel.co.uk*. Offers the choice of a cycling holiday or a wine-tour holiday in the Loire.

Language
Euro Academy, 67–71 Lewisham High Street, London, SE13 5JX, **t** (020) 8297 0505, **w** *www.euroacademy.co.uk*. Contact about French courses in Tours.

Singles

Solo's Holidays, 54–8 High St, Edgware HA8 7EJ, **t** 0870 072 0700, **w** *www. solosholidays.co.uk*. Singles holidays throughout France.

Walking and Cycling

Belle France, 45 High Street, Tunbridge Wells, TN1 1XL, **t** (01892) 55 95 95, **w** *www. bellefrance.co.uk*. Walking or cycling holidays in the Loire and elsewhere.

The Chain Gang, 30 Prospect Park, Exeter EX4 6NA, **t** (01392) 66 22 62, **w** *www. thechaingang.co.uk*. Guided cycling tours visiting Loire châteaux and vineyards.

Headwater Holidays, The Old School House, Chester Road, Castle, Northwich, Cheshire CW8 1LE, **t** (01606) 720099, **w** *www. headwater.com*. Cycling, walking, and wine-tasting holidays.

Sherpa Expeditions, 131a Heston Rd, Hounslow, TW5 0RF, **t** (020) 8577 2717, **w** *www. sherpa-walking-holidays.co.uk*. The Loire Valley walking holiday is probably one of the very easiest in their brochure.

Susi Madron's Cycling for Softies, 2–4 Birch Polygon, Rusholme, Manchester M14 5HX, **t** (0161) 248 8282, **w** *www. cycling-for-softies.co.uk*. Mixes a cycling itinerary in the Loire with culinary stops.

USA and Canada

General Interest

Abercrombie & Kent, 1520 Kensington Rd, Oak Brook, IL 60523-2156, **t** 800 554 7016, **t** (630) 954 2944, **w** *www.abercrombiekent.com*. Quality city and country breaks throughout France, taking in the Loire.

Maupintour, 10650 W. Charleston Blvd, Summerlin, NV 89135, **t** 800 255 4266, **w** *www.maupintour.com*. Barge cruises and escorted tours.

Ballooning

The Bombard Society, 333 Pershing Way, West Palm Beach, FL 33401, **t** 800 862 8537, **t** (561) 837 6610, **w** *www.bombardsociety.com*. Five-day luxury ballooning 'adventures' in Burgundy and the Loire.

Canal Tours and River Cruises

French Country Waterways, P.O. Box 2195, Duxbury, MA 02331, **t** 800 222 1236, **t** (781) 934 2454, **w** *www.fcwl.com*. Hotel barges.

Cooking and Wine

Off The Beaten Path, 7 Rue Surcouf, 29850 Gouesnou, France, **t** 06 77 67 35 67 (France), **t** 877 846 2831 (USA), **w** *www. traveloffthebeatenpath.com*. France-based company with offices in the USA offering a variety of tours.

Gay and Lesbian

Alyson Adventures, P.O. Box 1638, Key West, FL 33041-1638, **t** 800 825 9766, **w** *www. alysonadventures.com*. Bike tours.

Language

National Registration Centre for Study Abroad, 207 E. Buffalo St, Suite 610, P.O. Box 1393, Milwaukee, WI 53201 , **t** (414) 278 0631 or **t** (414) 278 7410, **w** *www.nrcsa.com*. Language and culture courses in Angers, Nantes, Amboise and Tours.

Walking and Cycling

Adventure Sport Holidays, 815 North Road, Westfield, MA 01085, **t** 800 628 9655, **w** *www.advonskis.com*. Biking in the Loire.

Backroads, 801 Cedar St, Berkeley, CA 94701-1800, **t** 800 462 2848, **w** *www. backroads.com*. Bicycling and hiking in the Loire Valley.

Brooks Country Cycling Tours, P.O. Box 20792 New York, NY 10025, **t** (212) 874 5151, **w** *www.brookscountrycycling.com*. Guided cycling tours in the Loire Valley.

Cross Country International, P.O. Box 1170, Millbrook, NY 12545, **t** 800 828 8768, **t** (914) 677 6000, **w** *www.equestrianvacations.com*. Organised horse-riding trails.

DuVine Adventures, 124 Holland Street, Suite 2, Somerville, MA 02144, **t** 888 396 5383, **t** (617) 776 4441, **w** *www.duvine.com*. Self-guided cycling tours through Loire vineyards.

Two Bicycles and a Map Ltd, PO Box 3142, Madison, WI 53704, **t** (608) 244 6598, **w** *www.twobicycles.com*. Small, 'pedal at your own pace' bicycle tours.

common colloquial word for a *bicyclette*. A *vélo tout terrain*, invariably abbreviated to VTT, is a mountain bike.

Be prepared to pay a fairly hefty deposit on a good bike. You may want to inquire about insurance against theft.

The Loire Valley countryside offers relatively easy riding, as it is only mildly undulating. One strong recommendation – avoid the busy N roads as far as possible.

Certain French trains (with a bicycle symbol in the timetable) carry bikes for free; otherwise you have to send them as registered luggage and pay a fee of around €50, with delivery only guaranteed within five days.

Maps and cycling information are available from the **Fédération Française de Cyclotourisme**, 12 rue Louis Bertrand, F-94207 Ivry-sur-Seine Cedex, t 01 56 20 88 88, *www.ffct.org*, or in Britain from the **Cyclists' Touring Club**, Cotterell House, 69 Meadrow, Godalming, Surrey GU7 3HS, t 0870 873 0060, *www.ctc.org.uk*.

See also the list of special-interest holiday companies, above.

On Foot

A massive 40,000km network of long-distance paths, or Sentiers de Grandes Randonnées (**GR** for short), marked by distinctive red-and-white signs, takes in some of France's most spectacular scenery.

The GR3 is the main walking path along the Loire Valley. The GR41 takes you along the Cher, the GR46 along the Indre. You can buy detailed but expensive guides to all routes in French (Topoguides), published by the Fédération Française de la Randonnée Pédestre, 14 Rue Riquet, F-75019 Paris, t 01 44 89 93 93, *www.ffrp.asso.fr*.

The complete set is available from Stanfords Map and Bookshop, 12–14 Long Acre, London WC2, t (020) 7836 1321, *www.stanfords.co.uk*.

In English, Bartholomew's, IGN and Robertson McCarta publish specialist books on walking along the Loire.

You can also find a few Loire walks recommended in books covering walking in France more generally.

For information on *la randonnée* (French for hiking) by *département*, contact the central tourist information office (*see* p.80).

Practical A–Z

07

Climate and When to Go

The first hardy cyclists tend to come out in March when the Loire roads are pretty well empty of other tourist traffic, depending on when Easter falls. In March you can see the landscape free of leaves, with large round clumps of mistletoe like winter baubles in many of the trees and the châteaux more clearly visible from afar. Although the weather along the Loire is pretty mild, it can be cold, grey and wet this early in the year. Remember also that before Easter many of the sights aren't open, apart from the major châteaux and museums.

Although the French for April showers is *giboulées de mars* ("March downpours"), April can be cruel in the Loire too. It can also be beautiful, especially with the fruit orchards in blossom. Surprisingly, May often turns out not much warmer or more reliable, but then the countryside looks at its freshest and greenest.

June gets a fair deal warmer and you avoid the main tourist season. July and August are generally nice and hot, and very crowded around the main tourist sights. As the flow of water in the Loire dwindles, life along the river and its tributaries comes into its own, with fishermen and Loire *barques* enlivening the river scenes.

September is a lovely month, the weather still generally good, but with far fewer tourists, and peace and quiet returning as children go back to school. The trouble is that the noisy French shooting season starts in September, an untamed passion for many French men. October tends to have its fair share of beautiful days, with foliage changing colour, and the many wispy asparagus plants on the sandy river banks turning particularly vibrant tones of orange and yellow. This is also the time of the grape harvest, the *vendanges*.

November, December, January and February are not really tourist months. Many sights close for the winter after All Saints' Day (1 November), or Remembrance Day (11 November).

Crime and the Police

France is a safe and very policed country, but it's important to be aware that thieves target visitors, especially their holiday homes and cars – they see foreign number plates or a rental car as easy pickings. Leave anything you'd really miss at home, insure your property, and be especially careful in large cities. Report thefts to the nearest *gendarmerie* or *police nationale* – it's not a pleasant task but the reward is the bit of paper you need for an insurance claim. If your passport is stolen, contact the police and your nearest consulate for emergency travel documents. Carry photocopies of your passport, driver's licence, etc. – it makes it easier when reporting a loss.

By law, the police in France can stop anyone anywhere and demand to see ID; in practice, they tend to do it only to harass minorities, the homeless and the scruffy. The drug situation is the same in France as anywhere in western Europe: soft and hard drugs are widely available, and the police only make an issue of victimless crime when it suits them – being a foreigner may be reason enough, and there is little that your consulate can or will do about it.

Disabled Travellers

When it comes to providing access for all, France is not exactly in the vanguard of nations, but things are beginning to change. The SNCF, for instance, now publishes a pamphlet, *Mémento du Voyageur à mobilité réduite*, covering travel by train for the disabled – see w *www.sncf.com* (French Railways) for details, or in France, phone

Average Maximum Temperatures in °C/°F						
	Jan	Feb	Mar	April	May	June
Centre-Val de Loire	8 / 46	7 / 44	10 / 50	16 / 61	16 / 61	24 / 74
Pays de la Loire	10 / 50	8 / 47	11 / 52	18 / 64	17 / 63	23 / 73
	July	Aug	Sept	Oct	Nov	Dec
Centre-Val de Loire	26 / 79	25 / 75	21 / 70	16 / 61	11 / 52	7 / 44
Pays de la Loire	26 / 79	25 / 75	22 / 72	17 / 63	12 / 54	9 / 49

t 08 00 15 47 53. All TGVs are equipped and, on non-TGV trains, if in a wheelchair, you can use the designated areas in first class carriages, even if you have a second class ticket – provided you book in advance. The Channel Tunnel (see p.65) is a good way to travel by car since disabled passengers are allowed to stay in their vehicle, and Eurostar gives wheelchair passengers first-class travel for second-class fares. Most ferry companies will offer facilities if contacted in advance.

Vehicles fitted to accommodate wheelchairs or modified for disabled drivers pay reduced tolls on *autoroutes*. For details, try contacting: **Ministère des Transports**, Grande Arche, Paroi Sud, 92055 La Défense Cedex, Paris, t 01 40 81 21 22, *www.transports.equipement.gouv.fr*.

The *Gîtes Accessibles aux Personnes Handicapées*, published by Gîtes de France, lists self-catering possibilities (see p.82 for their address).

The following organizations provide services for people with disabilities:

France

Association des Paralysés de France, Siège National, 17 Bd Auguste Blanqui, 75013 Paris, t 01 40 78 69 00, *www.apf.asso.fr*. A national organization with an office in each *département*, with in-depth local information; headquarters are in Paris.

Comité National Français de Liaison pour la Réadaptation des Handicapés, 236B Rue Tolbiac, 75013 Paris, t 01 53 80 66 66. Provides information on access, and produces useful guides to various regions in France.

UK

Access Travel, 6 The Hillock, Astley, Lancashire M29 7GW, t (01942) 888844, *www. access-travel.co.uk*. Travel agent for disabled people: special airfares, car hire and wheelchair-accessible *gîtes*.

Holiday Care Service, 7th Floor, Sunley House, 4 Bedford Park, Croydon, Surrey CR0 2AP, t 0845 124 9971, t (020) 8760 0072, Minicom t 0845 124 9976, *www.holidaycare.org.uk*. Publishes an information sheet on holidays for disabled and older people (£5).

RADAR (Royal Association for Disability and Rehabilitation), 12 City Forum, 250 City Rd, London EC1V 8AF, t (020) 7250 3222, Minicom t (020) 7250 4119, *www.radar.org.uk*. Campaigning organisation with some information about travel.

USA

Mobility International USA, PO Box 10767, Eugene, OR 97440, USA, t/TTY (541) 343 1284, *www.miusa.org*. Information on international educational exchange programmes and volunteer service overseas for the disabled.

SATH (Society for Accessible Travel and Hospitality), 347 5th Av, Suite 610, New York, NY 10016, t (212) 447 7284, *www.sath.org*. Travel and access information.

Other Useful Contacts

Access Ability, *www.access-ability.co.uk*. Information on travel agencies catering specifically to disabled people.

Access-Able Travel Source, *www.access-able.com*. Web-based database of city information, travel operators, cruise lines, hotels, equipment hire etc for the disabled traveller.

Australian Council for Rehabilitation of the Disabled (ACROD), PO Box 60, Curtin, ACT 2605, Australia, t (02) 6283 3200, t/TTY (02) 6282 4333, *www.acrod.org.au*. Information and contact numbers for specialist travel agencies.

Emerging Horizons, *www.emerging horizons.com*. International on-line (or mailed) quarterly travel newsletter for people with disabilities. Subscription-based.

Global Access, *www.geocities.com/Paris/1502*. On-line network for disabled travellers, with links, archives and information on travel guides for the disabled, etc.

Eating Out

The French tend to eat early, starting at 12 or 12.30 for lunch, and between 8 and 9pm in the evening. Brasseries and cafés are flexible and open long hours, but restaurants don't often like serving late. Most restaurants recommended in this book offer a choice of set-price menus, and these are the prices we provide to give a rough idea of cost. Most places post their menus outside the door so you know what to expect. Service should be included.

For further information about eating in the Loire Valley, including local specialities, wines and a menu decoder, see the **Food and Drink** chapter, starting on p.49.

Electricity

French electricity is all 220V. British and Irish appliances will need an adapter with two round prongs; North American appliances usually need a transformer as well.

Embassies and Consulates

Foreign Embassies In France
Australia: 4 Rue Jean Rey, 75724 Paris Cedex 15, t 01 40 59 33 00, www.austgov.fr.
Canada: 35 Av Montaigne, 75008 Paris, t 01 44 43 29 00, www.amb-canada.fr.
Ireland: 4 Rue Rude, 75116 Paris, t 01 44 17 67 00, irembparis@wanadoo.fr.
New Zealand: 7 Rue Léonard de Vinci, 75116 Paris, t 01 45 01 43 43, www.nzembassy.com.
UK: 18 bis, Rue d'Anjou, 75008 Paris, t 01 44 51 31 02, www.amb-grandebretagne.fr.
USA: 2 Rue St-Florentin, 75382 Paris Cedex 08, t 01 43 12 22 22, www.amb-usa.fr.

French Embassies Abroad
Canada: 42 Promenade Sussex, Ottawa, Ontario, K1M 2C9, t (613) 789 1795, www.ambafrance-ca.org; 25 Rue St Louis, Québec, QC G1R 3Y8, t (418) 694 2294, www.consulfrance-quebec.org; Suite #1100–1130, West Pender St, Vancouver, BC, V6E 4A4, t (604) 681 4345, www.consulfrance-vancouver.org.
Ireland: 36 Ailesbury Rd, Ballsbridge, Dublin 4, t (01) 277 5002.

UK: 21 Cromwell Rd, London SW7 2EN, t (020) 7073 1200, www.ambafrance-uk.org; 11 Randolph Crescent, Edinburgh EH3 7TT, t (0131) 225 7954, www.consulfrance-edimbourg.org.
USA: 4101 Reservoir Rd NW, Washington, DC 20007-2185, t (202) 944 6202; 205 North Michigan Avenue, Suite 3700, Chicago, IL 60601, t (312) 327 5200; 10990 Wilshire Bd, Suite 300, Los Angeles, CA 90024, t (310) 235 3200; 934 Fifth Av, New York, NY 10021, t (212) 606 3680, www.ambafrance-us.org, www.france-consulat.org.

Environment

The Parc Naturel Régional Loire-Anjou-Touraine (see p.349) has been created to protect this particular area's heritage and traditions, and to encourage both locals and visitors to take an interest in local nature and traditions.

Then there are the small Maisons de la Loire at Jargeau, St-Dyé-sur-Loire, Montlouis and St-Mathurin. They're run by people passionate about the river, and can provide further information on environmental issues.

Festivals

The Calendar of Events presents a fairly wide selection of festivals in the region covered in the guide. To find out about son-et-lumière shows, see 'Sports and Activities', below.

Each département publishes a booklet on the host of festivals in their area, down to the smallest events; contact individual CDTs (see p.80).

Useful Websites:
Music festivals throughout France: www.francefestivals.com
General information about festivals: www.whatsonwhen.com, www.culture.fr, www.franceguide.com.

Health and Emergencies

Ambulance (SAMU) t 15
Police and ambulance t 17
Fire t 18

Calendar of Events

Please note that dates can vary; contact local tourist offices to confirm details.

January

Jan–Feb *Rencontres Musicales de l'Est Tourangeau*. Classical music programme (contact Mairie in Montlouis-sur-Loire).

Late Jan *Festival Premiers Plans*. Festival of first-time European filmmakers, Angers, w *www.premiersplans.org*.

February

Early Feb *Festival de Danse Contemporaine*. Contemporary dance festival in Blois.

Late Feb *Fête des Vins d'Anjou*. A discovery of Anjou wines in Chalonnes-sur-Loire.

March

March *Le Printemps Musical de St-Cosme*. Classical concerts in a monastic refectory outside Tours.

1st Sat and Sun *Wine fair*, Bourgueil.

Last weekend *Fête des Plantes et des Jardins*. Brings together gardening professionals at the Château de Beauregard.

End March–late Oct *Cadre Noir*. Six horse shows and two galas at Saumur.

Easter

Easter–mid-Nov *Flower festivals* at the Parc Floral, Orléans-La Source. Events start with an Easter egg hunt on Easter Sunday.

Easter week *Festival de Paques*. series of concerts in the abbey of Fontevraud.

April

April–Sept *Rendez-vous Horticoles*. A variety of green-fingered associations in Anjou throw open their doors to the public.

Early April *Fête des Plantes et des Jardins de Touraine*. Garden festival at the Château de la Bourdaisière, Montlouis-sur-Loire.

3rd week *Journees Nationales du Livre et du Vin*. Literature and wine festival in Saumur.

Last weekend *Les Musicalies de Sologne*. Music festival in Pierrefitte sur Sauldre.

Late April *Championnat d'Europe de voltige equestre*. Acrobatic riding in Saumur.

End April–early May *Carnaval* in Cholet. Parades, floats and carnival festivities.

May

Early May *Fêtes Johannique*s (normally 7–9 May). Commemorates the freeing of the town of Orléans from the English, inspired by Joan of Arc.

Mid-May *Tour de Scènes* Regional musicians take to street platforms in Angers.

3rd weekend *Festival des Animaux de la Ferme* in Pruniers en Sologne.

Late May *Aucard de Tours*. Rock festival in Tours.

Late May *Concours Complet International*. International horse competition at Saumur.

Late May–early June *Florilège Vocal*. Choral music in Tours.

Late May–late June *Festival de Sully-sur-Loire*. Series of concerts with prestigious events.

June

June (among other dates throughout the year) *Le Chore-Graphique*. Festival of contemporary dance, Tours.

Early June (Pentecost) *Journées de la Rose*. A display and sales of roses at the Prieuré de St-Cosme outside Tours.

Early June *Festival des Atipiks*. Music festival in Blois.

Early June *Concours International de Brass Band*. French and international brass bands compete at Amboise.

2nd weekend RAM DAM – *Festival de Musique et d'Animation* in Blois.

Mid-June–mid-July *Festival d'Anjou*. Prestigious theatre festival in Angers and across Anjou.

Mid-June–mid-Oct *Festival International des Jardins*. Major annual show by around 30 leading international landscape gardeners, in the grounds of the Château de Chaumont.

3rd weekend *Journées Nationales de la Chasse et de la Pêche*. Game fair around the Château de Chambord.

3rd Sun *Fête du Velo sur la Loire*. Cycling routes along the Loire, beginning at Angers and Saumur.

End June *Fêtes Musicales en Touraine*, around Tours. Highly reputed festival specializing in chamber music.

End June–early July *Tous sur le Pont*. Lively music and dance events in Blois.

End June *Festival International de Musiques Militaires*. Military music in Saumur, held on odd years.

Late June *Solstice de Beaulieu-les-Loches*. Mix of classical, jazz and rock concerts.

Late June–early July *Festival les Orientales*. A big music festival at St-Florent-le-Vieil, combining Asian and Western music.

Late June–early July *Festival de Jazz* in Orléans.

Late June–early July *Festival Historique*. A son-et-lumière show on certain nights at the Château de Beaugency.

Late June–early July *Spectacle Théâtral 'Les Trois Mousquetaires'*. In the gardens of the Château de Meung-sur-Loire.

July

July *Festoyances Rabelaisiennes*. Medieval-style market in Chinon.

July and Aug *Heures Musicales de Cunault*. Music on the banks of the Loire in Cunault.

July and Aug *Angers l'Été*. Summer music and dance festival in Angers.

2nd week *Festival 'au Nom de la Loire'*. Street theatre and music on the riverbank in Tours.

13–14 July *La Parade Tourangelle*. Dance festival at Pouzay.

Mid-July *Journées de la Rose*. Rose festival in Doué-la-Fontaine.

Mid-July *Concours d'Attelage International*. Horse and carriage competition in Saumur.

Mid-July *Fête de la Peinture*. Art festival at Montrésor.

Mid-late July *Cléry Raconte Dunois*. Evening show at Cléry-St-André.

End July *Grand Prix Retro du Vignoble*. Classic car and bike rally in Le Puy-Notre-Dame.

August

Aug *Heures musicales du Haut-Anjou*. Concerts in châteaux and churches in northern Anjou.

Early Aug *Concerts à la Corroierie du Liget*. Classical music at Chemillé-sur-Indrois.

2nd week *Festival Cosmopolite*. Contemporary and world music at Genillé.

Mid-Aug *Musique et Jardins*. Classical music concerts in the gardens of the Château de Villandry.

Last Sun *Festival de la Nature en Val de Loire* in Richelieu.

September

Early Sept *Accroche-Coeurs*. Open-air street festival in Angers.

Early Sept *Festival de Jazz* in Touraine (for details, contact the Mairie in Montlouis, t 02 47 50 72 70).

Late Sept *Concours de Dressage International*. Dressage competition in Saumur.

Last weekend *Les Rendev-vous du Pain*. Bread festival in Montrichard.

End Sept *Marathon International de la Loire*. Race down the Loire in canoes and kayaks, starting from the village of Bouchemaine near Angers.

October

Oct *Floralies du Val de l'Indre* at the Moulin de Veigné near Montbazon.

First half *Sonates d'Automne* at Loches and Beaulieu-les-Loches. Concerts, exhibitions and educational workshops.

Mid-Oct *Mondial du Lion*. International horse-riding competition in Le Lion d'Angers.

Mid-Oct *Les Rendez-vous de l'Histoire* in Blois.

End Oct *Journées Gastronomiques de Sologne*. Food festival in Romorantin-Lanthenay.

November

First half *Festival International Acteurs*. Theatre, cinema and varied exhibitions in Tours.

Nov–May *Orchestre Symphonique de Tours*. Programme of concerts.

All Saints' week *Festhea*. National festival of amateur theatre in Tours.

Mid-Nov *Salon International Art et Metiers du Cheval*. Gathering of artists in Saumur.

3rd weekend *Les Rendez-Vous du Touraine Primeur à Montrichard*. Celebrates the arrival of the new wine (following the third Thurs in the month).

Last weekend *Festival de BD Boum*. Comic book festival held in Blois.

December

1st weekend *Grand Marché Animé de Noel*. The Château de Brissac is transformed into a winter wonderland.

Christmas Eve *Midnight Mass* at the abbey of St-Benoît-sur-Loire.

France has one of the best healthcare systems in the world. Local hospitals are the place to go in an emergency (*urgence*).

If it's not an emergency, pharmacists are trained to administer first aid and dispense advice for minor problems. Out of ordinary hours, in rural areas there is always someone on duty if you ring the bell of a pharmacy; in cities, pharmacies are open on a rota and addresses are posted in their windows and in the local newspaper. Tourist offices can supply lists of local English-speaking doctors.

In France, however you're insured, you pay up front for everything, unless it's an emergency, when you will be billed later. Doctors will give you a brown and white *feuille de soins* with your prescription; take both to the pharmacy and keep the *feuille*, the various medicine stickers (*vignettes*) and prescriptions for insurance purposes at home.

Citizens of the EU should bring an E111 form (available from post offices before you travel), entitling you to the same emergency health services and treatments as French citizens. After paying up front for ordinary medical care and prescriptions, only 70–75% of the costs of doctors' fees, and 35–65% of the cost of most medicines, are reimbursed about two months later. Keep copies of all documents and make sure you obtain receipts. In the UK, see the Department of Health web site at **w** *www.doh.gov.uk/traveladvice*. You may also wish to take out a travel insurance policy covering medical care completely (*see* below).

Canadians are usually covered by their provincial health insurance; Americans should check their medical insurance policies.

Insurance

Many of the larger credit card companies will also offer free travel insurance when you use them to book a package holiday or aeroplane/train tickets. Read the small print very carefully, especially if you're travelling with expensive equipment (laptops, cameras, etc.). If you're not covered on your credit card, you may want to consider taking out an insurance policy covering theft and losses and offering 100% medical refund and emergency repatriation if necessary; check to see if it covers extra expenses should you get bogged down in

airport or train strikes. Beware that accidents resulting from sports are rarely covered by ordinary insurance.

Money, Banks and the Euro

The French currency is the euro, made up of 100 cents. Banknotes come in denominations of €5, €10, €20, €50, €100, €200 and €500; coins in 1c, 2c, 5c, 10c, 20c and 50c, €1 and €2.

Beware of banks charging high fees for cashing cheques for euros from other countries.

Traveller's cheques are the safest way of carrying money, but the wide acceptance of credit and debit cards and the presence of ATMs (*distributeurs de billets*), even in small towns, make cards a convenient alternative. Visa is the most readily accepted credit card; American Express is often not accepted, however. Smaller hotels and restaurants and bed and breakfasts may not accept cards at all. Some shops, supermarkets and petrol stations experience difficulties reading UK-style magnetic strips (French credit cards now contain a chip, or *puce*, containing ID information), so arm yourself with cash just in case.

Under the Cirrus system, withdrawals in euros can be made from bank and post office ATMs, using your usual PIN. The specific cards accepted are marked on each machine, and most give instructions in English. Credit card companies charge a fee for cash advances, but rates are often better than those at banks.

In the event of **lost or stolen credit cards**, call the following emergency numbers:

Mastercard t 0800 901387 or **t** 01 45 67 84 84
American Express Paris, **t** 01 47 77 72 00 or **t** 01 47 77 77 77
Visa (Carte Bleue) **t** 01 42 77 11 90
Diners Club t 01 49 06 17 50 or **t** 01 47 62 75 00
Barclaycard t (00 44) 1604 230 230 (UK number)

Exchange rates vary, and most banks and bureaux de change take a commission of varying proportions. Bureaux de change that do nothing but exchange money, hotels and train stations usually have the worst rates or take the heftiest commissions.

For bank opening hours, *see* overleaf.

Opening Hours

Shops: While many shops and supermarkets are now open continuously Tues–Sat from 9 or 10am to 7 or 7.30pm, businesses in smaller towns still tend to close for lunch from 12 or 12.30pm to 2 or 3pm (even 4pm in summer). There are local exceptions, but outside the towns nearly everything shuts on Monday, except for grocers and *supermarchés*, which open in the afternoon. In many towns, Sunday morning is a big shopping time. Markets (often daily in the cities, weekly in villages) are usually open mornings only, although clothes, flea and antiques markets may run into the afternoon.

Banks: Banks are generally open 8.30am–12.30pm and 1.30–4pm. They close on Sunday, and most close either on Saturday or Monday as well.

Post offices: Post offices are open in the cities Monday–Friday 8am–7pm, and Saturdays 8am–noon. In villages, offices may not open until 9am, then break for lunch and close at 4.30 or 5pm.

Châteaux: The majority of châteaux are open between 10 and 12 in the morning and 2 and 5 or 6 in the evening through the spring, summer and autumn months. Many stay open through lunch in July and August. The more famous ones stay open all or most of the year, and have longer opening times than the rest in summer. You should leave at least 1 hour to visit any château. Many can still only be seen on guided tours, which often start on the hour, so bear that in mind. And really, you should arrive more than an hour before closing time to be sure of seeing inside a château. The term for a non-guided tour is *visite libre*. The very largest châteaux may offer the occasional guided tour in English. Virtually all can provide an English text to take with you on the tour. Admission is usually €4.50–6, but can be as much as €10 or as little as €2.

Museums: Most museums close for lunch, and often all day on Mondays or Tuesdays, and sometimes for the entire winter. Hours change with the season: longer summer hours begin in May or June and last through September usually. Most museums close on national holidays. Most museums give discounts on admission (which ranges from €1.50 to €4.50) if you have a student ID card, or are an EU citizen under 18 or over 65.

Churches: Churches are usually open all day, or closed all day and only open for Mass. Sometimes notes on the door direct you to the *mairie* or priest's house (*presbytère*), where you can pick up the key. There are often admission fees for cloisters, crypts and special chapels.

National Holidays

On French national holidays, banks, shops, businesses and many museums close, but most restaurants stay open.

1 January New Year's Day
Easter Sunday March or April
Easter Monday March or April
1 May Fête du Travail (Labour Day)
8 May VE Day, Armistice 1945
Ascension Day usually end of May
Pentecost (Whitsun and Monday) beginning of June
14 July Bastille Day
15 August Assumption of the Virgin Mary
1 November All Saints' Day
11 November Remembrance Day (First World War Armistice)
25 December Christmas Day

Post Offices, Telephones and the Internet

Known as PTT or La Poste, post offices are easily discernible by their sign of a blue bird on a yellow background. For opening hours *see* above. You can purchase stamps in tobacconists as well as post offices.

Nearly all public telephones have switched over from coins to *télécartes*, which you can purchase at any post office or newsagent for about €7.40 for 50 *unités* or €14.75 for 120 *unités*. If **ringing France from abroad**, the international dialling code is 33, then drop the first zero of the ten-digit number. For **international calls** from France, dial oo, then dial the country code (UK 44; US and Canada 1; Ireland 353; Australia 61; New Zealand 64), and then the local code (minus the o for UK numbers) and number. If calling from a public phone, the number should be marked, and people can ring you back. For directory enquiries, dial **t** 12.

Most cities and towns now have cybercafés, and the French have some of the most remarkable web sites on the information superhighway.

Sports and Activities

The central tourist information centres for each *département*, the Comités Départementaux de Tourisme (or CDTs for short), can supply a great deal of thematic information depending on what you're looking for. Sometimes they have a service, Loisirs Accueil, which organizes excursions and special events. The addresses for the CDTs are given in 'Tourist Information', below. You can also contact tourist offices for more detailed local information.

(Tour operators offering special-interest holidays are listed on p.68.)

Bird-watching: The Loire levee on the south bank between Gien and Sully is a good spot in season, as is the Ile de Parnay, east of Saumur. The Maison de la Loire at St-Mathurin, east of Angers, may be able to organize short trips with a local guide.

Boule de fort: Anjou's answer to English bowls, but played inside. *See* Saumur, p.360, for a description. An initiation into the art of the game may be available.

Canoeing and kayaking: The national centre for information is the Fédération Française de Canoë-kayak, 87 quai de la Marne, B.P.58, F-94340 Joinville Le Pont, **t** 01 45 11 08 50, *www.ffck.org*. There are a few places where you can go canoeing on the Loire itself, indicated in the touring chapters. You can also try some of the tributaries and the large lakes by the major towns.

Cycling: *See* 'Getting Around', p.65. Each *département*'s CDT should be able to supply a specific guide to *circuits à bicyclette* and may organize special cycling holidays.

Deer-watching: In the autumn rutting season, the Parc de Chambord is the place to try and catch a glimpse of the beasts (*see* p.140).

Falconry: You can watch displays of falconry at the Zooparc de Beauval (*see* p.209).

Fishing: A permit is required for fishing in Loire Valley rivers. Check what possibilities there

are and the terms and conditions with local tourist offices.

Flying over the Loire Valley: The tourist authorities for each *département* can give you information on helicopter, plane and hot air balloon trips.

Garden Festivals: The Château de Chaumont puts on the Festival International du Jardin (*see* p.225). Doué-la-Fontaine hosts a famous rose festival (*www.journeesdelarose.com*), as does the Prieuré de St-Cosme just outside Tours. The CDTs should be able to provide you with brochures listing the wide array of gardens open to the public.

Golf: There are usually a few golf courses per *département*. For further details, contact the CDT for the relevant information.

Horse-riding: Local tourist offices should have lists of *centres equestres/centres hippiques*.

River boats: The easiest places to go boating (sometimes on an old-style vessel) include Blois, Amboise, Saumur and Montjean-sur-Loire on the Loire; Briare in the Orléanais; Olivet on the Loiret; St-Aignan, Montrichard and Chisseaux on the Cher; Vendôme on the Loir; Angers on the Maine; and Chenillé-Changé on the Mayenne.

Son-et-lumière: These are popular night-time displays at some of the most famous châteaux, with illuminations and, usually, an historical play. The most important ones are: in the Blésois, at Blois and Cheverny; and in Touraine, at Amboise, Chenonceau and Azay-le-Rideau.

Walking: *See* 'Getting Around', p.65, for information on the GRs and other walks.

Water sports: The big towns all have a lake near to them where a variety of water sports are usually on offer. There are a few others dotted around the countryside.

Zoos: There are two excellent zoos in the Loire Valley, one near St-Aignan, close to the Cher, and one in Doué-la-Fontaine. There is also a major zoo outside La Flèche by the Loir.

Time

France is 1 hour ahead of GMT and BST, and 6 hours ahead of US Eastern.

Tourist Information

French Government Tourist Offices

On the web, look up the very useful *www.franceguide.com*.

Australia: Level 20, 25 Bligh St, Level 22, NSW 2000 Sydney, t (02) 9231 5244.

Canada: 1981 Av McGill College, No.490, Montreal H3A 2W9, t (514) 876 9881.

Ireland: 10 Suffolk St, Dublin 1, t (01) 679 0813.

UK: 178 Piccadilly, London W1J 9AL, t 0906 824 4123 (calls charged at 60p/min).

USA: 444 Madison Av, New York, NY 10022, t (410) 286 8310.

John Hancock Center, Suite 3214, 875 North Michigan Ave, Chicago, IL 60611, t (312) 751 7800.

9454 Wilshire Bd, Suite 715, Beverly Hills, CA 90212, t (310) 271 6665.

1 Biscayne Tower, Suite 1750 – 2 South B Tower, 2 South Biscayne Bld, Miami, FL 33131, t (305) 373 81 77.

Comités Régionaux du Tourisme

Regional tourist authorities for the Loire are:

Comité Régional du Tourisme Centre-Val de Loire, 37 Av de Paris, 45000 Orléans, t 02 38 79 95 00, *www.visaloire.com*.

Conseil Régional des Pays de la Loire, 44966 Nantes Cedex 9, t 02 28 20 50 00, *www.paysdelaloire.fr*.

Comités Départementaux de Tourisme

The following is a list of each Comité Départemental du Tourisme (CDT) relevant to this guidebook, excellent starting points for gathering information. The Loisirs Accueil sections can even offer planned trips and make reservations.

Comité Départemental du Tourisme du Cher, Maison Départementale de Tourisme, 5 Rue de Séraucourt, 18000 Bourges, t 02 48 48 00 10, *www.berrylecher.com*. **Loisirs Accueil Cher**, same address, t 02 48 48 00 18, *loisirsaccueil@cdt18.tv*.

Comité Départemental du Tourisme du Loiret, 8 Rue d'Escures, 45000 Orléans, t 02 38 78 04 04, *www.tourismloiret.com*. **Loisirs Accueil Loiret**, same address, t 02 38 62 04 88.

Comité Départemental du Tourisme du Loir-et-Cher, Maison du Loir-et-Cher, 5 Rue Voûte du Château, B.P.149, 41005 Blois Cedex, t 02 54 57 00 41, *www.chambordcountry.com*.

Comité Départemental du Tourisme de Touraine, 9 Rue Buffon, B.P.3217, 37032 Tours Cedex, t 02 47 31 42 58, *www.tourism-touraine.com*. **Loisirs Accueil Touraine-Val de Loire**, 38 Rue Augustin Fresnel, B.P.139, 37171 Chambray-les-Tours Cedex, t 02 47 27 56 10 or t 02 47 48 37 13, *www.loire-valley-holidays.com*.

Comité Départemental du Tourisme de l'Anjou, Place Kennedy, B.P.32147, 49021 Angers Cedex 02, t 02 41 23 51 51, *www.anjou-tourisme.com*.

Comité Départemental du Tourisme de la Loire-Atlantique, 2 Allée Baco, B.P.20502, 44005 Nantes Cedex 1, t 02 51 72 95 30, *www.cdt44.com*. **Loisirs Accueil Loire-Atlantique**, same address, t 02 51 72 95 31 or t 02 51 72 95 32, *loire-atlantique.resa@cdt44.com*.

Local Tourist Offices

Local tourist offices can go by the name of *syndicats d'initiative* as well as *offices du tourisme*. In smaller French villages this service is provided by the town hall (*mairie*). They distribute free maps and town plans, and hotel, camping and self-catering accommodation lists for their area, and can inform you about sporting events, leisure activities and wine estates open for visits. Addresses and phone numbers are listed in the text. Hours are generally Mon–Sat 9–12 and 2–6. Smaller ones often close Sun.

Where to Stay

Hotels

As in most countries, the tourist authorities grade hotels by their facilities (not by charm or location) with stars. Hotels with no stars are not necessarily dives: their owners probably never bothered filling out a form for the tourist authorities. Most hotels have a wide range of rooms and prices; a large room with antique furniture, a view and a bathroom will cost much more than a poky back room in the same hotel, with a window overlooking a car park and the WC down the hall.

Single rooms are relatively rare and usually cost two-thirds the price of a double; rarely will a hotelier give you a discount if only doubles are available (because each room has its own price). On the other hand, if there are three or four of you, triples or quads or adding extra beds to a double room is usually cheaper than staying in two rooms. **Breakfast** (usually coffee, a croissant, bread and jam) is nearly always optional.

Room rates rise considerably in the busy season (Easter holidays and summer), when some hotels with restaurants will require that you take half board (*demi-pension* – breakfast plus a set lunch or dinner). Many hotel restaurants are superb and are listed in the text; non-residents are usually welcome.

Your holiday will be much sweeter if you **book ahead**, especially from May to October, when rooms can be snapped up very early. Phoning or emailing ahead is always a good policy, although hotels will only confirm a room with the receipt of a credit card number covering the first night. Certain tourist offices will call around and book a room for you on the spot for free or a nominal fee.

Umbrella organizations such as Logis et Auberges de France, Relais de Silence or the prestigious Châteaux et Hôtels de France and Relais et Châteaux promote and guarantee the quality of independently owned hotels. Many are recommended in the text. Larger tourist offices usually stock their booklets, or you can pick them up before you leave from the French National Tourist Office.

Chambres d'hôtes, bed and breakfasts, are in private homes, châteaux or farms, or may be connected to restaurants or wine estates. Local tourist offices can provide listings. Prices tend to be moderate to inexpensive.

Also try **B&B France**, PO Box 66, Bell St, Henley-on-Thames, Oxon RG9 1XS, **t** (01491) 578 803, *www.bedbreak.com* (catalogue £15.25); or in France, Association Française BAB France and Bed & Breakfast (GB), 9 Rue Jacques Louvel Tessier, 75010 Paris, **t** 01 42 01 34 34.

Youth Hostels and *Gîtes d'Etape*

Most cities and resort areas have youth hostels (*auberges de jeunesse*) which offer simple dormitory accommodation and breakfast to people of any age for €8.50–25 a night. Most offer kitchen facilities as well, or inexpensive meals. They are the best deal if you're travelling on your own; for people travelling together, a one-star hotel can be just as cheap. A downside is that many hostels are either in the suburbs where the last bus goes by at 7pm, or miles from any transport at all in the country. In the summer the only way to be sure of a room is to arrive early in the day. Most require a Hostelling International card, which you can often purchase on the spot, although regulations say you should buy them in your home country from your national YHA.

A *gîte d'étape* is a simple shelter with bunk beds and a rudimentary kitchen set up by a village along GR walking paths or a scenic bike route. Again, lists are available for each *département*. They cost about €9–15 a night.

Camping

Camping is very popular in France and there's at least one camp site in every town, often an inexpensive, no-frills place run by the local authorities (*camping municipal*). Other sites are graded with stars from four to one: at the top of the line you can expect lots of trees and grass, hot showers, a pool or beach, sports facilities, a grocer's, a bar and/or a restaurant, for prices rather similar to one-star hotels.

Tourist offices have complete lists of camp sites in their regions. If you plan to move around a lot, pick up a *Guide Officiel Camping/Caravanning*, available in most French bookshops. A number of UK holiday firms book camping holidays and offer discounts on Channel ferries: try Canvas Holidays, **t** (01383) 629000, *www. canvasholidays.co.uk*; Eurocamp Travel, **t** (01606) 787000, *www.eurocamp.co.uk*; or Keycamp Holidays, **t** 0870 700 0123, *www.keycamp.co.uk*.

Gîtes de France and Other Self-catering Accommodation

The Loire Valley has a range of self-catering accommodation, from inexpensive farm cottages to history-laden châteaux, fancy villas, flats or even on board canal boats. The

Hotel Price Ranges

Note: Prices listed here and elsewhere in this book are for a double room.

luxury	€230 and over
expensive	€90–230
moderate	€60–90
inexpensive	€30–60
cheap	under €30

Self-catering Holidays

France

Château de la Guillonnière, La Guillonnière, Dienne 86410, **t** 05 49 42 05 46, *www. rent-a-castle.com*. Cottages, B&B and castles.

UK

Allez France, 27a West St, Storrington, West Sussex RH20 4DZ, **t** 0870 160 5743, *www.allezfrance.com*. Wide variety of accommodation, from cottages to châteaux.

Bowhills, Mayhill Farm, Swanmore, Southampton SO32 2QW, **t** (01489) 872727, *www.bowhills.co.uk*. Luxury villas and farm-houses, mostly with pools.

Chez Nous, Spring Mill, Earby, Barnoldswick, Lancashire BB94 0AA, **t** 08700 781 400, *www.cheznous.com*. Over 3,000 privately owned holiday cottages and B&Bs.

Dominique's Villas, 25 Thames House , 140 Battersea Park Rd, London SW11 4NB, **t** (020) 7738 8772, *www.dominiquesvillas.co.uk*. Large villas and châteaux with pools.

French Life, 26 Church Rd, Horsforth, Leeds, LS18 5LG, **t** 08704 44 88 77, *www. cottage-holidays-france.co.uk*. Selection of villages and cottages in the Loire region.

Owners In France, Harbour House, New Harbour Rd South, Poole, Dorset, BH15 4AJ, **t** 0870 901 3400, *www.ownersinfrance.com*. Privately owned properties in the area.

Vacances en Campagne, Bignor, Pulborough, West Sussex RH20 1QD, **t** (01798) 869 433, *www.indiv-travellers.com*. Farmhouses, villas and *gîtes* all over France.

VFB Holidays, Normandy House, High St, Cheltenham GL50 3FB, **t** (01242) 240340, *www.vfbholidays.co.uk*. From rustic gîtes to luxurious farmhouses and hotels; also provides river cruises.

USA

At Home in France, P.O. Box 643, Ashland, OR 97520, **t** (541) 488 9467, *www. athomeinfrance.com*. Apartments, cottages, villas and farm- and manor houses.

Families Abroad, 194 Riverside Drive, New York, NY 10025, **t** (212) 787 2434, **t** (718) 768 6185, *www.familiesabroad.com*. Sabbatical and vacation rentals, in apartments, villas and châteaux.

Hideaways International, 767 Islington St, Portsmouth, NH 03801, **t** 800 843 4433, **t** (603) 430 4433, **f** (603) 430 4444, *www.hideaways.com*. Villas, farmhouses and châteaux in the Loire.

Loire Tours, 158 Crosby St #3B, New York, NY 10012, **t** 800 755 9313. Studios, apartments and villas.

Fédération Nationale des Gîtes de France is a French government service offering accom-modation by the week in rural areas. Lists with photos arranged by *département* are available from the Maison des Gîtes de France, 59 Rue St-Lazaire, 75439 Paris Cedex 09, **t** 01 49 70 75 75, *www.gites-de-france.fr*, or in the UK from their official agents, Brittany Ferries, **t** 08705 360 360. If you want to stay in châteaux, request the *Chambres d'Hôtes et Gîtes de Prestige*.

Other options are advertised in the Sunday papers, or contact one of the firms listed in the box. The accommodation they offer will nearly always be more costly than a *gîte*, but the discounts holiday firms can offer on ferries, plane tickets or car hire can make up for the difference.

The Loire from Sancerre to Orléans

08

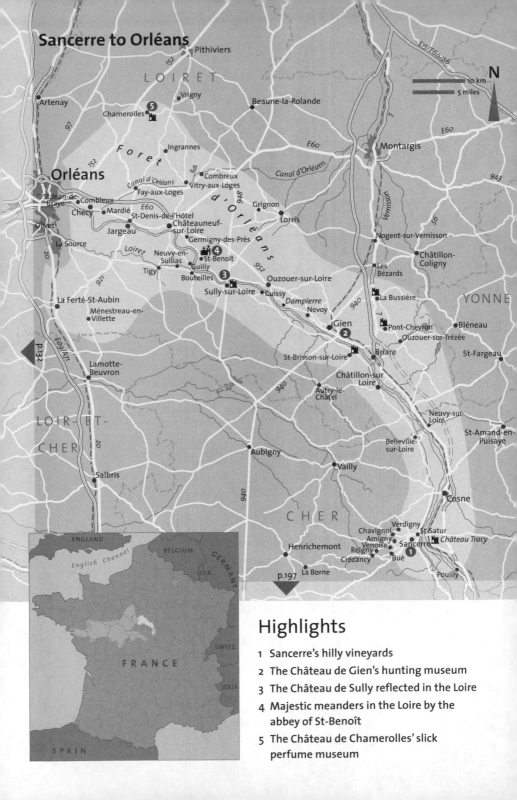

Sancerre to Orléans

N

to km
5 miles

LOIRET

Pithiviers
Vrigny
Artenay
Chamerolles **5**
Beaune-la-Rolande
Montargis
Ingrannes
E60
E60
Foret
Combreux
Orléans
Vitry-aux-Loges
Canal d'Orléans
Canal d'Orléans
Fay-aux-Loges
St-Jean-de-
Braye
Combleux
Grignon
Nogent-sur-Vernisson
Mardié
Checy
E60
St-Denis-de-l'Hôtel
Lorris
Châtillon-
Coligny
Olivet
Jargeau
Châteauneuf-
sur-Loire
d'Orléans
Germigny-des-Prés
Les
Bézards
La Source
Loiret
Neuvy-en-
Sullias
St-Benoît **4**
YONNE
Tigy
Guilly
Bouteilles **3**
Ouzouer-sur-Loire
La Bussière
Bléneau
Sully-sur-Loire
Cuissy
La Ferté-St-Aubin
Dampierre
Nevoy
Pont-Chevron
Ouzouer-sur-Trézée
Ménestreau-en-
Villette
Gien **2**
St-Fargeau
St-Brisson-sur-Loire
Briare
Lamotte-
Beuvron
Châtillon-sur-
Loire
Autry-le-
Châtel
Neuvy-sur-
Loire
LOIR-ET-
CHER
St-Amand-en-
Puisaye
Salbris
Belleville-
sur-Loire
Aubigny
Vailly
Cosne
Verdigny
Chavignol
St-Satur
Henrichemont
Amigny
Venoise
Sancerre **1**
Château Tracy
Reigny
Crézancy
Bué
p.197
La Borne
Pouilly

ENGLAND
English Channel
BELGIUM
GERMANY
LUX.
FRANCE
SWITZ.
ITALY
SPAIN

Highlights

1 Sancerre's hilly vineyards

2 The Château de Gien's hunting museum

3 The Château de Sully reflected in the Loire

4 Majestic meanders in the Loire by the
   abbey of St-Benoît

5 The Château de Chamerolles' slick
   perfume museum

The sensuous vine-covered hills of Sancerre produce one of the best-known white wines along the Loire. Take the winding road up to Sancerre town to get a full view over the Sancerrois area and a long stretch of the Loire before heading down to explore the wine villages tucked into the folds of the area's lovely rounded hills.

After Sancerre, the landscapes become more gentle as the Loire curves slowly up towards Orléans. Most of the châteaux open to visitors in this area are built of brick rather than the bright white limestone most often associated with the Loire Valley. Of the brick beauties vying for your attention, the tattooed Château de Gien contains an impressive museum on hunting, with enough material to interest even those opposed to the sport, while the Château de Chamerolles underwent a major facelift in the 1990s and is now devoted to the history of perfume. The one major white-stone château along this stretch of the Loire is that at Sully, at times magnificently reflected in the river's waters. The greying Château de St-Brisson has had a tougher time, abandoned by the Loire, but now puts on displays of medieval war machines.

You should always bear in mind that the religious legacy along the Loire is as strong as the lordly one; the Loire Valley boasts as many fine churches as fine châteaux. The major religious stop along this section of the Loire is the abbey of St-Benoît, in medieval times one of the most significant religious institutions in France, whose reputation was built on the bones of that greatest of influences on Western monasticism, the Italian saint Benedict.

Smaller curiosities to seek out in this chapter include: the mosaics of Briare, together with that town's elegant Eiffel bridge; the appealing pottery works of Gien; and the waterside villages which may have lost their river trade, but which have kept their atmospheric cobbled quays. The Loire and its tributaries acted for centuries as the major transport routes of the region, and this fact is well recalled at the museum dedicated to Loire mariners and river trading at Châteauneuf-sur-Loire. Since the war, the Loire has sadly seen several nuclear power stations sprout up along its length; if you follow this chapter along its course, you'll be treated to two. This hasn't stopped the river west of Sully being classified part of a UNESCO World Heritage Site; it's just odd that Sancerre has been left out, as it occupies one of the prettiest spots along the whole of the great river.

Sancerre and the Sancerrois

Such is the attention lavished on the famous white wine of Sancerre that the beauty of the town of Sancerre is often overlooked. The wine of the Sancerrois has become so successful since the war that the herds of goats that once grazed in these parts have been pushed west into the hills of the neighbouring Pays Fort as the vines have taken over almost every square inch of land. However, the area's goat's cheese, like the wines, still enjoys an international reputation.

Getting There

A train line from Paris passes through Cosne-Cours-sur-Loire; change there for the short bus link up to Sancerre. It isn't easy to reach Sancerre from west along the Loire using public transport; from Orléans, take a bus to Gien, then join the rail network.

Tourist Information

Sancerre: Office de Tourisme, Rue de la Croix de Bois, **t** 02 48 54 08 21, *www. ville-sancerre.fr*.
St-Satur: Office de Tourisme, Place de la République, 18300 St-Satur, **t** 02 48 54 01 30, *www.sancerre.net/saint-satur*.

Market Day

Sancerre: Sat morning and Tues morning.

Where to Stay and Eat

Sancerre ✉ 18300

Le Panoramic, 18 Rempart des Augustins, **t 02 48 54 22 44, *www.panoramicotel.com* (*inexpensive*). The spectacular views surpass the dullish modern architecture of this very well-located, comfortable hotel on the slopes just below Sancerre centre. The place has a good restaurant, **La Tasse d'Argent**, **t** 02 48 54 01 44 (*menus €15–32; closed Wed out of season*). *Closed Jan.*

La Tour, 31 Nouvelle Place, **t** 02 48 54 00 81, *www.la-tour-sancerre.fr* (*menus €30–53*). The swishest restaurant among the many choices on Sancerre's main square, with a smart beamed dining room. It's a good place to try regional specialities, such as goat's cheese and Berry lentils. *Closed over Christmas and New Year's Day.*

Auberge La Pomme d'Or, Place de la Mairie, **t** 02 48 54 13 30 (*menus €14.50–34; closed Tues pm and Wed summer, Tues–Wed rest of year*). In an interesting corner of gabled houses in a quieter area by the classical town hall, a reputed restaurant with small but well-chosen menus and an excellent wine list. *Closed over Christmas.*

St-Satur ✉ 18300

***Hôtel de la Loire, 2 Quai de la Loire, **t** 02 48 78 22 22, *www.hotel-de-la-loire.com* (*€60–90*). This newly reopened, lovingly restored hotel stretching along by the river offers the most characterful and appealing accommodation in the whole area. Each of the 10 stylish bedrooms has a view of the Loire waters flowing by. Georges Simenon, the Belgian author of the Maigret detective stories, who worked at the Château de Tracy on the other side of the river, apparently wrote some of his works here.

Le Jardin de St-Thibault, 7 Rue des Ponts, **t** 02 48 54 12 28 (*menus €14.50–33.50; closed Mon and Tues*). This restaurant may lie on the busy road from the Loire bridge towards Sancerre, but it has a delightful walled patio on which to savour quite gourmet local cuisine – including *couilles d'âne*, 'donkey's balls' (actually eggs in red wine!), and goat's cheese fritters. *Closed Nov.*

Verdigny-en-Sancerre ✉ 18300

L'Auberge du Vigneron, **t** 02 48 79 38 68, (*inexpensive*). Simple local favourite tucked away in this winemakers' village close to Sancerre. Lots of the dishes feature ingredients cooked in wine (*menus €14–21*).

Sancerre

The hilltop town of Sancerre dominates the Sancerrois and provides visitors with magical views down on to the Loire, the meanders to the south like a river disappearing into the background of a Gothic painting. To the north, you may be able to make out the huge chimneys of the nuclear power station of the unfortunately named Belleville-sur-Loire, churning out artificial clouds of vapour into the sky and marking the northern frontier of the old province of the Berry along the Loire.

During the Hundred Years' War, Sancerre acted as one of the important frontier posts of the shrivelled French kingdom, facing Burgundy, its enemy and poisonous ally of the English. Jean de Bueil of Sancerre became familiarly known as the Scourge of the English and was a loyal companion to Joan of Arc. What's more, in the 1460s he recorded his experiences from some of his later campaigns in *Le Jouvencel*, often described as the first French historical novel.

In the 16th century Sancerre became a powerful little Protestant stronghold during the French Wars of Religion. Catholic revenge followed in a terrible siege led by the Maréchal de la Châtre in 1573. The great 19th-century French historian Michelet described this siege as one of the most dreadful events in French history; the citizens of Sancerre were reported to have been reduced to eating crushed slate in their desperation. A further show of Protestant sympathies led Henri II de Bourbon, the early 17th-century aristocratic governor of the province of the Berry, to destroy most of the town's remaining fortifications, including its castle, leaving just one flint tower.

Sancerre's Vines of Success and Some Delicious Goats' Droppings

The lines of vines reach up and stretch around the Sancerrois like glorious patterned cloth fitted on the hillsides. Sancerre is known far and wide for the fine, crisp white wines these vines produce. Made from the Sauvignon Blanc grape variety, they frequently contain hints of gooseberry. A small amount of red wine is also produced in these parts, generally fetching a high price because of its rarity and its popularity in trendy Parisian restaurants. The reds are made from Pinot Noir grapes and can be delicately fruity.

A tour of the Sancerrois' wine villages is well worth undertaking. Verdigny and Chavignol, just northwest of town, are two highly regarded names in the Sancerrois. In very vinous **Verdigny**, one of the best wine estates to visit is that of the **André Dezat** household (*t 02 48 79 38 82; closed Sun and public hols*). André Dezat was one of the locals central in bringing Sancerre its postwar wine success, making sure that producers went for quality, although in recent years wine critics have complained that the wines of the area as a whole aren't always up to scratch.

Chavignol is the king of the *crottins* (meaning "droppings"), the affectionate name given to the goat's cheeses of these parts. You'll find cheese shops vying for attention with the wine cellars in the village. Among the latter, you might try **Roger Moreux** (*t 02 48 54 05 79; closed Sun*). The *cave* is small and charming, the wine excellent, some of it aged in oak. On a larger scale, **Henri Bourgeois** (*t 02 48 78 53 20, www. bourgeois-sancerre.com*), is a big Sancerre producer who can offer a wide range of quality wines and a nice tasting.

Other particularly appealing Sancerrois wine villages to head for include the batch just west of Sancerre town – look out for **Amigny, Venoize, Bué, Reigny** and **Crézancy**, for instance, where you can seek out cellars at which to taste and buy wines. **Pouilly-Fumé**, another very popular Loire white-wine producing *appellation*, lies east just across the Loire from Sancerre, on the Burgundy rather than the Berry side of the river. The reputed, and to English-speakers comically named, **Château Tracy** is a very well-known, aristocratic Pouilly-Fumé estate. It's not open to passing visitors, but stands above the Loire almost opposite Sancerre and is worth going to take a look at just for its charming location.

On the pinnacle of the town's hill, it still stands apart in its own clump of trees. The houses around it appear to have been shoved unceremoniously together on the hilltop as though they were a terrible inconvenience for the winemakers, who have otherwise colonized almost every centimetre of ground around Sancerre with vines.

Sancerre is a wonderful town to wander around. But beyond the winemakers and their shops it doesn't have any major cultural sites. The **Tour des Fiefs** of the château is rarely open (*check opening times with tourist office, or* **t** *02 48 78 51 52*). It looks dark and forbidding above the town, like the reflection of an evil lord dominating his subjects. Anyway, you can enjoy almost as good views from many of Sancerre's streets. **Nouvelle Place**, the main square, looks unselfconsciously charming without being over-prettified or over-restored, although its name hints at the peculiar sunken bunker of a building in the middle, housing the tourist office. Walk down some of the steep streets that lead away from this square to admire the houses provided with entrances the size of barn doors, awaiting the grape harvest. The two big winemaking names to visit in Sancerre itself are Mellot and Vacheron, with highly visible shops.

Other specialities you can find in town include goat's cheese, local biscuits known as Croquets de Sancerre, and local stoneware pottery, for instance at the Atelier d'Art de la Tour, just off one corner of Nouvelle Place, made on the spot. In the tourist season there are exhibitions by artists from further afield.

St-Satur

St-Satur is the town right by the Loire below Sancerre. Its two central grain silos the size of substantial churches may be ugly, but the riverside area of St-Thibault has plenty of appeal. On top of that, St-Satur has good sports facilities, including an outdoor swimming pool. The **Golf du Sancerrois** (**t** *02 48 54 11 22, www.sancerre.net/ golf*), lies just a stone's throw away. The place also has a boating harbour. You might be tempted to go on an **accompanied canoe trip** on the Loire – contact **Loire Nature Découverte**, Quai de la Loire, 18300 St-Satur, **t/f** *02 48 78 00 34, www.pays-sancerre-sologne.com/randonnees/canoe.htm*. It can be an exhilarating way of seeing the Loire from really close quarters.

The Loire Around Briare and Gien

Coming north along the Loire from Sancerre and the old province of the Berry into the Orléanais, head swiftly past the ugly brute of a power station at Belleville-sur-Loire to Briare and Gien. Although these two towns lie just outside the main Loire Valley tourist trail, they are each proud of their artistic attractions. We also suggest a few somewhat ignored châteaux to visit nearby.

Briare

Briare, unusually for the Loire, is marked more by the 19th century than the medieval and Renaissance periods. It's best-known for its **Pont-Canal**, a bridge built in the Belle

Getting Around

There are **train** services to Briare and Gien from Paris, but not a wide choice of trains. For the area west of Gien, use local bus services run by Rapides du Val de Loire (t 02 38 61 90 00, *www.rvl-info.com*), passing through Sully-sur-Loire and Châteauneuf-sur-Loire.

Tourist Information

Briare: 1 Place Charles de Gaulle, 45250 Briare, t 02 38 31 24 51, *tourisme.briare@wanadoo.fr*.
Gien: Place Jean Jaurès, B.P.13, 45501 Gien, t 02 38 67 25 28, *www.gien.fr*.

Market Days

Briare: Friday morning.
Gien: Saturday morning; food market Wednesday morning.

Where to Stay and Eat

Briare ✉ **45250**
**Le Cerf, 22–24 Bd Buyser, t 02 38 37 00 80, f 02 38 37 05 15 (*inexpensive*). Close to the sweet port, the rooms quite recently redone.
**Auberge du Pont-Canal, 19 Rue du Pont-Canal, t 02 38 31 24 24, *www.auberge-du-pont-canal.com* (*inexpensive*). You can't get closer to the water to eat than at this inn (€13–29; *restaurant closed Sun pm and Mon Jan–May*). Closed Oct–24 Dec.
Bateaux Croisières, contact the Maison Eclusière, Port de Plaisance, B.P.58, t 02 38 37 12 75, *www.bateaux-touristiques.com*. You can actually eat *on* the water if you take this cruise (lunch available every day early April–Oct; dinner Sat only mid-May–Aug). The journey lasts 3½ hours (€33–35). (They also offer a cruise without food; 1½ hours; €15–17 adults; no children under 3.)

Les Bézards ✉ **45290 (Boismorand)**
****Auberge des Templiers, entrance on the N7, t 02 38 31 80 01, *www.lestempliers.com* (*expensive*). The height of luxury and expense in the area. The entrance may stand uncomfortably close to the busy road, but the rooms and luxurious facilities are dotted around in the extensive grounds beyond.

The cuisine has an absurdly high reputation, for which you'll pay through the nose (*menus €53–114*). *Closed Feb.*

Autry-le-Châtel ✉ **45500**
Auberge Les Trainats, south of St-Brisson, off the road from Autry to Châtillon-sur-Loire, t 02 38 36 80 64, *perso.wanadoo.fr/trainats*. A country inn close to the borders of the Berry and Sologne regions. In the restaurant (*open Fri pm–Sun lunch only and you must book; menus €15.50–21.50*), try such specialities as duck with peaches, guinea fowl with cabbage, or the Berry favourite, pâté of potatoes. Also gîtes for rent. *Closed Jan.*

Gien ✉ **45500**
**La Poularde, 13 Quai de Nice, t 02 38 67 36 05, f 02 38 38 18 78 (*inexpensive*). Overlooks the plane trees by the Loire. It has comfortable rooms and offers fancy cooking (*menus €25–41; closed Sun pm and Mon lunch Feb–Nov, Sun pm and all day Mon Nov–Jan.*) Closed first two weeks of Jan.
**Sanotel, 21 Quai de Sully, t 02 38 67 61 46, *www.perso.wanadoo.fr/sanotel* (*inexpensive*). The best views in town if you ask for a room overlooking the Loire, as this hotel is on the south bank, looking across to old Gien. The rooms are comfortable modern boxes, with decent-sized bathrooms. You'll find a choice of basic restaurants and hotels by the busy Loire north bank road.

Nevoy ✉ **45500**
Auberge du Tranchoir, t 02 38 67 51 98, *www.aubergeetfermeauberge.com* (€34). The cow shed has been converted into a simple restaurant at this former farm on the edge of the sprawling forest of Orléans. Vegetable terrines, leek tarts and ewe's milk cheeses count among the specialities (*menu €17*). Book in advance to sleep and eat here.

Ouzouer-sur-Loire ✉ **45570**
L'Abricotier, 106 Rue de Gien, t 02 38 35 07 11, f 02 38 35 63 63. A haven of good cuisine on a triangle of land just slightly off the busy north-bank D952 between Gien and Sully (*menus €21.50–49; closed Sun pm, Mon, and Wed pm*). Closed mid-Aug–early-Sept, and over Christmas.

Époque to carry a canal over the Loire, enabling boats to avoid the danger of crossing the great river itself. The bridge was constructed by none other than Gustave Eiffel's company; it's rather surprising Briare hasn't baptized the thing the Pont Eiffel. While Eiffel's great Parisian erection sticks so vulgarly into the air, this bridge extends elegantly over the Loire. Spacious footpaths were thoughtfully provided either side, embellished with period lamps which give it a rather incongruous metropolitan feel in the midst of its rural town setting. The huddle of houses along the nearby levee, though, gives a typical picture of a long-established little Loire-side community.

Closer to the centre of town, you'll come to Briare's appealing **port de plaisance** (marina). The Canal de Briare on the north side of the Loire was ordered by King Henri IV's dynamic minister Sully (*see* p.98) in the first half of the 17th century; it was particularly significant as it linked the Loire with the Seine and hence Paris. The **Maison des Deux Marines** (*open June–Sept 10–12.30 and 2–6.30, Mar–May and Oct 2–6; 58 Boulevard Buyser, t 02 38 31 28 27, maison-2-marines@wanadoo.fr; adm*), a small affair, explains well how important both the Loire and the canals were to these parts in centuries past. Briare is a good place to hire a **river boat**; contact **Loisirs Accueil Loiret**, 8 Rue d'Escures, 45000 Orléans, t 02 38 62 04 88, *www.tourismloiret.com*.

When the industrialist Jean-Felix Bapterosses set up in Briare in the middle of the 19th century, the town became a large producer of buttons, beads and then mosaics. Jean-Felix Bapterosses' commercial tricks and triumphs are charted in detail at the **Musée de la Mosaïque et des Emaux** (*open June–Sept 10–6.30 and Feb–May and Oct–Dec 2–6; 1 Boulevard Loreau, t 02 38 31 20 51, musee.mosaique@wanadoo.fr; adm*) opposite the Maison des Deux Marines. Only a small number of mosaics are displayed here, but the exhibits include a splendid strutting cockerel designed for the 1910 Universal Exhibition, a Grasset depiction of St Michael and, from the 1970s, a series of pieces by Victor Vasarely, whose obsession with geometrical abstraction lends itself well to the art. The story of the beads on show proves surprisingly interesting; as well as becoming fashionable with the likes of the great actress Sarah Bernhardt, they were also exported to Africa, where they were used for bartering.

The **church of St-Etienne** in the centre of town, built by Bapterosses' heirs at the end of the 19th century, is crammed with mosaics. A frieze of them runs round the outside of the whole edifice, enlivening the rather dull stone. Inside, in the heady confusion of neo-Byzantine, neo-Romanesque and neo-Renaissance architecture, mosaics proliferate too. The aisles are covered with a swirling river of little tiles, apparently symbolizing the Loire or the river of life, designed by Eugène Grasset of Larousse fame. Even the sad panels in the apse commemorating Briare's numerous war dead have been given mosaic backgrounds. The altar is decorated with beautiful Botticelli-style mosaic angels, but the results in the separate sacristy aren't as successful – two deer come to drink in what has been made to feel suspiciously like a bathroom.

Châteaux between Briare and Gien

Mosaics continue as a theme at the **Château de Pont-Chevron** (*open May–Aug Wed–Mon 2–6; t 02 38 31 92 02; adm*), a handful of kilometres north of Briare, off the D122 between the N7 and Ouzouer-sur-Trézée. Here you get a much earlier little lesson in their decorative uses. The chic neoclassical château itself was only built in 1900 for the d'Harcourt family, but its grounds conceal two excellent, if damaged, Gallo-Roman works, dated to the 2nd century, one showing a splendid tender-faced masculine sea-god's head. On the other side of the château the lawn leads to a romantic lily-covered lake.

A few kilometres further up the N7, the brick **Château de la Bussière** (*open July–Aug daily 10–6, April–June and Sept–11 Nov Wed–Mon 10–12 and 2–6;* **t** *02 38 35 93 35, www.coeur-de-France.com/labussiere.html; adm*) long lay on the main route from Paris to Lyon. One side of the courtyard stands a superb outbuilding, with lozenged decorations. This huge barn was constructed to receive the tithe, payment in kind from vast estates. It gives a good indication of how wealthy the La Bussière lords must once have been. A walled kitchen garden has been lovingly re-created nearby.

The château proper, the oldest parts dating back to the 14th century, has been over-restored, but the first view of it standing on a lovely lake (apparently planned by Le Nôtre) is delightful. Inside, 19th-century tastes prevail. The present proprietors have chosen fish as the theme of the visit. The most surprising exhibit lies in Damien Hirst pose in formaldehyde, a massive primitive albino fish known as a coelacanth.

The **Château de St-Brisson** (*open early April–mid-Nov Thurs–Tues 10–12 and 2–6; the demonstration of medieval war machines takes place roughly 5 July–16 Aug Thurs–Tues at 3.30 and Sun at 3.30 and 4.30;* **t** *02 38 36 71 29, www.coeur-de-France.com/st-brisson-chateau.html; adm*), on the south bank of the Loire opposite Briare, once lorded it over the river. Time has sadly distanced the two; the Loire has moved many hundreds of metres due to the effects of the building of the Briare canal, combined with the Loire's natural wandering tendencies. The castle remains dramatic though, particularly seen sticking out on its rock in such flat county.

The medieval stronghold developed into a hexagonal fort, well constructed to resist bombardment with its mixture of towers and angled walls. Parties in the Wars of Religion and the Revolution took destructive swipes at the place, and the wounds had to be patched up. The château was left to the parish at the end of the 1980s and is looked after by a team of enthusiastic local volunteers who are restoring parts of the sprawling structure bit by bit.

The interior is surprisingly old-style, the visit starting with a workaday kitchen dating back to the 16th century and an indoor well – looking down it, you can easily imagine secret passageways disappearing off into the countryside. The grand listed room in the château is the dining room. The arms of the various families who owned St-Brisson are painted on the beams and cleverly used by the guides to tell a little of the place's history. The most exciting figures to emerge are a medieval lord who became a ruthless pirate on the Loire and another who was so influenced by Rousseau's ideas that he went off to live in the woods in an attempt to convert back to the state of a noble savage – Rousseau persuaded him to come home to his château! You're taken up to see the servants' rooms and the fine roof timbers. The woodwork was apparently executed by Loire mariners, who often sought employment as carpenters in periods when the river was unnavigable.

To help compensate for the loss of its strategic position, the Château de St-Brisson now also flexes its little tourist muscles with demonstrations of medieval war machines, while its façades are dramatically lit up at night.

Gien

Pretty brick-patterned Gien, site of a river crossing over the Loire since ancient times, was bombed to smithereens in the Second World War, by the Germans in 1940 and by the Allies in 1944. Eighty per cent destroyed, the town was harmoniously restored after the conflict. The splendid hump-backed stone bridge was patched up and river-side façades were re-created using traditional brick patternings of trellises and chevrons.

Meanwhile, by a stroke of good fortune, the Château de Gien up the hill escaped the bombs. It has witnessed a few interesting moments in its history. Joan of Arc stopped here on her way to King Charles VII's coronation in Reims in 1429. The place was then rebuilt in the 1480s for Anne de Beaujeu, daughter of King Louis XI. She would serve a short while as regent of France for her brother, the young Charles VIII (*see* Amboise). A little later, King François I handed the regency to his mother, Louise de Savoie, here when he went off on his early 16th-century Italian campaign. And at points during the 16th-century Wars of Religion the royal family took refuge in the château, as did Louis XIV and Anne d'Autriche at the time of the Fronde uprising.

From the terrace in front of the château you can enjoy extensive views over the Loire, even taking in two nuclear power stations on a good day, Belleville to the south, Dampierre to the north. Surprising patterns picked out in black brick adorn some of the castle's outer walls like medieval masonic tattoos. The symbols include a stretched-out Star of David and, most appropriately given the modern museum inside, an arrow. A bronze deer expresses its surprise at your arrival out on the lawn.

Before those of you who detest hunting dismiss the **Musée International de la Chasse** (*open June–Sept 9–6, Jan–May and Oct–Dec 9–12 and 2–6; Château de Gien B.P. 99, t 02 38 67 69 69, www.coeur-de-france.com/gien-museedelachasse.html; adm*), it must be said that this place proves surprisingly interesting both historically and aesthetically. It shows extraordinarily well the excesses to which their love of the killer sport pushed the aristocracy, as it attempts to trace the history of hunting down the ages. It contains some international exhibits, including a collection of very fine German crossbows and guns encrusted with figures of running deer and dogs chasing rabbits, 19th-century Algerian guns, and falconry pieces from as far away as Qatar and Japan. French displays dominate though, the highlights being the paint-ings by Desportes, Louis XIV's specialist hunt artist – hunting was controlled by royal order for much of French history.

Horns – one over 4.5m long – pipes, engravings, decoy ducks, powder horns, buttons from hundreds of hunts... a wealth of hunt-related objects fill the rooms, and are all very well exhibited. Among the more curious items are an umbrella made of 'wood, silver and wolves' teeth' – one of the last wolves in the Berry was shot in 1900, you are informed; a shaving bowl with a deer painted in the bottom – one only hopes the owner never cut his throat in an overenthusiastic gesture thinking of the kills to come; and a hunting scene in that supremely elegant French porcelain, Biscuit de Sèvres – two beautiful women lie back with satisfaction after the killing of a deer, not the best of images for encouraging gentle masculine manners. Hunting legends recur, of the goddess Diana, of course, and of St Hubert. The story goes that the latter was so bitten by the hunting bug that he even ignored the observance of religious days to indulge his passion. Out in the forests one Good Friday, he had a vision of a deer with a crucifix between its antlers; the admonitory sign set him back on the straight and narrow and he stopped ignoring his religious duties.

One room is dedicated to the works of the sculptor Florentin Brigaud. His smooth, exotic, deliberately overpolished animal forms don't appear to be linked with hunting; his inspiration came instead from the Paris Colonial Exhibition of 1931 and the zoo in the capital's Jardin des Plantes. The château's great hall with its beautiful rafters contains some 80 paintings by Desportes. Some of his works are simple studies of animals, beautiful and undisturbing; others show the savagery of hunting. And then there are the tranquil scenes from after the hunt – dead ducks and hares draped over aristocratic balustrades like gorgeous decorative objects. Celebrity pieces also feature in the museum, among them three guns that belonged to Napoleon. Bonaparte is also represented in an extraordinary painting of the emperor hunting in Fontainebleau, ladies looking on from carriages as the deer trapped by the chase awaits the megalomaniac's bullet. A separate series of 19th-century bronzes acts as a reminder of how cruel the animal kingdom can be too, with panthers and lions overwhelming their prey.

Beside Gien's château stands the **church of Ste-Jeanne d'Arc**. The bombs only left the soaring entrance tower of the earlier 15th-century church. The exterior of the new edifice, by the architect André Gélis, reflects the traditional regional interest in brick-work with its rich patternings, but the window tops have been given the modern twist of triangular shapes, rather than rounded or lancet arches. Red brick reigns within as well as without, but a slightly sickly orange glow lights up the interior, emanating from the predominantly red and yellow stained glass by Max Ingrand. Gien potters created the striking ceramic plaques showing the Stations of the Cross, and the intriguing elongated religious statues perched around the choir and transepts. Look out for the particularly tender and unusual rendering of the Virgin and Child, the baby Jesus caressing and almost kissing his mother. Behind the organ, Joan of Arc puts in an appearance in the modern stained glass by François Bernard, her face interpreted in Cubist style. Soldiers stand out in one panel, depicted in the vivid colours traditionally reserved for figures of devils in medieval stained glass.

It's worth wandering down into town from the upper plateau, as the centre below can be quite lively, even if the cafés and restaurants along the riverside are somewhat blighted by the noise of the traffic passing right in front of them.

The **Gien Musée de la Faïencerie and Factory** (*pottery museum open early May–Sept 9–12.30 and 1.30–6.30 (opens 10 on Sun), Oct–Dec 9–12 and 2–6 (opens 10 on Sun), Jan–Apr 2–6; pottery factory open Mon–Sat; 78 Place de la Victoire, t 02 38 67 00 05,* *www.gien.com; adm*) lie a little west of the centre of town. It was an Englishman, Thomas Hall, who acquired a former convent here in 1821 and converted it into his pottery factory. The first room of the small museum contains a collection showing the diverse influences on the Gien factory's early production, demonstrating how derivative Gien pottery was. It became best known for its blue decorations, called, not very originally, '*bleu de Gien*'. A video explains, in English or French, how the pottery is made. Some of the exhibits likely to catch your eye in the museum are the magnificent oversized vases, over 6ft high, made for the 1900 Universal Exhibition, as was the superb Louis XIV-style clock, dripping with turquoise pendants and gymnastic putti holding the globe of the clock. Among further curious items are several *barbotines* – shiny-looking ceramic paintings. In the extensive factory shop you can see the range of today's output and search through seconds, including dinner services decorated with St-Exupéry drawings for his much-loved children's book, *Le Petit Prince*.

To get from Gien to Sully, consider avoiding the main road along the north bank, which passes in front of Dampierre nuclear power station. Instead, follow the south bank and branch off to Cuissy, the bumpy narrow riverside road a delight once you leave the four huge power station chimneys behind. This way you get close to the **Ile de Cuissy** in the middle of the Loire. Panels beside the road give details on the common species of birds to be found on the river and in particular on the terns that favour this spot, their eggs and their young merging with the very beige gravels here.

From Sully to the Outskirts of Orléans

The great annual gathering of Gaulish druids is supposed to have occurred in a sacred site somewhere around St-Benoît, along this stretch of the Loire, only the mysterious location (as with so many details on this culture) has been lost in the mists of time. Traces of the seemingly vibrant Carolingian life of the late Dark Ages in these parts have survived a little better, with a small but splendid mosaic from the period preserved at Germigny. The glories of this area, though, apart from the river itself, are medieval: the Romanesque abbey church of St-Benoît and the Gothic Château de Sully. It's also worth taking a look at the old Loireside quays in virtually all the towns and villages along this stretch, often wonderfully atmospheric if a little neglected. Châteauneuf-sur-Loire's museum on Loire river trading will teach you a thing or two about the life of the Loire's mariners.

Château de Sully

*Open April–Sept 10–6, Feb–March and Oct–Dec 10–12 and 2–5;
t 02 38 36 36 86, www.coeur-de-france.com/sully.html; adm.*

Enjoy, Sir, the pleasures of Paris while I am, by order of the king, in the most agreeable château and with the best company in the world.

Voltaire, in a letter to a friend, during his
royal-imposed exile at Sully from 1716 to 1719

Getting Around

Public transport seems about as unlikely in this area now as it was in the druids' days and, where it does exist, is as slow as going by boat. No trains serve the area. There is the occasional bus each day plying its way between Orléans and Gien, stopping at Sully-sur-Loire and Châteauneuf-sur-Loire run by Rapides du Val de Loire (t 02 38 61 90 00, www.rvl-info.com).

Tourist Information

Sully-sur-Loire: Place de Gaulle, B.P.12, 45600 Sully-sur-Loire, t 02 38 36 23 70, www.sully-sur-loire.fr.

St-Benoît-sur-Loire: 44 Rue Orléanaise, 45730 St-Benoît-sur-Loire, t/f 02 38 35 79 00, www.saint-benoit-sur-loire.fr.

Châteauneuf-sur-Loire: 3 Place Aristide Briand, 45110 Châteauneuf-sur-Loire, t 02 38 58 44 79, www.chateauneuf-sur-loire.com.

Jargeau: La Chanterie, B.P.19, 45150 Jargeau, t 02 38 59 83 42, www.jargeau.fr.

La Ferté-St-Aubin: Place des Cadets de la France Libre, B.P.3, t 02 38 64 67 93, f 02 38 64 61 39.

Lorris: 2 Rue des Halles, 45260 Lorris, t 02 38 94 81 42, www.ville-lorris.fr.

Market Days
Sully-sur-Loire: Monday.

Châteauneuf-sur-Loire: Friday.
Jargeau: Wednesday afternoon.
Lorris: Thursday morning.
Fay-aux-Loges: Wednesday morning.

Where to Stay and Eat

Sully-sur-Loire ✉ 45600
**Le Grand Sully, 10 Bd du Champ de Foire, t 02 38 36 27 56, f 02 38 36 44 54 (*inexpensive*). Doesn't look particularly grand actually, but the cuisine here has a solid reputation (*menus €26–35; closed Sun pm, Mon, and first fortnight in March*).

**Hôtel de la Poste, 11 Rue du Faubourg St-Germain, t 02 38 36 26 22, f 02 38 36 39 35 (*inexpensive*). The place is prettier approached by the shaded gravel courtyard at the back than by the entrance on the busy main road. The rooms are dull, but the food again comes recommended (*menus €15–33*).

St-Benoît-sur-Loire ✉ 45110
**Hôtel du Labrador, 7 Place de l'Abbaye, t 02 38 35 74 38, f 02 38 35 72 99 (*inexpensive*). Standing calmly close to the abbey church, the Hôtel du Labrador has typical, rather dull, local architecture, with openings characterized by brick surrounds, plus a modern section. The rooms aren't bad, some with beams or with a view over the country-side. *Closed Boxing Day to 20 Jan.*

This château makes one of the most beautiful pictures along the whole of the Loire, even if the landscape around it is rather flat. The sparkling white-stoned castle stands close enough to the Loire to be splendidly reflected in it at times, although its moats are supplied by a tributary called the Sange. The sturdy towers with their pepper-pot tops look a model of their medieval kind, but they actually had to be rebuilt in 1908.

Three great families owned the Château de Sully. From the 10th to the 14th centuries it was the barons of Sully. Maurice Sully was from this family, the bishop who went off to order the building of Paris' famed cathedral of Notre-Dame. Then the dukes of La Trémoïlle transformed the place, living here from the end of the 14th century to the start of the 17th. The rectangular Vieux Château giving onto the Loire was commissioned by the first dukes of this family. The Hundred Years' War was raging when work began on this great keep for Marie de Sully and her husband Guy de la Trémoïlle. They had a fine architect though, the plans being by Raymond du Temple, responsible in Paris for the remodelling of the Louvre for King Charles V and for the Château de Vincennes. Joan of Arc's lightning campaign against the English

Retreat at the abbey, t 02 38 35 72 43, www.abbaye-fleury.com. For men wishing to go on a spiritual retreat for a day or more, write to the *père hôtelier de l'abbaye*, or call him. You are given a simple cell, can join the services and eat in the refectory.

Châteauneuf-sur-Loire ✉ 45110

Hôtel du Parc and Restaurant de la Capitainerie, 1 Square du Général de Gaulle, t 02 38 58 42 16, *lacapitainerie@libertysurf.fr* (*inexpensive*). Appealing small hotel, delightfully located by the gates to the castle grounds. The little rooms are rustically furnished, while the restaurant serves classic French cuisine. On warm days, you can eat outside (*menus €22–39; closed Sun pm and Mon lunch*).

Auberge du Port, t 02 38 58 43 07, f 02 38 58 98 31 (*inexpensive*). Also nicely located, with just four basic rooms in the quiet area beside the Loire, this inn lies just a stone's throw away from the river (*menus €14–30; closed Sat lunch, Sun eve, and Wed eve*). Closed 15 days in Aug.

St-Denis-de-l'Hôtel ✉ 45550

**Le Dauphin, Avenue des Fontaines, t 02 38 46 29 29, f 02 38 59 07 63 (*inexpensive*). Quite a comfortable accommodation option, with a characterful old-style wood-beamed restaurant (*closed Sun pm, most of Aug, and 1 Dec*).

Chécy ✉ 45430

Les Courtils B&B, Rue de l'Ave, t 02 38 91 32 02, www.france-bonjour.com/les-courtils (*inexpensive*). The stocky tower of the village church peers down protectively onto this charming walled property where you can hear the church bells singing merrily through the daytime. The small, slightly awkward, but tastefully decorated rooms are under the eaves, in a specially converted barn. In the large reception room below, the owner displays some of her art. From the private garden you can appreciate a lovely, peaceful view down onto the Loire.

Combleux ✉ 45800

La Marine, t 02 38 55 12 69, www.residence-la-marine.com. Beautifully located in a peaceful waterside hamlet by a weir where the Canal d'Orléans meets the Loire, the utterly charming restaurant looks as if it belongs to another era. It has a terrace by the water where you can make the most of the waterside in summer (*menus €21–28*). You can also stay here in new studios (*from €145 for 3 nights*).

La Ferté-St-Aubin ✉ 45240

***Château Les Muids, Les Muids N20, t 02 38 64 65 14, www.chateauxhotels.com/muids (*moderate*). A splendidly patterned late 18th-century brick château 4km south of town, just off the N20. Not outrageously expensive

was halted here after her victory at Patay, when the Lorraine upstart was kept at Sully against her will by the fractious Georges de la Trémoïlle, son of Guy and favourite of Charles VII – not all the French proved to be fans of the Maid of Orléans.

In 1602 the château became the property of Maximilien de Béthune, one of the greatest ministers in French history (*see* box overleaf), who worked in the service of King Henri IV. He received the title of Duc de Sully, but French history prefers to refer to him simply as '*le Grand Sully*'. His descendants lived here until they sold the château to the *département* of the Loiret in 1962. By then the massive family home lay almost empty.

Since 1962, the new administration has been progressively restoring the château and buying up pieces linked to Le Grand Sully to embellish its rooms. Some of the chambers in the Vieux Château are on a vast scale. A splendid and much-needed focus has been given to one of these great halls by a series of tapestries illustrating the legend of Psyche, Cupid and the envious Venus. Its marbled effects are superb. The borders carry the de Béthune arms. The series was bought from another of the Duc de

for such an elegant stop, with swimming pool and tennis court in the grounds. Fine restaurant, including home-smoked specialities (*menus €20–42*).

La Ferme de La Lande, northeast out of town, **t** 02 38 76 64 37, **f** 02 38 64 68 87 (*inexpensive; closed Sun pm, Mon, and Wed pm*). Very tempting, sophisticated little country restaurant in an immaculate miniature 18th-century farm, once part of the Château de La Ferté-St-Aubin's estates.

Ménestreau-en-Villette ✉ 45240

La Ferme des Foucault B&B, off the Route de Sennely (D64), **t/f** 02 38 76 94 41, *www.france-bonjour.com/ferme-des-foucalt* (*moderate*). Lost in typical Sologne countryside some way out of the village are these splendid and spacious B&B rooms in a farmhouse restored by an enthusiastic American, Rosemary Beau, and her French husband.

You'll also find a number of good places around the Forest of Orléans:

Lorris ✉ 45260

Le Sauvage, 2 Place du Martroi, **t 02 38 92 43 79, **f** 02 38 94 82 46 (*inexpensive*). This hotel is well placed on the old square (menus €21–50; *restaurant closed Fri, and Sun eve*). *Closed Feb and most of Oct.*

Guillaume de Lorris, 8 Grande Rue, **t** 02 38 94 83 55. Some snazzy dishes here, where the zander may come with a *fumet de homard*, or the moules in profiteroles (*menus €21–46*). *Closed Mon, Tues and Sun pm, and first week in Jan, third week in Feb and last two weeks of Aug.*

Combreux ✉ 45530

L'Auberge de Combreux, 35 Rue du Gâtinais, **t 02 38 46 89 89, *www.auberge-de-combreux.fr* (*moderate*). Looks like an archetypal French village inn (some of its cosy rooms even have a fireplace), but it has modern attractions, such as a heated swimming pool, a tennis court and a golf range. Traditional French fare (*menus €29–36; closed Mon lunch*). *Closed mid-Dec–Jan.*

Vitry-aux-Loges ✉ 45530

Château du Plessis-Beauregard B&B, **t** 02 38 59 47 24, *plessisbeauregard@minitel.net* (*moderate; no smoking*). Extremely comfortable, elegant rooms in a long brick wing completed at either end by a tower. The large garden ending at the canal is delightful. Good value for this level of comfort, the rooms are provided with old furniture, *toile de Jouy* wallcoverings, crucifixes over the bed, and tasteful personal touches. You can meet the traditional French family that owns the château at the *table d'hôte*, when you can sample refined French family cooking (*table d'hôte €30.50*). *Closed at Christmas.*

Sully's castles, Rosny-sur-Seine, his birthplace. A room of similar dimensions above is given over to portraits of the Sully family, including one of Maximilien's brother, Philippe, governor to King Henri IV's son Gaston, who became the rebellious Gaston d'Orléans. Look out for the remnants of sumptuous wall paintings around the upper room. You can also visit the Grand Sully's bedroom, while a little oratory contains a copy of the tomb made for him and his second wife; their remains were transferred here from Nogent-le-Rotrou in 1934. Climb to the top of the Vieux Château to admire the 600-year-old rafters and to tread gingerly along the machicolated walkway with its views down on the Loire. The atmosphere changes in the wing where Sully had his private apartments. One ceiling is decorated with remarkable detailed images symbolizing Sully's devotion to the king, such as the eagle carrying Jupiter's bolts. Further paintings reflect major events involving Sully and Henri IV.

The Château de Sully offers a varied cultural programme through the year. The **Festival de Musique de Sully** brings classical music to the château at weekends from the end of May to mid-June; prestigious international players come to perform. Look

France in Sully's Safe Hands

Trusted companion of Protestant Henri de Navarre, the man who would reunite France at the end of the fanatical follies of the Wars of Religion, Le Grand Sully was given a succession of important posts when, in 1589, his master became King Henri IV of France, and the first French Bourbon royal. Having been made Grand Maître de l'Artillerie and Grand Voyer de France, in 1598 Sully was appointed *Surintendant des Finances*. As finance minister he became a vastly powerful man. He is commonly portrayed as a solid, reliable figure who did much to help revive the French economy after deeply troubled and divisive times, keeping a tight rein on the journey to recovery. Some of the greatest successes overseen by Sully under Henri IV's rule were the development of new roads and of the silk industry in France, the latter helping the country avoid paying for expensive foreign imports.

Henri IV was assassinated in 1610. From that period, Sully's star was in decline. Distanced from power under the new administration, he devoted himself to his estates and to expounding his theories. The very name of his oeuvre reads like the title of an accountant's diary, *Les Sages et Royales Oeconomies d'Estat*. In this work dedicated to his former boss 'Henri le Grand', he put forward his ideas on developing the economy through increased agricultural activity – probably a bedtime book for the more serious historians among you. The weighty tome was printed at Sully's expense, in one of the towers of the castle. Louis XIII did eventually confer on Sully the illustrious title of Maréchal de France in the man's old age, in recognition of his services to his father Henri IV.

out, too, for special themed visits round the castle – in costume, for children, or by candlelight on certain nights.

In summer, a large sandy beach stretches out indolently by the Loire in front of the château. As in so many such spots along the great river, campers set up home here during the tourist season. As for the **town of Sully** beside the château, it was heavily bombarded during the war, some 80 per cent being destroyed. It wasn't as well restored as neighbouring Gien, but is quite pleasant. Wandering around town you may spot a couple of statues honouring Sully, while the church of St-Ythier contains interesting stained-glass windows, one showing a tree of Jesse, another the story of a pilgrim on the way to Santiago de Compostela. Down around the semi-abandoned church of St-Germain, a cluster of Loire mariners' houses remains. The Loire froze over in 1985 and the postwar suspension bridge snapped under the pressure. So now Sully has one of the most recent crossings over the Loire.

Church of the Abbey of St-Benoît-sur-Loire or Fleury

Open to visitors 8am–9pm except during services (free). Guided tours (adm) 10.30 and 3 weekdays, 3.15 and 4.15 Sun and festivals. No tours first Fri Jan/Feb, Sun am, Easter weekend am; t 02 38 35 72 43, www.abbaye-fleury.com.

Old saints' bones held a particularly powerful fascination for the religious-minded societies of the Dark and Middle Ages which it is hard to emphasize strongly enough today. They weren't just viewed as physical reminders of the saints' exemplary lives; they were thought to work miracles and to be closely linked to divine powers.

Around 672, a band of monks who had settled at the recently founded Benedictine abbey at Fleury, by the Loire, decided to go in search of the bones of the saintly Benedict (Benoît in French). He was the Italian of the first half of the 6th century who founded the great Western European monastic order named after him. His *Regula Monachorum* set down the general rule for monasticism in the West, making him an extraordinarily important figure in the development of the Church in Western Europe. He had died at his monastery of Monte Cassino near Naples around 547, but this had been destroyed by Lombards in 580.

The group from Fleury went all the way to Monte Cassino to scour the ground and recover what they could find by way of relics of the saintly man. They carried back to their abbey on the Loire what they claimed to be Benedict's bones. Outraged Italian monks protested at this action, but a papal declaration accepted that the remains should stay at Fleury. The abbey consequently became an extremely venerated site in western Christendom. The 11 July, known as the day of the *translation* of Benedict's bones, is still celebrated by the Benedictine order as a whole.

In Carolingian times, towards the end of the 8th century, Théodulfe, a renowned theologian and close adviser to Charlemagne, became abbot of Fleury, or St-Benoît as it would later become better known. The abbey blossomed as one of the centres of what has been described as the Carolingian renaissance. It was a place of great importance for teaching and learning in Charlemagne's empire, and also one that produced superb illuminated manuscripts. Nothing remains of those times, the abbey of that period having disappeared, the surviving manuscripts and treasures from it dispersed in the 16th-century Wars of Religion, when Abbot Odet de Coligny, brother of the leader of the Protestants, suddenly and treacherously converted from Catholicism and revealed the hide-outs of the abbey's riches to the Protestants. At nearby Germigny (*see* below), however, a mosaic from Théodulfe's private oratory can still be seen, among the oldest pieces of decorative Christian church art in France.

The abbey of St-Benoît amassed considerable territories and wealth down the centuries. The early Capetian kings were generous patrons in the 11th and 12th centuries, the period in which much of the church you can still see today was built. In return, they benefited from the international reputation of St-Benoît's network of schools and teaching, as well as from the widespread popularity of the pilgrimage to see St Benoît's relics. King Philippe I, ruling at the end of the 11th century, even decided to be buried here. A little later, in 1130, a famous meeting took place at St-Benoît between Louis VI, Pope Innocent II and St Bernard, the latter founder of the rigorously reforming Cistercian order. By contrast, a manuscript from the end of the 12th century records liturgical dramas being performed here, an early flowering of French theatre! The devoutly bellicose 13th-century French king known as St Louis visited St-Benoît repeatedly to stock up on saintly support.

A relative decline in importance followed, but the monastic order, the pilgrimage and the powerful significance of the abbey remained. In 1429, Joan of Arc and the soon-to-be Charles VII of France stopped here on the way to the latter's triumphant sacred crowning in the cathedral of Reims. After the early 16th century, when abbeys became the gift of French kings to grant as they wished, the most famous 'abbot' of St-Benoît was Cardinal Richelieu. He introduced the authoritarian reform of St-Maur here, which enabled the place to prosper for a good century more. However, the massive monastic ensemble that had grown up to the south of the church was demolished during the Revolution. The church itself was saved and for a brief period became a parish church until a monastic order was re-established in the mid-19th century.

Dominating the sweep of the Loire known as the Val d'Or, or Golden Valley, and the plain around it, today the imposing **abbey church** in its light Loire stone topped by slate looks more impressive than beautiful, the weight of its history and symbolism adding substantially to its gravity. Architectural historians consider it one of the most important Romanesque churches in France due to a handful of distinctive elements.

The most outstanding of these is undoubtedly the **early 11th-century narthex**, or entrance porch, with its carved Romanesque capitals. Some of them are decorated with Corinthian leaves or with animals, others with figures from the Apocalypse, others still with stories from other New Testament or early Christian texts. The most characteristic feature is the dramatic way the sculptors have made use of the curves of the capitals, so that the men of stone lean forward to stare right down at you or animals rear up dramatically. As you arrive, on the right-hand central pillar, Christ appears to John of the *Book of Revelations* with the messages he is to transmit to the seven Churches, symbolized by the candelabra. On the inside of this pillar, the Lamb, symbol of Christ, opens the book of the seven seals, and the four horsemen of the Apocalypse emerge. On the outside of the pillar, the good are seen being separated from the evil. Along the right-hand row of columns, you can decipher various animal scenes including big birds lining up, seemingly to drink, and a horseman pursuing what looks like a stag. A couple of further scenes that are relatively easy to interpret stand out close to the church door: St Martin seen slicing his cloak in two for a beggar (*see* Tours) and, opposite, the Holy Family fleeing to Egypt, Mary on a donkey.

Inside the church, past the bright nave with its Gothic arches, admire the second rare feature of the abbey church, the **Byzantine mosaics floor** of the choir, a many-patterned, multicoloured crazy paving. On it lies the tomb effigy of King Philippe I, with an apologetic note on his misbehaviour; he ran off with a married woman when he was already wedded to another. In the transept close to Philippe I's figure, spot another cartoonish face carved high up in the wall opposite the Virgin, either cheek pierced by a hole; this curious stone portrait apparently represents Raynaldus, a Viking who devastated the area before the new medieval abbey was built.

The third extraordinary feature of the church is its sombre, atmospheric **crypt**, where the bones of St Benedict still rest, according to the monks of today. Their medieval counterparts who guarded the precious bones were very wary of pilgrims who might be tempted to try to steal a piece for their personal benefit; they stood vigilantly by the relics as the visitors processed round the crypt. These relics were just visible to the pilgrims through a few slits in the protective wall of the martyrium, the inner sanctum, recreated a few decades ago.

The monks nowadays run a large souvenir shop next to the church. From the abbey you can walk down to the Loire, passing behind the Hôtel Labrador, to the site of St-Benoît's former **port**, once full of activity thanks to the abbey's vast estates and the large community it sheltered. Now the village, with its little old stone mariners' houses and their well-tended miniature gardens, makes one of the most charming riverside scenes in the area. In summer, you may see fishermen wading through the shallow waters here.

It was in this village that the poet and painter **Max Jacob** settled for much of his life after 1921. A great friend of Picasso in his early adulthood – the two shared a Parisian room when they were setting out on their careers – Jacob was considered a brilliant mind by his generation, particularly for his poetic work *Le Cornet à dés*, a daring, mysterious work once described as 'Cubist poetry'. Jacob had all the makings of a troubled figure, a gay Breton Jew who converted to Christianity after a mystical experience, but he had a great sense of humour too. Leaving Paris for the peace of St-Benoît, he served as a sacristan here. In 1944, despite efforts by the abbey to intercede on his behalf, the Nazis ordered his deportation from St-Benoît for being Jewish. Already a sick man, he died in the Drancy transit camp outside Paris.

Carolingian Oratory at Germigny-des-Prés

Church open April–Sept 8.30–7, Oct–March 8.30–6; t 02 38 58 27 03, f 02 38 58 24 12; free. Museum open April–Sept 9–12.30 and 2–7, Oct–Dec and Feb–March Wed–Mon 9.30–12.30 and 2–5.30; t 02 38 58 27 97; adm.

The treasured **Dark Ages mosaic** commissioned by Bishop Théodulfe may be relatively small in size, but it has its place in French art history. Théodulfe wasn't one to deprive himself, it seems. He is said to have sought out the architect of Charlemagne's great chapel at Aix-la-Chapelle to plan the delightful little building which houses the mosaic, as well as a now vanished villa nearby. The oratory was built early in the 9th century. Originally it took the shape of a Greek cross, each of its arms of equal length and ending with a horseshoe-shaped apse. Only three apses remain today, while a nave was tacked on to the fourth side in the 11th century.

The interior would once have been covered with many mosaics, but just one survives. It lay hidden under paint for centuries, but now the glorious blues and golds shine once more. In the style of the Ravenna School, the piece represents the Ark of the Covenant, above which hover two cherubs, watched over by a couple of stern-faced, great bird-winged angels. Between their wings, the hand of God reaches down from a crack in the sky. The Latin inscription is a heady cry to prayer, with an expression of Théodulfe's vanity tacked on, which reads like a heartfelt plea coming directly to you from down the centuries. Roughly translated, it reads: 'See here and contemplate the holy oracle and its cherubs. Here shines the ark of the divine testament. In front of this vision, try with your prayers to move the master of thunder, and please, do not forget to include Théodulfe in your wishes.' The church also contains some beautiful statues and sweet little foliage-decorated capitals.

The small Musée de la Grange Germignonne next door gives more details on the oratory; ask there to see an exquisite Limoges enamel reliquary.

The South Bank of the Loire from Sully to Châteauneuf
The abbey of St-Benoît is most impressive seen from the south bank of the Loire. From Sully, follow the D951 as far as Bouteille. From there, take the riverside road north to Guilly. Then, up on the levee, enjoy expansive views onto the Loire and the abbey church, as well as passing a mariners' cross, the **Croix Tibi**.

Where the Druids of Gaul Gathered?
The druids of Gaul may well have held their great annual gathering near St-Benoît. Caesar made some fascinating observations about them and their customs in his *Conquest of Gaul*. His views are particularly helpful, as the druids themselves forbade the transfer of their knowledge through writing. Caesar's account, though, should be read with reservations, precisely because the druids managed to keep their activities and beliefs so cloaked in mystery.

Caesar records:

On a fixed date in each year they hold a session in a consecrated spot in the country of the Carnutes which is supposed to be the centre of Gaul. Those who are involved in disputes assemble here from all parts and accept the druids' judgements and awards.

He then offers his insights into the druids' practices and beliefs:

The druids officiate at the worship of the gods, regulate public and private sacrifices, and give rulings on all religious questions. Large numbers of young men flock to them for instruction, and they are held in great honour by the people. They act as judges in practically all disputes, whether between tribes or between individuals... Any individual or tribe failing to accept their award is banned from taking part in sacrifice – the heaviest punishment that can be inflicted upon a Gaul...

... The druids are exempt from military service and do not pay taxes like other citizens. These important privileges are naturally attractive: many present themselves of their own accord to become students of druidism, and others are sent by their parents or relatives. It is said that these pupils have to memorize a great number of verses – so many, that some of them spend 20 years at their studies...

... A lesson which they take particular pains to inculcate is that the soul does not perish, but after death passes from one body to another; they think that this is the best incentive to bravery, because it teaches men to disregard the terrors of death. They also hold long discussions about the heavenly bodies and their movements, the size of the universe and of the earth, the physical constitution of the world, and the powers and properties of the gods; and they instruct the young men in all these subjects.

These observations, speculative as they may be, help to show what a highly developed and deeply complex society the Celts of Gaul had developed.

Just west of Bouteille and Guilly lies Neuvy-en-Sullias, where an extraordinary cache of Celtic bronze animal statues – of a horse, bulls, deer and wild boar, among others – was found in 1861. These sophisticated and beautiful treasures, dated to the early Gallo-Roman period, are now displayed in the Hôtel Cabu museum in Orléans). Little is known about them or what they were doing on this land. It's no doubt coincidence that the great Celtic annual druids' meetings are known to have been held some-where in the area.

Châteauneuf-sur-Loire

Unfortunately for the small town of Châteauneuf-sur-Loire, it lost most of its château in the Revolution and, in the course of the 19th century, virtually all of the Loire river trade on which it once thrived. During the Second World War it was badly bombed, causing it to be largely rebuilt in dull and hasty style. And yet the place still has two charming corners, its castle grounds and its riverside quays. The château's stables, which survived the Revolution, have been converted into an appealing modern museum celebrating the life and work of the Loire mariners. Châteauneuf-sur-Loire also offers the unexpected pleasure of one of the most repellent tombs in France.

Musée de la Marine de Loire in the Château of Châteauneuf

Open April–Oct Wed–Mon 10–6, rest of year except major hols Wed–Mon 2–6; t 02 38 46 84 46; adm.

You get a definite whiff of the grandeur of the Ancien Régime Château de Châteauneuf-sur-Loire from the stables left standing. They formed part of a lavish ensemble ordered in the late 17th century by the extravagant Louis Phélypeaux de la Vrillière, an important courtier under Louis XIV, serving for a time as master of cere-monies for a man unmatched in the history of France for his love of pomp.

In the museum, just a little space is dedicated to the castle's history. In fact, a fort stood on this spot from the 11th century, certain Capetian and Valois kings even devoting it some attention through the medieval period. It was destroyed during the anti-royalist Fronde uprising in the middle of the 17th century, leaving the way clear for Phélypeaux to erect his little Versailles. The owner after Phélypeaux, the Duc de Penthièvre, grandson of Louis XIV and Madame de Montespan, left his mark too with certain additions, including the elegant rotunda that stands out on the end of the only wing left from the Ancien Régime château itself.

The museum concentrates on the common people of Châteauneuf-sur-Loire rather than its lords, and more specifically on the many Loire mariners who once formed a very important part of the local community. A census of 1780 recorded this little town as having the fifth largest number of mariners along the Loire after the major ports of Orléans, Tours, Angers and Nantes. In the entrance hall, a helpful large-scale map gives visitors a clear picture of the immense size of the Bassin de la Loire, the area of France covered by the Loire and its tributaries. Read the introduction to the river in

Topics (p.40) to learn more about its great trading past, how it was used by Celts, Greeks, Romans and Vikings, and, from the Middle Ages, how its mariners formed a community to protect their interests which lasted almost to the Revolution.

All manner of goods were transported along the Loire, notably wine and salt, stones and coal, and pottery. In colonial times, much of the sugar from the French Caribbean islands was shipped up from Nantes to Orléans, while *indiennes*, patterned fabrics, were sent down the Loire. The mariners had a tough job, having to deal with the unpredictable conditions of an untamed river and spending a long time away from home. They gained a widespread reputation for being a troublesome lot when they weren't sufficiently occupied, regarded all too often as foul-mouthed drinkers, brawlers and *coureurs de jupons*, running after the girls. However, this museum is dedicated to respecting their memory. One of their sayings went: '*Si vilains sur terre nous sommes, nous sommes seigneurs sur l'eau* (However mean we may be on dry land, we're lords on the waters).'

The museum contains models of the different types of boats they used. Some excellent film shows how these worked and the skill required to manoeuvre them, particularly to pass under the many bridges along the Loire. Engravings and pottery from Nevers (further upriver) depict how busy the river once was, whole caravans of boats strung together on some trips. Depending on the weather, a journey downriver from Orléans to Nantes might take five or six days, but a trip in the other direction might last three or four weeks. While the prevailing southwesterly winds normally gave a helpful push to boats travelling up against the current, when they reached Orléans they generally had to be tugged, using manpower, not horsepower. For a big boat, up to 40 men might be needed.

The Loire mariners certainly formed a community apart, the profession often passed on from father to son. While the vast majority of them led a pretty basic existence, the odd one made his fortune. A big divide existed between the boat owners and the majority of poor sailors who were paid by the trip. The mariners wore distinctive clothes and jewellery, held special celebrations through the year, and their prayers and processions were devoted to particular saints, notably St Nicholas, their patron. In their houses, their furniture was marked with symbols of their profession, such as anchors and stars. While rivalry might have existed between mariners from different localities, those from the same community appear to have supported each other. At certain times of year the river wasn't navigable; many turned their hand to carpentry and woodcarving. They also played a key role in evacuating the local population when floods occurred. With their sailing skills, the mariners could even be called upon to serve on different waters in times of war; a number joined the French fleet to help the Americans in their War of Independence from Britain.

Loire river trade was still thriving in the early decades of the 19th century, as was river transport. A charmingly named firm, the Companie de Navigation Accélérée sur la Loire, even started to run the first steam boats along the Loire in the 1820s – one of them, *Le Vulcain*, tragically exploded at Tours in 1837; in an unsubtle publicity ploy to try and win back its customers, the company named its next model the *Inexplosible*!. But trains would rapidly supersede this mode of transport after railway lines were laid along the Loire in the late 1840s, and Loire river trade and transport dwindled rapidly. By the close of the century the profession of the Loire mariner had practically disappeared. Many went to work for the ground-breaking bridge-maker Ferdinand Arnodin, who set up here.

Other people whose lives revolved around the river are also recalled in the museum, such as the professional Loire fishermen who, during the period of the Grande Pêche from January to June, used to erect barrages across two-thirds of the river's width in order to catch the salmon, shad and eels coming upstream from the sea. As to the *passeurs*, they spent their days ferrying people, cattle and goods across from one side of the river to the other. The *lavendières* were the women who washed clothes in the Loire's waters on specially built boats moored to land, the *bateaux-lavoirs*. Lastly, a few local artists inspired by the river have also been given their place in the museum.

The Loire river was the centre of attention for a place like Châteauneuf, and for the whole Loire Valley region, for so long. Now that the river has been abandoned and left to its own devices, the mariners thrown off its wild back, the memories cherished by this museum act as an important reminder of how closely men worked with the Loire in centuries past.

To Châteauneuf's Repellent Tomb and the Riverside

Along Châteauneuf-sur-Loire's main street, poke your nose inside the **church of St-Martial**, split in two by war bombing. The architecture may not be particularly special, but the interior conceals the deliberately, brilliantly horrible **tomb of Louis Phélypeaux de la Vrillière**, a Baroque work attributed to the Italian Domenico Guidi. The pathetic, foppish Phélypeaux kneels between two atlantes holding up an arch in pink and black striped marble – but these figures, rather than being muscle-bound as is usually the case, are fully unfleshed, grinning skeletons.

Phélypeaux wears an imploring look, hand on heart, ornamental flower on his garter. He looks like a gushing actor who knows his time is up and just hopes that the critics won't be too harsh; but here the obsequious courtier's entreaties are addressed to God.

The town has a fairly good selection of shops selling local produce such as pear liqueur and forest pâtés, but you may think it excessive for such a small place to have treated itself to two covered markets. One in fact turns out to be a 19th-century shed for Loire boats, its elegant form now put to different uses.

Today the main centre of Châteauneuf's activities lie some distance from the Loire, but do go and see the **old riverside quarter**, which retains a character all of its own with its old cobbled quays.

You should be able to take a look at one or two reconstructed traditional mariners' boats here, including a *gabare* called the *Gaillarde*. Or there's a lovely peaceful walk you can take to a quieter stretch of the river if you follow the track down from the château's rotunda.

The Loire Between Châteauneuf and Orléans

North Bank

Heading along the north side of the Loire from Châteauneuf-sur-Loire towards Orléans, avoid the busy N60. Stick as closely as possible to the river instead, heading for **St-Denis-de-l'Hôtel**, the lofty entrance tower to its church so characteristic of the religious buildings along this stretch of the Loire, and matching that of Jargeau, across the river. St-Denis's little museum, the **Musée Maurice Genevoix** (*open weekends and public hols 10–12 and 2–6;* **t** *02 38 59 12 80,* **f** *02 38 46 00 30; free*), is dedicated to a 20th-century writer of some distinction. Genevoix, once permanent secretary of that august French literary body, the Académie Française, hailed from here and loved the area. The start of his autobiographical book, *Trente Mille Jours*, reveals a mass of interesting details on Loire-side life when he was a child at the start of the 20th century, at a time when merchandise and barrels were still rolled along to and from the Loire.

Which brings us neatly to the village of **Chécy**, which has an amusing **Musée de la Tonnellerie** (*closed until at least end 2004; adm*), devoted to coopers and vine-growers. Genevoix claimed that in the 1920s, vines still ran along the banks of the Loire practically from Sancerre to Nantes. Coopers formed an important part of the Loire-side community as well as mariners. Chécy also has the obligatory typical imposing church tower of these parts.

Do stop at the pretty, well-flowered former mariners' village at **Combleux**, just a bit further west; it's wedged between the Canal d'Orléans and the Loire, and well known to the people of Orléans as a picturesque place to which to escape from the big city.

The one good reason for stopping in busy, built-up St-Jean-de-Braye, effectively an eastern suburb of Orléans, is to visit the **Bollée bell foundry** (*open Fri–Sun 2–6; 156 Rue du Faubourg Bourgogne,* **t** *02 38 86 29 47; adm*), along the main road. Modern blocks may be going up around it, but this foundry remains firmly fixed in the 19th century, making bells in the traditional way, for instance using horse manure to aerate the earth for the hand-made moulds, and brushing on the necessary tallow with goose feathers. Enter the scruffy workshop with its earth pits where the bells are fired and you feel like you're stepping back into the pre-industrial age. Before that you're treated to a tour of the small modern museum on bell-making which Dominique Bollée set up in the early 1990s. A film explains the processes involved in making a *cloche*.

You can also admire many finished pieces in the museum, including one made for the bicentenary of the French Revolution – and in memory of the 100,000 bells which apparently disappeared then, a telling reminder of the destruction wrought by that traumatic upheaval. Dominique Bollée is the eighth generation of his family to make bells on this site. He and his colleagues produce about 100 a year, half of which are exported, mostly to churches in Africa and Asia, although in decades past the foundry has made bells for the likes of the cathedrals of Ottawa and Buffalo.

South Bank

Following the south side of the Loire from Châteauneuf-sur-Loire towards Orléans, at **Jargeau** by the river, the **Maison de Loire** (*open Tues–Sat 2–6; t 02 38 59 76 60, perso.wanadoo.fr/mdloire45*) holds small temporary exhibitions on various aspects of the great river. Jargeau, apart from enjoying the distinction of having been liberated from English occupation by Joan of Arc in 1429, is known locally for its *andouillette*, or chitterling sausage.

A Dip into the Sologne via La Ferté-St-Aubin

A vast forest dotted with hundreds of lakes fills the land between the Loire's arc through the Orléanais and the Cher river to the south. This is the Sologne. Silver birch, pine and heather thrive across its flat lands. The Sologne is a hunter's paradise, teeming with rabbits, boar, deer, birds, ducks and fish. Although some find the Sologne melancholic, others respond to its mysterious, misty atmosphere. The area features in a couple of famous French works – the magical party in Alain-Fournier's *Le Grand Meaulnes* is held in the Sologne, while an even more eccentric *fête étrange* takes place here in Jean Renoir's *La Règle du Jeu*, one of the most important films in the history of French cinema.

The Sologne occupies an island of clay in the midst of the Loire Valley's limestone. As there's no stone locally, the houses are built of brick. The big gap between the dwellings of the wealthy landowners and the poor villagers stands out: while the villages consist of low, meagre cottages, large châteaux hide out in the countryside. The regional writer Maurice Genevoix wrote movingly about the social divide in the Sologne, particularly in his tale of the likable rogue of a poacher *Raboliot*. Whether modest or posh, Sologne homes are often embellished with brick patterning.

La Ferté-St-Aubin, south of Orléans, is one of the most important gateways into the Sologne. Its pale brick **château** (*open April–Sept 10–7, mid-Feb–Mar and mid-Sept–mid Nov 10–6; t 02 38 76 52 72, www.chateauxcountry.com/chateaux/fertesaintaubin; adm*) is one of the most appealing in the region, although it is run down. The entrance has comical bell-hatted pavilions flanking a curious classical arch. One architectural historian has compared the pavilions to deerstalkers, which seems all the more appropriate as the castle served as the setting for the tragic hunting party in *La Règle du Jeu*. The moats are fed by the Cosson river, which later flows past the Château de Chambord, one of the many famous châteaux on the western edge of the Sologne (*see* p.140). The two sections of the main building went up in the 17th century, while two elegant wings providing stables and outbuildings were added later. You can visit the château's two top floors unaccompanied. The musty rooms are in a bad state of repair, but are filled with sometimes amusing bric-a-brac. A bell calls you on the guided tour through the better-preserved apartments on the ground floor. You finish with a modest cookery demonstration in the basement kitchens. The owner has a lot of work on his hands in restoring this place, but a visit here proves quite entertaining, and it's good to find the stables still in use.

To appreciate the Sologne's flora and fauna, visit the **Domaine du Ciran** (*open April–Sept 10–12 and 2–6, Oct–Mar Wed–Mon 10–12 and 2–5;* **t** *02 38 76 90 93, www.domaineduciran.com; adm*), an estate set in typical woodland near **Ménestreau-en-Villette**, east of La Ferté-St-Aubin. This reserve provides a haven for animals in this hunting-crazy area. You can walk through the grounds, with a fair chance of spotting deer at the very least. In the house, ask to see some of the wonderful short nature videos kept here, entries from the Festival International du Film de la Faune Sauvage (Wild Animals) held every November at Lamotte-Beuvron a little way south. (For further sights in the southern Sologne, *see* p.203 in the chapter on the Cher valley.)

Through the Forêt d'Orléans

A vast swath of woodland shadows the north side of the Loire from Gien to Orléans. This is the **Forêt d'Orléans**, the largest state-owned forest in France and the second largest in the country at around 35,000 hectares. Several place names here finish with the words 'aux-Loges', referring to the simple lodges that were built for the forest workers up until the start of the 20th century.

On the eastern edge of the forest, **Lorris** was the birthplace of Guillaume de Lorris, who wrote the first part of the great 13th-century *Le Roman de la Rose*, a classic of chivalric literature. The poem became a medieval bestseller, not for years but for centuries. An allegorical work, loaded with symbolism, it recounts how a young man finds his way into an enchanted garden, '*Qu'il i avoit d'oisiaus trois tans/Qu'en tout le remanant de France* (Where there were three times more birds/Than in all the rest of France)', peopled by magnificent courtiers. In this entrancing place he falls in love with a rose (*see* Meung, p.133, for the second author of the poem).

The town's church of Notre-Dame, hemmed in by houses, has several interesting features on the outside and, inside, one of the oldest organs in Europe. Dating from the 16th century, it perches somewhat precariously high up on one side of the nave. There's a little organ museum nearby. A splendid Renaissance-windowed, black-brick patterned Hôtel de Ville and an old covered market in brown tiles sloping down towards the ground add appeal to the centre of town. A war museum in the former railway station commemorates Resistance fighters killed here in August 1944.

The **Canal d'Orléans** passes not far from Lorris and crosses the forest. **Grignon**, **Combreux** and **Fay-aux-Loges** make up a string of quite pretty villages by the canal (Fay is a good place from which to take a boat trip along it). Half-a-dozen kilometres north of Fay-aux-Loges, go to **Ingrannes** to see the **Arboretum des Grandes Bruyères**, only rarely open (*Sundays and public holidays April–Nov 10–6, closed last Sun July to second Sun Aug;* **t** *02 38 57 12 61, www.parcsdefrance.org; adm*), but with atmospheric grounds inspired by the 19th-century gardener Gertrude Jekyll, full of heathers, old-fashioned roses and magnolias. The arboretum also presents a collection of trees from temperate climates around the world, arranged geographically.

Château de Chamerolles

Open July–Aug 10–6, April–June and Sept Wed–Mon 10–6, Feb–Mar and Oct–Dec Wed–Mon 10–12 and 2–5; t 02 38 39 84 66, www.coeur-de-france. com/chamerolles.html; adm.

Midway between Orléans and Pithiviers, on the northern edge of the forest (east of Chilleurs-aux-Bois on the N152), the Château de Chamerolles long lay forgotten and abandoned, a Sleeping Beauty of a building. It has been brought back to life in a commercial fairytale kind of way. To be honest, rather than being a Sleeping Beauty, the Château de Chamerolles had aged very badly when the *département* of the Loiret bought it from the Paris town council for one franc, but the authorities have revived the place with a strong dose of smelling salts, transforming it into a museum of perfumes and scents. The project was supported by some of the big-name perfume manufacturers, many of which have factories around Orléans. Every year an exhibition is devoted to a different perfumery.

The original castle on which the restoration was based was finished in 1522 under the magically named Lancelot du Lac, royal councillor and chamberlain, and one-time governor of Orléans. Although Chamerolles is clearly something of an ersatz-château now, it looks very pretty indeed and the restoration work has been carried out with great relish. A sturdy round tower marks each corner of the moated square. Inside the courtyard, the typical lozenge-patterned brick façades of the region dominate.

Within, local craftspeople have made a good number of imitation period pieces, and the Orléans fine arts museum has also lent a few fine pieces to embellish the interiors. The odd original feature has survived. The chapel with its ornate entrance contains Huguenot inscriptions, apparently the oldest to be found in France. They record the Protestants' ten commandments, and are in old French, the language, ironically, now rather Rabelaisian-sounding, comical and coarse, which isn't particularly surprising as it dates from the 16th century.

A series of rooms concentrates on *toilette* over the centuries, and in particular developments in the search for the perfect scent. The word *toilette* derives from the French word *toile*, meaning cloth – scent used to be put on a piece of linen, not on clothes or the skin; the guides admonish visitors that it is quite wrong to apply perfume directly to the skin. *Toilette*, in French, came to refer to washing one's person generally, and also to one's attire and presentation. There's a representative section for each of the 16th, 17th, 18th and 19th centuries. The disappearance of the bath tub during the 17th apparently wasn't occasioned by a lack of hygiene, but because doctors began to think bathing might be bad for the health, so people followed the fashion of the *toilette sèche*, dry washing!

Perfume bottles started to be mass-produced at the end of the 19th century, contributing their own share of glamour to scent. A sizable section of the château is devoted to superbly designed perfume bottles in the 20th century, with star contributors including the likes of Dali and Lalique. The great creators of perfumes are known rather unflatteringly as *nez* (noses), a name they dislike. Apparently some 80 per cent of the *nez* working for the big fashion names are French. In the château's attics you can amuse yourselves concocting your own perfume, or test each other on recognizing the different scents provided, a mixture of the natural and the artificial.

Chamerolles' sumptuous formal gardens were redrawn according to Renaissance records, the fine detail observed down to the planting and the carpentry work. Some visitors find the whole place too phoney, too Disney-like; it's certainly the slickest château you'll see along the Loire and has its own heliport awaiting its privileged seminar guests, as well as a large boutique well stocked with scents.

A few kilometres east of Chamerolles, at **Vrigny**, the more traditional little French museum of **La Maison du Père Mousset** (*open May–Oct weekends only 2.30–6; t 02 38 34 18 16; adm*) stands in comical contrast to the Château de Chamerolles, the peasant next to the posh aristocrat. Your French needs to be good to cope with the deliberately strong provincial accent in which the guide tells of life here in the 19th century.

Orléans

09

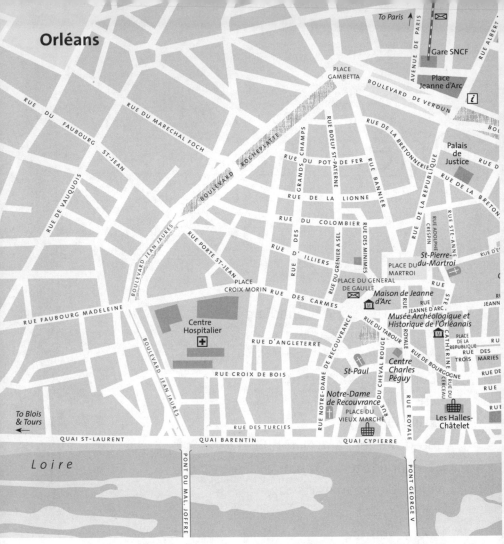

Orléans

At the crowning point of the Loire, Orléans could have been king of French cities. Under the Capetians, it was one of the French monarchs' great seats of power, vying for attention with its rival on the Seine, a little more than 100km to the north. Orléans lost out to Paris, which managed to lure the sovereign family away, while later French royalty would quite bypass the city to scamper down the Loire, its tail between its legs, with the arrival of the English armies in the second half of the Hundred Years' War. The English, however, came to lay siege to Orléans in 1428 and the town was only saved with the arrival of the heroic maid, Joan of Arc.

Orléans has been growing apace in the last couple of decades, spreading out in all directions. It has greatly benefited recently from its proximity to Paris, picking up a lot of spill-over trade from the capital. One area outside town has been dubbed Cosmetics Valley, as so many big-name houses (such as Dior) have set up factories here. Despite economic success, Orléans seems to lack a bit of self-confidence in its

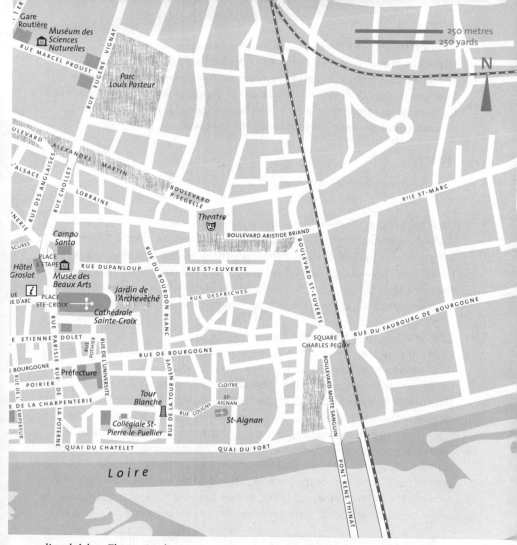

cultural riches. The centre, however, proves very interesting, although badly bombed in the Second World War.

So what can Orléans tempt you with apart from her Maid and the cathedral, the latter dominating the skyline of the centre? The Musée des Beaux-Arts is one of the finest provincial fine arts museums in France; it substantially helps fill a big chronological gap in French art history along the Loire, the Ancien Régime (that is, the 17th and 18th centuries), with its excellent collections. The unpretentious Musée Archéologique et Historique de l'Orléanais in the Hôtel Cabu takes you much further back in time, its unsung highlights a fabulous array of Celtic bronze animals, the pieces of such a sophistication and beauty that they're likely to shatter many preconceptions about the culture of that period – the statue of the horse dedicated to the god Rudiobus is one of the greatest pieces of art to be seen along the Loire. Meanwhile, tributes are paid to Joan as much at the Hôtel Groslot, part of the town hall, as at the so-called Maison de Jeanne d'Arc, while the Centre Jeanne d'Arc keeps all manner of books and films on her. The extraordinary early Romanesque crypt of St-Aignan hides under a church in an eastern quarter sloping down to the Loire. Strangely though, Orléans turns its back on the river, with virtually no use made of its banks when for so long the city flourished from its quayside trade. For waterside pleasures, head for Olivet just to the south, on the Loiret.

History

Ah! They remember me still in Orleans.

Joan of Arc in Bernard Shaw's *Saint Joan*

Remember? They're *obsessed* by Jeanne la Pucelle; unhealthily so, some might say. Orléans' memory is dominated by the days in 1429 when Joan of Arc so famously helped to break the English siege of the town. That week tends to be viewed rather too simplistically as a decisive moment in the Hundred Years' War, in French history and in the cementing of the French national identity. So let us widen the history of the town somewhat, as it was the setting for many other major events.

Caesar Slaughters the Carnutes

Cenabum, as Orléans was known to Caesar, was an important settlement of the Celtic Carnute tribe, lying at a strategic point on trade routes through Gaul. It had a fine bridge spanning the Loire by the time Caesar came to wreak his revenge on the place. The Celtic tribes had united in 52BC to rise up against the recent Roman conquest of their territories. A group of Carnutes were the unfortunate foolish first to rebel. They slaughtered a number of Roman merchants who had established themselves in the city, running off with their property. Caesar came speedily to teach the Carnutes a lesson, arriving towards nightfall one day. Lacking time to attack immediately, he made camp outside the town, but reckoned that the inhabitants might try to escape in the night. This they did, falling into his trap – he had kept two legions under arms close to the bridge. He dispassionately recounts the success of his stratagem:

Shortly before midnight the people of Cenabum moved silently out of the town and began to cross the river. Apprised of this by the patrols, Caesar set the gates on fire and sent inside the legions he had kept ready for action. The town was captured and all but a very few of the enemy taken prisoner – for the narrow street and bridge were blocked by the crowd of fugitives. After plundering and burning Cenabum, and distributing among his soldiers the booty it contained and the prisoners, Caesar marched across the Loire...

The plan of the Gallo-Roman town that grew up afterwards is still evident. The Rue de Bourgogne and Rue Parisie/Rue de la Poterne correspond to the main thoroughfares of that time. By the end of the second century the confines of the city were fixed pretty much as they would remain for a millennium. At the end of the third century the town became capital of the administrative region of the Civitatis Aurelianorum and was renamed Aurelianis, from which its modern name stems. A century later, a

Getting There and Around

By Train

Note that Orléans has two train stations, the central Orléans Gare SNCF, and Les Aubrais to the north of the centre. If you arrive at Orléans-les-Aubrais, either take the *navette* (free shuttle service) for the centre, the new Orléans tramway or a taxi. From Paris, trains for Orléans leave from Gare d'Austerlitz. Orléans has good connections with Blois and Tours.

By Bus and Tram

Orléans has local bus and tram networks (freephone **t** 0800 012 000). The main Gare Routière for buses is near the central railway station.

By Car and Bicycle

Orléans is well served by motorways. From Paris, take the A10, which goes almost to the centre of town. The main non-paying road from Paris to Orléans is the N20, passing via Etampes. Historic Orléans lies on the north bank of the Loire.

Car Hire

Avis, 13 Rue des Sansonnières, **t** 02 38 62 27 04, **f** 02 38 68 01 30

Europcar, 81 Rue André Dessaux (Nord), Fleury-les-Aubrais, **t** 02 38 73 00 40, **f** 02 38 73 46 90

Bicycle Hire

Kit Loisirs, 1720 Rue Marcel Belot, 45160, Olivet, **t** 02 38 63 44 34, *www.kitloisirs.com*

By Taxi

Taxis d'Orléans, **t** 02 38 53 11 11, runs a 24-hour service.

Tourist Information

Tourist offices: Office de Tourisme, 6 Rue Albert Ier, 45000 Orléans, **t** 02 38 24 05 05, *www.orleans.fr. (Note that they will move offices sometime in 2004.)*

Market Days

Les Halles-Châtelet: The town's covered market, with over 30 food stalls, is open daily (morning only on Sunday).

Place du Vieux Marché and the **Rue du Cheval Rouge**: A *marché forain*, where you'll find a whole mishmash of things on sale; Saturday.

Quai du Roy: Fruit and veg market; Saturday morning.

Boulevard Alexandre Martin: Antiques market; Saturday.

Place de la République: Flower market; Tuesday, Thursday, Saturday and Sunday mornings.

Festivals

The **Fêtes Johanniques** are the week-long festivities Orléans lays on in the first week of May to celebrate Joan of Arc's part in the liberation of Orléans. These Fêtes are an enormous, cheerful, all-embracing family affair – as the Orléanais themselves say: 'Half the population comes out to watch the other half parade'! Every year a new local Joan is picked to attend ceremonies around town. Her equestrian skills are put to the test, but *mauvaises langues* (gossips) question whether the selectors test her virginity nowadays. The main Parade of Nations is the most colourful event of the week, focusing around the Place du Martroi. The illumination of the cathedral, flypasts, tanks trundling through town and a large medieval fair on the Campo Santo count among other highlights.

The Orléans **jazz festival**, end of June/start of July, has drawn big names such as Gillespie and Hancock to the Campo Santo in the past.

Shopping

Mementos of Joan of Arc abound in the souvenir shops but are probably best avoided, except as a humorous present 'in the best possible taste'.

Among the culinary specialities of the Loiret to buy in Orléans, there's **pear liqueur** – believe it or not, the pears from the Loire Valley's

strong defensive wall was erected around it, a few vestiges of which can still be seen to one side of the cathedral.

orchards actually grow up in bottles placed on the tree! **Cotignac**, a quince jelly sweet, is made at nearby St-Ay. Other Loire Valley fruits go into making the new Orléans **macaroons** sold in some of the city's *pâtisseries*. Orléans was once famous for its vinegar industry. This has almost died out now, but **Martin Pouret** still produces vinegar the old-fashioned way. You might also try out the local Orléanais **wines**, although they're no great shakes. **Goat's cheese from Olivet** may be to more people's taste.

Orléans being a big producer of perfumes, you'll find many *parfumeries* around town, for instance along Rue de la République and in the Place d'Arc shopping centre.

Sports and Activities

Although wandering by the Loire isn't very easy in Orléans, swimming, watersports and fishing are possible at the **Ile Charlemagne**, 3km southeast of Orléans (direction of St-Jean le Blanc).

At Olivet, the *bateau mouche Le Sologne* takes you along the Loiret – **t** 02 38 66 12 58, **f** 02 38 56 58 51 (*Apr–Nov Mon–Sat 3.30, Sun 3.30 and 5.30; Nov–Mar Sun 3.30 only*); the trip lasts 1½ hours.

You can also take a **cruiser** along the Canal d'Orléans, running April–Oct; call **t** 02 38 46 82 91 for times (**Syndicat du Canal d'Orléans**, 61b, Route de Nestin, **f** 02 38 46 82 92). You can board at Mardié, a few kilometres east out of the centre of town by the north bank road towards Jargeau; or at Donnery, Chécy, or Fay. The trip lasts about 1½ hours.

Where to Stay

Orléans ✉ 45000
Central Orléans caters better for business people than for tourists in hotel terms, with a mass of chain hotels. The suburb of Olivet, just south of town, has some delightful options beside the Loiret river.

Moderate
★★★Hôtel d'Arc, 37 Rue de la République, **t** 02 38 53 10 94, *www.hoteldarc.fr*. In an elaborate Belle Epoque building well situated on the biggest, pedestrianized shopping street leading north from Place du Martroi. Modern comforts have been neatly fitted into the rooms, a few of which are very spacious.

★★★Les Cèdres, 17 Rue du Maréchal Foch, **t** 02 38 62 22 92, *www.hoteldescedres.com*. 'The Cedars' lies just outside the broad, busy avenues encircling the heart of town, off Bd Rocheplatte. It's still close to the centre, but peaceful, with a little garden, the rooms spacious and decorated with personal touches. *Closed late Dec–early Jan*.

Inexpensive
★★Jackotel, 18 Cloître St-Aignan, **t** 02 38 54 48 48, **f** 02 38 77 17 59. Modern, but tucked into a courtyard by the lovely tree-shaded square beside the church of St-Aignan, this place has some pleasant rooms. *Closed Sun and holidays 2–6*.

★★L'Abeille, 64 Rue d'Alsace Lorraine, **t** 02 38 53 54 87, *hotel-de-labeille@wanadoo.fr*. Not only in the heart of town, right on the corner of Rue de la République; it offers good-sized rooms at a good price.

Olivet ✉ 45160
For these hotels on the north bank of the Loiret, take the N20 south from the central Orléans.

★★★Quatre Saisons, 351 Rue de la Reine Blanche, **t** 02 38 66 14 30, *www.les-quatre-saisons.com* (*inexpensive*). Looks more like a classic beach house than a town house, with bright clapboard, a treehouse over the river and a smart restaurant (*menus €17–33*). *Closed Sun pm and Mon, three weeks Nov and two weeks Feb*.

★★★Le Rivage, 635 Rue de la Reine Blanche, B.P. 222, **t** 02 38 66 02 93, *monsite.wanadoo.fr/le.rivage.olivet* (*moderate*). The rather dull roadside entrance gives you no idea of the

The Hand of God Beats Attila the Hun

The first mention of a Christian bishop of Orléans, Diclopetus, dates from around the same time as Aurelianis. Two later bishops stand out at the end of the period of

stylish-to-chic interiors that await you. The rooms are pretty swanky. On warm days you can eat seafood and game specialities on the splendid shaded terrace by the Loiret; otherwise there's the extravaganza of the modern dining room (*menus €26–54*). *Closed late Dec–mid-Jan. Restaurant closed Sat lunch all year and Sun pm Nov–April.*

Eating Out

Moderate

La Chancellerie, 95 Rue Royale, **t** 02 38 53 57 54 (*menus €23–28*). Has the good fortune of being located in the noble 18th-century building on the corner of Orléans' main square and Rue Royale that survived the bombing. The food is in uncomplicated brasserie style, with such Loiret specialities as Jargeau *andouillette*.

La Promenade, Place du Martroi/1 Rue Adolphe Crespin, **t** 02 38 42 78 10 (*menus €20–30.50; closed Sun and Mon*). Has another of the best seats looking onto Orléans' main square and serves excellent French dishes . For a simpler option, see the sister establishment below, Le Martroi.

La Petite Marmite, 178 Rue de Bourgogne, **t** 02 38 54 23 83 (*menus €18–29; closed lunchtimes exc weekends and public hols*). Timber-framed and geranium-fronted, serving traditional local dishes in an atmospheric setting.

La Dariole, 25 Rue Etienne Dolet, **t** 02 38 77 26 67 (*menus €18–30.50; closed Wed pm and weekends*). With its cross-timbered front on this very quiet street parallel to busy Rue de Bourgogne, this is a sweet restaurant with a small but appealing menu, offering nice touches, such as saffron in the *poule au pot*. *Closed 12–20 April, 2–25 Aug and Christmas.*

Cheap

Le Martroi, Place du Martroi/Rue Adolphe Crespin, **t** 02 38 42 15 00 (*menu €15; closed Sun and Mon*). Fashionable rendezvous, a colourful brasserie on one corner of the Place du Martroi, with stylish outdoor seating.

Les Chineurs, 253 Rue de Bourgogne, **t** 02 38 54 00 79 (*menus €9–25*). Very simple options of traditional French dishes made using fresh produce. The setting is appealing, with pottery on display in the entrance cabinets. *Closed Sun.*

Le Brin de Zinc, 62 Rue Ste-Catherine, **t** 02 38 53 38 77. An amusing little restaurant (*menus €13.50–23*) filled with all sorts of bric-a-brac, run with verve. Offers a vegetarian menu and organic choices in summer. The place also has half a dozen simple rooms (*€31–44*).

For **cheap** ethnic options just have a wander along Rue de Bourgogne.

Entertainment and Nightlife

Cinemas

UGC, Centre Commercial, Place d'Arc, **t** 08 36 68 68 58

Les Carmes, 7 Rue des Carmes, **t** 02 38 62 02 96

Le Sélect, Rue Jeanne d'Arc, **t** 08 36 68 69 25

L'Artistic, Bd A Martin, **t** 08 36 68 69 25

Theatre

For details on what's on at the grand main **theatre** of Orléans, call **t** 02 38 62 75 30 (*pm only*), or go to *www.ville-orleans.fr/ scenenationale.*

Bars

There are plenty of bars in and around Place du Martroi.

Autour de la Terre, 7 Place Ste-Croix, **t** 02 38 54 59 15. Try this atmospheric tea house located opposite the façade of the cathedral for a more literary and trendy option than your normal French bar. Organizes cultural events.

BBC, 15 Rue de la Bretonnerie, **t** 02 38 53 38 14 (*open to 3am*). A central bar offering billiards and cocktails, as well as the bar (hence the name) and Internet access.

the Roman Empire. St Euverte is thought to have founded the first cathedral; legend has it that he was about to bless the building when the hand of God came down from between the clouds to do the job for him.

Orléans had another bishop as its great hero for almost a thousand years before Joan outshone him. For the 5th-century Hunnish invaders of Gaul, Orléans, more than Paris, was the centre of attention. St Aignan is the man celebrated for having Attila removed from the city's doorstep in 451. The story goes that the terrible warlord stormed the town, his troops gathering booty, but Aignan had sounded the alarm, calling on military help from the Roman Aetius, who managed to drive the Huns out.

Orléans and Early French Royals

In 498 the Merovingian Frank Clovis took the city. The Council he assembled here in 511 importantly established the strong relationship between French royalty and the Church. On Clovis's death, Orléans became capital for a time of one of the four smaller kingdoms into which Gaul was divided.

During the Carolingian period, Orléans flourished at the centre of a number of leading religious centres, with the cluster of nearby abbeys including St-Aignan and St-Benoît, or Fleury. One bishop of Orléans, Théodulfe (see Germigny-des-Prés, p.122), was one of the Emperor Charlemagne's closest councillors. Orléans' importance is further attested by the fact that Charles le Chauve (the Bald) was crowned king of the western Franks here in 848. The Viking raids along the Loire badly affected the city later in the century, but Orléans remained at the centre of French politics.

For the Capetians, Orléans was a place of enormous significance. Hugues Capet, from a line of counts of Orléans, founded the Capetian dynasty of French kings. In a vital act for the future of the French monarchy, he made Capetian kingship hereditary and indivisible with the crowning of his son Robert II le Pieux in Orléans cathedral in 987. The church of St-Aignan was consecrated in 1029. The Châtelet, the royal castle, watched over the bridge and river traffic. Robert stamped his royal and religious authority on the city on the infamous Jour des Saints Innocents in 1022, when he had a number of clerical intellectuals of the city branded heretics and burnt to death. Orléans couldn't precisely be described as the French capital at this period, but the royal retinue alternated between Paris and Orléans until Louis VI opted for the Seine rather than the Loire, even if he too was anointed in Orléans' cathedral.

Relations between Orléans and royalty became strained under Louis VII, a rebellion in 1137 leading the king to grant Orléans' merchants certain privileges. For those who may be under the false impression that classical learning was completely stifled for much of the Middle Ages, during the 12th century Arnoul d'Orléans had copious commentaries on classical authors published. An intellectual centre, the city became renowned for its civil law school. This was helped by the fact that Pope Honorius III banned the teaching of the subject in Paris in 1219. Greek was also banned in the capital, but taught in Orléans.

The majority of the 13th-century kings' lawyers were trained here. One student became Pope Clement V, elected pontiff thanks to King Philippe le Bel's bribes, and the pope who fled an anarchic Rome to become the first incumbent at Avignon in Provence. Clement V showed his gratitude to Orléans for his student days by granting the city the privilege of a university in 1306.

Joan of Arc's Finest Hour

The English brought terror to the region in the Hundred Years' War. Robert Knowles and his troops caused havoc from as early as 1358, and St-Aignan was destroyed. The town's most infamous troubles came in 1428, with the siege by Salisbury, who was killed in action and replaced by Glasdale. The English razed to the ground the churches and houses outside the city walls and erected a circle of English camps around Orléans. On 29 April 1429, Joan of Arc broke through the English defences to enter the city and give new hope to the hard-pressed population. She stayed a few days to spur on the citizens and then found another breach in enemy lines to go back out to the French army and play her part in the great attack.

The first English post was taken on 5 May. On 6 May a second was won, the Augustinian Convent. This stood in front of the main English position, the Fort des Tourelles guarding the southern end of Orléans' bridge. The fight for the fort raged all of 7 May. Joan, hit by an arrow, continued to rally the troops. She encouraged her soldiers to take to boats to help the attack from the Loire itself and, most importantly, she persuaded the troops with her to fight on rather than abandon for the day, as the French leader Dunois had proposed. Thanks to the Auld Alliance between France and Scotland, a Scottish contingent under Hugh Kennedy played an important part in the storming of the Fort des Tourelles. Late on 7 May, the French and their allies were victorious, and on 8 May the English gave up the siege of Orléans. This was to be Joan's supreme victory; it would still take a few decades for the French forces to oust the English from most of France, however.

Town Defences, the Wars of Religion and Explosive Protestants

In the second half of the 15th century Orléans was substantially fortified, for King Louis XI and then for Duke Louis d'Orléans, son of the famous chivalric figure Charles d'Orléans. (Despite their aristocratic family title, Blois, not Orléans, was the seat of the d'Orléans' court.) The beginning of the 16th century was a time of optimism for Orléans, with many fine new town houses being built. This prosperity would be shattered by the Wars of Religion.

In 1560 an Estates General was assembled at Orléans in a last desperate effort to avoid war between the rival religious factions, but it failed. To add to the woes, the sickly young King François II died in the Hôtel Groslot, not in a melodramatic poisoning as fiction would have it, but from an ear infection. He left as his widow the ill-fated Mary Stuart, Queen of Scots, who was actually brought up along the Loire, at the royal château of Amboise.

Orléans became infamous in much of France for serving as shortlived headquarters of the French Protestants during these wars. A Protestant theology college was created at the university where Calvin had previously taken his law degree, and one of the great Protestant leaders, Condé, took control of the town for a time from 1562. The powerful Catholic Duc de Guise besieged him, but was killed in front of the city. Catherine de' Medici stepped in, imposing peace, the promise of the Edict of Amboise offering the prospect of certain privileges for the Protestants. But Condé seized

Orléans again in 1567 after the frictions had worsened and this time Protestants attacked the churches. Most significantly of all, they blew up the cathedral.

The backlash was inevitable. King Charles IX had taken over authority for the town, and the terrible St Bartholomew's Day Massacres of 1572 were particularly bloody in Orléans, the Protestants savagely butchered and effectively silenced. For a while Orléans stood on the ultra-Catholic side of the Ligue. The Protestant King Henri IV would have to besiege the town in 1594 and win it back. In an important gesture of reconciliation, Henri IV ordered the cathedral's rebuilding, and in the old Gothic style.

The Grande Mademoiselle, a granddaughter of Henri IV and obstreperous niece of Louis XIII, participated in the aristocratic Fronde uprising, which defied royal authority in the mid-17th century. Such was her power that she gathered an army which briefly occupied Orléans, taking a leaf out of Joan's book, with the aid of boats.

From Ancien Régime Success to 19th-century Decline

The new Catholic religious orders of the Counter-Reformation were established in the town in the 17th century, while Fougeu d'Escures saw to the construction of a new quarter of very grand houses to be admired in the street named after him. Orléans experienced a time of prosperity from the mid-17th to the mid-18th centuries. The royal governor, or *intendant*, of the Orléanais became the administrator of an extensive region which at one time stretched from Orléans to the Atlantic. In addition to well-established industries such as tanning and textiles, new ones in Orléans thrived on trade from French possessions in the New World, especially the refining of Caribbean sugar cane. The loss of the French Caribbean and Canadian territories would bring decline, but in the meantime splendid new architectural developments such as the grand Place du Martroi and arcaded Rue Royale went up.

Orléans had a tradition of producing prints, and many Revolutionary ones were disseminated from here. But the Revolution had a less destructive impact on the city than one architect, Benoît Lebrun, so it's said. In 1793 the city was briefly outlawed because of pro-royalist intriguing.

At the end of Bonaparte's Empire in 1815, Prussian troops advanced for the first time as far as Orléans. They would come back in the Franco-Prussian War. Meanwhile, Orléans' economy was sliding downhill. Having counted among the six richest cities in France, its sugar, textile and Loire river trade collapsed (the last due to the appearance of the railway). The Prussian soldiers who took over the town in October 1870 stayed until March 1871, although the Armée de la Loire gathered by General Chanzy did manage to regain it for a brief month. One of the defiant, unifying figures in Orléans during these stressful times was bishop Monseigneur Dupanloup, a liberal religious and political figure.

Louis Pasteur, a frequent visitor to the area, became a bit of a local hero in Orléans' business circles when he found a more efficient way of making vinegar for the town's vinegar-makers. This had grown into an important industry, a rather bitter replacement for the sweet riches of Orléans' colonial days. Before the end of the century the old castle, one of the symbols of Orléans' royal past, was destroyed.

20th-century Destruction, Reconstruction and Regionalism

After economic decline came Orléans' decimation by bombs in the Second World War. Nazi attacks in June 1940 destroyed much of the historic centre. Further devastation of the area around the station was caused by American bombing in May 1943. One of the town's prominent prewar figures, Jean Zay, an important reforming minister of education, was imprisoned by the Vichy government and shot by its militia in 1944. The town was freed on 16 August 1944. Its liberating hero this time was General Patton. The work of reconstruction is plainly visible in many parts of the centre of Orléans, following plans laid down by the architect Jean Royer.

When the French regions were restructured at the start of the 1960s, the creation of the unimaginatively named administrative Région Centre was one of the more bizarre bureaucratic inventions. With its birth, Orléans became administrative capital for six *départements*, despite rivalry from Tours, and despite Orléans' proximity to Paris, in whose shadow some say it lives. A new university was created for the town in 1962, to the south of the old centre, close to the Loiret, a pretty river more frequented by Orléans' inhabitants than the sadly ignored Loire, and which has also given its name to the *département* of which Orléans is the capital.

Cathédrale Ste-Croix

Open 10–12 and 2–6, except during services; http://cdvorleans.free.fr.

From a distance, central Orléans is dominated by its cathedral and the tiers of its towers. In the centre, Rue Jeanne d'Arc was specially designed in the 19th century to create a spectacular vista up to the building's great Gothic-style façade, neatly compartmentalized by simple horizontal and vertical lines. Despite the monumental scale of the work, there is something delicate about it, particularly in the tracery of the windows and arches, and in the towers. Some have accused this cathedral of being over-pretty, while Marcel Proust seemingly took a violent dislike to it, disparagingly comparing the tops of the towers not to his beloved *madeleines*, but to vulgar strawberry gâteaux; such a reaction may strike you as a trifle oversensitive!

In fact, the tops of the towers resemble crowns, and crownings there were aplenty in the Cathédrale Ste-Croix under the Capetians. But the first basilica here was built way back in the Dark Ages, in the 4th century; it was for this building that the hand of God supposedly appeared to spare St Euverte the trouble of consecrating the place himself. A hand blessing the church is painted on the main boss of the apse. From the 7th century the cathedral was dedicated to the Ste-Croix, or Holy Cross. The structure grew in size as Orléans grew in importance, and Charles le Chauve (the Bald), Eudes, Robert le Pieux and King Louis VI le Gros (the Fat) were all crowned here.

Bishop Robert de Courtenay decided to commission a totally new building along the lines of Amiens cathedral late in the 13th century. This turned into a long-drawn-out affair. Work began in 1287, with the choir completed by 1329. The Hundred Years' War caused an extended pause in the building work. Thanks to the very strong links between France and Scotland through that conflict, a Scotsman, John Carmichael of Douglasdale, became a bishop of Orléans, while the great Scottish warrior John

Stewart Darnley was buried in the cathedral after he was killed at the Battle of Rouvray-St-Denis, north of Orléans, in February 1429.

The transept and nave were only added at the end of the 15th century and beginning of the 16th. They didn't last long – Protestants in 1568 almost entirely ruined the previous construction which had taken so many centuries to build. Only the radiating chapels around the choir and a couple of nave bays remained standing after one of the most monumental acts of destruction of the French Wars of Religion.

The first stone of the new, present building was laid by Henri IV in 1601. This cathedral took still longer to complete than the previous one, from 1601 to 1829 (excluding the steeple), the last date handily coinciding with the fourth centenary of Joan of Arc's liberation of Orléans. The choir and transepts are 17th-century, most of the rest 18th. The encroachment of certain Italianate elements shows that there was some tussle between the Gothic style and the neoclassical in the rebuilding. The most comical intrusion sticks out from the transepts: Louis XIV's face, and most notably his proboscis, form the centrepiece for the rose windows, together with his motto 'Nec pluribus impar' (crudely translated, 'Without equal'). The cathedral steeple was only added in 1858.

In the nave, the colourful-to-gaudy 19th-century windows in the side aisles commemorate the life of Joan of Arc, a well-known triumphalist feature, the work of Galland and Gibelin. The choir stalls have superb sculpted wood panels drawn by Jacques V Gabriel and carved by Degoullons. Interesting art works include the tomb of Monseigneur Dupanloup, and a *Pietà* by Michel Bourdin.

The tourist office organizes regular tours of the roofs and towers of the cathedral, from which you get good views of the architecture, in particular the great timbers which support the roof. You can also admire the few monumental statues on the towers themselves – one of the bells they contain is named after Joan, inevitably. And of course you can enjoy fine views over the city from such an elevated position.

Musée des Beaux-Arts

Open Tues–Sat 10–12.15, 1.30–6, closed Sun am and Mon, and public hols; t 02 38 79 21 55, www.ville-orleans.fr, adm.

The sober modern exterior of the imposing building next to the cathedral which holds Orléans' fine arts museum proves misleading. Inside, you are treated to an extravagant display of the arts. In the centre of one of the largest rooms, a sculpture by Germain Pilon shows Monseigneur de Morvilliers, one-time bishop of Orléans, in pensive sad reflection. It's as though he's dejected by the outrageous opulence that surrounds him. For the rest of the vast space is decorated with works from the Cardinal de Richelieu's sumptuous collection, once held in his vast château on the Touraine-Poitou border (*see* p.326). On great panels by Martin Freminet, the Evangelists and Fathers of the Church look vain as body-builders, draped in gaudy-coloured garments in the self-conscious poses of disco dancers. Below them, ornate fantasies by Claude Deruet depict the elements, aristocrats at play in the scenes: horse-drawn sleighs rush across an icy river in the snowy countryside depicting

Water; a city alight with flames illustrates Fire, and so on. Such works make complaints about the vanity of today's youth culture seem pretty petty by comparison. These paintings reveal the vanity of the leaders of France's Counter-Reformation.

The collections gathered together here from the churches and monasteries of the Orléans region during the Revolution scarcely give you a different impression. The works from the Monastère Notre-Dame de Bonne Nouvelle, the Couvent des Capucins and the Chapelle du Collège des Jésuites, among others, share the general characteristic of being outrageously extravagant. Typical pieces include Claude Vignon's *Le Triomphe de Saint Ignace* and Jean Senelle's *Saint François donnant le cordon du Tiers-ordre à Louis XIII*. A host of famous artistic names of the period are represented. All told, to severer Catholics and good puritan Protestants, the 17th- and 18th-century treasures of this museum might be regarded as a fair exhibition of the degenerate nature of French Ancien Régime art.

As with the cathedral, so here Louis XIV puts in an appearance or two. Another Deruet painting portrays the future Sun King as a child; so much lace can't have been good for the boy. A later portrait of the megalomaniac by Rigaud and his studio shows the king decadently aged, mouth puckered, baggy-eyed, weighed down by furs. With rather worrying undertones for European unity, in another room a picture by Jean-Baptiste Martin (alias 'Martin des Batailles') shows the 1673 siege of a Dutch town by Louis XIV's troops, the smoke of war rising in puffs around Maastricht.

Other classic French works include the *St Sébastien soigné par Irène* from the Georges de la Tour studio, in the immediately recognizable candle-lit atmosphere of that painter. Irène's eyes appear to be disconcertingly distracted from the arrow wound to the lightly covered groin of the beautiful young man she's tending. The more understandably raunchy Le Nain brothers' *Bacchus découvrant Ariane à Naxos* uses almost cloisonné colour effects. From an artist born in Pithiviers in the Orléanais, look out for Lubin Baugin's *La Déposition de Croix*, Christ's body painted in extraordinary white soft focus. Among some fine sculptures, a series of trials in terracotta by Jean-Antoine Houdon represents famous men of letters of the 17th and 18th centuries.

The 19th-century collections include typical Orientalist paintings and some notable Romantic ones. As for more experimental 19th-century artists, Gauguin went no further than Brittany, then considered foreign and exotic, for his *Fête Gloanec*. Alfred Johannot, meanwhile, tried a rendering of the Grande Mademoiselle's entrance into Orléans. Alexandre Antigna's depiction of women in *Les Baigneuses* caused a scandal in his day. The museum wouldn't be complete without its collection of works on Joan of Arc; many a 19th-century French artist went quite potty about her.

The more provocative early 20th-century Orléans sculptors Henri Gaudier-Brezska and Charles Malfray are also devoted space. Gaudier-Brezska was viewed as a precursor of much modern sculpture, a member of the Vorticist movement and friend of Ezra Pound. Another collection concentrates on Max Jacob (*see* St-Benoît-sur-Loire, p.98, for his connection with the area).

While we've focused on some of the best French paintings above, this excellent museum also contains a fair collection of works by foreign schools, Flemish, Dutch, Italian and Spanish, most famous among them the *Saint Thomas* by Velasquez.

Hôtel Groslot

Open Oct–Jun Tue–Fri 10–12, 2–6, Sat and Sun 4.30–6; July–Sept Sun–Fri 9–7, Sat 5–9; closed 7 and 8 May and during weddings and official receptions; t 02 38 79 22 30; free.

The Hôtel Groslot lies almost opposite the Musée des Beaux Arts. Its elegant patterned brick façades serve as the backdrop for many an Orléans wedding photo, the civil ceremonies taking place within. The *hôtel* was originally built for a *bailli* called Groslot, a high-ranking official under King François I. The renowned French Renaissance architect Du Cerceau probably played a part in its design. It was decorated with typically indecorous Mannerist-style statues, including a naked-breasted woman. After 1790 it served as Orléans' town hall. The extremities of the two wings were harmoniously added in the mid-19th century.

A double stairway sweeps up to the main entrance, in front of which stands a sculpture of Joan of Arc, clad in copper, designed by Princess Marie d'Orléans, daughter of the mid-19th-century King Louis-Philippe. The other sculptures in the niches are by Jouffroy, depicting famous figures in Orléans' history. The interior is in 19th-century neo-Renaissance style, sumptuously exaggerated. Joan dominates inside, clearly an inspiration if not an obsession for Marie d'Orléans; another sculpture by the princess shows the Maid on horseback, directing her steed to avoid a wounded soldier. There's no historical evidence that Joan was particularly gentle in war, although she said at her trial that she had never killed a man. A painting of her in the style of Ingres is also displayed. Yet another work depicts her wearing a gown, 19th-century decorum trying to dress her up as a woman. This is historically perverse; one of the main reasons for Joan's condemnation was her supposed 'unnaturalness' in refusing to wear women's clothing.

The room for wedding ceremonies is slightly disconcertingly the one in which King François II, short-lived husband of Mary Stuart, died. A painting hanging in the room morbidly recalls the event. It can scarcely be uplifting to be reminded of such a tragic, brief marriage as you pronounce your vows.

Hôtel Cabu and Musée Archéologique et Historique de l'Orléanais

Open July–Aug Tues–Sun 10–12.15, 1.30–6; May, June and Sept Tues–Sun 1.30–6; rest of year Wed and weekends 1.30–6; t 02 38 79 21 55; adm, but free on first Sun each month.

The Hôtel Cabu may also have been planned by Du Cerceau. Mainly built of brick, some decorative Renaissance details are picked out on its façades. Second World War bombing badly damaged the building, restored under the watchful eye of Paul Gélis. The interior houses the city's archaeological and historical museum, which holds a fabulous surprise.

The horse dedicated to the Celtic god Rudiobus, sometimes compared with the Roman god of war Mars, poses majestically as the centrepiece in a wonderful little collection on the ground floor, part of a cache unearthed east along the Loire at Neuvy-en-Sullias. The proud beast is thought to date from the 2nd century. Its dressage dignity, its flaming mane, its muscular tautness convey great power and poise. The wild boar, beautifully ugly brutes from the same find, were a great symbol for the Gauls, their ardent fighting spirit most admired by Celtic warriors. The animal was also associated for the Celts with the world of the dead. The splendid deer was made in molten bronze, the breast patterned with detail, its antlers removable. Deer antlers, which in the natural cycle fall in winter and grow again in spring, symbolized the cycle of death and rebirth, and the Celtic god Cernunos was traditionally represented crowned with them.

The Gauls' great spring carnival apparently began with a deer hunt and the ritual death of a deer. After the chase the hunters would don the skins of the dead animals and dance in them, before stripping to dance naked. These so-called 'Gaulish bacchanalia' were supposed to reflect the rebirth of nature. Human figures, too, are portrayed in the ground-floor room, a naked man running and women dancing, arms raised and full of movement. They appear much more primitive than the animals, but still make very powerful images. The site of Neuvy has thus far offered no clues as to the provenance of this cache. It may be that the pieces were hidden there at a time of barbarian invasions. The other collection of objects found at Neuvy are from the classical tradition. Among them stands a typical Gallo-Roman goddess mother figure, suckling a child on either breast.

On the first floor, carved fragments from vanished or damaged churches around the Loiret constitute the main feature, including bits of floral-patterned stuccowork from the Carolingian oratory at Germigny and five capitals originally from the abbey of St-Benoît, one featuring mermaids holding on to a fish. Joan of Arc is represented in yet more travesties of historical fact. Among old depictions of Orléans, one from the 17th century clearly shows the city walls built after the Hundred Years' War. Other rooms display local ephemera, including delicate Loire mariners' brooches and local pottery.

Maison de Jeanne d'Arc and Centre Jeanne d'Arc

The **Maison de Jeanne d'Arc** (*open May–Oct Tues–Sun 10–12.30; Nov–April Tues–Sun 1.30–6, closed public holidays; t 02 38 52 99 89, www.jeannedarc.com.fr; adm*) is a museum which retells Joan of Arc's short, dashing visit to Orléans and her role in its liberation (*see* 'History', above). It occupies a substantial brick-and-timberframe house on Place du Général de Gaulle. The building had to be totally re-created after the war. Despite the name, the place actually belonged to Jacques Boucher, the duke of Orléans' treasurer, and Joan only stayed a handful of days before the great attack.

You can follow the events in Joan's campaign in front of a large model of the town, the excited commentary provided in French or English. The video on the floor above, presenting the more general history of the times, is only in French, although further little models recreate scenes in the important towns through which Joan passed during her short military career. Otherwise, the museum contains a curious collection of memorabilia on Joan, such as commemorative plates. You may leave with the feeling that so many models and little mementoes don't do justice to one of the most extraordinary women in European history (*see* the box).

You can study Joan more seriously at the **Centre Jeanne d'Arc** (*open Mon–Thurs 9–12 and 2–6, Fri 9–12 and 2–4.45, closed public holidays; t 02 38 79 24 92, www.jeannedarc. com.fr; free*), near the cathedral at 24 Rue Jeanne d'Arc. This research centre, open to all, has its home in a grandly fronted school, and its rooms resemble a school library. All visitors are free to consult the volumes and papers written on Joan, classified by theme. If you telephone in advance, you might even consider spending a rainy afternoon in Orléans watching one or two of the many films about Joan.

A Walk Around Orléans

The obvious place to start a walking tour of Orléans is at Joan of Arc's feet, paying homage to her statue at the centre of **Place du Martroi**, heart of the modern Orléans. The bronze piece representing a standard-bearing Joan in formidable armour on her war horse was executed by Foyatier and dates from 1855. The panels below the statue depict scenes from Joan's life.

Place du Martroi gives some impression of the former Ancien Régime splendour of the city. It's very easy to tell the few prewar remnants from the newly built; the façade of the **Chancellerie du duc d'Orléans** typifies mid-18th-century grandeur. A good number of brasseries and restaurants spill out onto the square in summer and some of the town's liveliest streets lead off in various directions.

The two main shopping arteries head respectively north and south from Place du Martroi. **Rue de la République**, the grand thoroughfare leading up to the railway station, exudes Belle Epoque elegance. Its good array of shops include several specializing in perfume. **Rue Royale**, sloping south towards the Loire, recreates the sophisticated arcaded Ancien Régime street destroyed by war bombing; some very smart clothes shops and culinary stops are protected by its arches.

Rue Royale acts as something of a dividing line in the centre of Orléans. The quarter west of Rue Royale suffered terribly from war bombs and doesn't have the atmospheric appeal of the area to the east. For example, **Place du Général de Gaulle** is a chaotically rebuilt big triangle of a square. One one side of it you'll find the **Maison de Jeanne d'Arc** (*see* above), standing out with its brick and beam patterning.

Along **Rue du Tabour**, taking you back to Rue Royale, the substantial French Renaissance **Maison d'Euverte Hatte**, built for a wealthy 16th-century merchant, now houses the specialist, somewhat stuffy **Centre Charles Péguy** (*library open Mon–Thurs 9–12 and 1.30–6, Fri 9–12 and 1.30–5; museum open pm only; closed on public holidays; t 02 38 53 20 23, www.coeur-de-france.com/peguy.html; free*). An impassioned socialist and prolific writer of the Belle Epoque, among other massive labours, Péguy rewrote Joan of Arc's life in a huge three-volume dramatic work, *Jeanne d'Arc*, interpreting his native town's heroine according to his own ideals, turning her into a warrior for the oppressed against a leadership indifferent to suffering. After Péguy

Jeanne la Pucelle

O astonishing virgin!...Thou art the honour of the reign, thou art the light of the lily,
thou art the splendour, the glory, not only of Gaul but of all Christians.

Alain Chartier, 15th-century writer

After Mary, mother of Jesus, Joan of Arc is no doubt the most famous virgin in Western Christian history. Joan too received messengers from God, she said. Her voices were more modest than Mary's, simply telling her that she was to save the dignity of the French king and remove the English, who had taken over so much of the French royal territories in the Hundred Years' War. After persuading the Crown and French representatives of the Catholic Church to listen to her (they were desperate – *see* Chinon, p.333), Joan was given the royal and religious seals of approval and the troops to allow her to play her part in booting the English off the continent. Her whirlwind campaign lasted from May 1429 to May 1430.

Joan was then only a teenager, but hardly an innocent one. She had a plan, she had pigheaded ideas on how to execute it, and she had an unquestioning belief in her own calling. She was, it appears, a born leader, a captivatingly strong character for the war-weakened French, unhesitating and persuasive at a time when the French monarchy was in dire straits, and in need of positive thinkers, if not miracles. Uneducated and unabashed, Joan spoke her mind and managed to get her way to an almost incredible extent. Not that she always had it as she wanted it, mind you. Dunois led the French troops to Orléans, choosing a route which cantankerous Joan complained went against the advice of her voices.

Her part in the relief of Orléans, though, was her greatest moment. With this *tour de force* her credibility as a military leader was established, and she went on to play a crucial role in French victories across the Orléanais, bringing triumph at Jargeau, Meung, Beaugency and Patay. The English positions on the Loire were captured within weeks of Orléans' liberation. The details of Joan's precise military contribution are unclear. She claimed never to have killed a man, but as Marina Warner in her excellent book on Joan makes clear: 'whether or not Joan played a key part in the military manoeuvres fades into insignificance beside the historical truth that her contemporaries, on both sides, thought that she had.' Hers was in good part a victory in psychological warfare.

Joan became a legend in her own lifetime and has remained one for centuries. For the French side, she was a miracle worker. For the English she was inspired by the devil. But Joan's downfall was swift and no one in the French camp came to her rescue when she was captured by Burgundian troops, allies of the English, at Compiègne northeast of Paris on 23 May 1430. The Burgundians handed their precious prisoner to the English authorities in France, but people don't always

had been converted to mystical Christianity in 1909, he redrafted the drama of the Maid as *Le Mystère de la charité de Jeanne d'Arc*. As the threat of war grew, his idealistic hopes for a universal society yielded to the realities of the divisive situation in Europe and he became increasingly patriotic. He died fighting in the First World War.

realize that it was University of Paris theologians who put forward the request for her trial as a heretic. This complex event, of which the records remain, began in January 1431 in Rouen in Normandy; at the end of May Joan was found guilty of heresy and condemned to death. She briefly recanted, only to show her stubbornness one final, fatal time. She was burnt at the stake on 30 May 1431. The French Crown she had helped save hadn't lifted a finger to save her.

It took some time until her rehabilitation trial was held by the French, in 1456, once the English had been driven out of most of France. This retrial, which took place in Orléans, cleared Joan's name, but was also exploited in good part to reassert the French king's legitimate position.

Joan was a deeply controversial figure from the beginning. Her claims of contact with the divine made her extremely suspicious to the Church on both sides of the war divide. The Church in the French camp rigorously tested her religious views and virginity before accepting her. The assertion of her individual will and her claim to be able to execute the wishes of God directly, bypassing the Lord's bureaucratic institution on earth, have been seen by some as a kind of Protestantism before its day. She managed to assume a position of military authority despite being of lowly birth (although not as peasantish a shepherdess as romantics would believe). She wore men's clothes, which was particularly shocking. All round, she was a disturbing figure. She was also utterly extraordinary, managing to gain so much power in such a rigid society and acting as such an inspiration. Her claims were certainly not a unique occurrence in the medieval world (and wouldn't be in today's world, for that matter), but Joan got concrete results.

All sorts of causes have adopted Joan in a terrible confusion of ways. First and foremost, she's been seen as the symbol of a glorious France, a reunified country under a divinely ordained king. For many French people she's been *the* symbol of national pride.It matters little that in her day the leaders of many regions of what is now France wanted to remain independent of French royalty rather than become subservient to such an acquisitive and exploitative central power. Many tend to forget, too, the fact that it took a good many years after Joan's triumphs to get the English out of France. Confusingly, while the inhabitants of Orléans somewhat understandably recall and celebrate every year the town's liberation after the terrible siege, the right-wing Front National party organizes an alternative annual Joan of Arc march with more sinister undertones. As to the modern Catholic Church, it took a long time to recognize the supposed sanctity of this young military leader – Joan was after all condemned to death by one of its own most powerful branches – and she was not canonized until 1920. More recently, some have searched for the schizophrenic in Joan, while others have seen definite signs in her of a combative lesbian or bulimic, among a plethora of wildly speculative theories.

Rue Royale leads down to the **Pont George V**, Orléans' elegant central bridge across the Loire. Rebaptized in honour of an English king, it was in fact built under Louis XV; it's known to the locals as the Pont Royal. The modern quarters on the south bank of the Loire may look uninspiring, but it's worth crossing the Pont George V for the fine views back across the river to the historic town. On the south bank, set back from the Quai Fort des Tourelles, stands a **bronze statue of Joan of Arc**, from Napoleonic times, by Gois *fils*. This originally stood in Place du Martroi, but Joan's plumed, standard-bearing pose didn't go down well among the Orléanais (she does look rather combatively prissy in this version), so this version of her was removed to be replaced by Foyatier's. The siting of this statue is significant, though; it was here that the epic struggle to free Orléans of the English centred on 7 May 1429.

Crossing back to north of the river, the area immediately east of the Rue Royale has several very charming and lively streets. In their midst, the large modern shopping centre-cum-covered market known as **Les Halles-Châtelet** looks rather dull architecturally, but its stands and boutiques may draw you in. Several French Renaissance houses have been preserved in the streets around it, for instance the **Maison du Cerceau**, attributed to one of the best-known French architects of that period.

Rue de Bourgogne, one of old Orléans' liveliest streets, is packed with restaurants. Certain timberframe houses stand out along its length, as well as the round **Temple**, a 19th-century Protestant church. Take some time to explore the streets and little squares between Rue de Bourgogne and Rue Jeanne d'Arc as they are the most atmospheric in the city, containing fine Renaissance mansions and overseen by the belfry commissioned by the town's councillors in the 15th century.

From **Rue Jeanne d'Arc**, enjoy the most splendid vista onto the cathedral. On the north side of this broad, busy, very straight street you can seek out the **Centre Jeanne d'Arc** (*see* above). Rue Jeanne d'Arc leads to the big square in front of the cathedral, **Place Ste-Croix**. Head north from here, past the **Musée des Beaux-Arts** and the **Hôtel Groslot** (*see* above), to take a look along **Rue d'Escures**, which contains some of the smartest, largest houses in town, including the grandiose Pavilions d'Escures. These were commissioned by a dynamic mayor of Orléans who became a close friend of King Henri IV and they reflect the period taste for mixing brick and slate, as in the Place des Vosges in Paris. The imposing **church of St-Pierre-du-Martroi**, just off Rue d'Escures, was also rebuilt in brick after the 16th-century Wars of Religion.

Back near the cathedral hides the enormous, curiously vacuous **Campo Santo**. This site served for many centuries as Orléans' main cemetery. Arcades resembling cloisters were built around it from the 15th century, but by the 18th century the place was declared a danger to public health and closed. Restored in recent times, the place regularly serves as a venue for all manner of cultural events.

Do walk all the way round the **cathedral**. On the north side stand a few vestiges of Orléans' 4th-century Gallo-Roman wall, while from the walled garden of the Ancien Régime **bishop's palace** you can appreciate the flying buttresses around the cathedral's choir end particularly well. Off the south side of the cathedral, Rue Pothier leads to the **Préfecture**, the smart administrative seat of the Loiret *département*.

East of the Préfecture, you enter a quieter old district, with atmospheric streets sloping towards the Loire from Rue de Bourgogne. Down one, you'll be drawn by the slightly neglected medieval forms of the **church and cloister of St-Pierre-le-Puellier**, now converted into a venue for exhibitions and concerts. Down another, the **Tour Blanche** stands out, a medieval tower built on Gallo-Roman foundations. Down a third, seek out the **Fonds Régional d'Art Contemporain du Centre** or **FRAC** (*12 Rue de la Tour Neuve*, *t 02 38 62 52 00*, *www.frac-centre.asso.fr*), where contemporary art pieces acquired by the region are put on display. The big new glass building close to the Loire is a **covered Halles**, as yet empty most of the time.

But the most appealing attraction in this quarter is the sunken, tree-lined Square du Cloître St-Aignan with the **church of St-Aignan** looming over one side. This mutilated Gothic church isn't open to the public, but its large, atmospheric crypt is (*contact tourist office for tours; adm*). Already in Carolingian times, St-Aignan was a collegiate church, but it was rebuilt in the 11th century for King Robert le Pieux. The crypt is all that has survived from his time. However, it is on a grand scale, built to house not just bones belonging to St Aignan but also those of half-a-dozen other saints. The crypt's remarkable carved capitals were only rediscovered in 1953. They are cleverly presented, still encased within the supporting pillars added at a later date. Some feature plant decoration, with superbly carved acanthus leaves; others depict violent scenes – monsters spit fire, while a man with a sword is seen fighting, no doubt against evil, on one side of a capital, but running away on the other side! The *martyrium* was the protected inner sanctum reserved for the venerated relics. It was provided with small slits in the wall through which the pilgrims could look or pass objects such as a piece of cloth on a stick to benefit from the miraculous touch of the reliquary.

Take a car or bus south across Pont George V for **Olivet** and the pretty **Loiret** banks. A walk along the delightful tow path takes you past old watermills and along the backs of the houses, with boathouses and landing jetties at the bottom of the garden. At **Orléans-La Source**, next to Olivet, La Source refers to the fact that the Loiret river emerges here, in what is now the **Parc Floral** (*open April–mid-Nov 9–6, rest of year 2–5; t 02 38 49 30 00, www.parcfloral-lasource.fr; adm*). This is a beautifully tended public garden. Opposite lies the university campus, with several interesting modern buildings.

The Loire from Orléans to Blois

10

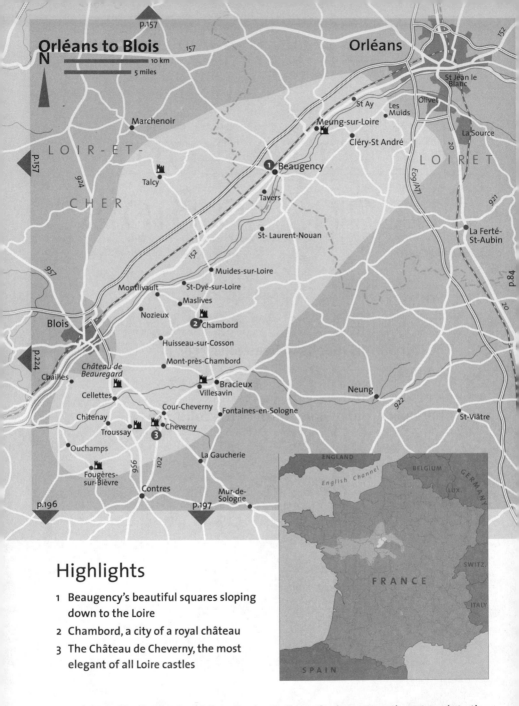

N

10 km

5 miles

p.157

157

p.157

Orléans

St Jean le Blanc

St Ay

Les Muids

Olivet

La Source

LOIR-ET-

Marchenoir

Meung-sur-Loire

Cléry-St André

LOIRET

924

Talcy

1 Beaugency

CHER

Tavers

152

St-Laurent-Nouan

La Ferté-
St-Aubin

957

Muides-sur-Loire

Montlivault

St-Dyé-sur-Loire

Maslives

Nozieux

2 Chambord

Blois

Huisseau-sur-Cosson

Mont-près-Chambord

p.224

Château de
Beauregard

Chailles

Cellettes

Bracieux

Villesavin

Neung

922

Cour-Cheverny

Fontaines-en-Sologne

Chitenay

3 Cheverny

St-Viâtre

Troussay

Ouchamps

La Gaucherie

956

102

Fougères-
sur-Bièvre

p.196

Contres

Mur-de-
Sologne

p.197

ENGLAND

English Channel

BELGIUM

GERMANY

LUX.

SWITZ.

FRANCE

ITALY

SPAIN

Highlights

1 Beaugency's beautiful squares sloping
   down to the Loire
2 Chambord, a city of a royal château
3 The Château de Cheverny, the most
   elegant of all Loire castles

The Loire begins its slow, determined marathon of a descent southwestwards to the
Atlantic once past Orléans. In this chapter we cover the river between Orléans and
Blois. On the north bank, the little towns of Meung-sur-Loire and Beaugency now

offer delightful Loire-side havens off the commercially scarred N152. Their protected slopes made them sought-after sites in the early medieval period, hence their legacy of châteaux and vast churches. On the south bank, opposite these two hillside towns, the fertile land is flat as a pancake, making the huge church of Notre-Dame de Cléry, chosen burial place of King Louis XI, stand out all the better.

At the massive nuclear power station at St-Laurent-Nouan you leave the Orléanais (now the *département* of Loiret) for the Blésois (the *département* of Loir-et-Cher). Passing swiftly along the south bank you arrive at St-Dyé-sur-Loire, the port which served the building site of that mammoth among Loire Renaissance châteaux, Chambord. The castle, surrounded by the thickest of forests, was commissioned in part as a hunting fantasy by outsized 16th-century French king, François I. It's a mesmerizing fairytale palace. A handful of much more modest but very appealing châteaux nearby can also be visited: Villesavin, Beauregard, Troussay, Fougères-sur-Bièvre and Cheverny – Loire châteaux don't come any more refined than the last.

The Loire from Orléans to Beaugency

Beaugency, with its clutch of impressive medieval monuments, is the highlight of this stretch of the Loire river, although Meung-sur-Loire also has its moments. The Basilique de Cléry-St-André and the Château de Talcy offer less well-known surprises.

Meung-sur-Loire

The bishops of Orléans chose Meung-sur-Loire for their out-of-town residence in medieval times and 'The Bishops' Castle' might be a suitable nickname for the château at Meung. They weren't ones to deprive themselves, clearly. The town also boasts a vast abbey church quite out of keeping with its present scale.

The **Château de Meung** (*open mid Feb–Nov 10–12 and 2–7; Dec–mid-Feb weekends only, 2–6;* t *02 38 44 36 47, www.chateaudemeung.com; adm*) has changed hands recently and been substantially restored. Beyond the severe medieval-looking entrance, you can visit many rooms, including unusual centuries-old bathrooms, and a network of creepy underground corridors which bring to mind imprisonment and torture. Out in the garden, the *oubliette*, or dungeon, looks very much like the ice houses it was once fashionable to dig in one's château's grounds. Two famously sharp-witted medieval French poets are associated with Meung's history, and one, Villon, is said to have been locked up here for a time. Villon led a wild life in Paris, being found guilty of theft and murder on a couple of occasions. His charm and his poetry, the latter full of pathos, pain and puns, helped get him out of many a sticky situation. He's most famous for his mock wills written in verse, in which, as he had so few possessions, he would ironically distribute all he owned with great pomp, down to old egg shells and his hair clippings, reserved for the people he most detested.

Below Meung's château, the **church of St-Liphard** stands out like a cathedral in a village. Much of it was built in small irregular stone rather than big, tidy blocks, but

Getting Around

Meung-sur-Loire and Beaugency are well served by regular **trains** between Orléans and Blois.

Tourist Information

Meung-sur-Loire: 42 Rue Jehan de Meung, 45130 Meung-sur-Loire, t 02 38 44 32 28, *www.visitez-meung.com*.

Cléry-St-André: 111 Rue du Maréchal Foch, 45370 Cléry-St-André, t/f 02 38 45 94 33, *o-tourismedeclery@wanadoo.fr*.

Beaugency: 3 Place du Dr Hyvernaud, B.P. 44, 45190 Beaugency, t 02 38 44 54 42, *tourisme.beaugency@wanadoo.fr*.

Market Days

Meung-sur-Loire: Thursday afternoon and Sunday morning.

Cléry-St-André: Thursday and Saturday mornings.

Beaugency: Saturday, all day.

Tavers: Sunday morning.

Where to Stay and Eat

Meung-sur-Loire ⊠ 45130

★★**Auberge St-Jacques**, 60 Rue du Général de Gaulle (N152), t 02 38 44 30 39, f 02 38 45 17 02 (*inexpensive*). Well regarded for its cuisine (*menus €15–30*), this traditional French inn is where d'Artagnan was wounded in a skirmish in 1625, after which he was tended by the beautiful Milady. On the unattractively busy main road. *Closed second half Jan.*

Dix Sept Sur Vins, 17 Rue du Général de Gaulle, t 02 38 45 13 41 (*menus €19–25*). This ivy-clad restaurant has a certain charm within and serves good fish dishes.

Café du Commerce, t 02 38 44 32 35. On an historic square, with awnings above the green terrace chairs, a delightfully unpretentious place at which to try simple menus (*menus €9.50–37*). *Closed Sun eve and Mon.*

Les Muids/Mareau-aux-Prés ⊠ 45370

Le Clos des Muids B&B, 1045 Rue des Muids, t/f 02 38 45 63 16, *www.chambre-dhotes.com* (*inexpensive*). An energetic couple have been restoring the farm buildings around their courtyard in the village of Les Muids, close to

with its originally shaped trefoil choir end and its flying buttresses, it mainly dates from the Gothic period. The place does contain the odd older Romanesque feature; the base of the stone rocket of a steeple goes back to the 11th century, for example, while the north transept is distinctly from the earlier period. Inside, huge lancet arches hold up the nave, while the side-aisles are flanked by side chapels, in a couple of which ornate reliquary boxes sit perched high on brackets. The temple-reliquary boxes in St Teresa's chapel are adorned with gruesome scenes of martyrdoms. Cast-iron gates with angels mark the entrance to the side chapel containing St Liphard's relics.

The pretty shape of the church's trefoil end is emphasized by the splendid vaulting in the apse and transepts, the ribs falling down like so many spider's legs. Look out for the stained glass in one end chapel, representing not St Liphard, but St Joan, shown celebrating Mass here in this very Meung church after another of her Loire-side victories – adoring, kneeling onlookers are distracted from thoughts of God to stare entranced at the Maid in her armour. Once again Joan is represented sweeping all before her, here stealing the limelight from St Liphard and the Lord.

Leaving Meung's main square by the choir end of the church, head past the covered market, the splashing modern fountain and the mill stream to come out close to the riverside. Much of Meung's north bank lies in the shade of five splendid lines of plane trees (the scene is only slightly marred by the camp site). The Loire bridge is a relatively modest, modernish construction. You may notice a couple of rather bad statues around here. One of them represents Gaston Couté, a local boy who hit the

orchards a handful of kilometres north of Cléry-St-André, off the D951. They've introduced a few high-tech features into the comfortable rooms, such as electronic shutters. Not only are the bathrooms excellent here, there's even a lovely heated indoor pool you can use (*table d'hôte €17*).

Beaugency ✉ 45190

***Hôtel de l'Abbaye**, 2 Quai de l'Abbaye, **t** 02 38 44 67 35, *www.chateauxhotels. com* (*moderate*). Set in former abbey buildings dating back to the Ancien Régime and superbly located by the Loire, this large hotel has rooms with views of the river. The fine restaurant serves Loire cuisine (*menu €36*).

****Hôtel de la Sologne**, 6 Place Saint-Firmin, **t** 02 38 44 50 27, *www.hoteldelasologne.com* (*inexpensive*). A charming little labyrinth of a hotel. The rooms are lovingly looked after and a bargain. *Closed late Mar–mid April.*

****Le Relais des Templiers**, 68 Rue du Pont, **t** 02 38 44 53 78, **f** 02 38 46 42 55 (*inexpensive*). Makes a pretty picture, with a private garden and terrace. *Closed Feb.*

****L'Ecu de Bretagne**, Place du Martroi, **t** 02 38 44 67 60, **f** 02 38 44 68 07 (*inexpensive*). Not quite as charming to look at as the hotels above, with a modern annexe as well as the old posting inn, but its rooms are generally comfortable. The menus aren't cheap, but then the chef experiments with rich dishes such as rabbit with gingerbread and pork in honey (*menus €18–30*). *Closed Sun pm and Mon Nov–Mar.*

Le P'tit Bateau, 54 Rue du Pont, **t** 02 38 44 56 38 (*menus €21–30; closed Sun pm, Mon, and Tues pm*). In a typical Beaugency light white stone house, with a beamed dining room where you can try fish specialities. *Closed late Aug–early Sept, late Oct–early Nov, late Feb–early Mar.*

Tavers ✉ 45190

*****La Tonnellerie**, 12 Rue des Eaux-Bleues, **t** 02 38 44 68 15, *tonnellerie@chateauxhotels. com* (*expensive*). A luxurious hotel, but it keeps its pleasures well hidden behind its unassuming façade in this peaceful village southwest of Beaugency. Within, elegant rooms, a pretty terrace, a walled garden and a swimming pool await; the cuisine is stylish too (*menus €25–45; closed Mon lunch and Sat lunch*). *Closed Christmas–Feb.*

big time as a Montmartre crooner at the beginning of the 20th century, here interpreted in the Chinese workers' school of sculpture.

The other figure is the other great poet beyond Villon associated with Meung: Jean de Meun has been made to look like a straight-backed, tight-waisted, prim spinster of a man here, holding a rose in one hand. The flower makes reference to his famous work; he was the main author of that medieval bestseller *Le Roman de la Rose*, taking over where Guillaume de Lorris (*see p.108*) left off, writing the bulk of the composition and adding a much sharper, more prickly twist to it, turning the allegory into a critique of contemporary society and mores. However, Christine de Pisan, one of the great female writers of the medieval period in France, attacked the poem for being obscene and degrading to women, and a debate long raged over the work and the various ways of interpreting it. Chaucer, Dante and Petrarch were all familiar with the poem. It's written in beautiful old French, which looks harder to read than it sounds when read out loud, but you need a firm grasp of the language to tackle it.

One other prickly thing that shouldn't go unmentioned in Meung is the fine collection of holly bushes planted at the **Arboretum des Prés des Culands** (*open April–Oct, but only by reservation and you are taken round by a guide*; **t/f** *02 38 63 10 49, ilex@noos.fr; adm*), a national *conservatoire* of the species, set in the charming watery scenery of Les Mauves, the name given to the streams that congregate at Meung, in a quarter where the mills used to grind the corn from the Beauce plain to the north.

Basilique de Cléry-St-André

Cross to the very flat south bank of the Loire from Meung to reach the grand late medieval Basilique de Cléry-St-André, which stands out like a great vessel in a desert. It's thanks to a large dose of medieval superstition that the diminutive place was donated such a disproportionately vast church. In 1280 a local farmer ploughing his field supposedly dug up a statue of the Virgin and Child, said to have begun working miracles. Such was the impact that royal Capetian patronage was quickly in on the act. King Philippe IV's generous sponsorship allowed for the building of a splendid church which became an important stop on the pilgrimage route from Paris to Santiago de Compostela. The English army passing this way in the second half of the Hundred Years' War destroyed Philippe le Bel's church. Miracle of miracles, the Virgin and Child survived, and the powerful local Count Dunois, aided by King Charles VII, supported a rebuilding programme. The reputed architects Pierre Le Paige and Pierre Chauvin worked on it, but progress was slow, until the supremely superstitious King Louis XI spurred on the work after what he reckoned was an act of divine intervention by the Virgin of Cléry. As dauphin, or heir to the French throne, in 1443 Louis had been fighting the English up in Dieppe with Dunois. The battle was going against the French. The story goes that Louis prayed to the Virgin of Cléry for her assistance; she apparently heard him and interceded, so the future king believed, reversing the tide of the battle and bringing victory to the French. So Louis became personally involved in the rebuilding of the church at Cléry-St-André and showered money on the project. Most significantly, the king of superstitious paranoia decided to be buried here. So anxious was he to see the place completed before his death that he even spent a couple of months at Cléry in 1482 as the site was nearing completion but his health was failing. In the end, the church wasn't quite ready by the time of his death in 1483; but he was able to decompose here in peace, even though Protestants in the 16th-century Wars of Religion destroyed his tomb effigy.

The basilica's nave is a huge, light Gothic space. Louis XI's effigy was replaced in the 17th century, the fine new sculpture of him executed by the Orléans artist Michel Bourdin in 1622. The king kneels soberly in prayer, looking severe and ascetic despite his robes decorated with fleurs-de-lys and in contrast to the putti holding up a coat of arms on each corner. Nearby, steps lead down to a crypt holding the sarcophagi of the king and his wife. The original statue of the Virgin and Child still graces the church, perched high up in an over-elaborate 19th-century structure. The brown-robed Mary looks distinctly surprised by all the attention, and the elevation. Only a few stained-glass windows remain in the church, high up in the choir. On the left-hand side, you can see a representation of the lifting of the siege of Dieppe. The king in the central panel under the Virgin isn't Louis XI but Henri III, easily distinguished by his distinctive goatee beard; this 16th-century work depicts him creating the knightly Order of the Holy Spirit. Back at ground level, grotesques stare out from the choir stalls.

Two important side chapels lie off the south aisle. The Chapelle de Longueville, in Flamboyant Gothic style, was the burial place of Dunois and his wife Marie d'Harcourt. The Chapelle Saint-Jacques has typical elements of decoration from the transitional period from Gothic to Renaissance in France, at the start of the 16th century (*see* p.31). The walls have been showered with symbols representing the men for whom it was built, Gilles and François de Pontbriant (Shining Bridge), close to King François I. Also on the south side of the church, look out for a secretive staircase leading up to a comfortable chamber with a big fireplace and a little peep hole, made for Louis XI to observe Mass, unobserved, from up high.

Beaugency

A patched-up, bumpy medieval bridge, cobbled quays, vast plane trees shielding low waterfront houses, and behind them, soaring medieval monuments… Seen from the south side of its bumbling old bridge, the oldest one on the Loire, Beaugency is one of the most beautiful towns along the river. In medieval times it lay on the limits of the Blésois, the territory of the extremely powerful counts of Blois and was long a particularly important, strategic place because of its bridge, for centuries the only crossing over the Loire between Orléans and Blois.

Start a visit of Beaugency down by the Loire. Close to the bridge you can appreciate the extent of the gently sloping **quays** and imagine the busy trading activity that must once have enlivened this area. Beaugency's **medieval bridge** looks particularly magnificent from here, with its variety of arches and the visible hiccups in its construction. Behind the line of quayside plane trees, the long façade of a substantial 17th-century **abbey building** (now a hotel) looks out to the water.

Head up the slope to discover a surprising number of interesting old buildings packed close together around a series of interconnecting triangular-shaped squares. The most imposing evidence of Beaugency's medieval importance is the massive keep known as the **Tour de César**. There are a couple of other keeps like this along the Loire, for example at Montbazon and at Loches, which show the formidable nature of this type of early stone feudal military architecture. This one dates from the last quarter of the 11th century and still looks frighteningly severe – it rises to around 100ft – despite the beautiful colour of the stone and the mullion windows added in the 16th century to give it more light. Originally it had five levels of chambers within. A fire started by Protestants during the Wars of Religion caused the roof to burn; it was never replaced and the keep gradually fell into ruin. The place can't be visited as it's dangerous, having been abandoned for so long; plants have sprouted on it and crows are now lords of the manor. But it still makes an impressive sight. So, too, does the **Tour St-Firmin** beside it, a remnant of a church that has otherwise disappeared. On the shaded square below these massive towers stands the obligatory Loire statue of Joan of Arc, put up by a grateful populace – only in 1896, it turns out!

Not far down from the keep, and dating from the same Romanesque period, is the **church of Notre-Dame**. It too was badly damaged by religious fire in 1567, but was restored in 1642. In medieval times, this church served as the setting for the discussion of a couple of extremely difficult royal marital crises. The first major council at Beaugency was held to consider King Philippe I's excommunication from the Catholic Church – in 1092 he had repudiated his wife Berthe and taken off with Bertrade de Montfort, unfortunately already married to the count of Anjou (west along the Loire).

The second council, in 1152, was more serious still, deciding on the annulment of King Louis VII of France's marriage to Eleanor of Aquitaine. The reason given was consanguinity, but this was an excuse. The irrepressible Eleanor and pious Louis were incompatible; furthermore they had not produced a male heir, and there were even rumours of Eleanor committing adultery in Antioch when the couple had gone off on a Crusade. As a result of the annulment of the marriage, Eleanor took back the vast inheritance of southwest France she had brought to the French Crown, and promptly married Henri Plantagenêt, count of Anjou and future King Henry II of England. In a way, it could be argued that the decision taken at Beaugency led to the centuries of war between France and England that ensued.

Inside the church, massive Romanesque columns hold up the nave and aisles, with bold capital designs, some representing primitive foliage, others fighting or humorous figures. One capital has been cleverly turned to form a man's magnificently large nose! Walk round the lovely open ambulatory at the choir end and back up to the organ at the entrance, its front adorned with finely carved wood panels.

A gateway to one side of the church leads into the small, urban Château Dunois, housing a cluttered museum, the **Musée Régional de l'Orléanais** (*temporarily closed for repairs; check opening with tourist office; adm*). This château was the seat of Jean, Bastard of Orléans, illegitimate son of Louis I Duc de Orléans (brother of King Charles VI) and Marguerite d'Enghien. Being a bastard in those times didn't mean social ostracism, and on the tour you can see fleurs-de-lys proudly displayed on Jean's coat of arms, only with a prominent diagonal bar across it, symbolizing his illegitimacy. Jean had the principal parts of his château built from 1440 and lived here for 17 years. A great warrior, he most famously fought alongside Joan of Arc – in fact, it was he who led the French troops to free Orléans with Joan. After her death he continued the successful fight against the English, beating them at Montargis, Chartres and St-Denis, and playing his part in recapturing Paris.

The architecture within the partly arcaded courtyard looks slightly disappointing. Cement has been spread about in slapdash manner during restoration work. In the past, you were herded through the museum rooms without much time to linger in front of the 8,000 or so objects apparently on display, a small number interesting. Special collections include representations of the Loire in the region, and items on life on the river; religious robes and statuary; and most cosmopolitan, sculpture by the American John Storrs.

Of course the museum wouldn't be complete without a set of plates telling the life of Joan of Arc.

The **town hall** (*tours organized by the tourist office; normally open for visits May–Sept Mon–Fri 11am, 3, 4, 4.30pm and Sat 11am; Oct–April Tues–Fri 3, 4 and 4.30pm. Closed Sun and public holidays; adm*), on a higher square, boasts an unmissable over-decorated, over-restored French Renaissance façade – the building was badly damaged in the Revolution and had to be substantially repaired; the excess of decoration is quite mesmerizing. The outstanding feature is the fleurs-de-lys scattered on the front, *semées à pleine main*, 'sown by the handful', as the delightful and accurate French phrase has it.

Inside, eight exquisitely executed embroideries are displayed, their original provenance and precise symbolism a mystery, although they were brought here from the abbey and are reckoned to date from the 17th century. Four of them appear to illustrate curious scenes of sacrifice, richly coloured and distinctly disturbing. The others show allegories of the continents, each rather approximatively symbolized by a beautiful woman and by absurd, exotic animals.

Further up the slope still, you come out on the bright and often bustling **Place du Martroi**. The stumpy little medieval **church of St-Etienne** stands timidly to one side. It once formed part of a a priory dedicated to the Holy Sepulchre and dates back to the 11th century. The pleasing sunken interior now serves as a venue for exhibitions.

A Detour to the Château de Talcy North of the Loire

The north bank of the Loire from Beaugency to Blois is best avoided, as the A10 motorway and the unattractive N152 hardly make it possible to appreciate the valley. However, one detour worth considering due west of Beaugency is to the **Château de Talcy** (*open Oct–April Wed–Mon 10–12 and 2–5, May–Aug Wed–Mon 9.30–12 and 2–6; closed on public holidays; t/f 02 54 81 03 01; adm*), a stern-looking castle standing guard over an isolated village on the edge of the huge flat cereal plains of the Beauce, often referred to as the grainstore of Paris.

The Florentine banker Bernardo Salviati bought the Château de Talcy in 1517, to be close to the French court, largely based at Blois at the time. There's nothing Italianate about the castle though; the stocky 15th-century keep looming over the village pavement looks severely medieval, although slightly mellowed by subsequent embellishments. The delicately decorated interiors, dating from a later period, prove

The Death of Two Poets' Passions

Two great French literary figures of the 16th century became closely associated with Talcy. Pierre de Ronsard and Agrippa d'Aubigné, both to become acclaimed poets, fell madly in love with Salviati girls. Bernardo Salviati had a daughter, Cassandre, who quite turned the tonsured head of the young Pierre. He met her at a Blois ball in 1545, when he was a stripling of 21, she a mere 15. *Les Amours de Cassandre* are the only certain fruits of Ronsard's passion, 183 sonnets to the Salviati girl of his dreams from the most lyrical of all French poets. Cassandre, unfortunately, was married to someone else the year after they met. But rumour has it that Ronsard and Cassandre continued to see each other and that one of her children was in fact fathered by the poet.

It was Cassandre's brother Jean who inherited the Château de Talcy. His daughter Diane was called upon to tend a soldier wounded in fighting in the Wars of Religion. The warrior she cared for was none other than the hot-headed Huguenot, Agrippa d'Aubigné. He was driven to poetry when hit by amour's *coup de foudre*: 'My love for Diana turned my mind to poetry,' he wrote. Unfortunately, the passion these lovers shared was destroyed by family religious differences. Diane's relatives were strictly Catholic and strongly disapproved of Protestant d'Aubigné. It was the man who went off to be married this time, breaking Diane's heart.

much more charming than the grey façades. Wood panelling in light greys and greens, family portraits, embroidered chairs, games tables, *objets* from the French colonies, bureaux with secret drawers all conjure up the refined Ancien Régime good living enjoyed here by the Burjects. This Protestant family held on to the castle until 1932, when it was sold, fully furnished, to the state.

Châteaux Around Blois South of the Loire

Between Beaugency and Blois, it's much more rewarding to follow the south bank of the Loire. The riverside becomes prettier the nearer you get to the city, but the main tourist attractions hide out in the woods to the south.

St-Dyé-sur-Loire once thrived as the port which served the massive building site of the Château de Chambord. Today, wandering along its abandoned river front, imagine the bustle and excitement that once gave life to the place. St-Dyé has a **Maison de la Loire** (*open Feb–mid-Dec; t/f 02 54 81 68 07, maison-de-loire.41@wanadoo.fr; adm*) which puts on little exhibitions on river themes.

A few kilometres after St-Dyé towards Blois, just past Montlivault, the view opens onto the **Château de Ménars**, a superb riverside castle on the north bank, remodelled in good part for Louis XV's celebrated mistress, the Marquise de Pompadour. In 1760 she had the king's architect Jacques-Ange Gabriel, genius of Versailles' Petit Trianon, reshape the château. She died in 1764, but her brother, the Marquis de Marigny, carried on with the property's expansion, notably calling on the architect Soufflot for embellishments. Tantalizingly inaccessible to visitors, the château presents a wonderful perspective from the south bank. Magical Chambord lies just half-a-dozen kilometres southeast of here, hidden in its massive oak forest.

Château de Chambord

Open April–Sept every day 9–5.15, Oct–Mar 9–4.15; closed public hols; t 02 54 50 40 00, www.chambord.org; adm.

The Château de Chambord is a palace, rather than the traditional cottage, in a glade. King François I's 'hunting lodge' is one of the great symbols of European royal megalomania, a truly glorious and absurd monster of French architecture. From whichever way you approach Chambord through the long alleys of the mysterious walled forest that encircles it, it makes a staggering sight, looking like a riotously exuberant yet self-contained royal city. On first seeing it you immediately realize you've arrived at one of the greatest buildings in France.

Work began on Chambord in 1519, but it's something of a mystery as to whom the original architect was. The name of Leonardo da Vinci, who spent the last few years of his life at Amboise, down the Loire, is tantalizingly associated with Chambord, without firm evidence. A name more concretely linked with it is that of another extremely talented Italian, Domenico da Cortona. He had come to France in King Charles VIII's retinue and made models of various constructions for François I as early

Getting Around

It's not easy to get to the clutch of châteaux in this section if you're relying on public transport – Transports du Loir-et-Cher (t 02 54 58 55 60, www.tlcinfo.net) runs services for Chambord and Cheverny May–Sept.

Tourist Information

St-Dyé-sur-Loire: 75 Rue Nationale, 41500 St-Dyé-sur-Loire, t 02 54 81 65 45, f 02 54 81 68 07.
Bracieux: Siège social, Hôtel de Ville, 41250 Bracieux , t 02 54 46 09 15, f 02 54 46 09.15.
Cour-Cheverny: 12 Rue du Chêne des Dames, 41700 Cour-Cheverny, t 02 54 79 95 63, f 02 54 79 23 90.
Cellettes: 2 Rue de Rozelle, 41120 Loire-et-Cher, t/f 02 54 70 30 46.

Market Days

Bracieux: Thursday afternoon.
Cours-Cheverny: Tuesday afternoon.
Contres: Friday.

Where to Stay and Eat

Here we've moved into major Loire château and tourist country, which means lodgings don't come quite so cheap, but good places proliferate.

Muides-sur-Loire ✉ 41500

Château de Colliers B&B, t 02 54 87 50 75, **f** 02 54 87 03 64 (*expensive*). Low curving wings greet you like open arms at this very charming but modest château right by the Loire just west of Muides. The rooms are delightful, the hosts charmingly professional, the painted dining room memorable.
La Chanterelle, 21 Av de la Loire, **t** 02 54 87 50 19 (*menus €13–32; closed Sun pm, Mon, and Tues pm*). By the banks of the Loire beside Muides' bridge and camp site, this is an obvious place to try Loire fish specialities. *Closed mid–late Mar, late Sept–mid-Oct and early–late Jan.*

St-Dyé-sur-Loire ✉ 41500

★★Manoir de Bel Air, 1 Rte d'Orléans, **t** 02 54 81 60 10, www.manoirdebelair.com (*moderate*). Spectacularly located, renovated old manor above the Loire, many rooms with views down onto the river. There's a large dining room with views as well (*menus €22–41*). *Closed mid-Jan–mid-Feb.*
La Bourriche aux Appétits, 65 Rue Nationale, **t** 02 54 81 65 25 (*menus €22–30; closed Mon–Thurs exc. public holidays*). There's a good selection of river fish specialities to sample in this pleasing, simple new restaurant in the centre of St-Dyé, the dining room rustically decorated with old pots and pans. Try such tasty recipes as *sandre* with chives, pike in chervil, carp with saffron, shad with sorrel, or lamprey or eel stew. The delightful adjoining shop (*closed Mon*) offers a wide selection of river fish terrines and specialities, as well as a kind of casual exhibition on Loire fishing and more general gifts.

Chambord ✉ 41250

★★Hôtel du Grand St-Michel, Château de Chambord, **t** 02 54 20 31 31, **f** 02 54 20 36 40 (*inexpensive; closed Wed Dec–Mar*). You'll need to book well ahead to get a room at

---

as 1517. One model was a version of Chambord. This included the extraordinary **Greek cross plan** (a Greek cross has four arms of equal length extending out symmetrically from a central point) for the main building. The overall basic structure was fixed. Important details would prove quite different from the model, but much of the credit for Chambord seems to be due to Domenico da Cortona.

François I wasn't a man afraid of advancing his own ideas, so it's quite possible that he too had a major influence on the planning, for instance maybe insisting on some of the features which have a traditional French feel. For although Chambord contains a panoply of Italianate Renaissance features, its general forms actually hark back a lot to medieval architecture. The formidably solid round towers at the corners, in

this hotel as it's in the exclusive position of having many rooms looking out on to the château. The restaurant has a solid reputation. The terraces may be crammed with tourists during the day, but early or late you can enjoy the pleasure of relative peace by the magnificent palace. The strangely artificial street on which this hotel stands is filled with a choice of simpler restaurants (*menus €19–25*). *Closed mid-Nov–mid-Dec.*

Restaurant du Château de Chambord, t 02 54 33 34 71 (*€15–26*). Interesting new restaurant in the very castle itself, serving traditional Loire fare, and with terrace. *In Jan, just open Fri, Sat and Sun, otherwise open every day.*

Maslives ✉ 41250

✶✶L'Orée de Chambord, 14 Route de Chambord, **t** 02 54 81 42 42, *www.oreedechambord.com* (*inexpensive*). A cheap and cheerful address at which to stay and eat, just a few kilometres northwest of Chambord (*menus €17–45*). *Closed late-Jan–Feb and 25 Dec.*

Huisseau-sur-Cosson ✉ 41350

Château de Nanteuil, 16, Rue de Nanteuil, **t** 02 54 42 61 98, *www.chateau-nanteuil.com* (*moderate*). Lies prettily on the Cosson just a few kilometres west of Chambord, with a handful of spacious B&B rooms, plus restaurant (*menus €28; must reserve in advance; closed Mon*). *Openings variable Nov–Mar.*

Bracieux ✉ 41250

✶✶La Bonnheure, 9 Rue René Masson, **t** 02 54 46 41 57, **f** 02 54 46 05 90 (*inexpensive*). Very pleasant, modern, flowered place to stay.

Bernard Robin/Le Relais de Bracieux, 1 Av de Chambord, **t** 02 54 46 41 22 (*menus €60–115; closed Tues and Wed outside July and Aug*). Highly reputed if rather overpriced restaurant run by an illustrious chef. From the roadside the place looks deceptively normal, even old fashioned; however, the dining room is modern and bathed with light from the garden. The cooking is classic stuff, but with interesting touches such as the use of flambéed Loire *marc. Closed late Dec–Jan.*

Mont-près-Chambord ✉ 41250

✶✶Le Saint Florent, 14 Rue de la Chabardière, **t** 02 54 70 81 00, *www.hotel-saint-florent.com* (*inexpensive*). This place makes a pleasant stop, with light bedrooms and two dining rooms which serve up reasonably priced regional cuisine (*menus €13.50–39; closed Mon lunch*). *Closed Jan–mid-Feb.*

Manoir de Clénord B&B, Route de Clénord, **t** 02 54 70 41 62, *www.clenord.com* (*moderate*). Highly regarded, very pretty and very well-established B&B, in an 18th-century manor. *Closed Dec–Feb.*

Cellettes ✉ 41120

La Roselle, 15 Rue de la Rozelle, **t** 02 54 70 31 27 (*menus €27–40; closed Sun eve, Mon, and Tues eve*). Rich, delicious French cuisine served in a big, bright conservatory elegantly fitted onto the end of an 18th-century manor. It's set in its own grounds just above this village on the D956 south of Blois. *Closed late-Jan–early March.*

Cheverny and Cour-Cheverny ✉ 41700

✶✶✶Château du Breuil, Route de Fougères-sur-Bièvre, outside Cheverny, **t** 02 54 44 20 20,

particular, with their roofs like great upturned funnels, could come from a textbook image of a chivalric castle.

But Chambord is also an obsessively ordered building, neo-classical Renaissance ideas imposing symmetry and precise proportions on the façades. Chambord has virtually none of the idiosyncratic crooked and comical quirks of medieval castles, instead being a rigorous mathematician's delight.

Why build so magnificently in the marshy middle of a vast forest? Chambord certainly wasn't built simply for royal hunting. 'It was like a great royal advertising campaign,' the guides wittily explain. Bear in mind what an important royal centre the nearby town of Blois was at the time. Chambord was also a deliberate

www.chateauxhotels.com (*moderate; closed Sun pm and Mon*). The driveway through the densely wooded park to this delightful little château puts you into a dreamlike state. It is set in a glade-cum-garden; the reception rooms, in Louis XVI style, are superbly refined, the bedrooms extremely comfortable. *Closed mid-Nov–mid-Mar.*

Ferme des Saules B&B, south of Cheverny, just off the D102 road to Contres, t 02 54 79 26 95, *merlin.cheverny@infonie.fr* (*inexpensive*). With a little white tower attached to the sweet house, a little well in front of it, and a little swimming pool beyond, this is a cute B&B option close to a camp site (*table d'hôte Fri, Sat and Mon €22*).

**Hôtel des Trois Marchands, Place de l'Eglise, Cour-Cheverny, t 02 54 79 96 44, *www.hoteldes3marchands* (*inexpensive*). In a sprawling mass (or mess) of buildings around the church, this place is a bit of an institution, with functional rooms and naff paintings, but a comfortable large dining room serving reliably good meals (*menus €25–35*). *Closed Mon and Feb–mid-Mar.*

**Le Saint-Hubert, Rue Nationale, Cour-Cheverny, t 02 54 79 96 60, *www.hotel-sthubert.com* (*inexpensive*). Rather similar to the above, but on a smaller, more family scale (*menus €13–36.50*). *Hotel closed early–late Feb; restaurant closed Sun pm mid-Nov–mid-Mar.*

Le Grand Chancelier, 11 Av Chênes des Dames, Cheverny, t 02 54 79 22 57 (*menus €17–50*). Close to the château, a traditional French restaurant offering some tasty options, the chef generous with fine vegetables to accompany well-cooked meat dishes.

Closed Jan–early Feb and Tues pm–Wed pm in season: Mon pm, Tues and Wed Nov–April.

Chitenay ✉ 41120

**Auberge du Centre, Place de l'Eglise, t 02 54 70 42 11, *www.auberge-du-centre.com* (*inexpensive*). Some nicely done rooms and a garden in which you can eat in summer, just west of Troussay (*menus €19–38.50; closed Mon lunch and Tues lunch May–Sept*). *Closed Feb and Sun pm–Tues pm off season.*

Contres ✉ 41700

***Hôtel de France, 37–39 Rue Pierre-Henri Mauger, Route de Blois, t 02 54 79 50 14, *metivier@mond.net* (*moderate*). If you're seeking modern luxuries such as a heated pool, a sauna and a gym, then this might be the place for you. The practical rooms are set in a typical local building (*menus €17–44; closed Sun pm and Mon Oct–Easter*). *Restaurant closed late Jan–late Mar.*

La Botte d'Asperges, 52 Rue Pierre-Henri Mauger, Route de Blois, t 02 54 79 50 49 (*menus €11–27; closed Mon*). Rustic restaurant, whose name is a good indicator that serving seasonal local produce is the chef's main concern here. *Closed 24–27 Dec, and Sun pm Sept–June.*

Ouchamps ✉ 41120

***Relais des Landes, t 02 54 44 40 40, *www.relaisdeslandes.com* (*moderate*). An old converted manor. You could work off a sumptuous lunch here (*menus €19–39; closed Mon and Tues lunch Mar–Nov*) by hiring bikes, playing tennis, or taking a siesta in your spacious room. *Closed mid-Nov–Mar.*

---

demonstration of royal magnificence and power at a time when Western Europe witnessed a clash of titanic leaders; François I came to the throne not long after the young King Henry VIII had started ruling England, while soon Charles I of Spain would outbid them both (thanks to the massive financial backing of the German banker Jacob Fugger) in the stakes to become Holy Roman Emperor (Charles then became better known as the Emperor Charles V.) These three monumental kings competed with each other in outrageously expensive games of power politics and prestige.

Inside, you visit what the guides like to describe as one of the first apartment blocks in modern Europe! In the fillings between Chambord's Greek cross arms, hundreds of rooms repeat the same patterns. Chambord has a staggering 85 staircases: 70 lesser

Chambord, a Fantasy Château Where the Living Was Hard

A very substantial portion of Chambord was completed by 1547, the year in which François I died. But the palace was virtually never lived in; as it was a building site for almost the entire span of François' reign, he was scarcely able to spend much time here beyond the odd extravagant reception. And then there were the disasters of the mid-1520s which kept him away, notably his capture by the Holy Roman enemy at the Battle of Pavia in Italy, which forced him to remain a pampered prisoner of Charles V's in Madrid for some time. On top of all this, he had lost his first wife. During his imprisonment, it was agreed between François and Charles that he should marry Charles' sister, Eleanore of Austria, and he organized a sumptuous reception for her at Chambord in 1530. In 1532 and 1534 he stayed in the palace for hunting parties. Then in 1539 he laid on the most dazzling show for Charles V, who was travelling through France from Spain to his northern territories, Flanders. This was no doubt Chambord's finest evening.

It took until the pomp of Louis XIV's court to bring a further spark of royal life to the château. Not surprisingly, Chambord appealed to the Sun King, who felt at home with its preposterously vain scale, and came with his massive court retinue to hunt and play. He was also amused here; Molière staged the first performances of his plays *Monsieur de Pourceaugnac* and *Le Bourgeois Gentilhomme* at Chambord, in 1669 and 1670 respectively, converting one of the arms of the Greek cross into a theatre. Louis XV, however, proved uninterested in the château. In 1725, in an act of dubious generosity, he gave the place to his father-in-law, the exiled king of Poland, Stanislas I Leszcynski. Such were the insanitary conditions that one summer 50 of his servants were put out of action! After Leszcynski's death Louis XV offered the Maréchal de Saxe the honour of Chambord in recognition of his services to the crown. This eccentric military man had crazed delusions of grandeur and kept the place in flamboyant

ones, 14 major ones, and one considered a work of genius, a monument in itself, its intriguing double ramps possibly designed by Leonardo.

This masterpiece of a central staircase takes you up to the amazing **roofs**, where you can wander around the fabulous chimneyscape. (Be aware that on the way up or down you may be swept aside by packs of schoolchildren racing round the castle.) The towers and chimneys, which at first appear like a triumphant medieval riot, are actually meticulously ordered behind the wild visual fireworks. Similes have rained down on these wonderful roofs: they've been compared to an overcrowded chessboard, an exotic Eastern palace and even, by the rather excessive French Romantic author Chateaubriand, to a woman's locks dishevelled by the wind! Our favourite description, which seems in fact to sum up the whole of Chambord best, is that of '*un gigantesque bouquet de pierres* (a gigantic bouquet of stones)'.

Chambord is so vast that most of its interiors have stood empty for ages. But in recent times, more and more has been done to fill the chambers. On the first floor you can visit a series of sumptuously furnished **royal apartments**, where you'll learn more about the various owners of the castle (see box) and see paintings of them, as well as

style. A bodyguard of negroes from Martinique accompanied him round it on white horses. Parties would visit him from court and he would hold dinners for a modest 150 people. But the marshal reflected on the insalubrious living conditions which continued to blight those who tried to settle in this château in its marshy forest: 'Chambord is a hospital,' he once wrote. 'I have more than 300 sick, several dead, and others have the look of exhumed corpses.' Royal governors then appointed to look after the dilapidated vastness could do little to stop Chambord's decay.

The Revolution saw most of the interiors stripped of their contents, including the wood panelling that had been added for Louis XIV, but Napoleon's era had pretensions to the absurd grandeur needed to revive the place. In 1809 the emperor donated Chambord to Maréchal Berthier, for whom the title of Prince of Wagram was created. It was symbolic of the times that one of this man's ambitions was to replace the innumerable F motifs at Chambord, referring to François I, with Ws, to stamp the honour of his newly acquired title on the place! He was dead by 1815, leaving his widow with a simply impossible house to run. Louis XVIII permitted her to sell the estate, and it was bought by public subscription to be donated to King Charles X's heir. This was his grandson, Henri, Duc de Bordeaux, whom it was hoped would become King Henri V of France. He took on the title of Comte de Chambord. First though, his mother, the endlessly intriguing Duchesse de Berry, had to fight for Chambord's survival, stopping the dismantling of the building for the selling of its stone. But with the 1830 revolution the Orléans royal family had to flee, and the Comte de Chambord stayed in Austria for the next 41 years, returning to spend his one and only night in Chambord in July 1871. His nephews, the Duc de Parme and the Comte de Bardi, tried to stem some of the damage to Chambord after 1883. Finally the French state bought the property in 1930. Someone has calculated that the château, in all its existence, has only been lived in for 20 years.

personal items. On the second floor, the **Musée de la Chasse**, focusing on hunting, was redone in 1997. Hunting objects, tapestries and paintings bring the drama of the hunt inside, including one particularly startling scene where a fleeing deer comes racing into a dining room. In 2001 the castle also started to put on exhibitions on architecture.

All sorts of special tours of the castle and its grounds are organized at various times of year. The main one is **Les Métamorphoses de Chambord** (*late June–Aug every evening except Sun; Sept Fri and Sat only, although in 2004 these evenings will not take place as a major exhibition, De l'Italie à Chambord, running July–Oct, will mean an exceptional change in events at the castle; adm*), when you can wander freely round the castle at night, swept along by sound-and-light shows.

To check out other possibilities, such as **boating** on the Cosson river, **cycling** round the grounds, **riding** in a horse and carriage, or going to see the **deer rut** in autumn, call t 02 54 50 40 00; it's highly recommended to organize such special trips in advance, given the crowds.

Château de Villesavin

Open Feb–Dec 10–7 daily except Christmas Day; t 02 54 46 42 88,
chateauvillesavin@wanadoo.fr; adm.

Construisez bien, construisez beau, mais construisez modestement (Build well, build
beautifully, but build modestly).

François I to his friend Jean le Breton

The delightfully modest Château de Villesavin lies discreetly on the southern edge
of Chambord's forest, near Bracieux. A chip off the old block of Chambord is the way
the château is frequently described – it might be more apt to compare it to a little
piece of the Chambord's roof that miraculously blew off in the wind and landed in the
middle of these charming woods close to the Beuvron river. Some say it was no
miracle, but that the man for whom Villesavin was built, Jean le Breton, diverted
funds and workers from the king's building site to construct himself a nice little
château on the side.

King and courtier were very close. Jean le Breton fought for François I at the Battle of
Pavia. Both men were captured and shared a period of captivity for around 14 months.
François I greatly appreciated Le Breton's company, and once they were released he
made him administrator of the County of Blois, among other positions. His tasks
included overseeing the works at Chambord. During the king's imprisonment, work
had stopped on the great château, so the project, involving hundreds of employees
(maybe around 1,800 of them), had to be set in motion again.

It is clear that Jean le Breton made the most of the fine workmanship so close at
hand to help build his relatively modest shack. Construction of Villesavin began at the
end of 1526 or beginning of 1527 and was finished within 10 years. The place may seem
something of a half measure of a château in size, but even if it does look rather top
heavy – the single storey is only 9m high, the roof over 11m – it is full of charm.

Many of the château's features are enchanting. Several stand out in the **central
courtyard**. First, there are the almost pyramidal tops to the pavilions on the corners of
the *cour d'honneur* which give the place its delightfully idiosyncratic character. These
roofs were early precursors of an architectural fashion which grew enormously in
popularity under Louis XIII. The second outstanding feature is the Loire *lucarnes*, or
dormers, superb examples of their kind. The ones on the right are carved with
symbols of the arts, with an Italian mandoline symbolizing music, comedy depicted
with three lilies, and tragedy, typically, stabbing herself. Worn by time, these sculptures are the originals.

Then a beautiful Renaissance fountain embellishes the centre of the courtyard. It
has been claimed that this superbly carved work in Carrara marble may have been
destined for Chambord but diverted here. Villesavin's guides loyally describe it as a
gift from the Florentine craftsmen of Chambord to Jean le Breton, and it certainly
fits in elegantly. It's covered with typical Renaissance devices and faces, the bottom
of the bowl simulating fish scales, with lion's heads protruding discreetly from
among them.

The tour inside the château is relatively short but sweet. You visit three out of the four pavilions and a few other rooms. The diminutive **chapel** is covered with frescoes badly worn by time, but still evocative. The style of the major wall paintings is strikingly 16th-century Italian, and they have been attributed to the reputed court artist Niccolo dell'Abate. He's known to have lived in France from 1552, assisting Primaticcio in the decorating of Fontainebleau. The depiction of the Flagellation of Christ is particularly moving, if you're not wincing at the cruelty of the scene. The 17th-century putti on the vaults rather clash with the sobriety of style below. They were ordered by Jean Phélypeaux (*see also* Châteauneuf-sur-Loire, p.105), a later owner of Villesavin and counsellor to Louis XIII, and may be the work of Jean Mosnier, who decorated so much of Cheverny's interior. Among the interesting details, St Veronica is depicted in putto guise, the shroud showing the vague outline not so much of an imagined Christ's face, but more, apparently, that of Phélypeaux himself, with his goatee beard.

Entering the main building, the hall and restored pavilion room on the south façade prove particularly elegant rooms. The first includes a Chardin and a study for the Comédie Française's statue of Poquelin, alias Molière. The second contains niches for statues and oval portraits. Moving to the kitchens, these have a rich rustic feel. A substantial collection of wedding garments and accoutrements, mainly dating from the 19th century, has recently been acquired by the château to try and add a distraction to please large groups of visitors. But Villesavin will always remain on an intimate scale. Beyond the wedding collection you're also shown the dovecote, with its hundreds of holes for pigeons, and the long back façade of the castle with its 19th-century inscription and rather neglected air – the unpretentious but devoted young couple who've inherited this place clearly need the aid of more tourists.

Le Breton was something of a rarity in François I's service, a councillor who died without being disgraced or framed and who held on to his châteaux until the end, rather than having them confiscated by the Crown. He didn't limit himself to this one château, and passed away at another, much more famous and rather larger one which he had built in the Touraine, the Château de Villandry (*see* p.306).

Château de Beauregard

Open July–Aug 9.30–6.30; April–June and Sept daily 9.30–12 and 2.30–6.30;
mid-Feb–Mar, Oct–Nov and late Dec–early Jan Thurs–Tues 9.30–12 and 2–5;
closed public hols; t 02 54 70 40 05, www.beauregard-loire.com; adm.

This shy château hides down a long, dark, deeply wooded alley off the busy D765 linking Blois with Romorantin-Lanthenay. Its sober, almost dull exterior gives no clue as to the highly decorated series of rooms that await within. Beauregard's outward sobriety stems from the fact that it's a château of what's termed the second French Renaissance, dating from around the middle of the 16th century. Any lingering playful influences of Gothic were wiped out by this time.

Although the lordship of Beauregard was granted by François I to his uncle René de Savoie, the building you see now was ordered by the owner who succeeded René's widow in 1545, one Jean du Thier, Seigneur de Menars. This man served as secretary of state to the treasury under King Henri II. A patron of the arts, he was the sponsor of two of the famous Pléiade poets, Pierre de Ronsard (see Tours, and Talcy) and Joachim du Bellay (see Liré). The outside of the château is disappointingly covered in roughcast for the most part, rather than being in seductive blocks of Loire limestone. At least the decoration of the pilasters and the medallions stands out pleasantly on the main façade, while the slate encrusted in the dormer windows and chimneys imitates decorative features from Chambord.

Florimond Robertet came by the château in 1566. He held some of the same political posts as his predecessor. But as he also owned the much grander (now vanished) Château de Bury, west of Blois, he paid little attention to Beauregard. The family which wrought the biggest changes on Beauregard after du Thier were the Ardiers. Paul Ardier, one-time controller-general of wars and treasurer of the royal savings bank, retired to Beauregard having served three French kings – Henri III, Henri IV and Louis XIII. It was he who ordered the **Galerie des Illustres**, the highlight of the interiors, in the 1620s. This gallery offers a wonderful lesson on the leading figures in western European history across several centuries, as well as on the looks and fashions of those times. It is covered with rank upon rank of portraits of famous people, a staggering 327 in total, going from the reign of the first Valois, Philippe VI, through to Louis XIII. Beauregard's gallery is now unique along the Loire, but at one time there was in fact something of a vogue for such galleries in the 17th century. It's an Italian, Paulo Jove, who's credited with launching the fashion in his villa near Lake Como. He donated one manuscript on his collection to the future Henri II of France, which contained miniature reproductions of the portraits in his house.

Faced with such a daunting number of historical figures, it can be hard to know where to focus your attention. But the groupings are chronologically displayed for the most part (proceeding round left from the fireplace) and well ordered by series of 12 portraits according to each reign, the monarch featuring last in each cycle, except in the cases of Henri IV and Louis XIII, each given special prominence. As well as all the great men, 21 women feature, including Joan of Arc, Catherine de' Medici, Diane de Poitiers (rival in her husband's affections), and Elizabeth I of England. Americans should have little difficulty spotting Amerigo Vespucci, the Florentine explorer who gave his name to their continent – he features in the Louis XII section.

The artists aren't known, although Jean Mosnier of Cheverny fame (see opposite) is associated with the project. It's probable that most of the panels were painted in Paris and are copies (or copies of copies) of original portraits. All the faces are painted against a black background, full on, in semi-profile or in profile. The collection of ruffs alone impresses. The reds of the cardinals and popes also stand out prominently. Among the hats you may remark a Turkish one, a reminder of the alliance between François I and Suleyman II which so shocked Christian Europe at that time. These may not be great works of art, and through time they've been more or less badly restored, but the general effect is wonderful.

The guides sometimes use the room to give you a very long and elaborate history lesson, darting from one figure to another, so the advice is to study hard the section on the Valois and early Bourbons in the History chapter at the beginning of this book. Underneath the triple ranks of portraits, allegories and arms symbolize the mottoes of the French kings. The most relevant to English visitors is that under Louis XIII, showing a snail pierced by an arrow with the inscription *'Esto domi'* ('Stay at home'), a dig at the English navy, whose fleet was too slow to come to the rescue of Huguenot La Rochelle. As to the floor, it is covered with an army on the march, painted on Delft tiles from the 17th century.

The library, or south gallery, has beams embellished with the painted busts of Pléiade poets. Among the notable objects here are a late 16th-century Brussels tapestry showing the marriage of King Henri IV, in the guise of Solomon and his 1,000 wives; 17th-century Spanish chairs inlaid with ivory depicting hunting scenes; and a grotesquely decorated Lyon Mannerist cupboard, whose doors are opened by placing a finger up a lady's skirts. The **Cabinet des Grelots** next door is another splendidly decorated room, this time small in scale. It dates back to the days of du Thier, who commissioned the finely carved gilt oak panelling from the Italian Scibec de Carpi. The three golden *grelots*, or bells, featured on the du Thier family arms are here repeated in great number. Along with the sumptuous details of the carving and the glowing colours of the wood, painted panels depict the artistic and scientific pursuits of the day, including the art of war. The tour finishes by bringing you down to earth with a copious display of copper kitchenware in the servants' quarters.

Beauregard's grounds were given added appeal by the creation of a sunken garden in the mid-1990s, the **Jardin des Portraits**. The forms here play on the famous portrait gallery within, the garden divided up into 12 boxes containing a wealth of plants.

Château de Cheverny

Open July–Aug 9.15–6.45, April–June and Sept 9.15–6.15, Jan–Feb and Nov–Dec 9.30–12 and 2.15–5, Mar and Oct 9.30–12 and 2.15–5.30; t 02 54 79 96 29, www.chateau-cheverny.fr; adm.

Cheverny is the most refined Loire château of the lot, a lesson in French architectural and aristocratic good taste. Ironically, this splendid, pristine-looking 17th-century masterpiece was built following a terrible family scandal (*see* box overleaf). Henri Hurault, who commissioned the castle, was descended from an illustrious line of aristocrats close to the French Renaissance kings. His ancestor Raoul Hurault, a minister of finances under François I, had in fact had an earlier castle built at Cheverny at the start of the 16th century, but this was entirely wiped away by his descendant. As for Henri's father, Philippe Hurault, he served as chancellor to both kings Henri III and Henri IV.

It's sometimes said that Henri Hurault destroyed the family home that already stood at Cheverny to try and forget the past. But it was over 20 years after the infamous events that work began on the new château. The main building programme lasted from 1626 to 1648, the year in which Henri Hurault died. His best-loved daughter Elisabeth, Marquise de Montglas, oversaw completion of the castle.

Cuckoldry at Cheverny

King Henri IV was inadvertently the cause of the scandal which shook the Hurault household to its core. The story goes that one day when Henri Hurault was at court, he spotted the king in a mirror poking fun at him, making the sign of the cuckold behind his back. The proud and fiery Hurault left that instant, riding through the night to reach Cheverny, arriving at five in the morning, his anger at boiling point. The Burgundian gentleman in bed with his wife Françoise Chabot was quick enough to jump from a window into the garden, but broke his leg and lay there injured; Henri Hurault put a definitive end to his amorous misconduct by running him through on the spot. Having summoned the local priest, Henri then offered his wife the choice of ending her days by poison or the sword. Parish records note that she died 'poisoned, as the common rumour has it, for her adultery'. She was apparently carrying a baby boy in her womb. Such was the hierarchy of justice in that period that Henri Hurault was simply exiled to Cheverny for a time by way of punishment. In 1604 he was remarried to Marguerite Gaillard, and the two had many children together, as well as re-creating the Château de Cheverny.

The main architect associated with the château is Boyer, or Jacques Bougier, of Blois, who worked with the likes of the eminent Salomon de Brosse, best-known for his royal Palais du Luxembourg in Paris. Although the Château de Cheverny was built on a relatively small scale, the architecture was at the forefront of its time, adopting the so-called Louis XIII style – classicism mixed with extravagant roofing and decoration that became typical of Ancien Régime France. Boyer died in 1632. It isn't certain who continued his work, but it's thought that his successor stuck to his plans. The exterior has scarcely been altered since it was built, although some of the interiors, notably on the ground floor, were modified in the 19th century. A descendant of the Huraults, the count of Vibraye, still owns and lives in the castle.

A generous smooth lawn leads to the Château de Cheverny's immaculate front. The main façade looks so clean and white, and the stones are laid in such a seamless manner, that many have mistaken the effect for whitewashed clapboard. Some regard it as a weakness that such an expensive cut-stone façade should resemble a less noble material. Other critics have complained that the central section and the two adjoining pavilions stand uncomfortably squashed in by the two great curving-roofed end pavilions, with their mansard windows like bulging frogs' eyes. Despite such quibbles, this is a great piece of Loire architecture. The building is slimly elegant, the whole château only one room thick, light pouring through it. The ensemble is also pleasingly symmetrical. On the main façade, a pediment tops each window like a stylized eyebrow. Along the first floor, a series of busts of 12 Roman emperors runs across the façade.

Cheverny is the Loire château which probably boasts the finest collection of paintings and tapestries. In this respect it resembles a fine arts gallery, but it is also still clearly lived in and lovingly maintained. On the self-guided tour round the château you visit much of the ground and first floors. Among the outstanding features of the interiors are the allegorical classical wall paintings by Jean Mosnier. This accomplished artist hailed from Blois, like the architect Boyer, and was also involved in preparing the Palais du Luxembourg in Paris. Much of the decorative ensemble he and his team executed at Cheverny has been well preserved. For example, in the dining room on the ground floor, Mosnier panels illustrate the tales of Don Quichotte (Quixote) – Cervantes' Spanish comic masterpiece was the height of fashion at the time. The embossed Cordoba leather covering the walls of the dining room is stamped with the Hurault family coat of arms.

Still on the ground floor, the western rooms contain splendid works of art. In the antechamber hangs an exquisite 17th-century Flemish tapestry showing a fishing scene after Téniers. Alongside royal portraits, several fine depictions of Hurault family members are displayed in the great drawing room, including those of Philippe Hurault and his wife Anne de Thou, as well as a rendering of a later countess of Cheverny by Mignard. But these works are eclipsed by a portrait of Cosimo de' Medici attributed to Titian and one of Jeanne d'Aragon by the school of Raphael. Don't miss the splendid portraits in the more cramped vestibule. Three by the most renowned French court painter of the mid-16th century, François Clouet, represent Philippe Hurault, his wife, and his brother Jacques. The château also displays four works by that great portraitist under Louis XIV, Hyacinthe Rigaud. American visitors may also spot the small equestrian statue of George Washington by Baron Carlo Marochetti; the château even owns a document signed by the great president witnessing the membership of Charles de Loménie de Brienne, an ancestor of the Vibrayes, in the Order of Cincinnati, founded to celebrate the role of high-ranking French officers who played a part in the American War of Independence. On the ground floor you may also notice one portrait of the infamous Henri Hurault.

Take the steps up the main staircase slowly to admire the finesse of the carved work around it, executed by the mysterious F.L., who signed his oeuvre in 1634. Then enter the substantial **Salle des Gardes**, the largest room in the château, its extravagant fireplace flanked by gilded wooden statues, the caryatids surmounted by figures of Mars and Venus. The central painting, by Mosnier, represents the death of Adonis. Old armour hangs on the walls around the room, but below, along the wainscoting, the anachronistic images depict flowers, with pithy Latin sayings associated with them: 'Self-love was my downfall', reads that by the narcissus. Mosnier supposedly sent his assistants into the surrounding countryside to pick many of the plants from which the illustrations were painted.

Beyond the Salle des Gardes lies the most sumptuous room of all, the **Chambre du Roi**, made in preparation for a royal visit, although none was ever received at Cheverny. Here several decorative features vie for your attention: the dazzling main wall paintings by Mosnier illustrate the classical legend of Perseus and Andromeda, the smaller ones depict episodes from the tale of Chariclea and Theagenes (made popular by a period bestseller), while the amazingly fine tapestries from Paris show the labours of Ulysses after cartoons by Simon Vouet. On the bed, the most exquisite Persian silk cover is embroidered with flowers and figures. After such a lavish artistic feast, the simple and charming private rooms you can also visit on the first floor make for a pleasant, intimate few minutes of relaxation.

The Wines of Cheverny and Cour-Cheverny

A friend whom I introduced to a red Cheverny wine looked up with surprise from her wine glass and said: 'It tastes like the dust from moths' wings.' Somewhat alarmed by the comparison, I asked whether it was unpleasant. 'No, but distinctly unusual.' I'd agree with that. I've noted on the occasions that I've drunk Cheverny red that I've found it 'musty'. Is this, I wonder, roughly the taste that one wine critic famously described as 'wet foxes in the undergrowth'? You can certainly imagine foxes running around the rather flat lands of the Cheverny *appellation*, on the edge of the Sologne forest; this wine area is even known unofficially as the Sologne *viticole*. The red Cheverny wines aren't really powerful enough to go with game and strong sauces, however. They're very pale in colour, distinctly light and quite transparent, with orange tints, but in the best ones the fruit flavours, even dried fruit tastes, emerge young. Gamay is combined with Pinot Noir to make these reds, just a touch of Cabernet Franc or Côt sometimes added. The major white grape variety here is Sauvignon, which can be pleasantly aromatic, complemented by Chardonnay and sometimes a touch of Menu Pineau. This white wine could make a crisp accompaniment to the ubiquitous *sandre*, or other river and lake fish.

The Cour-Cheverny wine area is a curiosity, awarded AOC status in the 1990s. The white wine which can carry the AOC label is made from Romorantin, a rarity of a grape variety. Its origins aren't local, but they are royal. François I, whose family owned the castle of Romorantin in the Sologne, had 80,000 vines brought over from Burgundy to plant in this region in 1519. The variety adapted well to the move, while in time it dwindled in importance in its homeland; so it then took on the name of the place to which it had been transplanted. The Romorantin wines, dry whites, tend to have a lively start and a long, lingering flavour.

The obvious name to cite for a visit is Christian Tessier at the **Domaine de la Desoucherie** (*t 02 54 79 90 08, summer Mon–Sat 8–12 and 2–6; rest of year, phone for a visit*), between Cour-Cheverny and Fontaine-en-Sologne. Not only does he produce the range of local still wines, he also makes a good sparkling *crémant*.

Cheverny's park is best known for it pack of **hunting dogs**, to be seen chasing across the lawn in most clichéd images of the place. Ordinarily you can go and watch the doleful mutts lazing around in their cages. They're a mix of English fox hounds and French Poitevins dogs, and are tattooed with V for Vibraye. Between September and March they go hunting twice a week. Otherwise, you can watch them being fed in the afternoon, their trainers keeping the scrum under control. Near the dog pens, a room is dedicated to the hunt, hung with hundreds of trophies and given colour by a large stained-glass window. Between April and November you can also hire little **buggies** and **boats** to enjoying the extensive shaded grounds.

On an amusing last note, readers of Tintin may feel that the Château de Cheverny looks rather familiar – that's because it served as Hergé's model for Captain Haddock's home ('Marlinspike Hall' in the English translated version)! There's even an exhibition on the matter.

An international 18-hole **golf course** (*t 02 54 79 24 70, www.golf-cheverny.com*) hides down a track just south of the château. The course, set around a typical Solognot lake, takes you round delightful countryside and you can eat at the clubhouse.

Troussay

Open Easter–Oct; t/f 02 54 44 29 07; adm.

Troussay, just west of Cheverny, is in fact a *gentilhommière*, or manor house, rather than a château. It provides a good example of the architecture and living arrangements of the minor nobility of its period. But its comparatively modest frame contains some rather grand pieces of decorative art rescued from other, larger Loire châteaux and houses that fell into disrepair or disappeared off the map.

The pretty house was built in the 15th century. Alterations were made to it in the 16th. The fine quality of the decorative display within is due to historian Louis de la Saussaye, who inherited the property in 1828 and called upon Jules de la Morandière to restore it. The idea was not just to help the house but also to create a fitting home for works of art saved from dilapidated châteaux. Several of the most important pieces came from the very sorry remnants of the Château de Bury, one of the first great Renaissance châteaux in France, situated west of Blois. The carved wooden door to Bury's oratory is the finest piece on display, but there are also excellent fragments of stone carving from there. The porcupine on the back of the house, symbol of Louis XII, was taken off the Hôtel Hurault de Cheverny in Blois. The stained-glass windows, from the early 16th century, come from the Hôtel Sardini in Blois. The Louis XII tiling in the manor is one remaining original interior feature.

The other collection at Troussay is connected with peasant Sologne rather than courtly Blois; everyday household and farming implements are displayed in the outbuildings, and there is a small exhibition on traditions of witchcraft in the region.

Château de Fougères-sur-Bièvre

Open daily April–Sept, Jan–Mar and Oct–Dec Wed–Mon, closed public hols; visits can be made with or without a guide; t/f 02 54 20 27 18; adm.

The Château de Fougères-sur-Bièvre is a bit of an odd man out in this area. Most of the other châteaux around these parts are characterized by openness, generally constructed of sparkling clean-cut blocks of white stone, the towers roomy and decorative. Fougères looks defensively medieval with its massed turrets, its small irregular stones and its inner courtyard paranoiacally enclosed on all four sides. Despite this stern exterior, the château you see surprisingly dates from the last quarter of the 15th century. It was constructed on the foundations of an earlier fort for Pierre de Refuge, a financier who built his fortune serving the royal family and who obtained permission from King Louis XI, a few years before the latter died, to re-establish Fougères 'as a *château-fort*'. Some additions were perhaps made for his grandson Jean de Villebresme, who inherited the place in 1497.

Fougères hasn't survived intact down the centuries. The moat was filled in and for most of the 19th century a spinning mill was installed here, the course of the Bièvre stream even being diverted under the château for this work. In the 20th century the place became a poor-house before the state acquired it in 1932. During the Second World War, Fougères served as a depot for some of the country's great art collections.

Past the imposing north wing you come into the wonderfully atmospheric courtyard. Here the mixture of different styles – Gothic, Renaissance and plain idiosyncratic – stands out. Through time, the interiors have been stripped and converted. You can see this immediately on entering the chapel, where nothing much remains apart from a couple of *culs-de-lampe* and a mill wheel, placed here in the château's spinning days. Many of the rooms stand empty, with just their volumes to please the visitor. Climb right to the top, however, for the most enjoyable part of the tour, with interesting displays under the fine rafters on the various building trades involved in the construction of the Loire's châteaux.

Chartres and the Loir Valley to Angers

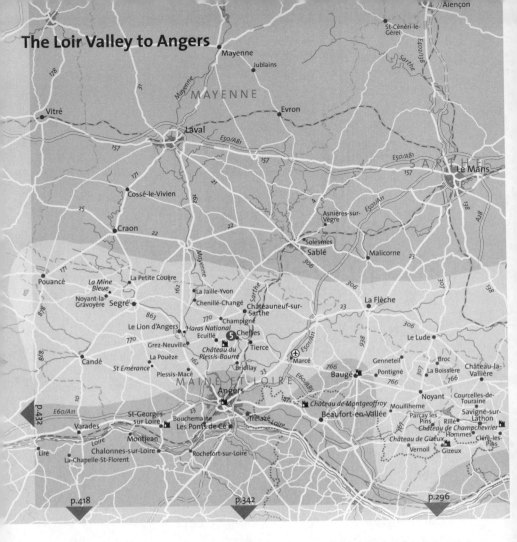

The Loir Valley to Angers

Another river Loir, this one spelled without an 'e', runs down through a delightful valley almost as far as Angers, for much of its length paralleling its far greater cousin, also offering beautiful white-stoned waterside towns and village, numerous châteaux large and small, even a scattering of *appellation* wines too, although all these attractions remain a pretty well-kept secret. But this Loir does rise close to one of the most famous of all French cities, known to foreigners across the world. Chartres is still completely dominated by its cathedral, the symbol *par excellence* of the way medieval culture has left its mark so powerfully on France.

Chartres

With the gift of the supposed blouse of the Virgin Mary, the Sancta Camisia, in the late Dark Ages Chartres became one of the greatest pilgrimage cities of Western

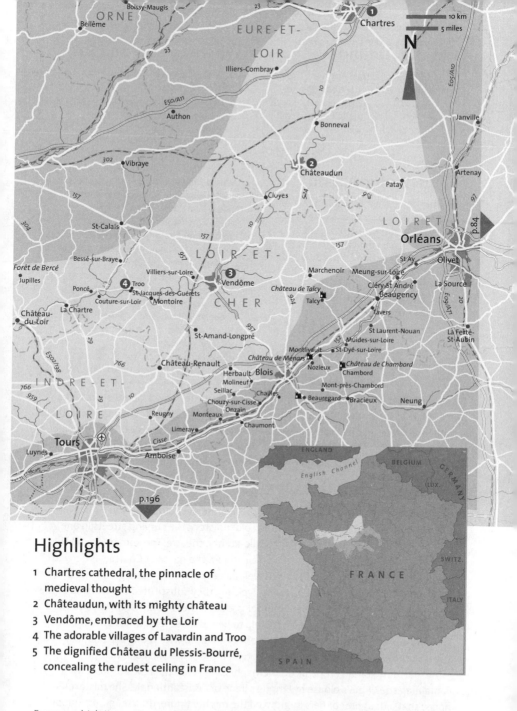

Highlights

1 Chartres cathedral, the pinnacle of medieval thought
2 Châteaudun, with its mighty château
3 Vendôme, embraced by the Loir
4 The adorable villages of Lavardin and Troo
5 The dignified Château du Plessis-Bourré, concealing the rudest ceiling in France

Europe, which it remains to this day. What a mesmerizing sight its medieval cathedral must have made for pilgrims through the Middle Ages, rising as it does from afar above the flat surrounding landscape. Even today, this stupendous Christian symbol

Getting Around

Chartres has good **train** links with Paris-Montparnasse (1hr) and the odd train to Orléans. Vendôme has excellent high-speed train services to Paris, the TGV station well outside the centre. Slower trains serve Châteaudun.

Tourist Information

Chartres: Place de la Cathédrale, **t** 02 37 18 26 26, www.villechartres.fr.
Bonneval: 2 Square Westerham, **t** 02 37 47 55 89, www.bonnevaltourisme.com.
Châteaudun: 1 Rue de Luynes, **t** 02 37 45 22 46, www.villechateaudun.com.
Vendôme: Hôtel du Saillant, 47 Rue Poterie, **t** 02 54 77 05 07, ot.vendome@wanadoo.fr.
Montoire-sur-le-Loir: 16 Place Clemenceau, **t** 02 54 85 23 30, www.montoire-sur-le-loir.net.
La Flèche: Bd de Montréal, **t** 02 43 94 02 53, www.ville-lafleche.fr.

Where to Stay and Eat

Chartres ✉ 28000
★★★Le Grand Monarque, 22 Place des Epars, **t** 02 37 18 15 15, www.bw-grand-monarque.com (expensive). Chartres' best hotel, distinguished-looking and comfortable, close to the cathedral, if on a very busy traffic square. Posh restaurant (€25–45; closed Sun pm and Mon) and cheaper but stylish brasserie (€19; open daily till late).
★★de la Poste, 3 Rue du Général Koenig, **t** 02 37 21 04 27, www.hotelposte-chartres.com (moderate). Reasonable if lacking character, on a busy road but close to the cathedral. Big restaurant (€15–26; closed Fri pm & Sun pm).
Le Buisson Ardent, 10 Rue au Lait, **t** 02 37 34 04 66. Perhaps the best dining option up by the cathedral, in an historic building, offering good regional cuisine at a more reasonable price than the more renowned Vieille Maison opposite.
Le St-Hilaire, 11 Rue du Pont St-Hilaire, **t/f** 02 37 30 97 57 (€15–38; closed lunchtimes Sat and

appears almost isolated on the immense horizon of the Beauce cereal plain. It's as though the city around it didn't exist. In fact, a major medieval town grew up at the cathedral's feet, and round the now-vanished castle of the counts of Chartres, jealous rivals of the bishops of the city from the 10th century. Down by the Eure river, a multitude of trades established themselves, competing in smelliness.

History

Explore Chartres' delightful lower town beside the river Eure, and you'll discover that this famed medieval city has a much older history, the curving streets in one quarter following the lines of a major Gallo-Roman theatre. The Romans found this part of Gaul inhabited by the Carnutii, from whom the name of Chartres is derived. Their settlement, built around a sacred well, already had religious significance and as such was a key target for the Christians. Typically, they substituted the worship of the Virgin Mary for that of the ancient mother goddess. The first Christian basilica went up in the 4th century, this place of worship to be rebuilt several times after fires. One early bishop, 6th-century Lubin, is traditionally credited with fixing the boundaries of the vast diocese of Chartres stretching between the Seine and Loire valleys.

The first Holy Roman Emperor, Charlemagne, was given the relic purportedly containing the Virgin's blouse by Empress Irene of Constantinople. She mistakenly hoped that a daughter of hers might wed the mighty figure, thus reuniting Europe's Eastern and Western empires. Charlemagne kept the precious cloth at his main court church in Aix-la-Chapelle, or Aachen, but with the division of his empire between his

Mon). One of several enchanting restaurants in old houses down in the Basse Ville by the Eure. The chef goes to the great efforts to prepare regional dishes using the finest local ingredients. *Closed late July–early Aug and Christmas period.*

Moulin de Ponceau, 21 Rue Tannerie, t 02 37 35 30 05 (*€20–40; closed Sat lunch and Sun pm*). Converted 16th-century tanning mill with pretty dining rooms and terrace over the Eure, excellent settings for an enjoyable meal. *Closed mid-Feb–early March.*

St-Prest ✉ 28300

Manoir des Prés du Roy, t 02 37 22 27 27, *www.manoirdespresduroy.com* (*moderate*). Just 7km north of Chartres, by the Eure river, a delightfully restored manor house in spacious grounds, with beamed restaurant (*€23–36*)

Frazé 28120

Auberge du Château, 5 Place du Château, t 02 37 29 54 14. Appealing traditional restaurant on the village square opposite the castle. *Closed Sun eve Oct–Easter.*

La Ville-aux-Clercs ✉ 41100

**Manoir de la Forêt, Fort-Girard, t 02 54 80 62 83 , *www.manoirdelaforet.fr* (*inexpensive-expensive*). Big block of a hunting lodge in lovely grounds, with traditional rooms and a delightful restaurant (*€25–46*).

Troo ✉ 41800

Château de la Voûte, t 02 54 72 52 52, f 02 54 72 52 52 (*moderate*). A gem of a B&B on Troo's slope, with lovely rooms and splendid views.

Le Petit Relais, Place du Château, t 02 54 72 57 92. Adorable one-woman restaurant in the upper village.

Luché-Pringé ✉ 72800

**Auberge du Port-des-Roches, t 02 43 45 44 48, f 02 43 45 39 61 (*inexpensive*). Sweet little roadside inn west of Le Lude. Lovely terrace by the river for summer dining (*€20–38; closed Sun pm and Mon*). *Closed Feb.*

sons, the piece then travelled. For his grandson King Charles the Bald to have donated such a precious object to the cathedral of Chartres in the mid-9th century shows the importance of the city's religious community by that time. The official reason for the gift was in compensation for a substantial portion of land closer to Paris, which Charles' ancestor Pépin had taken by force from the bishopric. The relic may have been donated for the consecration of a new cathedral, rebuilt during the times of the destructive Norse raids. The story goes that when the Viking Rollo came to lay siege to the town in 911, Bishop Gantelme exposed the Virgin's tunic on the ramparts; the Norseman supposedly fled, made peace with the Frankish king, and settled down as first duke of Normandy.

Towards the end of the 10th century, a brilliant religious student by the name of Fulbert came to Chartres from Reims, where he had been taught by the enlightened scholar and scientist Gerbert d'Aurillac, the future Pope Sylvester III, the first-ever French pontiff. Fulbert in turn made the Chartres cathedral school into one of the greatest centres of Christian learning and became bishop of the city in 1006. As well as encouraging scholarship, he promoted the cult of the Virgin. For two centuries, during a period sometimes described as the First Renaissance, the Chartres cathedral school's reputation radiated far and wide; only with the founding of the University of Paris would its importance decline.

Unfortunately, the Carolingian cathedral burned down during Fulbert's time. The influential man managed to persuade many leading figures across France, as well as the likes of King Canute in England, to donate generously towards the building of a

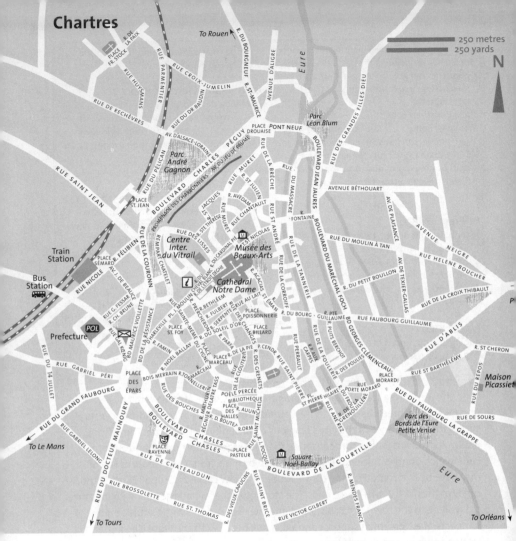

Chartres

To Rouen

R. DE LA PAIX
PLACE FL. STOCK
R. DE PARMENTIER
RUE HUYSMANS
RUE CROIX JUMELIN
RUE DE RECHÈVRES
RUE DU DR BAUDIN
R. DU BOURGNEUF
R. ST-MAURICE
AVENUE D'ALIGRE

Eure

250 metres
250 yards

N

PLACE PONT NEUF
DROUAISE
PLACE PÉGUY
AV. D'ALSACE-LORRAINE
BOULEVARD CHARLES
AV. DU JEU DE PAUME
RUE DU PÉLICAN
RUE SAINT JEAN
Parc André Gagnon
PLACE ST. JEAN
BOULEVARD
PROMENADE DES CHARBONNIERS
JACQUES
R. AVEDAM
RUE CHANTAULT
RUE DE LA BRÈCHE
RUE DE LA
RUE MURET
RUE ST-JULIEN
Parc Léon Blum
BOULEVARD JEAN JAURÈS
RUE DES GRANDES FILLES DIEU
AVENUE BÉTHOUART
AV. DE PLAISANCE
AVENUE NEIGRE
RUE HELENE BOUCHER

Train Station
PLACE SÉMARD
RUE NICOLE
AV. J. DE BEAUCE
RUE DE LA COURONN
RUE DE FÉLIBIEN
RUE DES LISSES
Centre Inter. du Vitrail
REMPART CHÂTELET
CHEVAL BLANC
R. DE STE-THÉRÈSE
PL. SAINTE-MÊME
R. ST-NICOLAS
Musée des Beaux-Arts
RUE ST-ANDRÉ
R. FONTAINE
BOULEVARD DU MARÉCHAL FOCH
RUE DU MOULIN À TAN
AV. DE TEXIER-GALLAS
R. DU PETIT BOULLON
RUE DE LA CROIX THIBAULT

Bus Station
RUE NICOLE
R.G. FESSARD
R. CH. BRUNE
RUE J. MOULIN
Cathedral Notre Dame
R. BETHLÉEM
R. DE SERPENTE
RUE AU LAIT
PLACE POISSONNERIE
RUE DE LA TANNERIE
RUE DE LA CORROIE
R. DU BOURG
RUE DE LA PÉROUSE
RUE FAUBOURG GUILLAUME
RUE D'ABLIS
R. ST CHERON

Prefecture
POL
RUE G. FESSARD
HARLEVILLE PL.
PLACE ST. FOY
R. DU SOLEIL D'OR
PLACE BILLARD
R. PARFA
PLACE DE LA PIE
P. CENDR
R. PUITS BERCHOT
BD GEORGES CLÉMENCEAU
PLACE MORARD
RUE ST BARTHÉLÉMY
Maison Picassiet

RUE DU 14 JUILLET
RUE GABRIEL PÉRI
BD MAURICE VIOLLETTE
R. FAMIN
R. NOEL BALLAY
PLACE MARCEAU
R. DES GRENETS
RUE SAINT PIERRE
R. DES POULIES
PLACE MORARD
RUE DU REPOS

PLACE DES ÉPARS
BOIS MERRAIN R. TONNELLERIE
R. ARTHURIN
RUE DES BOUCHES
RÉGNIER D. BOUTEAU
POÊLE PERCÉE
BIBLIOTHÈQUE
PLACE DES HALLES
R. AUUN
ST PIERRE HILAIRE
PTE. PORTE MORARD
R. GRENOUILLÈRE
Parc des Bords de l'Eure Petite Venise
RUE DU FAUBOURG LA GRAPPE
RUE DE SOURS

To Le Mans
RUE GABRIEL LELONG
RUE DU DOCTEUR MAUNOURY
BOULEVARD CHASLES
BOULEVARD CHASLES
PLACE RAVENNE
PLACE PASTEUR
R. ORM
RUE SAINT MICHEL
R. POCQUE
Square Noël-Ballay
BOULEVARD DE LA COURTILLE

RUE DE CHATEAUDUN
RUE BROSSOLETTE
RUE ST. THOMAS
R. DES VIEUX CAPUCINS
RUE SAINT BRICE
RUE VICTOR GILBERT
R. MENDÈS FRANCE

Eure

To Tours

To Orléans

more magnificent Romanesque edifice, carried out under the architect Béranger, roughly on the scale of the current cathedral, if a little shorter and lower. The crypt holding the Virgin's relic was greatly enlarged for pilgrims to parade past it easily.

Great men succeeded Fulbert, and promoted the teaching of classical authors. Bernard de Chartres famously compared the scholars of his day to dwarves perched on the shoulders of giants (that is, the philosophers of antiquity) allowing them to see further. The scholars of the time striving to unite the ideas of these great pagan thinkers with Christian thought, they even honoured some of the major philosophers of antiquity by having them carved on the west front of the cathedral when it was extended in the mid-12th century.

Medieval Chartres, meanwhile, was growing into a city about the same size as the present version, and consequently of far greater significance. But another terrible fire in 1194 destroyed much of the town and severely damaged the cathedral. The populace feared the Virgin's relic had been destroyed, and that they would lose her protection. It seemed a miracle when three days after the conflagration, a procession appeared carrying the precious object, rescued from the crypt by attentive priests. A huge wave of enthusiasm swept across the city, and the whole populace set about helping in the construction of a new, more brilliant Gothic cathedral. Chartres' position as a prime religious centre of learning and pilgrimage was assured for centuries to come, and a rich city endowed with a staggering array of religious houses as well as many fine merchants' quarters expanded around the cathedral. The grain from the Beauce plain surrounding the city went to feed Paris, adding to Chartres' riches.

In the Wars of Religion, the city remained staunchly Catholic, but at the end of the conflict, in February 1594, the reconciling Henri IV came to the cathedral to be crowned king of France. Chartres continued to prosper through to the Revolution, which spelt disaster for many of the religious establishments in town, although you'll see that many churches did survive, together with the cathedral. Paris was brought even closer with the building of a railway line this way as early as 1841, and from that time, tourists began to vie in number with the pilgrims.

Cathédrale Notre-Dame

Open 8.30–7.30; free. Mass is held on Mon–Fri at 11.45 and 6.15, Sat at 11.45, Sun at 9.15 (Gregorian), 11 and 6.

The rebuilding of Chartres' cathedral represents one of the most impressive communal endeavours of medieval Europe. Everyone who could pitched in with labour, for example helping extract stone from the Berchères quarries 8km away, or giving funds for the inspired new 'Palace of the Virgin' – even kings Philippe Auguste and Richard Coeur de Lion, who were then fighting over the area. Over the next decades, donations poured in from rich nobles in France and abroad, but the wealthy city corporations also gave generously – after all, the Virgin had brought them great prosperity through the mass of pilgrims.

By 1260 the building was nearly complete. The relative rapidity of the work allowed Chartres to have a stylistic unity seen in few other medieval cathedrals. It perfected the concepts of roof vaulting and the flying buttress, enabling it to carry large expanses of glass-filled sides. Inside, carving the thick pillars into apparent bundles of slender columns accentuated the building's verticality and lightness.

The façade's south tower is a Romanesque survivor; the northern one was struck by lightning in 1506 and rebuilt, more ornately, to the plans of Jehan Texier de Beauce in the early 16th century; he followed the Flamboyant Gothic style, but also added a little Renaissance building below. In medieval times, the cathedral roof would have been covered with lead, but this was stolen at the Revolution. Then yet another fire in 1936 destroyed the forest of timbers holding up the roof. A new, bold metallic structure replaced them, topped by copper tiles, giving the distinctive green colour.

Joyously, most of the cathedral's medieval decoration has survived down the centuries. In the words of the eminent French art historian Emile Mâle, 'Chartres is medieval thought in visible form'. More than 10,000 figures in stone or glass make this cathedral a period encyclopedia. It would take a thorough knowledge of the Scriptures and of medieval philosophy, and a lifetime's work, to decipher all the scenes.

The mid-12th-century **west porches** escaped the 1194 fire relatively unscathed. It is generally said that various schools of French sculptors, from St-Denis, Etampes and Chartres, carved the supremely serene tall Romanesque statues which flank the doors, although an Australian scholar has recently speculated as to whether Italian masons might have executed these works. The statues are supposed to represent Old and New Testament figures, although certain researchers suspect that some might also bear a likeness to medieval royals, for example Eleanor of Aquitaine and her sons. The central tympanum shows the Christ of the Apocalypse being crowned by two angels, hence the nickname of the Portail Royal. Mary sits enthroned in the right-hand portal, holding out the baby Jesus; above them, note the fascinating depiction of classical scholars, together with the instruments most associated with their areas of learning. In the left-hand portal, as well as the Ascension scene in the tympanum, the signs of the zodiac and associated labours of the month prove engrossing.

Down the cathedral's sides, the substantial protruding **north and south porches** contain just as great a concentration of sculpted figures, but from the Gothic period, with more of a sense of movement and drama than in the west front Romanesque pieces. On the south portal, the central tympanum represents Christ and the Last Judgement, that to the left, St Stephen's stoning, set above other Christian martyrs, that to the right, the generosity of St Martin (*see* Tours) and St Nicholas in particular. The big statues below feature the apostles.

The recent cleaning of the north portal has really brought the Old and New Testament figures here to life. The three tympanums present a delightful Nativity, the Virgin's Assumption and seating beside Christ, plus the more alarming tale of Job on his pile of manure, the last among several Old Testament prefigurations of Christ brought to the fore across the whole portal. Below humiliated Job unfolds the Judgement of Salomon. The big statues further down represent a wide variety of biblical characters. Traces of the original colouring of these statues have reemerged with the cleaning, particularly noticeably with the black figures. The Queen of Sheeba is even shown standing on a black lad. Black people were, unfortunately, generally reserved evil roles in medieval Christian iconography, and the executioner in the Salomon story, ready to slice the disputed baby in two, is black.

Inside blaźe the finest **stained-glass windows** in the world, 173 of them, mostly original. As was the custom, different trade guilds as well as wealthy individuals supported the making of these pieces. Look at the bottoms of the windows and you'll see goldsmiths, bakers, weavers, tavern-keepers, furriers, blacksmiths and others at work below the biblical stories and saintly tales. Particularly outstanding are the tall windows in the west front picturing the life of Christ, the stunning rose windows, and the distinctive Notre-Dame de la Belle Verrière celebrating the Virgin. The northern rose window and lancets were donated by Queen Blanche of Castille, the southern rose window and lancets by Pierre Mauclerc, the latter Duke of Brittany, but also count of nearer Dreux. Thibault VI of Chartres gave some of the brilliant windows around the choir.

On the floor of the nave, look out for the labyrinth (fully revealed on Friday mornings). Many other Gothic cathedrals once had a similar one, but this is a rare survivor, its much disputed significance encouraging all sorts of flaky interpretations. You can visit the vast, complex Romanesque **crypt** *(April–Oct 11 (exc Sun and bank hols), 2.15, 3.30 and 4.30; rest of year 11 (exc Sun and bank hols) and 4.15; adm)*, sanctuary of the Virgin's blouse spared by the fire of 1194, and climb the **north tower** *(May–Aug Mon–Sat 9.30–12 and 2–5.30, Sun 2–5.30; rest of year Mon–Sat 9.30–12 and 2–4.30, Sun 2–4.30; adm)*.

Chartres' Museums and Shopping Streets and Squares

Very fine houses from a variety of periods surround the cathedral as you'll discover wandering all the way round it. Beyond the cathedral's north portal, the **Centre International du Vitrail** *(open Mon–Fri 9.30–12.30 and 1.30–6; weekends and public hols 10–12.30 and 2.30–6; adm)* occupies a major medieval timberframe building, built to stock produce brought in as tax in kind from the cathedral's extremely lucrative territories. The upper floor received grain, the lower floor, with grand columns and carved capitals fit for a church, wine. Now the place is devoted to stained-glass-making up to the present day, several studios still thriving in the Chartres area.

Behind the cathedral, the **Musée des Beaux-Arts** *(open daily exc Tues 10–12 and 2–5; adm)* occupies the former bishops' palace. The brick and stone Ancien Régime facade may look rather plain, but Baroque puts on quite a show as you enter, with a dramatic main staircase and chapel. Certain notable religious objects have been brought here from the Chartres church of St Peter, including the exquisite 16th-century enamels of the apostles, originally given by King Henri II to his mistress Diane de Poitiers, but much of the fine religious statuary comes from further afield, while the so-called Charlemagne glass is reckoned to be 12th-century Syrian enamel work. Among the collection of paintings, Zurbaran's *St Lucy* is the most highly regarded religious work. Remarkable portraits include Molière by Mignard, the Duc de St-Simon by Largillère, and Erasmus, attributed to Holbein. Chardin's monkey scenes provide more surprising entertainment. The modern art sections range from a Courbet nude bather to dramatic pieces by Soutine and Vlaminck – the latter lived a good deal of his life north of Chartres. Henri Navarre's heady sculptures also feature prominently. Alarming depictions of Chartres dotted around the museum include a bird's eye view of the city besieged in 1568, during the Wars of Religion, and the cathedral on fire in 1836. Local crafts are also represented, along with collections of arms, and ethnography from as far afield as Oceania.

Beyond the cathedral's south portal stand the characterful **main shopping streets and squares** of the upper town, filled with grand houses, several with elaborately carved creatures clambering over their beams. Some of the prettiest corners are to be found around **Place de l'Etape du Vin** and **Place de la Poissonnerie**. The centre of nearby **Place Bilange** is taken up by a graceful steel-covered roof, these late-19th century Halles serving as centrepiece for the magnificent Saturday morning food market. Local culinary specialities which you can find in Chartres' many gastronomic shops any day of the week include *cochelins*, pastry men often filled with jam or marzipan; *pâté de Chartres*, a generally crust-covered mixture made with venison or duck meat, often with a foie gras kernel; *mentchikoffs*, oversweet pralines coated in white meringue; and Chartres beer, made from Beauce grain.

From around the terraced gardens at the back of the cathedral, steep paths plunge down to the river Eure. One even carried the nickname of Rue Glisse Putain – Slipping Tart Street – as prostitutes going down to serve the barracks supposedly tended to slide down in the mud on rainy nights. Explore the **Basse Ville** by the Eure, often completely missed by visitors, but exceptionally picturesque, packed with old churches and converted mills, numerous medieval bridges spanning the river, on which you can go boating in season.

For a really different, wacky view of Chartres cathedral, head out into the suburbs for the **Maison Picassiette** (*open April–Oct daily exc Sun am and Tues 10–12 and 2–6; adm*), so called after the nickname given to Raymond Isidore, describing someone who nicks things from other people's plates. Isidore, working as a cemetery sweeper, in fact developed an obsession with collecting shards of broken plates, pots and glasses, saving the pieces, which he then used in plastering every inch of his house with naive, colourful mosaics, the rough artistic endeavour continuing from 1930 until 1962, two years before he died. Flowers, birds, animals and human figures pop up all over the place, along with many holy places and cities such as Jerusalem. But Chartres cathedral features most of all, naturally.

The Loir Valley

The Loir (without an 'e') meanders down through four French *départements* from below Chartres almost to Angers, its wide, flat valley often seeming to be cut too big for its slender size. The names Loir and Loire suggest there might be a connection between the two, and similarities do exist: limestone in lovely whites and beiges for the picturesque waterside architecture; troglodyte villages; Romanesque churches; and characteristic châteaux.

The source of the Loir lies southwest of Chartres, close to dilapidated, melancholic small town of **Illiers-Combray**, with its museum and public garden dedicated to Proust, whose aunt and uncle had a house here. The place served as inspiration for the magically detailed descriptions of the narrator's childhood in the early parts of the greatest French masterpiece of the 20th century, *A La Recherche du temps perdu*, and the **Maison de la Tante Léonie** (*open mid-Jan–mid-Dec daily exc Mon, guided tours 2.30 and 4, plus 11am July–Aug; adm*) has kept a good deal of period atmosphere, thanks in part to the legacy of Proust's beloved servant and her family, who donated lots of the objects. The guides mournfully show you round the rooms, and bring to life Proust and his social circle, represented by photographic copies up in the attic. The big barrel-roofed church in the centre adds to the gloomy appeal of this depressed little town.

To the west, the village church at **Méréglise** holds more Proustian memories for literary pilgrims, while the disparate array of buildings at the **Château de Frazé** a couple of villages further west make for a delightfully picturesque detour.

Continuing down the Loir past **Bonneval** behind its ramparts, and the secretive **Conie river**, an enjoyable place to go boating, **Châteaudun** imposes a halt. Its vast grey-stoned fortress soaring way above the Loir stops you in your tracks. While the locals love to mess about in boats on the waters below, the historic upper town has a more hushed air, its bright-stoned, big central square and well-ordered grid of streets recently scrubbed clean, as though in readiness for the visit of some dignitary. The big church near the castle has been given a going over too, even if it looks vacuous inside.

The entrance to the **château** (*open July–Aug 9.30–7; April–June and Sept 9.30–6.15; Jan–March and Oct–Dec 10–12.30 and 2–5; adm*) stands discreetly tucked away in an extremely picturesque corner of the upper town. With its magnificent mix of Gothic and Renaissance wings, this castle can lay claim to being the most northerly of the typical greater Loire Valley châteaux. The word *dun* comes from a Celtic word for a rocky promontory, and the natural site was an obvious spot for Thibault le Tricheur and subsequent counts of Blois to fortify through the Middle Ages. The huge round Grosse Tour or keep, over 100 feet high, went up for Thibaud V at the end of the 12th century. In 1391, Louis d'Orléans, son of King Charles V of France, acquired the castle. His illegitimate child Jean d'Orléans was the bastard Dunois who led the French troops to end the English siege of Orléans, aided by Joan of Arc. He would receive many estates and titles in recognition of his military services, becoming Count of Longueville (near Dieppe) as well as Count of Dunois. He and his wife had the **Sainte Chapelle** built from the 1450s. The relic it held of a supposed piece of wood from Christ's cross may have vanished, but fifteen dignified Gothic statues still stand proudly inside, helpfully presented on panels.

Splendidly ornate stair towers protrude from the **two main wings** of the castle. The Dunois one, built for Jean d'Orléans, has been given over to a contemporary exhibition on the importance of food and feasting in medieval times. The presentations are a bit hit and miss, with few original objects and too many poor copies, but there's lots of entertaining material to eke out. The most unusual dishes featured include pustulant old whores served in a green sauce, and buggers in a grand Parisian concoction, both part of a banquet given by the King of Hell, as imagined by 13th-century poet Robert de Houdereau. Regular cookery demonstrations and tastings take place, but not of these particular recipes. The soberer Longueville wing went up in the 16th century for Jean's son and grandson. Here too, the chambers are embellished with substantial fireplaces, while impressive tapestry cycles enliven the walls of the two immense main galleries.

The attractive historic heart of **Vendôme** is tightly embraced by the arms of the Loir and overseen by the remnants of a ruined castle, from which, in the 11th century, Geoffroy Martel of Anjou and his wife Agnès de Bourgogne witnessed what they thought to be three stars falling in a fountain. They took these as a sign to order a magnificent house in God's honour. The massive Abbaye de la Trinité which arose and was much transformed down the centuries still dominates the centre of town. The most precious relic it held was a supposed tear of Christ, donated by the papacy for Geoffroy's military services to the Church. Much of the abbey church may be

Romanesque, but its splendid façade is a last blaze of Gothic, the great window alight with fiery tongues of stone licking their way skywards. The choir and side chapels contain some of the oldest stained glass in France (one piece dating from *c*. 1140) and an exceptional 14th-century scene showing Geoffroy Martel receiving the tear of Christ. The other remaining abbey buildings, dating from the 17th and 18th centuries, contain the local **Musée du Cloître** (*open daily exc Tues 10–12 and 2–6; adm*), while some vivid Romanesque frescoes have survived in the old chapterhouse. One floor of the museum presents works by Louis Leygue, a 20th-century sculptor from the town.

Nearby spacious, lively, café-lined **Place St-Martin** is overseen by a soaring tower to rival that of the abbey, all that remains of a late 15th-century church, and by a statue of the Marquis de Rochambeau, the man to whom the USA in large part owes its independence, thanks to his crucial role in the Battle of Yorktown. He died back at his château close to Vendôme in 1807. Characterful historic streets lead off this main square, while in the height of summer you can take a boat tour on the branches of the Loir passing through the centre of town.

West of Vendôme, seek out the extraordinary wall paintings in the 15th-century church of **St-Hilaire** at **Villiers-sur-Loir**, but the prudish should avert their eyes from the choir stalls with their bawdy scenes. In this area, you enter **Coteaux du Vendômois** wine territory, granted *appellation* status in 2000. At **Thoré-la-Rochette**, head for the railway station either to look at the wine museum and shop, or for a return trip to Troo on board an old train (*open June–mid-Sept, weekends and public hols at 2.25, July–Aug additional Sun trips 9.30 and 5.30; adm; t 02 54 72 80 82*).

At **Montoire**, a pact with the devil was sealed with a handshake in the **railway station** (*exhibition open mid-April–mid-Sept Mon–Fri 11–12 and 3–6; adm*) – here, Pétain met with Hitler in October 1940 to accept officially the German occupation of France and his collaborative role. On a much happier note, the town holds a vibrant annual world folklore festival and has opened a museum on unusual instruments. By the charming south bank of the river, the tiny truncated 11th-century **Chapelle St-Gilles** (*open April–Sept daily exc Mon 10–12 and 3–7, Sun 11–3; adm*) conceals three over-whelming depictions of Christ. Nearby, **Lavardin**'s ruined hillside castle looks like a Romantic painting. The church below is plastered with further wall paintings, including a queue of naked people waiting to enter paradise.

The secretive village of **Troo** climbs the steep bank of the Loir west of Montoire, its cliff punctured with troglodyte caves turned into houses, a couple open to visitors in summer and certain weekends. The upper village conceals several attractive elements: semi-ruined ramparts, a large church, a 'speaking well', and an earth fort with a path snailing up to the top. Looking down into the valley, the enchanting box-like **St-Jacques-des-Guérets** is decorated with fine Romanesque art. Make a detour north to see the **Château de Courtanvaux**, on the outskirts of Bessé-sur-Braye, offering a storybook vision of a late-Gothic silhouette above lovingly tended gardens.

The supremely lyrical French Renaissance poet Pierre de Ronsard (*see* Tours) was born near Couture-sur-Loir, at the **Manoir de la Possonnière** (*open July–Aug daily exc Mon and Tues 3–7; April–June and Sept–15 Nov weekends and hols 3–6; adm*). Learning is literally written all over the house here, the windows graced with Latin inscriptions.

Many of these were ordered by Ronsard's father in celebration of his marriage. In the hillside opposite, seven cave entrances stand out, further inscriptions engraved over each, recalling their various uses for the medieval pilgrims who stopped here.

The Loir continues through **Poncé**, partly colonized by craftspeople. At the put-upon **Château de Poncé** (*open April–Sept 10–12.30 and 2–6; adm*), the great Renaissance staircase is the highlight, its coffered stone ceiling filled with a plethora of sculptures, while a bust of Ronsard stands at the top of the stairs, accompanied by a delicious poem he wrote to the Loir, as though to a rumbustious friend. A small museum is in the cellars.

Just west, the valley vineyards produce intriguingly rare white **Jasnières** *appellation* wine. The more ordinary if pleasant **Coteaux du Loir** whites, reds, and rosés come from around the little market town of **La Chartre-sur-le-Loir**. Bending up northwards from here around the village of Jupilles, the **forest of Bercé** conceals mighty oaks, some 300 years old. **Jupilles' Maison du Sabot et de l'Artisanat du Bois** (*open Easter–mid-Nov Mon–Sat 10–12 and 2.30–6.30, Sun 2.30–6.30; adm*) is devoted to woodworking, especially clog- and toy-making. A little further north, two gardens call for a visit, that at **Pruillé L'Eguillé** (*open mid-March–mid-Nov daily exc Thurs 2–6; adm*) specializing in conifers, that at the **Château du Grand Lucé** (*open May–Sept Tues–Sun 10–7; adm*) laid out in the formal French style beside a fine 18th-century castle.

Back close to the Loir, beyond the orchards of Vaas, the **Château du Lude** (*open April–Sept gardens daily, exc Wed outside mid-June–Aug, 10–12 and 2–6; château daily, exc Wed outside mid-June–Aug 2.30–6; adm*) competes in scale with some of the grandest of all Loire Valley châteaux, each corner marked by a massive round tower covered with Renaissance decoration. The place was substantially modified in the 18th century for the finance minister the Marquis de Talhouët, given a grand classical façade, plus an inner courtyard which has something of the air of a great Parisian town house. The interiors are very grand. From the spectacular ballroom, with its floral marquetry floor, you trip through a series of spacious salons. An intimate surprise awaits in a little jewel box of a room covered with paintings and grotesques in the Italian Mannerist style.

Take the prettier Loir north bank from Le Lude to reach **La Flèche**, lying in a pleasingly open spot on the river. Here, the first Bourbon king, Henri IV, founded an exceptionally grand Jesuit school, the Collège Royal, now the **Prytanée National Militaire** (*open July–late-Aug 10–12 and 2–6; adm*). Philosopher René Descartes was its star pupil. Henri IV requested that his heart and that of his tempestuous wife Marie de' Medici be buried in the school's stunning Chapelle St-Louis, but these were ceremonially burnt in 1793. Napoleon turned the college into an élite military training school, which it has remained to this day. Honours boards list pupils who became marshals and generals, and the many who have died in conflicts. Outside town, the big zoo is a popular attraction.

Two last memorable châteaux open to visitors lie by the banks of the Loir before Angers, the rustic little **Château de Bazouges** (*open mid-June–mid-Sept Thurs–Sun 3–6; adm*), its concentration of adorable towers just popping up out of the trees on the river bank beside a village full of fishermen and river boats, and the **Château de Durtal** *(open July–Aug 10–12 and 2–7; April–June and Sept weekends and public hols 2–6; adm)*, a self-important edifice with fat towers lording it over the little town grovelling below. By Durtal, you have entered Anjou.

The Loir into Northern Anjou

Just a short way north of Angers, the Loir joins the Sarthe, which immediately joins the Mayenne to form the very short, fat river Maine, by which Angers stands. Two important but contrasting late-medieval châteaux lie in this well-watered area, both confusingly carrying the name of Plessis. Le Plessis-Bourré is a welcoming château built in fine white limestone, while Le Plessis-Macé is a forbidding schist fortification. You can go boating up the Sarthe and the Mayenne from various picturesque villages on their banks. The historic border with Brittany lies to the west.

Château du Plessis-Bourré

Open July–Aug daily 10–6; April–June and Sept Fri–Tues 10–12 and 2–6, Thurs 2–6; Feb–March and Oct–Nov Thurs–Tues 2–6; t 02 41 32 06 72, www.plessis-bourre.com; adm.

The invitingly formal Château du Plessis-Bourré stands near Ecuillé between the Mayenne and the Sarthe rivers. Inside, it offers the shock of the weirdest ceiling in the Loire Valley. As you approach this château along an alley of tall, noble trees, imagine King Charles VIII's representatives arriving on horseback at this somewhat remote but extremely refined country house to greet the king of Hungary's emissaries in 1487; the place would have provided a suitably ambassadorial setting. A cavalcade consisting of some 200 horses came, the Hungarians bringing their own musicians to provide entertainment.

In 1487 Le Plessis-Bourré was the recently completed swanky modern home of Jean Bourré, faithful minister to King Louis XI, 'most trusted master of an untrusting king', as the writer Ian Dunlop summarized him neatly. Under Louis XI, not only was Bourré given the royal finances to oversee, he was also put in charge of the education of the Dauphin, the future King Charles VIII. What's more, he was asked by the king to organize the construction of the Château de Langeais by the Loire. Meanwhile, the minister went ahead with two châteaux for himself, Le Plessis-Bourré and Jarzé, the latter east of Angers, sadly disappeared. Busy man that Bourré was, he appears to have had a great zest for the good things in life.

The nature of Bourré's work meant that he was usually running after the king, and he left it to his wife, Marguerite de Feschal, to manage the building site. Their tender correspondence has survived, providing some idea of the way the building of the château progressed. Begun in 1468, it was completed by 1473, and demonstrates a much more advanced taste in planned architecture than Plessis-Macé close by.

Although set in flat, slightly uninspiring land, the château makes for the prettiest of moated pictures. The moats were once even more elaborate than they are today, but you still have to cross three bridges to reach the main entrance. These waters

Getting Around

Bus lines from Angers serve the Sarthe valley, with stops at Cheffes and Châteauneuf-sur-Sarthe; the Mayenne, with stops at Grez-Neuville and Le Lion d'Angers; and the Segréen, with stops at Segré, Noyant-la-Gravoyère and Pouancé. The rare bus stops at Le Plessis-Macé.

Tourist Information

Le Lion d'Angers: Square des Villes Jumelées, 49220 Le Lion d'Angers, t 02 41 95 83 19, *otintercom-leliondangers@wanadoo.fr*.
Châteauneuf-sur-Sarthe: Quai de la Sarthe, 49330 Châteauneuf-sur-Sarthe, t/f 02 41 69 82 89, *tourismechateauneufsursarthe @wanadoo.fr, www.cc-payschateauneuf.fr*.
Segré: 5 Rue David d'Angers, 49500 Segré, t 02 41 92 86 83, *www.ville-segre.fr*.
Pouancé: 2 bis Rue de la Porte Angevine (in season) or Mairie (out of season), 49420 Pouancé, t 02 41 92 45 86 or t 02 41 92 41 08 (out of season).

Market Days

Segré: Wednesday.
Pouancé: Thursday.

Where to Stay and Eat

Briollay ✉ 49125
★★★★**Château de Noirieux**, 26 Route du Moulin, t 02 41 42 50 05, *www. chateaudenoirieux.com* (expensive). The height of luxury in Anjou, in a soberly elegant castle above the Loir. Refined cuisine. Swimming pool, tennis court and helipad in the grounds (*menus €49–92*).

Châteauneuf-sur-Sarthe ✉ 49330
Hôtel de la Sarthe, 1 Rue du Port, t/f 02 41 69 85 29 (inexpensive). With a terrace looking on to the river. You can try a steak of Maine-Angevin here, a special breed developed across the two regions (*menus €14–32; closed Sun pm out of season, and Mon*). Closed Oct.

Champigné ✉ 49330
Château des Briottières B&B, t 02 41 42 00 02, *www.briottieres.com* (expensive). Extremely elegant 18th-century property. Heated swimming pool (*table d'hôte €46*).

Grez-Neuville ✉ 49220
La Croix d'Etain B&B, 2 Rue de l'Ecluse, t 02 41 95 68 49, *www.anjou-et-loire.com/croix* (moderate). Delightful 19th-century property by the banks of the Mayenne.

Chenillé-Changé ✉ 49220
La Table du Meunier, t 02 41 95 10 83/98 (*menus €23–34; closed Mon pm–Wed Sept–Oct and April–June; closed Sun pm–Wed Nov–Dec and Mar*). A restaurant in an intriguing schist property close to the river, with curious sculptures set around it. Not only do Anjou wines feature in certain sauces, but also cider, reflecting the closeness of cider-producing Maine. *Closed Jan–Feb; open daily July–Aug.*

La Jaille-Yvon ✉ 49220
Château du Plessis-Anjou B&B, t 02 41 95 12 75, *www.chateauxhotels.com/plessis* (expensive). A really appealing mix of 16th- and 18th-century architecture, just north of Chenillé-Changé on the Mayenne. You can go up in the château's hot air balloon as well as playing tennis in the grounds (*table d'hôte €48*).

Pouancé ✉ 49420
Le Vieux Logis, 53 Rue de la Libération, t 02 41 92 40 15. An unpretentious restaurant by the Breton border, with inexpensive and tasty food on offer (*menus €12–27*). *Closed Mon and Feb hols.*

provided one form of defence, the château itself sitting on an island. Each corner is marked by a round tower, one more imposing than the others, referred to as the donjon and providing a viewing post for the countryside around. While defence certainly wasn't ignored, nor were the possibilities for gracious living. The walls were pierced with generous mullion windows, making the rooms light and airy. In the main *corps de logis*, the windows were neatly arranged in vertical rows, even if symmetry of the whole façade doesn't appear to have been an objective. All in all, it is an extremely attractive house in late-Gothic style. A particularly light stone from a quarry near Saumur was chosen for its construction. As you enter the large inner courtyard, the Lord's Wing confronts you, its three storeys topped by a row of plainish *lucarnes*, three bearing arms: those of France, of the Roi René and of Jean Bourré. Although Jean Bourré seems to have had the interior decorated, he and his family spent little time at Le Plessis-Bourré, making Jarzé their main residence.

Most of the rooms have been substantially altered since Bourré's time. The wood panelling in the Louis XV and Louis XVI salons was put in by the family that acquired the château at the start of the 20th century and still lives here. The floral carvings in the Louis XVI room were made by David d'Angers, father of the renowned 19th-century sculptor of the same name (*see* Angers). The high-relief wood carving in the Grand Salon elaborately depicts hunting scenes. By contrast, the Salle des Parlements, vaulted with splendid stone ribs, the floor of tiles made at Les Rairies near Durtal on the Loir, takes you back to Bourré's period. The monumental fireplace off centre apparently bears symbols of alchemy.

Upstairs, the strangest painted ceiling in the Loire Valley awaits you in the Salle des Gardes. For those of a delicate sensibility, it might be better not to look up too carefully. The hexagonal panels in the coffered wood include pictures of a woman sewing up a magpie's anus and of Venus peeing, standing up, into a bowl a man holds out below her. One prudish owner's wife covered up the offending ceiling before the Revolution, which may explain how it survived that period. Her husband was not so lucky; despite local pressure and protests in his defence, he was executed in Angers in 1794. In the middle of the 19th century the château was put up for sale and almost fell into the hands of ruthless opportunists wanting to sell off the stone, but an Angers lawyer stepped in to buy it. He ordered much restoration work in the castle, not always in the best taste, but also had this ceiling restored.

The meanings of the 24 very bizarre scenes still remain shrouded in mystery. They're thought to date back to Bourré's day and to reflect the period taste for alchemy. The booklet available at the château gives a rather abstruse and inadequate reading of the symbols. Eight of the panels apparently illustrate popular old French sayings. These include further absurd scenes, such as a goose which a couple are earnestly trying to shoe, and eels which another couple are attempting to break in two.

After such strangely absorbing decoration, the hotchpotch of articles in the last few rooms prove a bit of an anticlimax. You're rushed through the wing connecting the lord's dwelling to the chapel, converted into a library, but also containing a large collection of fans and ephemera. A memorably naive depiction of the Last Supper is displayed in the chapel.

Up the Sarthe

A little north of Le Plessis-Bourré, at Cheffes and Châteauneuf-sur-Sarthe, you can take a **river trip** with a commentary giving you the history of river navigation, trade and the life of mariners in the past across Anjou. The highlights along the Sarthe river lie just across the border, in the *départements* of the Sarthe and the Mayenne, roughly equivalent to the medieval province of Maine, sandwiched between the Loire Valley and Normandy. The bright riverside town of Sablé, the renowned plain-chant-singing abbey of Solesmes, the splendid tiny medieval village of Asnières-sur-Vègre and the pottery town of Malicorne are just a short drive away.

Château du Plessis-Macé

Open July–Aug daily 10.30–6.30, Sept–Oct Wed–Sun 1.30–5.30, early March–June Wed, Thurs, Sat and Sun 1.30–5.30; t 02 41 32 67 93; adm.

Le Plessis-Macé stands on the edge of a plateau just west of the Mayenne river above Angers. The name Macé refers to an 11th-century lord. On arrival outside the castle, you're confronted by forbidding schist fortifications, and an overgrown moat with just a trickle of a stream running through it. The outer defences date back as far as the 12th century. At the end of the Hundred Years' War, the château proper was in good part devastated, but the substantial keep survived, overdone with later decoration. Rebuilding work took place in the 1450s. Once past the imposing outer defences, a much more graceful, light, expansive courtyard opens up before you, although the architecture isn't harmonious or unified; in fact it looks an appealing shambles. The castle follows a traditional plan, with the lord's chambers on one side, his followers' and servants' quarters on the other. This inner château mixes rugged schist with smooth limestone in almost comical fashion, the latter used to frame the windows and corners, but also for odd bits and pieces of decoration.

Louis de Beaumont was the most significant of Le Plessis-Macé's 15th-century lords. He served King Louis XI as chamberlain and as *seneschal* of Poitou, and devoted quite some attention to his château. A knight of the Order of St-Michael (created by Louis XI at Amboise in 1469), his chapel is dedicated to the dragon-slaying military saint. The bottom half was built in rough schist, the top half in well-prepared limestone.

During Louis XI's time the independent province of Brittany a short distance west of here was a force to be reckoned with for the French Crown. Louis XI is recorded setting out from the castle to attack Pouancé to the northwest and to take Ancenis, west along the Loire, then the major town on the Anjou's frontier with Brittany. That obstreperous region would effectively be joined to the French royal possessions by the marriage of Louis XI's successor, Charles VIII, to Anne de Bretagne. The guides claim that in one of Le Plessis-Macé's rooms, in 1532, King François I signed the last clause of the Treaty of Vannes, definitively joining Brittany to the royal French realms.

Le Plessis-Macé became a country residence for the powerful du Bellay family, serving the house of Anjou and the Valois, from the mid-16th to the mid-17th centuries. The 1627 inventory gives an idea of the wealth of the interiors, listing Aubusson tapestries, Turkish rugs, fine furniture, bookshelves and a mass of gold brocade and crimson velvet. What you see today is less ostentatious, much altered by the 19th-century owners, with many window openings added along the outer château walls and defences to let in more light. The furniture varies in quality. Among the more interesting pieces, you'll see a rare tapestry with a red parrot, one of the oldest pianos in France, and a great bookshelf containing vast tomes on Egypt, reflecting the 19th-century fascination with that place. The chapel preserves original late-Gothic carved wood panelling, the lords' box on the first floor an exceptional piece of carpentry work. In the over-cemented outhouses, space is given to local exhibitions, while during the Anjou theatre festival in June and July, the courtyard serves as a venue for performances.

A short way west of Le Plessis-Macé, the little **chapel of St-Emérance** is delightfully decorated in Flamboyant Gothic style in royal recognition of the relief the saint apparently brought Louis XI when he was caught short while out hunting.

Into Northwestern Anjou

Above Le Plessis-Macé, the Mayenne river has a couple of particularly attractive little riverside villages from which you can take a river cruise. **Grez-Neuville** lies just east of the N162 a few kilometres north of Le Plessis-Macé. At the confluence of the Mayenne and Oudon, by **Le Lion d'Angers**, stands a national stud farm, the **Haras National** (*open Easter–mid-Sept daily 10–12 and 2–6, tours at 11, 3 and 4.15; mid-Sept–Easter weekends only 2–5.30, tours at 2.45 and 4; t 02 41 18 05 05, www.haras-nationaux.fr; adm*), with a beautiful race course. Even outside the racing season you can go and visit the stud. There's no guide, but details on the wide variety of stallions in their stalls are clearly stated. Continuing up the Mayenne, the village of **Chenillé-Changé** makes a particularly picturesque river stop. The Mayenne is a beautiful river, with wooded banks protected from roads, and towpaths you can walk along. You can take a cruiser from Chenille-Changé to discover it. Contact **Maine-Anjou-Rivieres** (*t 02 41 95 14 23; www.maine-anjou-rivieres.com*).

Some way further up the Oudon, a tributary of the Mayenne, the **Domaine de la Petite Couère** (*open May–Aug 10–7, March–April and Sept–Oct Sun and public hols only 10–7; t 02 41 61 06 31*) is a rural museum on rural ways outside Châtelais, north of the town of Segré. It recalls ordinary life in the countryside, as well as displaying some more curious collections. The vast array of objects is well presented and includes horse-drawn carriages, tractors, old engines, old cars and model cars, most of them lined up in long, purpose-built barns. You can then walk or take a little train to the farm turned fake olde village.

The character of northwestern Anjou turns markedly Breton around **Pouancé**, with its landscape of agricultural ridges broken up by hedgerows and its much darker stone. Fragments of an extremely ruined **château** (*open mid-June–late Sept Tues 2–6.30, Wed–Fri 10–12 and 2–6.30, Sat 1.30–7, Sun 2–7.30, groups by appt all year; t 02 41 92 45 86 or, out of season, t 02 41 92 41 08; adm*) are being restored little by little each year by enthusiastic young volunteers. The vestiges date from the 13th to the 15th centuries. The castle was abandoned when Brittany was attached to the French Crown after Anne de Bretagne's marriage to Charles VIII in 1491.

Blois

12

Blois

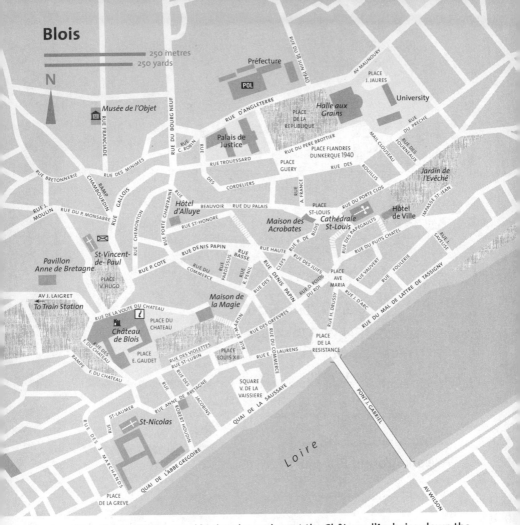

King Charles VIII bumped his head on a door at the Château d'Amboise, down the Loire, and died. So it was that in 1498 Charles' cousin, Louis, duke of Orléans, but based at Blois, became the new king, Louis XII, and his town the centre of French politics – a big role for what now seems like a modest provincial town. Blois had been a place of great importance through medieval times, though. In the early Middle Ages, the powerful counts of Blois had their headquarters for their substantial territories here and built a large castle. Louis XII commissioned a new one to his tastes, to which his successor, François I, added a grandiose new Renaissance wing. After François, in the Wars of Religion, the château became the setting for one of the most memorable bloody murders in French history, instigated by King Henri III no less. In fact, several important ghosts of France's past wander round the Château de Blois.

For years, the château was the only thing that was easy to visit in town, and contained most of Blois' museums, though its layers of grime were hardly appealing. A magic wand was waved over the place in the 1980s. Blois' fairy godmother took the flamboyant form of the high-profile mayor, Jack Lang, for many years France's trendy graffiti-art-friendly socialist Minister for Culture, later Minister for Education. The château's contrasting façades were scrubbed clean and the interiors completely reorganized to house a whole array of new museums. As a mark of gratitude, a likeness of Jack Lang in medieval style was carved on the castle. Still more surprisingly, a museum of magic suddenly appeared on the château's esplanade in the late 1990s, although its start has been somewhat shaky. Another startling recent apparition in Blois is the Musée de l'Objet, dedicated to the object as work of art.

A handful of the town's churches made it through the Revolution, most noticeably that dedicated to St Nicholas, which punctures the Blois skyline with its very sharp slate towers. The cathedral has recently received controversial modern glass. In between these two main churches, up the steep Loire-side slopes of the town, the sumptuous houses of many royal courtiers have survived the centuries, giving an indication of just how grand Blois was at its height.

History

The name of Blois apparently stems from the Celtic word for a wolf, *bleiz*, conjuring up the picture of a thickly forested area around the early settlement. Indeed, forests still surround Blois to this day. The emergence of a powerful dynasty of counts of Blois dates back to the time of the Norman invasions of the mid-9th century. A century later, it was the Thibaud family, first viscounts of Tours, then of Blois, which asserted its supremacy. This became an extremely important aristocratic dynasty in the Loire region and in France in the early Middle Ages. At the start of the 11th century the line was pitted against the ambitious Foulques Nerra of Anjou, who pushed east and managed to take much of the Blois counts' territories in Touraine. Count Eudes II of Blois made up for these losses by inheriting the region of Champagne, east of Paris. With their two centres of power, the subsequent counts were often absent from Blois, but a *prévôt* was left in charge of the town. Trade prospered and the main Blois fair at the end of August became one of the most important on the Loire, its date marking the time when vassals had to pay their dues to their lords.

By the time of Thibaud IV, in the first half of the 12th century, the counts of Blois were very much figures to be reckoned with – Thibaud IV's territories effectively surrounded the southern boundaries of the very small holdings of the kings of France in the Ile de France. Thibaud IV's brother, Etienne de Blois, like him a grandson of William the Conqueror, became King Stephen of England, a disastrous monarch. The power games between the great families of the Loire continued across the Channel; Henri Plantagenêt of Anjou made Stephen declare him his rightful successor to the English throne, and as a result became King Henry II. Meanwhile, Adèle de Champagne, daughter of Thibaud IV, was the woman who married the French King Louis VII after he had divorced Eleanor of Aquitaine (*see* Beaugency).

In the second half of the 12th century, Blois' Jewish community was subjected to a terrifying persecution, apparently due to the jealousy of a countess who suspected her husband of having an affair with a Jewish woman. The Jews were accused of ritually murdering children, and some 30 were burnt in Blois on trumped-up charges in 1171.

Getting There and Around

By Train

Trains from Paris to Blois leave the capital from Gare d'Austerlitz. Blois SNCF train station (t 08 91 67 68 69) is fairly central, west of the château. It has regular connections along the Loire to Orléans, and to Tours and towns further west. Remember that Tours airport, with its Ryanair flights, is just 50km away.

By Bus

For information and tickets for local buses, the Point Bus office is at 2 Place Victor Hugo (t 02 54 78 15 66).

By Car

The A10 Paris–Bordeaux motorway passes Blois. The main non-toll road route from Paris to Blois is the N20 to Orléans, then the N152 along the northern bank of the Loire.

By Taxi

Taxi-Radio Blois, Place de la Gare (t 02 54 78 07 65); they will also do private excursions. Other taxis are also available from the station.

Car and Bicycle Hire

Car hire companies include:
ADA Location de Véhicules, 108 Av Maunoury, t 02 54 74 02 47, f 02 54 74 02 97.
Avis, Av de Vendôme, t 02 54 74 48 15.
Budget, Rue Gutenberg, t 02 54 33 33 03. They rent out minibuses as well as cars.
Europcar, 105 Av de Vendôme, t 02 54 43 22 20.
Ligérienne de Location, Route Nationale, La Chaussée St-Victor, t 02 54 78 25 45.
For bicycles try:
Cycles Leblond, 44 Levée des Tuileries and 17 Rue du Sanitas, t 02 54 74 30 13, cycle.leblond@caramail.fr.

Carriages and Helicopters

Old Blois is small enough to explore by foot, but it is full of steep and awkward stairways. To take the pressure off your feet, you could always take a ride in a **horse and carriage** from the château entrance (*April–Sept daily*). For those of you on a *châtelain*'s budget, contact the tourist office about **helicopter rides** above the châteaux (*June–Sept, Thurs–Tues*).

Tourist Information

Tourist office: 23 Place du Château, 41000 Blois, t 02 54 90 41 41, *www.loiredeschateaux.com.*
Maison du Loir-et-Cher: Comité Départemental du Tourisme, 5 Rue de la Voûte du Château, B.P. 149, 41005 Blois Cedex, t 02 54 57 00 41, *www. chambordcountry.com.* Provides information on the whole *département* of Loir-et-Cher.

Market Days

Rue Pierre et Marie Curie: Wednesday morning.
Parc des Expositions, south of the river: Wednesday afternoon.
Rue Chateaubriand: Thursday morning.
Place Louis XII: Monday, Thursday and Saturday mornings.
Quartier Croix Chevallier: Saturday morning.
Mail and **rue Jeanne d'Arc**: Flea market; every second Sunday in the month.
Marché de Chez Nous, Place du Château: Market for regional specialities, local farmers and craftsmen coming into town to sell their wares; Thursday afternoon (*July and Aug*).

Festivals

Blois holds a **carnival** every year one Sunday in mid-March.
Le Festival Paroles Plurielles at the end of March revolves around storytelling; t 02 54 45 34 32.
Tous sur le Pont is a popular new festival of diverse musical and cultural events taking place late-June–early July.
The end of November sees the **BDBoum cartoon festival** at the Halle aux Grains and

---

The Thibaud line came to an end in 1235 and the Châtillons took over. This family retained power until 1392, when, strapped for cash, the last in the line sold the Blésois to Louis d'Orléans, brother of King Charles VI. It was from this time, and for several centuries to come, that the town of Blois confusingly served as the seat of power for a

Bibliothèque Abbé Grégoire; **t** 02 54 42 49 22, *www.bdboum.com*.

Sports and Activities

Boat trips on an old-fashioned Loire vessel are organized July–Aug; contact the tourist offices. If you're tempted to go **canoeing** on the Loire here, call **t** 02 54 42 95 60.

ULMs are **microlights**, and if you feel that wafting above the châteaux of the Blésois might be the best way to tempt you into trying such means of flight, the Lac de Loire base (**t** 02 54 20 68 51; *jymy@club-internet.fr*) is the place to ask.

Where to Stay

Blois ✉ 41000
The choice of characterful places to stay in Blois is a bit disappointing; you may find more exciting places outside the city.

Expensive–Moderate
***Mercure, 28 Quai St-Jean, **t** 02 54 56 66 66, *www.mercure.com*. A big chain hotel, but here done with some style and located close to the château. Some parts have views onto the Loire. A pool and *espace fitness* count among the extras. The restaurant is well regarded (*menus €15–29*).

***Holiday Inn Garden Court, 26 Av Maunoury, **t** 02 54 55 44 88, *www.holiday-inn.com/blois*. Another high-standard chain hotel with a solid reputation, even if it looks like a shopping mall from the outside. Inside, it offers such little luxuries as a pool and sauna, along with well-equipped rooms. Reasonable food served (*menus €14.50–23*).

***Le Médicis, 2 Allée François Ier/Route d'Angers, **t** 02 54 43 94 04, *www.le-medicis.com*. It overlooks an uninspiring roundabout west of the train station, but has some quite elaborately decorated rooms and some nice

touches. High-quality traditional French cuisine is served in the smart dining room (*menus €22–65; closed Sun pm low season*). *Closed Jan.*

Coffart B&B, 195 Rue Albert I, **t** 02 54 43 80 08, *leplessisblois@wanadoo.fr*. High-quality B&B close to the Forest of Blois, in a peaceful residential quarter on the edge of town, rooms in a former wine-making building. Also with a swimming pool.

Inexpensive
Hôtel Anne de Bretagne, 31 Av Jean Laigret, **t 02 54 78 05 38, *annedebretagne. free.fr*. Only a few hundred metres from the château, with pleasant enough though somewhat noisy rooms. *Closed early Jan–early Feb.*

Le Savoie, 6–8 Rue Ducoux, **t 02 54 74 32 21, *www.citotel.com*. An unpretentious family-run hotel.

Le Monarque, 61 Rue Porte Chartraine, **t 02 54 78 02 35, *annedebretagne.free.fr*. Awkwardly situated on a busy hillside junction; the rooms and restaurant are rather dull, but the place has some good-value rooms and food (*menus €11–25*). *Closed mid-Dec–early Jan.*

Cheap
*Hôtel du Bellay, 12 Rue des Minimes, **t** 02 54 78 23 62, *hoteldubellay.free.fr*. A pleasant little surprise, a miniature 18th-century cottage with bright rooms that are a complete bargain. *Closed at Christmas and New Year.*

*A la Ville de Tours, 2 Place de la Grève, **t** 02 54 78 07 86, **f** 02 54 56 87 33. Another surprisingly characterful cheap address, close to the river and the centre of town, with the quirky kind of bathroom facilities you should expect in French hotels of this category. *Closed 1 Jan.*

Auberge de Jeunesse, Les Grouëts, 18 Rue de l'Hôtel Pasquier, Blois 41000, **t/f** 02 54 78 27 21, *www.fuaj.org*. A youth hostel 4km from

string of men of royal blood carrying the title of Duc d'Orléans. This royal connection caused Blois to grow rapidly in political importance in the 15th century. Louis d'Orléans was infamously assassinated in 1407 by the men of Jean sans Peur (the Fearless), duke of Burgundy. Louis' wife, Valentine Visconti, from Milan, took refuge in

Blois at Les Grouëts, in the direction of Tours. *Closed mid-Nov–Feb.*

Eating Out

The choice of appealing restaurants in town is much more extensive than that of hotels, but beware: some of the best are curiously closed at the height of the season, in mid-August.

Expensive–Moderate

L'Orangerie du Château, 1 Av Jean Laigret, t 02 54 78 05 36 (*menus €22–34; closed Sun pm, Mon lunch and Wed Easter–Oct, Sun pm, Tues and Wed Nov–Easter*). Formerly in the castle grounds, now set back from a main road by a spacious courtyard, this restaurant in a swish building offers an elegant setting for a meal, facing the façade of the château. *Closed mid-Feb–mid-Mar, second week Nov and 01 May.*

Au Rendez-Vous des Pêcheurs, 27 Rue du Foix, t 02 54 74 67 48 (*menu €24–38; closed Sun, and Mon lunch*). The restaurant with the best reputation in town. Set in a small town house close to the river, it is crammed, even slightly cramped, with good things. The food is extremely refined and rich without being heavy, the speciality being river fish and seafood. *Closed public hols, first two weeks of Jan, and 3 weeks in Aug.*

L'Espérance, 189 Quai Ulysse Besnard (west along the river out of town), t 02 54 78 09 01 (*menus €21–52; closed Sun pm and Mon*). Although it's fronted by a terribly quirky and messy façade, inside you can appreciate much more harmonious, inventive cuisine in a bright, raised dining room overlooking the Loire, perhaps contemplating herons and other river birds as you eat. Fish is the appropriate savoury speciality, but the chef also pays tribute to Poulain's legacy with delicious chocolate puddings. *Closed Feb school hols and 10–25 Aug.*

Moderate–Cheap

Le Bistrot du Cuisinier, 20 Quai Villebois-Mareuil, t 02 54 78 06 70 (*menus €18–24*). It's worth finding a little extra energy to cross Blois' old bridge to enjoy the appealing combination of good food and good setting here. A dash of alcohol enlivens many of the sauces, while the historic town across the river forms the best of backdrops. *Closed late Dec–early Jan and 1–10 Sept.*

Le Castelet, 40 Rue St-Lubin, t 02 54 74 66 09. With beamed dining room; a wide choice of menus, including local specialities in Les Gourmandises du Val de Loire, and even that French provincial rarity, a *formule végétarienne* (*menus €14–25; closed Wed and Sun*). *Closed late Feb and late Oct.*

L'Embarcadère, 16 Quai Ulysse Besnard, t 02 54 78 31 41 (*€13–20; closed Mon pm mid-Nov–mid-April*). A lively, popular address by the river, west along the nothern quays, serving simple food such as mussels and chips.

Entertainment and Nightlife

Blois' main summer night-time attraction is the son-et-lumière at the château, called '*Ainsi Blois vous est conté*' – mug up on your history of Blois and the Loire to understand what's going on. For information and bookings, call t 02 54 78 72 76, but there's no real need to book seats in advance. The show takes place virtually every night from April to mid-Sept, with a version in English every Wednesday night.

Blois' main **theatre, dance and music** activities take place at the Scène Nationale, La Halle aux Grains, t 02 54 56 19 79.

You can choose from two **cinemas** in town: **Cap Ciné**, Rue des Onze Arpents (new complex by the motorway exit), t 08 92 68 73 40 (*€33/min*), *www.cap-cine.fr*.

Les Lobis, 12 Avenue du Maréchal Maunoury, t 02 54 74 08 43, *www.cap-cine.fr*.

Blois. Her Italian blood would later prove crucial to French royal claims across the Alps, leading to the Italian campaigns which brought Renaissance ideas across to France.

One of Valentine's sons was the famed Duke Charles d'Orléans, captured by the English at Agincourt in 1415 and held prisoner in England until 1440. Joan of Arc showed a particular attachment to the cause of this cultivated, chivalric poet-knight, and stopped at Blois on the way to liberate Orléans in 1429. On his release from prison, Charles d'Orléans settled back in Blois, and made changes to the medieval château. The court he gathered round him brought both prosperity and culture to the town. Charles became a patron of the arts and was greatly acclaimed as a versifier himself. The merchants of Blois catered to the aristocrats' tastes, many becoming wealthy from trade on the Loire and some changing career to serve Charles as financiers and advisers. As early as 1462, Florentine ambassadors visiting the Blois court praised the beauty of the town, its bridge and its fountains. When Duke Charles was nearly 70, his wife bore him a son, named Louis, like his kingly cousin Louis XI.

Louis XI was succeeded by his son Charles VIII. The male heirs produced by Charles and his wife, Anne de Bretagne, didn't survive early childhood, and when Charles met his fate with a door at Amboise, the young Louis d'Orléans became the new king of France as Charles VIII's closest cousin. He immediately divorced his crippled wife on the grounds that the marriage hadn't been consummated and married Charles VIII's widow. Blois became the centre of the royal court in place of Amboise and Louis XII, with Anne, decided to make the Château de Blois grander. The builders who had been employed at the Château d'Amboise were transferred here. The glorious days of royal Blois followed, wealth pouring into the town. Many of the main acts of Louis XII's reign were signed at the castle.

Louis wished to claim his Italian inheritance, through his grandmother Valentine Visconti, in the region of Milan, and followed the example of the forays Charles VIII had led into Italy in the late 1490s. Charles had brought back Italian booty and artists from his campaigns, but Italian influences were only just beginning to show at the end of his reign. Under Louis XII and at Blois, they were to affect ways of living and building more profoundly, although late Gothic French style and new Italianate forms coexisted for a period. The powerful men under Louis XII would commission new town houses and country seats near Blois. Florimond Robertet, one of the king's closest advisers, for example ordered both the Hôtel Alluye in Renaissance style in Blois itself and the sumptuous Château de Bury (sadly vanished) a little west of the city. The population of Blois grew by a massive 20,000 during Louis XII's reign. Purveyors of luxury goods thrived in the town, notably goldsmiths and clockmakers.

Louis XII and Anne had a daughter, Claude, who married François d'Angoulême. As Anne had no male heir, on Louis XII's death in 1515 François d'Angoulême became king of France, the outsized François I. François had been brought up largely at the Château d'Amboise, and on his enthronement he and the queen decided to share their time between the respective châteaux of their youths. At Blois, they commissioned one of the most famous examples of early French Renaissance architecture, although the most monumental of François' self-glorifying building projects, the Château de Chambord, lay only a few miles east across the Loire (see p.140).

Through the first half of the 16th century, many influential figures in Blois were won over to the Protestant, Church-reforming cause. When François I's son, King Henri II, began to persecute Protestants, or Huguenots, they started leaving for Geneva and other more tolerant havens. Crisis came with the rule of Henri's sons François II,

Charles IX and Henri III, and the outbreak of the vicious Wars of Religion. A terrible massacre of Protestants in 1562 led to the first uprising and Blois was among the towns taken by the Huguenots for several weeks. Catherine de' Medici, Henri II's widow and the hugely influential Queen Mother, came to the town in 1563 to negotiate with the Protestant leaders, Condé (held prisoner for a time at the château) and Coligny. But dialogue couldn't stop the second outbreak of war. This time, in 1568, Blois was ravaged. The town then served as the setting for talks gathering together the Estates General at the end of 1576.

In the meantime, the extremist Catholic Ligue was asserting its power in many parts of the country, especially in Paris, and its leaders, the Duc and Cardinal de Guise, had amassed enough power to threaten royal authority. Henri III took desperate action. Forced to flee Paris in the face of his formidable adversaries, he repaired to the château of Blois in 1588. His bloody solution to the problem was to call a meeting of the Estates General to which his opponents were invited; he then proceeded to have the de Guises assassinated in the castle. While Paris, in the grip of the Ligue, went wild on hearing news of the king's actions, Blois remained on his side. It would also support his successor, France's reunifying King Henri IV.

Henri IV's trouble-making widow, Marie de' Medici, was exiled to the castle for a time by her son Louis XIII. A still more troublesome royal figure closely associated with Blois was Louis XIII's brother Gaston, a rogue of a royal. In 1626 he received the duchy of Orléans as an appanage. For some time, Louis XIII and his wife didn't produce male offspring, making Gaston the heir presumptive. He wasn't content to wait in the wings. Gaston plotted against the king and was exiled to his Blésois capital. Here the fractious man set about planning the destruction of the former royal château in favour of a grand new scheme to his greater glory, designed by the most famous of 17th-century French architects, François Mansart. One wing was built, but Gaston's funds ran out, leaving much of the 16th-century royal palace standing. Gaston was an active patron of the arts in Blois, however, and also saw to the founding of new religious communities and a hospital.

Blois finally became a cathedral city under Louis XIV. But the latter's Revocation of the Edict of Nantes made life intolerable for the Protestant contingent in town. One of those who left for England was the renowned scientist, Denis Papin, after whom the main street and great stairway of Blois are now named. He has the distinction in the world of French *haute cuisine* of being considered the inventor of the pressure cooker, but his experiments with the use of steam power were much more widely influential. In the early 18th century, a couple of notable architectural features were added to the cityscape by Jacques V Gabriel, notably the archbishop's palace and the town's beautiful central bridge.

Blois has been described as 'moderately revolutionary'; some of its inhabitants were revolutionary enough to destroy virtually all the parish churches. However, a certain Abbot Henri Grégoire of Blois distinguished himself during the period as a strong advocate of the rights of man; he also became member of parliament for the region and president of the National Assembly in 1791. Blois became the capital of the Loir-et-Cher, one of the new *départements* into which France was divided. Notable

19th-century commercial successes in town included Auguste Poulain's chocolate-making business – Poulain is a household name in France, but the company was acquired by Cadbury-Schweppes not long ago – while Blois potters successfully specialized in mock-Renaissance ware. The town also developed as a centre with an increasingly large working class in an essentially rural *département*.

In the Second World War, Blois was badly bombed, both in 1940 and in 1944. Much in the historic quarter between the foot of the château and the river was destroyed. The architect Nicod was put in charge of the reconstruction. Since then, Blois has developed into a city with an unusually high proportion of social housing, but culturally it has become much richer in recent decades. Fairy godmother Jack Lang finally lost his grip on the town at the start of the new millennium when a young upstart from the centre-right, Nicolas Perruchot, beat him to become mayor.

Château de Blois

Open daily July–Aug 9–7, early Apr–June and Sept–Oct 9–6, Jan–Mar and Nov–Dec 9–12.30 and 2–5.30; closed 25 Dec and 1 Jan. You can go round the château by yourself or on a 1-hour guided tour. The special **Visite Insolite** *2hr tour takes you on a different circuit, to the cellars and attics, July–Aug daily at 10.30 and 3, rest of year Sat only at 3. For further information, call t 02 54 90 33 32; www.ville-blois.fr; adm.*

The mismatched wings of the Château de Blois resemble an architectural game of Misfits, pieces of four clashing styles shoved next to each other. The effect is by no means unattractive; it's even rather amusing. Each piece offers a sumptuous example of its period's style, and some of France's finest builders and craftsmen worked on the different wings. Meticulously restored, the place now contains: an archaeological museum; a Musée Lapidaire, or museum of old stones; the François I wing with its collections of furniture and objects; and Blois' fine arts museum, in the Louis XII wing. All these elements combine to make this one of the richest buildings in provincial France, a major royal château once properly lived in by a king and princes (unlike Chambord), and one still left standing in far greater part than Amboise downriver.

The legacy of historic tales at the Château de Blois is weighty as well. All told, the place crams rather too much in for just one visit. The museum of fine arts would merit a separate visit to appreciate it fully, rather than being treated as an impossibly rich dessert at the end of a banquet. This description begins with the château's architecture. Major historic tales and résumés of the museums inside follow.

The Architecture of the Château de Blois

Before plunging into a chaos of architecture and anecdote, pause to take a deep breath in front of the château, on the open **esplanade**, a high platform above the Loire. The main remnant of the castle's medieval structures is the **Salle des Etats**, one end clearly visible, its pale stone attached to the splendid brick-patterned Louis XII wing.

Although begun in 1499, this **Louis XII wing** is essentially late Gothic, not Renaissance. Just the odd Italianate element managed to creep in. Work on this wing started very shortly after Louis had ascended to the throne. Symmetry was clearly not a major consideration; even the entrance gateway lies off centre. The windows, generous in size and showing the greater openness of late Gothic, were decorated with the typical exuberant motifs of that period and topped by characteristically extravagant Loire *lucarnes*, or dormers. The trellis patterning in brick, with only trimmings in stone, follows the architectural fashion of the time. But there are notable elements of French Gothic missing here; no sturdy corner towers, no battlements, no fortified gateway, no drawbridge. Colin Biart, who had worked for Charles VIII at Amboise, may have been the master builder here. The 19th-century statue in the niche represents a young Louis XII riding a splendid horse sporting formidable armour-plated headgear, as though ready to charge to war; and charge to Italy he would.

Once through the entrance to the castle, it comes as quite a shock to emerge in the **inner courtyard**; the Château de Blois is just such an architectural hotchpotch. To the right, the salamander-strewn François I wing, with its twisting outer staircase, vies for attention with the powerful classical bulk of Mansart's building straight ahead. Turn your back on these for a while to concentrate on the already familiar Louis XII wing first. On this inner side it has an arcaded gallery; peer closely at its columns and you'll notice the subtle inclusion of Italian Renaissance motifs, such as candelabra, vases and long-beaked birds appearing in among the bravura of the late Gothic detail. Look up to see the crowned porcupines on the end tower – they're the main emblem associated with Louis XII. The notion was that porcupines could use their quills both for immediate protection from close up, and in long-range ripostes, by firing them (although in truth they're not able to do so). Among the figures carved high up, see if you can spot the one representing Jack Lang, shown baring his backside at visitors!

Before contemplating the two flashiest inner wings, don't ignore the most neglected side of the courtyard. Beyond the remnant of a gallery topped by a curious Flemish gable stands the **Chapelle St-Calais**. Royal emblems decorate the rooftop, while the little spire is suitably gilded. This so-called 'chapel' is in fact only a choir end which survived from a much larger church built under Louis XII and consecrated in 1508. During Louis and Anne's reign it was apparently filled with the most magnificent paintings of the time. With Gaston d'Orléans' ambitions to totally transform the château in the 17th century, the nave was destroyed in preparation for Mansart's work to start along this side too, but the masons never got this far. The choir has lost much of its interest. The façade is a 19th-century invention, while the stained-glass windows date from even later, commissioned from Max Ingrand in the 1950s. These windows do, however, usefully illustrate some of the major figures in Blois' history.

Opposite the chapel rises the **François I wing**, with its extraordinarily decorated stair tower. The François I inner façade makes a lavish display of Gothic style fusing with that of the Renaissance. It was begun in 1515, almost immediately after François had inherited the throne. Symmetry is still not especially sought. The salamanders, François I's favourite emblem, plastered over the walls may be a Gothic-looking flourish, but many other details are very much Italianate. A grid of horizontal lines, an

Italian influence, breaks the traditional vertical movement of French Gothic architecture. The shape of the steep roof may remain traditionally French, with the proud *lucarnes* a feature not to be found in Italy, but the niches added in these dormer windows, a putto placed in each, are a typical device of classical fashions.

The **François I stair-tower** is a celebrated Loire monument in its own right, although the staircase at Chambord runs away with first prize in the category. The protruding spiral stair-tower was a well-established feature of French Gothic architecture, not of the Italian Renaissance, the latter preferring straight ramps more discreetly incorporated into the main building. The openwork sides, though, impart an Italianate touch, allowing for fine courtly display – just try to resist any temptation to practise your own royal wave when you walk up the ramp. The openings and balustrades, rather than concealing the angle of the stair ramps, reflect it with their sloping shapes and friezes. The procession of sculpted salamanders add to the sense of movement. The swans shot through by an arrow were the melodramatic symbol of Louise de Savoie, François I's influential mother. During grand ceremonies, the loggias at the top were used to observe events below.

No one is sure who conceived the plans for this famous façade, nor for the **outer façade of the François I wing**, which has a totally different character, facing the town. It consists of a series of arcaded storeys much more in Italian Renaissance style. Curiously, the architect didn't make the balconies interconnect, giving the feel of some snooty Renaissance hotel, each window given its exclusive terrace. Henry James, visiting the château towards the end of the 19th century, wrote of them being 'repainted with red and blue, relieved with gold figures; and each of them looks more like the royal box at a theatre than like the aperture of a palace dark with memories'. Elaborately sculpted panels also adorn this outer façade, but they're very hard to decipher from a distance; the Musée Lapidaire can help you appreciate such fine detail.

Actually, the so-called François I wing might just as well be known as the Queen Claude wing, as François' wife was personally involved with the plans, the king being frequently absent. When she died in 1524, shortly before François was captured at the disastrous Battle of Pavia in Italy, work at Blois was halted. On his eventual return, François moved his attentions elsewhere; his heart had gone out of the project.

In the 1630s, Gaston d'Orléans decided to knock down the whole Château de Blois, which he found outmoded and disordered. He wanted to replace it with a magnificent, coherent, fashionable classical model to rival the Palais du Luxembourg in Paris, the latter conceived for Marie de' Medicis by Salomon de Brosse in 1615. Gaston's architect was the most famous of the French classical period, François Mansart. The one **Mansart wing** that was completed before funds ran out stands in stark, ordered contrast to the delightfully eccentric, slightly chaotic other wings. Symmetry and the classical orders triumph in the bright, light stone. Gone are the joyously individualistic elements of Gothic decoration. Gone are the elevating, exuberant Loire *lucarnes* which stretch the gaze skywards. But there is playfulness to Mansart's design, even if it comes in the subtle use of the double pilaster and other such humorous classical copybook elements. Henry James wrote of this wing that 'taken in contrast to its flowering, laughing, living neighbour, it marks the difference between inspiration and calculation'. This wing reflects the triumph of classicism in France, but also how inventively certain French architects treated it.

The Museums and Collections in the François I Wing

On the ground floor of the François I wing, the **Musée Lapidaire** displays interesting carved stones from the château. When Félix Duban set about restoring the decayed

An Evil Queen Mother, Scarface Guises, and the End of the Valois Line

To appreciate a tour round the Château de Blois, and the François I wing in particular, it's important to understand something about Catherine de' Medici, the three sons of hers who became the last three kings of the Valois dynasty, and the formidable dukes and cardinals of the aristocratic De Guise family who threatened the stability of the French monarchy in this period.

Catherine de' Medici is a figure who continues to fascinate the French, and is generally thought of as the most evil of queen mothers. At the outset of the Wars of Religion in the 1560s she did in fact attempt to bring together the feuding parties. But forces were far beyond her control and she and her sons became caught up in the violent maelstrom. Most infamously, she is held in large part responsible for giving the go-ahead to her son King Charles IX for the St Bartholomew's Day massacres of 1572, when leading Protestants were brutally murdered in the night in several major French cities. Catherine de' Medici was forced by the circumstances of the turbulent Wars of Religion to stay at the Château de Blois from time to time.

Looking at the decoration in the royal apartments you may notice Catherine's initials painted here and there. The pretty interlinking initials C and H refer to her and her husband King Henri II. It's rather unfortunate that the Cs laid back to back within the initials also form Ds, the initial of Henri II's mistress, Diane de Poitiers (*see* Chaumont and Chenonceau). Catherine de' Medici died at the Château de Blois on 5 January 1589, very soon after the infamous assassinations arranged by her son King Henri III here in the royal apartments.

Who were the dangerous de Guises whom the king felt he had to do away with so dramatically? Henri de Guise came from a line of formidable dukes of Lorraine who amassed extraordinary power in the course of the 16th century – to such an extent that they became a threat to royal power during the Wars of Religion. The Maréchale de Retz is said to have written of them in the late 16th century: 'These Lorraines had such an air of distinction that alongside them the other Princes looked plebeian.'

Henri's grandfather, Claude de Lorraine, had been a staunch supporter of François I, and was conferred some of the powers of regent during the king's captivity after the Battle of Pavia. Claude was ennobled with the title of duke in honour of his crushing of a peasants' revolt in Lorraine in 1527. His daughter Marie would marry King James V of Scotland, by whom she gave birth to the ill-fated Mary Queen of Scots. Claude's son François de Guise was the second duke in the line, and the first family member to be called Le Balafré – Scarface. The contemporary writer Brantôme described him as towering above the other officers of the realm 'as a great and sturdy oak has pride of

castle in the mid-19th century, he was confronted by crumbling masonry and beautiful sculptural details eaten away by time. He had the good sense to keep the very worn originals as well as plastercasts of the replacements, enabling us now to observe some of the fine details of decoration from close up, such as monk gargoyles from Louis XII's time, and the fat salamanders and the labours of Hercules from the François I wing. Duban is devoted a special room up in the royal apartments. Down in

place in a plantation'. A brilliant military man, he it was who successfully wrested Calais from the English in 1558.

The following year, the French king, Henri II, died. His and Catherine de' Medici's eldest but very sickly young son became King François II. The Queen Mother and the de Guises struggled for dominance. The de Guises were supremely well placed; François de Guise's niece, Mary Queen of Scots, was now queen of France. François de Guise and his brother, Cardinal Charles de Guise, became the most influential figures in French politics along with Catherine de' Medici.

Persecution of the French Huguenots, or Protestants, had increased under Henri II. Ardently anti-Protestant, the de Guises led the Catholic side in the persecution of their enemy, beginning in earnest with the bloody repression of the Huguenot conspiracy of the Conjuration d'Amboise in 1560 (*see* p.230). Full-scale civil war in the form of the first War of Religion broke out two years later, in 1562. By this time, the minor Charles IX was on the throne, Catherine de' Medici was acting as regent, and the rival factions were out of all control. François de Guise died, killed by Huguenots while besieging Protestant-held Orléans in 1563.

François's son Henri became the second family Scarface and the third in the line of dukes. He pursued his father's anti-Protestant hatred with even greater zeal, not only fighting the Huguenots in battle, but also acting as one of the main instigators of the St Bartholomew's Day massacres in 1572. He went on to command the Ligue, the Catholic league founded in 1576 against the Huguenots, the latter headed by Henri de Bourbon, king of Navarre. Henri de Guise, whose power cannot be underestimated, was closely supported by his brother, Cardinal Louis de Guise.

After Charles IX's death in 1574, a third son of Henri II and Catherine de' Medici took the crown as Henri III. Married but childless, Henri III was left with no Valois heirs on the death of his brother, the Duc d'Anjou, in 1584, but he had promised the crown to Protestant Henri de Navarre. Henri de Guise, though, appeared to have aspirations to find a new Catholic monarch, if not to become king himself. By 1588, Henri III was in desperate straits. He called the Estates General of the realm, with representatives of the nobles, the clergy and the bourgeoisie, to meet at the Château de Blois to try and work out the terrible national crisis. But while they were gathered here he resorted to the most cowardly and vicious of means to do away with Henri and Louis de Guise.

Three months after the gory events of the 23 and 24 December 1588 in which they died, the widowed Duchesse de Guise was granted her request that formal statements by witnesses be recorded by the Court of Parliament. The events have been pieced together by historians from those reports. On the bitterly cold morning of 23

the basement, there's an **Archaeological Museum** in the former castle kitchens, with displays on the history of Blois, concentrating on medieval finds.

You enter the **royal apartments** of the François I wing via the great staircase, which sweeps you up to the first floor. Just as the exteriors of the château have been scrubbed clean, the interiors have been given a thorough going-over. The swirling dark patterns splurged all over the walls and beams were commissioned by Duban,

December 1588, during the gathering of the Estates General at Blois, the king called Henri de Guise to his chambers. Henri III had prepared his trap meticulously, disposing the men he had picked for the mission (a bunch subsequently known as the notorious 'Quarante-Cinq') around the royal apartments. Two priests were ordered to repair to the royal oratory and told in vague terms to pray for the successful outcome of a project the king had embarked upon to ensure peace in his realm. As Henri de Guise passed through the king's bedroom he was savagely attacked. He put up a strong resistance, but set upon by a whole pack of assassins, he was mercilessly stabbed by them. Such was his phenomenal strength, the apocryphal story has it that he managed to drag himself across the room to fall accusingly by the king's bed.

Immediately after the murder, the royal side declared that an attempt had been made on the king's life. They spread the rumour that a purse had been found on Henri de Guise containing a treacherous note revealing his collusion with France's enemy Spain and declaring that to keep the civil war going in France it was necessary to raise 700,000 livres a year with Spanish aid. Several men were arrested, including the merchants' provost of the town of Blois. He reported being taken to the place of the assassination and seeing two pools of blood still so hot that they were steaming.

Louis de Guise was among those arrested. Henri III wanted to do away with him as well, but it's said that no one from Henri III's personal guard would accept the order to kill a religious man, especially one of such high rank. Other soldiers had to be found to carry out that dirty deed. Louis was assassinated the following day. The same provost of Blois doubtless didn't need a keen nose to smell the horrific stench of burnt flesh in one staircase up which he was taken – he reported that he was told by a guard that the bodies of the de Guises had been burnt there.

In Paris, in the hands of the Ligue, hysteria followed news of the murders. The de Guises were conferred an almost saintly status by many supporters around the land. Henri III had had his archrivals butchered in his very own royal apartments, by what some French history books call 'Florentine means', supposedly passed on to him by his Medici mother, as though this were another of the features exported to France from Renaissance Italy. Henri would very soon get his comeuppance; he was assassinated in his turn the following year, in Paris, by a fanatical Catholic monk. So the Valois dynasty, which had ruled France since 1328, came to its bloody end, and the head of the Bourbon family, Henri de Navarre, the pro-Protestant leader, became the reconciling King Henri IV, although the Wars of Religion raged on until 1598.

the big leaves and flowers inspired by forms he'd found on illuminated manuscripts and old cloth. The apartments were recently provided with new tile floorings; they may look brash, as much fit for a modern bathroom as an old royal castle, but apparently they do follow the spirit of the original decorations. The fine pieces of furniture displayed don't date from the French Renaissance, but are mainly extravagant 19th-century interpretations of the style of that period.

One or two original elements have remained in some of the royal apartments, including some panelling and parts of certain fireplaces, plus, most engrossingly, the **Cabinet de Travail**, an Italianate study, the finest room in the wing. It has retained its rich array of original carved wood panels. Don't bother trying to count the overwhelming number of Renaissance motifs depicted – apparently there are 237 in all. This room has been described as a kind of copybook of Renaissance designs: masks, dolphins, cornucopia and many other familiar emblems abound. Cabinets lie discreetly behind certain of the panels. As to their uses, the 19th-century novelist Alexandre Dumas spread the notion that they were caches for poison. This idea delighted the popular imagination, such was the poisonous reputation of Catherine de' Medici and her final Valois sons. But the cabinets were probably used more prosaically for storing and displaying curios and the most beautiful objects of the royal collection; some exquisite pieces are now on show in them.

Through the Other Wings of the Château de Blois

The **Salle des Etats Généraux** is the name given to the early 13th-century medieval hall, although the Estates Generals referred to are those of 1576 and 1588. Somewhat squashed into a corner between the Louis XII and François I wings, it's hard to appreciate the hall's architecture from the outside, but inside, the huge space gives an indication of the power of the medieval counts of Blois and Champagne. A row of alarmingly slender columns divides the massive chamber into two. The ceiling is of painted wood. Again, the polychrome designs are 19th century.

Blois' **fine arts museum** takes up the first floor of the Louis XII wing. It doesn't contain the collections of royals – the Loire Renaissance kings transported their movable items (their *mobilier*, as the French call furniture) as they went from château to château (the architecture being what French estate agents would call *immobilier*), and then the monarchy went off to Paris, carting its riches off to its châteaux there.

There is an amusing tale about the way the Blois fine arts museum was founded. The story goes that Napoleon III had fallen for an actress from the Comédie Française. Called away on imperial business, he was overcome by the desire to see her again and wrote to her telling her to meet him at the museum of Blois. He then sent word to the town to expect him for a visit to the august establishment. The Blois authorities were mightily embarrassed, however, because of one important detail – the town had no museum! The wealthy citizens are supposed to have gathered round and generously donated some of the finest pieces of their private collections, hung within 48 hours, in time for the royal visit and assignation. All supposedly went off smoothly.

The speed of the museum's creation is only mildly exaggerated in this comic tale. Early in the 19th century, the château was serving as a barracks. In middle of the century a town mayor managed to persuade the French army to cede at least the François I wing for the town to start displaying a fine arts collection. In 1850, the local council called for donations of works. Pieces flowed in, the town acquired more, and it put in a few successful requests to the state for additional paintings. New barracks were built in town so that by 1867 the army had a new home, leaving the authorities free to use all the château's interiors as they wished. The Louis XII wing was chosen as the best setting for the collections.

Among the 16th-century pieces, two typically bizarre Mannerist works stand out: *L'Enlèvement d'Europe* by Jean Cousin Le Fils, Europa holding on tight to the garlanded bull-god's horns in this weird rush of love; and Martin de Vos's Flemish Mannerist *La Mort d'Adonis*, dogs posing with swans. English visitors may be moved by the French painting depicting Thomas More being taken to the Tower, his distraught daughter trying to embrace him. Of particular interest given the Blois royals' designs on northern Italy, Lombard early 16th-century art is represented by the *Vierge à l'enfant et anges musiciens* by Marco d'Oggiono, a pupil of Leonardo da Vinci (*see* Amboise).

The museum possesses a couple of engrossing series of portrait panels, famous figures painted in rows, removed from châteaux in the wider region. (One is still in place in the Château de Beauregard a short way south of Blois). The art work may not be of the highest order, but what a fine way of giving one's children a history lesson at home. Another striking donation from a château, this time Cheverny, close to Blois, is *La Force, la Fortune et le Temps*, a rich work by Jean Mosnier, the mid-17th-century artist who substantially helped create the most refined château interiors along the Loire. Among other 17th-century pieces, look out for the pouting Grande Mademoiselle, Gaston d'Orléans' difficult daughter, in her blue décolleté dress, with her curls, pearls, and slightly manly nose... she certainly looks like she'd be a terrible handful. Among other notable Ancien Régime pieces, seek out Sébastien Bourdon's Poussin-like, bustling *Eliézer et Rébecca*, Claude Vignon's tenderly melodramatic *La Mort de Lucrèce*, the dagger deep in Lucretia's breast, and François Boucher's *Psyché recevant les honneurs divins*.

Three 17th-century tapestry cycles also feature. The most impressive, woven in Paris in the tapestry workshops Henri IV set up with Flemish experts, represents scenes from the life of the Emperor Constantine, after cartoons by Reubens. The *Histoire d'Artémis*, from the same workshops, were executed after cartoons by Antoine Caron. Finally, the third series has a French royal theme, the life of Louis XIV, produced between 1663 and 1675 at the recently created Gobelins works, following Charles Lebrun's cartoons.

Some splendid clocks and watches recall a skilled craft for which Blois was long famous. Portrait medallions feature prominently in a separate room; one of the museum's curators acquired almost 60 medallions by the 18th-century artist Jean-Baptiste Nini, closely associated with the Château de Chaumont. Among them you can see Benjamin Franklin represented wearing his glasses and Voltaire looking like a smug Roman emperor. The interesting 19th-century French Romantic sculptor Auguste Préault gave some of his own works to the Blois museum, including *Lélia*, a rendering of a character in one of George Sand's novels, and a Gaulish soldier, his face full of grim determination. Daniel Dupuis, another 19th-century sculptor, donated around 500 works of his to his town museum, including medallions illustrating many famous figures of his day. There are also a few sculptures of famous Blésois figures by that rare phenomenon, an 18th-century female sculptor, Julie Charpentier.

Among the 19th-century paintings, famous French historical figures are delivered into the hands of the 19th-century troubadour stylists, for example Hippolyte Lecomte with *Jeanne d'Arc et Charles VII*; of course the artist couldn't resist giving the Maid an overfeathered hat and a prominent bust line. King François I, too, sports an absurdly overdone plumage, fit for a transvestite show, in Louis Ducis' *François I armé chevalier par Bayard*.

Finally, moving to the other side of the castle's courtyard, don't miss the sensational interior of the **Mansart wing**. Baroque sweeps into the building, creating a heady feeling of melodrama in the magnificent lobby – just look up to the splendid oval cupola, framed through the shape of a cross. Ornate sculptures were meant to add still more to the wondrous effects, but the work was never completed, although in certain spots you can see drawings on the ceiling indicating where the pieces were to go. Blois' town library was housed in this wing until quite recently, but now the rooms here are given over to temporary exhibitions relating to the castle.

A Walk Around Blois

Historic Blois spreads over two hills, the western one crowned by the castle, the eastern one by the cathedral. We start this walking tour on the upper esplanade outside the castle, known as the **Place du Château**. This triangular, gravel-covered square is full of wealthy-looking houses and has a couple of clusters of restaurants and tourist shops. The **Maison de la Magie** (*open daily July–Aug 10–6.30; April–June, 26 Oct–4 Nov, 21 Dec–6 Jan, and Sept 10–12 2–6. Closed on Mondays in May, most of June, and Sept, and 25 Dec and 1 Jan; t 02 54 55 26 26; www.maisondelamagie.fr; adm*) occupies a splendid renovated brick mansion opposite the castle. The museum was inspired by and pays particular homage to the 19th-century Blois-born magician Jean-Eugène Robert-Houdin, the name almost as complicated as some of his tricks. So far did his fame spread that Robert-Houdin even gave a private performance at Buckingham Palace in 1849, showing off his Cabalistic Clock, The Wonderful Orange Tree and The Ladies' Favourite (whatever that might have been), among other tricks. In his colonializing century, Robert-Houdin apparently felt a calling to add his powers to those of the French military, which had recently conquered Algeria, and went off there to show some of the North African religious leaders just how weak they were in the face of his magic tricks. As impressive as the modern presentations of this centre are the regular magic shows.

Among the other façades on the Place du Château, look out for the **Maison du Vin** if buying Loire wine appeals. On the esplanade's open side, views stretch out over the town roofs, but beyond the formal flowerbeds and row of clipped trees, the Loire is barely visible from up here. The church of St-Sauveur, where Joan of Arc had her banner blessed in April 1429, stood on this terrace until the church was destroyed during the Revolution.

Close to the Musée de la Magie, look down the grand stairway leading to Blois' main shopping quarter. If you can avoid being tempted in that direction, turn back and descend from the esplanade via the **Rue de la Voûte du Château**, next to the Salle des Etats Généraux. Along this sloping street you might stop for tourist information on the whole of the Blésois (known nowadays as the *département* of the Loir-et-Cher) at the swish **Maison du Loir-et-Cher**. Also cast an eye over the temporary art exhibitions held in the smart galleries downstairs.

Rue de la Voûte du Château will take you down past the layers of loggias of the outer façade of the château's François I wing and into **Place Victor Hugo**, round which cars race. In the square, with its great sequoia and cedar, the Fontaine Corbigny is decorated with a bas-relief by Julie Charpentier depicting the Loire, although by now you have completely turned your back on the river. Across the square stands the **church of St-Vincent-de-Paul**, a grandiose 17th-century building. The central classical façade with its rose window is bordered by sides finished with lavish scrolls, the lantern topped by a fleur-de-lys. The scent of royalty hangs over this church. Henri III founded the Collège de Blois in 1581, served by the Chapelle St-Louis on this site. The Jesuits were given control of this institution in 1622 and their most celebrated architect, Père Martellange, drew up a plan for a new church in 1624. But it was his successor in overseeing so much Jesuit architecture, Frère Turmel, whose design was used, building work beginning in 1634. Both Gaston d'Orléans and his obstreperous daughter gave generously for the construction, which continued slowly through the century. Their arms and initials can be made out on the front. You can also make out signs of how the church was re-dedicated to St Vincent de Paul after the Revolution.

The interior was restored in the 19th century and daubed in paint mimicking marble. The architectural style within remains predominantly 17th-century classical, although a hideously vulgar Virgin over the altar will distract your attention from everything else at first. The venerated medieval French king Louis IX, or St Louis, is represented by initials placed here and there and by a carving in the choir; the sculpture in this section is by Gaspard Imbert. The monument to the left representing Faith, Hope and Charity once held Gaston d'Orléans' heart. That to the right depicting Religion, Pity and Generosity was a modest memorial to his daughter La Grande Mademoiselle.

Some may find the **Musée de l'Objet** (*open mid-May–mid-Sept Tues–Sun 1.30–6.30, mid-Sept–mid-May weekends only 1.30–6.30; 6 Rue Franciade, t 02 54 55 37 40, musee.objet@wanadoo.fr; adm*), the other new museum opened in Blois in the 1990s apart from the Musée de la Magie, even more esoteric than its counterpart. Established in the town's school of fine arts, it is reached by taking the Rampe Chambourdin, just north of Place Victor Hugo. The museum concentrates on, well, objects. But objects turned into art. With its roots in surrealism, this is provocative modern art, often ironic, conceptual, commenting on contemporary life. While many of the titles of the pieces may seem facile or silly, their deliberate placing or misplacing, manipulation or metamorphosis gives them new, often more profound or surprising, meanings.

Back at Place Victor Hugo, Avenue Jean Laigret leads you past the castle's former **orangerie**, a greatly altered 16th-century building turned restaurant. It once lay in the splendid château gardens, which covered a wide area here until they were abandoned upon the death of Gaston d'Orléans. The **pavillon Anne de Bretagne**, a little further up, is another fragmentary remnant from the château's once-glorious grounds. With its heavily restored brick façade and balustrade, and the symbols of Louis XII and Anne de Bretagne, it retains its Gothic outlines, but the interior shows the fusion of Gothic and Italianate styles. Avenue Jean Laigret leads up to the train station; cross south into the **Jardin des Simples et des Fleurs Royales**, behind the ugly institutional façade of the former Ecole des Garçons opposite the pavilion. This public garden is a successful conversion of the school gardens, now planted on the theme of royal and medicinal plants.

Next, head for the sharp, soaring spires of the **church of St-Nicolas**. This church's spiky twin entrance towers with their defensive look, and the crossing with its sharp needle of a spire to match, form the easiest landmarks to spot in town, puncturing the Blois skyline. To reach the church from the Jardin des Simples you pass below the imposing outer façade of the château's Gaston d'Orléans wing. This way leads you down into what used to be the old commercial riverside part of Blois, the **Quartier St-Nicolas**. It was badly bombed in the war, but luckily the church survived relatively unharmed. Cross **Rue des Trois Marchands** and **Rue St-Lubin**, two fine streets that were restored with care after the war, although other ones in the neighbourhood weren't so easily patched up. Still, the Quartier St-Nicolas has atmosphere, especially close to the looming church. A good number of restaurants hide out in this area.

St Nicholas' church has retained its medieval grandeur, even if it looks a bit grim in parts. You can get a good view of it along Rue St-Laumer, named after the previous saint to whom the edifice was dedicated before the Revolution. The building was begun in 1138, construction going from east to west. The choir end offers a harmonious demonstration of Romanesque geometry, with its radiating chapels. The choir is supported by very early examples of flying buttresses, probably from the end of the 12th century. Double flying buttresses hold up the later nave, mostly dating from the 13th century. The façade contains remnants of 14th-century sculpture, including the angels, prophets and saints of the central doorway. The west rose window was redone in Gothic style in the 17th century. As to the soaring spires, they actually only date from the 19th century.

Inside the dankness of this vast vessel, the eastern end has a rare Romanesque grandeur, with its impressive rib vaults and its series of chapels. This part also demonstrates very graphically how, in medieval times, the church authorities weren't averse to masons depicting the sinful ways of man; among the capitals are a few extremely bawdy carvings. Prudes avert your eyes. The wall paintings in the Chapelle des Fonts were an abortive 19th-century attempt to revive period decoration. The sculpture in the end chapel by the Blésois Gaspard Imbert represents the Assumption of the Virgin. The upper windows of the choir were decorated with stained glass by the postwar specialist Max Ingrand. The western section of the church shows how quickly the influence of the great cathedral building of Chartres reached Blois and the Loire. The style is of course more elevating and sober than the Romanesque part – no naughty sculptures here to deflect attention from the glorification of God.

Rue des Trois Marchands leads down to the river. At Place de la Grève, the small **Musée de la Résistance, de la Déportation et de la Libération** (*open Mon–Fri 9–12 and 2–6, Sat 2–6; t/f 02 54 56 07 02;adm*) is devoted to the memory of the Second World War anti-Nazi struggle in the Loir-et-Cher. South of here lie the quays, with views onto the old bridge. Head east along **Quai de l'Abbé Grégoire**, then turn up Rue Robert-Houdin. Attached to the southern side of St-Nicolas you'll see the remains of the **Ancien Couvent des Jacobins**. Once a large abbey complex, it was destroyed in the Wars of Religion, rebuilt in the 17th and 18th centuries by the Benedictines of St-Maur, and converted into a hospital after the Revolution. Only vestiges of the convent and the cloister were left standing.

Reached via Rue Anne de Bretagne off Rue Robert-Houdin, the **Musée Diocésain d'Art Religieux** (*open Tues–Sat 2–6; t 02 54 78 17 14; free*) contains religious artefacts, including statuary, robes, paintings and goldsmiths' work. Head north from here to rejoin **Rue St-Lubin**, with its collection of fine old houses, No. 41 displaying a statue of a bishop of Chartres, No. 31 boasting an unusual slate sundial.

Rue St-Lubin leads east into busy **Place Louis XII**, at the foot of grandiose stairs up to the château. The square was laid out in the 19th century, but had to be remodelled after the war, its principal feature the Louis XII fountain, a copy of the medieval one embellished for Louis XII, with its fleur-de-lys balustrade and spouting dolphins. By the stairs lie the ruins of another of Blois' churches, St-Martin-des-Choux.

The shopping quarters start in earnest here. It's a good area to pause at one of the many cafés or pâtisseries. Some of the liveliest **shopping streets**, the Rue du Commerce and Rue Denis Papin, lie just northeast of the square. **Rue Denis Papin** is the town's main thoroughfare, with a 19th-century Parisian air. The perspective along it ends to the north with the dramatic flight of stairs up to the 19th-century statue of that steamy scientist Papin. The way south leads to busy **Rond Point de la Resistance**, with its big-town feel and bustling cafés next to the bridge.

The **Pont Jacques V Gabriel** is surely the most refined bridge over the Loire. It replaced the medieval one swept away in 1716. Its famous architect is honoured in its name. An Egyptian-style needle adds ornamental grandeur to the central point. Blois **south of the river** doesn't have many interesting sites, but cross the river to appreciate the splendid views of the historic town from the **cobbled southern quays** and to visit the **church and cemetery of St-Saturnin**; these are set in a pleasantly quiet corner off Quai Villebois-Mareuil. The church was a popular place of pilgrimage in the Middle Ages. Visitors came to pray to Notre Dame des Aydes, Blois' patron. The church was commissioned in late-Gothic Flamboyant style by Anne de Bretagne to replace an earlier medieval one. The *ex votos* to Notre Dame des Aydes and the mariners' chapel count among the curiosities inside. The cemetery of St-Saturnin is often described as a cloister, given its form. The graves have disappeared and the space is now used to display fragments of local sculpture from across the centuries. Rue du Poinçon Renversé, just north of the cemetery, contains several low old Loire mariners' houses.

Back north of the Loire, on the hillside to the **east of Rue Denis Papin** you can explore many of Blois' most atmospheric, smart old **residential streets** leading up towards the cathedral. They contain a good number of fine old town houses with appealing features: intimate courtyards with wells, stair-towers, galleries and Gothic sculptures, sometimes a touch of Renaissance decoration, and even the odd royalist symbol from Louis XII's period that survived the Revolution. Many royal courtiers took up home in this quarter. Seek out such streets as Rue du Puits Châtel and Rue Pierre de Blois. **Place Ave Maria** forms the charming meeting point of a handful of tracks up the hillside.

The **Maison des Acrobates**, further north on Place St-Louis, is the most appealing of all Loire town houses, full of late-Gothic humour, comically covered with wooden beams carved with figures of playful jesters.

A hurricane in 1678 destroyed much of the church on what is now the site of the **Cathédrale St-Louis**. So this is essentially a late 17th-century building, funded by the Colberts – the wife of Louis XIV's famous minister, Marie Charron, hailed from the Blésois. The great bell tower acts as the historic town's eastern landmark. The façade is actually mostly 16th century, a survivor of the inclement weather. Its classical motifs once again show the Italianate style mixed with the traditional French. But Gothic designs dominate elsewhere, evidence of that style persisting in religious architectural aesthetics; as at Orléans cathedral, this church demonstrates that classicism didn't take over completely in Ancien Régime France. Inside, several of the side chapels contain obtrusive tombs from the 17th and 18th centuries. The 19th-century stained glass by Lobin of Tours throws a rather sickly light over some of the interior, while the very recent additions of stained glass by the Dutch artist Jan Dibetts, although controversial, prove anodyne, Christian phrases in Latin placed at strange angles like colourful transfer lettering. The descent into the crypt offers a sobering experience.

East of the cathedral lies the **Jardin de l'Evêché**, a very pleasant 18th-century garden, ending with a belvedere and containing a 1921 statue of Joan of Arc by the American artist Anna Huntington Hyatt. The garden gives good views over the town and onto the Pont Jacques Gabriel. That architect also designed the **bishop's palace** by the cathedral. Since the Second World War, it has housed the town hall, as the previous one was destroyed. Rose enthusiasts may appreciate the lower terrace in season, planted as it is with hundreds of rare varieties.

A detour up via the Mail Clouseau northeast of the cathedral leads you to the plateau of **Place de la République** and **Place Jean-Jaurès**, surrounded by their mix of 19th- and 20th-century civic buildings. The 1850 **Halle aux Grains**, or corn exchange, has been converted into the main town theatre. The water towers date from roughly the same time. Among recent buildings are the conference centre, the 1990s university buildings and Blois' ultra-modern public library. The Loir-et-Cher administrative buildings and law courts are also up here. So too, curiously, is the **Haras National de**

Blois (*open Mon–Fri 10–12 and 2–4.30, Sat 2.30–4.30. In July and Aug Sun also, 10.30–3. Special presentations on Thurs mid-Aug–mid-Sept pm; 62 Avenue Maunoury, **t** 02 54 55 22 82, www.haras-nationaux.fr; adm*), Blois' national stud farm, on Avenue Maunoury. In the vast, specially built 19th-century buildings, bordered with brick, some fifty stallions, thoroughbreds, draught horses and ponies are pampered for breeding.

Bourges and the Cher Valley

13

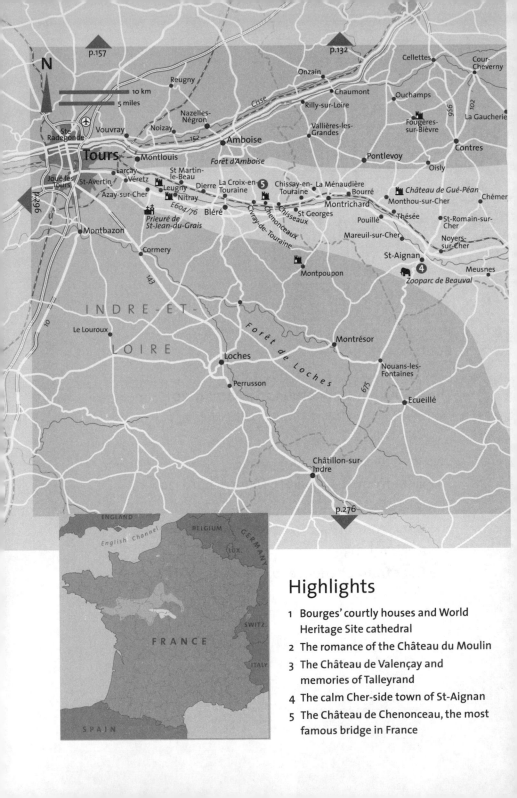

N

p.157
p.132
p.296
p.276

10 km
5 miles

Reugny
Onzain
Cellettes
Cour-Cheverny
Chaumont
Ouchamps
Rilly-sur-Loire
Cisse
Nazelles-Négron
Vallières-les-Grandes
Fougères-sur-Bièvre
La Gaucherie
Ste Radegonde
Vouvray
Noizay
Noilois
Amboise
Pontlevoy
Contres
Tours
Montlouis
Forêt d'Amboise
Oisly
Joué les Tours
St-Avertin
Larçay
Véretz
St Martin-le-Beau
Dierre
La Croix-en-Touraine
Chissay-en-Touraine
La Ménaudière
Château de Gué-Péan
Chémer
Leugny
Nitray
Bourré
Monthou-sur-Cher
Azay-sur-Cher
Chisseaux
St Georges
Montrichard
St-Romain-sur-Cher
Prieuré de St-Jean-du-Grais
Bléré
Chenonceaux
Pouillé
Thésée
Montbazon
Civray-de-Touraine
Mareuil-sur-Cher
Noyers-sur-Cher
Cormery
St-Aignan
Meusnes
Montpoupon
Zooparc de Beauval
INDRE-ET-LOIRE
Le Louroux
Forêt de Loches
Montrésor
Loches
Nouans-les-Fontaines
Perrusson
Ecueillé
Châtillon-sur-Indre

ENGLAND
English Channel
BELGIUM
GERMANY
LUX.
FRANCE
SWITZ.
ITALY
SPAIN

Highlights

1 Bourges' courtly houses and World Heritage Site cathedral

2 The romance of the Château du Moulin

3 The Château de Valençay and memories of Talleyrand

4 The calm Cher-side town of St-Aignan

5 The Château de Chenonceau, the most famous bridge in France

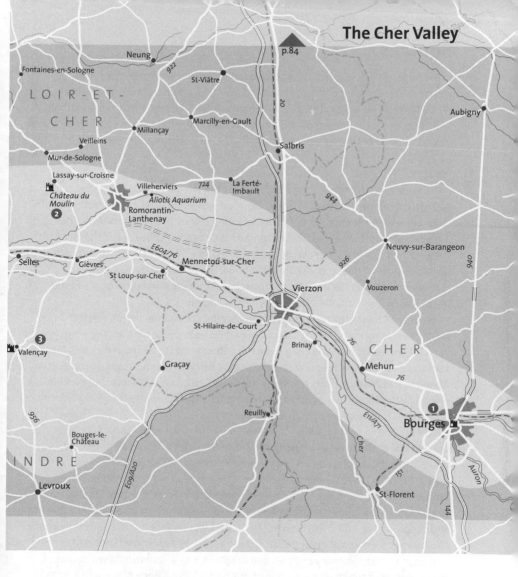

p.84

Neung

Fontaines-en-Sologne

St-Viâtre

922

LOIR-ET-

Marcilly-en-Gault

Aubigny

CHER

Millançay

Veilleins

Salbris

Mur-de-Sologne

Lassay-sur-Croisne

Villeherviers   724   La Ferté-Imbault

Château du Moulin   *Aliotis Aquarium*

2   Romorantin-Lanthenay

Neuvy-sur-Barangeon

E604/76

Selles   Gièvres   Mennetou-sur-Cher

St Loup-sur-Cher

926   940

Vierzon   Vouzeron

St-Hilaire-de-Court

3   Brinay   CHER

Valençay   Graçay   Mehun   76

956   E11/A71   Cher

Reuilly   **1**

Bourges

INDRE

Bouges-le-Château   E09/A20

Levroux   St-Florent   Auron   151

144

Rising out of the Berry plains like a huge spiritual silo, the cathedral of Bourges rivals that of Chartres in greatness. It dominates an exceptionally beautiful, compact, historic city, built by tributary rivers a little east of the Cher. This chapter starts with the splendours of the Berry's capital. It ends with an even more celebrated highlight, in Touraine: the most famous Loire Valley château of them all – Chenonceau's gallery actually spans the Cher, a little east of Tours.

In between these two magnificent places you can seek out restful, rustic little towns such as Selles, St-Aignan and Montrichard, and surprisingly delightful châteaux such as Valençay, Bouges or du Moulin. Wine and goat's cheese add further tasty attractions to this stretch of the Cher river.

Bourges

'The huge, rugged vessel of the church overhung me in very much the same way as the black hull of a ship at sea would overhang a solitary swimmer,' wrote Henry James of Bourges cathedral. 'It seemed colossal, stupendous, a dark leviathan.' UNESCO was just as impressed and made Bourges cathedral a World Heritage Site in 1992. The rest of the city is packed with fine historic streets and museums.

History

Avaricum, capital of the Bituriges tribe, was one of the glories of Gaul. Caesar destroyed it after a siege in 52 BC and chillingly described how his troops dealt with the Celts: 'None of our soldiers thought about making money by taking prisoners. They were exasperated by the massacre of Romans at Cenabum [Orléans] and the labour of the siege and spared neither old men, nor women, nor children. Of the whole population – about forty thousand – a bare eight hundred... got safely through to Vercingetorix.' Under the Romans, the town became of great importance, for a time the capital of the vast Gallo-Roman province of Aquitania.

The French Crown took possession of the viscounty of Bourges in 1101, when Philippe I bought it, making eastern Berry one of the earliest holdings of the Capetian kings outside the Ile de France. Work began on the Cathedral of St-Etienne in 1195. In 1360, Jean, a son of King Jean le Bon, was made Duc de Berry and would later also control the Auvergne and Poitou. He was a ruthless ruler, and fleeced his subjects to support his refined taste in the arts. In 1412 he tried to negotiate with the English, causing French royal troops to besiege Bourges. The duke submitted.

After his death, the future King Charles VII inherited the territories and Bourges became one of the bases of his peripatetic court. Charles was a weak, indecisive figure, often mockingly referred to as '*le petit roi de Bourges*' while Paris lay in English hands. Two vital figures came to his rescue. One was Joan of Arc. The other was Jacques Coeur, one of the most successful merchants in French history, who had one of his main bases in Bourges and grew fabulously wealthy from trade with the Orient and supplying the court with luxuries. As Charles VII's finance minister, Coeur worked the miracles economically which Joan of Arc had inspired militarily. However, his influence earned him many enemies and in 1451 he was arrested on false charges of having poisoned the king's mistress. Just as Charles VII had done nothing to aid Joan of Arc, so he did nothing for Coeur. Coeur escaped to work for the pope while his money helped to finance the expulsion of the English from France.

Charles VII's son, Louis XI, was born in Bourges and saw to the founding of Bourges University in 1463. It became known for law and theology; German students brought with them the seeds of Luther's preaching and planted them in the brain of Jean Calvin, a student here in 1530. By the 17th century, following the Wars of Religion, Catholicism was ascendant again, although more friction was inevitable, with the rebellious Condé family based here. When Louis XIV came to the city, he destroyed the Grosse Tour – a symbol of Condé power – and authority passed to the monarchy. Bourges declined, and would only really pick up with what might be described as an

Getting There and Around

There are **trains** to Bourges from Paris via Orléans and Vierzon; also from Bourges to and from Tours and the southern Berry.

Tourist Information

Bourges: 21 Rue Victor Hugo, 18000 Bourges, t 02 48 23 02 60, *www.bourges-tourisme. com*. The tourist office organizes a whole range of themed tours of town. For a wonderful night walk round Bourges which you can do by yourself, follow **Les Nuits Lumière** (*nightfall–about 11.30pm: July–Aug nightly; May–June and Sept–Oct Fri and Sat; free*), a trail of blue lights along the ground from the cathedral gardens, taking you past the city's monuments, all beautifully lit.

Where to Stay

Bourges ✉ **18000**
★★★**Hôtel de Bourbon**, Bd de la République, t 02 48 70 70 00, *www.alpha-hotellerie.com* (*moderate*). The smartest hotel in Bourges, set in a converted 16th-century abbey, with a fine restaurant, **L'Abbaye St-Ambroix**, t 02 48 70 80 00, in a former chapel (*menus €23–80*).

★★★**Hôtel d'Angleterre**, 1 Place des Quatre Piliers, t 02 48 24 68 51, *www.bestwestern.fr* (*moderate*). Excellent location and elegant exterior, but the comfortable rooms turn out to be unimaginatively decorated. *Closed 24 Dec–1 Jan.*

★★**Le Christina**, 5 Rue de la Halle, t 02 48 70 56 50, *www.le-christina.com* (*inexpensive*). In a dull modern block, but in a pretty good central location with a few rooms furnished with character, and views on to old Bourges rooftops.

Eating Out

Jacques Cœur, 3 Place Jacques Cœur, t 02 48 70 12 72, *www.tablegourmandeduberry.com* (*menus €23–64*). Reasonably priced traditional French fare, in a grand neo-Gothic dining room.

Le Bourbonnoux, t 02 48 24 14 76 (*menus €12–28; closed Fri, Sat lunch, and Sun pm in winter*). On an atmospheric street for restaurants and food shops, vibrant, stylish address serving inventive regional cuisine.

d'Antan Sancerrois, t 02 48 65 96 26 (*no menus; reckon c. €24 for 3 courses; closed Sun pm and Mon*). Atmospheric white-stoned dining-room, and dishes with a strong Berry flavour.

explosion in its arms industry under the Second Empire, which, by the First World War, employed more than 20,000 people. It has remained a major centre of the French arms industry, yet its population has been strongly left wing since the war.

Cathédrale St-Etienne

The roughly almond-shaped old town boasts the first French Gothic cathedral built south of the Loire, begun in 1195 under Archbishop Henri de Sully. His brother was archbishop of Paris, and Bourges cathedral is just as large and grand as Notre-Dame. Consecrated in 1324, its five-portalled façade is unique. Below the arches stands a wealth of sculpture – almost all from the 13th century – depicting the Last Judgement, the lives of St Etienne, St Just, St Ursin, the Virgin and St William, the last a Bourges archbishop. Between the portals, at the level of the niches, a series of bas-reliefs represents scenes from the life of Christ and from Genesis. The magnificent rose window above was added at the end of the 14th century by order of Jean Duc de Berry.

Unfortunately the ground wasn't strong enough to support the weight of the cathedral towers. On the south side, the Tour Sourde (Mute Tower – it has no bells) is propped up by an enormous pillar which was once a church prison. To the north, the

Tour de Beurre (financed by patrons in return for a dispensation to eat butter and milk during Lent) fell down in 1506 and had to be restored. Like Chartres, St-Etienne spectacularly demonstrates the engineering and visual possibilities of the flying buttress, which allows for much glass, and hence light, for the interior. The north and south side portals protect Romanesque sculptures from an earlier cathedral. The north presents the story of the Virgin but was badly damaged by Protestants. Owls and monkeys add a lighter note. The south portal shows dignified Old and New Testament figures.

Inside, the rows of Gothic lancet arches up to the apse reach higher than the arches of Notre-Dame. Don't miss the complex astronomical clock from 1424. Many fine tombs and works of art adorn the side chapels. Originally, nave and choir would have been separated by a *jubé*, or rood screen. The famed 13th-century stained-glass windows in the ambulatory feature a fabulous array of geometrically patterned settings for biblical and saintly stories.

You can only visit the crypt on a guided tour which allows you to see vestiges of the 13th-century rood screen, the Duc de Berry's tomb, a magnificent work by Jean de Cambrai, and several tall statues from the towers. After visiting the crypt, the ticket allows you to climb the Tour de Beurre for views of the old city.

Palais Jacques Cœur and the Bourges Museums

The most playful Gothic sculpture adorns the **Palais Jacques Cœur** (*open Jul–Aug 9–1 and 2–7, May–June 9.30–12 and 2–6, Sept–April 9–12 and 2–5; closed public holidays; 10 bis Rue Jacques Cœur, t 02 48 24 79 42, www.monum.fr; adm*), a truly palatial town house full of carved delights. Above the entrance doorway look out for the false windows with stone people in them who – as Henry James wrote – 'appear to be watching for the return of their master, who left his beautiful house one morning and never came back'. Cœur had a finger in every pie: real estate, mining, banks and the arms trade. Appointed Charles VII's Minister of Finance in 1439 and ennobled in 1441, he became the king's councillor in 1442 and began this house in 1443. The bitter tale of Cœur's demise (legend has it that he was killed by the Turks, with a weapon he had sold to them) contrasts with the lightheartedness of the sculpture in his homes. Exceptionally entertainingly carved fireplaces are highlights of the otherwise sadly empty interiors, while in the magnificent little chapel Jacques Cœur and his wife were each provided with a private oratory.

The Hôtel Cujas housing the **Musée du Berry** (*open July–Aug 10–6.30, rest of year 10–12 and 2–6, closed Sun am and Tues; 4 Rue des Arènes, t 02 48 57 81 15, www.ville-bourges.fr; free*) was built around 1515 for Durand Salvi, a Florentine trader. It contains two extraordinary exhibits: a re-created Gallo-Roman necropolis and some extremely moving marble *pleurants* (mourners) from Jean Duc de Berry's splendid tomb. As well as the Gallo-Roman and medieval sections, several rooms are given over to artefacts of Berrichon life in the 18th and 19th centuries.

A rich merchant family of German origin built the fine Hôtel Lallemant (1490–1518), now the elegant **Musée des Arts Décoratifs** (*open July–Aug 10–6.30, rest of year 10–12 and 2–6, closed Sun am and Mon; 6 Rue Bourbonnoux, t 02 48 57 81 17, www.ville-bourges.fr; free*). Its fine Renaissance features include a loggia, frescoes and an oratory with an engrossing coffered stone ceiling, each square decorated with an angel or symbol. Another joyous late Gothic house, the Hôtel des Echevins, built as a new town hall in 1487, contains the riot of 20th-century colour of the **Musée Estève** (*open July–Aug 10–6.30, rest of year 10–12 and 2–6, closed Sun am and Tues; 13 Rue Edouard Branly, t 02 48 24 75 38, www.ville-bourges.fr; free*), displaying the abstract works of Maurice Estève, a native of the Berry. The **Musée des Meilleurs Ouvriers de France** (*open July–Aug 10–6.30, rest of year 10–12 and 2–6, closed Sun am and Mon; Place Étienne Dolet, t 02 48 57 82 45, www.ville-bourges.fr; free*), in the 17th-century classical archbishops' palace, encourages modern craftsmanship.

Between Bourges and Vierzon

Northwest of Bourges, between the Berry's capital and Vierzon, a few little stops might appeal. Quiet **Mehun-sur-Yèvre** contains the meagre ruins of one of the great vanished medieval castles of France, built for Jean Duc de Berry. Cross the Cher, and you can discover the tiny but intriguing wine territories of **Quincy** and **Reuilly**.

By the Cher, just before Vierzon, **Brinay**'s church of St-Aignan stands by the village green. The choir contains some of the most moving Romanesque wall paintings in France. The east wall – normally the location for a Christ in Majesty – is occupied by a harrowing Massacre of the Innocents here. On the south wall, Christ is shown overcoming the Devil's temptations and turning water into wine at the feast of Cana.

The Cher from Mennetou to St-Aignan

This is a quiet stretch of the Cher, offering the calm provincial pleasures of Mennetou, with its crafts shops, and Selles, best known for its goat's cheese. Delightful but overlooked châteaux lie north and south of Selles. To the north, heading into the Sologne, the Château du Moulin has the prettiest brick façade of all the châteaux in that peculiarly atmospheric forest. It lies a dozen kilometres west of Romorantin-Lanthenay, capital of the Sologne. To the south of Selles, the Château de Valençay is a typical Loire hulk in blonde limestone, with a vineyard running down from it. Head some way further south for the jewel-box Château de Bouges.

Mennetou-sur-Cher to Selles-sur-Cher

Mennetou-sur-Cher, some way west of untouristy Vierzon, is a meagre slice of a medieval town, its crooked houses and cobbled streets encircled by run-down ramparts now sadly sandwiched between a railway line and a main road. In the Middle Ages the Cher ran just past the gateway known as the Porte d'En Bas, roughly along what is now the *camion*-clattering N76, but the river has shifted south since then and now it's the Canal du Berry that's more central. Bridges over this canal lead to the pretty riverbanks, where locals seek the shade of the weeping willows in

Getting Around

A **train** line runs along the Cher valley from Vierzon to Tours-St-Pierre-des-Corps, with stations at Gièvres and Selles-sur-Cher. To reach Valençay by train you need to change at Gièvres.

Different **bus** lines from Blois serve Romorantin-Lanthenay, Selles-sur-Cher, St-Aignan and Valençay, but these are mainly geared to school times, so leave very early in the morning.

Tourist Information

Mennetou-sur-Cher: 21 Grande Rue, 41320 Mennetou-sur-Cher, t/f 02 54 98 12 29, otsi.mennetou@infonie.fr.

Selles-sur-Cher: Place Charles de Gaulle, 41130 Selles-sur-Cher, t/f 02 54 95 25 44.

Romorantin-Lanthenay: 32 Place de la Paix, 41200 Romorantin-Lanthenay, t 02 54 76 43 89, www.tourisme-romorantin.com.

Valençay: 2 Av de la Résistance, t 02 54 00 04 42, www.pays-de-valencay.com.

Market Days

Mennetou-sur-Cher: Thursday morning.
Selles-sur-Cher: Thursday morning.
Romorantin-Lanthenay: Wednesday all day and Saturday morning.
Valençay: Tuesday morning.

Where to Stay and Eat

Selles-sur-Cher ✉ 41130

**Hôtel du Lion d'Or, 14 Place de la Paix, t 02 54 97 40 83, ph.lauraire@club-internet.fr (inexpensive). This old house benefits from the historical bonus that Joan of Arc is said to have stayed here. Inside it's quite bright and cheerful, with clean, reasonably priced rooms and both traditional regional Berrichon-Solognot cuisine and more original dishes combining meat with shellfish (menus €15).

The following are a few suggestions close to the Château du Moulin, taking you into the Sologne:

Mur-de-Sologne ✉ 41230

***Domaine de Fondjouan, Route de Lassay, t 02 54 95 50 00, www.domaine-de-fondjouan.fr (inexpensive). Recently restored 19th-century château offering simple accommodation and relaxation, and a restaurant that even caters for vegetarians (menus €13–38). Open all year.

Chémery

Château de Chémery, t 02 54 71 82 77, www.chateaudechemery.fr.st (inexpensive). At this picturesque run-down château some of the rooms have been converted into chambres d'hôtes. The price is a bargain for an eccentric night in a château. The kind hosts can offer table d'hôte for around €20 on request.

Romorantin-Lanthenay ✉ 41200

****Grand Hôtel du Lion d'Or, 69 Rue Georges Clemenceau, t 02 54 94 15 15, www.hotel-liondor.fr (expensive). The soberly smart façade in the centre of town conceals a fabulously luxurious restaurant run by Didier Clément, and some truly delightful luxury rooms (menus €79–115; closed Tues lunch). Closed mid-Feb–Mar and late Nov–early Dec.

**Le Colombier, 18 Place du Vieux Marché, t 02 54 76 12 76, f 02 54 76 39 40 (inexpensive). Down-to-earth central option (menus €17–32; closed Sun pm–Mon). Closed in Feb and on public holidays.

summer. Craftspeople have been tempted to settle in Mennetou – have a look at the **Salle Artisanat d'Art** at the tourist office. And visit the Gothic church of St-Urbain.

On the south side of the Cher from Mennetou, the Romanesque church at **St-Loup** contains some worn frescoes which you'll need to strain your eyes to decipher. They probably date from the end of the 12th century or early 13th. A particularly spectacular Catherine wheel of doves, gifts of the Holy Spirit, radiates out from the Virgin's heart.

The name of white-stoned **Selles-sur-Cher** conjures up snow-white goat's cheese to those in the Loire. The place has a central **château**, prettily reflected in the river.

Recently acquired by new proprietors, it is uncertain whether it will be open for visits in the future (*check with tourist office or on www.chateaudesellessurcher.com*). Also in the centre of Selles, the **former abbey of St-Eusice** has been roughly handled through time. The foundation may date back to the Frankish period, but Normans destroyed the first abbey, and Protestants wrought much damage on the Romanesque architecture that replaced it. Heavy 19th-century restoration has exacted its own toll, in the choir in particular. Fragments of Romanesque decoration do survive, including rare, imaginative and amusing late 11th-century friezes carved on the outside of the apse. One series tells the life of the hermit Eusice and another depicts scenes from the New Testament, all in the raw Romanesque style.

The best time to see Selles-sur-Cher is at the spring **goat's cheese festival**. The little **Musée du Val de Cher** (*future uncertain; was open June–Aug Tues–Sun 10–12 and 2.30–6; t 02 54 95 25 40 or t 02 54 95 25 44; adm*), with the church cloister attached, explains how the cheeses are made and other local traditions.

Heading from Selles to St-Aignan via the south bank of the Cher, you might pass through **Meusnes**, with its very early Romanesque **church of St-Pierre** housing lovely statues from the 16th and 17th centuries. The place also has a small museum on gunflint; this whole little area was devoted to production of the stuff in Napoleonic times to serve the vast armaments needs of the emperor's troops.

Into the Sologne

Château du Moulin

Open April–Sept Thurs–Tues 10–12.30 and 2–6.30, in Oct by arrangement; t 02 54 83 83 51, f-de-marcheville@wanadoo.fr; adm.

The Château du Moulin, lost in Sologne woods 12 kilometres west of Romorantin-Lanthenay, is the romantic star of the brick châteaux of the Sologne. It's a dreamy place, hidden in the countryside, reached by an alley of oaks you have to walk down, and surrounded by trees dipping their branches into the moat. Swans swim elegantly in its waters. The buildings that remain are fragments of a once more solid ensemble. The brick changes colour here and there, going from orange to purple. The typical Sologne lozenge patterns give way at one point to an intriguing configuration of squares within squares. The slim cylinders of the entrance towers convey elegance, despite the horizontal crossbow slits, mean eyes of defence. The little chapel has twisting Gothic tracery windows, while Renaissance decoration encroaches in other parts, with shells above certain windows.

As the mix of architectural elements indicates, this is one of those Loire Valley châteaux built at the time of the transition from Gothic to Renaissance styles, at the turn of the 15th to the 16th century. The name Moulin here refers not to a mill, but to the man who commissioned it, Philippe du Moulin, a loyal servant of Charles VIII. Charles VIII was the first French king to go campaigning in Renaissance Italy; du Moulin rescued him on the disastrous return journey when the French came close to complete humiliation at the Battle of Fornovo in 1495.

The main *logis* is still very much lived in as you'll discover on the guided tour. It was restored at the start of the 20th century for M. de Marcheville, ancestor of the present owner, who turned it into an extremely liveable country retreat. The interiors are very light and agreeable. It seems only appropriate in this hunting forest that several pieces of furniture should depict animals being chased. The chapel contains some lovely period stained glass. Among the more unusual objects on display in the side buildings are a formidable crossbow – the arrows apparently shot off at 200 kilometres an hour – and an enormous, curious spit, apparently once worked by a dog running round in the wheel!

If you go to the village church of St-Hilaire at **Lassay-sur-Croisne**, just north of the château, you can see an early depiction of the castle as it looked originally, in one of the wall paintings in Philippe du Moulin's chapel, his monument desecrated during the Revolution.

Some way west of the Château du Moulin, the much put-upon **Château de Chémery** (*open daily 10–nightfall; t 02 54 71 82 77, chateaudechemery@libertysurf.fr; adm*) had become very dilapidated and has now come under attack from the advance of the new, nondescript modern village houses of Chémery. But the courageous owners have taken on the battle to try and save some of this little castle's dignity, patching it up as best as they can, organizing cultural events in the courtyard in summer and taking in B&B guests (*see* p.202).

Romorantin-Lanthenay and Aliotis

If Leonardo da Vinci's outrageously ambitious plans had gone ahead to transform Romorantin-Lanthenay for King François I, the town would no doubt have become one of the most famous in France. François had spent some of his childhood at Romorantin, and once crowned king decided to have a sumptuous new castle built here in his beloved hunting Sologne. Leonardo, who had come to France at François' behest, began drawing up ideas for this wonderful palace in 1517. Among other magnificent Renaissance features, the château was to have a series of arcaded galleries looking over the Sauldre river.

As it happened, unfortunately, in 1518 an outbreak of the plague struck the town and the king decided to have his fabulous new hunting lodge built a bit to the north, in the forests of Chambord. Romorantin-Lanthenay was left to play a rather minor part as isolated capital of the Sologne, hardly a very exciting role considering what might have been. Although the fair number of mills built along the Sauldre and its islands brought economic activity to the place, Romorantin came to be viewed as a symbol of *la France profonde*, backward, provincial France. Things have changed somewhat in recent times. The centre has been spruced up, and the townspeople have enjoyed a certain prosperity since Matra cars set up a factory here in 1968; the Renault Espace model is made here and you can visit the **Espace Matra Automobile** (*open Wed–Mon 9–12 and 2–6, Sat and Sun from 10; closed public hols; 17, Rue des Capucins, t 02 54 94 55 55, www.romorantin.fr; adm*).

A new museum, the **Musée de Sologne** (*open June–Aug Wed–Mon 10–6, Sun am only; rest of year Wed–Mon 10–12 and 2–6; closed 1 May, 1 Jan, 25 Dec; t 02 54 95 33 66,* *www.romorantin.fr; adm*), has been created in some of the renovated Sauldre mills and pays its respects to the area. A wall painting gives you a picture of Leonardo's dreams for Romorantin, while a Renault Espace counts among the museum exhibits. In addition, the town has its ambitious Pyramide, rural rival to that of the Louvre in Paris; this Espace François I is used for cultural events. On a more old-fashioned note, the **Musée Archéologique** (*open summer daily exc Thurs and Sun 2–6; adm*) occupies one of the finest old timberframe houses in Romorantin.

Aliotis (*open early Feb–Oct daily 10–early evening; rest of the year afternoons only; times very variable, t 02 54 95 26 26 , www.aliotis.com; adm*), the Sologne aquarium, lies near Villeherviers, just a few kilometres east of Romorantin. The complex is protected by a curious funky permanent tent-like structure. The development of soggy Sologne for fishing dates back at least to early medieval times, when monks began regulating the waters with a whole network of lakes. A Sologne lake stopper made out of oak and reckoned to be 800 years old counts among the most ancient of objects on display. Now the Sologne has a staggering 3,000 lakes in all, covering some 12,000 hectares. In the aquarium's tanks you can see the fish that thrive in these lakes, and in the rivers of the Loire Valley more generally.

You might head north from here via the likes of **Millançay** or **Marcilly-en-Gault** to explore the major area of lakes, although most are in private hands and are difficult to appreciate close up. A bit further northeast, the village of **St-Viâtre** has more displays devoted to this lakeland at the **Maison des Etangs** (*open 15 June–15 Sept 10–12 and 2–6, otherwise by appointment; t 02 54 88 23 00, www.coeur-de-france.com/ st-viatre-tourisme.html*), along with panels suggesting walks in the area.

South from Selles-sur-Cher

Château de Valençay

Open July–Aug 9.30–7.30, April–June and Sept–Oct 9.30–6; grounds open until nightfall; t 02 54 00 10 66, www.chateau-valencay.com; adm.

'Shit in a silk stocking' was the not entirely flattering way in which Napoleon apparently once referred to Talleyrand, the most significant historical figure associated with the splendid Château de Valençay. But this massive castle, which stands aloof to one side of a pretty little town due south of Selles-sur-Cher, is once again the typical Loire Valley mix of late Gothic and French Renaissance forms, dating mainly from the 16th century. The two features which immediately stand out when you arrive are the château's ornate keep and the great pepper-pot towers on one side, the latter the hallmark of Valençay. The keep, really something of a redundant military element left over from medieval architectural design, was here embellished with Renaissance features. It would almost be worth using binoculars to admire the wealth of sculptural details on the frieze placed high up around it.

Walk into the inner courtyard and the scene changes somewhat. The most imposing wing within was built at the start of the 18th century. To the south, views open onto the little Nahon valley, while to the east lie the château's vineyard and the town.

The entertaining guided tour around the grand interiors focuses on Talleyrand. Napoleon also said of this brilliant man: 'He was the most capable of all my ministers.' He became the emperor's massively powerful foreign minister, and was allowed to entertain foreign dignitaries at Valençay. Talleyrand married Catherine Worlée, whose beauty is clearly shown in a beautiful portrait of her at the château, painted by the reputed female artist Vigée Le Brun. But Catherine's stupidity was as great as her looks. She was said to have had '*pas plus d'esprit qu'une rose* (no more intellect than a rose)'. Although she became Princesse de Talleyrand, she was easily supplanted in her husband's affections by the wife of Talleyrand's nephew, his '*chère nièce*', as she was euphemistically known. She was an intelligent, driven woman who eventually came to reign with Talleyrand at Valençay. They entertained royally and liberally, the famous cook Carême cooking up sumptuous dishes for their guests.

After taking in the pompous Napoleonic interiors, wander round Valençay's grounds, which are populated with a whole menagerie of animals, while a makeshift outbuilding also holds an extensive collection of old cars.

Château de Bouges

Open July–Aug 10–1 and 2–7; June Wed–Mon 10–12 and 2–7; April–June and Sept Wed–Mon 10–12 and 2–6; March and Nov weekends 10–12 and 2–5; 15 Rue du Château, t 02 54 35 88 26, www.monum.fr; adm.

You'll find pure elegance at the Château de Bouges, east off the D956 between Valençay and Levroux. A simple classical rectangle, it is sometimes compared with Versailles' Petit Trianon. The château was built in 1762 for Count Charles Le Blanc de Marnaval, an owner of ironworks. His family didn't benefit from it long, and it too fell into Talleyrand's grasping hands for a time.

It is furnished with the elegant accoutrements of noble life from the 18th and 19th centuries: a man's dressing table for powdering his wig; a *voyeuse* chair for women in vast crinolines to watch the society games comfortably; a *table à ouvrages* around which a family could sit, each member carrying out his or her own occupation, a locking drawer in front of every seat; a library ladder which folds away impeccably into a leather-covered stool; and a rent-farmer's table, with a turning drawer to avoid the vulgarity of passing money from hand to hand.

In season, beautifully arranged cut flowers from the garden adorn many rooms, while the generous grounds visible out of the windows beckon for a stroll.

The Cher from St-Aignan to Montrichard

St-Aignan is the nicest spot on the Cher after the Château de Chenonceau. It's a very appealing little town, although its major tourist attraction is a well-run zoo to the south. Montrichard, dominated by modern tower blocks as well as its medieval keep, makes an interesting historical stop too. Between St-Aignan and Montrichard lie Cher valley vineyards and discreet attractions such as the Château du Gué-Péan, lost in its woods, the Gallo-Roman finds of Thésée, and the quarries of Bourré, reputed to have provided the purest stone in the Loire Valley. The eccentric remnants of Pontlevoy abbey come as a big surprise rising out of the plain north of the Cher valley.

St-Aignan

Like a decadent parody of a Jacob's ladder, a magnificent monumental staircase climbs from St-Aignan's church up to the **château of St-Aignan**. The interiors aren't open to the public, but you can appreciate the grand exterior, and from the splendid terrace, enjoy good views down onto this delightful town. One side of the town tumbles down the slope to the Cher. On the other side, the old town roofs, a mix of brown tiles and slate, are crammed together in the cramped valley of a tributary of the Cher.

Aignan, after whom the town is named, was the bishop of Orléans who saved that city from Attila the Hun. An island in the middle of the Cher here is known as **L'Ile aux Trois Evêques**, 'the island of the three bishops', indicating the ancient divide between the territories of the dioceses of Orléans, Tours and Bourges that lay here. The hillside above became a site of strategic importance in the territorial struggles between the counts of Blois and Anjou at the start of the second millennium. A southern fort for the Blois family, the place was attacked by the dreaded Foulques Nerra of Anjou, who extended his vast domains down the Cher valley in the early 11th century.

Descending the château staircase, you're led straight into the great narthex of the **church of St-Aignan** below. The soaring tower is a 19th-century addition to the large Romanesque building beyond. (You can climb the tower in summer for a small fee.) On the front of the church, note the words '*République française*', left from the time the holy place was forcibly converted to secular use at the Revolution. Inside, 19th-century restorers have had their cleansing way, giving the spaces an almost hospital-like whiteness. The capitals in the choir look absurdly sparkling and new, although the figures are in the entertaining Romanesque tradition. For a recorded commentary on the church, on the left as you enter there's a button which activates a 15-minute recorded guided tour.

The high point of the church interior is the **crypt**. This is in fact an older church upon which the larger one above was later plonked. The dark, dank place contains some fine vestiges of Romanesque wall paintings and capitals; it offered excellent conditions for a local wine merchant to keep his stock in the last century, saving this level from the clinical restoration work carried out above. The most original painting depicts events not from the life of St Aignan but from that of St Gilles; here he performs acts of charity and miracles, clothing a beggar, healing a man bitten by a snake and even praying powerfully enough to rescue a ship from being wrecked. A grandiose Christ in Majesty was painted in the inner chapel. He is flanked by St Peter and St James the Minor, who appear to bow before his glory thanks to the curve of the ceiling. At the feet of their robes, cripples grovel, one with a stick holding out a

Tourist Information

St-Aignan: 60 Rue Constant Ragot, B.P.41, St-Aignan 41110, t 02 54 75 22 85, www. ot-val-du-cher.fr.st.

Thésée-la-Romaine: Rue Romaine, 41140 Thésée-la-Romaine, t/f 02 54 71 45 45 (high season), t/f 02 54 71 70 24 (low season).

Montrichard: 1 Rue du Pont, 41400 Montrichard, t 02 54 32 05 10, f 02 54 32 28 80.

Market Days

St-Aignan: Sat morning for food; Sat all day for clothes.

Montrichard: Monday afternoon and Friday morning.

Where to Stay and Eat

Noyers-sur-Cher ✉ 41140

***Clos du Cher, 2 Rue Paul Boncour, t 02 54 75 00 03, www.closducher.com (moderate). This very pleasant hotel hides on the north bank of the Cher outside St-Aignan, in a private park off the main road. It has characterful rooms furnished with antiques. The cuisine has style too (menus €16–34; closed Thurs lunch out of season).

St-Aignan ✉ 41110

**Grand Hôtel St-Aignan, 7–9 Quai J-J Delorme, t 02 54 75 18 04, grand.hotel.st. aignan@wanadoo.fr (inexpensive). With large windows looking onto the Cher, this ivy-clad building is the archetypal old-fashioned French hotel (menus €15–34; closed Sun pm, Mon and Tue am Nov-Mar). Closed mid-Feb–mid-Mar and last two weeks in Nov.

Chez Constant, 17 Place de la Paix, t 02 54 75 10 75 (menus €11–23). With its old painted beams and its bright red plush seats, this is a lively new restaurant in a rather splendid old setting, professionally run and offering good local dishes.

Mareuil-sur-Cher ✉ 41110

Ferme Auberge La Lionnière/Bouland B&B, t 02 54 75 24 99, perso.wanadoo.fr/ frederic.bouland (inexpensive). Lost in the countryside (follow the signs carefully from Mareuil's boulangerie) is this charming little country farm B&B with restaurant attached. The good-value rooms, neatly set under the eaves, are bright and fresh, with the rural pleasure of the farmyard just outside. It helps to like goat in all its forms if you come and eat, as it predominates on the very filling menus. Lamb, duck, guinea fowl and freshwater fish can also be on the menu – check when you ring. On sunny days you can eat out on benches in the delightfully unkempt garden (menus €17–21). You must book in advance.

Thésée ✉ 41140

**Moulin de la Renne, 15 Impasse des Varennes, t 02 54 71 41 56, www. moulindelarenne.com (inexpensive). This place's setting is its main charm, with fishing and walking. The rooms are rather

coin, another moving along on walking irons. The frescoes to the side of this scene are much later, from the 15th century, but also show penitent, frail mortals, the lord of St-Aignan, Louis II de Chalon, and his second wife, Jeanne de Perellos. They caused a terrible scandal in 1420 when they eloped from the Burgundian court – Louis was unfortunately already married to Marie de la Trémoïlle. Look out too for a 16th-century interpretation of the Last Judgement, illustrating what Louis and Jeanne might well have lived in fear of.

The cobbled streets and squares in the little town below the church are full of old houses, a few with crooked medieval frames and carved beams, others in more controlled 16th- or 17th-century styles.

There are several possibilities for going **boating** on the Cher from St-Aignan. The **Syndicat du Cher Canalisé**, t 02 54 75 08 51, offers little barges and river boats. For canoes, contact either the **Base Nautique des Couflons**, t 02 54 75 12 31, or

bare, but the cooking's good value (*menus €15–37; closed Sun pm, Mon and Tues lunch out of season*). *Closed mid-Jan–mid Mar.*

Oisly ✉ 41700

Le Saint Vincent, southwest of Contres (via the D675 and the D21), **t/f** 02 54 79 50 04 (*menus €21–45; closed Tues–Wed*). This may not look anything special on the village square, but inside the chef is devoted to his cuisine. Original dishes include the likes of guinea fowl served in aromatic wine and pork *confit* with rhubarb cream. *Closed mid-Dec–Feb.*

Pontlevoy ✉ 41400

★★Hôtel de l'Ecole, 12 Route de Montrichard, **t** 02 54 32 50 30, **f** 02 54 32 33 58 (*inexpensive*). The flower- and ivy-covered façades have an immediate charm, set back just off the main street in this calm little town. There's a pleasant garden where you can eat in summer – the food is well executed (*menus €16–45.50; closed Sun pm–Mon exc public hols and July–Aug*). *Closed mid-Feb–mid-March and mid-Nov–mid-Dec.*

Montrichard ✉ 41400

★★★Le Bellevue, 24 Quai de la République, **t** 02 54 32 06 17, *www.hotels-montrichard. com* (*inexpensive*). Big and modern, it has some comfortable rooms with good views of the river. The restaurant serves filling fare (*menus €14–45*).
★★★La Tête Noire, 24 Rue de Tours, B.P.03, **t** 02 54 32 05 55, **f** 02 54 32 78 37 (*inexpensive*).

Offers slightly cheaper but good quality rooms, while the annexe has a shaded garden leading down to the Cher (*menus €16–37*). *Closed Jan.*

Chissay-en-Touraine ✉ 41400

★★★Château de Chissay, Chissay-en-Touraine, **t** 02 54 32 32 01, *www.chateaudechissay.com* (*expensive*). A pure white château that stands out proudly among the woods above the Cher valley road. Its architecture has been mutilated in parts for visitors' comfort and commercial expansion, but it has many attractions, in particular characterful, bedrooms furnished with antiques, a tiny chapel and fine vaulted reception rooms. In the superb dining room try imaginative avant-garde cuisine on curiously shaped plates. The swimming pool lies down the slope, the railway line close by a slight irritation amid such luxuries (*menus €18–51*). *Closed mid-Nov–mid-Mar.*

La Ménaudière ✉ 41401

★★★Château de la Ménaudière, Route d'Amboise (D115), B.P. 15, **t** 02 54 71 23 45, *www.chateaumenaudiere.com* (*moderate-luxury*). Another luxurious choice, on the D115, this dates back to the 16th century, like nearby Chenonceau. The château's rooms are spacious and stylish, the setting peaceful. There is a heated swimming pool and a tennis court, and the restaurant is of a high quality (*menus €23–53; closed Sun pm and Mon out of season*). *Closed mid-Nov–Feb.*

M. Roussineau, **t** 02 54 75 00 57. The organization **AVAC Environnement**, **t** 02 54 71 40 38, has run boat trips in the past.

Zooparc de Beauval

Open April–Nov 9–nightfall, Nov–April 10–nightfall; **t** 02 54 75 50 00, *www.zoobeauval.com; adm.*

This top-class zoo (clearly marked south from St-Aignan) started with an innocent-sounding request which should act as a cautionary tale to all parents. Madame Delord was asked by her three-year-old daughter whether they could keep a couple of birds in their Paris apartment. Now she runs this large zoo with her children – fortunately still impassioned about animals now that they've grown up. Some of the species kept and bred here and some of the pens built for them in this quiet, well-tended little valley make Beauval compare favourably with the most respected zoos in the world. More than a dozen of the animals are part of the European Endangered Species Programme (EEP).

One of the strengths of the park is its sizeable **aviary** full of tropical birds. Outside, the vultures, owls and parrots are limited to more conventional little pens. The parrots tend to come from Parisian owners who got sick of their pets, as do a few of the more dangerous animals – Beauval doubles as something of an animal sanctuary. Parrots were prized as possessions rarer than many a fabulous jewel by the Loire Valley kings of France. Along with the booty and artists which Charles VIII brought back with him from his Italian foray at the end of the 15th century was a Moor from Naples, recruited to serve as royal parrot-keeper!

In the mammals section of the zoo, the **wild cats** are particularly impressive. The most famous inmates are the white tigers, their shaggy coats striped with brown lines. The mature ones reach the size of small bulls and are infinitely more awe-inspiring. White lions, snow panthers, black panthers, pumas and jaguars – in all a collection of around 30 types of big cats – also laze in their enclosures. In the house for apes and monkeys, the gorillas and the mournful-faced orang-utangs don't look as though they would hurt a flea, but the chimpanzees are generally completely out of order, the males outrageously aggressive. A major investment of recent years has been in the large **seal pool**, a commercial venture to increase the number of visitors. In season there are displays of seal acrobatics, as well as of falconry. The 'savannah' beyond, a largish section of hillside cut out in the shape of Africa, has also been developed to hold a selection of animals from south of the Sahara, such as giraffes, zebras, antelopes and rhinos. Panels throughout the park impart educational information about the animals.

The Cher from Thésée to Bourré

Vineyards begin to hold their own on the Cher's southern slopes west of St-Aignan. The D17 leads to Pouillé, where you can cross north to **Thésée-la-Romaine**. This place has a rather grand name to indicate the small Gallo-Roman finds made here. The town hall, a tall, sparkling white building in a pleasant park, has a small **Musée Archéologique** (*open July–Aug Wed–Mon 2.30–6.30, April–June weekends and public hols only 2–6, Sept–Feb by appointment, exc public hols; t 02 54 71 00 88, http://thesee.tourisme.free.fr; adm*) on the top floor. The Gallo-Roman objects on display include some pieces of quite ornate pottery. These fragments came from the ancient settlement of the ruined **Tasciaca**, or **Les Maselles** as it's now known, 1km west of the village (*open July–mid-Sept daily 10–12 and 2–6; Sept–June by appt*). Small vestiges of Gallo-Roman walls still stand there.

The **Château du Gué-Péan** (*open April–Oct 9–7, Nov–Dec and Feb–Mar weekends and hols 10–6, Jan weekends and hols 10–5; t 02 54 71 37 10*) is a Sleeping Beauty of a castle, not quite cut off by impenetrable woods and brambles, but lost down dark wooded tracks beyond the village of Monthou-sur-Cher and its undulating vineyards. Gué-Péan means 'paying ford', but it's hard to imagine anyone forking out money to pass via such obscure back roads in centuries past.

Goat's Cheese and Wine in the Cher Valley

It's not just wine that can get an *appellation d'origine contrôlée* label along the Cher valley: the goat's cheese can too. Good places to try it or buy it include the *fromagerie* (cheese shop), on the church square at Selles-sur-Cher, the *ferme-auberge* at Mareuil-sur-Cher, where you can go and visit the goats before tasting their produce (*see* p.208), or the Ferme de Bellevue at Pontlevoy, with a choice of *appellation* cheeses on offer, which you can taste at a small charge, along with Touraine wine.

From St-Aignan west to the Touraine border, vineyards prettify the banks of the Cher valley. A large percentage of the grapes go for vinification to the Oisly et Thésée *confrérie* (rebaptized Wally and Teazy by some in the British wine trade). This cooperative, based at Oisly, has established a solid reputation for improving the quality of the local wines since it was founded at the start of the 1960s.

Slightly confusingly, the best wine produced in this part of the Loir-et-Cher is categorized as AOC Touraine. A small number of vinegrowers vinify and bottle their own production, reds, rosés and whites, and very occasionally sparkling wine too. The characteristic Loire grape varieties feature and are most often stated on the label to differentiate the types. Gamay dominates in the reds, with Cabernet France and Côt added in varying amounts. Sauvignon wins out in the whites, possibly supplemented by Chenin Blanc or Pineau de Loire.

A fine address to start tasting at would be the **Clos Roche Blanche** (*t 02 54 75 17 03*) at Mareuil-sur-Cher, splendidly located overlooking the valley, with a cellar in the cliff face where they sell their organic wine.

Slightly northeast of St-Aignan, the **Domaine du Chapitre** (*open daily; 82 Rue Principal, t 02 54 71 71 22; free*) at St-Romain-sur-Cher has been run by the same family for a couple of centuries.

The **Domaine Joel Delaunay** (*open daily Mon–Sat exc public hols 9–12 and 2–6.30; t 02 54 71 45 69; free*) at Pouillé, on the south bank opposite Thésée, benefits from magnificent views. Here you can appreciate the recently installed modern vat house for vinification.

At Pontlevoy, you could try **Michel Roy** (*open daily exc public hols 9–7; 3 Rue Franche, t/f 02 54 32 51 07, domaine-des-roy@wanadoo.fr; free*), who welcomes you in an unpretentious little reception room.

In Montrichard, the **Caves de Monmousseau** (*t 02 54 71 66 66, www.monmousseau. com*) is the well-known name (*see* p.214). Also in Montrichard, Paul Buisse, a professional cook turned winemaker and merchant, will enthuse to you in his cliffside cellars, the **Caves de la Boule Blanche** (*open Mon–Fri 9–12 and 2–6; 69 Route de Vierzon, t 02 54 32 00 01, www.paul-buisse.com; adm*), on Route de Vierzon.

Finally, there are a couple of vineyards you might visit at St-Georges-sur-Cher close to Chenonceaux. At the panoramically sited **Domaine Guenault/Maison Bougrier** (*t 02 54 32 31 36, www.bougrier.fr*), Noël Bougrier is a vinegrower and wine merchant who sells a wide variety of Touraine wines. The substantial **Domaine de la Rablais** (*open daily Mon–Sat exc public hols 9–12 and 2–6.30; t 02 54 71 36 14, www.isasite.net/ caves-simoneau/; free*) is also well used to receiving tourists.

A joy to look at as you arrive, the château seems somewhat dejected when you get closer, even badly run down at the back. It is full of charm though. Each corner is marked by a solid tower, one curious one standing out from the rest – like a bell, or a pepper-pot, or even a German military helmet. The front sections of the buildings beyond date from the middle of the 16th century. These parts were built for François Alaman, a high-ranking royal taxman. He amassed enough of a fortune to transform the previous château on the spot, which his family had owned for over a century. Further back still, the two main wings were redone in the 17th century, in plain but noble style. Decayed elegance has been the main feature of the *cour d'honneur* until recently, especially with its disused pool in the centre. And inside, the string of *salons* wore an air of jaded beauty. But the castle has been acquired by new owners who may bring the place the new lease of life it needs.

Oisly, northeast of Gué-Péan, is known for its wine cooperative (*see* box on p.211). Northwest of Gué-Péan rises the **Abbaye de Pontlevoy** (you need to book to visit, either by calling Robbie on his mobile, *t 06 32 95 13 83*, or by calling the abbey, *t 02 54 32 99 39*), an extraordinarily large and imposing religious complex seemingly set in the middle of nowhere. Approached from the south, the top of the abbey church looks like a lovely little Gothic chapel tossed high into the air. The structure in front of it, by contrast, has the sturdy neoclassical appearance of a military school. It turns out that the abbey did serve that purpose for a short time, during the reign of Louis XVI. Before that, it long had a reputation as a major centre of religious education. Now American-owned, it offers study programmes for the Consortium of American Universities (*www.euramcenter.com*).

You can visit the Gothic church, but its nave has gone AWOL. That's why the choir seems to soar so strangely by itself into the air when you see the abbey from a distance. However, the choir alone is the size of a decent church. Its impressive architecture dates from the end of 13th century to the beginning of 15th, with heavily restored Gothic tracery windows and side chapels radiating out from the centre. Inside, the decoration is 17th century, an indication of the establishment's revival after Cardinal Richelieu became its abbot. Look out for the splendid choir stalls and a couple of superb, excessive Baroque altarpieces. A very worn older fresco of St Martin was also uncovered relatively recently.

Troglodyte Bourré

Bourré sits back on the Cher's north bank, just east of the town of Montrichard. Its name is synonymous with some of the finest-quality stone in the Loire. Across the region, château guides will cite the name of Bourré with pride if it's been used in the construction of their particular architectural treasure. It's astonishing to hear that in the course of four centuries, some 400 kilometres of quarries were carved out in the area around Montrichard. The best tufa in these parts lay around 20–30m under the earth, and was known as *le blanc royal*, royal white – the stone of Bourré apparently whitens with age as the water in the stone evaporates. The most famous buildings to use Bourré blocks include some of the most illustrious Loire châteaux, notably Chambord, for which some 450,000 pieces were required.

To appreciate Bourré's picturesque cliffside setting, it's worth taking a look at it from the south, in the valley. No longer exploited for stone, the former quarries have been converted to other uses. Mushrooms are cultivated in vast caverns you can visit – follow the signs for the **Caves Champignonnières des Roches** (*open April–Nov daily 10–6; 40 Route des Roches; t 02 54 32 95 33, f 02 54 32 42 99; adm*).

The newest troglodyte site in Bourré has been created by the young and dynamic Maurice de Lalande, whose family own the mushroom farm, and some of whose ancestors were stone quarriers. On a tour of the **Carrière de Tuffeau and Ville Souterraine** (*open daily April–Nov; 40 Route des Roches; t 02 54 32 95 33, f 02 54 32 42 99; adm*) you can not only learn about the centuries of quarrying that went on in these parts, but also see the work of a couple of present-day sculptors who have created a fake village in stone in a corner of one quarry. The main artist, Christian Lhermite, working with an assistant, Luc Bodin, has spent an enormous amount of time shaping façades, human figures and animals. There are even vines in stone down here. It's a slightly curious enterprise, to have carved out such a static place in rock when there are so many pretty real villages above ground in these parts.

At **La Magnanerie** (*open April–Aug Wed–Mon, visits at 11, 3, 4 and 5; Sept–Oct Thurs–Mon, visits at 3, 4 and 5; 4 Chemin de la Croix Bardin, t/f 02 54 32 63 91; adm*) the guided tour teaches you about further uses to which the caves were converted, both for human habitation and for silk worm production.

Montrichard

The authorities at Montrichard clearly decided to place housing above tourism at one time in the town's not-too-distant past. The result is the provocative siting of an army of modern apartment blocks on the hillside beyond Montrichard's splendid remnant of a medieval keep. Judge for yourselves how successful the decision was. The keep still manages to hold its own on the skyline, though. It has stood the test of time rather better than the ruined fortifications around it. The whole medieval complex recalls the period when Montrichard was fought over by the great regional counts and by English and French royalty. Yes, Foulques Nerra of Anjou raises his ugly head again. He only had a wooden fortification built here, however; the stone keep went up a century after him. The keep itself is now too structurally unsafe to enter. A narrow, cramped tower among the fortifications manages though to squeeze in the **local museum** (*open Easter–Sept daily 10–12 and 2–6, plus lunchtimes mid-June–Aug; adm*) on its different levels. Displays on archaeology, history and local explorers who headed for wider horizons (notably the Sahara) are neatly fitted into the tiny spaces.

Popular legend has it that the town's name, Mount Richard, derives from Richard the Lionheart's connection with the place (he was apparently responsible for ordering the fortifications surrounding the foot of the keep, as well as the town walls, late in the 12th century) – but in fact the name of Montrichard preceded his arrival. The town experienced a further flurry of royal activity in the 15th century, under King Louis XI, who brought the fief into the French royal possessions the year of his accession, 1461.

Superstitious to a fault, he couldn't resist getting control of the **church of Notre-Dame de Nantheuil**, whose statue of the Virgin and Child was said to work miracles and attracted a large number of pilgrims. As with the Notre-Dame de Cléry, Louis lavished money on this building to his beloved Virgin. He had it restored, but the old Romanesque forms were respected, with the addition of elaborate Flamboyant doors, whose admirable decoration includes Louis' arms.

Beyond fortifications and church, Montrichard boasts quite a fine legacy of medieval buildings. It's worth going to the tourist office just to take in its grand brick façade. The other houses worth a look at stand close by. A fair amount of the life of the town is concentrated down by the river, with its little cobbled quay leading to the water. On the eastern edge of town, the **Caves de Monmousseau** (*open April–mid-Nov daily 10–7, mid-Nov–Mar Mon–Fri 10–12 and 2–5; t 02 54 32 35 15, www.monmousseau. com*) are impressive quarries on several levels turned into wine cellars for a firm which produces Loire bubbly wine on a grand scale. The guided tour through an impressive labyrinth of limestone corridors takes you to the Musée des Confréries Européennes, devoted to the mass of wine fraternities across France, and ends with a tasting. West of Montrichard, in the village of **Chissay-en-Touraine**, the alcoholic curiosity is a strawberry liqueur distillery. From Montrichard, take to the Cher on the *Léonard de Vinci*, a grandiosely named little boat (*daily July–Aug; t 02 54 75 41 53*).

The Cher from Chenonceaux to Tours

The Château de Chenonceau (without an 'x') by the village of Chenonceaux (*with* an 'x') is the star of this stretch of the Cher, of course. Lost in woods to the south of it, the Château de Montpoupon has housed a museum on hunting in the outhouses. A few splendid little villages lie along the Cher valley west of Chenonceau before the suburbs of Tours.

Château de Chenonceau

Open daily mid-March–mid-Sept 9–7, rest of Sept 9–6.30, early March and first half of Oct 9–6, rest of Oct and mid–end Feb 9–5.30, first half Feb and first half Nov 9–5, mid-Nov–Jan 9–4.30; t 02 47 23 90 07, www.chenonceau.com; adm.

As the royal party passed by, trees burst into cascades of fireworks and fountains gushed with wine. The later fêtes were more licentious; in 1573 women dressed as men and Henri III and his acolytes were gorgeously dressed as girls.
Marcus Binney on parties at Chenonceau, in *Châteaux of the Loire*

Most glamorous of all the Loire Valley châteaux, with its galleries spanning the Cher, the Château de Chenonceau incites decadence, it's so irresistibly gorgeous. It's said to be the most visited castle in France after Versailles. You can well believe it when you see the crowds crammed into its relatively small spaces. Those of you who feel put off

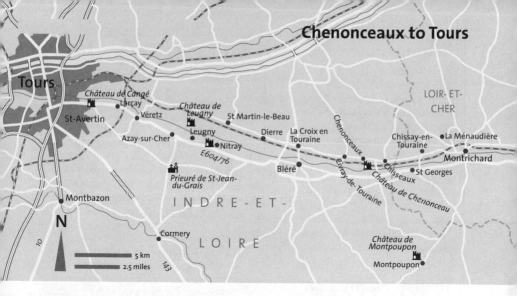

by the chattering, cluttering groups might try using your imaginations to re-create the atmosphere of those 16th-century royal parties.

You approach the château through a dramatic alley of vast plane trees, at the end of which you can make out the entrance façade romantically filling the view. There are two distinct parts to the château itself. The square block you get a glimpse of from afar is the earlier part. With its splendid corner turrets and windows, it was built for Thomas Bohier, an inspector of finances for kings Louis XII and François I. He had bought the property in 1512 from the bankrupt Marques family. who had been the owners of the estate here from the 13th century, in 1423 replacing a manor house with their château. Thomas Bohier had this medieval castle destroyed, save the sturdy Tour des Marques. It still stands, on your right as you arrive in front of the castle.

Bohier decided to build his château on the Cher itself, using the foundations of a mill on the river. Construction began in 1515, the year of François I's accession. A regional builder, Pierre Nepveu, known as Le Trinqueau, directed the work. He would also play an important part in the building of Chambord (*see* p.140) for François. As Thomas Bohier accompanied the king on his expeditions, including to Italy, it was his wife Katherine (née Briçonnet) who oversaw many of the developments. The initials TB and TK to be seen in numerous locations around the château refer to Thomas Bohier and Thomas and Katherine. The Bohiers' magical residence was completed by 1521, the year in which Thomas' brother Antoine, archbishop of Bourges, came to consecrate the chapel.

Bohier's 'keep', as this first château is sometimes rather misleadingly called, has splendidly elegant proportions and rooms. On the eastern side built over the river, two prows of stone protrude, the first containing the chapel, the second, a delightful library. The pillars of the arch under Bohier's building were ingeniously fitted with kitchens, a little stairway leading down to a platform at which boats could dock to unload deliveries.

Getting Around

Chenonceaux is on the slow Tours–Romorantin **train** route, which also stops occasionally at some of the towns and villages along the way, notably Bléré.

By **road**, the south-bank N76 is slightly prettier than the north-bank D140 between Tours and Chenonceaux.

There are a couple of very slow **buses** a day between the Château de Chenonceau and Tours (Touraine Fil Vert ligne C). Bléré, Athée-sur-Cher and Azay-sur-Cher lie on Touraine Fil Vert Ligne D.

Boat trips are possible from Bléré and Chisseaux.

Tourist Information

Chenonceaux: B.P.1, 1 Rue Dr Bretonneau, **t** 02 47 23 94 45, **f** 02 47 23 82 41.
Bléré: B.P.43, 8 Rue J-J Rousseau, 37150 Bléré, **t/f** 02 47 57 93 00, *www. blere-touraine.com*.

Market Days

Bléré: Tuesday morning and Friday afternoon.

Where to Stay and Eat

Chenonceaux ✉ **37150**
★★★**Le Bon Laboureur**, 6 Rue du Dr Bretonneau, **t** 02 47 23 90 02, *www.amboise.com/laboureur* (*moderate*). An 18th-century coaching inn, now the closest place to stay to the château in this village packed out with hotels and restaurants. The rooms are actually spread out in four different buildings, and are comfortable. On sunny days you can eat out on the terrace (*menus €29–69; closed Tues and Thurs lunch*). Closed *mid-Nov–mid-Dec and early Jan–early Feb*.
★★★**La Roseraie**, 7 Rue du Dr Bretonneau, **t** 02 47 23 90 09, *lfiorito@aol.com* (*inexpensive*). This wasn't as well looked after as its neighbour, but new owners have recently taken over and have been giving the place a face-lift. The rooms are simpler. The cooking is hearty and generous (*menus €16–32; closed Tues lunch and Mon in Mar and mid-Oct–mid-Nov*). Closed *mid-Nov–Mar*.
★★**La Renaudière**, 24 Rue du Dr Bretonneau, **t** 02 47 23 90 04, *gerhotel@club-internet.fr* (*inexpensive–moderate*). Furthest of the bunch from the château, but it isn't far, and it has a chic brick façade and a garden. One of its menus recreates old recipes (*menus €19–39*). Closed *mid-Nov–mid-Dec and early Jan–early Feb*.

The king had granted the Bohiers permission to construct a bridge over the Cher, but they both died in the mid-1520s, before any work on one could be started. Financial scandal ruined the families of many of François I's financiers and the builders of many of the Loire's most famous châteaux. After Thomas Bohier's death, he was found guilty of embezzlement and his son was forced to hand over the château to the crown in 1535 by way of repayment. So the extravagant François I gained possession of yet another beautiful Loire Valley castle, and Chenonceau was temporarily reduced to serving for the occasional hunt. The Holy Roman Emperor Charles V, during his visit to France in 1539, was brought to see Chenonceau on the tour of royal properties François organized to impress him.

François I's successor, his son Henri II, gave away Chenonceau as a token of his love – unfortunately not to his wife, Catherine de' Medici, but to his mistress, Diane de Poitiers, instead. The deeds described the donation as one of gratitude towards Diane's late husband, Louis de Brézé, for his services to the king. It's perhaps not surprising that this unsubtle ruse might have galled the formidable Catherine. Diane had many ideas for Chenonceau and had her architect, the famous Philibert de l'Orme, draw up plans. Arches were built over the Cher to reach the other bank and

**Hostel du Roy, 9 Rue du Dr Bretonneau, t 02 47 23 90 17, *hostelduroy@wanadoo.fr* (*inexpensive*). A pleasing little turret marks the façade of this cheaper option. The rustic touches have been laid on a bit heavy-handedly here, but the food is copious, fitting the setting (*menus €12–32*). *Closed mid-Nov–mid-Feb*.

Au Gâteau Breton, 16 Rue du Dr Bretonneau, t 02 47 23 90 14 (*menus €11–19*). The small dining room expands in summer to the larger terrace outside. You can try Touraine specialities here for a good price. *Closed Tues eve and Wed eve in main season; closed every eve Nov–mid-April*.

Civray-de-Touraine ✉ 37150

**Château de l'Isle, 1 Rue de l'Ecluse, t 02 47 23 63 60, *chateaudelisle@wanadoo.fr* (*moderate*). This modest 18th-century manor, set in private grounds which go down to the Cher river, takes you well away from Chenonceaux's bustle, even though it lies just a little west of the château. Each room has its own character and the cuisine is well prepared (*menus €27–32; closed at lunchtime*). *Closed mid-Nov–mid-Feb*.

Bléré ✉ 37150

**Le Cheval Blanc, 5 Place de l'Eglise, t 02 47 30 30 14, *le.cheval.blanc@wanadoo.fr* (*moderate*). Has a good reputation locally for its inventive cuisine, and cosy rooms are in an 18th-century house (*menus €17–56; closed Fri lunch and Sun pm out of season, and Mon*). *Closed Jan–mid-Feb*.

*Hôtel du Cher, 9 Rue du Pont, t 02 47 57 95 15, f 02 47 30 26 35 (*inexpensive*). By the bridge, a basic, unpretentious address at which to stay, with lively restaurant (*menus €11–40*). *Closed mid-Feb–mid-March, and Sun eve and Mon in winter*.

Maison Pommé, 21 Rue Paul-Louis Courier For a special tasting of Touraine charcuterie specialities, which are something of a local institution. Try *rillons, rillettes* and *andouillettes* washed down with local wine.

St-Martin-le-Beau ✉ 37270

**Auberge de la Treille, 2 Rue d'Amboise, t 02 47 50 67 17, f 02 47 50 20 14 (*inexpensive*). Serves good traditional French dishes in its beamed interior (*menus €11–40; closed Sun pm and Mon out of season*). *Closed mid-Nov–early Dec and mid-Jan–early Feb*.

Larçay ✉ 37270

La Planchette, 46 Rue Nationale, t 02 47 50 54 73. Set in a 17th-century barn, this restaurant serves copious portions of barbecued meats and local wines at bargain prices (*menus €8–18*).

the intention appears to have been to construct a gallery on top of them, but this wasn't done. Some of the garden designs Diane approved were carried out at vast expense. She herself virtually never came to Chenonceau, preferring her stunning château at Anet, much closer to Paris.

Catherine de' Medici had her revenge on her husband's death in 1559. Henry James called it 'the most pardonable of all the revenges with which the name of Catherine de' Medici is associated'. She forced Diane to give up Chenonceau and accept in exchange the only slightly less gorgeous Château de Chaumont on the Loire. Under Catherine, Chenonceau underwent its most important transformation. It was she who ordered the second wing of Chenonceau to be built, with its beautiful galleries over the Cher. The name of the architect remains uncertain, but it seems most likely that Jean Bullant was responsible for the work. The construction is extremely graceful. Dating from the 1570s, it's much more soberly classical in design than the square 'keep'. There is, though, a wonderful rhythm to the galleries' bays and details, for example the *œil de bœuf* windows in the roof. The ceaseless swirling waters of the Cher beneath it add movement, light and excitement to the architecture.

Catherine also greatly altered the appearance of the earlier Bohier château, some say rather grossly, adding great caryatid figures in the grotesque Mannerist style favoured at the time. These changes were removed at a much later date. Most extravagantly, Catherine had plans for two great wings fanning out from the Bohiers' building. These would have dwarfed the château as we know it today, but were never constructed. Outbuildings were added in the outer courtyard, though.

So often portrayed as a totally wicked witch of a Queen Mother, Catherine de' Medici held sumptuous festivals here, the *triomphes de Chenonceau*. Henry James isn't sparing in his estimation of her selfish capacity to enjoy parties, writing of 'the terrible daughter of the Medici, whose appreciation of the good things in life was perfectly consistent with a failure to perceive why others should live to enjoy them'. Like so many other writers, he got a bit carried away by his own rhetoric of vilification. But the parties do appear to have been outrageous.

The first of Catherine's Chenonceau *triomphes*, described in the opening quote, was held for her sickly son King François II and his wife, Mary, to go down in history as the unfortunate Queen of Scots. The artist Primaticcio masterminded the ceremony, which stood in such ironic contrast to the recent bloody repression of the Protestants involved in the Amboise Conspiracy. Cannon salvos greeted the young royals, while black banners recalled the Queen Mother's mourning for her recently dead husband. The courtyards and gardens were decked out with follies – a triumphal arch, obelisks, false altars and statues – while poets had prepared adulatory texts. Spectacular entertainments were laid on. Actors appeared as classical figures declaiming in grandiose fashion. One fountain splashed out claret. All in all, the entertainment was extraordinary.

On François II's early death, King Henri III's gay abandon enlivened the place. Some have speculated that his mother tried to tempt him with wild parties here into making love to his wife and thus making more of an effort to continue the Valois line. Apparently more successful were the seductresses of Catherine de' Medici's 'flying squad' of beautiful and intelligent aristocratic young women, trained to entice the leading nobles of the realm, all the better to spy on them for the Queen Mother! But as to Henri III's wife, Louise de Lorraine, she remained devout and devoted. It was to her that Catherine de' Medici would in fact leave Chenonceau. After Henri III's assassination in 1589, Louise became a recluse, mourning in white, as was the royal tradition. When she passed away, the château was pretty well neglected for a century and more.

It was an ancestor of the writer George Sand, a tax gatherer by the name of Dupin, who restored some dignity to Chenonceau after he had bought it in 1730. His wife gathered together many figures of the Enlightenment in parties at the château. Jean-Jacques Rousseau even served for a while as teacher to the Dupins' son. At the Revolution, an attempt to dismantle this once-royal home is said to have been averted by the subtle reasoning of a local priest; he advanced the purely utilitarian argument that it would be a disservice to the community to get rid of the only river crossing between Montrichard and Bléré! So Chenonceau survived unscathed.

Another in a line of important women in Chenonceau's history, one Madame Pelouze, bought the château in 1863. She asked the architect Felix Roguet to follow as closely as possible the engravings of Chenonceau drawn by the architect Du Cerceau at the end of the 16th century, in order to try to restore the château to its Renaissance appearance, and the original forms re-emerged.

The Interiors of the Château de Chenonceau

Within, evocative 19th-century decoration was made to complement what was left from the 16th century. This has since been added to by the private owners since 1913, the Menier family, who built their big fat fortune on chocolate bars. The interiors of the château hold many delights, particularly on sunny days, when the sparkling light reflecting off the Cher's waters jumps around the rooms. The tour is easy to follow off the single central corridor.

You enter via this eccentric corridor with highly decorated key stones. The first room, the so-called **Salle des Gardes**, sets the tone for the chambers that follow, decked out with 16th-century tapestries and chests. Off it lies the little **chapel**, retaining its original door and graffiti scratched by the Scots guards who protected the French royal family. It was a captain of the Scots guard, Gabriel Montgomery, who accidentally killed King Henri II in a jousting tournament. The next room is described as **Diane's bedroom** and has an extraordinary fireplace by Jean Goujon, decorated with lions and putti and flanked by caryatids. A modern portrait of Catherine de' Medici is framed in the centre of it. Ironically, one of the tapestries depicts *The Triumph of Charity* and another *The Triumph of Power*. The *Virgin and Child* is attributed to Murillo. Off this room, the interlaced Cs of the magnificent ceiling make clear who made the green cabinet her own. Powerful paintings also decorate the room. The **library** jutting out over the river has a coffered ceiling which recalls the Bohiers with their initials. It's a perfect little room, even if there are no books in it.

Heading on to the **gallery** over the Loire, despite its magical light, it's slightly disappointing to find the long, elegant room empty. The place is so patently made for celebration that nothing short of candles, moonlight and dancing would make the atmosphere live up to the imagination. In the First World War, the gallery served as a makeshift hospital. During the Second World War, up until the end of 1942, Chenonceau lay on the frontier between German-occupied France and Vichy France, formed by the Cher at this point. The gallery is said to have been used at the time by members of the Resistance to pass from one zone to the other. The place was then occupied by the Germans and even targeted by Allied bombs in 1944.

The so-called **François I room** has a fireplace covered with Bohier's motto 'S'il vient à point me souviendra', roughly interpreted as meaning that if he completed his work (the château) he would be remembered. But the royal past predominates. Diane de Poitiers is recalled here in a painting by Primaticcio, said to have been executed at Chenonceau when Diane was proprietor. The *Three Graces* by Van Loo depict the des Nesles sisters, favourites of Louis XV. Signs of royalty decorate the place, the salamander and full ermine on the fireplace referring to François I and Claude de France, while Louis XIV, always generous about donating paintings of himself to the provinces, left a Rigaud work surrounded by an overelaborate gilded frame. Rubens' *Baby Jesus with St John* contrasts with it.

The finely wrought stonework of the staircase leads to the simpler corridor on the first floor, lined with exquisite 17th-century Audenaarde tapestry scenes of a hunt. Fine furnishings abound on this upper level. The names given to the four main chambers recall royal figures and events: one is named after Catherine de' Medici; another, that of the Five Queens, after her five well-married girls (her two queenly daughters and three queenly daughters-in-law); yet another after Henri IV's favourite, Gabrielle d'Estrées. A morbid room on the top floor re-creates the tearful surrounds in which the White Queen, as Louise de Lorraine became known because of her attachment to white mourning clothes, lived her last 11 years.

You can wander along the river banks and through the relatively small but well-tended **formal gardens**. The **Galeries des Dames de Chenonceau** outbuildings contain a waxworks museum, recreating some of Chenonceau's historic moments, and a tea house. The château's **son-et-lumière** (*July–Aug nightly 10pm–11.30pm*; *t 02 47 23 90 97 for bookings*) also recalls the importance of the women in Chenonceau's history.

From **Chisseaux**, east of Chenonceaux, you might consider joining a boat trip or gourmet cruise on board *La Bélandre* (Maison Eclusière, B.P. 4, 37150 Chisseaux, *t 02 47 23 98 64, www.labelandre.com*), which takes you along the river and under Chenonceau's arches. When Henry James came to visit Chenonceau, he was most surprised to encounter a gondolier he had met in Venice, and who had been brought to the château, gondola in tow, to paddle decoratively in the Cher.

Château de Montpoupon

Open daily July and Aug 10–6; April–June and Sept 10–12 and 2–6; Feb–Mar and Oct–Dec 10–12 and 2–4; t 02 47 94 21 15, montpoupon@ louvencourt.com; adm.

Montpoupon feels far from the madding crowds of Chenonceau, although it lies only a little way south. The château looks picturesque on its charming rise above three diminutive valleys. A pleasant Gothic-to-Renaissance gateway stands in front of the much-restored main building. Montpoupon once lay on the royal road to Spain. Owned by the De Prie family from the early 14th to the mid-17th centuries, the place thrived on hunting. It is still devoted to the sport, with a smart hunt museum, the **Musée du Veneur**, set up in the outhouses. As at the Gien hunt museum, the exhibits are good enough to be of interest even to visitors unsure about hunting. Inscribed antlers, costumes, buttons, weapons, a generous collection of topical scarves from Hermès, prints and memorabilia give a full picture of the long-established aristocratic pastime.

From Chenonceaux to Tours

Before you reach the sprawling outer suburbs of Tours, the Cher valley has several pleasant spots along its banks. **Bléré**, a pretty little town with nice shops in the historic centre and a classified church, comes to life in the summer. On the north bank, **La Croix-en-Touraine** and **Dierre** each have charming village churches, the latter's restored partly thanks to a donation from the British Queen Mother, who must have been moved by her visit to the place. **St-Martin-le-Beau**, with its mixture of brown and slate-tiled roofs like its bigger wine cousin Montlouis, to the west, also produces wine under Montlouis' *appellation* (*see* p.250). Five extraordinary layers of foliage and geometric Romanesque decoration surround the doorway to the village church. Inside, the refined white marble Virgin is attributed to the great Tours Renaissance sculptor Michel Colombe.

Cross back south over the river here to appreciate the Cher's sloping bank. A string of châteaux line the way, best seen from the GR41 national walking route. After the château in **Nitray**, whose park you can visit and whose wines you can taste, you carry on west past the châteaux of Beauvais (neo-Gothic), Leugny (late 18th century, copying Versailles' Petit Trianon) and Coteau. **Azay-sur-Cher**, by the latter, is yet another pretty riverside village.

Do seek out the **Prieuré de Saint-Jean-du-Grais** (*open July–mid-Sept daily 2.30–6, Mar–Oct for groups on request; t/f 02 47 50 73 00; adm*). It presents the most delightful ensemble of disused religious buildings, set in the quiet countryside just a few kilometres south of Azay-sur-Cher. An enormous forest covered this area in early medieval times, and two hermits, Renaud Fremaud and Geoffroy Paissonnel, chose to settle in it in 1120. They were on the vast territories of Count Foulques V of Anjou. The count was away crusading at the time, but his forest guards were busily enforcing his rights and insisted that the two hermits pay their taxes. When Foulques V returned to France, he lifted these taxes and even donated land to the hermits, but soon left on another campaign against the so-called infidel. He never returned, becoming King of Jerusalem and dying in the Middle East.

From 1163, the little religious community that had grown up at Grais began to construct priory buildings in stone. Now the prior was given powers over the local area, and was able to dispense justice in these parts, but soon the nearby abbey of Cormery (*see* p.279) and the deanery of St-Martin in Tours wrangled over who should have control over the place. The papacy was asked to intervene, and resolved the situation by putting the priory under its direct control, following which its history was relatively uneventful for centuries. At the Revolution, the buildings were sold off to wealthy farmers, who turned the priory to agricultural uses. Inevitably the place was badly damaged. Although a stone rocket of a church tower still stands out from the ensemble, the rest of the church was brought down, its stone sold off. Around the courtyard, you're shown a few empty but evocative chambers, including the lovely chapterhouse, the dormitory above, with traces of intriguing medieval graffiti, and the refectory with its beautiful oak timbers, its protruding pulpit and a fragment of badly damaged fresco representing Christ surrounded by the Evangelists. You're also shown round the separate 15th-century prior's lodgings, which the owners, the Darrasse family, plan to restore. It was Raymond Darrasse who did much to rescue the priory from total neglect from 1927. There's a tea shop to incite you to linger just a little longer.

Back by the Cher, the Eglise Notre-Dame at **Véretz** contains fine Renaissance art, with 16th- and 17th-century murals, and Christ and the Disciples depicted in terra-cotta medallions. **Larçay** plunges you right back into Gallo-Roman times; the ruins of a *castrum*, with its eight defensive towers, date from the 3rd century when barbarian hordes were invading from the east. The name of the Château de Cangé at **St-Avertin** is associated with a French government in desperate straits in 1940 as the Germans swept through the country at the start of the Second World War. Winston Churchill dashed over to the meeting here at which the French decided on their terrible, humiliating armistice.

The Loire from Blois to Tours via Amboise

14

Blois to Tours

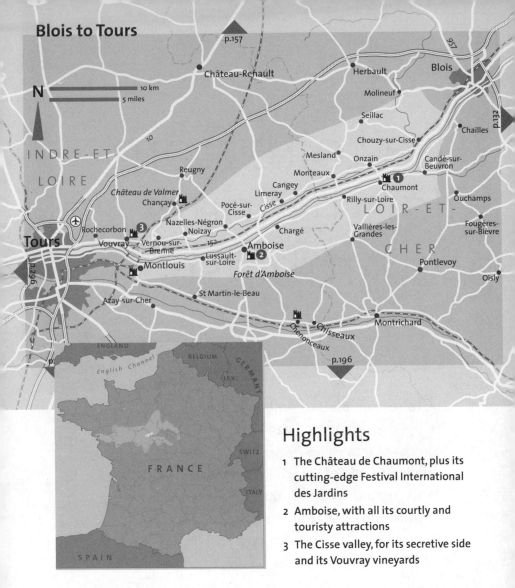

p.157

Château-Renault

Herbault

Blois

Molineuf

N 10 km
   5 miles

Seillac

p.132

Chailles

INDRE-ET-
LOIRE

Mesland

Chouzy-sur-Cisse

Onzain

Candé-sur-
Beuvron

Reugny

Monteaux

Château de Valmer

Cangey

Chaumont ❶

Ouchamps

Chançay

Limeray

Rilly-sur-Loire

LOIR-ET-

Pocé-sur-
Cisse

Cisse

Fougères-
sur-Bièvre

Nazelles-Négron

Vallières-les-
Grandes

CHER

Rochecorbon ❸

Noizay

Chargé

Tours

Vouvray

Vernou-sur-
Brenne

Amboise ❷

Pontlevoy

p.296

Lussault-
sur-Loire

Montlouis

Oisly

Forêt d'Amboise

Azay-sur-Cher

St Martin-le-Beau

Montrichard

Chisseaux

Chenonceaux

p.196

ENGLAND

BELGIUM

GERMANY

English Channel

LUX.

FRANCE

SWITZ.

ITALY

SPAIN

Highlights

1 The Château de Chaumont, plus its cutting-edge Festival International des Jardins
2 Amboise, with all its courtly and touristy attractions
3 The Cisse valley, for its secretive side and its Vouvray vineyards

Châteaux abound in this area. Many are in private hands, like Mick Jagger's, or have been turned into posh hotels. But two very mighty ones which are open to the public survey the Loire majestically from their heights: first Chaumont, then Amboise. The town of Amboise is the major attraction along this stretch of the Loire, the royal castle dominating the riverside while the Clos Lucé, a splendid house on the outskirts of town, was where Leonardo da Vinci spent the last few years of his life. Funnily enough, though, it's the modern aquarium at Lussault, a little west of town, which gets the largest number of tourists in these parts. Amboise is surrounded by further surprising attractions, including the Parc des Mini-Châteaux, presenting miniature versions of the most famous Loire Valley châteaux. You can get a rather more authentic feel for the former aristocratic grandeur of the area from a visit to the forlorn clown of the Pagode de Chanteloup, sole remnant of a vast 18th-century palace.

Shadowing the north bank of the Loire between Blois and Tours, the river Cisse is lined with delectable little villages as well as castles. A few châteaux here, such as Valmer and Jallanges, have opened their grounds to the public. Follow the Cisse and the Loire westwards and you come into major Touraine wine and troglodyte territory around Vouvray. Vouvray is renowned in France for its range of Chenin Blanc white wines, from dry and sparkling to the super-sweet. Montlouis, opposite on the south bank of the Loire, also produces good Chenin Blanc. The Château de la Bourdaisière on Montlouis' outskirts is devoted to stranger fruit for the Loire, the tomato.

The Loire from Blois to Amboise

The splendidly located Château de Chaumont is the first major stop along this stretch of the Loire. We also introduce you to the Cisse valley here.

Château de Chaumont

Open 15 Mar–Sept 9.30–6, Nov–14 Mar 10–5; closed 1 Jan, 1 May, 1 and 11 Nov and 25 Dec; t 02 54 51 26 26, f 02 54 20 91 16; adm.

The Château de Chaumont boasts one of the best locations of all the châteaux along the Loire, looking dramatically down onto the river. You can best appreciate the place, standing proudly on its hillside, from the north bank. 'Hot mount' appears at first glance to be the translation for 'Chaumont'. There is certainly quite an invigorating walk up the slope to reach the castle, but it turns out that the name derives from the Latin for 'bald hill'. Today the château is surrounded by woods.

The counts of Blois had a fortress here around the year 1000, at a time when they were in direct conflict with the counts of Anjou to the west. That keep has vanished, but Chaumont does have a medieval chivalric feel to it, even if it is in fact another of those transitional Loire châteaux, built in period when Italian Renaissance features were merging with French late Gothic forms. Construction began at the start of the 1470s, after the previous castle had been destroyed on King Louis XI's orders as punishment for the owner Pierre d'Amboise's part in a rebellion. Pierre was subsequently pardoned and allowed to build a new château on the spot. The north and west wings went up before his death in 1473. His grandson Charles II d'Amboise inherited Chaumont in 1481. Charles II was an enormously influential figure in French politics in his day, serving as governor of Milan for a period, and being appointed marshal and admiral of France under King Louis XII. Thanks to his money, from 1498 to 1510, a vital period in the change in French architectural styles, the rest of the château was completed.

Two massive but charming towers flank the main gateway, which cuts diagonally across the southeast corner of the castle. The frieze running along the outside sports interlacing Cs, referring to Charles d'Amboise, while the motifs between them

Getting There and Around

Occasional **trains** on the Blois–Tours line stop at Chouzy, Onzain and Limeray. There's a **bus** service between Amboise and Tours.

Tourist Information

Chaumont-sur-Loire: 24 Rue du Maréchal Leclerc, t 02 54 20 91 73, *www. chaumontsurloire.info*.

Where to Stay and Eat

On the south bank of the Loire between Blois and Amboise:

Candé-sur-Beuvron ✉ 41120

**La Caillière, 36 Route des Montils, t 02 54 44 03 08, *lacailliere@mageos.com* (*moderate*). Looks a picture, with cosy rooms in the old inn and parasols in the garden. And it serves interesting dishes; for example you might be able to try *sandre* served with an original citrus and ginger sauce to pep it up (*menus €17–49; closed Thurs lunch and Wed*). *Closed Jan and Feb*.

Chaumont-sur-Loire ✉ 41150

La Chancelière, 1 Rue de Bellevue, t 02 54 20 96 95 (*menus €14–32; closed Wed and Thurs*). Restaurant tucked under the Loire cliffside, offering quite refined, good-value cuisine in its two cosy dining rooms. *Closed mid-Nov–early Dec and mid-Jan–mid-Feb and major public hols pm*.

On the north bank of the Loire between Blois and Amboise:

Molineuf ✉ 41190

La Poste, 11 Av de Blois, t 02 54 70 03 25 (*menus €17–28; closed Wed, Tues pm Oct–April and Sun pm Sept–June*). Up the picturesque little Cisse valley, serving experimental as well as traditional cuisine. *Closed mid-Feb–early Mar and mid-Nov–early Dec*.

Herbault/Landes-le-Gaulois ✉ 41190

***Château de Moulins, t 02 54 20 17 93, *www.chateauxhotels.com/moulins* (*expensive*). Still further up the Cisse, a little south of the D957 from Blois to Vendôme by the D138, this posh and very appealing little ivy-clad château sits nobly in its vast grounds. Inside, you should be delighted with the grand salons, coffered ceilings and antique furniture. *Open all year*.

Chouzy-sur-Cisse ✉ 41150

***Hostellerie les Couronnes, by the N152, t 02 54 20 49 00, *www.lacarte.com.fr* (*moderate*). An old farm converted to offer comfortable modern rooms set in a golf course, with tennis court and swimming pool. The dining room is charming. The food is better value than the rooms (*menus €12*). *Closed Nov–mid-Mar*.

Onzain ✉ 41150

****Domaine des Hauts de Loire, Route de Mesland, t 02 54 20 72 57, *www. domainehautsloire.com* (*expensive*). Another hunting pavilion disguised as a château, this one 19th century and full of luxuries,

represent burning hills, an amusing if slightly silly pun on the words 'hot mount'. The symbols of a cardinal's hat pay their respects to Charles II d'Amboise's uncle, the vastly powerful Georges d'Amboise. He oversaw much of the work at Chaumont, as well as at his sumptuous early Renaissance Château de Gaillon in Normandy. He was clearly a cardinal with a taste for the temporal in his spare time. A powerful figure in his day, he was a one-time contender for the papacy, and effectively served as King Louis XII's top minister for a period. Further symbolic lettering on the building apparently refers to Diane de Poitiers, the mistress of King Henri II, who beat his wife, Catherine de' Medici, in the battle for the king's affections. Diane is represented not just by 'D's, but also by a Greek delta and by depictions of the accoutrements of the goddess Diana the Huntress.

situated well above the rather ugly little town below. It has beautiful rooms with painted beams. In the restaurant, sample refined regional cuisine, such as crispy eel salad and beef poached in Montlouis wine. Tennis court, pool and, of course, helipad in the grounds. You could splash out on a trip over the Loire by helicopter or hot-air balloon from here – just ask at reception (*menus €60–121; closed Mon and Tues exc public hols*). *Closed Dec–mid-Feb.*

***Château des Tertres**, 11 Rue de Meuves, t 02 54 20 83 88, *www.chateau-tertres.com* (*moderate–expensive*). For a much more reasonably priced stay in another 19th-century château, try this place, set on the wooded hillside a couple of kilometres west of Onzain, its grounds providing a very peaceful setting. *Closed mid-Oct–early April.*

Seillac ✉ 41150

Domaine de Seillac, at Seillac, north of Onzain on the D131, t 02 54 20 72 11, *www.hotel-seillac.com* (*moderate*). Reflected in its lake, this smart Ancien Régime and 19th-century manor house makes a pretty picture. But note that only a small number of the Domaine's rooms are in the manor; most are in bungalows set around the large grounds, which also include the luxury of three tennis courts and a heated swimming pool (*menus €20–55; closed Sun pm Nov–Mar*). *Closed mid-Dec–mid-Jan.*

Cangey ✉ 37530

Le Fleuray, Route Dame Marie-les-Bois (along the D74), t 02 47 56 09 25, *www. lefleurayhotel.com* (*moderate*). Run by an enthusiastic British couple who have put great effort into turning this Touraine farm into a tasteful country hotel; they also prepare and serve the food, on a terrace in summer, by a log fire in winter (*menus €26.50–36.50; dinner only*). *Closed early Nov–mid-Nov, mid-Dec–early Jan and mid-Feb.*

Limeray ✉ 37530

Auberge de Launay, Le Haut Chantier, t 02 47 30 16 82, *auberge.de.launay@ wanadoo.fr* (*moderate*). With reasonable rooms, this place serves tasty popular local dishes such as Tourangeau kid with Gratin Dauphinois, or eel pie marinated in white wine and cognac. In summer you can eat out in the garden (*menus c.€20–31; closed Mon and Tues lunch out of season*). *Closed mid-Dec–early Feb.*

Pocé-sur-Cisse ✉ 37530

La Croix Verte, Route d'Amboise, t 02 47 57 03 65. A pleasant restaurant just outside Pocé-sur-Cisse, with a good choice of menus (*menus €20–32; closed Mon and Tues*). *Closed a fortnight in Oct.*

Nazelles ✉ 37530

Château des Ormeaux B&B, Route de Noizay, t 02 47 23 26 51, *www.chateaudesormeaux. com* (*expensive*). A very posh B&B, this gorgeous hillside property is a square-sided little château with cute slender corner turrets. The rooms were redone in 1998 in grand style and have lovely views and excellent bathrooms. There's a pool in the grounds. The place doubles as an antiques shop (*table d'hôte dinner €39, all included*).

The tale of how the beautiful Diane came to receive Chaumont isn't a particularly pretty one – Henri II died in 1559 and she was forced by his jealous widow to exchange the romantic Chenonceau for the colder Chaumont. Some say that Catherine de' Medici bought Chaumont expressly to arrange this exchange and organized the swap even before she had paid for the place. In fact she had acquired this lucrative château with its large estate back in 1550. She appears barely to have stayed here at all, despite the legend (*see box p.229*). Nor did Diane, once she became the owner, although she had work carried out on the château in the 1560s.

In 1739 the proprietor knocked down the north wing of Chaumont, opening up the courtyard as you now see it, so that it looks out onto the Loire. Unfortunately, the views from here don't match those up to the château, as they take in the village's ugly modern bridge over the Loire and the dull flat plain to the north. Around the middle of the 18th century, Jacques-Donatien Le Ray bought Chaumont and turned it into something of a centre of artistic production. A glassworks in the outbuildings attracted the English glass painter Robert Scott Godfrey, and the pottery brought the Italian J. B. Nini. Among the latter's terracotta medallions, one represents a famous American visitor to France of the time, Benjamin Franklin.

This period of artistic activity at Chaumont was followed by one of abandonment at the start of the 19th century. But wealthy new owners came to the rescue. The Comte d'Aramon, who bought the château in 1833, ordered the first restorations. His widow married the Vicomte de Walsh from Anjou, who called upon Jules de la Morandière, that region's well-known restorer, to help here. However, the look of the place was most altered inside and out by another 19th-century architect-cum-restorer, Paul-Ernest Sanson. His work was commissioned for a spoilt young woman who supposedly spotted Chaumont when out on a day trip and asked her daddy to buy it for her. Monsieur Say, literally a sugar daddy, his massive fortune coming from the sugar-refining industry, duly did, in 1875. His daughter Marie married Prince Amadée de Broglie, who had just as extravagant tastes as she. They apparently acquired two hamlets just to knock them down to improve the view and extend Chaumont's park. They didn't like the village church either, so they changed that too. In addition, they had electricity installed in the village below, making it one of the first in France to boast street lamps. Back up in the château, the entertainment was lavish. One very enthusiastic maharajah, to thank the couple for his stay, gave them an elephant, Miss Pungi, whom Marie loved. The Say girl's story all ended in tears of course, the family sugar beet business going bankrupt. The château was sold to the state in 1938.

The interiors still bear the marks of 19th-century good living, however, with underfloor heating added at that time, along with the collection of fine art pillaged from a pot-pourri of places. You get a Victorian view of chivalric centuries past here, grand Gothic turned neo-Gothic. There are some sumptuous pieces of art to admire on the tour, like the late 16th-century tapestries depicting classical gods representing days of the week, hanging in the Salle de Conseil. Look out too for the Nini terracotta medallions in the library. The dining room is on a grand scale, while weapons set out in the shape of fans decorate the Salle des Gardes, making a formidable display. In the last rooms, Renaissance superstition and historical legend take over (*see* box opposite). You pass through the chamber known as Catherine de' Medici's room, the chapel and the Chambre de l'Astrologue, all restored, the brooding bedrooms heavily furnished.

The château visit also includes a separate guided tour of the extravagant 19th-century **stables** built by Sanson. Do go for a walk around the château grounds as well. The Princesse de Broglie called in the landscape architect Achille Duchêne to design the *parc à l'anglaise*, with its sweeping lawns and meandering paths through beautiful trees. Part of these grounds now serve as the setting for the prestigious annual **Festival International des Jardins** (*open late May–19 October 9.30–nightfall; t 02 54 20 99 22, www.chaumont-jardins.com; adm*); in the summer months, modern garden designers are given the chance to experiment with compact contemporary creations in this excellent, thought-provoking gardening extravaganza.

A Bad Heir Day

The story goes that, soon after her husband's death, Catherine de' Medici came to Chaumont with one of the famous astrologers of the day, either Ruggieri or Nostradamus. Contemporary writers allude to the horrifying vision of the future with which she was confronted in a magic mirror. Catherine's male children appeared one after the other, followed by Henri de Navarre, of Bourbon blood. The princes were said to have walked in a circle for as many times as they had years to reign. Thus the untimely death of Catherine de' Medici's sons and the downfall of the Valois dynasty were supposedly foretold to the Queen Mother at Chaumont. Henri de Navarre would become the first French Bourbon king after Henri III was assassinated.

However dubious the legend may be, it is true that, just as with certain members of the British royal family today, many of the kings and queens of France set great store by their astrologers.

Continuing west along the south bank of the Loire from Chaumont, you pass **Rilly**, a peaceful wine village, before arriving at **Mosnes**, just across the Touraine border. This sleepy village has been given a new lease of life by the creation of **Fantasy Forest** (*open April–Nov, t 02 47 30 50 90*), a well-designed outdoor activity centre offering assault courses through the treetops, buggy rides, bike hire, and paintball games.

Along the Cisse Valley between Blois and Amboise

The north bank of the Loire west of Blois sees the appearance of vineyards producing a sub-*appellation* of Touraine wines, allowed to carry the title AOC Touraine-Mesland, after the village of **Mesland**. Most of the vines grow on the sandy and gravel plateau above the river; maybe it's the good south-facing position of the vines that gives the local wines a certain durability. Gamay grapes dominate the red production; for the whites, Chardonnay and Sauvignon are blended with Chenin Blanc, while the Vin Gris is a quite enjoyable rosé. To get a taste of these wines, try visiting the Clos de la Briderie at **Monteaux**, west of Chaumont, where a characterful barn has been converted into a tasting and reception room, or the Domaine de Lusqueneau up in Mesland, where modern equipment dominates in the vat house, although some of the buildings date back to the 11th century.

As to the Cisse river north of the Loire, it 'slithers like a silvery snake through the meadow grasses', as Balzac poetically put it. The Cisse is so diminutive that you'd think it might have an inferiority complex when compared with its majestic neighbour, but in fact has developed a delightful character all of its own. While the N152 road offers grand views of the Loire along its way, the D58 and D1 along the Cisse are calmer and more charming. The pocket-sized French country vegetable plots of yesteryear still thrive here, flowers too grown in rows. The hillsides are peppered with caves. Past the concentration camp for poultry at Cangey (well known for rearing the fowl), **Limeray**'s peeling-whitewashed church interior is lined with an impressive array of statues, collected together by a priest in the 19th century. **Pocé-sur-Cisse** and **Nazelles-Négron** have characterful village churches before you reach Amboise.

Amboise, Cradle of French Renaissance Royalty

French towns don't come more royal than Amboise, and its dominating château remains in would-be French royal hands today. The place makes a splendid sight seen from the north bank of the Loire. Along with Saumur, in Anjou, Amboise is the most typical old limestone town on the very banks of the great river. A row of riverside houses runs along the foot of the massive château ramparts. These defences look austere to say the least, protecting a plateau above the town on which the remnants of the château stand, a line of typical Loire *lucarnes* ornamenting the roof overlooking the river. A large proportion of this once-vast royal castle has disappeared, but it still makes a fine impression, flags flying from the battlements.

Few French towns receive more Italian tourists than Amboise. This is in good part because Leonardo da Vinci spent the last three years of his life here. But Amboise is also where King Charles VIII, the first French king to invade Renaissance Italy, brought home his booty, even if these riches have long since been carted off elsewhere. After Charles VIII, the Château d'Amboise served as one of the principal residences of a string of French Renaissance kings and princes. It was that collector extraordinaire, King François I, who paid for Leonardo to come to Amboise and sit in attendance. Leonardo lived in the manor of the Clos Lucé, but was buried in the château's collegiate church. The church has disappeared. However, Amboise retains the genius' bones.

Amboise Before the Royals

Early man occupied the well-located, easily defended plateau above the Loire at Amboise. It seems that there was a Neolithic settlement here. Later, some of the Celtic Turones tribe made their home on the spot. Then a Gallo-Roman community developed. The plateau overlooks l'Ile d'Or, the Golden Isle, in the middle of the river. This is where, in 503, the Frankish King Clovis is supposed to have met with the Visigoth leader Alaric II to sign a peace 'for all time'. The story goes that they shook each other by the goatee beard, seemingly settling the disputes between them. A couple of years later Clovis slew Alaric near Poitiers.

Viking *drakkars* travelled up the Loire in the second half of the 9th century, terrifying the locals, the Norsemen pillaging Amboise several times. French counts then fought for supremacy over the region, and for a time the fiefdom fell to Ingelger, count of Anjou. Amboise became a divided town, however, when château and plateau came into the hands of the Amboise family, while the town became the property of the Buzançais.

The most successfully bellicose of the early medieval Loire feudal lords, Foulques Nerra of Anjou, swept in to take control. Around 1030 he built one keep here in his great ring of Touraine fortifications, as well as a collegiate church dedicated to St Florentin. Direct Angevin control came to an end in 1107, however, when Hugues I of Amboise and Chaumont became master of both château and town, his descendants maintaining their dominance until 1422. It then fell to a viscount of Thouars, who became Louis d'Amboise and fought against the English in the Hundred Years' War, notably supporting Joan of Arc. Unfortunately for him, he was also implicated in a plot against La Trémoïlle, favourite of King Charles VII. His life was spared but he was forced to hand over Amboise to the Crown in 1431 as a forfeit.

This is how the place acquired its royal owners. For the next century and a half, its château developed into a major centre for the peripatetic French royal family, and for lines of French royal children in particular.

Château d'Amboise

Open July–Aug 9–7; April–June 9–6.30; Sept–1 Nov and 15–31 Mar 9–6; Feb–14 Mar 9–12 and 2–5.30; 2 Nov–15 Nov 9–5.30; 16 Nov–Jan 9–12 and 2–4.45; t 02 47 57 00 98, chateau.amboise@wunuduu.fr; adm.

French would-be royalty is still just about alive and it owns the Château d'Amboise, under the guise of the Fondation St-Louis. Its head is the new Comte de Paris, who took over after his ancient father died in 1999, leaving something of an inheritance scandal behind him. The line descends from the Orléans branch of the Bourbon royal family; Louis-Philippe, their ancestor, was the last king of France, playing the part from 1830 until 1848, the latter being another French revolutionary year, one in which the king was forced to flee to Britain under the subtle pseudonym of 'Mr Smith'. The house of Orléans royal branch regained their French possessions, including Amboise, later in the 19th century, only to be expelled from France by a paranoid Republican government in the 1870s. The royal pretenders were only allowed to return in the 1950s. They do have controversial rival challengers to the throne, the Spanish Bourbon branch, but for the moment it doesn't look as if the French people are quite ready to accept any monarch back onto the throne, preferring to take an interest in the soap opera lives of the British and Monegasque royals presented to them in the popular press.

The royal presence at Amboise is discreet nowadays, but at one stage in French history the château became the animated centre of the French royals' life. Unfortunately, most of the sumptuous wings of the château that went up for them during the 15th and 16th centuries have vanished. The remnants, although impressive, can only impart a very partial picture of the grandeur of the place at its height, which witnessed many great events.

The First French Royals at Amboise – Charles VII and Louis XI

As the first royal to own the place after he had confiscated the old château in 1431, King Charles VII, although he held court principally in Chinon and Loches, did take some interest in the new stronghold, having the fortifications reinforced. Succeeding in 1461, King Louis XI chose Plessis-lès-Tours, just outside Tours, as his main residence. However, he developed Amboise into a castle much more befitting royalty, and it became one of the main centres of royal life. Louis ordered many developments to create a pentagon of defences around the sides of the plateau. For instance, a new Logis Royal on the southwestern side was completed by 1465, although it has now completely disappeared. In 1469, Louis retired to Amboise to work out the terms of peace after his humiliating defeat by the formidably independent duchy of Burgundy, then ruled by his relative and enemy Charles le Téméraire (the Fearless). That same year, in a much more positive act for the French monarchy, Louis established the

The Order of St Michael

The Ordre de St-Michel was to be a very select club, the most important clique in the French kingdom, with only 36 members, the king at its head, the knights of the order pledging their allegiance to him. The aim, while honouring these powerful vassals, was to unite them in their support for the French Crown and Church through flattery and favour at a time when several regions of what is now France were still fiercely autonomous, even if their nominal overlord was the king of France. The Order became one of the instruments by which Louis XI succeeded in cementing the French regions to the central kingdom.

The symbol of this exclusive chivalric society was a specially created gold chain of shells, with an effigy of St Michael, patron saint of France, killing the dragon. The Mont-St-Michel off Normandy and Brittany became the home for the order and its first chapter was held there, but it was instituted at Amboise and many meetings took place in the château here. The Order became slightly less exclusive in time, counting some 500 members by the start of the Wars of Religion, during which King Henri III decided to found the Ordre du Saint-Esprit as a much more select little grouping once more. These Orders lasted until the Revolution, and were briefly revived with the restoration of the French monarchy after Napoleon's come-uppance.

knightly order of St-Michel (see box) in Amboise's chapel of St-Florentin. Louis XI chose the Château d'Amboise as a place of safety for his wife Queen Charlotte to bring up the royal children. She stayed here pretty well permanently to look after them, while Louis travelled around on affairs of state and warring campaigns. The Château d'Amboise was the secure childhood home of his heir, the future King Charles VIII, born in the palace in 1470. Louis would become increasingly paranoid through his reign and was immensely protective towards his son. Those permitted to visit the castle and even the town were carefully vetted. Devoted servants were put in charge of Charles' education, notably Jean Bourré, Seigneur du Plessis (see p.168), who sent Louis regular reports on his progress.

Louis occasionally returned to the family home, in 1476 accompanied by a royal mistress on each arm, La Passe-Fillon and La Gigonne, two conquests from a visit to Lyon. They were set up in apartments in the château; it was quite normal for French kings to have mistresses. The queen didn't entertain greatly in the king's absence, but it can hardly be said that she lived frugally, having a budget of 37,000 livres for her housekeeping in one typical year – a huge amount. Rich materials and tapestries on classical themes embellished the castle's chambers. As well as having an extravagant penchant for shoes, Queen Charlotte liked her books, gathering together a rare collection of more than 100 manuscripts, including not only pious works, but also ones debating the role of women in society, such as Alain Chartier's *Débat de quatre dames* and Christine de Pisan's *Cité des dames*.

Louis reared his son carefully for kingship. Meanwhile, he paired off his daughters in politically arranged marriages, as was the way in those times. The eldest, Anne, was wedded to the influential figure Pierre de Beaujeu, a mere 21 years her senior. Another daughter, Jeanne, bright but severely crippled, was early betrothed to her royal cousin

Louis d'Orléans, her father thereby hoping to put an end to a potentially fractious rival line, imagining that Jeanne and Louis would never be able to have children.

King Charles VIII Rebuilds Amboise and Takes On Brittany and Italy

In 1482, important lords of the land gathered at Amboise to hear Louis XI lecture his heir Charles on his duties towards the realm and his subjects. The following year, the boy was formally engaged here to Marguerite d'Autriche, daughter of the Holy Roman Emperor Maximilian. If Charles was young, Marguerite was barely out of infancy. At three and a half years of age, she was known as '*la petite reine*' and was brought up at Amboise. Such early arrangements and preparations for royal marriages were commonplace at the time.

Louis XI died in 1483 and Anne de Beaujeu assumed the regency until the following year, when Charles turned 14, the age at which French kings were allowed to assume power. Charles wouldn't marry Marguerite, however. Brittany, an important independent duchy west of Anjou, had long been a thorn in the side of the French realm. The councillors of Anne de Bretagne, the young, ugly, but very desirable heir to the duchy, were organizing her marriage to the Holy Roman Emperor himself. Charles VIII's side, pursuing his father's campaigns to unify a greater France, saw the opportunity for bringing Brittany under royal control by getting Charles to marry Anne de Bretagne. He and his men went fully armed into her province to persuade her party to change her marriage arrangements, and Anne was in effect forced to accept Charles' hand. As to the young Marguerite d'Autriche, still not in her teens, she was sent packing tearfully back to Flanders with a heavy gold chain as consolation from the French king.

Work began on altering the Château d'Amboise as the 15th century came to a close. Having spent his childhood there, Charles VIII was deeply attached to the place, and under him it was to become the most favoured royal residence. He wanted something grandiose, and the plans were inevitably expensive. The building was financed by raising an additional levy on the existing hated salt tax, the *gabelle*, and started in 1492. The two first wings to be completed were the one you still see overlooking the Loire, flanked on one side by the enormous Tour des Minimes, and the wing on the opposite side of the courtyard, overlooking the Amasse valley, the arcaded Logis des Sept Vertus. This wing was named after statues adorning its façades – it has disappeared, save the massive Tour Heurtault matching the Tour des Minimes.

Hundreds of workers, especially stonemasons, were employed on the site and the accounts show that they even worked by candlelight through the winter, sometimes needing to make fires to unfreeze the building blocks. Charles VIII went on a great shopping spree for his new château, buying vast tapestry cycles which depicted Old Testament, classical and traditional French chivalric scenes. Also on display were magnificent arms and armour, including Joan of Arc's suit, the swords of several French kings, a dagger of Charlemagne, a weapon belonging to King Dagobert, Clovis' axe and Lancelot's sword, history becoming somewhat confused with legend in the typical medieval way! It's just a shame that all these precious objects have vanished.

On the self-guided visit round the château, you can admire the two enormous towers still standing from Charles VIII's time, the **Tour des Minimes** and the **Tour**

Charles VIII, His Italian Adventures, His Courtly Life at Amboise, and his Banal Death There

Very few signs of Renaissance architecture and decoration made it into Charles VIII's building programme at Amboise. But as it was underway, he set out on the first in a line of hot-headed French royal forays into Italy, which changed the course of French history, architecture and the arts, as successive monarchs tried to assert their inheritance claims there. Charles may have been seduced by Italy, but he didn't exactly woo it; he ravished it. In Charles' first Italian campaign of 1494–5, he and his troops may have captured the kingdom of Naples, but they were lucky to escape with their lives after being trapped at Fornovo on the way back. Some of the loot they had amassed, including castle gates and stained glass, was stopped from leaving the peninsula, but another load which did get through from Naples to Amboise in 1496 included 130 tapestries, 172 carpets, sculptures in marble and porphyry, and over 1,000 manuscripts from the king of Aragon's collection. Much of the art was destined to decorate the Château d'Amboise's Logis des Sept Vertus.

Charles didn't come back with booty alone. He also imported men. Among the group of around 20 Italians to come to France in his train were the famous architects Domenico da Cortona and Fra Giocondo, a scholar of Greek and a sculptor, along with couturiers, a gardener and a Moor to pamper the king's parrots! And so the refinements of the Italian Renaissance entered France. The history books have ascribed huge cultural significance to this first French royal adventure in Italy, which transformed the ways of the French monarchy and aristocracy, creating the French Renaissance of the 16th century. But these Renaissance influences arrived too late to much affect the Château d'Amboise's expansion under Charles VIII.

Records give a taste of what the royal daily life here was like under Charles VIII. After the serious attendance of Mass and the council on state affairs, much of the rest of an ordinary day would be given over to games. Dice, cards and chess were very

Heurtault. Rather than being purely defensive, these were in fact extravagant entrances, with wide spiralling ramps leading up from the valley to the plateau. Horses and even carriages could comfortably ascend this way.

The beautiful **chapelle St-Hubert**, another building from Charles VIII's time, has also survived. This jewel box of a chapel sits precariously on the edge of the fortifications. It's a delightful work from the late Gothic period, topped by a needle of a spire visible from afar. The lintel above the entrance depicts the legends of St Anthony, St Christopher and St Hubert (*see* Château de Gien, p.92, for an explanation of the last). The beautiful carving was executed by Flemish sculptors. Above, the tympanum was filled in in the 19th century with sculptures representing Charles VIII and Anne de Bretagne kneeling before the Virgin and Child. Inside, among the wealth of curling tracery, if you look hard you can make out little carved animals, such as serpents, toads and bats, concealed in the stone. The dinky fireplaces in the minute transepts show the comforts royalty allowed themselves even in prayer. The stained glass is by that prolific 20th-century artist Max Ingrand, made busy after the shocks from Second World War bombs destroyed so much of the older decoration. The life of

much the fashion among the courtiers, although the king disliked these pastimes, apparently beaten too many times by his sister Anne when he was a boy. The *jeu de paume*, or real (as in royal) tennis was more to his taste, along with falconry. Hunting was a great favourite, but it seems that the kings would be led astray by more than the wild animals they were out to capture. Anne de Bretagne is supposed to have accompanied Charles on long hunts even when she was pregnant, to check that if the party had to stay away from home the king shouldn't be tempted by a hostess's overgenerous hospitality. Animals of all sorts fascinated French royalty in this period. Pets were doted on. Rare animals were cherished, and lions were kept in the ditch on the château's plateau. Meanwhile, the fashion for monkeys was just taking off.

The king had two personal confessors and the same astrologer as his father, consulted for all important events as to the most propitious day on which to hold them. In painting, Jean Perréal and Jean Bourdichon continued to prepare royal portraits after Jean Fouquet. Poetry and reading were also pastimes, often singing the praises of noble princes, but sometimes being more bawdy in tone. Easter and May were the times for the colourful jousts.

A couple of Italians were commissioned to write the official chronicles of Charles VIII's reign, while Philippe de Commynes (or Comines) kept his diaries in secret. He records the bathos of Charles VIII's death. After all the care that had been taken to protect the king as a young man, after all the foolhardiness of his Italian campaigns, one day in 1498 in the midst of all the frivolous court entertainment, Charles bumped his head in Amboise castle's Haquelebac gallery overlooking the real tennis court, in a passageway where '*tout le monde pissait*' (we don't think you require a translation for that). The king got up and continued to talk on religious subjects, having recently entered something of a pious phase in his life. But he quickly collapsed again and lay on the ground in the same spot for some nine hours, only regaining consciousness three times to call upon God and his beloved saints before dying from a final stroke.

St Louis, alias pious, crusading King Louis IX, is recounted in these windows. A simple plaque in the chapel commemorates Leonardo da Vinci, whose bones were transferred here after the chapel of St-Florent was destroyed in the 19th century.

In fact, curiously, it was in Napoleonic times that much of the Château d'Amboise was destroyed. But the remaining **Charles VIII wing** has been beautifully restored and embellished in recent years, even if it looks over-scrubbed in some parts. You visit the guards' quarters first, with a sober vaulted room furnished with Gothic-style furniture and late 16th-century Aubusson tapestries. The walkway from here gives onto the Loire, an excellent viewing post. The palm vaulting of the Salle des Gardes Nobles is striking, while two 16th-century Milanese coats of armour stand empty guard. Above, the flooring in the Salle des Tambourineurs is stamped with fleurs-de-lys and leads to the superb council chamber with its double row of vaulted bays. The light central columns are flecked with fleurs-de-lys and ermine tails, the latter the symbol of Charles VIII's wife Anne. Try deciphering the amusing restored Gothic sculpture in the room. The four seasons are depicted down the central capitals. Some of the stone carvings illustrate proverbs, the big ears in one corner reminding courtiers of the fact that walls have ears! One Renaissance detail at least has crept in here, the marble medallion of Alexander the Great over one of the room's fireplaces.

Louis d'Orléans, married to Charles VIII's crippled sister Jeanne de France, succeeded to the throne as Louis XII after Charles' fatal accident at Amboise (*see* box p.235), as Charles and Anne de Bretagne had no heir. He immediately rid himself of the handicap that his wife represented to his ambitions. This was made relatively easy by the fact that Louis' marriage to Jeanne was unconsummated, and that Charles VIII, in his marriage contract with Anne, had stipulated that, in the case of their having no heir, she should be obliged to marry his successor. Louis took Anne to Blois – he was deeply attached to the château there, the place where his father had held court, and scarcely wanted to live in Charles VIII's shadow.

King François I at Amboise

The Château d'Amboise wasn't entirely neglected, though, and the second half of the château tour takes you into what's known as the **Louis XII-François I wing**, although it would be more appropriate to call it the Louise de Savoie wing. Louis XII gave Amboise to her and her children, François and Marguerite d'Angoulême, important figures in the royal circle. Louise herself had been brought up in part at the château by her aunt Anne de Beaujeu. In 1488 she had married Charles d'Angoulême of the Orléans royal branch. Much older than her, he died in 1496. But, vitally, by then she had had children by him. So long as Louis XII and Anne de Bretagne remained without male heir, Louise's son François stood first in line to inherit the French throne. A new wing was built on to the Château d'Amboise for Louise and her children.

From the outside, you can see how the upper part of its façade, heavily restored, bears the influences of the Renaissance. Compare, for example, the window decoration of this wing with that on the Charles VIII wing, this one with its Italianate columns, stylized capitals and pilasters. Within, many excellent pieces of furniture decorate the rooms, now beamed rather than vaulted.

The first chamber, the Salle de l'Echanson, contains pieces of furniture on which food would be placed and tasted, and extendable tables in the newly imported Italian fashion. The tapestries are 17th-century Aubusson works, the bold scenes made after cartoons by Le Brun. The Henri II chamber plunges you further into the Renaissance, with its very ornate bed sporting columns and pilasters and carved detail. Two great chairs show early examples of trompe-l'œil perspectival carving. More symbols of royalty and Brittany have been added around the window, as well as a symbolic pilgrim's staff and purse. The last period room is the Passage de la Cordelière. The fireplace is decorated with looping Franciscan chords, symbols of Anne de Bretagne's piety. Around the shield, the shell necklace is that of the Order of St Michel. The salamander on the wood panel above refers to François I, who came back to the Château d'Amboise for some very grand celebrations once he had become king (*see* box, p.xxx).

The French Wars of Religion and the Decline of Amboise

Monumental events were occurring in Germany at the start of François I's reign. Luther's devastating criticisms of the Catholic Church, its traditions and corruption,

François d'Angoulême's Golden Childhood

The venerated Italian priest François de Paule had been called by Louis XI to his deathbed. After the king passed away, de Paule stayed on to serve in the spiritual guidance of the French royal family. He apparently predicted to Louise de Savoie in 1489 that she would have a son who would become king of France.

François was born in 1494. Louise arranged for her children to have the finest education possible at Amboise. This went not just for François but also for his elder sister, Marguerite d'Angoulême. François was taught Latin and Italian, history and law. The château's library contained a rich collection of imaginative works which François later moved to Fontainebleau and which would go on to constitute one of the great founding collections of France's national library, the Bibliothèque Nationale. The boy's lessons in ethics were taught him by François du Moulin, who wrote down his instruction in the form of a book, the *Dialogue entre un jeune homme et son confesseur*. His sporting education was also carefully overseen and he was surrounded by boys of his own age to play with, first at ball games, then in hunting and mock battles. François was turning into a formidable but fun-loving figure. His extremely bright sister, Marguerite, went on to write the celebrated *Heptaméron*, following in Boccacio's style of story-telling. One of the tales relates how a prince (generally interpreted as her brother) came to the house of a beautiful lady who had stirred his passions to such an extent that he deliberately fell from his horse into the mud in front of her abode, just to be allowed into her house to be cleaned up and dressed in fresh clothes.

In 1507 François de Paule died. The mourning Louise de Savoie sent money to Rome to have him canonized, which happened in 1519. Meanwhile, in 1508, François was engaged to Claude de France, daughter of Louis XII and Anne de Bretagne. He left the Château d'Amboise for the court at the Château de Blois and began planning his real war games in Italy. Amboise for a time felt deserted to Louise and she abandoned it.

were rocking religious stability in Europe. Then the Holy Roman Emperor Maximilian I died in 1519, leaving the competition open for his succession. Massive amounts of money were spent in promoting their causes by Charles I of Spain, Henry VIII of England and François I of France. Charles won the contest. From this time on, François spent less and less time at Amboise, almost always on the move. But he would occasionally stay here. On the morning of 18 October 1534, while staying at Amboise, he woke up to find a pamphlet stuck to his door. It contained a stinging attack on the meaning of the Mass. The troubles of the Reformation had been spreading through France. The French king, defender of the Catholic faith, had remained moderate in his views towards the Protestants up until now. But such irreverent gall in an episode which became known as the Affaire des Placards (*placards* here meaning pamphlets, not cupboards) enraged him, and he decided to take action against the Huguenots. The persecution of the French Protestants was underway. This led to the terrible Wars of Religion which split the country in two during the second half of the 16th century. In the turmoil, the Château d'Amboise became a safe haven for bringing up the French royal children.

Courtly Celebrations at the Château d'Amboise

On his succession to the French throne in 1515, François I decided to retake the Milanese area, captured by Louis XII, but then won by the Holy Roman Emperor Maximilian. While he waited for the army to be prepared, François came to Amboise to hold great festivities.

Two major events were to be celebrated on 26 June 1515. First, François' wife Claude officially signed over her rights to the duchy of Milan to her husband, giving him the legitimate excuse to attack. Second, a very grand aristocratic marriage between Duke Antoine de Lorraine and Renée de Bourbon-Montpensier, sister of Duke Charles de Bourbon, Constable of France, was to take place here.

For the double celebration, the king sent for a wild boar to provide the entertainment within the château walls. The young show-off at first wished to take on the creature one-to-one to demonstrate his prowess. His wife and mother managed to put a stop to this foolhardy idea. Instead, dummies were placed in the courtyard for the enraged animal to attack. Pierre Sala, who had recorded royal events since Louis XI's time and would amass his stories in *Les Prouesses de plusieurs roys*, takes on the tale as the wild beast has pushed aside a barricade and ended up in the royal apartments: 'he [the king] wanted to wait for the boar alone and did so with the same total assurance as though he had been watching a young woman coming towards him'. The little scene turns into an heroic episode, the violent boar making for the king, the sovereign maintaining his poise, stabbing the creature to death. Three days later François I was off to conquer Milan.

It was in 1516 that Leonardo da Vinci came to live the last few years of his life at Amboise, persuaded to move to the French courtly town by François and his generous

As was the productive way in those times, Catherine de' Medici gave birth to ten children between 1544 and 1556. Although all of them were born outside the Loire, they all spent time being educated at the Château d'Amboise, where the air was considered particularly healthy and the surroundings safe. Their parents, even when they came to visit them, had little time to spare for them, what with the councils, diplomatic receptions and balls that followed in quick succession. The children were hardly neglected though. An army of attendants looked after them.

Diane de Poitiers, King Henri II's most famous mistress, played a significant role in overseeing the royal children. It wasn't just Henri II's legitimate children who were brought up at the château. Another Diane, a bastard royal daughter by Filippa Duci, six years older than the dauphin, also received her education here. Then in 1548 the six-year-old Mary Stuart arrived from Scotland, her hand promised to the future king of France. Her beautiful governess set Henri II alight again; the son they had, Henri d'Angoulême, had soon joined the numbers in this warren of a château. The great court painter of the period, François Clouet, was also occasionally sent down to Amboise. Beyond this innocent Amboise of pampered royal childhood, as Henri II's reign progressed, the troubles with the Protestant factions were growing out of hand, as was their persecution. By the end of his rule France was ready to slide into civil war. The bloody precursor, the Conjuration d'Amboise, occurred in and around the town.

terms. Further staggering celebrations were held in the castle in 1517 and 1518, and Leonardo may have played an important part in their organization. On 17 January 1517, the date of the anniversary of the Order of St Michael, not only was the inauguration of new members confirmed in the Chapelle St-Florentin and a joust held, but there was also the added violent attraction of an extraordinary animal fight. This time a lion was pitted against three huge hounds. Such was the aggression of the dogs' attack that they had to be pulled away from the lion to stop its being torn apart.

In April and May 1518 two particularly important events were to be marked, the joy of the baptism of the newly born Dauphin (or royal heir), also named François, and the deeply significant marriage of Lorenzo de' Medici to the very rich heiress, Madeleine de la Tour d'Auvergne. This Lorenzo de' Medici was a grandson of Lorenzo the Magnificent and nephew of Pope Leo X, whom he represented as godfather to the new French royal baby. He brought with him from Italy splendid works of art to honour the royal parents, including two Raphaels, the Holy Family for Claude, St Michael for the proud father (these paintings are now in the Louvre). After the baptism, ten days of celebration were given over to the wedding. Fleuranges, a great companion of François I, recorded the event, adding in a charming touch that Madeleine had married not just the Duke or Urbino, 'but with him the pox which he had freshly acquired' – many a prince who spread his liberalities wide was rewarded with a case of venereal disease, and in this period the king of France officially paid for a train of filles de joie to follow the court around. Lorenzo's wife would soon become pregnant; in April of the following year, Madeleine gave birth in Florence to Catherine de' Medici, to become the notorious queen of France when she married François' second son and eventual successor, Henri.

After the appalling period around the Amboise Conspiracy, the Château d'Amboise was more or less abandoned by royalty. For a time under the control of Louis XIII's brother Gaston d'Orléans, it was confiscated from him. As with many other Loire châteaux, it then served as a gaol – Louis XIV's finance minister Fouquet was briefly imprisoned here after he was accused of corruption on a massive scale. Napoleon's friend Pierre-Roger Ducos had most of the castle dismantled in the early 19th century.

In 1821 the future King Louis-Philippe regained royal possession of what remained, and some work was carried out to make this into a royal summer residence. The style changes completely in the **Louis-Philippe rooms** you visit on the first floor of the Louis XII wing. Rich red walls and drapery serve as the backdrop to royal family portraits, executed with the crisp stylization of Winterhalter, among others. Extremely elegant Restoration or Louis-Philippe furniture enriches the rooms still further, with a notable Récamier-style bed, its mahogany front decorated with delicate bronze work. From these apartments you can go out onto the roof of the Tour des Minimes for one of the most memorable views onto the Loire.

After Louis-Philippe fled into exile, the château served as a prison for a period, for example housing the Algerian chief Abd El-Kadr, who had tried to resist the French colonialists. Later in the century, what remained of the great royal castle was restored by Victor and Gabriel Ruprich-Robert. So much of the Château d'Amboise's architecture

The Amboise Conspiracy

By 1558, the dauphin François and Mary Queen of Scots were married. A year later the boy became King François II, after his father had died from a wound accidentally inflicted on him by one of his Scots guards in a jousting tournament. François II's reign was to be a short-lived, and ill-fated for Mary too. Mary's overbearing uncles, the de Guises (see Blois) had amassed considerable power for the Catholic cause. Through Mary, a much more powerful character than her sickly husband, they had become the controlling force in French politics. There were many Protestant sympathizers in high places, however. The most powerful were the Bourbons: Antoine, king of the little region of Navarre near Spain, and his brother Louis, Prince de Condé. They were outraged at the influence the de Guises had acquired at court. On their side stood Gaspard de Coligny, admiral of France. A major plot was hatched by Condé in 1559. The aim was to capture the de Guises from the royal court and put an end to their stranglehold on affairs of state. The main backing for this plot came from the disgruntled lesser nobles, the *gentilshommes*, led by Jean du Barry, lord of La Renaudie. He soon gathered a large number of supporters.

The Conjuration d'Amboise might be described as France's foreshadowing of England's Gunpowder Plot, but played out in reverse. In this case, Huguenots aimed to overthrow the controlling ultra-Catholic de Guises, it's said with the support of Protestant England. Arms depots for the rebels were set up at Tours, Orléans and Châteaudun. Initially, the plan was to capture the de Guises at the Château de Blois, some time between 6 and 10 March. But the de Guises were on the look out for trouble. And La Renaudie was too indiscreet. He confided the dates to des Avenelles, a Paris lawyer on the Protestant side, but who then switched allegiance. Des Avenelles informed the de Guise party of the plot and an extraordinary period of paranoia ensued.

The king had been out hunting with the court around the Loire. It was decided to retreat to the stronghold of the Château d'Amboise. The de Guises told François to summon Condé and Coligny to the château to persuade them to disassociate themselves from the conspirators. Only Coligny came. Already a little earlier in the decade he had met with Catherine de' Medici at Blois to work on an edict of pacification

has disappeared, but you can muse on the significance of this royal castle while wandering around the gardens, parts of which are now being transformed to reflect their original Renaissance design, or descending the monumental but finely decorated Tour Heurtault, offering some irreverent late-Gothic imagery, light relief after so much talk of serious royal goings-on, including one figure scratching its backside.

A Walk Around Amboise

Amboise grew fat at the château's feet. The town supplied the court with its vast needs and picked up the crumbs from its elevated table. Courtiers settled here, as did fine craftsmen, and some splendid town houses remain. Those along **Rue Victor Hugo**, running parallel to the formidable ramp you have to take to visit the château, are now

between the rival factions. This was now worked on again, and a declaration was issued that Protestants who peacefully agreed to live on Catholic terms would go unharmed. But the atmosphere of fear mounted as 6 March approached. Light relief was sought in a *bal travesti* in the gardens of the Château d'Amboise. When the dreaded day arrived, a Spanish ambassador at court described the trepidation at Amboise being 'as great as though there were an army at the gates'. The whole household was armed to the teeth. Nothing happened, and a few days later the king went out hunting again. However, a further rebel defected from the Protestant side, and disclosed that a new date for the attack had been set for 15 March. He also revealed that many of the conspirators were gathering at the Château de Noizay, on the north bank of the Loire close to Amboise. This time the de Guise faction moved. Noizay was surrounded and the conspirators there captured.

On news of this blow, La Renaudie acted rashly. He ordered the scattered rebel troops to converge on Amboise, but without giving them a coherent plan. Arriving in dribs and drabs, they were easily captured. Condé, sensing trouble, had responded to the king's invitation and arrived at Amboise on 16 March. But the very next day an attack was launched on the town by the Huguenots. Rumour did its worst and the court thought that thousands of Protestants were at the gates. They didn't know that there were in fact just a couple of hundred outside, mounting a rather pathetic attack. Once they had been eradicated, the king's response was to name François de Guise lieutentant-general of France and to hand over to him the task of the suppression and punishment of the rebels.

Executions followed in nauseating waves at Amboise. It was written that the de Guises planned executions after dinner 'to give some entertainment to the ladies whom they saw getting bored having to stay for so long in this place'. La Renaudie was early captured and killed. His body was prominently displayed in town, hanging for a day before being chopped into five parts, one placed over each town gate. Other conspirators were tied up in sacks and thrown into the Loire to drown. The most famous image from the suppression of the Huguenots at Amboise is of bodies being left to hang from the château's battlements. The end of the Amboise Conspiracy was a very gory preface to the dreadful decades of the French Wars of Religion.

crammed with cafés, restaurants and shops; tourists have replaced the courtiers as the source of Amboise's revenue. Burrowed into the walls under the ramp, **Les Vignerons d'Amboise** offers a cave of a space where local winemakers present their production on a rota basis.

Approaching the river from the castle's ramp, the **Hôtel de Ville**, or town hall, looks out over the Loire. This grand town house of the early 16th-century went up for the then mayor of Tours. It contains some beautiful works of art, including Aubusson tapestries from the Château de Chanteloup and the statue of the Virgin which used to grace the Tour de l'Horloge. On the other side of the street rises the late medieval **church of St-Florentin**. Commissioned by Louis XI, it was formerly known as Notre-Dame-en-Grève (on-the-riverbank). Inside, it has been rendered unrecognisable by 19th-century restoration work, while it was given modern glass after the war.

Getting There and Around

Amboise is easy to reach, an important stop on the **train** line between Tours and Paris-Austerlitz passing via Orléans and Blois. You can also get **buses** from Tours to Amboise.

Tourist Information

Amboise: B.P.233, Quai du Général de Gaulle, 37402 Amboise Cedex, **t** 02 47 57 09 28, *www.amboise-valdeloire.com*.

Market Days

Amboise: Friday and Sunday morning.

Where to Stay

Amboise ✉ 37400
★★★★Le Choiseul, 36 Quai Charles Guinot, **t** 02 47 30 45 45, *www.le-choiseul.com* (*expensive*). This luxury hotel and restaurant by the Loire roadside, just east of the centre, is packed with interesting things. Its well-maintained gardens back on to the limestone hillside which contains superb former grain stores, the so-called **Greniers de César**, a tourist sight in themselves; contemporary art exhibitions are held in them April–Oct. The rooms in the neat 18th-century building are extremely comfortable and intimate. The cuisine is highly regarded – lunch menus are more reasonable than evening ones (*menus c.€46–80*). There's a pool in the grounds. *Closed mid-Dec–early Feb.*

★★★★Le Manoir Les Minimes, 34 Quai Charles Guinot, **t** 02 47 30 40 40, *www.manoir-lesminimes.com* (*expensive; closed Sun mid-Nov–mid-Mar*). Le Choiseul's immediate neighbour and rival, this beautiful, recently opened hotel occupies an 18th-century house built on the site of a convent founded by King Charles VIII just below the château. The first floor has superb suites, the second floor very smart rooms under the eaves (*no restaurant*). *Closed 1–19 Feb.*

★★★Le Clos d'Amboise, 27 Rue Rabelais, **t** 02 47 30 10 20, *www.leclosamboise.com* (*moderate*). Smart new hotel in a grand old 17th-century townhouse with spacious formal garden and pool. *Closed mid-Nov–mid-Mar.*

Take the Loire bridge opposite the town hall, and you can get onto the **Ile d'Or**, from which you can appreciate splendid views of the château, particularly from beside the rather silly bronze statue of a naked Leonardo, posing like an artistic river god. It is possible to go canoeing from the island; contact **Le Club de Canoë-Kayak** (*open all year, daily exc Sun and Mon in winter, t 02 47 23 26 52*).

Back on the town side of the Loire, the walk along the river bank is a favourite with the people of Amboise at weekends. Head west and you'll pass the **Max Ernst fountain**, a comical piece by the celebrated surrealist, featuring turtles and frogs. Ernst was helped to become a French citizen in 1958 by the then mayor of Amboise and leading politician Michel Debré – the Debré family political dynasty is still strongly associated with the town. Parallel to the riverside road, you can join Amboise's main shopping street, the **Rue Nationale**, from below the castle's ramp by walking under the impressive 14th-century **Porte de l'Horloge** topped by a late medieval belfry. You'll find a good range of shops along the street, including Loire et Terroir, specializing in regional produce. On the slope beyond this street, visit the **Collégiale St-Denis**, with elaborately carved capitals and a realistic 16th-century recumbent figure, said by some to be Marie Babou, a mistress of François I, who drowned in the Loire.

It's quite a long walk from the centre of town to Leonardo's last home, the Clos Lucé. Signs indicate the shortest way. Heading southwards, you could meander through the quiet old streets admiring ancient mansions. The large, pleasing **Place Richelieu** is

Le Blason, 11 Place Richelieu, **t 02 47 23 22 41, *www.leblason.fr* (*inexpensive*). A pretty timberframe and limestone building overlooking a busy square south of the centre, but some of the rooms could do with renovation. *Closed mid-Jan–mid-Feb.*

Chargé ✉ 37400

****Château de Pray, **t** 02 47 57 23 67, *www.chateauxhotels.com/pray* (*expensive*). A thoroughly delightful and intriguing little château just east along the Loire from Amboise, with a wonderful garden laid out on terraces over the Loire. The interior decoration is stylish, both in the rooms and in the splendid dining room. Pigeon in acacia honey sounds the appropriate kind of speciality for such a setting (*menus €28–50*). The place has a heated swimming pool. *Closed 2 Jan–mid-Feb.*

Lussault-sur-Loire ✉ 37400

Château de Pintray B&B, **t** 02 47 23 22 84, *marius.rault@wanadoo.fr* (*expensive*). This is a distinguished centuries-old winemakers' property south of Lussault along the D751. It

makes for a peaceful stop, and has woods as well as vineyards.

Eating Out

L'Epicerie, 46 Place M. Debré, **t** 02 47 57 08 94 (*menus €18–35; closed Mon and Tues Oct–June*). Set in a lovely timberframe house close to the intimidating ramp up the side of the château, this restaurant serves classic, reliably good and relatively good-value dishes.

La Table Riche Lieu, 14 Rue Joyeuse, **t** 02 47 57 69 79 (*€14–23*). Good traditional restaurant beside the Blason hotel. *Closed Tues, and Wed lunch, and Jan.*

Pâtisserie Bigot/Le Fournil, Place Michel Debré, **t** 02 47 57 04 46. Elegant, old-fashioned, proudly family-run pâtisserie which tempts you inside with its chocolate and cake displays, but you can also sit down to enjoy a savoury tart, a cake or a home-made ice cream. The cocoa specialities include the *ambroisines*, filled with Touraine grape liqueur. *Open daily Easter–All Saints' Day 9–7.30; rest of year Tues–Sun.*

presided over not only by a pompous statue of the interfering 17th-century cardinal, but also by a bad rendering of the royal painter Jean Fouquet.

Château du Clos Lucé

*Open July–Aug 9–8; late Mar–June and Sept–Oct 9–7; Feb–late Mar and Nov–Dec 9–6; Jan 10–5; **t** 02 47 57 00 73, www.vinci-closluce.com; adm.*

Don't expect any great art by Leonardo da Vinci at the Clos Lucé. The house is very fine, though. Originally constructed in 1477 for a royal forest warden, Etienne Le Loup, it was bought by King Charles VIII for his wife Anne de Bretagne to have a quiet retreat to which she could retire to pray in peace; a pretty oratory was added for her. François I then donated the house to Leonardo as one of his perks for agreeing to come to work for the French king at Amboise. The place is often swamped by tourists and you are only treated to disappointing copies of Leonardo's paintings inside the house. However, it is thought that Leonardo completed his famous painting of St John the Baptist in one of the rooms here, and it is known that he arrived at the Clos Lucé with his beloved *Mona Lisa* in his arms, which helps explain why it ended up in the French royal collection. The owners have tried to re-create a 16th-century atmosphere in many of the chambers. Others have an 18th-century feel; in that period, the Clos Lucé belonged to the d'Amboise family, who left their mark. One room contains magnificent gilded and marquetry furniture saved from the Château de Chanteloup (*see* below). Rich tapestries further adorn the rooms.

Among Leonardo's many creative talents, he proved a wizard at imagining new, ever more destructive weapons for his day. This is the side of his work brought out most clearly inside the Clos Lucé. The basement displays concentrate on models of many of his war machines, kindly recreated by IBM. Not all of Leonardo's drawings reproduced here are on the art of war, and they do show what a visionary engineer he was, although one very important ingredient was often missing to stop his inventions from actually working – a source of power.

Leonardo was also a great architect, who certainly drew up plans for a château for François I at Romorantin-Lanthenay in the nearby Sologne area. This was never executed, but it is widely believed that Leonardo played some part in the design of François's great Château de Chambord (*see* p.140). And he probably helped plan great entertainments for the court here at Amboise. He also delighted the king with his enlightened conversation and the breadth of his erudition. Legend even has it that Leonardo died in King François I's arms. With his insatiable desire for knowledge he wrote down all manner of his thoughts in his notebooks – in mirror writing. An interesting video in the outbuildings beside the château presents in French the amazing variety of Leonardo's intellectual pursuits. On a more playful note, the château has recently commissioned a panoply of giant models and backdrops, dotted around the spacious grounds below the castle. Commentaries you can listen to along the way imagine conversations between Leonardo and his much-loved pupil Francesco da Melzi allowing you to learn a little more about the Tuscan genius' interests in anatomy, botany and engineering as well as the arts. At the bottom of the garden, in an elegant building designed by Eiffel, videos and screens present more on the ultimate Renaissance man, as well as displaying a copy of his flying machine.

Tourist Attractions Around Amboise

The **Pagode de Chanteloup** (2.5km south of Amboise via the D31; *open July–Aug 9.30–7.30, June 10–7, May and Sept 10–6.30, April 10–12 and 2–6 (weekends 10–6), Oct–mid-Nov weekends, public hols and school hols 10–5; t 02 47 57 20 97, www.pagode-chanteloup.com; adm*) is the charming, comical, but also slightly melancholy remnant of the great Château de Chanteloup, a palatial 18th-century house whose most famous owner was the Duc de Choiseul, a figure of prime importance under King Louis XV. He served as Minister of Foreign Affairs, of War and of the Navy, and in 1768 organized the securing of Corsica for France. But by 1770 he had fallen out of favour, ousted by the king's controlling mistress, Madame Du Barry, and retired to Chanteloup, where he established an alternative court, attracting many influential European figures. This castle all but disappeared in the early 19th century.

You can climb the pagoda's seven decreasing circles, which end with a clownish hat of lead topped by a golden ball. An architectural Pierrot, the form is reflected in a half-moon of a pool. Beyond this, a great channel of water once led up to the château. One of the entrance pavilions before the pagoda houses a little museum on the history of the palace that once stood nearby. In summer you can picnic in the grounds around the pagoda, hire out a croquet set, or even take a trip in a hot air balloon.

Near Chanteloup, the **Parc des Mini-Châteaux** (*open April–mid-Nov; t 02 47 23 44 44 and t 0825 0825 22, www.mini-chateaux.com; adm*) inflates you to Rabelaisian giant proportions, displaying miniature versions of the most famous castles of the Loire Valley. Here you can get bird's-eye views of over 20 – the selection could perhaps help you choose which châteaux most take your fancy to then visit properly. (The real Château de Chenonceau lies only a short distance south from here – *see* p.214.)

Continuing along the south bank of the Loire river from Amboise to Tours, you come to what is surprisingly the most popular of all the tourist attractions along this stretch of river, not a château, but an aquarium, apparently the largest for freshwater fish in Europe. The **Aquarium du Val de Loire** (*open all year except 10 days at end of Nov and mid-Jan; t 02 47 23 44 44 and t 0825 0825 22, www.aquariumduvaldeloire.com; adm*) takes the form of a massive complex of tanks. It looks like a modern conference centre on the outside, but within a lovely light filters down into the very clean tanks on sunny days. You can see here all the fish you can eat along the Loire, plus many more, but they have the advantage of still being alive. Some tanks have been made to stretch right over the ceiling at certain points. Details are given on the fish presented.

The Loire and Cisse from Amboise to Tours

The delightful little Cisse river cheekily steals a ribbon of territory in the Loire's valley between Amboise and Tours. It's well worth following it through a string of pretty villages and past numerous cliffside châteaux. Westwards, you come into prime Touraine wine and troglodyte territory. The vineyards of Vouvray stretch up the north bank of the Loire, while those of Montlouis slope down from the south side.

From Amboise to Vouvray

The village of **Noizay** boasts two châteaux on its slope; the darker Château de Noizay is the one where the Huguenot conspirators of the Amboise Conspiracy gathered before they were butchered (*see* box, p.230). This little castle was transformed after a fire in the 17th century. This is also the village where the complex 20th-century French composer Francis Poulenc lived much of his life. **Vernou-sur-Brenne** is a rather larger but still attractive village, former country seat of the bishops of Tours.

Take the D46 north for Reugny and follow the signs for the **Château de Valmer**, near troglodyte Chançay. This is one of the few châteaux that you can visit along this stretch, but only for its gardens, only in high summer, and only in the afternoon (*open 2–7; July–Aug closed Mon; May–June and Sept weekends and public hols, Oct–April by appt; t 02 47 52 93 12, valmer37@aol.com*). It does, though, occupy one of those memorably picturesque corners of Touraine that is well worth seeking out. The château was built in the mid-17th century, but the main buildings have been sadly reduced. Three graceful matching outbuildings trip gaily down the slope to greet you. Above them lie

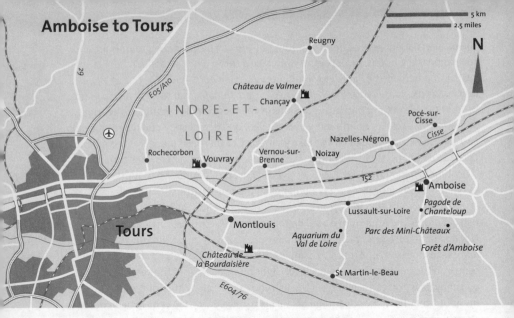

balustraded formal gardens, an archetypal picture of their period, with statues and urns scattered elegantly around. A 16th-century chapel is hidden in the rock face.

Reaching the town of **Vouvray** itself, the lower part looks a bit of a mess down in the valley. Signs signal *dégustations*, potential wine tastings, at every turn. There's also a renowned charcuterie down here, Hardouin; the family company's *charcutiers* add a dash of Vouvray wine to their array of specialities. Go up to explore the elegant upper village of Vouvray, with a terrace overlooking the valley.

Rochecorbon, towards Tours from Vouvray, also conceals a wealth of extraordinary troglodyte homes. You can occasionally get the chance to visit an elegant 18th-century troglodyte home, the **Manoir des Basses Rivières** (*open July and Aug Wed–Mon 2–7; also open Sat, Sun and public hols from Easter to June and in Sept; t/f 02 47 52 80 99; adm*). One room is actually thought to date from the 11th century, while a great staircase dug into the tufa links together the various levels. Book a cruise on *Le Saint-Martin-de-Tours* (*open Mar–Oct, t 02 47 52 68 88, georges.marchand@wanadoo.fr; adm*); you're treated to a commentary along the way, as well as exceptional views.

Just west of Rochecorbon is the cliffside where St Martin of Tours (*see* Tours) founded his famous Loire Valley monastery, **Marmoutier**, the second to be created in France, in the 4th century. The sacred place isn't open to visitors as it lies in the grounds of a religious establishment turned into a private school.

Montlouis and Around

The **Maison de la Loire** (*open May–Sept 10–7, Oct–mid Nov and April 10–12 and 2–6; t 02 47 50 97 52, www.ville-montlouis-loire.fr/mdl; adm*) in Montlouis-sur-Loire has information and puts on regular little exhibitions on the flora, fauna and geology of the Loire Valley. There are observation posts and the possibility of hiring binoculars.

Getting Around

Noizay and Montlouis are both served by **train** from Tours, Blois and Orléans. There are regular **bus** services between Amboise and Tours, and occasional stops at Rochecorbon, Vouvray, Vernou and Noizay on the north bank, and Montlouis and the aquarium of Lussault near the south bank; contact Touraine Fil Vert for times, **t** 02 47 47 17 18, *www.touraine-filvert.com*.

Tourist Information

Vouvray: N152 or Mairie, 37210 Vouvray, **t** 02 47 52 68 73 or **t** 02 47 52 70 48, *www.vouvray.org*.
Rochecorbon: Place de la Lanterne, 37120 Rochecorbon, **t/f** 02 47 52 80 22, *www.mairie-rochecorbon.fr*.
Montlouis-sur-Loire: Place de la Mairie, 37270 Montlouis-sur-Loire, **t** 02 47 45 00 16, *www.ville-montlouis-loire.fr*.

Market Days

Vouvray: Friday morning.
Montlouis-sur-Loire: Thursday morning.

Where to Stay and Eat

Noizay ✉ 37210

★★★★**Château de Noizay**, **t** 02 47 52 11 01, *www.relaischateaux.com/noizay* (*expensive*). A splendid little château. What with its private park, cliff caves, a tennis court, swimming pool and walks in the wood, Noizay has all the ingredients to help you relax in style, plus a fascinating history (*see 'Amboise'*). The chef cooks up memorable Loire dishes (*menus €40–65; closed lunch Mon and Thurs*). *Closed mid-Jan–mid-Mar.*

Vernou-sur-Brenne ✉ 37210

Château de Jallanges B&B, **t** 02 47 52 06 66, *www.chateaudejallanges.fr* or *www. chateauxhotels.com/jallanges* (*expensive*). This splendid brick château full of architectural interest is set in grand grounds up from the village of Vernou, in the winding valley of Vaugondy. You can stay in the grand rooms as a B&B guest and reserve the *table d'hôtes* (€45), meals served in lavish surrounds; finish the evening with a game of billiards. The place has a heated pool and the proprietors can organize luxury trips.

Vouvray ✉ 37210

Domaine des Bidaudières B&B, Rue du Peu-Morier, **t** 02 47 52 66 85, *www.bandb-loire-valley.com* (*expensive*). This is an Italianate dream of a place built on terraces along the Loire cliffside a little east of Vouvray. This is an utterly gorgeous 18th-century wine property, restored in the mid-1990s. The place actually feels more like a luxury little hotel, the owners very discreet. The rooms have been beautifully decorated with designer furnishings and tasteful fabrics. There's a wonderful conservatory by the pool.
★★**Le Grand Vatel**, 8 Av Brûlé, **t** 02 47 52 70 32, **f** 02 47 52 74 52 (*inexpensive*). This has a choice of dining rooms, one daubed with bawdy 1950s wall paintings, the other modern and bright. River fish and seafood

Château de la Bourdaisière

Salacious stories of royal mistresses hang around the Château de la Bourdaisière, an impressive, typical-looking Loire Valley château which has just about managed to keep apart from the modern suburbs stretching into southern Montlouis. Although the castle looks the very image of an early 16th-century French palace, it is in fact a 19th-century reinvention; the Baron d'Angelier, a massively wealthy mayor of Montlouis in that period, had his fantasy built on a site with many historical resonances. In medieval times a fortress stood here. The first traceable lord was a major warrior figure, Jean le Meingre, better-known as Boucicaut. Then in 1520, Philibert Babou, a finance minster to François I, commissioned his fine château. François appreciated not just Babou's housekeeping for the nation, but also the women in his household. The lusty royal often visited to enjoy the delightful company of Philibert's

are mixed on the one plate, with *sandre* served with a seafood coulis, and you may find more exotic touches such as lobster with mango (*menus €18–61; closed Fri lunch out of season, Sun pm and Mon exc public hols*).

Rochecorbon ✉ 37210

★★★★**Les Hautes Roches**, 86 Quai de la Loire, **t** 02 47 52 88 88, *www.relaischateaux.com/hautesroches* (*expensive*). This unique and magical cliffside hotel has some of the most extraordinary rooms along the Loire, luxuriously fitted in troglodyte hillside caves, with light window openings, fireplaces and canopied beds. The dining room and reception rooms lie in the neat 18th-century pavilion alongside. The only negative is the busy road separating the hotel from the Loire (*menus €38–70*). *Closed Feb–mid-Mar*.

Château de Montgouverne B&B, at St-Georges, just west of Rochecorbon, **t** 02 47 52 84 59, *www.montgouverne.com* (*expensive*). This delightful 18th-century home is set in splendid grounds in the Vouvray vineyards, with swimming, riding and cycling possible.

L'Oubliette, 34 Rue des Clouets, **t** 02 47 52 50 49 (*menus €22–51; closed Sun pm and Mon, and Wed out of season*). Also in a cave, and another address where attention is paid to detail. The menu is tempting and regional, with *croustillant de petits gris des Pays de la Loire* served with *rillons* and sweet garlic purée and *pommes de terre au Chinon*, while even the lobster comes in a sweet Vouvray sauce. *Closed late Aug–early Sept, late Oct–early Nov and late Feb–mid-Mar*.

Hostellerie de la Lanterne, 48 Quai de la Loire, **t** 02 47 52 50 02 (*menus €21.5–44.50; closed Sun pm and Mon, and Tues pm Oct–Jun*). This has the refreshing attraction of a garden by the whiter-than-white 18th-century posting inn. You can eat a grill outside in summer, take the three-course menu which includes a carafe of wine, or opt for such classic dishes as snails with mushrooms. *Closed 17–26 Nov and mid-Jan–mid-Feb*.

Montlouis-sur-Loire ✉ 37270

Château de la Bourdaisière, 25 Rue de la Bourdaisière, **t** 02 47 45 16 31, *www.chateaulabourdaisiere.com* (*expensive*). For a description of this grand Loire Valley château *see* below. The suites and rooms are very spacious and luxurious. Twenty are in the château itself, while a further six have recently been created in the eaves of the stables. Tennis court and pool.

★★**Hôtel de la Ville**, Place de la Mairie, **t** 02 47 50 84 84, **f** 02 47 45 08 43 (*inexpensive*). Neat rooms, plus a terrace and garden in the centre of the town (*menus €17–35; closed Fri pm, Sat, and Sun pm*). *Closed 20 Dec–10 Jan*.

Relais de Belle Roche, 14 Rue de la Vallée, **t** 02 47 50 82 43 (*menus €14.50–30.50*). The dining room here is cut into the Loire rockface, and a good choice of typical Touraine dishes is offered. *Closed Tues pm and Wed pm*.

La Cave, **t** 02 47 45 05 05 (*menus €17–40*). Truly cavernous; a very popular, sometimes loud former stone quarry along the riverside in which to eat meats cooked over a wood fire, as well as the usual Loire fare. *Closed Sun eve, plus Mon and Tues out of season*.

wife Marie Gaudin, and of her daughters. Moving on a few generations, Gabrielle, a great-granddaughter of Philibert's, may have been born at La Bourdaisière in 1565. She went down in history as King Henri IV's famed mistress, Gabrielle d'Estrées.

In the 18th century, when the Duc de Choiseul had been exiled to Amboise by Louis XV, he decided to expand his Château de Chanteloup (*see* p.244). He had most of the Château de la Bourdaisière demolished to use the stone for his new building. The story goes that he did this in part to spite his rival the Duc d'Aiguillon, who had an eye on La Bourdaisière, wanting to add it to his nearby estates at Véretz on the Cher.

The de Broglie family which now owns the château has put a great deal of effort into sprucing up the place in recent years. As well as developing the buildings as a hotel, they have had much work carried out on the gardens, open to the general public. The château forms the photogenic centrepiece. An Italianate gateway in the

Vouvray Wines

A tingling taste on the tongue, even with a dry, still Vouvray served as an apéritif, gives away this wine's natural leanings towards bubbles. The other defining element of Vouvray, apart from its very slight natural effervesence, is the Chenin Blanc grape variety. In fact, it's virtually the exclusive grape variety here, although a tiny percentage of Arbois may be found. Vouvray produces some of the finest of all Chenin Blanc wines. Vouvray is the largest producer of Chenin Blanc in France, made from 1,750 hectares planted with the variety.

The Vouvray vineyards extend across eight parishes (Vouvray, Rochecorbon, Ste-Radegonde, Parçay-Meslay, Vernou, Noizay, Chançay and Reugny), and importantly lots of them slope down the well-sheltered creases of five litte valleys coming down to the Loire. In many places the steep exposed tufa hillsides were quarried in ages past and provide some wonderful cellars in which the wines can be made and kept.

Some people find the tingle and tastes of Vouvray Chenin Blanc startling. It definitely has bite. Too much acidity is the enemy in bad years or bad wine-making here. The aroma can jump out at you as well, what with its touches of exotic fruits and fragrant flowers. With age, you can often detect hints of roasting or slight burning, either of nuts or of raisins. Honey, too, is often used to describe Vouvrays.

It's interesting to distinguish the different characteristics of the various types of wine produced here. The dry white makes for a powerful-tasting apéritif. In Touraine it could easily be served with fish and seafood. The demi-sec is the kind of sweet wine the French used to think the English loved best, but its flowery honey flavour is less popular these days – some suggest trying it with Touraine goat's cheese. The Chenin Blanc character often comes out to good effect when transformed into sparkling wine, Vouvray *mousseux*, its flavours strong enough to cope with the distraction of the bubbles, the honeyish aroma still present. The liquorous sweet *moelleux* is only made in special years, when noble rot sets in; these sweet wines are a completely different matter and can age for decades, even up to a century in rare vintages. They can have a mouth-filling richness and develop complex flavours.

A couple of estates have the irresistible appeal of a superb château along with their wine. The **Château de Valmer** (*open 2–7; July–Aug exc Mon, May–June and Sept weekends and public hols, Oct–April by appt; t 02 47 52 93 12, valmer37@aol.com*) at Chançay is mentioned elsewhere for its gardens, but also produces good wine. The **Château de Moncontour** (*t 02 47 52 60 77, www.moncontour.com*) standing proudly above Vouvray has a picturesque wine museum. A highly respected name among producers in Vouvray is that of Huet – **Domaine Huet** (*open 9–12 and 2–6 Mon–Fri; 11 Rue de la Croix Buisée, t 02 47 52 78 87, www.huet-echansonne.com*). A wider selection of the wines can be tasted at the **Cave des Producteurs des Grands Vins de Vouvray** (*open 9–12.30 and 2–7 exc 25 Dec and 1 Jan; 38 La Vallée Coquette, t 02 47 52 75 03, www. cp-vouvray.com*), which has hundreds of metres of galleries in the rock. At Rochecorbon, the **Etablissements Brédif** (*open 9–12 and 2–6; 87 Quai de la Loire, t 02 47 52 50 07; adm*) are well known for the quality of their wines, produced in superb caves, some dating back to the 10th century.

Montlouis-sur-Loire and its Wines

Former stone quarries have been converted into dramatic wine cellars by many wine producers in Montlouis. Most of Montlouis' vines grow on slopes facing south towards the Cher river rather than the Loire, in the parishes of Montlouis, Lussault and St-Martin-le-Beau. As with more famous Vouvray, only white wines are produced here, exclusively from the Chenin Blanc variety, also known in these parts as Pineau de Loire. The soils across the small 250-hectare *appellation* territory are lighter than on the north side of the Loire, a sign that the wines should reach maturity more quickly. The same range of whites is made, with some dry, some demi-sec, and in years when the noble rot allows it, some *moelleux*, which then needs to be aged for the acidity to melt. As at Vouvray, the Chenin Blanc comes out quite well, in the sparkling *mousseux*.

The **Chidaine** family (*t 02 47 45 19 14*), along Montlouis' Grande Rue, is very well respected for its wines. For a larger-scale introduction to the *appellation*, you could try the **Cave des producteurs des vins de Montlouis** (*daily July–Aug 8–12 and 2–7, Sept–June 8–12 and 2–6: best to visit between Mon and Thurs when there's more activity; 2 Route de St-Aignan, t 02 47 50 80 98, cave-montlouis@france-vin.com*).

The **Domaine Deletang** (*t 02 47 50 67 25, www.domaine-deletang.com; closed Sun pm*) gives you a good reason to visit the attractive little village of St-Martin-le-Beau. Close to the church, the family cellars have a good reputation. *Perruches*, flinty clays, are recognized for their part in producing good-quality wines here. The presence of these flints may explain why experts often describe Montlouis wines as more mineral than Vouvrays. See if you can spot nutty flavours too, almonds and hazelnuts regularly cropping up in tasting notes.

grounds has been attributed to Leonardo da Vinci. Up above the château, the walled kitchen garden has been transformed into a beautifully designed vegetable plot, the hundreds of varieties of tomato cultivated here the pride of the collection. Down in the sumptuous stables by the castle (one original feature to have survived from Babou's 16th-century château), the de Broglies have created the Conservatoire de la Tomate where you can learn about the history of tomatoes, and the great number of varieties that exist today. The euphemistic term for tomatoes in French is *pommes d'amour*, apples of love, which seems suitable enough given La Bourdaisière's history. A very tasty boutique allows you to buy all sorts of tomato products, while in season you can also sit down to a light tomato lunch. The castle's estates produce a respectable Montlouis wine.

Tours

Tours

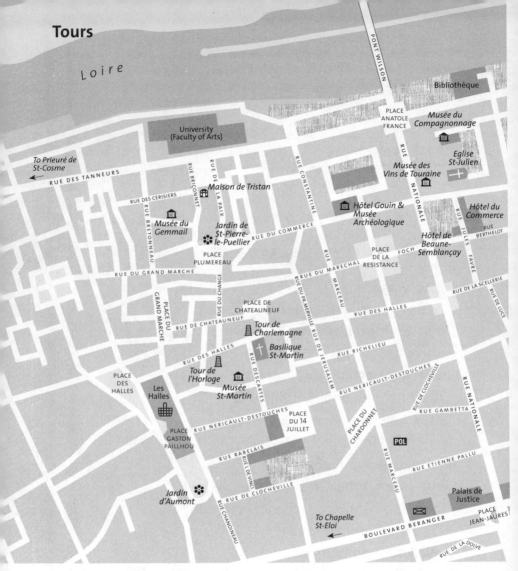

Bienheureux qui comme la Loire suit son cours dans son lit. (Happy those who, like the Loire, follow their course in their bed.)

graffiti at the University of Tours

Tours is the kind of glamorous French town where it's easy to enjoy a very laid-back French time, wandering idly through historic streets, browsing in tempting shops, sitting in cafés, watching the world go by. Certainly the courses must seem a distraction to the large number of students who pose a great deal around the centre. Back in the mid-19th century, Balzac wickedly wrote of complacent Touraine contentment in *Le Curé de Tours*, describing the place as 'an area where no one wants to be disturbed for any reason whatsoever, not even for a pleasure'. Nowadays,

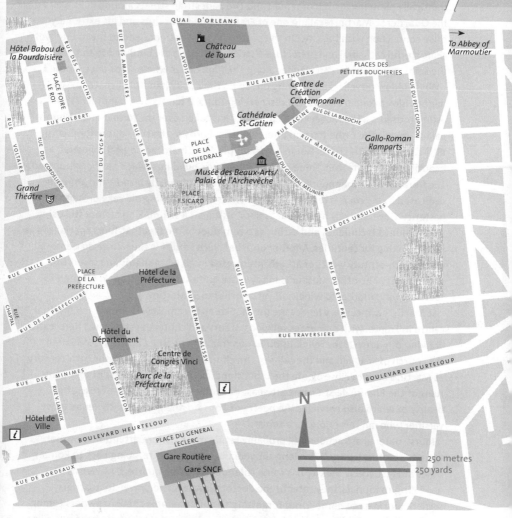

Loire

QUAI D'ORLEANS

Hôtel Babou de
la Bourdaisière

RUE DES CAPUCINS

RUE DES AMANDIERS

RUE LAVOISIER

Château
de Tours

To Abbey of
Marmoutier

PLACES DES
PETITES BOUCHERIES

PLACE FOIRE
LE ROI

RUE ALBERT THOMAS

Centre de
Création
Contemporaine

RUE DE LA BAZOCHE

RUE DU PETIT CUPIDON

RUE COLBERT

RUE

RUE DES CORDELIERS

RUE VOLTAIRE

RUE DU CYGNE

RUE DE LA BARRE

Cathédrale
St-Gatien

RUE RACINE

RUE MANCEAU

Gallo-Roman
Ramparts

PLACE
DE LA
CATHÉDRALE

Musée des Beaux-Arts/
Palais de l'Archevêche

RUE DU GENERAL MEUNIER

Grand
Théâtre

PLACE
F.SICARD

RUE DES URSULINES

RUE EMILE ZOLA

PLACE
DE LA
PREFECTURE

Hôtel de la
Préfecture

RUE JULES SIMON

RUE DU PETIT PRE

RUE CHAPTAL

RUE DE LA PREFECTURE

RUE BERNARD PALISSY

Hôtel du
Département

Centre de
Congrès Vinci

RUE TRAVERSIERE

RUE DES MINIMES

RUE DE BUFFON

Parc de la
Préfecture

RUE VLALOUX

Hôtel de
Ville

BOULEVARD HEURTELOUP

BOULEVARD HEURTELOUP

PLACE DU GENERAL
LECLERC

N

RUE DE BORDEAUX

Gare Routière
Gare SNCF

250 metres
250 yards

innumerable foreign students deliberately descend upon the town, coming here to
learn what's considered the purest French in France. So the feeling is cosmopolitan
and distinctly lively. Occasionally, apparently, Mick Jagger pops in from his château
not far off for a drink at his favourite bar on the Place Plumereau, the social hub.
Tours certainly has a great buzz to it.

Tours is an excellent central spot from which to visit the very famous châteaux to
east, west and south in the Touraine. It's also very much worth a stay in its own right,
a vibrant cultural centre with numerous attractions and attractive quarters, despite
the terrible damage inflicted on it in the Second World War, particularly by the river
and down its main drag. The heart of the historic part of town is divided in two by
the latter, the long, straight north–south Rue Nationale, and is located north of Place

Jean-Jaurès with its grandiose Hôtel de Ville. On the western side of the centre lie the frantically pumping Place Plumereau and the pedestrian streets around it, as well as the Quartier St-Martin, recalling one of France's greatest saints and his extremely close connection with the city. On the eastern side, the streets lead to the quieter yet characterful cathedral and *préfecture* district. Both parts are bordered to the north by the Loire, by which you can wander along the high quays where ships once moored.

While fellow travellers are rushing out to do their daily handful of châteaux, you might enjoy a couple of days just discovering Tours. It has its own handful of interesting museums. The Musée des Beaux-Arts has taken over the former archbishop's palace next to the cathedral and offers the peculiarity in the Loire of predominantly 18th-century art. The Hôtel Gouin holds a typically rich archaeological collection and beautiful fragments from some of the grand Tours buildings which have disappeared. The Musée du Compagnonnage, by contrast, proves distinctly bizarre and amusing, dedicated to the *chefs-d'œuvre* of master craftsmen, including old cake preserved for posterity. One relatively new attraction for visitors is a silk-making factory still using old-fashioned techniques and acting as a reminder of the fact that Tours specialized in silk-making for centuries. Another unusual place to visit is the Musée du Gemmail, where 20th-century works of art are interpreted in glowing shards and layers of stained glass. The other museums in town are quite small affairs, one dedicated to Tours' history, another to wine, and yet another to St Martin.

St Martin's 4th-century legacy meant that Tours became a very important spiritual centre in France, with numerous religious orders and churches established here, early drawing pilgrims. Of the religious buildings that remain, the Cathédrale St-Gatien, the church of St-Julien and the ruins of the church of St-Martin, with the 19th-century St-Martin's basilica close by, are the most significant. On the outskirts of town, the ruins of the Prieuré de St-Cosme are seasonally filled with the scent of roses, the beauty of which also pervades the poetry of Ronsard, the great French Renaissance versifier who ran this priory for a time.

Tours' material attractions will probably retain most visitors' attention now more than its spiritual legacy. It has long thrived as a trading centre, going back to Roman times at least. Today the city has some splendid shopping quarters. As well as appealing to tourists, they cater to the doctors, lawyers and university teachers settled here in large number, not forgetting the innumerable château owners coming in from the surrounding region to furnish their *salons* and stock up on *froufrous, foie gras* and *petits fours*.

History

The Gallo-Roman history of the town pales into insignificance compared with what's known of its early Christian history. However, the Gallo-Roman settlement, called Caesarodunum, founded in the first half of the 1st century AD, became an important city. It was one of the 50-odd towns created as heads of the districts of Gaul under the Roman emperor Augustus, roughly following the territorial divides of the Celtic tribes. The region around Caesarodunum had been the land of the Turones and the Roman region was named the Civitas Turonorum.

Getting There and Around

By Air

Ryanair flies daily from London Stansted to Tours. The small Tours Val de Loire airport (4 Rue de l'Aérogare, t 02 47 49 37 00, *www. tours-aeroport.com*) lies 6km northeast of town. A shuttle bus (c. €5 per trip) links it with the central railway station.

By Train

Be warned that Tours has two main stations, the central one and St-Pierre-des-Corps. A shuttle service links St-Pierre with the train station, a tourist sight in itself. Paris is only 1 hour from central Tours. Slower, slightly cheaper trains are also available.

By Car and Bicycle

The A10 motorway, the main route from Paris to Bordeaux and Spain, cuts through the eastern side of the city centre. If you arrive early you may find a space on the free bays on the Loire quays, otherwise there are car parks.

Car Hire

Avis, Place Général Leclerc, t 02 47 20 53 27. Also has an office at the airport.
Europcar, 76 Rue B Palissy, t 02 47 64 4 76.
Hertz, 57 Rue Marcel Tribut, t 02 47 75 50 00.
Citer, 24 Rue Marcel Tribut, t 02 47 05 94 95.

Bicycle Hire

Amstercycles, 5 Rue du Rempart, t 02 47 61 22 23.
Vélomania, 109 Rue Colbert, t 02 47 05 10 11.

By Bus

The intercity bus station is in front of the train station. The local bus station is on the nearby Place Jean-Jaurès, where Av Grammont enters the square from the south. There's a Kiosque Information, 5 Rue de la Dolve, or call Allo Fil Bleu, t 02 47 66 70 70.

By Taxi

Taxi Radio, 13 Rue de Nantes, t 02 47 20 30 40.

Tourist Information

Tours: Office de Tourisme, 78–82 Rue Bernard Palissy, B.P.4201, 37042 Tours Cedex, t 02 47 70 37 37, *www.ligeris.com*. The Carte Multi-Visites allows you to visit the town's six municipal museums for a mere €7.62. The tourist office organizes a programme of *visites à thèmes*; these tours in French concentrate on topics such as ancient Tours, St Martin, Renaissance Tours, the cathedral, Victor Laloux, and the silk-making works.

Market Days

There are traditional French markets in different parts of town every morning of the week except Monday – the tourist office can supply listings. Other regular specialist markets include:
Place de la Résistance: the *Marché gourmand*, first and third Friday in each month, 4–10am.
Place des Halles: Wednesday and Saturday.
Place de la Victoire: second-hand junk markets; Wednesday and Saturday.
Rue de Bordeaux: antiques; first and third Friday of month.
Boulevard Béranger: flower market; Wednesday and Saturday.
Boulevard Béranger: antiques; fourth Sunday in month.

Shopping

Rue Nationale has the big chain shops. The streets either side, but especially to the west, offer an excellent array of smaller boutiques. East of Rue Nationale, between Rue Colbert and Rue de la Scellerie, lies the main antiques quarter.

Where to Stay

Tours ✉ 37000

Expensive

★★★★Château Belmont Jean Bardet, 57 Rue Groison, t 02 47 41 41 11, *www.jeanbardet. com*. A name known across France for the highest standards of cuisine, but recently rocked by a scandal over misleading customers about wines. However, this is still a chi-chi restaurant and hotel. The substantial town house stands in the posh part of the suburbs on the north bank of the Loire, east off Av de la Tranchée. The rooms are charming. The garden is lovingly tended, and has a pool. If you don't want to spend too much on a meal, there's a quite reasonable value menu. The one jarring note is the boutique – avert your eyes; here bad taste reigns (*menus €60–138; closed Sun pm Nov–Mar, Mon exc pm April–Oct, and Sat and Tues lunch*).

****Hôtel de l'Univers**, 5 Bd Heurteloup, t 02 47 05 37 12 *hotel-univers-sa@wanadoo. fr*. At the heart of the town, a grand Belle Epoque building where the famous automatically used to stay in Tours, as the portrait gallery on the ground floor flaunts. Churchill counted among the number to grace one of its 85 relatively luxurious rooms. The restaurant isn't bad, the prices quite reasonable (*menus €25–30; closed Sun Nov–Mar and lunchtimes mid-July–mid-Aug*).

Moderate

***Le Grand Hôtel**, 9 Place du Général Leclerc, t 02 47 05 35 31, *www.bestwestern.fr*. Large and by the railway station, but has a certain charm and is quite reasonably priced. *Closed mid-Dec–end of Dec.*

***Kyriad**, 65 Av de Grammont, t 02 47 64 71 78, *kyriad.tourscentre@wanadoo.fr*, *www.kyriad.fr*. On the big bustling artery south of Av Jean-Jaurès. It has a peculiar mix of contemporary and old-fashioned rooms, again at reasonable price.

Inexpensive

Hôtel du Cygne, 6 Rue du Cygne, t 02 47 66 66 41, *perso.wanadoo.fr/hotelcygne.tours*. There's a lovely old-fashioned character to this very centrally located, exceptionally good-value little hotel. *Closed Christmas and New Year.*

Le Moderne, 1–3 Rue Victor Laloux, t 02 47 05 32 81, *hotelmoderne37@wanadoo.fr*. On a quiet, central street corner with well-kept rooms and an owner who doubles as a good cook in the evenings (*menus €12.50 and 15.50; closed Sun mid-Dec–late Jan, and lunchtimes*).

Le Balzac, 47 Rue de la Scellerie, t 02 47 05 40 87, *hotel.balzac@9online.fr*. Another well-located small hotel with some charm, including a little inner courtyard where you can have breakfast in summer.

Châteaux de la Loire, 12 Rue Gambetta, t 02 47 05 10 05, *perso.wanadoo.fr/ hoteldeschateaux.tours*. West of the Rue Nationale, this has some spacious rooms and a bar. *Closed mid-Dec–mid-Mar.*

*Mon Hôtel, 40 Rue de la Préfecture, t 02 47 05 67 53, f 02 47 05 21 88. Well located for such bargain prices, in one of the chicest parts of Tours, close to the railway station, but with most of the rooms you have to share the toilet and washing facilities.

*Le St-Eloi, 79 Bd Béranger, t 02 47 37 67 34, f 02 47 39 34 67 (*closed Sun afternoon*). A small town house further out on one of the main thoroughfares cutting through town, but set back from the road with its front garden and parking.

Eating Out

Expensive

Jean Bardet, *see* 'Where to Stay', above. The crème de la crème for cuisine in Tours.

Charles Barrier, 101 Av de la Tranchée, t 02 47 54 20 39 (*menus €23–75; closed Sat lunch and Sun exc public hols*). The other really exceptional sophisticated restaurant north of the Loire and Pont Wilson, named after the chef who originally made its name. Stylishly redecorated.

Moderate

Les Tuffeaux, 21 Rue Lavoisier, t 02 47 47 19 89 (*menus €19–35; closed Sun, Mon lunch and Wed lunch*). Opposite Tours' now meagre château, with beams as well as tufa walls, offers warm traditional Touraine cooking, several dishes usually coming with Touraine wine sauces.

La Rôtisserie Tourangelle, 23 Rue du Commerce, t 02 47 05 71 21 (*menus €16–45; closed Sat lunch, Sun pm, and Mon*). This is a well-established restaurant with impeccable manners.

Cheap

Le Petit Patrimoine, 58 Rue Colbert, t 02 47 66 05 81 (*menus €11.50–26; closed Sun lunch*). Lively narrow little restaurant down a very pleasant shopping street, serving traditional Tourangeau dishes.

Chez Jean-Michel – Le Charolais, 123 Rue Colbert, **t** 02 47 20 80 20 (*menus €18.50–25; closed weekends and public hols*). Wine bar specializing in Loire *appellations*, and also offering a simple selection of Touraine dishes. *Closed 30 Sept–11 May, 11–31 Aug and 21 Dec–5 Jan.*

Brasserie Buré, Place de la Résistance, **t** 02 47 05 67 74 (*menus c.€18*). A big Belle Epoque-style brasserie.

Le Singe Vert, 5 Rue Marceau, **t** 02 47 20 02 76 (*menus 13–34; closed Sun and public hols*). A madly cluttered brasserie named after what was once a house of low repute. A place to go if you like your charcuterie and grilled meats.

Au Bistrot des Halles, 31 Place Gaston Pailhou, **t** 02 47 61 54 93 (*menus €12–27*). By the covered market, busy brasserie serving traditional French fare.

Comme Autrefouée, 11 Rue de la Monnaie, **t** 02 47 05 94 78 (*menus €10–20; closed Sun and Mon, and Sept–May lunch Sun–Thurs*). Serves the Loire equivalent of calzone pizzas, dough balls stuffed with various fillings.

Entertainment and Nightlife

Look out for *L'Agenda culturel*, the quarterly cultural magazine for the town, listing events, or look at the cultural pages at *www.tours.fr* or *www.ligeris.com*.

Cinema

Cinémas Studio, 2 Rue des Ursulines, **t** 02 47 20 27 00 or **t** 0892 682 015, *www.studiocine.com*. Excellent programme of classic and contemporary films in original versions.

CGR Rex, 45 Rue National, **t** 02 47 66 91 69 or **t** 0836 680 445, *www.cgrcinemas.fr*. Has disabled seating.

CGR Mega, 42 Av Marcel-Merieux, **t** 0836 680 445, *www.cgrcinemas.fr*.

Pathé Tours, 4 Place François Truffaut, **t** 0892 696 696, *www.pathe.fr*.

Events

Centre de Congrès Vinci, 26 Bd Heurteloup, **t** 02 47 70 70 70, *www.vinci-conventions.com*.

Major contemporary centre for cultural events as well as conferences.

Theatre

Grand Théâtre, 34 Rue de la Scellerie, **t** 02 47 60 20 20, *theatre@ville-tours.fr*. Theatre venue in 19th-century grandeur, where concerts, dance and other events are also staged.

Le Nouvel Olympia, 7 Rue de Lucé, **t** 02 47 64 50 50. Specializes in contemporary theatre.

Dance

Centre Chorégraphique National de Tours, 47 Rue du Sergent Leclerc, **t** 02 47 36 46 00, *www.ccnt-larrieu.com*.

Classical Music

Salle Jean de Ockeghem, 15 Place de Châteauneuf, **t** 02 47 20 71 95, *mact@wanadoo.fr*. Main stage for classical concerts, although several churches in Tours put on interesting classical concerts.

Contemporary Music

Le Petit Faucheux, 5 bis rue du Mûrier, **t** 02 47 38 29 34, *www.petitfaucheux.com*. The city's main jazz venue.

Le Bateau Ivre, 146 Rue Edouard Vaillant, **t** 02 47 44 77 22, *www.bateau-ivre.org*. Another well-known jazz address.

Les 3 Orfèvres, 6 Rue des Orfèvres, off Place Plumereau, **t** 02 47 64 02 73. Rock, reggae, blues and jazz.

Bars and Clubs

For bars and clubs, the area around Place Plumereau is very lively and quite chic. Down Av Grammont are bigger, more popular places.

Music Festivals

Aucard is a rock festival held on the main island in the Loire in central Tours. It was recently held in late May, but you should check for current dates (Radio Béton are the current sponsors: **t** 02 47 51 03 83, *www.radiobeton.com*).

Florilège Vocal is a choral singing festival in late May or early June. For info, call **t** 02 47 21 65 26, or email *florilege.vocal@free.fr*.

Fêtes Musicales en Touraine, **t** 02 47 21 65 08, is a highly reputed chamber music festival held in late June.

It seems strange that the town should have been built on the flat south bank of the Loire, liable to floods, rather than on the hillside to the north. But with the Cher river to the south, perhaps this gave the location something of the protection of an island. A few vestiges of the Gallo-Roman town have been discovered in digging foundations for new buildings around the cathedral area. The clearest trace of Gallo-Roman times is in the straight line of the former main street, or *decumanus*, now the Rue Colbert. A curving street behind the cathedral apparently follows the line of a Gallo-Roman arena. Invasions from the east led to the building of the town's first fortifications – a few vestiges can be seen by the remnants of the medieval château.

Tours had an important Christian community early on by French standards. Gatien is the first recorded bishop, at work before the Roman emperor Constantine, who would proclaim Christianity as the Empire's religion from 324, came to power. A first cathedral was begun in 337 under Bishop Lidoire, but the present one is named after Gatien. The city's most important bishop, Martin, was appointed in the 370s. He stands out as one of the most important figures in French Christianity (*see* box).

With the popularity of the cult of St Martin and the magnetic magnificence of the early basilica, a whole new quarter of town grew up slightly to the west of the older city, becoming known as Martinopolis. Tours formed an early strong royal connection when Clovis, king of the Franks, stopped at the shrine in 496 and said that he would convert to Christianity if he beat the Alamanni. This he managed and he went on to be baptized at Reims, a decisive step in the establishing of the divine right of the French kings. Clovis then defeated the Visigoths under Alaric II in 507. St Martin was considered to have played his part in such victories and he became a particularly cherished figure for the Merovingian dynasty.

Pilgrims flocked to the new town, including Gregory, a nobleman from distant Auvergne. He stayed in the place and was nominated bishop of Tours in 573. His great historical work, the *Historia Francorum* (*The History of the Franks*), is one of the most important texts of the Dark Ages in Europe, a riveting read about those centuries of turmoil, crammed with details of the events, superstitions and prejudices of the period and depicting its ruthlessness. Tours' Benedictine abbey of St-Julien was founded at this time.

The Carolingian dynasty maintained strong links with Tours. Charlemagne's third wife, Luitgarde, died here in 800 – the so-called Tour Charlemagne close to St-Martin's basilica is really named thus because of her. The great Carolingian scholar Alcuin of York was named abbot in Tours in 796 and founded a brilliant school. The curriculum centred on grammar, rhetoric and dialectics, and its method of teaching set the model for many great medieval centres of learning. Alcuin also established a centre for producing manuscripts which became one of the finest schools for Carolingian illuminated works. For some time, in fact, Tours was one of the major intellectual centres of the West.

The abbey of St-Julien survived the Viking raids in the mid-9th century, but the St Martin's quarter of the city was devastated. The abbey of St Martin had to be reconstructed and a timber fortification was replaced by one in stone, while the whole area was given defences and became known as Châteauneuf. With the

Miraculous St Martin Cuts His Cloak in Half

Here ends the first book, which covers five thousand, five hundred and ninety-six years from the beginning of the world down to the death of St Martin.
Gregory of Tours, *The History of the Franks*, written in the 590s

The line ending Gregory of Tours' first book on the history of the Franks makes clear the massive importance ascribed to St Martin in the Dark Ages. Martin came originally from Hungary and fought as a soldier for the Roman Empire, although he was to abandon his military ways. He's most famously represented as a fighter on horseback, putting his sword to charitable use. Travelling through Amiens in Picardy, northern France, he came across a wretched, naked beggar; he was so moved, he divided his cloak in half to give protection to the suffering man. The oft-reproduced image makes a touching scene, even if Martin doesn't get down from his mount and may seem less magnanimous than St Francis of Assisi, by half a coat at least. But St Martin is said to have been a great inspiration for the famous medieval Italian, as well as for innumerable Christians through the Dark Ages.

Apparently, in the night after the incident of the cloak-cutting, Christ appeared to Martin, holding the other half of his mantle. The mercenary was converted to the Christian faith, his mission clear. With Hilary, Bishop of Poitiers, he created the first monastery in France, at Ligugé in the Poitou, in 360. He then travelled to Tours, where he founded a second monastery, Marmoutier, its present incarnation now on the eastern outskirts of town, north of the river. Martin was made bishop of the city around 371. He also continued to organize missionary activities said to have had a profound impact in converting many parts of France to the new faith. Patrick, who became the patron saint of Ireland, may have received spiritual guidance from Martin.

The extraordinary circumstances of Martin's death, related in Gregory of Tours' history, occurred in Candes, a village to the west of Tours (*see* p.344). His body was boated back along the Loire to Tours and a cult to St Martin began to grow in town. Miracles were said to have taken place at the cemetery where he was buried. His tomb was moved to a specially constructed chapel by St Brice, which was replaced by a grand basilica by Bishop Perpet and became an important place of pilgrimage.

Gregory of Tours had good reason for regarding St Martin so highly – he believed that he himself had been cured from sickness by his visit to the holy man's shrine in the 560s. Miracles continued to occur. The power of his relics is even said to have repulsed one Viking invasion in the 9th century. The Norsemen had made a breach in the city walls and were about to enter to ravage the place when St Martin's bones were held up in front of them. They immediately turned back. With such incredible powers ascribed to Martin, it's no surprise that Tours pays homage to its greatest historical figure; a special basilica, a museum and a set of stained-glass windows in the cathedral stand out as the most important Martinian legacy in the city. The power of his life and miracles drew the pope to Tours in 1996. In countless churches not just across the Loire Valley but also throughout France and Europe, you will see representations of St Martin on his charge, dividing his cloak in two for the pauper.

breakdown of the Carolingian empire, the regional feudal counts feuded over these territories. Under Count Eudes of Blois in the first part of the 11th century, a new bridge was built over the Loire. The neighbouring counts of Anjou, however, overran Touraine in the first half of the 11th century and the region fell totally under their control in 1044. New walls went up in the mid-12th century.

Touraine was absorbed into the so-called Plantagenet empire for some time, but would be won by the French king Philippe Auguste early in the 13th century. In that period, further expansion of the town occurred with the establishment of the mendicant orders of the Franciscans and the Dominicans, while the port thrived. With the start of the Hundred Years' War, the two main parts of Tours were finally joined behind one single defensive wall.

The fact that Tours had become such a fortified town no doubt helped paranoid King Louis XI decide to choose it as his capital after the Hundred Years' War ended in 1453. Son of Charles VII, Louis had been brought up in the Berry and in Touraine, after his father was hounded out of Paris by the English. Louis became king in 1461. His centre of power was the Château de Plessis-lès-Tours, which he developed into a regal residence; a sad remnant of it now lies choked by Tours' western suburbs. With the court's presence, trade and culture flourished in the city. Jean Fouquet, from Tours, continued as the great 15th-century court painter. The superb musician Ockeghem was appointed treasurer of the cathedral; of Flemish origin, he would serve as court composer to three successive French kings, Charles VI, Charles VII and Louis XI. Luxury crafts, such as goldsmiths' work, took off in Tours. So too did printing, while Louis XI particularly encouraged the development of the silk industry, having mulberry bushes planted around the town.

When Louis XI died in 1483, the court under Charles VIII moved to Amboise, but Tours continued to enjoy a time of great prosperity and administrative and trading importance, the royal court frequently châteaued nearby for a century to come. Fine town houses were built. Although this period was on the cusp of the final glorious Gothic extravaganza and the sobering symmetry of the Renaissance, most of the Tours town houses of the turn of the century were Gothic in style. The odd grand Renaissance façade stands out, in particular those of the Hôtel Gouin and the Hôtel de Beaune-Semblançay.

In the second half of the 16th century, Protestantism had many converts among the merchant class of which Tours was so full and the town was inevitably shaken by the bloody Wars of Religion. King Henri III took refuge in Tours after he had had the overpowerful de Guise brothers murdered in his castle at Blois in 1588. He called a meeting of the Estates General here and held talks with the Protestant leader who was to become his successor, Henri de Navarre, seeking reconciliation with him.

After the new Bourbon French royal family had abandoned the Loire Valley of the Valois, the 17th and 18th centuries were quieter for the city which had previously played such a central role in the kingdom's history. The ministers Richelieu and Colbert tried to revive the silk industry and tapestry-making. The Revocation of the Edict of Nantes in 1685, though, caused many of the successful Protestant merchants to pack up shop and emigrate, draining the town of much wealth. One Catholic to emigrate from Tours was Marie de l'Incarnation, leaving the Ursuline convent to go and heavy-handedly help convert the natives of Québec. With its port on the Loire, Tours still remained a significant trading town through this period.

In the Ancien Régime, the French provinces were administered by centrally appointed *intendants*. In the second half of the 18th century the royal administrator of Touraine, the *intendant* du Cluzel, controlled the vast Généralité de Tours, extending over several modern-day *départements*. He was supported by the powerful minister, the Duc de Choiseul, and raised the finances to build the magnificent Rue Royale (now the much duller postwar Rue Nationale), cutting north to south through Tours' centre, part of the grand new royal route from Paris to Spain.

By the Revolution, the citizens of Tours appear for the most part to have been a tame lot. The tendencies of this potentially prosperous region were towards conservatism and deep-rooted Catholicism. In 1790 the town became the capital of the new *département* of the Indre-et-Loire, the new name for Touraine. The stately plans for the town drawn up for du Cluzel continued to be developed through the 19th century.

'Balzac invented the 19th century,' Oscar Wilde wrote of the stupendously ambitious Tourangeau writer born along Rue Royale in 1799, just as the turmoil of the French Revolution was being replaced by the lunatic dictatorship of the Napoleonic Empire. Several of Balzac's works, including *Le Lys dans la vallée* and *Le Curé de Tours*, expose the petty-minded shenanigans of the citizens of the city in the early 19th century. With the end of Napoleon, the Prussians came as far as Tours and French royalty was re-established. Steam ships were now paddling their way up and down the Loire, but the arrival of the railway in 1845 changed France's transport and trade practically overnight, stimulating the town's economy. Tours' grand central station was designed by Victor Laloux, who also made the Gare (now Musée) d'Orsay in Paris. Terrible floods in the second half of the century caused passing difficulties for the town.

In the Second Empire, a new town centre began to emerge further from the river and closer to railway transport, around what's now Place Jean-Jaurès. Grand public buildings went up. They briefly received the French government fleeing the Prussians, who had advanced on Paris in 1870. Léon Gambetta famously got round the blockade by leaving Paris for Tours by hot air balloon, going on to act as distanced dictator in southwest France for five months, the Prussians having pushed as far as Tours again. The Belle Epoque from the close of the 19th century to the start of the 20th left a happier mark on the city, best seen in the grandiose architecture of the town hall.

In the First World War, Tours was the seat of the USA's services of supply, which played such a vital role in the final victory. The monument by the Loire recalling this American contribution stands on a piece of land donated to the USA by a grateful French nation. It comes as a surprise to learn that conservative Tours was the birthplace of the French Communist party. In December 1920, the Congrès de Tours, the 18th conference of the Section Française de l'Internationale Ouvrière, was being held in the city. Delegates had to decide whether or not to adhere to the Komintern founded by Lenin in Moscow in March 1919. Léon Cachin, who ran the newspaper *L'Humanité*, led those in favour of joining, Léon Blum those against. The latter went off to found the French Socialist Party, Cachin to lead the Communists. Thus the divide in French left-wing politics of the 20th century was decided.

At the start of the Second World War, Tours once again became the capital for a French government on the run. On 10 June 1940 the ministers arrived. On 13 June Churchill flew over for a final meeting with the French. The Germans were heading apace towards Tours for a third time in such a short period, and the French government fled to Bordeaux, in a move which was becoming a distressing recurring pattern. Fighting broke out along the Loire in Touraine. Thousands upon thousands of refugees flocked to Tours to try and escape by rail, but bombing was beginning and the line was cut. On 18 June an artillery battle caused the outbreak of a terrible fire and 12 hectares of the historic centre burned to the ground. A small band of some 300 North African snipers kept the Germans at bay for a couple more days, but then the town fell into enemy hands, to remain in occupied France throughout the war. Further bombing in 1944, this time by the Allies, wrought yet more catastrophic damage before the area was liberated in September.

Virtually nothing remained of Tours' old riverside quarters. But the city was one of the first places in France to benefit from concerted attempts at careful postwar renovation promoted by the Loi Malraux of 1965. The reconstruction programme had many successes, as well as some inevitably hasty and shoddier results. After the war, Tours' image may have remained a predominantly conservative one. But from 1959 to 1995 it was run by the energetic Jean Royer, an independent mayor, if basically to the right. He helped make Tours the vibrant, lively city it undoubtedly is today. Things moved a liberal stage further with the 1995 elections, when a left-wing mayor won Tours, although in 2001 the city swung again to the right. One important development in the 1990s was the arrival of the TGV fast train line as far as Tours. Paris is now just an hour away, and although it makes their critics laugh, those proud of Tours now like to say that it's just a month behind the French capital's fashions.

Cathédrale St-Gatien

Open 9–7; Mass at 10 and 6.30 on Sunday, and at 7pm on weekdays; free.

There are many grander cathedrals, but there are probably few more pleasing; and this effect of delicacy and grace is at its best toward the close of a quiet afternoon, when the densely decorated towers, rising above the little place de l'Archevêché, lift their curious lanterns into the slanting light...

Henry James,
A Little Tour in France

The lantern tops of St-Gatien still stand out gracefully on the Tours skyline today. The façade below contains a mass of Flamboyant Gothic detail, with a rose window from the early 16th century. A little later in the century, during the Wars of Religion, the statuary in the Gothic niches was destroyed by Protestants, but was replaced in the 19th century.

Behind the façade, the rest of the cathedral offers a lesson in the evolution of the Gothic style, working west from the choir to this Flamboyant front. So as you walk through to the choir, you go progressively back in time. While the façade is mainly 15th-century, the nave and north transept are 14th-century. The choir contains superb 13th-century stained glass. Just small portions of an earlier Romanesque building remain visible here and there.

On the way down the church, look out for several contrasting images of St Martin shown dividing his cloak in two with his sword. In one transept you can spot him in a remnant of medieval fresco. In the other transept, he is depicted in a grand imperialist painting, riding a splendid white horse. He also features in stained glass in the splendid choir, built under the mason Etienne de Mortagne. The tracery and the richness of the glass have led some art historians to make connections between it and Paris's celebrated Sainte Chapelle, dating from slightly earlier.

The oldest glass, from the 1240s, stands in the three radiating chapels at the end of the apse. In the central one, scenes depict Christ's life. The stained glass in the neighbouring chapels, though of the same period, wasn't in fact made for this building; on the south side, the pieces come from the abbey of St-Julien and illustrate the life of St Férréol. To the north, the life of St James originally appeared in the abbey of St-Martin, and serves as a reminder that Tours lay on a major pilgrimage trail from Paris to Santiago de Compostela.

The upper windows, mainly from the 1260s, depict the lives of a number of other saints, including Julian and Maurice, as well as Martin; in fact, until 1498, the cathedral was named after St Maurice, whose remains were brought here in 1267. The cathedral was later rededicated to underline the see's long history. Some of the glass here is painted in grisaille, alternating with the coloured glass.

The transept rose windows contrast tellingly with each other, the southern one a perfect picture, the outer circle displaying the arms of St Louis and his mother Blanche de Castile. A bulky column passes right through the northern transept rose window, quite spoiling its effect – this whole section was in danger of collapsing and had to be propped up when it was rebuilt in the 14th century.

The most beautiful and moving work of art in St-Gatien is a tomb, ordered for two royal children. Commissioned in 1499, it displays the effigies of Charles-Orland and Charles, the two ill-fated sons of Anne de Bretagne had by King Charles VIII, whom she had married in 1491. The sculptures around the tomb are thought to be by the Florentine, Girolamo da Fiesole, the sarcophagus sculptures from the workshop of the famous Tours sculptor, Michel de Colombe. Henry James described the monument rather unfeelingly as 'really a lesson in good taste', when it movingly commemorates royal family tragedies.

You can visit the **Cloître de la Psalette** (*small fee*) from within the cathedral. This cloister may have lost one side, but the 15th- and 16th-century remains are quite beautiful. The former library still shelters some earlier wall paintings. You can also climb the cathedral's south tower on special tours.

Musée des Beaux-Arts

Open Wed–Mon 9–12.45 and 2–6, closed public hols;
18 Place François Sicard, t 02 47 05 68 73, f 02 47 05 38 91; adm.

A beautiful concave triumphal arch leads into the grounds of the former archbishop's palace next to the cathedral, where a vast and splendid cedar spreads out its branches. Fritz the elephant is kept in the former stables to the right; he was a circus animal who went on the rampage in Tours at the start of the 20th century. Shot dead, his body was sent to Nantes to be stuffed and was then brought back up to Tours by boat. Formal French gardens lie on the far side of the courtyard.

The big gate and wall protecting the splendid archbishop's residence were put up just before the Revolution, but didn't stop the place from being taken over for the benefit of the people. The main Ancien Régime buildings house the Tours fine arts museum. In 1792, Charles-Antoine Rougeot, who had founded the town's art school, was given the task of gathering together works from abandoned Touraine abbeys, churches and the homes of aristocrats who had emigrated. Paintings were brought in from such august religious institutions as those at Marmoutier, Bourgueil and La Roche, while works from the Château de Chanteloup outside Amboise (*see p.244*) also arrived here.

To add to this sudden influx of fine art from the region, in the Consulate period (just before Napoleon became emperor) the museum became one of 15 across the country to benefit from donations from France's central national depot of art. Tours received 30 works, among which are the most famous international pieces in the collection. The magnificent Mantegna panels, *Christ in the Olive Grove* and *The Resurrection*, made for the church of San Zeno in Verona, came as booty from Bonaparte's Italian campaign. In the middle of these two panels should be a scene of the Crucifixion, actually in the Louvre, although a later room in the Tours museum contains Degas' approximative homage to the missing piece.

Rubens' *Ex-Voto of the Virgin Presenting the Child to the Donor Alexander Goubeau and his wife Anne Antoni* of 1615, another 'gift' to Tours from the nation, was commissioned by an Antwerp family. The artist depicts an extraordinarily intimate meeting, the picture dominated by the Virgin's red dress whose colour seems to be reflected in the donors' faces.

The other very famous name in the museum's collection is Rembrandt, represented by a small early painting of his, *The Flight into Egypt*, with a rather doe-eyed donkey, but the whole conveying a dreadful feeling of darkness, although the infant Jesus's head glows like a bright beacon in the night.

The collection's first stay in the archbishop's palace was short-lived, as the bishops regained their seat. It was only in 1910 that the town once more became proprietor of the palace, its peripatetic collection hung here again. In the meantime, further important donations had been made by leading families, to be considerably added to in the 20th century. Octave Linet left a collection of early Italian and Flemish paintings. State help and exchanges allowed the museum to acquire a very fair representation of 19th-century French neoclassicism, Romanticism, Orientalism (notably Delacroix's

Bouffons arabes) and Realism. The 20th-century collection includes challenging works by the likes of Olivier Debré, Michael Haas and Joe Davidson.

The main emphasis, however, is very much on the 17th and 18th centuries. And it isn't simply painting which is represented. Fine statues and furniture feature, for example the pieces from the Château de Chanteloup, including lacquer-work from the East. The overall atmosphere in the rooms is one of spacious elegance and calm, affording a more refined and more private experience than a visit to a Loire château. The Galerie de Diane has particularly splendid decoration to frame Jean-Antoine Houdon's 1776 bronze of the hunting goddess.

Views of Tours and the Loire are one interesting theme to follow. Again from Chanteloup, two interesting landscapes by Jean-Pierre Houel, painted in 1769, show a *View of the Loire Between Amboise and Lussault* and *Paradise View near Chanteloup*. One room is given over to Touraine in the 17th and 18th centuries, with an absorbing panorama by Charles-Antoine Demachy, who has somewhat exaggerated the hills south of the Cher, turning them into the foothills of mountains!

Among Touraine literary figures to be seen in portraits are Descartes, Racan, Destouches and Bouilly. The *intendant* François-Pierre du Cluzel is also well represented thanks to generous donations from his family. Most famous perhaps of all the great figures Touraine has produced, Balzac is shown in thoughtful pose in a study by Louis Boulanger for a painting commissioned by Balzac's great love, Madame Hanska. Balzac is also to be seen in a copy of Rodin's famous sculpture of him, bound in a swirl of draped stone; the piece appeared merely unfinished to many when it was shown at the Salon de la Société des Beaux-Arts in 1898, but it has since been viewed as a revolutionary work. Look out too for works by the Tourangeau François Sicard, an important French sculptor of the Second Empire, commissioned to produce a great number of monuments in Touraine.

Other Tourangeau artists whose work is well represented include Jean-Charles Cazin, who served as curator of the museum from 1869 to 1872; his best-known work is *Hagar and Ishmael in the Desert*. The works of the 19th-century ceramicist, Charles-Jean Avisseau, and the school that formed around him, are numerous, distinguished by a bright mix of colours and a delight in flora and fauna. But the most fascinating Tourangeau artist on show is Abraham Bosse. An engraver of the 17th century, he depicted all walks of society and all manner of trades, offering enlightening details on life under the reign of Louis XIII. A room in the basement displays a frequently changing series of his etchings, showing his eye for detail and satire. His series on the five senses, dating from around 1635, was interpreted in paint by an unknown artist, the enchanting pieces crammed full of symbolism.

Château de Tours

The truncated remnants of the Château de Tours lie not far north of the cathedral, close to the Loire, in a slightly ignored corner of town. All that now stands of Philippe le Hardi's late 13th-century fort are two towers, the northern one known as the Tour de Guise, named after the mighty Catholic family. Charles de Guise, son of the duke of Lorraine murdered on King Henri III's orders in Blois castle, remained imprisoned here for several years after the bloody death of his father, to stop him continuing the family power struggle. He would eventually escape. Other more illustrious events had taken place in this château before that time, including two French royal weddings. In 1413, Marie d'Anjou was married to the future King Charles VII here, and later in the century Margaret of Scotland's union with the future King Louis XI was celebrated at the château. The Logis du Gouverneur is the separate late 15th-century wing parallel to the Loire. Under it, you can make out remains of the Gallo-Roman town wall, used as foundations.

Within the Logis du Gouverneur the history of Tours is treated in serious fashion by the **Atelier Histoire de Tours** (*open Wed and Sat only 2–6; 25 Av André-Malraux,* **t** *02 47 64 90 52 and* **t** *02 47 70 88 42; free*). The archaeological and pictorial evidence, as well as models and videos, give some idea of how the town developed through history.

Saint-Julien Abbey and its Museums

The entrance to the large, grubby **Eglise Saint-Julien** is tucked away behind the postwar precinct of the Rue Nationale, close to Tours' historic bridge, the Pont Wilson. The church now seems somewhat contemptuously treated in such surrounds. Yet for centuries this was one of Tours' great monastic institutions, founded by Gregory of Tours. Gregory was from the Auvergne and Auvergne monks first settled here, having brought with them the relics of St Julien de Brioude, the revered patron saint of their region. The Vikings destroyed the first monastery, and a new one was built in the 10th century. The towering porch dates from this time, although it was so heavily restored in the 19th century that only the form remains original. A violent storm brought down the Romanesque building, which was replaced between 1243 and 1260 by the Gothic construction you see today. Inside, you can appreciate its pure, uplifting style. The beautiful tracery of the east window stands out. The stained glass didn't survive the war, but was replaced by modern works by Le Chevallier.

Two strange museums are to be found in the other remaining buildings from the monastic foundation. Old cake preserved for posterity counts among the most curious exhibits in the **Musée du Compagnonnage** (*open mid-June–mid-Sept daily 9–12.30 and 2–6, rest of year Wed–Mon 9–12 and 2–6, closed public hols; 8 Rue Nationale,* **t** *02 47 61 07 93, www.ville-tours.fr/compagnonnage; adm*), housed in the former 16th-century dormitory of St-Julien, above the cloister. This museum is surely one of the very strangest in France. As you enter you're faced with a chaos of information on the history of *compagnonnage*. The whole notion is made to sound most strange, but basically it involved different trade guilds encouraging their crafts and supporting their brothers, including through ritual and masonic-type ceremonies. Mysterious, legendary roots are cited, with Solomon, Jacques de Molay – the last persecuted leader of the Knights Templars, burned to death in Paris in 1314 – and Père Soubise mentioned as formative figures.

Following the mass, or rather mess, of bits and pieces on the history of *compagnonnage*, the chefs d'oeuvre beyond are clearly divided by craft. Many of the artisans represented won the prestigious prize of *meilleur ouvrier de France* (best craftsman in France). The staggering number of hours the pieces took to make is often stated. Most of the works are miniature examples of their profession, for example, intricate, perfectly executed small-scale timber roofs or wrought iron gates. Some of the exhibits are not so miniature for their trade, though, for instance the works by the *pâtissiers*, the bizzarest among the bizarre. 'Let them not eat my cake!' would be the all too appropriate motto for these proud fellows. In the food section, it's perhaps the culinary model of the Hospices de Beaune in Dijon which takes the biscuit. Made from 20kg of pasta, with 22,000 coloured tiles and leaves of gelatine (for the stained glass), it took 800 hours to complete and won the first prize at the cooking olympics of 1976 in Frankfurt. You can see why.

Down in the former cellars of St-Julien abbey lurks the **Musée des Vins de Touraine** (*open Wed–Mon 9–12 and 2–6; closed public hols; 16 Rue Nationale, t 02 47 61 07 93, f 02 47 21 68 90; adm*). Many excellent quotes on the wonders of wine scattered around the massive, vaulted room are the best thing about the place. Otherwise, the very old-fashioned displays are desperately in need of modernization.

Hôtel Gouin (Musée Archéologique)

Open April–Sept 9.30–12.30 and 1.30–6.30, rest of year 9.30–12.30 and 2–5.30; 25 Rue du Commerce, t 02 47 66 22 32; adm.

A riot of Renaissance detail has proliferated like brambles across the extraordinary façade of the Hôtel Gouin, west of the Rue Nationale and Pont Wilson. The front was the only part of the building to survive the war bombs. It had itself been added on in the 16th century to an earlier Gothic mansion for René Gardette, a wealthy silk merchant. The façade shows how Italian fashion had caught on in France at that period. The name of Gouin refers to a Breton banking family which later owned the house. After the war the family left the very badly damaged remnants of the house to the town on the understanding that it would be turned into a museum.

The Touraine archaeological museum within takes you from the prehistoric and everyday Gallo-Roman finds displayed in the basement, via the fine collection of medieval and Renaissance pieces, up to the 18th-century Enlightenment science cabinet from the Château de Chenonceau and a display of 18th-century pottery. Many of the fine pieces of medieval sculpture were saved from Touraine religious buildings that have been destroyed. The museum contains a whole array of beautiful sculptures of saints, including some from the Prieuré St-Cosme (*see* p.273) depicting the persecuted Syrian doctors St Cosme and St Damien, who came west only to be decapitated. The medieval trades are also represented in sculpture, but in much more humorous ways. One highly amusing post carries the sign of a *hongreur*, a castrator of horses, only here two women are depicted carrying out the painful operation on a poor creature half-man, half-chicken.

Engravings show interesting details of Tours in centuries past, with the Ile Simon (previously known as the Ile St-Jacques) a veritable village in its own right, sat in the middle of the Loire. You can also admire the grandiose 19th-century aspect of the area which once stood around Tours' main bridge before the Second World War devastation. The Cabinet de Physique et de Chimie from Chenonceau reflects the fashion among the 18th-century aristocracy for carrying out scientific experiments at home. Tours, a town where the liberal professions flourished, was quite an intellectual centre in centuries past, and learned societies became fashionable in the Ancien Régime.

Musée du Gemmail

Open April–mid-Nov Tues–Sun and public hols 10–12 and 2–6.30, rest of year weekends only; 7 Rue du Mûrier, t 02 47 61 01 19, f 02 47 05 04 79; adm.

The Musée du Gemmail, tucked away in its own courtyard in an early 19th-century house on Rue du Mûrier, close to glorious Place Plumereau, is another of Tours' stranger museums. It celebrates a radiant 20th-century development in the art of stained glass. The word *'gemmail'* was coined by Jean Cocteau, one of the many notable artists to rave about this art form; it derives from the amalgamation of the words *gemme* and *émail* (enamel). Of course gems aren't used, just coloured glass that takes on luminous qualities.

In the 1930s, the artist Jean Crottie had the idea of superimposing thick layers of coloured glass on top of each other to create vibrant works of art. A Touranageau called Roger Malherbe-Navarre then developed the necessary soldering technique. No leading is used and only very rarely is any paint added for a finishing touch. Rather, layer upon layer of glass, coloured in the mass, is cut and soldered together with enamel to compose a vivid and complex, textured picture. Each *gemmail* is executed by two people, the *maître d'œuvre* guiding the *gemmiste*; they work to a model on an easel, the former literally overseeing the latter from on high, the *gemmiste* placing the pieces of glass according to precise instructions. Roger Malherbe-Navarre can be seen directing a work in progress in the short explanatory video.

The museum contains an extraordinary collection of interpretations of works of art in this medium. Of several of Picasso's works transformed into stained glass, *Les Adolescents* and *La Tête Noire* stand out. Rouault is another modern master whose works have been well interpreted. Pollet's magnificent *Dinde* (Turkey) presents a riot of changing coloured plumage as you pass by. Jean Cocteau and Roger Malherbe-Navarre set up an annual international prize in 1957, the object being to select one contemporary work to be newly interpreted as a *gemmail*; the town has now taken over the prize-giving. Some of the more recent pieces may seem vulgar, but there have been notable successes, such as Margotton's Greek-inspired *L'Amphore*, lending itself wonderfully to the luminosity of the form. The museum offers the added curiosity of an **underground chapel** dating from the 12th century, which makes for a particularly atmospheric setting for some of the displays.

A Walk Around Tours

We start this tour in front of the cathedral. After admiring its façade, wander all the way round the outside. The area just behind the cathedral provided the backdrop for Balzac's tale of vicious petty religious rivalry leading to the persecution of an all-too-innocent priest in *Le Curé de Tours*.

The pretty, shaded **Place François Sicard** lies just to the south of the cathedral, outside the archbishop's palace. This square typifies Tours' civic elegance. Named after a Tourangeau sculptor, several other sculptors' works here honour other local figures. **Rue Bernard Palissy** leads down to the tourist office and train station. Two of France's greatest 16th-century artists, the painter François Clouet and the sculptor Michel Colombe, once had their studios along this street.

The quarter behind the cathedral is full of atmosphere. Take the curving **Rue des Ursulines**. The garden of Touraine's archives building contains Gallo-Roman ruins and the Brèche des Normands, where in June 903 the marauding Vikings supposedly fled in reaction to the holy flashing of St Martin's relics. Rue des Ursulines is also the site of the 17th-century **Chapelle St-Michel**, where Marie de l'Incarnation took her vows in 1633 before she set out to spread the Gospel in Canada. She and her sisters spent a great deal of time in Québec not just trying to wash off the native children's pagan 'sins', but also to wash them clean of the grease they traditionally wore to protect their skin. The chapel was restored by the Association Tours-Canada. Nearby, down Rue du Petit Pré, the **Centre Marie de l'Incarnation** (*open mid-June–mid-Sept 3–6, rest of year Wed only 3–5; t 02 47 66 65 95*) is a small museum devoted to the religious figure.

North of Rue des Ursulines, the high walls of old religious institutions give curving **Rue du Général Meunier** great atmosphere. The curve is attributed to the former site of a huge Gallo-Roman amphitheatre, said to have been bigger than the one in Nîmes, possibly built from the time when the Emperor Hadrian passed through Tours in the 120s. Many religious orders established themselves on this street just behind the cathedral, and a few are still based here, hidden from public gaze by their high walls. You're forced to loop back to Place Grégoire de Tours behind the cathedral. From here head up Rue Racine to Place des Petites Boucheries. Then head west along Rue Albert Thomas and Rue Colbert. The long straight line they form follows the track of the main street back in Gallo-Roman times. Where Rue Thomas and Rue Colbert meet, Rue Lavoisier leads up to the remnants of the Château de Tours and the river.

Rue Colbert, with a fair number of restored timber-framed fronts from the 15th and 16th centuries, is a fine street. Look out for the occasional beams and doorways carved with figures and animals. **Place Foire-le-Roi**, crammed with grand old town houses, was a market square back in medieval times. It was also here that public executions often took place. The most famous house on the square is No.8, the **Hôtel Babou de la Bourdaisière**. Philibert Babou was for some time treasurer to the young King François I at the start of the 16th century and had several fine homes built for himself, including the Château de la Bourdaisière (*see p.247*). His fine town house was much added to in subsequent centuries. Another remarkable house has slate-covered sides, a style you'll see in one or two other spots in Tours. Continuing along Rue Colbert, at No.66, look out for the little alleyway which gives you an inkling of what the medieval maze of the city must have felt like. No.39 is where Colas de Montbazon is supposed to have bashed out Joan of Arc's armour.

As you approach the abbey of St-Julien the old houses give way to the makeshift blocks put up after the bombing of this quarter in the Second World War. Head south down **Rue Jules Favre**. The splendid mid-18th-century Hôtel du Commerce was built for an association of Tours merchants. The most striking architecture here, though, is the ruins opposite, the shell of the façade of the great Renaissance **Hôtel de Beaune-Semblançay**, left standing like a theatrical backdrop after the bombardments. The place was built for Jacques de Beaune-Semblançay, treasurer to Louise de Savoie and then to her kingly son, François I. Unfairly blamed for François' huge debts, Semblançay was executed, at the ripe old age of 80. On the square, the magnificently carved fountain, the work of Martin and Bastien François, and the perched Sainte-Chapelle were also made for him.

Rue de la Scellerie, stretching between Rue Nationale and Place François Sicard, is lined with fine buildings. The most imposing is the 19th-century **theatre**. Beyond it, off the side streets, you'll find the town's best antiques shops. **Rue Corneille** leads down from the theatre to the square with the **Préfecture**, the administrative centre of Touraine, its offices installed in Napoleonic times in the buildings of a former convent. Busts of Roman emperors from Richelieu's great vanished château in southern Touraine have been placed here.

Rue de Buffon leads south from Place de la Préfecture towards the central train station; take it and at the end you can't miss Jean Nouvel's striking 1990s creation, the **Centre de Congrès Vinci**, with a visor at the front like the peak of a baseball cap. Opposite it, across the major boulevard of Heurteloup, stands the splendid old train station, designed by Victor Laloux, the builder of the Gare (now Musée) d'Orsay in Paris. The **Centre de Création Contemporaine** nearby at 55 Rue Marcel Tribut offers a generous space for contemporary art exhibitions.

Victor Laloux also designed the grandiose façade of the Hôtel de Ville on **Place Jean-Jaurès**, the bustling heart of Tours. The colossal atlantes shouldering the weight of the town hall's balcony were sculpted by François Sicard. Two figures of river gods recline on either side of the great clock, symbolizing of the Loire and the Cher which embrace the centre of Tours. Other grand buildings on the square include the law courts and the Hôtel de l'Univers. The major arteries serving Tours head off from here, Boulevard Heurteloup and Boulevard Béranger going east and west respectively, and Rue Nationale and Avenue de Grammont north and south. The wide, tree-lined Avenue de Grammont heads straight as an arrow down to the Cher river.

Rue Nationale, the largest shopping street in Tours, leads up to the Loire. Although the big stores along it attract large numbers, the street itself isn't beautiful, as it all had to be rebuilt after the war. However, the chic shops may tempt you into the prettier streets off its length. At the northern end of Rue Nationale, Place Anatole France looks rather soulless, despite statues of Rabelais and Descartes. It's surprising not to find a statue of Balzac, who was born along Rue Nationale. By the river, the intriguing copper-roofed building in Moroccan style is Tours' Bibliothèque (municipal library), a gilded statue beside it recalling the contribution of the American services of supply based at Tours during the First World War and expressing French gratitude.

You can get down to the lovely **Loire-side quays** here and go for a walk along the river. Tours' main historic bridge, the **Pont Wilson**, is of beautiful white stone and known as the *pont de pierre* by the townspeople; but it's collapsed so often in its history that it might almost be built of sand. The last time part of it fell down was in 1978. Walk westwards along the cobbled riverside and you pass below the university arts faculties. The steep riverside walls cut with narrow stairs and the mooring rings still in place are a reminder of the river trading that once took place in Tours. It seems unbelievable that large ships once stopped here. In the middle of the Loire lies the Ile Simon, now an uninhabited island on which you can go for a walk by crossing the Pont Napoléon, west of Pont Wilson.

Back at Rue Nationale, head into the western half of Tours' historic centre. Rue du Commerce leads into an area packed with bars and restaurants heralding the superbly restored **Place Plumereau**. The network of streets around it is filled with remarkable beamed houses, the woodwork sometimes carved with figures, the court-yards embellished with splendid stair towers. This was the quarter where many of Louis XI's courtiers lived in the second half of the 15th century (there are many later additions of course). Restaurant and café tables stand at the ready on the pavements for the waves of arts students leaving their lecture halls. The liveliness doesn't abate in the holidays, when tourists take the students' places. The Place Plumereau quarter is the most famous area of postwar restoration in Tours, and the most successful, although immediately after the war it wasn't considered a desirable corner of town, many immigrants living in poverty here. Some complain that the area was then prac-tically cleansed. Today it is extremely sought after. Place Plumereau was the hat-makers' domain in medieval times, but its plumed name derives from that of a Tours councillor who had a mansion in the middle of the square.

Explore the streets towards the river via the breach in the north side of the square. You first stumble upon the **Jardin de St-Pierre-le-Puellier**, where some of the ruins of a medieval church have been left exposed in a pit in the ground while others have been incorporated into a variety of idiosyncratic buildings. This is apparently a spot with an extremely distinguished Christian history, as Clothilde had a convent founded here in the Dark Ages. She was the wife of Clovis, the first Frankish king to convert to Christianity, in good part thanks to her powers of persuasion. To the west of this curious and charming garden, **Rue Briçonnet** contains some particularly fine houses at its northern end.

Just south from Place Plumereau lies the once strongly religious quarter of Châteauneuf, with its links with St Martin. Make for the **Place Châteauneuf** via Rue du Change and Rue de Châteauneuf. On the north side of the square you can admire the remnants of a 14th-century château, once the residence of the counts of Touraine, now given over to the Conservatoire de Musique.

Many churches have succeeded each other on St Martin's burial site. Gregory of Tours described Perpet's basilica, built between 466 and 470, as the finest in Gaul. Several centuries on, Charlemagne appointed Alcuin as abbot of St-Martin and he set up his famed school here. A couple of 10th-century fires destroyed the church of that time. In 1014 a new structure was consecrated. Two immense towers still standing along Rue des Halles, the **Tour Charlemagne** and the **Tour de l'Horloge**, give a very good impression of the vastness of the edifice, one of the most significant early Romanesque buildings in France. One 12th-century writer, Aimery Picaud, compared it to the great pilgrimage church of Santiago da Compostela in northern Spain. Through the medieval period this mammoth building suffered from numerous fires. By the time of the Revolution the place was already badly run down and most of it was subsequently destroyed. The Tour Charlemagne is the mightier of the two towers left, the remnant of the north transept of the great church. At its foot you can see a plan of the whole ensemble as it once stood. The Tour de l'Horloge was one of the two towers on the main west front, added at the end of the 12th century.

Although these soaring towers are extremely impressive, it's hard for them to convey the significance of the site below them now, as the area around is given over to tempting shops. However, the old church of St-Martin was, with Notre-Dame de Paris, Reims and Chartres, one of *the* most important centres of Christian learning in medieval France. The **Musée St-Martin** (*open mid-March–mid-Nov Wed–Sun 9.30–12.30 and 2–5.30; closed 1 May and 14 July; 3 Rue Rapin, **t** 02 47 05 68 73 and t/f 02 47 64 48 87; adm*) occupies the former Chapelle St-Jean on Rue Rapin and gives historical details both on St Martin and on the previous churches on the site. It's a small museum, but contains fragments of sculpture and even one or two murals. Off it lie the beautiful remnants of the **cloister of St-Martin's**. There are traces of Gothic work on the west side, but the 16th-century Renaissance east gallery is the real attraction.

The tomb of St Martin was rediscovered in the course of an archaeological dig in 1860. This gave cause to celebrate with the creation of the **Nouvelle Basilique St-Martin**, a self-important white whale of a building from the outside, with a large dome topped by a statue of Martin in triumphant pose. The plan was by Victor Laloux, and it was built between 1887 and the start of the 20th century. The interior glistens with polished Vosges granite columns, surmounted by capitals in neo-Byzantine style. A bronze statue of St Martin decorates the interior of the dome, while at the back of the crypt below, François Sicard's sculpture of Cardinal Meignant pays tribute to the man who ordered the building of this new basilica. The crypt contains St Martin's tomb. His cult is very much alive and well, to go by the number of people who come to pray here.

Just west along Rue des Halles or Rue Rapin, you come to the modern **covered market** and the western end of Tours' major historic quarter.

North of the Loire: Les Trois Tours Silk Factory

One good reason to cross to the north bank of the Loire from the centre of Tours is to visit the fascinating old-fashioned silk-making factory known as Les Trois Tours, or La Maison Le Manach (*at 35 Quai Paul Bert, but you need to go via the tourist office*). To take this step back in time, you will be taken across the Loire to the Quai Paul Bert via the foot bridge known as the Pont de Fil, which serves the Ile Aucard, this island given over to sports grounds, and in summer the venue for a lively rock music festival.

Lyon may be the French city most closely associated with fine silk production, but Tours also became a specialist centre from the late 15th century, encouraged by King

Louis XI and his courtiers. Les Trois Tours, set up in 1829, has continued to use old-fashioned techniques and machines in the main. The tour offers an extraordinary insight into traditional silk-making. Walking through the entrance into the courtyard, you're confronted by a striking image of 19th-century industry. An array of old looms is lined up in the building at the back of the courtyard. The company owns almost 80 old models, almost all in working order, and listed. Many are famous Jacquard looms, named after the Lyon silk-weaver who invented an ingenious system of punch cards to facilitate the copying of complex patterns in the early 19th century. Les Trois Tours has kept its records, including over 4,000 designs, and the vast majority of its work is now in reproducing these, to old-fashioned methods and standards.

A short video (available in English) explains the various stages in traditional silk-making. Les Trois Tours workers carry out virtually all the processes in silk-making, apart from the dyeing, in-house. On the tour, you'll learn about the great variety of qualities of silk that can be produced. Seeing the expert silk-weavers in action is both impressive and deafening. Using the old-fashioned machines, they can create around 2m of silk a day. At the end of the tour you can admire an exhibition of silks; there are also pieces to buy, such as cushions and bags, or, more simply, framed silks.

Prieuré de St-Cosme

Open daily April–Sept 9–7, Oct–Mar 9.30–12.30 and 2–5; closed 25 Dec; t 02 47 37 32 70 and t 02 47 31 43 27, f 02 47 37 25 20; adm.

Drive west out of the centre of Tours following the south bank of the Loire and the route to the Prieuré de St-Cosme is well signposted. The confusion of roads surrounding this ruined priory may be unprepossessing, but once in the grounds you find yourself in a delightful spot. The figure most closely associated with the place is the great 16th-century French Renaissance Pléiade poet Pierre de Ronsard. But the priory dates back to well before that period. A little chapel dedicated to saints Cosme and Damien already existed in the 10th century. At the end of the 11th century the chapter of St-Martin in Tours took control and established a priory with five canons following the Augustinian rule. Many of the vestiges left today are from the 11th and 12th centuries. King Louis XI had his favourite château of Plessis-lès-Tours very close by – unfortunately only a sad wing of his palace remains.

Charles de Ronsard became prior in the mid-16th century. But his poetic brother was apparently so taken with the place that in 1565 Charles agreed to swap it with one of Pierre's benefices. The first main building you come to, the Logis du Prieur, has been turned into a museum on Ronsard, with details of his life and loves (four major ones). Mainly thought of as a lyrical versifier on the human passions and nature these days, in his time he was also a political poet. He composed much of his *Franciade* here, an epic work singing the praises of France. The supreme lyricist of the French language, whose verse flows like water, is buried in the priory grounds, a tombstone to him lying in the sorry remnants of the church. The refectory and guesthouse have survived much better. The former, entered via triangular teeth of stone, appears totally out of proportion for the needs of the dozen religious men who made up the core of the religious community here. But the place also served as a stop for pilgrims heading down to Santiago de Compostela.

The gardens contain superb collections of roses, appropriately enough, as Ronsard is famed for his descriptions of these flowers, which serve as such powerful symbols of the transience of love and life in his verse – the lines in *A Cassandre* count among the most famous in the French language:

> *Mignonne allons voir si la rose*
> *Qui ce matin avait declose*
> *Sa robe pourpre au soleil*
> *A point perdu ceste vesprée*
> *Les plis de sa robe pourprée,*
> *Et son teint au vostre pareil.*

(Darling, let us go and see if the rose / Which this morning had disclosed / Its scarlet robe to the sun / Might not this eventide / Have lost its folds so crimson-dyed / And its hue so similar to you.)

The Indre South of Tours

16

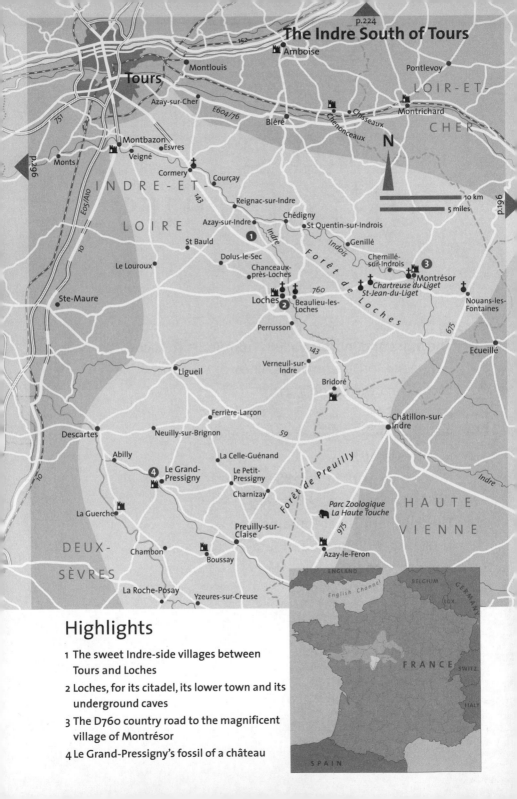

Tours

LOIR-ET-

CHER

INDRE-ET-

LOIRE

N

10 km

5 miles

Amboise

Montlouis

Pontlevoy

Azay-sur-Cher

Montrichard

Bléré

Chisseaux

Chenonceaux

Montbazon

Esvres

Veigné

Monts

Cormery

Courçay

Reignac-sur-Indre

Chédigny

Azay-sur-Indre

St Quentin-sur-Indrois

St Bauld

Genillé

Dolus-le-Sec

Chemillé-
sur-Indrois

Le Louroux

Chanceaux-
près-Loches

Montrésor

Chartreuse du Liget
St-Jean-du-Liget

Ste-Maure

Loches

Beaulieu-les-
Loches

Nouans-les-
Fontaines

Perrusson

Forêt de Loches

Indrois

Indre

Écueillé

Verneuil-sur-
Indre

Ligueil

Bridoré

Châtillon-sur-
Indre

Ferrière-Larçon

Descartes

Neuilly-sur-Brignon

Abilly

Le Grand-
Pressigny

La Celle-Guénand

Le Petit-
Pressigny

Forêt de Preuilly

Charnizay

HAUTE

VIENNE

La Guerche

Parc Zoologique
La Haute Touche

DEUX-

Chambon

Boussay

Preuilly-sur-
Claise

Azay-le-Feron

SÈVRES

La Roche-Posay

Yzeures-sur-Creuse

ENGLAND

English Channel

BELGIUM

GERMANY

LUX.

FRANCE

SWITZ.

ITALY

SPAIN

Highlights

1 The sweet Indre-side villages between
Tours and Loches

2 Loches, for its citadel, its lower town and its
underground caves

3 The D760 country road to the magnificent
village of Montrésor

4 Le Grand-Pressigny's fossil of a château

This chapter leads you into some of the quietest and most enchanting little valleys not just in Touraine, but in the whole region covered by this guidebook. The main cultural centre is magnificent little Loches, briefly a courtly town under King Charles VII in the 15th century. It had fallen back into sleepy rural life by the time Descartes spent his childhood around these parts in the early 17th century; he headed off to wake up the European mind to modern thinking. Now Loches and the Lochois are utterly charming backwaters, the countryside strung with the loveliest of quiet villages and the most picturesque remnants of religious establishments, showing how monks once sought out the area's inspiring tranquillity. Beyond Loches, the highlights are Montrésor, with its stuffy old château, and Le Grand-Pressigny, its castle converted into a museum of prehistory – Neolithic man loved this corner too.

The Indre and Indrois Valleys from Tours to Loches

Travelling down from Tours to Loches, avoid the busy N143 rushing through flat and uneventful cereal land and follow a much quieter, winding route along the Indre's intimate, enclosed valley. It's been nicknamed the Vallée Verte, the Green Valley, and offers a delightful mix of pretty villages, châteaux, water mills, pastures and copses, shimmering plantations of poplars standing out.

Between Montbazon and Loches

We start at **Montbazon**, on the Indre river due south of Tours. This attractive place is rather spoilt by being split in two by the N10 main road, once the royal route to Spain. The centre of Montbazon is overseen by the ruins of a substantial **keep** (*open Easter–Oct daily exc Tues off season 10–6; adm*), one of the many built for that indefatigable Loire campaigner, Foulques Nerra of Anjou. This may even be the first stone donjon he had erected, and it fights it out with that in Langeais (west along the Loire) for the title of the oldest stone keep built in France. Montbazon's is certainly much more impressive; parts of its cracked, herringbone-patterned walls still reach almost 100ft in height. Eleanor of Aquitaine and Richard the Lionheart apparently counted among its owners. The building is capped by a spectacular sour-looking copper Virgin carrying the baby Jesus. Weighing in at 20 tonnes, she was put up here on the insistence of a mid-19th-century priest. It's thanks in good part to William Dudley, a US soldier who came over to France to fight in the First World War, that the keep is standing. He settled here after the war and carried out vital repair work. Now an enthusiastic British Canadian and his French wife have bought the ruin. They have ambitious plans to transform it into a tourist sight, bringing out its history and using it as a dramatic backdrop for events. Pay them a visit to see how they're getting on.

Veigné stands in a picturesque riverside setting. A handful of wine producers in neighbouring **Esvres** make one of the least-known of Touraine wines, Noble-Joué, an intriguing *vin gris*, or rosé. It once graced the French royal court, Louis XI having a particular liking for it. The Noble-Joué of Touraine has the distinction of being the

Getting There

Many of the villages along the Indre between Tours and Loches are served both by local **bus** and **train** services.

Tourist Information

Montbazon: O.T du Val de l'Indre, B.P.2, 37250 Montbazon, **t** 02 47 26 97 87, *ot-valdelindre@wanadoo.fr*.

Cormery: 13 Rue Nationale, 37320 Cormery, **t** 02 47 91 82 82/02 47 43 30 84, **f** 02 47 43 18 73.

Genillé: 17 Place Agnès Sorel, 37460 Genillé, **t/f** 02 47 59 57 85.

Chemillé-sur-Indrois: Mairie, 37460 Chemillé-sur-Indrois, **t** 02 47 92 60 75, **f** 02 47 92 67 98.

Market Days

Montbazon: Friday afternoon and Tuesday morning.

Cormery: Thursday morning.

Where to Stay and Eat

Montbazon ✉ 37250

★★★★Château d'Artigny, Route de Monts, along the D17, **t** 02 47 34 30 30, *www.artigny.com* (*expensive–luxury*). This outrageously sumptuous castle west of Montbazon looks out over the Indre valley. The image of an elegant château of the Ancien Régime, it was actually built at the start of the 20th century. The rooms, divided between the château and outhouses, are immaculately decorated and there are enough of them to receive large parties of American and Japanese tourists. It's all very chichi. The frescoes on the central dome may repel sensitive tastes, but the cuisine is extremely elegant, the wine list vast. In the gardens *à la française* are a swimming pool, two tennis courts and a helipad (*menus €47–80*). *Closed mid-Dec–late-Jan.*

La Chancelière and **Le Jeu de Cartes**, 1 Place des Marronniers, **t** 02 47 26 00 67 (*menus €25–35; closed Sun pm and Mon*).

La Chancelière is a highly regarded, exclusive, refined little restaurant in the centre of Montbazon, Le Jeu de Cartes its simpler, cheaper little brother. *Closed late Aug–early Sept and early Feb–start of Mar.*

Auberge de la Courtille, 13 Av de la Gare, **t** 02 47 26 28 26 (*menus €17–35; closed Sun pm, Tues pm and Wed*). A good option for traditional Tourangeau food. *Closed mid-Jul–mid-Aug.*

Veigné ✉ 37250

★★★Domaine de la Tortinière, Les Gués-de-Veigné, 10 Route de Ballan-Miré, **t** 02 47 34 35 00, *www.tortiniere.com* (*expensive*). A sparkling-white little Second Empire château with grounds sloping down to the Indre. The delightful rooms have lovely views onto the valley. You can go boating on the river, or swimming in the heated pool. The chef does stunning things with goat's cheese, using it to stuff Touraine pigeon or to add to his sorrel soup (*menus €38–68; closed Sun pm Nov–Mar*). *Closed 21 Dec–Feb.*

★★Le Moulin Fleuri, Route du Ripault, **t** 02 47 26 01 12, *www.chateauxhotels.com/fleuri* (*inexpensive*). If any place were appropriate for eating frogs' legs, this hotel's modern dining room right by the river would be it. The cuisine is of a high order. The rooms in this mill, which dates in part from the 16th century, are more ordinary, but it's quite fun being so close to the water (*menus €21–49; closed Mon, Thurs lunch exc public hols, and, out of season, Sun pm*). *Closed Feb–early March and Christmas hols.*

Azay-sur-Indre ✉ 37310

Le Moulin de la Follaine B&B, **t** 02 47 92 57 91, *www.moulindefollaine.fr.st* (*inexpensive*). Set on an island in the Indrois just before it joins the Indre and just below a little medieval castle, this delightful watermill has been converted into a romantic B&B, some of the decorative details perhaps a touch over-romantic for some tastes. The owners are passionate about this lovely property; the main waterwheel is beautifully displayed.

only wine in France made from three varieties of Pinot grape, Pinot Noir, Pinot Meunier and Pinot Gris. It can accompany light meats and fish.

The Benedictine **abbey of Cormery**, a step further east, was once an important French religious institution, founded with the blessing of Pope Leo I and Alcuin of York, its constitution dating back to 800. The Vikings laid waste to the place in 853. Fragments of later buildings spanning the medieval centuries remain, although much was destroyed after the Revolution. Many parts of the abbey were transformed to personal use by the villagers. For example, the 15th-century Lady Chapel has long served as a barn! The main vestige of the abbey is the Tour St-Paul, while Rue de l'Abbaye follows the line of the former nave. To get an overall understanding of the place and to appreciate its quirkiness, follow a tour organized by the local tourist office. The monks may have left Cormery long ago, but their macaroons remain, their shape said jokingly to resemble the religious brothers' belly-buttons!

Courçay makes the pretty next little stop, with an extraordinary rough-stone 12th-century spire to its church and a picturesque windmill. Only the monstrous old watermill on the river disturbs the picture. Along the south bank, at the Rocher de la Pinone, Rabelais would have us believe that the first-ever rainbow was witnessed here when Gargantua stopped to pee! **Reignac**, with its château and mill, has a very old church tower and, within the church, the peculiarity of a choir at the west end instead of the traditional east. An attraction up by the N143 in recent summers has been the **Labyrinthus** (*open mid-July–end Aug 10–7.30; t 02 47 37 47 80, www.labyrinthus.com*). Each year a portion of the dull agricultural plain by this main road has been turned into a vast maze, to the delight of children in particular.

Two châteaux dominate the well-located village of **Azay-sur-Indre**, neither open to the public. Here, the Indrois joins the Indre, having travelled west from Montrésor via a string of picturesque villages, Chemillé, Genillé, St-Quentin and Chédigny.

Loches and the Lochois

...elle fait vivre mille ans en un jour (it brings to life a thousand years in one day)
Onésime Reclus, 19th-century traveller, on Loches

Loches is a splendidly imposing model of medieval defence sweetly named after the little fish found in the Indre river. Now viewed as an extremely picturesque tourist spot, Loches must have made a formidable sight for centuries, its walls and keep standing proud on a spur of rock above the plains that surround it. Loches is in fact one of the most important medieval strongholds left standing in France. Rather than there being one single château, the place has a whole upper city, entered via the steep Rue du Château and Porte Royale. The citadel contains an exceptional variety of interesting buildings from different centuries, including not just a castle, but also a separate, soaring keep. The four towers on the medieval church of St-Ours also cut an extraordinary figure. The elegant houses within the ramparts date mainly from the 17th and 18th centuries; one contains a museum devoted to a 19th-century landscape painter from Loches, Emmanuel Lansyer. The hill below the citadel contains a warren of caves from which stone was quarried for centuries; you can go on an extraordinary visit through some of them at the Carrière Troglodytique de Vignemont.

Getting There

The **bus** service between Loches and Tours is more regular than the train service. Both bus and train stations at Loches are located centrally.

Tourist Information

Loches: Place de la Marne, B.P.112, 37601 Loches Cedex, t 02 47 91 82 82, *www.lochesentouraine.com.*

Montrésor: 43 Grande-Rue, 37460 Montrésor, t 02 47 92 70 71, *www.montresor-village.com.*

Market Days

Loches: Wednesday all day and Saturday morning.

Montrésor: Saturday morning.

Festivals

Loches' **son-et-lumière** at the château takes place on Friday and Saturday nights through the summer. Opera is staged in the splendid setting of the '*théâtre de verdure*' up among the fortifications in the **Festival de Théâtre Musical** in July.

Where to Stay and Eat

Loches ✉ 37600

★★★**Hôtel George Sand**, 39 Rue Quintefol, t 02 47 59 39 74, *www. hotelrestaurant-georgesand.com* (*moderate*). In a house once used by 19th-century female novelist George Sand as stables, sandwiched between the river Indre and a narrow busy road. The Fortins have converted it into an extremely attractive, well-kept hotel. It's a lovely place for sunny lunch or summer dinner, as it has a terrace overhanging the river, as well as good food (*menus €16–38*).

★★**Hôtel de France**, 6 Rue Picois, t 02 47 59 00 32, f 02 47 59 28 66 (*inexpensive*). Smart old town house, some rooms with views onto the medieval city. It does quite good food too, at quite a good price (*menus €15–46; closed Sun pm, Mon, and Tues lunch exc July–Aug). Closed mid-Jan–mid-Feb.*

Beaulieu-lès-Loches ✉ 37600

★★**Hôtel de Beaulieu**, 3 Rue Foulques Nerra, t 02 47 91 60 80 (*inexpensive*). Lodging in 12th-century convent buildings, with a simple brasserie next door. *Closed Oct–Mar.*

East of Loches the beautiful route along the D760 is strung with many fragments of religious buildings. These important foundations must once have brought a good deal of life to this area, now so calm. There are medieval fortifications too, particularly in the perfectly picturesque village of Montrésor. Head for Nouans-les-Fontaines for a major artistic surprise. Southeast from Loches, the little-known Château de Bridoré boasts a defensive speciality of its own, the *caponnière*.

Loches

Logis Royal et Donjon de Loches

Open April–Sept 9–7, rest of year 9.30–5; closed 25 Dec and 1 Jan.
Logis t 02 47 59 01 32, keep t 02 47 59 07 86, logisroyalloches@cg37.fr; adm.

The counts of Anjou won Loches through marriage, not war, in the 10th century. Given Loches' easterly position in their territories, it became an important outpost in their conflict with the counts of Blois. Its hill was an obvious place to build fortifications and the first remaining ones probably date from the great Foulques Nerra of Anjou, dating possibly from as early as the 1030s. Royal connections came with Henri Plantagenêt of Anjou, later Henry II of England. He added to the earlier defences, in particular with the building of ramparts and the digging of a great ditch, still to be seen. His rebellious son Richard the Lionheart rose against him, in collusion with the French King Philippe Auguste. Richard took Loches from his father's troops in 1189, but when Richard was later trapped in prison, Philippe Auguste decided to add the place to his possessions. Richard, on his angry return, is said to have recaptured the citadel in three hours; the probable explanation is that the gates were opened to him.

Philippe Auguste's men won Loches back from King John and the English Crown in 1205 after a terrible one-year siege. The end of the siege brought to a close Plantagenet control in the region, and Philippe Auguste donated Loches to Dreux de Mello, the son of his victorious captain. In 1249, King Louis IX bought the place back to form part of the French royal domain. Through the 13th century, Loches' fortifications were reinforced by beak-pointed towers, and further military architecture was added in the course of the 14th and 15th centuries. The royal lodgings, at the other end of the outcrop, date from this time. Expansion also continued around the keep. The great Tour Neuve is something of a second keep in its own right, added in the 15th century. Nearby, the Martelet, from Charles VII's reign, burrows underground into former quarries to provide three levels of dungeons. These towers have a very dark reputation in history, associated with Louis XI's cruelty. A further surround of 16th-century positions completed the hilltop defences.

The Donjon, the Tour Ronde and the Martelet

It makes sense in historical terms to start the tour with the 11th-century **donjon**. With black jackdaws circling round its sheer walls, the place looks forbidding and impregnable. It's considered the finest example of a keep in France. The holes puckering the outer walls were apparently used for beams to hold up the scaffolding. You enter via an arrowhead-shaped *barbacane* and a drawbridge. The stairway in an abutting tower leads to the first floor of the main structure, which served as headquarters. The space below was used for cooking and storage. The second floor was reserved for sleeping and the top level for the guards. Originally this keep would have been roofed, with a walkway on the outside of the top floor. A small chapel was squeezed into the side tower along with the stairs.

Loches' keep and adjoining towers have been converted into something of a museum on torture and imprisonment. Louis IX formalized the use of torture, considered an improvement on the otherwise unregulated practice. Medieval procedure for the euphemistically named *question* (for *question* read torture) was quite painstakingly codified. If a suspect refused to confess, the judge could proceed to the *question préparatoire*, divided into an 'ordinary' and an 'extraordinary' torture. Its form varied according to region. The *question ordinaire* might involve 9 litres of water being forced down the prisoner's throat by funnel, the *question extraordinaire* 18 litres. Another common method of torture was stretching on the rack. For the guilty, there were also various methods of death. At the end of the 15th century, one Louis Secretin was sentenced to burn to death in boiling water in Tours, having been found guilty of counterfeiting. The executioner failed to heat the water sufficiently and Secretin got out relatively unscathed; the executioner was beaten and Secretin went on to marry and have five children.

After the death of King Charles VII, who had held court at Loches, his son King Louis XI, clearly harbouring bad memories of the place, converted it in good part into a prison, which it remained for centuries. One of the terrible iron and wood cages Louis XI ordered for the prison has been recreated in the keep. Their bizarre euphemistic nickname was *fillettes*, little girls. One of the figures supposed to have languished in such a cage was Cardinal La Bahue, servant of Louis XI, but punished for treacherously supporting the king's great enemy, Duke Charles the Bold of Burgundy.

Terrible tales survive of men holed up in Loches' *oubliettes* (from *oublier*, to forget). Numerous tunnels disappear under the citadel. A governor of Loches a little after Louis XI's reign is said to have explored these and to have come across a seated man holding his head in his hands; as the governor approached, the man disintegrated where he had rotted. A researcher of more recent times has revealed that a lot of the supposed haunted *oubliettes* were probably dug for sanitation purposes.

The prisoners' graffiti on the walls of the keep and the great round tower nearby, the **Tour Ronde**, are being carefully preserved for posterity. Some date back to the 12th and 13th centuries, although deciphering and dating them is difficult. Among the crude engravings, religious symbols, a hunting scene and a flat-bottomed riverboat stand out. Outside, the Tour Ronde has great machicolations with gargoyles and superb views onto the citadel and the lower town.

Next you come to the **Martelet**, with its three levels of cells. It isn't as grim inside as might be expected. Its most famous prisoner was Ludovico Sforza, duke of Milan and patron of Leonardo da Vinci. Sforza was a pragmatic, ruthless politician as well as a man of culture who amassed great power in Italy at the end of the 15th century. Ruler of Naples, which he defended against King Charles VIII of France's attack, he came by his position as ruler of Milan through usurping power from his young nephew. In 1500, during Louis XII's Italian campaign to claim his rights over Milan, Sforza was captured and brought to France. Sforza was apparently well treated as an aristocratic prisoner and used the resources of his culture in what must have been dark days. His cells were decorated with insignia and inscriptions. You can clearly make out the murals on the wall of the larger chamber, with its fireplace, which apparently also carried his portrait. Even the latrines were decorated, with cannons, deer and hearts. Sforza was later transferred to the top of the Tour Ronde, but the legend of his terrible treatment doggedly survived. The old story went that after years and years deprived of seeing any daylight, he died from the shock of seeing the sun on finally being taken outside. The circumstances of his death are uncertain.

Loches' defences continued to serve their purpose as a prison, for Huguenots after Louis XIV's Revocation of the Edict of Nantes, and for local lords at the Revolution. In the 20th century, an enthusiastic prison director even got his inmates involved in archaeological excavation of the site. Ironically, the continued if degrading use of these medieval buildings as a gaol probably stopped them from falling into ruin.

The Logis Royal

To appreciate the easier side of life in the citadel, head over to the Logis Royal. The amusing statues of dogs greeting you at the entrance are 19th century. The lodgings

Agnès Sorel, King Charles VII's Scandalous Mistress

Agnès was a woman who stirred the passions. She was both greatly loved and profoundly hated in her time. She had been in the service of Isabelle de Lorraine, wife of René d'Anjou (*see* Angers), when in 1444 she entered the royal court retinue as a lady-in-waiting to the queen. Soon it was the queen, Marie d'Anjou, who would have to wait to see the king as she continued to devote her life to producing offspring for Charles – she gave birth to 14 royal children in all, many of whom died in infancy.

Agnès' beauty was famed, even if the oft-copied depiction of her by Jean Fouquet may not match our present notions of aesthetics. For instance, the fashion of her day was to pull the hair harshly up to display the forehead prominently, plucked of excess strands, in a style known as *le front épilé*. Breaking with traditional etiquette, the king had Agnès served like a princess, allowing her a retinue of her own. One chronicler remarked that the trains of her dresses were longer than those of any other woman at court, which probably says a great deal about her position and her extravagance. Agnès' nickname of La Dame de Beauté, while playing on her looks, came from one of the many expensive gifts the king lavished upon her, the estate of Beauté-sur-Marne. Agnès also gave prominence to the extremely influential courtiers and patrons Jacques Cœur (*see* Bourges) and Etienne Chevalier; she was one the best clients of the former, the greatest merchant in France. Winning the king's affections, Agnès exercised political as well as emotional power over him. And she bore Charles three daughters.

Royal scandal is nothing new. Agnès Sorel shocked many in her day with her extravagant and unabashed ways and fashions. The future Louis XI, son of Charles VII, detested her. He wasn't the only one. The pope railed against her; she made the Church see red, and many others complained about the outrageous expense of her circle and the manner in which she distracted the king's attention from the queen. The weakness of Charles VII seems more to blame than anything. He it was who decided on the fortune to be spent dressing the court ladies, the money coming from taxes raised from the common people. Agnès tried to deflect some of the venom directed at her by making numerous generous charitable donations to the poor and to religious institutions. That is why she was allowed to be buried in Loches' church of St-Ours. However, for three centuries following her death, the canons of the church pressed for the removal of her tomb, permission being granted during Louis XVI's reign. The beautiful alabaster work now rests in the Logis Royal. Agnès died as a result of a miscarriage in 1450. Once again dark rumour steps in and says that she was poisoned. All three of her daughters were publicly recognized by Charles VII.

were much restored in that period. They consist of two adjoining wings of different style, the first originally built at the end of the 14th century, the other at the end of the 15th to the beginning of the 16th.

The main section was the celebrated home of King Charles VII's powerful mistress, Agnès Sorel (*see* box), she of the single bared breast memorably immortalized in pictures by France's greatest known 15th-century painter, Jean Fouquet.

Agnès Sorel wasn't the only influential woman to leave her mark on Loches. Two more of the most memorable women in French history are associated with the castle. Before Agnès, Joan of Arc came to Loches after the French victory freeing Orléans from the English siege, and spurred Charles VII to go through English-occupied territory to be crowned in the sacred French royal ceremony at Reims cathedral. Anne de Bretagne, the third great 15th-century woman connected with Loches, was the pious wife of two French kings, Charles VIII and Louis XII. Her oratory is the best preserved of the rooms in a quite disappointingly bare series in the Logis Royal, several containing rather uninspiring copies of famous paintings. Henry James described the oratory in a typically American way as being 'hardly larger than a closet'. So it may be – but it is a sumptuously decorated one. The splendid Grande Salle is the hall where Joan of Arc was received after her triumphs in the Orléanais and is now embellished with fine 17th-century Flemish tapestries. Beyond Agnès Sorel's tomb, its two lambs playing on her Christian name, look out for a beautiful late 15th-century triptych, brought here from the nearby Chartreuse du Liget. It appears to be the work of the great period artist Bourdichon.

Church of St-Ours

Even if you don't buy a ticket to visit Loches' keep and castle, you can wander round parts of the citadel and see inside the church of St-Ours. This is a curious, charming building, much commented on by architectural historians. Between the quite normal entrance tower and crossing tower, the bays of the nave have each been covered with a quirky tower, upturned cones dubbed *dubes*. These unique features date from the middle of the 12th century, like the rest of the church. Under the entrance porch, you can admire some fine Angevin vaulting. Imaginative sculptures, on the usual themes of Romanesque carving, with monsters and semi-human creatures, draw attention to themselves. Somehow packed in under the vault is a further collection of early Gothic sculptures. The church was the proud owner of a supposed piece of the Virgin's girdle, a relic donated by Geoffroy Grisegonelle, the count of Anjou who founded the place in the late 10th century. The relic encouraged pregnant women to come here to pray for an easy childbirth, a custom that continued into the 20th century.

La Maison Lansyer

Open April–Sept daily 10–12.30 and 2–6.30, rest of year Mon–Sat only 10–1 and 2–5; closed 25 Dec and 1 Jan; Rue Lansyer, t 02 47 59 05 45; adm.

On the main street leading out from the citadel down into the centre of town, this pretty house was once owned by the 19th-century landscape painter Emmanuel Lansyer (1835–93), a prolific artist. Brought up in the Vendée, south of the Loire estuary, he went up to Paris to try and make a career in the arts. He first studied briefly under the architect Viollet-le-Duc and then under the fiery painter Courbet, who promised that he would teach his fervent followers of realism to paint faster than you could take a photograph! But Courbet's skill didn't live up to the rhetoric, and Lansyer found a better teacher in lesser-known Harpignies. He went on to be represented at the famous alternative Salon des Refusés of 1863. Lansyer then headed off on trips to Brittany and other provinces, where he found inspiration for his rather sweet interpretations of the French countryside. He won a first prize for his work in 1865.

Lansyer was no starving artist, as you can tell from his comfortable house. He became close to the likes of Princess Mathilde, a cousin of Napoleon III. His works were even sold to the emperor himself as well as to many aristocrats. He lived along Quai Bourbon on the Ile St-Louis, in the centre of Paris. Lansyer spent some time, too, in his picture-pretty family home in Loches. He painted some delightful canvases of the town and the area around it. He died childless and a large number of paintings were left to Loches. His house has recently been restored. Inside, you can watch a slide show on Lansyer's life and times, featuring early photographs he took, before wandering round the picturesque 19th-century-style salons filled with paintings by the artist, including a good collection of Lochois and Breton scenes. Lansyer was also a collector of engravings, from works by Piranesi and Canaletto to pieces by the likes of Gustave Doré and Victor Hugo. An exotic touch is added by his Japanese collection.

A Tour of Loches

Wandering down through the winding old streets of the town proves a real pleasure. The feel is mainly 15th and 16th century. The Rue du Château turns into the **Grande Rue**, off which lies the town hall square, a wonderfully atmospheric corner. The **Porte Picois** is the very image of a late Gothic town gate. It formed part of another line of Loches fortifications, built to protect the lower town. Further pieces of these ramparts still survive. The splendid house tucked into the corner next to this gateway is the **Hôtel de Ville**, built in 1535 in the then still young Renaissance style.

Venture out of the gateway, turning left into the Place des Blés and then right down the Rue Descartes, and you come out at **Place de Verdun**. The church of St-Antoine stands on the site of the former Ursuline convent. Opposite it lies the neoclassical 19th-century Palais de Justice, or law courts. In the centre of the square, the statue by respected regional sculptor François Sicard honours a famous son of Loches, the great Romantic writer Alfred de Vigny, born here in 1797 (though he actually spent little time in the town).

Alternatively, take the Rue St-Antoine out of the town hall square to reach the **Tour St-Antoine**, an imposing mid-16th-century belfry, one of the town's landmarks. It was once attached to a church, but that was destroyed. Continuing round, cross the river and you come to the pretty public garden, the Indre flowing gently past the houses. From here you get lovely views onto the château's Logis Royal.

La Carrière Troglodytique de Vignemont

Open Easter–All Saints' Day daily; call t 02 47 91 54 54 to book a time for the 1-hour guided tour. They normally leave at 10, 11, 2, 3, 4 and 5; also 12 and 6 in July and Aug. 52 ter, Rue des Roches; adm.

These former quarries below the citadel count among the most spectacular you can visit in the Loire Valley region. The owners lead you on a didactic tour round the place. The quarries themselves only date back to the 18th century, but on the visit you're taken through the history not just of quarrying in France, but also of the geology of these parts. The 80m of tufa limestone stacked up under the earth of Touraine took 4 million years to form, during a time when the whole region lay under the sea. Billions of crushed shells are the main constituent of this sedimentary rock.

Separate corners of the quarries are dedicated to the ways the stone was extracted in different periods, and the uses to which it was put. The Gallo-Romans employed a lot of limestone blocks, but they extracted them from open-air quarries. It seems that it was the Merovingians who started quarrying underground. They had a particular penchant for making stone sarcophagi or tombs. Although the medieval period is sometimes regarded as backwards, it was during this age that there was an explosion in building in stone, for the construction of forts, churches and all manner of houses, such as those in Loches.

The quarries of the Loire Valley weren't only used for stone extraction. They could also serve as refuges in times of war. Not only would the population go down to hide in the underground tunnels, they would also bring their cattle with them. All sorts of defensive tricks were incorporated into the architecture of these refuges. Some 150 of them have been identified in Touraine and a portion of one has been recreated in the Carrière de Vignemont. The entrance to these quarries once served as a troglodyte home, its domestic features still clear, including a wine press and even a dog's kennel. A display of sculptures in stone has been added recently.

Religious Forests East of Loches

Beaulieu-les-Loches is Loches' near neighbour and once-important rival down in the plain. Its Abbaye de la Sainte-Trinité, of which only dislocated fragments remain, was founded by the fearsome Angevin count, Foulques Nerra. Foulques Nerra was a man of extreme passions, often exceedingly cruel and destructive, but also clearly concerned about the state of his soul, as was quite typical of his age. He ordered Beaulieu's abbey so that monks could pray night and day for his salvation, and donated the precious relic of a supposed piece of Christ's tomb to the place. Some might ask whether it was divine punishment that the abbey's great nave burnt down the day after its consecration in 1007. Foulques Nerra was buried here in 1040. Destruction by fire was to return as a theme, but only after the abbey had enjoyed several centuries of prosperity, the town around growing large enough to have three parish churches, the markets providing thriving trade. The Hundred Years' War brought disaster in the form of a couple of further major conflagrations. It was decided to move the market from Beaulieu to better-protected Loches, effectively sounding the death knell for commercial life in the town.

A few kilometres outside Beaulieu on the D760 you enter what was once the ancient royal forest of Loches. You may spot a surprising obelisk along the way, one in a line set up through the woods as elegant markers for the hunt in the 18th century. Signs point to **L'Etang du Pas d'Ane**, a lake in the forest around which you can go walking. At **Couroirie**, the gorgeous mellow medieval buildings were once the dwellings of the lay brothers of the charterhouse of Liget, separated by some distance from the monks' quarters, as was the tradition in the very strict Carthusian order.

The main monastery or **Chartreuse du Liget** (*open daily summer 9–12 and 2–7; rest of year 9–12 and 2–5.30; t 02 47 92 60 02; adm*) is still protected by great lengths of walls marked by the occasional little turret. The sophistication of the entrance gateway seems particularly out of place in the quiet wooded surrounds, but it looks so enticing that it tempts you to stop. Up close, it's very strange to be confronted by the elaborate artificiality of Baroque decoration in this landscape. On the front of the gateway the monk flying to the altar is St Bruno, founder of the Carthusian order. On the other side, John the Baptist (patron saint of the monastery) looks rather self-consciously desperate, a dove descending towards him through a cascading cloud.

King Henry II Plantagenet is said to have founded the original institution in 1178 as part of his penance for the murder of Thomas à Becket in Canterbury Cathedral in 1170. But the entrance gate is pure 18th century and the bulk of the collection of buildings descending the slope date from the Ancien Régime. At the bottom of the valley, at an angle to the other architecture, the substantial remains of a late 12th-century church still stand, close to the vestiges of a vast 17th-century cloister.

At the Chartreuse you can ask for the key to the tiny circular chapel of **St-Jean du Liget**, set in the midst of a field among the woods a kilometre back west, signposted off the D760. It looks almost as though someone has deposited this little round box of a building here for safekeeping. It has been scrubbed clean on the outside. Within, murals depict six scenes from the New Testament, from the tree of Jesse to the Assumption of the Virgin, saints and bishops depicted in between.

The **Ermitage Ste-Trinité de Grandmont-Villiers** is a tattier yet charming vestige of another religious establishment. It lies a bit east of the Chartreuse du Liget off the D760, and is still occupied by a few religious men. An old track takes you to the peaceful dilapidated buildings, including the truncated, heavily restored chapel, set around a grassy courtyard. The Grandmont order, founded in the Limousin region of southwest France by Etienne Muret in the early Middle Ages, emphasized absolute poverty and charity, together with humble manual labour. Unlike in other orders, the father isn't divided from the brothers, but leads the same religious life as them.

Montrésor

Montrésor exudes charm from every stone. A delightful village of brown-tiled houses, it's located in a curve in the Indrois, a tributary of the Indre, and overseen by a fortified castle. It thoroughly deserves its membership of the association of Les Plus Beaux Villages de France. The feel is late medieval, although the place was much developed in the early 16th century, when Imbert de Bastarnay gave it its imposing church and had the château enlarged. A legend ascribes the name of the village, Mount Treasure, to the unlikely emergence from the local rock of a lizard covered in gold. Today at the château you'll find unexpected treasures from Eastern Europe; the many Polish street names in the village are explained by the fact that a family of Polish origin has long owned the castle.

You pass through the early medieval fortifications of the **Château de Montrésor** (*open daily April–Oct 10–12 and 2–6; t 02 47 92 60 04; adm*) via an impressive, partly ruined Gothic gateway which gives you a feel for the age of the place. One of Foulques Nerra's associates, the disturbingly named Robert le Petit Diable (Little Devil), built an early medieval keep here around the turn of the first Christian millennium, but this was dismantled in the 19th century. After Robert le Petit Diable, Henri Plantagenêt added his fortifications, sturdy remnants of which are also to be seen down below in the village. The place was taken from the Plantagenets in 1198 by the French King Philippe Auguste. The buildings within the curtain walls date from much later and were ordered in the main by Imbert de Bastarnay after he came by the castle in 1493. He served several French kings and was one grandfather of King Henri II of France's great lover, Diane de Poitiers. At the Revolution, much of the castle was burnt down.

Count Xavier Branicki was a Polish émigré who fled from the Russians and bought the castle in 1849, as the French Second Empire was getting under way with Napoleon III. The count was a friend of the new emperor and a leading financier of the time. His descendants still own and live in the château, which has been preserved in 19th-century Polish aspic inside. It's crammed with mementoes of Poland, including, apparently, the stuffed wolf, one of the most startling of innumerable trophies hanging from the dining room walls. Some of the Polish objets d'art are magnificent, a plate showing Warsaw particularly memorable. Trophies from war with Turkey add a further surprising note. Family portraits and busts look at you from all around, stamping the family character on the place. Further interesting paintings adorn the refined interiors, showing that the Branickis were collectors of taste, with works from Italian schools and by Elisabeth Vigée-Lebrun. Finely wrought furniture also features.

The **collegiate church of St John the Baptist** stands a little outside the castle precinct. It looks disproportionately splendid for such a small village. Built in neat white stone, it was completed in 1541. The main restored tomb is that of the lordly de Bastarnay family, with fine effigies of the lord, his wife and his son. They look like a family tucked up in bed, their heads deep in their stone pillows. The sculptures have been attributed to the famous master Jean Goujon. The choir contains amusing contemporary misericordes, figures with their tongues hanging out. Two early French Renaissance stained-glass windows have also survived. The aisleless nave is hung with four Italian paintings donated by the Branickis, who also gave the 17th-century work in the north choir chapel, the *Annunciation* painted by Philippe de Champaigne, artist to the French royal family in his time. It comes as a surprise to find such artistic riches hidden away in such a quiet corner of Touraine.

Nouans-les-Fontaines

Still more surprising is the great work at Nouans-les-Fontaines, a one-painting village a little east of Montrésor. The picture is breathtaking, dominating the perspective as you enter the otherwise unremarkable old **church of St Martin** (*open 9–8 except during services; a small contribution will allow you to see the panel lit up and to listen to a sensible commentary in English while you survey the painting*). Known as the **Nouans *Pietà***, the work ranks among the finest masterpieces of late medieval French art, its rediscovery an exciting event not just for the village, but also for art historians.

In 1931 the painting was sent to be cleaned. As the restorer removed the grime of ages it suddenly became apparent what a great work it was. Its history remains something of a mystery. The extremely large panel is generally agreed to be the work of the 15th-century royal court painter Jean Fouquet, intended as the central part of an altarpiece. Fouquet, born in Tours around 1420, died there probably at the start of the 1480s. He probably trained in Paris. He's generally considered to be the first known great French artist to be remembered in history. He combined the delicacy of the northern International style of painting with more monumental and classical influences from Renaissance Italy. Fouquet may be referred to in French as a *primitif* (which doesn't sound too complimentary, but in French art history, it simply means that his work dates from before the Renaissance period), but he had travelled to Italy and absorbed lessons there. His example demonstrates how painting was ahead of architecture in its adoption of Italianate forms in 15th-century France, but also how French artists could find a style of their own. He had gained such a fine reputation by his 20s that he was commissioned by King Charles VII and Pope Eugenius IV to paint their portraits. Best remembered for his depiction of Agnès Sorel as the Virgin (*see* Loches, above), he also executed a miniature self-portrait, a rare early portrait of an artist.

As soon as you open the church door, you perceive the body of Christ ghostly white in the distance, stretched out, pale from death, his body just brought down from the cross. The figures are superbly characterized. Jesus, his eyes closed, looks calm in death, youthful, smooth-skinned, with elegant hands, while the Virgin resembles an exhausted Meryl Streep, drained by emotion, hands clenched, feelings of suffering so evident. Nicodemus and Joseph of Arimathea are lowering Christ's body on to a shroud in front of her, his bent form stretching diagonally across the panel. All the accompanying figures concentrate the attention on the sombre event, conveying the power and pain of the moment.

The identity of the important donor, who's depicted kneeling on the right-hand side, represented on the same large scale as the religious figures in the painting, remains a mystery. The mass of his white robe, seen from afar, rather disconcertingly connects him to the white Christ. One theory is that the painting was made for the chapel in the palace in Bourges of the fabulously wealthy merchant Jacques Cœur. However, Jacques Cœur died in 1456 and most scholars date the painting to the 1470s. What makes the Jacques Cœur theory tempting still, apart from the vast wealth and power this councillor-cum-merchant commanded until his disgrace, and the fact that he was known as a patron of the arts, is that the donor is overseen by St James the Pilgrim (St Jacques in French). Scholars continue to search for another suitably rich patron to link to this superb work.

West and South of Loches

Head northwest from Loches for **Chanceaux-près-Loches**, a delightful place with the ruins of a medieval fortress, a Second Empire château built for the hugely wealthy ironworks industrialists, the Schneiders, and a main street protected by vast plane trees. From Chanceaux continue via Dolus-le-Sec and St-Bauld to reach **Le Louroux**.

This fortified village has preserved its medieval character and is exceptionally unspoilt by 20th-century encroachments. The place was owned from the end of the 10th century to the 18th by the wealthy abbey of Marmoutier outside Tours. An impressively large 15th-century barn divides it in two. The church tower is the oldest remaining building, from the 12th century. To the east lie the lord's lodgings. The great 19th-century artistic prodigy Eugène Delacroix came to stay in the village as his brother had a house here, and he started his fascinating journal here in 1822, collecting his first recorded thoughts by the moonlight of Louroux.

Heading south from Loches, the village church of **Perrusson** is one of the most ancient in Touraine, with portions of 10th-century walls still standing and a couple of Merovingian sarcophagi in the choir. **Verneuil-sur-Indre**, off the N143, has a restored Romanesque church and two contrasting private châteaux. The little-known **Château de Bridoré** (*open daily June–Sept 1–7;* **t** *02 47 94 72 63, www.chateau-bridore.com; adm*) is impressively fortified. To reach it turn southwest off the N143 after Oizay Cerçay. The soaring keep separates two courtyards. The buildings mainly date from the 14th century, supplemented by Renaissance windows and defensive elements added in the Wars of Religion. The visit is short but reasonably interesting. The originality of the château lies in its *caponnières* in the dry moat. Bridoré claims to possess four out of the eight that exist in France. You may have spotted one at Loches. Nantes has another. These 16th-century defences attached to the corners of the main building, protrude like outsized armoured feet. The château also boasts a sauna from the 14th century, the idea imported from the Middle East during the Crusades. You can climb the keep – latrines at all levels – to reach the top, where you'll get superb views.

The Southern Tip of Touraine

Ce coin de terre ignoré et exquis (This unknown, exquisite corner of land).

André Theuriet

Touraine's sharp southern tip is extremely attractive. Not many tourists come down this way, but the area has profound charm thanks to numerous little wooded valleys. Along the Claise river you come to the most substantial sight in these parts, the Château du Grand-Pressigny, housing Touraine's museum of prehistory. But there are also plenty of very attractive rural villages to potter round, with their Romanesque churches, châteaux and little local museums, as well as the odd dolmen, proof of a much earlier thriving human presence.

The Villages of Southern Touraine

Ferrière-Larçon, some way southwest of Loches, plunges you into the mood of this deeply rural region. For such a quiet village, you may well wonder why it has such a substantial rocketing spire shooting out over the brown-tiled roofs. It's said that the church of St-Mandet and St-Jean was built with proceeds from the Crusades by

Getting Around

Trains don't come this far. Just a couple of buses a day link Le Grand-Pressigny with Tours. Strangely, there are a few more connections a day between the villages of Preuilly, Le Petit-Pressigny, La Celle-Guénand and Ferrière-Larçon. Descartes, La Guerche and Yzeures are served by a separate line.

Tourist Information

Le Grand-Pressigny: Mairie, 37350 Le Grand-Pressigny, t/f 02 47 94 96 82, *www.le-grand-pressigny.net*.
Descartes: Pl Blaise Pascal, 37160 Descartes, t 02 47 92 42 20, *www.ville-descartes.fr*.

Market Days

Le Grand-Pressigny: Thursday morning.
Descartes: Sunday morning.

Where to Stay and Eat

Le Petit-Pressigny ✉ **37350**
Dallais-La Promenade, 11 Rue du Savoureux, t 02 47 94 93 52 (*menus €34–69; closed Sun*

pm, Mon and Tues exc hols). This place is reason in itself for many Tourangeaux to come and discover southern Touraine, as you can taste gourmet cuisine at a bargain price in this former inn. *Closed 2 weeks end Sept–start Oct and early Jan–early Feb.*

Preuilly-sur-Claise ✉ **37290**
★★Auberge St-Nicolas, 6 Grande-Rue, t 02 47 94 50 80, f 02 47 94 41 77 (*inexpensive*). Basic but welcoming stop (*menus €18–35; closed Sun pm and Mon out of season*). *Closed 4 weeks Sept–Oct.*

Yzeures-sur-Creuse ✉ **37290**
★★★La Promenade, 1 Place du 11 Novembre, t 02 47 91 49 00, f 02 47 94 46 12 (*inexpensive*). Quite stylishly decorated rooms in a former posting inn. The proprietor also cooks up a good meal (*menus €20–37; closed Mon and Tues*). *Closed mid-Jan–mid-Feb.*

Chambon ✉ **37290**
Le Vieux Fournil, Place du 11 Novembre, t 02 47 91 02 23 (*menus €14.50–25; closed Sun pm and Wed*). The old village bakery has been transformed into a cheerful restaurant, offering local cuisine.

wealthy Knights Templars. Typical Romanesque carving decorates the west end. The tower dates from the second half of the 12th century, quite out of proportion with the place, while in the nave a 13th-century Gothic section dwarfs the early 12th-century one. The outsized, splendidly vaulted choir was never completed, possibly because funds ran out. In the village, Rue des Caves contains more modest buildings, with some semi-troglodyte houses where weavers once worked.

From Ferrière-Larçon, one option is to follow the Brignon river along the D100 towards Descartes, looking for the dramatic defensive site of the **Fortresse du Châtelier** on its steep spur, the dolmen known as **Pierre Chaude** (Hot Rock) and the beautiful mill of Aunay at **Neuilly-sur-Brignon**. Then you're almost at Le Grand-Pressigny.

Alternatively, head down from Ferrière-Larçon for **La Celle-Guénand**, tucked into another typical southern Touraine valley, with a charming church and château. The church is late Romanesque, its doorway decorated with bearded heads, the château late Gothic, with bold towers. You may be able to walk into the château's grounds, which include a picturesque ensemble of early 17th-century houses and barns known as La Juiverie; it's said that Jews were protected by the lord here in times past. The village museum, the **Musée de l'Outil et des Vieux Métiers** (*open daily July–Aug 2–6.30, May–June and Sept Sun and public hols only 2–6; t 02 47 88 05 26 and t 02 47 94 45 27; adm*), celebrates old trades, with thousands of objects on display.

The D50 leads southeast to **Le Petit-Pressigny**, down in another valley, that of the Aigronne, with wash houses by the stream and a Romanesque church. A detour east along the D103 takes you to **Charnizay**, whose Ancien Régime château belonged at the start of the 20th century to Comte Robert de Montesquiou-Fezensac, a Paris society figure and poet, model for the Baron de Charlus in Proust's *A La Recherche du temps perdu*. On a height a couple of kilometres northeast of the village seek out the **dolmen de Charnizay**, also known as **Les Palets de Gargantua**, the Rabelaisian story having it that giants threw these massive Neolithic stones down here.

Preuilly-sur-Claise lies a little further south. The main, startling monument in this slightly larger place is the abbey church of St-Pierre, a once-grand Romanesque structure very heavy-handedly restored in the 19th century. The restoration included re-roofing a bell tower with coloured tiles in the Dijon style, surprising in Touraine, but you can still admire the skill of the Romanesque builders of the choir with its many apses. Inside, the place is decorated with carved capitals. The Cleveland museum in the USA bought another set from a second Romanesque church in Preuilly, that of Ste-Melanie, attached to the Château du Lion and partly destroyed by the ruling 16th-century Protestant family here. The early fortress ruins remain next to a 19th-century château. The **Musée de la Poterne** (*open July–Aug Tues–Sun 2.30–6.30, and weekends in Sept; adm*), in the medieval gatehouse, contains archaeological and traditional regional displays, including of Touraine lace and embroidery. The forest of Preuilly stretches eastwards. Taking the D725 through it you reach **Azay-le-Ferron**, just in the Berry, but its heavily restored château owned and run by the Tours town authorities. North from here in the forest, the **Parc Zoologique de la Haute Touche** protects a splendid and varied collection of deer in its substantial grounds. Many other animals from around the world are also to be seen in the spacious runs.

Back at Preuilly, cross the Claise and head immediately west for a pretty detour past the beautifully framed **Château de Boussay**. A couple more turns south bring you to **Yzeures-sur-Creuse**, where the **Musée de Minerve** (*open 9–12 and 2–5; free*) presents interesting fragments of Gallo-Roman art from the 2nd century in the form of carvings of classical mythological figures and other archaeological pieces. This isn't the only museum in this little spot. The other consists of a dressing room dedicated to Mado Robin, an opera singer who died in 1960; she was particularly famed for her interpretation of Delibes' Lakmé, a sublime piece of music hijacked by British Airways advertising. Stage costumes she wore accompany recordings of her singing at the **Musée Mado Robin** (*open 8–6; t 02 47 94 55 01; free*). A statue of the singer stands in the village.

If you've come this far south, we'd thoroughly recommend that you cross into Poitou to visit the gorgeous village of **Angles-sur-l'Anglin** (*www.anglessuranglin.com*), another dozen kilometres south. Its name is supposed to derive from 5th-century Angles who settled here. The ruins of the medieval château (*open July–Aug Wed–Mon 10–12.30 and 2.30–6.30; adm*) present romantically crumbling towers and lodges rising out of the limestone cliff. Steps hewn into the rock help in the walk up to a Romanesque chapel, converted into a showroom for local embroidery and cutlery. The embroidery is known as Les Jours d'Angles because of its openwork effects.

Heading north from Yzeures along the Creuse valley, the D750 road is a joy, as the countryside opens up. While most of the châteaux in this area are private and not open to visitors, the **Château de la Guerche** (*open late June–late-Sept Mon–Sat 10–1 and 2–7, Sun 1–7; t 02 47 91 02 39 or t 01 46 51 47 73, www.chateaudelaguerche.com; adm*), overlooking the Creuse, is a rare exception, and occupies a marvellous riverbank spot. Go onto the bridge to get the best view on this beautiful stretch of river. The castle dates from the end of the 15th century. From the bridge you can see the Gothic aspect of the building, which was constructed at a time when comforts were beginning to be thought of as well as defence. The upper floors were for the lord's apartments – few of these are included in the visit. Instead the tour concentrates on the castle's defensive elements. You're shown the two lower floors of the river wing. The bottom one contains the artillery rooms, finely built, with vaults and sturdy towers, as were the interconnecting store rooms of the level above. On sunny days the shifting light reflected off the Creuse fills these chambers with brightness. The château prison was also on this level. It contains several touching pieces of graffiti.

Château du Grand-Pressigny

Open daily April–Sept 9.30–7, Feb–Mar and Oct–Dec 9.30–12.30 and 2–5; closed 25 Dec; t/f 02 47 94 99 60; adm.

This château, a dozen kilometres southeast of Descartes, is a pure delight. The site was chosen for its defensive potential at the close of the 12th century. From this position on top of a plateau, the valleys of the Aigronne and the Claise could be surveyed and the countryside controlled. The local lord took the French king's side against the Plantagenets of Anjou. The fortifications were made more elaborate through time, with the addition during the 15th century of a barbican and, in certain parts, machicolations and a *chemin de ronde*. In the second half of the Hundred Years' War, the troops of Jean sans Peur, duke of Burgundy and ally of the English, took the castle in 1417, although the French dauphin, the future King Charles VII, won it back in 1418.

In 1523, René de Savoie, half-brother of Louise de Savoie (mother of King François I), became owner of the château. His son Honorat de Savoie-Villars was the one to order the classical gallery, built some time between 1550 and 1580. This classical block splits the medieval buildings neatly in two. It isn't in the tentative style of the first French Renaissance, but much more assuredly Italian in influence and order. Its stone looks somewhat grey and coarse, however, which gives the whole a rather heavier appearance than the Renaissance châteaux to the north.

The classical gallery contains the main section of the **Musée de la Préhistoire**. But starting in the first courtyard, the Salle de Paléontologie contains a massive collection of marine, plant and animal fossils, showing the geological and natural prehistory of the area. The exhibits are extremely neatly and clearly laid out. You can climb the stairs in this large room; they lead out onto the *chemin de ronde*, an amusingly crooked outer walkway. In another corner of the courtyard you can climb the thin stick of a tower known as the Tour Vironne for an even better panorama of the surrounding area and the brown-tiled village houses tucked into the valley below.

The rooms of the Renaissance wing house thousands of artefacts demonstrating the substantial presence of prehistoric humans in the area. Important communities settled here from the Stone Age; they churned out flint instruments on a massive scale. The flint blades could be employed for all manner of agricultural uses. Such was the quality of the implements produced here that they were exported across Europe; finds of Pressigny flints have been unearthed in Belgium and Switzerland. From a much later period relatively speaking, but still very ancient, a few other objects complement these collections, including swords and jewellery and a fine ancient Gaulish religious statue with a necklace. Through the central arch of the Renaissance building, the second courtyard has a charming little Renaissance pavilion dwarfed by an early medieval keep. This donjon hasn't kept so well recently, as two walls fell down one day in 1988, but it is the oldest part of the fortifications remaining, dating from the late 12th century. What you now see does give you a fine cross-section of this type of building, while the open spiral staircase looks, rather fittingly, fossil-like.

To get some impression of a prehistoric flint works in action, take the D42 from Le Grand-Pressigny for Descartes. Along the way, at **Abilly**, is the **Archéolabe** (*open mid-June–mid-Sept 2.30–6.30, otherwise by appt;* **t** *02 47 59 80 82 or* **t** *02 47 91 07 48; adm*). An archaeologist will explain the site, which was exploited between 2800 BC and 2400 BC.

Descartes

René Descartes didn't live for long in the small sleepily attractive Touraine town that's taken his name, and his childhood years here were his least significant, intellectually speaking. But the place has done him and itself the honour of setting up a small museum, the **Musée Descartes** (*open June–Sept Wed–Mon 2–6;* **t** *02 47 59 79 19; adm*), dedicated to this towering genius of mathematics and philosophy. The town was known in Descartes' day as La Haye and lay just in the Poitou region. Although born in Châtellerault, the prodigy was baptized here and spent his early years in La Haye. Probably around the age of 10 Descartes left the town to go and study at the prestigious Jesuit college just founded by Henri IV at La Flèche, north of Anjou. Later, it was to Holland that he would go to produce his famous works.

Descartes is generally regarded as the founder of modern philosophy. His best-known work, his *Discours de la Méthode* of 1637, proves a highly entertaining read. In it he describes how he tried to overcome the terrible doubts over the self and the problems arising from people's differing opinions and faiths. Among the more important notions he elaborated on were the dualism of mind and matter, and the idea that God equalled absolute perfection, plus he came up with the rather famous idea 'cogito ergo sum (I think therefore I am)'. The museum also contains memories of another writer of a rather different complexion, who tackled issues of a rather less profound and mysterious nature. René Boylesve (real name Tardiveau, 1867–1926) offered insights in his novels into the pettiness of provincial life. Who could be cruel enough to look for a reflection of his themes in the dopey old town of Descartes?

Western Touraine

17

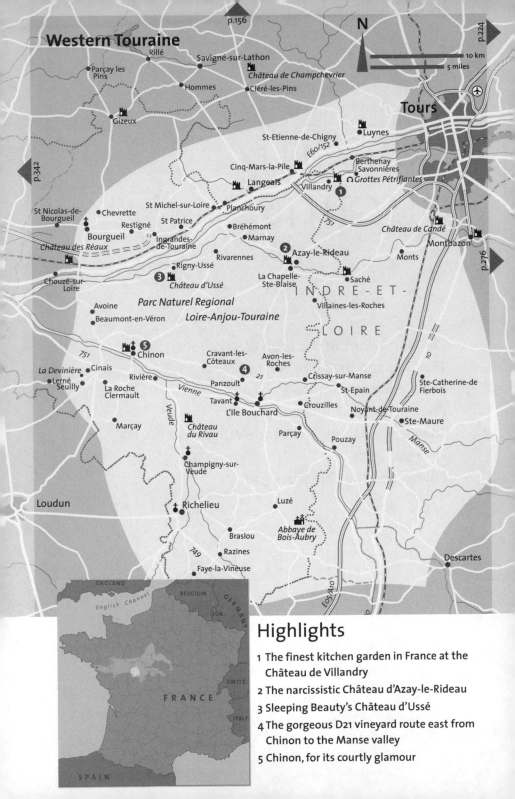

Highlights

1 The finest kitchen garden in France at the Château de Villandry

2 The narcissistic Château d'Azay-le-Rideau

3 Sleeping Beauty's Château d'Ussé

4 The gorgeous D21 vineyard route east from Chinon to the Manse valley

5 Chinon, for its courtly glamour

The châteaux of Villandry, Azay-le-Rideau and Ussé count among the most famous castles in all of France. The three don't stand by the Loire, but by its great tributaries of the Cher and the Indre. These two rivers and that of the Vienne reach the Loire in western Touraine. Beyond being rich in châteaux and churches, their valleys are particularly beautiful and fruitful. As you head west, the orchards give way to dense vineyards, Bourgueil north of the Loire, Chinon south of it, along the Vienne. Much of splendid western Touraine now forms part of the Parc Naturel Régional Loire-Anjou-Touraine created in the 1990s (*see* p.349). Touraine's neighbour Anjou was the original territory of the Plantagenets, who went on to form a dynasty of English kings. But one of King Henry II Plantagenet's favoured royal residences was the Château de Chinon, now an impressive ruin stranded above a splendid town. Several other of France's best-known national figures have close links with western Touraine, notably Joan of Arc, Rabelais, Richelieu and Balzac, all with a museum to their name.

Western Touraine is full of delightful villages and smaller sights. And if most of our attention focuses south of the Loire, we would also encourage you to consider visiting the posse of intriguing lesser-known castles just to the north of it.

The North Bank of the Loire West of Tours

While the châteaux south of the Loire from Tours to the Anjou border are famously light and gay, those just to the north of the mighty river look much more severe. However, Luynes, Langeais, Champchevrier and Gizeux all prove surprisingly fresh within. West beyond them you come into the wine-making territory of Bourgueil.

Château de Luynes

Open daily 29 Mar–Sept 10–6; t 02 47 55 67 55.

Standing guard high above the Loire in the first town west of Tours along the river's north bank, the formidable medieval Château de Luynes first opened its gates to the public in the mid-1990s. From the outside it looks forbidding. The grey medieval armour of its exterior dates back to the 13th century in the main. Large stone pimples protrude from several of its towers. In the medieval period, settlement and château were known as Maillé, and in the second half of the 15th century, one of the lords of the Maillé family brought a great deal more light to their castle with the addition of an array of windows. Charles d'Albert acquired the property in 1619. He had been brought up with King Henri IV's son, the future Louis XIII, and the two had become particularly firm pals through their love of falconry. Their friendship would become less innocent as they grew up: in 1617, when Louis XIII came of age, the two of them conspired to have Concini, the powerful Italian adviser-cum-lover to the Queen Mother Marie de' Medici, assassinated. Charles took on the title of Duc de Luynes, after a place in Provence, and the name of the Touraine château and town changed to reflect his new appellation. He went on to become Constable de France and the most important minister in the land, in particular fighting Protestantism – Richelieu would take his place soon after he died. Descendants of the duke still live in the château. Modifications were made through the 17th century, and again in the 19th.

Getting Around

Cinq-Mars-la-Pile and Langeais lie on the **train** line from Tours to Saumur, but don't expect a wide choice of trains. A very limited **bus** service from Tours passes through Cinq-Mars, Langeais, Planchoury, St-Patrice, Ingrandes, Restigné to Bourgueil. Another line serves Luynes, Cléré-les-Pins, Savigné-sur-Lathan, Rillé, Hommes, Gizeux and Parçay-les-Pins.

Tourist Information

Luynes: 9 Rue Alfred Baugé, B.P.1, 37230 Luynes, **t/f** 02 47 55 77 14, www.luynes.fr.
Cinq-Mars-La-Pile: Mairie, 37130 Cinq-Mars-la-Pile, **t** 02 47 96 20 30, **f** 02 47 96 38 52.
Langeais: Place du 14 Juillet, B.P.47, 37130 Langeais, **t** 02 47 96 58 22, www.tourisme-langeais.com.
Bourgueil: 16 Place de l'Eglise, 37140 Bourgueil, **t/f** 02 47 97 91 39, www.ot-bourgueil.fr.

Market Days

Luynes: Saturday morning.
Langeais: Sunday morning.
Bourgueil: Tuesday and Saturday mornings.

Where to Stay and Eat

Luynes ✉ 37230
****Domaine de Beauvois, Le Pont Clouet, **t** 02 47 55 50 11, www.beauvois.com (*expensive*). Very elegant manor set in a pretty wooded valley. The rooms are excellently furnished. The large Louis XIII-style dining room gives onto the smart front garden. A lake and a swimming pool lie down below, and there's a tennis court in the grounds (*menus €43–68*). *Closed Feb–mid-Mar.*

Courcelles-de-Touraine ✉ 37330
****Château des Sept Tours, **t** 02 47 24 69 75, www.7tours.com (*expensive*). A castle which cuts quite a dash northwest of the Château de Champchevrier, its grounds turned into a golf course. It all looks very grand; just the odd bit of tasteless decoration lets it down (*menus €35–50; closed Sun pm, Mon, and Tues–Thurs lunchtimes in Jan*). *Closed Feb and 24–26 Dec.*

Langeais ✉ 37130
***Errard Hosten, 2 Rue Gambetta, **t** 02 47 96 82 12, www.errard.com (*inexpensive*). The exterior isn't unpleasant, but it isn't harmonious either, and doesn't do justice to what awaits you inside. The rooms are smartly

Once across the dry moat, which has been planted as an enchanting garden, you enter a surprisingly sophisticated courtyard. Inside, you visit a series of grand rooms, finely furnished, some with splendid views onto the Loire. Particularly memorable is the vast sunken Salle des Jeux, with its traditional ochre walls, and above it the Grand Salon, with an elaborate fireplace thought to be the work of Jean Goujon. Look out for the portraits, sumptuous furniture and very well-preserved tapestries.

Fine medieval houses and a 15th-century covered market are the main attractions down in the town. Maillé had a Gallo-Roman ancestor, Malliacum. Archaeological digs on the plateau above the town have brought to light remnants of early civilizations, including an isolated piece of aqueduct to which a pink house has attached itself.

Cinq-Mars-la-Pile

A brick *pile*, or tower, rises slightly east of the village of **Cinq-Mars-la-Pile**. For a long time its original purpose remained a mystery. Some speculated that it had been constructed as a lighthouse for boats on the Loire, others as a marker for pilgrims travelling along the great river, others still as some grandiose milestone. It's now reckoned to have been erected as a mausoleum for a rich 2nd-century merchant. It stands an impressive 100 Roman feet high.

and tastefully decorated, while you can sample very fine cuisine in the elegant dining room (*menus €26–42; closed Sun pm, Mon and Tues lunch Oct–mid-Mar*). *Closed mid-Feb–Mar.*

★★La Duchesse Anne, 10 Rue de Tours, **t** 02 47 96 82 03, *eric.billi@wanadoo.fr* (*inexpensive*). A notch less expensive, with clean rooms and a delightful town garden, as well as solid traditional French fare (*menus €13.50–33; closed Sat lunch and Mon lunch high season, and weekends out of season*).

Hommes ✉ 37340

Vieux Château d'Hommes B&B, near Savigné up the D57 from Langeais, **t** 02 47 24 95 13, *www.le-vieux-chateau-de-hommes.com* (*expensive*). A 15th-century barn converted to give five high-standard *chambre d'hôte* rooms. Swimming pool (*table d'hôte €30*).

St-Michel-sur-Loire ✉ 37130

Château de Montbrun B&B, 47 Route du Coteau, Domaine de la Riboisière , **t** 02 47 96 57 13, *www.chateauxhotels.com/montbrun* (*expensive*). A delightful 19th-century Loire-style little château with lovely views over the Loire valley. You're likely to have an entertaining time here, with swimming and archery possible in the grounds and a host

who's sung at the London Palladium. The swimming pool is heated and *table d'hôte* is offered (*€40–50*).

St-Patrice ✉ 37130

★★★★Château de Rochecotte, **t** 02 47 96 16 16, *www.chateau-de-rochecotte.fr* or *www.chateauxhotels.com/rochecotte* (*expensive*). Absolutely splendid 18th-century aristocratic country house with formal French gardens hidden on the wooded Loire bank. This became one of the homes of Talleyrand, close associate of Napoleon. The spacious rooms are decorated in period style, and the elaborate cuisine is served in the colonnaded dining room. Heated swimming pool (*menus €37.50–58.50*). *Closed mid-Jan–Feb.*

Chouzé-sur-Loire ✉ 37140

Château des Réaux B&B, Le Port-Boulet, **t** 02 47 95 14 40, *www.chateaureaux.com* (*moderate–luxury*). Utterly enchanting historic castle described in the touring section below. The woman who runs it is a bit of a character, and together with her husband she has lovingly restored the château and turned it into a B&B. The rooms are full of individual character and many are rather romantic. The place is a real delight.

The ruined medieval **Château de Cinq-Mars-la-Pile** (*open March–Oct Wed–Mon 9–nightfall, rest of year Wed–Mon 11–nightfall*; **t** 02 47 96 40 49, *chateau-cinq-mars@wanadoo.fr*) was famously decapitated in the 1640s along with its young owner, Henri Coiffier de Ruzé d'Effiat, Marquis de Cinq-Mars. A protégé of Cardinal Richelieu, he quickly rose to high rank and became a favourite of Louis XIII, possibly even sexually intimate with him. The seductive young upstart amassed such influence that he then conspired with Gaston d'Orléans, the king's brother, to get rid of Richelieu. The plot was discovered and Cinq-Mars executed at the age of 22. The château was partially revived during the 19th century. Today, you can visit a couple of semi-ruined 12th–13th-century towers and admire the 16th-century moat.

Château de Champchevrier

Open mid-June–mid-Sept daily 10–6; **t** 02 47 24 93 93, *www.chateau-champchevrier.com; adm.*

A pack of hounds barks wildly as you arrive at this stocky grey château (*take the D34 from Cinq-Mars-la-Pile for Château-la-Vallière; it's just after Cléré-les-Pins*) surrounded by alleys of towering plane trees that line up in ranks like giant guardsmen. The hounds indicate how important hunting is in the history of Champchevrier. The very name of the place reflects this, *chevrier* apparently derived from *chevreuil*, the French word for roe deer. The first castle went up in the forests here back in the 11th century. In late medieval times, Louis XI, one of the keenest among the hunting-mad Loire kings, stopped to indulge in his pleasure here.

In the 16th century the estates came by marriage into the de Daillon family, which already owned the mighty Le Lude castle (*see* p.167) a bit further north, on the Loir (without an 'e'). Jean de Daillon had much of the medieval castle demolished and new Renaissance façades built. If the architecture looks distinctly messy on the side facing the road, you'll find a much greater harmony to the main façade giving onto the large grass-covered courtyard. A boxy chapel was added off one corner. An extremely long line of outbuildings was later attached to the main wing in the 17th century, when the château was in the hands of the de Roquelaure family, one of whom became a leading military figure of his day, elevated to the ultimate height of marshal of France.

But the de Roquelaures soon sold the place to one Jean-Baptiste de La Rüe du Can, in 1728. This man served as Secretary of Buildings to Louis XV and was honoured with the title of baron of Champchevrier in 1741. At the Revolution, the drawbridge was destroyed and some of the architectural refinements hacked off, including the dormer windows. But otherwise the château remained relatively untouched, even if some of the family had to flee or face imprisonment. The present owners, the Bizards, are descendants of the baron of Champchevrier, and very much devoted to their château. Through the 1990s they opened up an increasing number of rooms in the château.

On the guided tour inside, after the old hunting trophies and carriages, you're treated to an array of family portraits and, above all, a splendid display of tapestries. These have been superbly preserved. Some were made in Flanders, others in Picardy, in Amiens and Beauvais. The oldest shows a hare hunt in naive 16th-century style. The most famous are a series made from cartoons by Simon Vouet. This superlative French 17th-century artist was greatly influenced by his classical training in Italy and worked for Louis XIII. He was commissioned to make cartoons for a series of magnificent classical cycles; the one at Champchevrier illustrates the mythological Loves of the Gods, some with exceptional movement and energy. Adonis fleeing from Venus, Neptune and Ceres, Bacchus and Ariadne and the rape of Prosperina by Pluto are the main scenes. Mars, Jupiter and Hercules are represented in further tapestries.

A few minor events in Champchevrier's war history may interest British and American visitors. At the outbreak of the Second World War, the castle was chosen as the place to which the British embassy should retreat, though they only stayed a week before having to flee. And at the end of the conflict, an American bomber accidentally dropped a bomb somewhere on the estate; the crater it caused has become a drinking hole for deer!

If you don't want to go on the guided tour inside, you can buy a cheaper ticket just to wander round the outbuildings on your own, and look in at the old-fashioned rustic kitchens and laundry. A video of about an hour concentrates on hunting and hunting horns. Visitors can also go and admire the pack of mutts lounging around. They have a fine pedigree, their history going back to 1804.

Château de Langeais

Open 14 July–20 Aug 9.30–8, April–13-July and 21-Aug–15 Oct 9.30–6.30,
16 Oct–Mar 10–5.30; closed 25 Dec; t 02 47 96 72 60, f 02 47 96 54 44; adm.

A kitsch 1950s neo-Gothic bridge spans the Loire at Langeais. The town's formidable château is the real thing, however. In fact there are two castles or forts here, the grey Gothic monster's walls concealing the ruins of one of the very oldest stone keeps in France. If the main Château de Langeais looks a villain of a Loire château, then it comes as no surprise to learn that the severe King Louis XI ordered its building after the end of the Hundred Years' War. There's none of the usual exuberance of so much late Gothic architecture here.

Langeais' sternness does impress, though, from the outside, and as you gaze up at the towering mass, the machicolations and double layer of *chemins de ronde* look defensively down on you. The castle's tall walls and towers cast their sinister shadows over the town houses around them. Yet inside the picture is entirely different, the warmth of the rooms utterly contrasting with the coldness of the exterior. The château turns out to have one of the richest interiors along the Loire, full of fine furnishings and, in particular, glorious tapestries.

First, cross the sturdy 19th-century reconstruction of a drawbridge and enter the castle via its imposing gateway. The earlier **keep** comes into view on the hillock beyond the open courtyard whose formal garden has suffered badly from an overdose of cement. The ceaselessly combative and constructing Foulques Nerra, Count of Anjou, ordered the old hillside stronghold, possibly before the end of the 10th century, so this may be the oldest stone keep in France (*see* Montbazon's claim on p.277). What remains is a truncated shell. You need to imagine a structure that would have towered above the trees with sheer cliff-faces of masonry for walls. The Plantagenets added to the fortifications before they lost their lands to the French King Philippe Auguste, but during the Hundred Years' War many of these defences disappeared.

Louis XI asked his trusted servant Jean Bourré (*see* the Château du Plessis-Bourré p.168) to oversee the building of a new château here in 1465, guarding the Loire at the western entrance to Touraine. The original plan was probably for a four-sided château, but only two were built. In fact, Bourré seems to have handed over charge to Jean Briçonnet, a mayor of Tours and another close confident of Louis XI, soon after 1465. At roughly the same time the king gave the castle under construction to his cousin and brother-in-law François Dunois d'Orléans (son of the Dunois who fought with Joan of Arc). Building work continued under Dunois and was practically completed by 1490. It was in this castle that the fate of Brittany's independence was effectively sealed when the French King Charles VIII forced Anne de Bretagne to marry him here in 1491. Dunois helped organize the celebrations, but died before the event took place in December.

The interior like the exterior was heavily restored in the 19th century. In 1886 the wealthy entrepreneur and banker Jacques Siegfried bought the place, and with his wife devoted himself to creating a warm Gothic feel. Although the pieces aren't originally from Langeais, the Siegfrieds' good taste gave harmony to the rooms. The Petit

Salon sets the tone, panelled with polychrome carved wood taken from a Normandy church, an exquisite Flemish triptych adding to the strong Gothic atmosphere. The main artistic theme of the interiors, fine tapestries, starts in the *millefleurs* drawing room. The walls of the rooms that follow are embellished with stylized 19th-century neo-Gothic painting, the floors decorated with elaborate tiles, while splendid coffers and pieces of furniture line up along the sides. The Salle des Jeux offers a good example of this neo-Gothic decoration, with linenfold panelling too. The initials A and K refer to Anne and Karolus (Charles), the cords to Anne's pious attachment to the Franciscan order. Some of the tapestries are particularly entertaining in the Guards' Room with its monumental fireplace.

The first room on the first floor has a beautiful Flemish tapestry depicting Christ's crucifixion. Next door, the Salle des Aristoloches has the most curious tapestry of the château's whole collection, with Oriental-style birds set against a background of bizarre large curling leaves after which the room is named. The Blue Room continues with the rich variety of tapestries. Here the *millefleurs* are almost overwhelmingly dense with petals, of which there must indeed be many thousands. Another great hunting scene continues the collection on that theme.

The Salle Anne de Bretagne is on a different scale. Huge tapestries celebrating heroes from antiquity, the Bible and the Dark Ages are hung around the walls. Joshua, David, Hector, Alexander, Caesar, Arthur and Godefroy de Bouillon (11th-century crusader elected ruler of Jerusalem after the holy city was taken in the First Crusade) feature. These large-scale tapestry panels rather eclipse the slightly repellent waxwork models commemorating the marriage of Anne to Charles VIII on 6 December 1491. A barge brought Anne de Bretagne's dearest personal possessions up the Loire from the Château de Nantes, her home in the then capital of Brittany. Although the region had been run down by warring, the pious Anne loved her luxuries and she found the money to pay for what is surely one of the most extravagant wedding dresses in French history. True, the weather was likely to be cold, but to pay 58,000 livres, as some estimated! The attendants wore silk and velvet. Even the horses were decked out in black and crimson.

Up above, the Salle de la Chapelle has a splendid wooden ceiling in the form of an upside-down ship's hull, while a superb reliquary chest also draws the attention. After a breather walking round part of the castle's *chemins de ronde*, a couple more furnished rooms with yet more fine tapestries await. Fittingly, the visit ends with a room where tapestries are exhibited and sold.

To Bourgueil

From Langeais the N152 runs close to the Loire up to the Anjou border. However, you can also follow the D35 high road to Bourgueil if you turn off at Planchoury. The road along the valley ridge via St-Michel to St-Patrice offers some wonderful views. Ingrandes-de-Touraine used to stand on the border with Anjou before the Revolution. You're now entering Bourgueil wine territory. **Bourgueil** itself is a pretty market town. Its abbey is its most significant historic building. Its origins date back to the days when the counts of Blois ruled this far west, at the end of the 9th century. Count

Thibaud le Tricheur's daughter Emma founded the institution in 990, and it prospered more or less until the Revolution, when most of it was done away with. Much of what's left is still occupied. Tourists can go via the vestiges of a late-medieval cloister and an 18th-century refectory up a magnificent staircase to the cluttered displays of the **Musée Arts et Traditions Populaires** (*open July–Aug Wed–Mon 2–6, April–June and Sept–Oct weekends and public hols only 2–6; t 02 47 97 72 04; adm*). Heading from Bourgueil to the Loire, make a small detour to marvel at the geometric patterns adorning the façades of the **Château des Réaux** (*Mar–mid-Nov 9.30–6.30; t 02 47 95 14 40; you can wander around the exterior for a small fee*). Past the pea-soup moat, the chequered brick and tufa walls make this one of the most astonishing-looking of Loire châteaux. In all, several buildings of different ages and styles have been joined together. The original château was built for a Touraine notable in the first half of the 16th century. The name of the place was changed in the mid-17th century from Le Plessis-Rideau to Les Réaux, after the all too little-known memorialist and moralist who lived here. Arriving back at the great river, **Chouzé-sur-Loire** once thrived as a port. The place wistfully remembers its lucrative past with a little **Musée des Mariniers** (*open June–Aug weekends and public hols 3–5; 4 Rue St Pierre, adm*).

The Wines of Bourgueil and St-Nicolas-de-Bourgueil

The *appellations d'origine contrôlée* (AOC) areas of Bourgueil and St-Nicolas-de-Bourgueil lie just north of the Loire, pretty well opposite the Chinon vine-growing area. The two *appellations* produce red wine, almost exclusively from the Cabernet Franc variety (a tiny amount of Cabernet Sauvignon has crept in). Around 1,200 hectares are planted in the Bourgueil territory; St-Nicolas-de-Bourgueil forms an enclave within it of some 800 hectares. The vines here mainly extend over a plateau of more or less sandy, gravelly and limestone ground.

What tells the Bourgueils apart from Chinon reds and from each other? Some Bourgueils may be more tannic, those from limestone ground giving meatier aromas; those from the gravelly terrain may have a more distinctive aroma of raspberries (although violets, as at Chinon, are also traditionally associated with the Bourgueil bouquet). With good vintages, they could be left to age a bit longer than they are, but as ever along the Loire, reds tend to be drunk very young. The St-Nicolas-de-Bourgueils are generally lighter wines from lighter soils, and pleasantly fruity.

The name of Bourgueil is well known to the average French drinker. The wine became trendy in Paris from the 1980s, but has never been as well recognized as Chinon abroad. To find some good Bourgueils you could try **Lamé Delille Boucaud** at Ingrandes-de-Touraine or **Joël and Clarisse Taluau** (*open weekdays; t 02 47 97 78 79, joel.taluau@wanadoo.fr*) at Chevrette. Also in Chevrette, at the **Cave Touristique de la Dive Bouteille** (*open April–Oct daily 10–12 and 2–7; www.histoires-en-scene.com; adm*) for a small fee you get a museum display on the local wines as well as a tasting; look out too for events staged here. An up-and-coming producer at Restigné, Jean-François Demont's wines from the **Domaine des Mailloches** (*telephone in advance if you want to visit in the week; open Sat, closed Sun, 9–12 and 2–7; t 02 47 97 33 10, www.domaine-mailloches.fr*) are highly regarded.

Château de Gizeux

Open May–Sept Mon–Sat 10–6.30, Sun and public hols 2–6;
t/f 02 47 96 50 92, www.lapastiere.com; adm.

North of Bourgueil along the D749 stands another isolated but impressive Loire castle. The long driveway up to the Château de Gizeux befits such a massive home, probably built in the 16th century for René du Bellay. The main building is almost eclipsed in extent and beauty by the stables, added in 1741. The round tower you see before reaching the château is a remnant of an earlier du Bellay castle finished in 1415.

Inside the château, on the ground floor you're taken through an enfilade of rooms with an 18th-century feel, including in the grey-painted woodwork. The first salon contains a portrait of the Marquis de la Contade, proprietor at the time of the Revolution. He didn't die by the guillotine, but apparently from a fit brought on when he thought one of his servants had supported the uprising. Although he looks as though he must have been a difficult character, he is much appreciated in the culinary world for making foie gras fashionable. A bastard son of his, Héros de Seychelles, became something of a Revolutionary hero, but he did end up going to the guillotine for promoting a relatively moderate stance. Here he's represented as a sweet-faced youth. The Salon des Dames has an intimate feel, with embroideries executed by the present owner's grandmother. Two dining rooms follow, one chic, the other for *la chasse* – this one often smells of cooking, showing how lived-in the château still is.

On the first floor you're even sometimes allowed to poke your head into the owners' bedroom! But your attention will be drawn away by splendid views down two long galleries lying at right angles to each other. Both are elaborately decorated. One contains a vast number of painted bouquets, each different, and scenes of courtly life. The walls of the other, the **Galerie des Fresques**, were seemingly used as practice space by a school of painters. It seems incongruous, in the midst of the region of great Loire châteaux, that the panels should depict royal châteaux of the Ile de France around Paris. Art historians reckon that pupils from the Ecole de Fontainebleau were given free reign to hone their skills here. Among the scenes, the one of Fontainebleau leaves the most delightful impression, with ships sailing in the moat. One Loire château does make it into the gallery, royal Chambord. Go to the village church to admire the splendid kneeling effigies of the du Bellays.

An Artistic Detour into Eastern Anjou

North of Gizeux, cross the border into Anjou to visit the peaceful village of **Parçay-les-Pins**, which has opened the modern **Musée Jules Desbois** (*open 15 June–15 Sept daily exc Tues 10–12 and 3–6; Easter–June weekends 10–12 and 3–6; t 02 41 82 28 80, www.cg49.fr; adm*), crisply presenting the life and works of an accomplished sculptor born here in 1851. Though he never worked in his home village, and was sad not to be commissioned to make its First World War memorial, Desbois was trained at Angers before going to Paris. There he was spotted by Rodin, who took him into his studio.

Desbois' biographical story is told in the museum's first room, setting him in his period. Then follow rooms with small-scale and decorative works concentrating in particular on the female form, full of sensual to gymnastic curves, most beautifully shown in *La Dryade*, at their most exaggerated in *L'Arc*. Desbois' interest focuses on the forms more than the faces, the latter often somewhat stern and cold. One of his greatest inspirations as a model was Alda Moreno, who appears repeatedly. He died childless, and left her many of his works. The most spectacular and seductive sculpture on display in the museum is the classical *Léda et le Cygne*, the beautiful woman and swan shown in their strange intimacy. Much more disturbing works follow in the later rooms, concentrating on the decay of the body, most chillingly in *La Mort casquée*, bringing to mind the horrors of the First World War. This fine little provincial museum ends with pieces Desbois executed for major commemorative works.

Just north again, outside the village of Breil, the **Parc du Château de Lathan** (*open April–Oct Tues only, 10–6; t 02 41 82 31 00, parcdelathan.lc@wanadoo.fr; adm*) with its architectural follies is undergoing interesting restoration work.

The Cher and the Indre West of Tours

The staggering vegetable garden of the Château de Villandry is the mouth-watering *pièce de résistance* along the final stretch of the Cher west of Tours. But do go exploring the atmospheric, ignored isthmus between the Loire and the Cher on the way from Touraine's capital to the château. The last stretch of the Indre river from Montbazon south of Tours to the Loire is packed with fairytale châteaux. The most famous are the romantic Azay-le-Rideau and Ussé, but others have strong stories to attract you, notably the Château de Saché, where that stupendous 19th-century Touraine writer Balzac wrote his greatest romance, *Le Lys dans la vallée*, and the Château de Candé, where the Duke and Duchess of Windsor got married.

To the Château de Villandry from Tours

The land between the Loire and the Cher west of Tours narrows into a thin, flat peninsula. It's a rarely explored but wonderful spit of sandy land. There are no châteaux to visit, although these territories once formed part of the estates of the **Château de Plessis-lès-Tours**, the centre of King Louis XI's world, its sad remnants now swallowed up by the western outskirts of Tours. A number of Italian visitors continue to visit the little chapel housing the tomb of St François de Paule (*see* Amboise) near the Château de Plessis-lès-Tours.

Take the D88 road along the **south bank of the Loire**. From the quiet, patched-up levee road you get an excellent chance to observe the Loire flowing by. The river looks at its most typical along this stretch, the sandbanks and different varieties of trees easy to observe. Instead of encountering thundering traffic, as you do on the Loire's north bank opposite, you may meet men going out fishing or, in season, hunting, or farmers picking their asparagus.

The Loire and the Cher then converge and you can turn back in the direction of Tours' southern suburbs, now following the **north bank of the Cher**. The first bridge

Getting Around

Azay-le-Rideau lies on the **train** line between Tours and Chinon.

Tourist Information

Villandry-Savonnières: Le Potager, 37510 Villandry, **t** 02 47 50 12 66, *www. tourisme-en-confluence.com*, *officetourismevillandry@ wanadoo.fr*.
Azay-le-Rideau: B.P.5, Place de l'Europe, 37190 Azay-le-Rideau, **t** 02 47 45 44 40, *www.ot-paysazaylerideau.com*.

Where to Stay and Eat

Berthenay ✉ 37510
La Grange aux Moines B&B, **t** 02 47 50 06 91, *grangeauxmoines.free.fr* (*inexpensive*). A traditional Touraine farmhouse on the delightful spit of land between the Loire and Cher west of Tours. The farmhouse has been very nicely converted to offer extremely comfortable *chambre d'hôtes* accommodation. There's also a swimming pool in the back garden (*table d'hôtes possible*).

Savonnières ✉ 37510
Prieuré des Granges B&B, 15 Rue des Fontaines, **t** 02 47 50 09 67, *www.chateauxandcountry. com/chateaux/prieuredesgranges* (*expensive*). Private rooms and a pool.

Villandry ✉ 37510
L'Etape Gourmande - Domaine de la Giraudière, **t** 02 47 50 08 60, *www. etapegourmande.com* (*menus €13.50–26*). For the ultimate goat meal experience, head southwards out of Villandry towards Druye to this goat farm. *Closed 12 Nov–15 Mar.*

Bréhémont ✉ 37130
***Le Castel de Bray et Monts, Place du Village, **t** 02 47 96 70 47, *www. castelhotel-bray.com* (*moderate–expensive*). A charming hotel set in a wealthy Loire house from the 18th century, with spacious grounds and a tennis court. It's a lovely place to try Loire fish and other specialities (*menus €19–42; closed Sun pm*). *Closed Nov–mid-Feb.*
La Clé d'Or, **t** 02 47 96 70 26, **f** 02 47 96 73 13 (*inexpensive*). Unpretentious, clean and restored, a bargain hotel in a fine position close to the village church and the Loire quays, with a raised terrace which allows you to eat almost on the Loire (*menus c.€12*).

you come to following this itinerary takes you over to the very pretty riverside village of **Savonnières**, its church covered with typical Romanesque carvings.

The road west from Savonnières leads to the **Grottes Pétrifiantes** (*open April–Sept daily 9–6.30, Oct–mid-Nov daily 9.30–12 and 2–6, early Feb–March and mid-Nov–mid-Dec Fri–Wed 9.30–12 and 2–6 ; t 02 47 50 00 09, www.grottes-savonnieres.com; adm*). The streams trickling through the former stone quarries here are particularly rich in limestone, which will quickly coat objects left in the water. The sparkling sugary look is definitely an acquired taste, which you can take or leave in the shop, but the tour of the caves is quite amusing.

Château de Villandry

Château open daily July–Aug 9–6.30, April–June and Sept–mid-Oct 9–6, Feb 9.30–5, Mar 9–5.30, mid-Oct–mid-Nov 9–5. Garden open May–mid-Sept 9–7.30, April and mid-Sept–mid-Oct 9–7, March 9–6, rest of year 9–5.30; t 02 47 50 02 09, www.chateauvillandry.com; adm.

Vegetables are transformed into art at the Château de Villandry. They're the enticing main attraction of the place. But in truth it isn't simply the vegetables but also the complex geometrical and symbolic calculation of the whole ensemble of gardens

Monts ✉ 37260
L'Auberge du Moulin, Au Vieux Bourg, t 02 47 26 76 86. Traditional seasonal cooking in a pleasant modern interior (*menus c.€15–30*).

Azay-le-Rideau and La Chapelle-Ste-Blaise ✉ 37190
***Le Grand Monarque, 3 Place de la République, t 02 47 45 40 08, www. legrandmonarque.com (*moderate–expensive*). Set in a former posting inn, with good food and accommodation. Every day the restaurant serves a different regional dish (*menus €26–50; closed out of season Mon, Tues am, Fri am and Sun pm, otherwise open every day*). Closed mid-Dec–Jan.
**Biencourt, 7 Rue Balzac, t 02 47 45 20 75, biencourt@infonie.fr (*inexpensive*). Charming rooms divided between an 18th-century town house and a 19th-century school, with a patio. *Closed mid-Nov–mid-Feb.*
**Hôtel des Trois Lys/ *Hôtel Le Balzac, t 02 47 45 42 08, www.traiteur-touraine.com (*inexpensive*). Simpler twin establishments, also in atmospheric town houses. Restaurant (*menus €16–23*). Closed Mon out of season, and Jan.
L'Aigle d'Or, 10 Av Adélaïde Riché, t 02 47 45 24 58 (*menus €17–56; closed Sun pm and Wed 3*

July–15 Sept, Sun pm, Tues pm and Wed 15 April– 2 July and 16 Sept–15 Nov, rest of year Sun pm, Mon pm, Tues pm and Wed). A good place to eat out in summer. Local Azay wines make it into some of the sauces. *Closed second fortnights in Nov and Feb.*
Les Grottes, 23 ter Rue Pineau, t 02 47 45 21 04 (*menus €20–32; closed Wed and Thurs low season, Wed and Thurs lunch high season*). Atmospheric troglodyte restaurant which also has a walled terrace where you can try the refined cuisine in summer. *Closed mid-Dec–mid-Feb.*
Manoir de la Rémonière B&B, La Chapelle-Ste-Blaise, t 02 47 45 24 88, www.chateauxhotels. com/remoniere (*expensive*). A joy for anglers as it borders a good stretch of the Indre; a renovated 15th-century manor with a handful of high-standard rooms. There's a pool in the grounds.

Saché ✉ 37190
Auberge du XIIe Siècle, 1 Rue de Château, t 02 47 26 88 77 (*menus €27–58; closed Sun pm, Mon, and Tues lunch*). Splendid beamed house, an inviting place with its great fireplace. The chef is inventive rather than rooted in tradition, despite the setting. *Closed 10–18 June, 1–9 Sept and 6–28 Jan.*

that create a sense of wonder and delight. The château itself shouldn't be overlooked, a fine piece of French Renaissance architecture.

Villandry's Gardens

Villandry's gardens only date from the start of the 20th century, but they follow the spirit of formal Renaissance design. They were conceived by a Spanish-American couple, Dr Joachim Carvallo and Anne Coleman (the latter from Pennsylvania), who bought Villandry in 1906. The late 16th-century bird's-eye views of noble French estates drawn by du Cerceau in his *Les Plus Excellents Bastiments de France* served as a particular source of inspiration. These showed clearly the almost architectural qualities of the gardens at that time, concentrating on carefully constructed patterns. This formal French style had developed out of two traditions: the French medieval monastic garden and the Italian noble estate, ideas on the latter brought over by the likes of Dom Pacello da Mercogliano, one of the gifted Italians to come back with King Charles VII from the latter's daredevil adventure there at the close of the 15th century. However, several important elements in Villandry's gardens date from the 18th century, such as the formal pools used for irrigation.

The gardens are laid out on various levels. The famous **potager**, or vegetable garden, on the lowest level, must surely be the most enviable kitchen garden in France.

Flowers and fruit trees have for once to bow to the beauty of the beet, the charm of the comely cabbages, the perfection of the peppers. Some of the vegetable visions at Villandry are unforgettable: a dense bed of leeks sprouting among rose bushes, or an intense crowd of celery against a backdrop of pruned pear trees. Of course the range of vegetables and colours on show depends on the season, but apart from in winter, there's almost always a dense and colourful patterning of plants to admire.

An hilarious little booklet, *The Gardens of Villandry – Techniques and Plants*, will give you some understanding of the seven gardeners' tasks through the year. It also relates some wonderful, sometimes absurd little vegetable tales rendered more comical by poor translation. The sinister solanine-poisoned aubergine 'is, in a manner of speaking, the loose, smooth-thighed woman of the plant world... A Turkish legend refers to it as being responsible for the constant fainting of one of their imams when he ate it in the presence of his naked concubines.' The carrot is 'inclining towards the phallic inwardness of its root, its regenerative power, source and channel of the active principle of the seed. In this it is the reverse of the standing stone (a reversed acupuncture of the soil)... The Gaulois made it their national plant.'

The little booklet also tackles the small *jardin des simples*, or **medicinal herb garden**, on the next level up from the *potager*. On the opposite side of the vegetable gardens, below the hillside, you come to the magnificent **ornamental gardens**. Here, box hedges have been carefully cut into splendid symbols of the different forms of chivalric love. You'll need to climb up past the *jardin d'eau*, or **water garden**, swans gliding on the mirrored pools, to get a good view down onto the chivalric designs. Tender love is reassuringly represented by complete hearts encasing the romantic allusions of a masked ball. Fickle love takes the form of fans, objects of dissimulation, interspersed with the horns of the cuckold, while love letters remind of the potential deception of words, and a lover's absence. Daggers and swords evoke the duels of tragic love, red flowers symbolising spilt blood. In the last square, the hearts have been broken by the disruptive dance of mad, passionate love. To the left of these four interpretations of love, crosses and fleurs-de-lys have been cut out in further box hedges. Beyond, you can make out musical topiary, with stylized lyres, harps, notes, and even candelabra to light the sheet music. The whole effect is quite magical.

The Château

A château already stood here in the 12th century; it was at the medieval Villandry, on 4 July 1189, that Henri Plantagenêt, alias Henry II of England, signed a peace with the French Capetian King Philippe Auguste, with whom Henri's own son Richard the Lionheart had entered into an alliance. Philippe Auguste gained the Berry and the Auvergne through this treaty. It went down in history as the Paix de Colombiers, as Villandry was then known. King Henry died two days later in Chinon, and was buried at the abbey of Fontevraud, close by in Anjou. In the 16th century, Jean le Breton, a minister and close friend of King François I (*see* the Château de Villesavin), used the remains of the medieval castle to start his Renaissance château. Its three wings were set on the irregular base inherited from the previous fort, with a water-filled moat on a couple of sides, while the southwest tower was kept from the earlier castle. This new Villandry went up through the 1530s, and its architecture displays many of the features of the elegant new Renaissance style derived from Italy – regular window openings, these windows framed by pilasters, strong horizontal bands dividing up the façades, elegant colonnades on the ground floor. Certain French tastes remain evident, such as the splendid array of Loire *lucarnes* in the slate roofs – one carries Le Breton's arms. Descendants of Le Breton held on to the château until the 1750s, when it came into the hands of the Castellane family. French nobles of the neo-classical period frequently wanted to modernize Renaissance châteaux. The new marquis decided on transforming the windows, embellishing the oldest tower, filling in the moat and adding neo-classical outbuildings. The latter still exist, but when Dr Carvallo bought the place, he set about restoring the original Renaissance features. You cross the watery moats that Carvallo reopened to come into the enchanting cobbled *cour d'honneur* for a tour of the interiors.

Inside, first you might watch the slide show presenting the gardens through the four seasons. Many of the rooms that follow were remodelled during the 18th century for the Castellane family. Two other striking features characterize the interiors: instead of freshly cut flowers, there are beautiful displays of vegetables in bowls; and Spanish art is very much in evidence, brought in by the Carvallos. Several disturbing works from the school of Goya stand out. In the Petit Salon, the *Décapité pendu par les cheveux* is a disturbing reminder of the terrible massacres of Spanish civilians carried out by the French army in 1807. The Grand Salon looks as though the *châtelains* have just left before you arrived. Two Spanish 17th-century still lifes stand out here, as does the *Temptation of St-Anthony* by the school of Tintoretto. The portrait of Isabella de Bourbon is interesting in terms of French royal genealogy, as this daughter of King Henri IV and Marie de' Medici married King Philip IV of Spain, giving birth to Marie-Thérèse, future wife of Louis XIV. In the Salle à Manger, the Castellanes added a touch from their native Provence with the cooling fountain. Further Spanish works adorn the staircase and the first floor. The gallery is given over to temporary exhibitions and leads to a curious room with a Moorish ceiling, taken from a 13th-century Spanish mosque. Climb the tower, with its exhibition of old photos of Villandry revealing just how much the Carvallos changed the place. From the top you get splendid views.

West of Villandry, turn at Le Moulinet to follow the Loire riverside road, a beautiful route little-known to most tourists. The village of **Bréhémont**, with its great quays, makes a magical sight; the 19th-century church seems ready to slip into the river.

The Indre from Montbazon to Ussé

To join this section of the Indre from Tours, head towards Montbazon along the N10, then turn west onto the D87 just north of Montbazon to reach the Château de Candé.

Château de Candé

Open May–Oct 10–12 and 2–6, t 02 47 26 61 10; adm.

Wallis Simpson's 28 pieces of luggage containing 66 dresses arrived a few weeks after she did at the Château de Candé in May 1937. She had come here to be married for the third time, to the man who had abdicated as King Edward VIII of Britain the year before because of his love for her. The wedding of the Duke and Duchess of Windsor, as they became known, took place at the Château de Candé on 3 June 1937. The property served as the backdrop in the famous images of what some called the most sensational marriage of the 20th century.

This was the main moment in the Château de Candé's history. Otherwise the story of the castle is a fairly modest one. A first fortification was built in the 10th century on this high spot overlooking the valley. The name Candé derives from an old word for a confluence, the St-Laurent stream joining the Indre at this point. The medieval lords of Candé were vassals of the lords of Montbazon close by. In 1499, François Briçonnet, a powerful courtier and one-time mayor of Tours, bought the property and transformed the fort into a charming country hunting pavilion. This new building was on quite a small scale by Touraine standards. Numerous families then owned the property, including, very briefly, a Huguenot Guillaume Bertrand, one of the many victims of the terrible St Bartholomew's Day massacres of Protestants of 1572. In the 18th century, a gunpowder factory was built by the Indre river below the castle, and still mars the valley. Several proprietors owned the castle after the Revolution, until in the mid-19th century a flamboyant Cuban by the name of Drake del Castillo bought the property and decided to substantially enlarge the château. The Tours architect Jacques-Aimé Meffre drew up the plans, tripling the size of the place. It became a pastiche of a Loire Valley castle, but on an impressive scale. Drake's son Jacques served as a much-loved mayor of nearby Monts, but his son in turn sold the castle, this time to a Frenchman who had gone off to make his fortune in America.

Charles-Eugènes Bedaux made a mint with his model for labour efficiency in industry. He became a US citizen, although in the First World War he enlisted for foreign service. In 1927 he bought Candé and installed all manner of modern comforts that he had come to enjoy in America: efficient heating, luxurious bathrooms, the latest telephone systems. A wheeler-dealer on an international scale, he courted the powerful of all persuasions, including the likes of Citroën in France and, much more notoriously, Hitler and Mussolini in Fascist Europe. In the meantime, Edward, heir to the British throne, had met Wallis Simpson in 1931 and fallen under her spell. After his father died, he became King Edward VIII in January 1936. But his love for Wallis was too strong, and he decided that in order to marry her he would abdicate (as head of the Church of England he was forbidden to marry a divorcee). He had to leave Britain and the couple wanted to find a place in which to get married in France. They had recently met Bedaux, who suggested his castle. So arrangements were quickly made. Some sumptuous evenings took place here before the wedding, the chef Legros preparing dishes in the grand Ancien Régime style, the great organist Marcel Dupré playing for the guests.

Bedaux made sure that the wedding day was carefully planned, and managed to arrange for the ceremony to take place at the château itself rather than at the local town hall, as is the normal legal requirement in France. Madame Bedaux roped in the locals to play their parts as servants and lackeys dressed in elaborate uniforms. Tales of the event still thrill many of the families involved. A certain number of press people attended, but many were thrown off the scent by heading for the Château de Candé in neighbouring Anjou. A priest from Britain defied the Archbishop of Canterbury's orders, and came and presided over the religious ceremony.

As you arrive for the short tour inside the château, you may recognize some of the architectural details from the celebrated wedding photos. Above the doorway, the ceramic scene represents St Martin dividing his cloak in two, somehow a symbol fraught with ambiguities with regards to the duke and duchess. Within, the look is predominantly neo-Gothic, with heavy wood panelling and big painted beams. Bedaux's library with its organ was where the wedding ceremony took place. The fireplace carries graffiti supposedly scratched by the duke and duchess to record their romantic day. You can also see a few other grand rooms, now used by the county council of Touraine. The council has owned the place since 1974, Madame Bedaux having left the château to the French state after her husband had killed himself in gaol, awaiting trial on charges of collaborating with the Nazis. For the moment, the guided tour in fact concentrates more on a walk around the grounds rather than the castle, but there are plans for the council to develop the château as a more significant tourist centre, possibly opening more rooms and presenting a video on the famed Windsor wedding.

Keep to the north bank of the Indre beyond Monts to appreciate the beauty of the valley to the full along this stretch. Balzac sang its praises in *Le Lys dans la vallée*. He portrayed it there as a '*vallée riante* (a laughing valley)', where '*la sensibilité coule à torrents* (sensitivity runs in torrents)'. The restful village of **Saché** has an amusing Alexander Calder sculpture. The American renowned for his large-scale mobiles took to this area and one of his metal monsters surveys the old village square.

Château de Saché and Musée Balzac

Open daily April–Sept 9–7, rest of year 9.30–12.30 and 2–5.30; closed 25 Dec and 1 Jan; t 02 47 26 86 50; adm.

Behind the intriguing long walls of its estate, the Château de Saché proves a rough, rugged 16th-century manor rather than a pretty castle. What gives the house its fame is that Balzac frequently stayed here. In 1952 it was converted by the owner into a museum to commemorate Balzac, or as the guide puts it, 'to pay homage to his excesses'. It should be said that while the interiors and grounds have an easily appreciated charm, those who aren't already familiar with the rampant writer might appreciate an introduction (*see* box p.313) before facing the mass of books and information on Balzac provided at the museum.

Although Balzac didn't spend substantial periods at Saché, they proved to be particularly productive times. This place provided an oasis of tranquillity in his storm of a life. He worked like a maniac, at the bizarrest of hours, often getting up between 2 and 5am and working through to 5pm. Coffee, toast, fruit and more coffee was his basic diet. He would occasionally go downstairs to give a reading. The results were large portions of *Le Lys dans la vallée*, *César Birotteau* and *Le Père Goriot*.

The house is full of memorabilia about the man and his works, not just focusing on what Balzac wrote at Saché, but also collecting items to give glimpses of his chequered life and loves and his multitude of other works, although giving special prominence to those incorporating recognizably local detail. Visitors who've worked in publishing may particularly appreciate Balzac's agonies over copy and be horrified by the number of amendments and additions he scribbled on in brown ink, sometimes on as many as nine sets of proofs! The museum also attempts to recreate the early 19th-century atmosphere which would have surrounded Balzac. Of course, adulatory pieces have been added, such as the bronze of the author by the Tourangeau sculptor Sicard and details of other memorials to him. On the top floor, Balzac's little guest bedroom has been done up as he might have known it. Caricatures of the literary giant and his characters help lighten the tone.

Villaines-les-Rochers

Southwest of Saché the village of **Villaines-les-Rochers** displays wacky sculptures made by local basket-weavers. The place has a long tradition in this craft, with a cooperative, the Vannerie de Villaines, which dates back to 1849. This is well worth a visit as you can see how the basket-weavers handle the willow wicker, and the shop has an good collection of wicker objects for sale. The village is typically Tourangeau and attractive, stretching along the narrow valley, caves dug into the rock.

Château d'Azay-le-Rideau

Open daily July–Aug 9.30–7; April–June and Sept–Oct 9.30–6; Nov–Mar Tues–Sun 9.30–12.30 and 2–5.30; closed hols; t 02 47 45 42 04; www.monum.fr; adm.

...almost a rival of Chenonceaux...

Henry James, *A Little Tour in France*, 1884

The beauty of Azay-le-Rideau's château reflected in its moat encourages extravagant comparisons. Balzac likened it to a 'diamond with its multiple facets set in the Indre'. Like that other supremely romantic image of the Loire, Chenonceau, Azay-le-Rideau is built on the water. Although the word Rideau (the French for curtain) in the name in fact refers back to the name of a medieval lord, a curtain of trees does separate the château from the delightful town outside. The site by the Indre was important in medieval times as a crossing point over the river. An earlier construction was burnt to the ground on the orders of the future French King Charles VII who, passing through in 1418, apparently took revenge on Burgundian troops here who insulted him. The town was known for a long time as Azay-le-Brûlé (the burnt).

The château you see now was started in 1518 for Gilles Berthelot, a treasurer of France for King François I. Only the large tower as you arrive in the courtyard survived from the earlier medieval building. Gilles being so often away on business, his wife Philippa, née Lesbahy, oversaw much of the work. The man in charge of the architecture appears to have been one Etienne Rousseau. Azay is so often cited as the example par excellence of French Renaissance architecture, but in fact it dates from that transitional early 16th-century period during which Gothic elements lingered on.

Balzac, Slave to Words

Balzac was by turns a saint, a criminal, an honest judge, a corrupt judge, a minister, a fop, a harlot, a duchess, and always a genius.
André Maurois in *Prometheus: The Life of Balzac*, 1966

His mother's infidelity led Honoré de Balzac to Saché. She had a liaison with the owner, Monsieur de Margonne, and a child by him, Balzac's half-brother Henri. Balzac was always very well received by de Margonne and came to stay here, seeking refuge to write and to avoid his creditors in more or less brief stays in the 1820s and 30s.

Honoré himself had been born along Tours' main street in 1799. His father, of peasant origin, had managed to climb the social ladder to become a civil servant, got a post in Tours and married an 18-year-old when he was 50. Balzac's mother was particularly fascinated by the occult, but not especially interested in her first son. He was sent packing to boarding school and saw little of her. He took solace in literature from an early age. A large amount of semi-autobiographical childhood detail creeps into the start of *Le Lys dans la vallée*.

The Balzacs moved to Paris in 1814. Honoré trained there to become a lawyer, but wished to be a writer. He deliberately avoided finding a job in the law and devoted himself to more imaginative word play, starting out with several pieces that he himself admitted were literary filth. The coarse Rabelais was a great influence on the exuberant young man. So too were several older women, guiding spirits-cum-lovers. One of his first important liaisons was with Laure de Berny, whose mother had served Marie Antoinette as a lady-in-waiting before her royal mistress got the chop.

Balzac embarked on a business venture in printing in the mid-1820s which soon ended in bankruptcy. He was left with huge debts, in particular to members of his family. But his writing rapidly began to earn him literary success. At the age of 30, *Les Chouans* brought him his first critical acclaim. From this time on a flood of novels poured from his pen; Balzac was to prove one of the most prolific writers in French letters. The advances on his books couldn't keep up with the debts he continued to accumulate, however, and his life reads like a race to dash off more and more novels to meet deadlines and stem financial crises. Although this inevitably meant that his writing was rushed, he cared deeply for the detail. Just look at the extent of the corrections he made to his proofs, on display at Saché, an editor's nightmare.

Between times Balzac carried on torrid love affairs and burning correspondences, in particular with 'L'Etrangère', as a mysterious correspondent from Eastern Europe signed herself in her first letter to him. It was the start of a passionate friendship. A Balzac enthusiast has calculated that the author's lifetime of letters to Mme Hanska add up to a quarter of the length of his *Comédie Humaine*!

The pepper-pot towers, the guards' *chemin de ronde*, the steepness of the roof, its finial tips, all give a Gothic twist to the whole. The Italian influence can be seen in the move towards symmetry, in the pilaster-framed, standardized windows, and in many typical decorative details, such as medallions and candelabra. The famous staircase too was built in the Italian manner, with spacious straight ramps as opposed to a

This *Comédie Humaine* was Balzac's grandiose scheme, from the early 1830s, to make the bulk of his works into a coherent whole, giving a full picture of early 19th-century French society. The works in *La Comédie Humaine* bring to life almost 2,500 characters, the more important ones cropping up in several books, be it only in cameo parts or by reference.

Readers who enjoy Balzac tend to get addicted to him, although there are several different styles to his writing. The *Contes drolatiques*, for example, are a collection of bawdy tales set in the Touraine, 'the chronicle of the old manors and abbeys of this region' as Henry James described them, inspired by Rabelais, but sub-Rabelaisian in seriousness, lacking the same substance. Balzac also wrote several books in which the supernatural plays an important role, such as *La Peau de Chagrin*, *Louis Lambert* and the daring *Séraphita*.

But Balzac is generally considered as a writer whose stories are rooted in 19th-century reality – to such an extent that in French editions of his works, the academics tend to put in a good number of footnotes explaining that such and such an event occurred in reality on this or that day, not the one given by Balzac. Balzac was more interested in the broader issues behind different types and individuals and behind French society in his period. The breadth of his coverage is phenomenal. That giant of American literature Henry James summed it up when he wrote admiringly that 'Balzac, in the maturity of his vision, took in more human life than any one since Shakespeare.'

It's not a pretty picture that Balzac paints. France had just emerged shaken to the core and deeply scarred by the massive upheaval of the Revolution followed by the Napoleonic Empire. While Rabelais covers up the complexities and horrors of his 16th-century times beneath a thick surface of absurd humour, the barbs stick out of Balzac's works. His humour is ironic, cruel, pitiless. He kicks his characters when they're down, and in the world he creates, fate shows no pity for the weak. Time and again in his plots, those who are tender and emotionally vulnerable are trampled on for their weakness and punished.

Touraine appears as a prominent background in several of Balzac's works, most notably the *Contes drolatiques*, *Le Lys dans la vallée* and *Eugénie Grandet*, the last set just across in Saumur in Anjou. A fair number of his shorter stories also take place in Touraine, such as that of the persecuted Birotteau in *Le Curé de Tours*, or *La Grenardière*, named after a house which Balzac once rented for Mme de Berny.

Some say Balzac was killed by the coffee he drank in such quantities to keep him going, although the complications caused by gangrene seem a more plausible explanation of what, in 1850, put an end to this '*galérien de la plume et de l'encre* (galley slave of pen and ink)', as he once described himself.

cramped French stair tower. The emblems of the salamander and the ermine on the building pay tribute to the royal couple François I and Claude de France. This is somewhat ironic, given that the building work wasn't entirely completed in 1527 when Berthelot had to flee to avoid being caught up in the financial scandal caused by the indictment of his cousin by marriage, Jacques de Beaune-Semblançay, François I's main treasurer. (Semblançay was later cleared of the charge, but it came rather too late, as he had already lost his head.) François I grasped Berthelot's possessions and so yet another exquisite Loire château, albeit not quite complete, fell under his control. He handed it to his captain of the guards, Antoine Raffin. A number of refinements would only be finished as late as the 19th century. However, standing in the courtyard, the ensemble may still not feel quite complete to you. Unusually, there are only two wings to the château, forming an L-shape. A third wing may have been planned originally.

Before going inside, it's worth wandering round the château to enjoy the splendid view of it across the Indre. The château isn't reflected in this river moat at all times of the year. Sometimes the water is too fast-flowing, at others it may be covered with plant life, but when the calm mirror of the water does reflect its form, it makes a delightful sight, elegant, light and sparkling. While the traditional dried-blood colour of the top floor shutters jars slightly, the chimneys in brick, stone and slate give an elegant finishing touch to the château's exterior. Within, the rooms are somewhat empty and unexciting, but you start the visit down in the kitchen, which has some hilarious Gothic touches in the *culs-de-lampe*, including a dog chewing on a bone and a man mooning at visitors. After that it's the usual round of tapestries, chests and, generally speaking, bad copies of paintings. A few 16th-century royal and noble portraits are the exception. The tapestries are particularly atmospheric in the Grande Salle, bathed in a shimmering light reflected off the Indre on sunny days.

You can wander round the gardens, which in the past few years have been used as the setting for an idiosyncratic *son-et-lumière* show, **Les Imaginaires d'Azay-le-Rideau**, where visitors walk round to see and experience the effects at their own pace (*weekends in May, June and Sept, daily in July at 10.30pm and in August at 10pm; contact the château, t 02 47 45 42 04, or the tourist office for further details; adm*).

Leaving the château through the elegant 17th-century outbuildings with their gilded tops, it's only a short walk to the **church of Saint-Symphorien** with its extraordinary Romanesque façade. Three sets of diminutive statues stand in niches. No one knows exactly when these figures were made or whether they were meant as part of this church. Around them, crisscrossed and diagonal stonework adds to the curiosity.

Around Azay-le-Rideau

In the midst of this major château country, seek out **Les Goupillières** (*open July–Aug daily 2–7; Easter–June and Sept–Oct weekends and public hols 2–7; t 02 47 96 60 84; adm*) to learn about how farmers used to live in these parts. However, hidden in its cute, quiet little valley, this is no ordinary farming hamlet, as virtually all the dwellings and stables lie underground. The caves may have been used in times of war originally, but then the families here developed a whole maze of well-laid-out chambers in which to live and keep their animals and provisions. Farm animals are still kept in this beautiful spot, but the owner now specializes in growing apples.

West of Azay-le-Rideau, the Indre draws closer and closer to the Loire. After passing the splendid private Château de l'Islette by the river, look out for signs to the **Château de la Chatonnière**, discreetly standing at the bottom of its own little valley. This intimate castle presents an enviable picture of Touraine comfort. A half-dozen small, charming themed gardens have recently been created around it. While you can't enter the defensive walled building itself, wandering around the sloping terraces you can spy on the château and its enclosed courtyard below.

At **Marnay**, the **Musée Maurice Dufresne** (*open Feb–Nov; peak season 9.15–7, otherwise 9.15–6; t 02 47 96 60 84, www.musee-dufresne.com; adm*) contains a massive collection of old agricultural machines and the tools of many other trades (including a guillotine for your professional executioner). The place reflects the passion of a zany collector. All the pieces are immaculately presented in massive buildings on an estate which includes a mill on the Indre. At **Rivarennes**, the **Musée de la Poire Tapée** (*open June–Aug 3–6, May and Sept Sat only 3–6; t 02 47 95 47 78; adm*) revives the traditional craft of pear-drying and bashing – the British Navy used to be a customer for this practical, nutritious food.

Château d'Ussé at Rigny-Ussé

Open daily April–Aug 9.30–6.30; mid-Feb–Mar and Oct–mid-Nov 10–12 and 2–5.30; t 02 47 95 54 05; adm.

To the French, the Château d'Ussé is a symbol of romance. This is the castle said to have inspired the tale of Sleeping Beauty. The picture-book château nestles on the wooded bank of the Indre leading up to the forest of Chinon. The architecture combines a series of elements from different periods. Any trace of the Viking Gelduin I, who settled here in Foulques Nerra's time, has disappeared. So too has the 12th-century fortress that then went up. The de Bueil family, supporters of kings Charles VII and Louis XI in the second half of the 15th century, ordered a third construction. The substantial southwest tower is the oldest surviving part. The south wing and some of the west wing had gone up by the time the château was sold to Jacques d'Espinay, servant of Louis XII. By the 1520s the d'Espinay family had completed the east, west and north wings, some Italianate details creeping into the overall Gothic design. In the course of the 17th century, the Marquis de Valentinay ordered profound changes, especially adding to the lightness of the interiors. Off came the north wing, while the south wing was given much more generous windows. A whole new section to the west brought a completely different style into the picture, without towers. The slope down to the water was beautifully transformed by formal terraces, orange trees shipped in to add an exotic touch.

The tale linking the Château d'Ussé with the writing of *Sleeping Beauty* goes thus. Charles Perrault, 17th-century author of the romance, apparently stopped in this area on his way back to Paris and was offered hospitality here by the count of Saumur. Put up in the château, Perrault was moved to pen notes for this most famous of fairytales. If you can't remember the story exactly, before the tour of the apartments you can try to piece it together from the scenes re-created with waxwork models at the top of the greatest of the château's towers. They seem to be quite out of sequence. As this version would have it, the princess is first revived and rescued by a handsome prince from her century of sleep, even before the evil witch has had time to cast her spell on her or the princess to prick her finger on an old woman's spinning wheel. To leave your head reeling further, walk around the towers' *chemin de ronde*, which looks rather daunting, with chunks of stone missing, although these gaps provide splendid views over the village of Rigny-Ussé.

Before the guided tour inside the castle, you can also visit the separate chapel, a gem of an early French Renaissance building. High relief carvings of the apostles in medallions frame the entrance. Worn memento mori add to the effect, only slightly spoilt by some unfortunate graffiti. The interlaced initials C and L refer to the couple for whom the chapel was built, Charles d'Espinay and Lucrèce de Pons. The interior has an almost marble-like whiteness. Nuns and a reptilean man with a beaded backbone count among the fine carvings on the pews. Two great cedars of Lebanon stand next to the many towers and turrets of the château, a gift from the great 19th-century writer René de Chateaubriand to the owner of Ussé in his day, the Duchesse de Duras. Inside the castle, the duchess' daughter contributed her own modifications to the many 17th-century alterations made for the Marquis de Valentinay. A potpourri of styles and objects fills the rooms, reflecting the changing tastes and increasingly exotic travels of the line of Ussé's aristocratic owners.

Extravagant trompe-l'oeil painting covers the ceiling of the Salle des Gardes, with its collection of arms and Oriental pieces brought back in the 19th century by Count Stanislas de Blacas, ancestor of the present owner. In what was the original chapel, among the 16th-century Flemish tapestries and the Ancien Régime furniture, lie mementoes of French Romanticism, including a portrait of Chateaubriand, the greatest of French Romantic writers. The Duchesse de Duras was a novelist herself, her works *Edouard* and *Ourika* little known now, but successful in her day. Secret passageways dug into the rock disappear off from the kitchen; one tapestry hides a passageway. A great series of further tapestries adorns the long gallery. These fine 18th-century Flemish works were made after cartoons by David Teniers, and ironically depict peasant scenes. The architecture of the grand staircase is all refinement, planned by François Mansart, the most illustrious French architect of the first half of the 17th century. The little steps were made to take into consideration the great big dresses that were the fashion for ladies back then. The best is saved until last. During Louis XIV's reign, leading aristocrats had to decorate one room of their château in sumptuous style in case of a visit from the king. Ussé's Chambre du Roi has been splendidly rejuvenated, with gold-leaf detailing and rich reds framing exquisite pieces of furniture such as the Boulle bureau in red tortoiseshell and copper. Royal portraits of Louis XIV and of Mademoiselle de Blois, Princesse de Conti, the daughter of the Sun King and Louise de la Vallière, add to the wealth of the room. But the king never came.

The Pays du Véron

West of Ussé you come into the Pays du Véron, the arrowhead of land between the Loire and the Vienne. It's a curious spit, with sandy terrain and pine landscapes which at times make you think you might be approaching the coast. Typically pretty old Touraine houses embellish the vine-growing countryside – the Chinon *appellation* extends this far. But the clouds of the nuclear power station near Avoine on the Loire hang over the place, somewhat spoiling the tranquillity of the picture.

The Vienne, Manse and Veude Valleys

The Vienne river enters Touraine south of Ste-Maure on its plateau, the name of Ste-Maure synonymous for French people with goat's cheese. To the west, the Manse valley is a well-kept secret, offering a delightful alternative route to Chinon from the better-known Vienne valley. The Vienne's banks are so dotted with Romanesque churches that you have to conclude that this area was much more popular and populated in medieval times than now. Vines appear on the gorgeous gentle Vienne valley slopes as you approach Chinon. South of the great Plantagenet courtly town, you can follow the Veude and Mable valleys further south for a detour past some startling castles to the model 17th-century town of Richelieu.

Ste-Maure-de-Touraine and Ste-Catherine

Ste-Maure simply means **goat's cheese** to your average Frenchman; the long cylindrical type with a piece of straw sticking through the middle, so highly regarded that it's been awarded its own *appellation d'origine contrôlée* status to protect its exclusivity. In town, what remains of the 14th- and 15th-century château has been converted into a local museum, the **Musée de la Ville** (*open weekdays April–mid-Sept 10–11.30 and 2.30–5; t 02 47 65 66 20; adm*), which sings the praises of the cheese (tasting included), as well as presenting local history and ways. Perhaps the greatest attraction of the town is the Friday morning market, the place to buy the local speciality. The market spreads over two squares divided by the splendid **Halles**, or covered market, built in 1672 for the powerful Rohan family, its coat of arms visible over a couple of the entrances. You might also like to visit the vast 11th–12th-century crypts under the church, but they're only open on Thursday mornings.

A few kilometres north of Ste-Maure, **Ste-Catherine-de-Fierbois** is the village which, it is claimed, provided Joan of Arc with her sword. Her trusted weapon with its five crosses came from here, she said at her trial. Legend also claims that this was the sword of Charles Martel, the 8th-century king who so significantly beat the Moors on a site between Tours and Poitiers in 732, putting a stop to the Arabs' great northern advance. Some maintain that the battle took place on the plateau of Ste-Maure. The story continues that Charles Martel left his sword in a nearby chapel dedicated to Catherine of Alexandra, offering thanks to her for his great victory.

Ste-Catherine certainly lay on a pilgrims' route from Chartres to Santiago de Compostela. Before Joan's day, a blind paralytic who visited the dilapidated chapel in 1375 was cured here and had the place restored by way of thanks. Apparently, a tradition then arose for passing knights to leave a sword in the chapel in thanksgiving to St Catherine. This could explain the presence of a spare sword lying in the chapel when Joan came by. The lord Boucicault payed for the creation of a hospice to St

James here in 1415 and this is where Joan stayed nearing the end of her journey from Lorraine to seek out the Dauphin Charles at Chinon. The present **church** was built after her rehabilitation in the 1450s by order of Hélie de Bourdeilles, the Franciscan whom Charles VII appointed to re-examine her condemnation for heresy so long after her death. The village also has a **Musée de Traditions Populaires** full of local bric-a-brac (*open June–Aug Tues–Sat 11–12.30 and 4.30–6.30; t 02 47 65 43 46; adm*).

The Manse and North Bank of the Vienne

The Manse valley west of Ste-Maure makes for a memorable little trip. **St-Epain**, with its collection of 15th- and 16th-century houses and earlier medieval church provided with Angevin vaults and 16th-century misericordes, sets the tone. The Maison du Pays sells regional produce from one of the fine houses. An early medieval keep and a church spire topped by a Renaissance dome stick out above another fine collection of 15th- and 16th-century houses with mullion windows, rounded stair towers and old wells at **Crissay-sur-Manse**. Most of the church dates from the 15th century, and has Flamboyant Gothic decoration. It was built for a member of the powerful local family, the Turpin-de-Crissés, lords here from 1120 to 1632. Lancelot and Antoine Turpin, both of whom served as royal chamberlains, erected the château in the 15th century. Vestiges remain, including some of the dependencies built into the rock. The whole village is lovingly cared for. Art exhibitions, antiques displays and a theatre company bring life to this little place in summer.

Nearby, the **Collégiale des Roches Tranchelion**, a dramatically perched and picturesque ruin of a church, was originally built at the start of the 16th century, as is clear from the predominantly Renaissance features of the entrance façade, although a statue of the Holy Father as a blessing bishop seated on high shows Gothic influence. Very much in a state of romantic abandonment, the skeletal remains of the choir vault cast black shadows in the sunshine, which may bring out guardian hornets. The château that once stood here has all but disappeared. However, in 1449 King Charles VII and his councillors met at this spot to decide on a further campaign against the English which would lead to the final French victory in the Hundred Years' War. The name of Tranchelion apparently refers back to a cruel crusading legend, the local lord supposedly returning from the Holy Land with a lion to whom he served serfs who displeased him. Continue on to the next village, **Avon-les-Roches**, its village church embellished with ornate Romanesque portals.

The Manse joins the Vienne at L'Ile-Bouchard. Following the D21 through Panzoult to Cravant-les-Côteaux you enter utterly enchanting vine territory on the slopes above the Vienne. This is arguably the prettiest wine route in Touraine. In **Cravant**'s Vieux Bourg, the disued church with its remarkable chequerboard exterior decorations said to date back to Carolingian times, has been converted into a **Musée Lapidaire** (*open 9–7; for the curator t 06 07 04 43 34; adm*), a curious little thing. Among the fragments of sculpture inside, a collection of old carved pillars stand out. Charles VII's favourite, George de la Trémoille, added on a southern side chapel in which he is

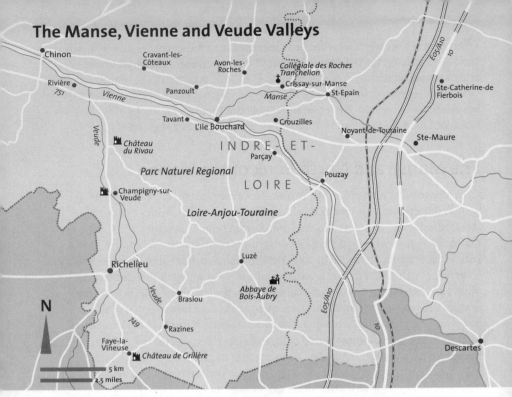

The Manse, Vienne and Veude Valleys

represented with his daughters kneeling in prayer to the Virgin, the period fashion in evidence. From Cravant, vines accompany you to Chinon's outskirts.

The South Bank of the Vienne to Chinon

Parçay has one of a whole string of charming Romanesque churches along the Vienne river banks as it arrives in Touraine, this one rich in sculpture inside and out and reflecting the strong influence of the Poitou region on the valley.

The island which gives the small town of **L'Ile-Bouchard** its name proves slightly disappointing. It could be charming, with many weeping willows lining the riverside, but the bald square where the château once stood isn't pretty. However, on the south side of the river, the truncated priory **church of St-Léonard** comes as a delightful surprise. Only the choir end has survived. Its ambulatory, with its wings and its little roof, looks like a diminutive semicircular theatre. The columns are decorated with superb Romanesque carvings of New Testament stories. The wave-like long hair and finger-pointing of the human characters is typical of mid 12th-century carving, executed with a feeling for drama. The **church of St-Maurice**, also south of the river, is a much more substantial affair, standing out with its hexagonal belfry and spire dating from 1480. Although **St-Gilles**, on the north bank, is the oldest church in town, thought to date back to the late 10th century possibly, the stone of its vegetal decorated entrance eaten away, the interior presents a naff 19th-century restoration.

Close to L'Ile-Bouchard, the village of **Tavant** is reputed for an extraordinary Romanesque fresco cycle in the crypt of the **church of St-Nicolas** (*open by appointment only March–Nov Wed–Sun 10–12 and 2–6; closed first Sun each month; t 02 47 58 58 01 – the town hall; adm*). The church doesn't look particularly impressive from the outside, nor is its site very remarkable. However, the frescoes in the crypt are outstanding. They may lie buried in a restricted little columned coffer of a space, but the figures spring full of life from the walls. Art historians have waxed lyrical about these paintings, considered by some to be the most refined frescoes of Romanesque Europe. Instead of the normally rather static poses of Romanesque art, here the highly expressive gestures of outstretched arms and hands and the curves of the bodies convey great movement. It's as though characters in a medieval passion play had been caught in their poses. The chronology of the stories moves from Old Testament scenes in the west to New Testament ones in the east, but the variety of people represented between the scenes breaks up any notion of a coherent narrative. Several typical medieval characters feature: a knight in armour who fights with a devil; a pilgrim; and a woman piercing her own breast, one of the Middle Ages's most favoured and most disturbing visions of sin, Luxuria or lust. The frescoes in the church above, which include a Christ in Majesty and pieces from the New Testament, are later works.

Getting Around

There's an exit off the A10 motorway at Ste-Maure.

Coming by **bus** from Tours, two lines serve the area; one goes to Ste-Maure and Ste-Catherine, the other, very limited indeed, goes through St-Epain, Crouzilles, l'Ile Bouchard, Champigny and Richelieu.

Tourist Information

Ste-Maure-de-Touraine: Rue du Château, 37800 Ste-Maure-de-Touraine, t 02 47 65 66 20, f 02 47 34 04 28.
Ste-Catherine-de-Fierbois: Mairie, 37800 Ste-Catherine-de-Fierbois, t 02 47 65 43 46.
St-Epain: Maison de Pays d'Accueil, 33 Grande-Rue, 37800 St-Epain, t 02 47 65 80 21, f 02 47 65 80 42.
Richelieu: 6 Grande Rue, 37120 Richelieu, t 02 47 58 13 62, *www.cc-pays-de-richelieu.fr*.

Market Day

Ste-Maure-de-Touraine: Friday morning.
Richelieu: Friday morning

Where to Stay and Eat

Ste-Maure-de-Touraine ✉ 37800
★★★Les Hauts de Ste-Maure, 2 Avenue Générale de Gaulle, t 02 47 65 50 65, *www.hostelleriehautsdestemaure.fr* (*expensive*). The town's 16th-century posting inn, with comfortable rooms with beams and old furniture, traditional French fare served in the restaurant, a shady garden with a heated pool, and a collection of old cars (*menus €35–58; closed Sun Oct–April and Mon lunch*). *Closed Jan.*

Noyant-de-Touraine ✉ 37800
★★★Château de Brou, t 02 47 65 80 80, *www.chateau-de-brou.fr* (*expensive*). 15th-century castle with turrets set on a large estate west of Ste-Maure. *Closed early Jan–late Mar.*
La Ciboulette, 78 Route de Chinon, t 02 47 65 84 64 (*menus c.€15.50–24.50*). May be rather close to the motorway, but it has a terrace which gives onto vines and the forest and serves tasty Loire specialities.

Pouzay ✉ 37800
Le Gardon Frit, t 02 47 65 21 81 (*menus c.€20–34.50; closed Tues and Wed exc hols*).

St-Nicolas was one of two churches built in the village, both attached to the powerful abbey of Marmoutier near Tours. St-Nicolas was the parish church, while **Ste-Marie** served a priory. It was built from around 1070. It hasn't been so much neglected as swallowed up by village houses, along with vestiges of other priory buildings. Virtually all its sculptural decoration has been stripped away, the portals sold to an American woman in 1927. The belfry was rebuilt in the 15th century, with one of two carved 11th-century stone slabs incorporated into the building, which once went down to the river.

Rivière is a another sweet, tranquil spot along the Vienne. Head down to the water's edge in summer and you may well see locals fishing from their traditional brightly coloured little boats. Wander round the outside of the Romanesque **church of Notre-Dame** to appreciate its 11th-century exterior decoration, including its chequerboard work and bas-reliefs. Within, you'll be startled by the gaudy mock-medieval decoration, the 19th-century work of the Comte de Galembert; it's worth remembering that medieval churches were filled with colour. The sculpted capitals of the choir have been painted too, as is virtually every millimetre of wall. River scenes feature, among others. Down in the dark crypt-like lower chapel the atmosphere is much more sober and moving, a small arch framing the tomb of the lords of Basché, their 16th-century effigies decapitated.

Close to a bridge over the Vienne, well known for its fish and seafood dishes. *Closed 3 weeks at start of Jan, 1 week at end of Mar and 2 weeks at end of Sept.*

L'Ile-Bouchard ✉ 37220
Auberge de l'Ile, 3 Place Bouchard, t 02 47 58 51 07 (*menus €23–37; closed Tues and Wed*). Bathing in the Vienne, a restaurant done up in elaborate Louis XVI style. The cuisine is refined. *Closed Jan–mid-Mar.*

Panzoult ✉ 37220
Domaine de Beauséjour B&B, t 02 47 58 64 64, *www.domainedebeausejour.com* (*moderate*). Accommodation in a lovely winemakers' property on a hillside covered with vines. The rooms are charming and there's a pool you can use.

Cravant-les-Coteaux ✉ 37500
Le Domaine de Pallus B&B, t 02 47 93 08 94, *bcpallus@club-internet.fr* (*moderate*). A very refined address. The rooms, which are stylishly decorated, have gorgeous views over the vineyards and there's a swimming pool in the garden.

Champigny-sur-Veude ✉ 37120
Domaine de la Pataudière B&B, t/f 02 47 58 12 15, *www.lapataudiere.com* (*inexpensive*). Can offer an afternoon's introduction to truffle hunting in winter, otherwise simply a pleasant rural retreat (*table d'hôtes €18*).

Richelieu ✉ 37120
La Maison B&B, 6 Rue Henri Proust, t 02 47 58 29 40, *www.lamaisondemichele.com* (*expensive*). Smart early 19th-century town house with a lovely garden. *Closed 11 Oct–14 April.*
Madame Leplâtre's B&B, 1 Rue Jarry, t 02 47 58 10 42 (*moderate*). Another town house with a garden, and the owner can tell you a lot about the history of Richelieu.
Auberge du Cardinal, 3 Rue des Ecluses, t 02 47 58 18 57 (*menus from €12*). At the gate into town by the statue to the cardinal, a friendly traditional inn serving good regional cuisine, and with terrace. *Closed Sun pm and Mon.*

Razines ✉ 37120
Château de Chargé, t 02 47 95 60 57, *www.chateauxcountry.com/chateaux/charge* (*moderate*). Once the country château of the governors of Chinon and Richelieu, now with three *chambre d'hôtes* rooms and pool.

Down the Veude and Mable to Richelieu

Chinon lies only a few kilometres away, but consider a wonderful detour south along the D749 to the Château du Rivau, Champigny-sur-Veude, Richelieu and Faye-la-Vineuse. This road offers a typical view of southern Touraine's delights, white-stoned châteaux and manors scattered prettily about the open, undulating countryside.

Château du Rivau

Open July–Aug 1–7; June and Sept Wed–Mon 1–7; May and mid-Oct–early Nov weekends and public hols 2–7; t 02 47 95 77 47, www.chateaudurivau.com; adm.

The Château du Rivau makes a fantastic picture of a medieval fort, a white castle rising out of the wide, rolling Touraine fields off the D749 from Chinon to Richelieu. It was built in the mid-15th century for the Beauvaus, an ancient aristocratic family from Anjou, closely linked to French royalty of the period. Pierre de Beauvau served as Grand Chamberlain to King Charles VII. Several descendants also worked for French kings, one François Beauvau acting as Grand Ecuyer to King François I. The Beauvaus were a warrior family and their castle was provided with magnificent royal stables where war horses were reared. Many horses from here went into battle in François I's campaigns. Le Rivau's fortified stables, built in surprisingly sumptuous Italianate style, have been listed as an historic monument in their own right, along with the château. The place played a significant part in the 16th-century Wars of Religion.

The Beauvaus stayed at Le Rivau up to the very end of the 17th century. Then from 1695 to the Revolution, the Castellane family of the Château de Villandry owned the fort and its massive estates. At the Revolution the lands were broken up and sold. The buildings weren't demolished, but they did fall into a state of disrepair. From 1960 to 1990, Brenot, a well-known poster artist, lived in the crumbling castle. At the start of the 1990s, the Laigneaus, a dynamic couple, bought Le Rivau to restore it. They've poured an impressive amount of money into the work. Monsieur is an architectural expert, while Madame is a designer who has recreated the gardens. Our guide described the place as 'in effect a big farm'. What a farm! The whole ensemble is surrounded by tall, thick white stone walls. The place looks impressively solid from afar, but get up close and you can see how it has been battered by time. The white stone blocks have become chipped and stained like old teeth. A vast amount of dental work has already had to be carried out to give it a new, self-confident look.

Pass through the imposing walls and you come into the spacious outer farm courtyard surrounded by agricultural buildings. They're on a very grand scale. The outstanding portion is the stables. One story has it that Joan of Arc came this way to collect horses on her famed Loire campaign in 1429. But she wouldn't have seen these refined 16th-century buildings. These stables may have been designed by the great Italianate architect Philibert de l'Orme. The details are very cleverly conceived. For example, look at the keystones over the windows; they've been given the stylized form of horse's heads. Several massive barns also surround this farm courtyard. In one corner you can see the grape-pressing area, held up on wooden pillars, where the fruit from 45 hectares of vines were once turned into wine. In the centre of the courtyard, the sunken pool is a *pédiluve*, where the horses were washed. A kitchen garden has now been created around it, the vegetables protected by wicker sides.

A huge white keep stands guard at the entrance to the turreted castle. Although very imposing, look closely and you can see how the stone has been eaten away at the base. A drawbridge takes you over the dry moat into the castle's courtyard. The *logis* here dates from the mid-15th century and has typical Gothic features. All the rooms were provided with fireplaces, showing the desire for comfortable living inside. When the Laigneaus bought the property, all lay empty. The big chambers with their stone floors and massive beams have been restored in the last few years. The most interesting, the **Salle du Festin de Balthazar**, contains a fresco showing the biblical scene, the feast depicted as a Rabelaisian event of excess – Rabelais himself knew the château. A daunting array of hunting trophies from Europe and North America stare out from the walls of many of the other chambers.

Despite all the work recently carried out on the buildings, the main focus for visitors is on the gardens. They've been divided into ten sections and play on medieval and Renaissance themes and on the senses. Beyond the chequerboard of roses and old-fashioned fruit trees stands a small wood with alleys lined with ewes and new plantations of truffle oaks. Homage is of course sculpturally paid to Rabelais.

The area around the Château du Rivau, although now deeply rural, is peppered with white-stoned châteaux, many still in private hands. Not far east of Le Rivau, for example, stands the impressive Château de Brizay, protected behind substantial walls. Head south from Le Rivau and you come to the village of Champigny-sur-Veude, with a castle that could boast even finer stables than Le Rivau.

Champigny-sur-Veude

The honours are evenly divided between the Almighty and the family of Bourbon-Montpensier.

               Ian Dunlop on Champigny-sur-Veude's Sainte-Chapelle, *Châteaux of the Loire*.

You can be forgiven for mistaking the dazzling outbuildings in the centre of Champigny-sur-Veude for a château. They're just so grand; and with their particularly distinctive corner towers, they certainly look the part. It's somewhat disingenuous to describe these aristocratic remnants as outbuildings, though, as they in fact formed part of the outer court of a once much larger ensemble built here in the 16th century.

Louis I de Bourbon inherited the estate, which included an old castle, in the 1470s. Having accompanied King Charles VIII on his mad dash to Italy, and once married to Louise de Montpensier in 1504, he decided to build a sumptuous new château, including a princely chapel. Work progressed slowly on the vast project, much of it completed under Louis' son, Louis II de Bourbon, and his wife, Jacquette de Longwy.

So what happened to the main portion of the splendid, vast edifice? Gaston d'Orléans, King Louis XIII's awkward brother, inherited it through his marriage in 1626 to Marie de Montpensier. His enemy, the king's political servant Richelieu, whose family seat lay close by, wanted to put Gaston d'Orléans down a peg or two. Historically, the lords of Richelieu had owed allegiance to the lords of Champigny. In typical fashion, in the 1630s Richelieu ordered both that Gaston d'Orléans swap this château for another and that Champigny-sur-Veude be destroyed. What a waste. Richelieu had at least embarked on his own vast new castle just a few kilometres south, and some of the stone from Champigny may well have headed that way. The outbuildings and chapel survived, the latter, it's said, through the intervention of Pope Urban VIII. He had once celebrated Mass there and in response to Richelieu's request for a demolition order, sent an envoy (the future Pope Innocent X) to check out the place. The chapel was declared to be magnificent and in good repair, and not to be destroyed.

These outbuildings aren't open to the public, but the place has recently been acquired by new American owners. You can, however, visit the freestanding **Chapelle St-Louis** (*open July–Sept Wed–Mon 10–12 and 2–6; t 02 47 95 71 46; adm*). A clean, neat white building on the outside, it transforms into a jewel-box inside. Most of the exterior, begun in 1508, clings to late Gothic outlines, although the details are interpreted in unusual shapes signalling a forward-looking architect. The porch, tacked on later, has totally assumed Renaissance features, which have also crept inside the building. The stained glass was commissioned by the Cardinal de Givry, as a staggering wedding gift for Louis II and Jacquette in 1538. It is thought to have been executed through the 1540s, perhaps by Robert Pinaigrier. This glass counts as one of the great Renaissance works of the Loire. The scenes have a brilliant clarity. The bottom strip depicts figures from the Bourbon and Valois families, as well as Jacquette and the Cardinal de Givry. The main sections concentrate on the life of St Louis, the ultra-pious and crusading King Louis IX. For viewers unclear about what's going on, French inscriptions in the windows give explanations. The lozenge-shaped windows at the top follow Christ's Passion and Resurrection, except for the Crucifixion, where his suffering takes on grander proportions.

Richelieu

King Louis XIII's great political fixer, Cardinal Richelieu, has the disgraceful reputation of having acted as a vandal of major proportions in the French regions. Stamping on provincial independence, he had many a powerful piece of provincial architecture pulled down, asserting the central authority of the royal state and his own will with ruthless purpose. But he also commissioned two outrageously ambitious architectural plans to his greater glory here, in an out-of-the-way corner of France. Ironically enough, one of the two achievements, his château, has been almost entirely demolished, whereas the other – a whole new town built from scratch to provide courtiers and merchants to kowtow to the châtelain – survives as a fairly unspoilt 17th-century utopian vision, albeit with a somewhat neglected air today. The plans for both came to fruition in the 1630s.

Why build so grandly in so distant a corner on the Touraine–Poitou border (engravings refer to Richelieu as being in the Poitou) by a meagre river called the Mable? The principal reason was that this had been the Richelieu family seat and that a château belonging to the cardinal's ancestors already stood here. The family had fallen on hard times, but the cardinal bought the château and lordship back for himself in 1621. Born into a family of impoverished aristocracy, regaining the family honour and leaving his stamp on posterity surely contributed to the scale of his ambitions. The family château remained standing on the other bank of the Mable until the cardinal's new château was well on the way to completion, but then it was eradicated.

Park of the Former Château de Richelieu

Open July–Aug 10–7, rest of year Wed–Mon 10–7; t 02 47 58 10 09; adm.

We begin with the cardinal's none-too-modest mansion, embarked upon before the town. Richelieu started dreaming up the château in 1624, and the following year the architect Jacques Lemercier came up with plans. The castle's splendour would more or less eclipse just about every previous château of the Loire, maybe even rivalling Chambord. Building continued through the 1630s and 40s, with Jacques Lemercier's brothers Pierre and Nicolas taking over from him.

The Château de Richelieu was without doubt one of the most ostentatious buildings of 17th-century France, adorned with a fabulous art collection, now dispersed. So too are the stones which housed it. A pavilion, of doll's house proportions compared with the château when it was complete, is all that remains. This humiliatingly small remnant consists merely of one tower from the south wing of the middle of three great courtyards. But as sole survivor from such a vast palace, it still manages to impress a little. Inside, past a lonely polychrome ceramic parrot, the models and engravings which recall the full architectural event should make you gasp. The place was clearly staggering.

Cardinal Richelieu's ghost hangs over the place. He didn't see his work completed, as he died in 1642. But to furnish the castle he had acquired one of the most eye-watering collections of art ever amassed in France. Many of the divided spoils have ended up in the Louvre or at Versailles. The Louvre, for example, received the two statues by Michelangelo known as the *Dying Slaves*, made for the tomb of Pope Julius II and bought by Richelieu on his home-buying spree. A fair number of other pieces can be seen in the fine arts museums at Orléans and Tours.

The Revolution didn't put an end to the château, but the Richelieu family, having battled to regain possession of the place after the turmoil, briefly won it back only to have to sell it on in 1805 to a certain Bourton. This entrepreneur then took it to pieces. In 1930 the last so-called duke of Richelieu, Odet-Armand de Jumilhace, donated the property to the Sorbonne. The Richelais complain that it has sadly not shown much interest in the place. You pay a small entrance fee to wander in the park, with its towering shaded plane tree alleys, its fine perspectives and its lingering scent of grandeur. Apart from the isolated pavilion, you can visit the wine cellar and the orangery.

Richelieu's Model Town

To accompany his château, Richelieu wished for a model town where courtiers would buy a retreat and gather to enjoy cultivated, exclusive society. Jacques

Lemercier planned an ideal classical town. Maths dominates. So close to all the idio-
syncracies of most Loire architecture, the rectangle is god here. It's all too precise for
words. The plan employed the measure of the *toise*, roughly 2m in length. Just look
down the principal street, the **Grande Rue**, and you'll appreciate the symmetry
imposed. Each property occupies a 10-*toise* plot. The obsession with order can
perhaps be seen to reflect the cardinal's obsession with imposing order on
everything.

You might think that there would be something lifeless about a plan so coldly
mathematical, that it wouldn't leave much leeway for quirks of the imagination. But
it's hard not to find something pleasing about the order of the place. The symmetry
gives a rhythm to the streets, and a certain playfulness. There's pleasure in playing
with numbers in this way, and a perverse pleasure too in looking for spots where the
maths don't quite add up.

Not all the buildings are alike. The two outstanding ones stand on Place du Marché,
with the **Halles**, or covered market, on one side, its splendid timber frame covering a
sizable space, the **church of Notre-Dame** on the other. Pierre Lemercier planned the
latter, also rectangular of course. Statues pose in the niches of the church's classical
façade. Curiously though, the façade is on the east, rather than the traditional west
end. The interior appears disproportionately large for such a small town church, but a
fair congregation still packs the boxed stalls on a Sunday. The small **Musée de l'Hôtel
de Ville** (*open July–Aug 10–12 and 2–6; rest of year Wed–Mon 10–12 and 2–4; t 02 47 58
10 13; adm*) in the town hall contains further details and drawings on the construction
of town and château.

None of the courtiers at the time of Richelieu bought into his dream. But by the
start of the 18th century, 3,000-plus people were installed, which is more than there
are nowadays. Today there's a desolation to the place, the grand social ideals behind
the plan undermined by an air of apathy. It feels like a grand town that has become a
backwater in a rather remote corner of France. Individuality has managed to find a
place through time. Spot the house fronts and roofs which have modified a detail
here or a detail there! But generally speaking little has been altered.

Around Richelieu

South of Richelieu, the feel of the landscape is more like Poitou than the Loire Valley,
with big farms scattered on their rises, their large, gently sloping open fields baked by
the sun in summer. The local white crystalline stone is known as *galuche* and rings if
you knock pieces of it together. **Faye-la-Vineuse** stands prettily atop its gentle hill, a
typical old-fashioned village. It looks undisturbed by modern development, except for
the water tower, which reaches higher to the heavens than the church. The place
seems virtually lifeless now, but it was once fortified for Foulques Nerra of Anjou and,
later, suffered terror in the Wars of Religion. The Collégiale Saint-Georges survived
harassment by the Huguenots, but suffered at the hands of a restoring priest in the
19th century. It boasts the largest crypt in the Indre-et-Loire, which has the appearance of a Romanesque church (plus modern cement flooring), and typical capitals.

East of Richelieu you can follow little roads through scarcely inhabited lands via Braslou and Luzé to **Bois-Aubry** for a look at the ruins of the abbey there. Dating back to the 12th century, the place appears bombarded by time. In 1978 a number of Orthodox monks reinhabited the buildings that remained. The top of the great octagonal spire dates from the 15th century. Within lies a remarkable 12th-century effigy thought to be that of Clement, the abbot who had much of the abbey built. The restored chapter house contains Romanesque capitals.

Chinon and the Chinonais

The Plantagenets, Joan of Arc, Rabelais and red wine have brought this irresistible part of Touraine more than its fair share of fame.

Chinon

With fine medieval houses as close knit as chain mail fighting for space down between the hillside and the Vienne river, Chinon is dominated by the secure walls of one of the great ruined castles of the Plantagenet kingdom. The town may appear distinctly provincial today, but Chinon is still a place that retains more than a spark of old courtly glory. It's a magnificent little spot, with charming streets behind the busy riverside road and its pruned trees. For the most dramatic view of the town lorded over by its hilltop fortifications, take in the scene from the south bank of the Vienne.

Arriving through the Chinonais vineyards from the plateau to the north, by contrast, the sturdy curtain walls of the castle remain concealed until the last minute when you suddenly get a view of the risibly thin Tour de l'Horloge rising above the edge of the plateau. This tower is now devoted to the memory of *the* greatest visitor to Chinon, Joan of Arc, who came here to find the Dauphin Charles (heir to the French crown), who had run off from the English in the Hundred Years' War. But the person who most marks the tourist town today, more even than Joan, is a brilliant and bawdy 16th-century monk, doctor and writer born in the Chinonais, François Rabelais, one of the outstanding figures of the French Renaissance period.

History

Way before the glitter of the medieval courts and Renaissance times, the protective white cliff and the shimmering waters of the Vienne were reasons enough for Gallo-Romans to settle here. The place was then known as Caïno. Despite building a *castrum* for walled protection against the descending barbarian hordes, the town was taken by Visigoths around 400 AD.

But Christianity also established a firm foothold. St Martin came to preach in the neighbourhood, while Brice, his successor as bishop of Tours, established a church in honour of him in the middle of the 5th century. Visigoths and locals were united in their efforts to repel the Roman governor of Gaul, Aegidius, when he lay siege to the town. Lacking water, Chinon's defenders were reduced to desperation. When the rains came with a thunder storm, the miracle was attributed to another follower of

St Martin, Maxime, also known by his abbreviated name Mexme. He founded a second church and a monastery at Chinon. A third religious institution was established in the Dark Ages in honour of a Breton hermit, Jean, who was consulted by Queen Radegonde about her troubled marriage to Clotaire. Such an early concentration of religious activity helped make Chinon an attractive, active trading town and in the 6th century a Merovingian mint was producing coins here. The Norman invasions of the 9th century put paid to the town of the Dark Ages.

Provincial power then became concentrated in the hands of formidable counts. First the counts of Blois occupied the site and erected a keep as early as the middle of the 10th century. Their Anjou rivals were pushing to expand their territories eastwards, however, and in 1044 Geoffroy Martel of Anjou took Chinon and proceeded to add to its defences. The town's first great courtly age came with Henri Plantagenêt of Anjou. Actually the town didn't form part of his inheritance, but that of his brother Geoffroy, from whom Henri seized the place. He decided that Chinon was excellently situated to administer the vast territories he had acquired, known as the Plantagenet or Angevin empire. These possessions included not just Anjou, Maine and Normandy, but also Aquitaine and, let's not forget it, England. The château was enlarged to become the largest fortress of its time in Europe. Henri, or King Henry II of England, loved the place and spent a great deal in it. This was the principal stopping point for his peripatetic court.

Henri died at Chinon in 1189 and a struggle then raged between his sons – Richard the Lionheart, followed by John – and the Capetian French King Philippe Auguste. Richard the Lionheart may have died in one of Chinon's town houses after being mortally wounded at the Battle of Châlus in Poitou, to the south. As for John, he was married to Isabelle d'Angoulême at Chinon. Philippe Auguste's forces triumphed over John's in a one-year siege of the town, and the ill-fated English king had subsequently to relinquish virtually all his Plantagenet lands in France in the first few years of the 13th century. Chinon lost the importance it had briefly acquired in these early Middle Ages, although further building work on the château was carried out for the French Crown. Philippe Auguste, Louis IX (alias St Louis) and Philippe III would stay at the château from time to time.

A couple of particularly gruesome incidents stain the history of Chinon in the first half of the 14th century. The Knights Templars had acquired massive power in France through their role as bankers for the Crusades and the special privileges accorded them. King Philippe IV le Bel decided to wipe them out, and the Templars were rounded up in 1308, many being sent to Poitiers. On the way there, several of their leaders, including the Grand Master, Jacques Molay, fell ill and were kept prisoner at Chinon instead. Cardinals came to the town to hear them confess. The commonly held belief is that they were tortured by the Inquisition, or threatened with torture, and admitted to heresy, idolatry, witchcraft, profanity and sodomy, among the most serious crimes of the time. They were sent to be burnt in Paris. In 1321 prejudice towards the Jewish community at Chinon led to a terrible extermination of Jews in the town. They were accused of poisoning the town's water supply by throwing the excrement from lepers down a communal well, and were taken onto the island on the river and burnt alive.

Getting There and Around

With a combination of **train** and **bus** services, Chinon can be said to have a regular link with Tours. Trains and buses arrive at the train station, about 1km east of the centre.

Tourist Information

Chinon: Office du Tourisme du Pays de Chinon, B.P.141, Place d'Hofheim, 37501 Chinon Cedex, t 02 47 93 17 85, www.chinon.com.

Market Day

Chinon: Thursday.

Where to Stay and Eat

Chinon ✉ 37500

You can choose from a lovely selection of mid-range hotels in town, even if there's nowhere particularly grand to stay.

***Hôtel de France, 47–49 Place du Général de Gaulle, t 02 47 93 33 91, www.bestwestern.com/fr/hoteldefrancechinon (moderate). Set back in the leafy, calm northern corner of this central square, the rooms neat and comfortable (menus €24–56; closed Fri lunch, Sat lunch and Mon lunch in summer, Sun pm and Mon otherwise). Closed 17 Feb–11 Mar, 17–30 Nov and 21 Dec–6 Jan.

**La Boule d'Or, 66 Quai Jeanne d'Arc, t 02 47 93 03 13, f 02 47 93 24 25 (inexpensive). This former posting inn has some nicely decorated rooms overlooking the river and an interior courtyard where food is served in summer. The menu Gargantua is huge, interesting and relatively heavy, given the old-style dishes it recreates (menus €16–29; closed Mon lunch). Closed mid-Dec–Jan.

**Hostellerie Gargantua, 73 Rue Voltaire, t 02 47 93 04 71, www.hostelleriegargantua.com (inexpensive–moderate). Occupies one of Chinon's most famous historic houses. It has some very comfortable rooms, a medieval-style dining room serving quite modern cuisine, and a pretty courtyard where you can eat on warm days (menus c.€27.50; closed Wed pm and Thu out of season). Closed mid-Nov–mid-Dec.

**Hôtel Diderot, 4 Rue Buffon, t 02 47 93 18 87, www.hoteldiderot.com (inexpensive–moderate). The rooms are set around a delightful courtyard, in buildings which include a lovely 18th-century ivy-covered house. This place offers peace in the centre of town, except for early-morning footsteps across the gravel. Closed mid-Dec–mid-Jan.

**Agnès Sorel, 4 Quai Pasteur, t 02 47 93 04 37, www.agnes-sorel.com (inexpensive–moderate). A delightful small hotel looking

A royal court was re-established here with the Dauphin Charles, but under rather less auspicious circumstances than Henri Plantagenêt's. Rather than being expansionist, the king was for a time uncrowned and his territories much reduced by the double-pronged attack by the English and the Burgundians in the second period of the Hundred Years' War. The French court shifted to Chinon after a time in Mehun-sur-Yèvres and Bourges in the neighbouring province of the Berry. Despite the difficult times, a superb courtly and trading town full of sumptuous medieval houses developed at the foot of the château. But our attention first focuses on the castle.

Château de Chinon

Open April–Sept 9–7, rest of year 9.30–5; closed 25 Dec and 1 Jan; t 02 47 93 13 45, f 02 47 93 93 32; adm.

Looking steeply up from the town, the castle seems to consist of little more than a string of beautiful battered towers and fortifications nowadays. It's worth making the climb up the winding, treacherous paths to it, however, not just because the castle offers wonderful views over the town and the Chinonais; it also has a few rooms of

onto the river, rooms in a variety of styles. It's run by a hospitable young couple.

Hôtel de la Treille, 4 Place Jeanne d'Arc, **t** 02 47 93 07 71, **f** 02 47 93 94 10 (*inexpensive*). For cheaper options, a basic, cheerful hotel with six rooms in what was once a medieval episcopal house. You can also eat well here (*menus c.€11–30; closed Wed*). *Closed part Sept, and Christmas hols.*

Au Plaisir Gourmand, 2 Rue Parmentier, **t** 02 47 93 20 48 (*menus €27–59; closed Sun pm, Mon, and Tues lunch*). The outstanding restaurant in town, reputed far and wide, discreetly set back from the river and with its own little garden. Jean-Claude Rigollet mainly prepares traditional French cuisine to perfection, such as oxtail in a deep, dark Chinon sauce, but also the odd newer dish, for example snail-filled ravioli with garlic cream. *Closed mid-Feb–mid-Mar.*

L'Océanic, 13 Rue Rabelais, **t** 02 47 93 44 55 (*menus €20–50; closed Sun pm and Mon*). Excellent seafood. *Closed Jan.*

La Maison Rouge, 38 Rue Voltaire, **t** 02 47 98 43 65 (*menus €13–30; closed Fri*). Serves both as a fine foods store and as a restaurant where you can sample regional specialities. *Closed mid-Dec–mid-Jan.*

Beaumont-en-Véron ✉ 37420

Hôtel La Giraudière, off D749 on the way from Chinon to Avoine, along the Route to Savigny, **t 02 47 58 40 36, *www. hotels-france.com/giraudiere* (*inexpensive– moderate*). A slightly unkempt, eccentric manor house, but it offers charming rooms within its 17th-century architecture. The atmosphere is very calm. It's a nice place to linger over a long lunch (*menus c.€27; closed Sun out of season*). *Closed mid-Dec–mid-Jan.*

Château de Coulaine B&B, **t** 02 47 93 01 27 (*moderate*). Yet more eccentric, a wonderful-looking restored 16th-century château with bathrooms in the round towers. The rooms may not be sophisticated, but the place is great fun. This is also an excellent wine-making property. *Closed mid-Nov–mid-Mar.*

Marçay ✉ 37500

****Château de Marçay, **t** 02 47 93 03 47, *www.relaischateaux.fr/marcay* (*expensive*). A perfect picture of a Loire castle of the late medieval period, set in restful countryside due south of Chinon along the D116. Rooms are split between those in the château itself, some a bit jaded, and the ones around the courtyard, freshly decorated and with private little gardens. Make the most of the delightful terraces or salons for an apéritif before going in to dinner. You'll also find that there's a heated swimming pool and tennis court (*menus €46–75; closed Mon lunch, Tues lunch, and Thurs lunch*). *Closed mid-Jan–mid-Mar.*

interest and great ruins to clamber around. Three separate medieval fortifications were combined into one in the castle's heyday. In one of the rather bare rooms you can visit, a model recreates the place at its apogee, giving you a bird's-eye view of the three parts, making them look like a stylized fish. You enter the main, central part, the Château du Milieu, through the thin **Tour de l'Horloge**, the only tower to remain virtually intact and roofed, its slender side looking quite out of keeping with the great length of castle walls. It now houses an interesting museum on Joan of Arc.

So many of the myths of the Joan of Arc story are the stuff of nonsense on which the tourism trade has all too happily thrived in the past. The presentation of Joan of Arc's life in the Tour de l'Horloge is mercifully sensible. The narrator on the English tapes – one to listen to on each level of the tower – has the stern voice of an academic giving short shrift to wild speculation. It's rather pleasurable to sit on the stone ledges in the tower's rooms overlooking the town, listening to a voice of reason debunking absurd notions rather than peddling them, all the while conceding that Joan was clearly a very remarkable woman indeed, in fact one of the most remarkable in European history. Detailed maps marked with crayon arrows follow her various journeys across France, commemorative plates recall scenes from her life, and documents show how monuments have been erected to her around the world. You might like to be reminded of the details of Joan's vital visit to Chinon castle when she famously managed to pick out the would-be French king from the courtly crowd and convince him of her mission to rescue France from the English invaders (*see* box opposite).

Back outside, head west for the **main hall** and royal apartments, past the well through which stone for the château was quarried. The great hall was added for the Dauphin Charles and it's in this building that Joan of Arc recognized him in the crowd. The history of the place is much more remarkable than the contemporary displays. The visit of the interiors is certainly not particularly taxing, with only a few pieces of sculpture, including a Gallo-Roman funerary stone, a gauche wooden statue of St Martin (where the beard of the pauper he's supposed to have helped appears unfortunately to be stuck to the horse's bottom) and some classical busts from Richelieu's castle (*see* p.326). A few tapestries, some tacky copies of works of art, a video on the genealogy of the kings of France and the interesting model of the Château de Chinon as it once stood add to the meagre pickings through this part of the castle.

So the interiors aren't the Château de Chinon's strongest point. But back out in the leafy courtyard of the **Château du Milieu**, it is a pleasure to walk to the ramparts on the other side, which include the Tour des Chiens (the Dogs' Tower), a 12th-century construction where the royal dogs were once pampered, and the Tour d'Argenton, added for the château's governor at the end of the 15th century, Philippe de Commines, the famed chronicler of Louis XI's reign. The two further forts are separated by large ditches from the Château du Milieu. The eastern ditch spanned by the entrance bridge was dug by order of Henri Plantagenêt, providing further internal defences for the vast complex – as you entered the castle you may have spotted the reconstructions of medieval siege machines displayed in the eastern ditch. Little remains of the **Fort St-Georges** and it isn't open to the public.

You can visit the better-preserved **Fort du Coudray** to the west. Philippe Auguste ordered these mighty defences. The Tour du Moulin marking the westernmost point was in fact Chinon's original keep, but the most daunting of the many towers is the later Coudray keep, a splendid piece of architecture. Inside, you can admire a fantastic fan of arrow slits and intriguing medieval graffiti. From this end of the fortifications, Charles would apparently later keep discreetly in touch with his mistress. He saw to it that Agnès Sorel (*see* p.283) had a house close to the château easily accessible via underground tunnels.

After Charles VII's reign, the château was used mainly as a base for military operations and as a state prison. Governors of Chinon also lived up in the castle. At the very end of the 15th century, following Charles VIII's untimely death, it was at Chinon that the new king, Louis XII, received the news of Pope Alexander VI's official granting of the annulment of his marriage to the infertile Jeanne de France. Great celebrations were held by the king for this event.

On a couple of occasions during the 16th-century Wars of Religion the château was used by royal forces, but the place was gradually falling into a state of disrepair, patchily restored during the short time the Prince de Condé owned it early in the 17th century. Cardinal Richelieu acquired the property in 1633, when King Louis XIII sold it to him. In his usual manner, his first thought was to demolish the place. Instead it was simply left to fall further into ruin by him and his descendants.

When Prosper Mérimée, the writer-cum-influential inspector of historical monuments, visited the castle in 1855, he realized the importance of saving what remained of the fortifications. A local architect from Saumur, Joly-Leterme, was called upon to consolidate what he could, so that many of the towers and ramparts were spruced up in the 19th century. It's a joy that they were rescued.

A Tour of Chinon Town

The thin wedge of land below the castle between cliff and river is crammed with splendid architecture. The most striking element of the buildings is the variety of stair towers, some round, some square, some in timberframe and brick, others in local limestone. Several of the finest buildings house hotels, restaurants or museums, notably in the main string of streets.

But first, on the western end of the quays, the very clean-looking former abattoir has been turned into the Chinon riverboat museum, the **Maison de la Rivière** (*open*

Joan of Arc Won't be Fobbed Off by a Blue Beard and Persuades the Gentil Dauphin to Listen to Her Voices

La Trémouille: I wonder will she pick him out!
The Archbishop: Of course she will.
La Trémouille: Why? How is she to know?
The Archbishop: She will know what everybody in Chinon knows: that the Dauphin is the meanest-looking and worst-dressed figure in the Court, and that the man with the blue beard is Gilles de Rais... [Joan appears.]
The Duchess [to the nearest lady-in-waiting]: My dear! Her hair! [All the ladies explode in uncontrollable laughter.]
From *Saint Joan* by George Bernard Shaw, 1923

Joan came to Chinon in late winter 1429, the reputation of her divine messages preceding her. She said that the voices of several saints were transmitting orders from God which declared that with her help Charles would be crowned king in the sacred royal ceremony at Reims and that the English would be expelled from France. The French leaders were in desperate straits, in terrible need of divine intervention. Although sceptical about Joan's claims, they were willing to put them to the test.

Once Joan appeared in town, where she took up lodgings and set to praying, she was quickly granted an audience. But a trap was set for her. Charles' courtier Gilles de Rais (later to be infamously condemned to death for paedophilia and killing children on a massive scale) was made to pretend to be the king. Joan of Arc is said to have seen through this ruse immediately – perhaps not as difficult as it may sound if Gilles really did sport 'the extravagance of a little curled beard dyed blue at a

*July–Aug Tues–Fri 10–12.30 and 2–6.30, weekends 3–6.30; April–June and Sept–Oct Tues–Fri 10–12.30 and 2–5.30, weekends 2–5.30; closed 1 May; **t** 02 47 93 21 34, maison.de.la.riviere@free.fr; adm*). The displays give you some notion of what daily life must once have been like for the ordinary folk living by the Vienne, in particular the mariners, ferrymen and fishermen. An interesting range of models of the different sorts of boats that were used on the river is displayed in cabinets. Old postcards of Chinon show it in the days when *bateaux-lavoirs*, laundry boats, were moored to the river bank. Now in the tourist season, you can book to go on a river boat from the quays outside the museum, while the museum shop offers river-related gifts.

It isn't a long walk through the old town. Start at the western end of the **Rue Haute St-Maurice**. The **church of St-Maurice**, with its soaring spire, looks as though it's been painstakingly squeezed in between the narrow side streets here. Both the belfry and the north aisle date back to the 12th century, when Henri Plantagenêt donated money for the building. Typically, 19th-century restorers insensitively renovated the place. The north aisle used to be the nave and is covered with Angevin vaulting and little sculptures. The south aisle is of much later date, mid-16th century, paid for by prosperous Chinon merchants.

---

clean-shaven court' as Shaw has it. She picked out the Dauphin without any difficulty and soon persuaded him of the importance of her mission.

'The recognition scene at Chinon has been depicted, in paint and in words, as a secular equivalent of the Annunciation to Mary, with Joan as Gabriel announcing to Charles that he is himself France's Messiah,' writes Marina Warner in her meticulous analysis of Joan in *Joan of Arc: The Image of Female Heroism*. It's a meeting that has acquired mythical, and for many who wish to look no further, supernatural significance in French history. Joan herself at first didn't admit during her trial to seeing an angel picking out Charles. But as she became more confused, she elaborated on this tale. Then the fictionalizers of history took up the case, not content with Joan's elaboration, or simply ignoring the trial transcripts. Extraordinary explanations have been advanced for why Joan was so readily accepted by Charles. A whole series turn on the wild notion that she was an illegitimate royal child sent away from court but later able to return and impart family secrets to Charles. These theories ignore the evidence about Joan from the witnesses at the rehabilitation trial after her death.

The medieval French leaders weren't as superficial as you may have been led to think. Joan wasn't immediately allowed to assume a position of power and a military post unchallenged. She had first to be thoroughly examined, not just theologically, but physically too. She was sent to Poitiers to undergo these tests to check that she wasn't an impostor and came out with flying colours, her reputation intact, confirmed as the French virgin sent by God to restore the integrity of the French kingdom. Once back at Chinon she was supported by the royal figure of Yolande d'Aragon, given her own band of men to lead into battle and, donning men's armour, set out for Orléans.

Just east of the church, the **Hostellerie Gargantua** may have a real connection with Rabelais, as this was once the Palais de Baillage, where Rabelais' father may have carried out some of his legal business. A little further east you come to the **Musée du Vieux Chinon** in the **Maison des Etats Généraux** (*open April–Sept 10.30–12.30 and 2–7; t 02 47 93 18 12 or, off season, t 02 47 93 12 80, www.chinonhistoire.org; adm*). This local history museum is situated in one of the most significant historic houses in town. Richard the Lionheart may have died here from his battle wounds in 1199. It's also the house where King Charles VII called the Estates General of France to meet in 1428, after the English had begun to lay siege to Orléans. The local archaeological and historical society has turned it into a small museum.

Undoubtedly, the most moving piece of sculpture within is a mould of the Crucifixion Christ taken from Chinon's 11th-century church of St-Mexme, one of the most painfully emotional depictions of Jesus' suffering from French medieval art, his face that of an exhausted old man, stretchmarked by agony. Older fragments of civilization have been unearthed in Chinon, including Merovingian *deniers*; these silver coins were adopted in 675 and were to last six centuries as the basis of the French monetary system.

The big hall where the Estates General met has some further interesting religious sculpture, contrasting with some tacky copies of works of art, including a notably hideous rendering of Joan of Arc. The portrait of Rabelais by Eugène Delacroix for the 1834 salon isn't one of the artist's greatest works. Among a further eclectic range of objects, the most exceptional is the **chape de St Mexme**, or St Mexme's cope. This turns out in fact to be a piece of Arab, possibly Egyptian, silk from the 11th century, thought now to have been made for a horse! It's decorated with an eye-catching pattern of chained wild cats. Other displays include a particularly tortured *Pietà* and 19th-century Loire pottery from Langeais, a 19th-century taste.

The road down from this museum leads to the start of the main shopping street, **Rue du Commerce** (later turning into the Rue Rabelais), and then to the bridge. Keeping on the higher streets, though, at the start of the **Rue Voltaire** stands the brick façade of the **Maison Rouge**, the original building constructed around 1400. Joan of Arc must have seen it it, as she stayed in a house that then stood next door, called the Hostellerie du Grand-Carroi, when she first arrived at Chinon. As she recounted with such innocent conviction at her trial: 'I was almost always in prayer in order that God should send the sign of the king; and I was staying at my lodgings at a good woman's house close to the castle of Chinon when he [the archangel] came; and then we went together to the king; and he was well accompanied by other angels with him, which other people could not see.' Once Joan had convinced Charles and then the Church authorities in Poitiers, when she returned to Chinon she was upgraded, given the honour of being put up in the castle itself.

A little east along Rue Voltaire you come to a cul-de-sac with the **Musée Animé du Vin et de la Tonnellerie** (*open April–Sept 10.30–12.30 and 2–7; t 02 47 93 25 63, musee-vin-chinon@club-internet.fr; adm*), a display on wine-making in the Chinonais, set in a former quarry. The Chinonais vines grow almost up to the château walls on the plateau beyond the castle (*see box*). Life-sized models enact the laborious work

Chinon Wines

'*A boire! A boire! A boire!* (A drink! A drink! A drink!)', rang the immortal first screeches of the giant baby Gargantua as he was born through his monster of a mother's left ear, in a field in the Chinonais. And the baby wanted wine from the start, thirsting for a stiff drink, not your namby-pamby milk. The quest for the '*Dive Bouteille* (the Divine Bottle)' becomes the great objective of the spoof quest in Rabelais' giant cycle.

Wine-tasters most frequently discover violets and rubies hidden in Chinon wines, grown and produced along the final stretch of the Vienne river as it approaches the Loire. Chinon wines are almost exclusively red. Cabernet Franc (the soft, 'feminine' grape variety that makes up the most important ingredient in the great wines of Pomerol and St-Emilion in the Bordelais) makes up the major grape variety here. It's rather confusingly known as 'Breton' locally. Chinon's *appellation d'origine contrôlée* wine territory spreads over some 1,850 hectares in 19 parishes, going from around L'Ile-Bouchard to the Vienne's confluence with the Loire. The different soils along the valley produce different characteristics. The low gravels by the river give lighter, fruity wines with aromas that emerge very young. The vines on the slopes and the plateaux above, with siliceous-clay or limestone-clay ground, yield more powerful wines, some of which have a surprisingly good ability to age in fine years. But, as with all but the great sweet Loire wines, they tend to be drunk young.

In wine terms a 'château' often refers simply to an individual wine-producing property, which usually just has an ordinary house attached. With several of the best-known Chinon vineyards, however, you get a proper little Loire château thrown in. Among the most spectacular vineyards to visit for a wine tasting are: the **Château de la Grille**, a little north of Chinon, splendidly visible on the road to Ussé (*open July–Aug 9–7, otherwise Mon-Sat 9–12 and 2–6; t 02 47 93 01 95*), and the **Château de Coulaine**

involved in winemaking. To reward you for your attention, you're treated to a wine tasting at the end. An impasse next to this one contains the **Cave Paincte**, a painted cave mentioned by Rabelais and generally reserved for the meetings of Chinon's wine fraternity; but ask at the tourist office: a visit may be possible in July and August.

Rue Voltaire ends in the very pleasant 19th-century square of **Place du Général de Gaulle**, with the town hall on the northern end and a crowd of cafés at the southern end, by the proud statue of Rabelais. Continuing along from the northern end of the square, **Rue Jean-Jacques Rousseau** takes you on to several important Chinon churches. The west front of the **church of St-Etienne** carries the arms of Chinon, an archbishop of Tours and the late 15th-century governor Philippe de Commines. The interior is simple, without side aisles. Joan of Arc crops up twice; once in a white marble statue of 1900 by the Tourangeau François Sicard, and again in the 19th-century stained glass in the choir, by Léopold Lobin. Two further important religious figures for Chinon, St Mexme and Ste Radegonde, also feature in glass.

The **church of St-Mexme** (*contact the tourist office to join a guided tour inside*) lies just down the street from St-Etienne. Its sturdy slate-capped towers dominate this part of town, but below them the building hasn't fared well. It was quite

(Mon–Sat 10–12 and 2–6, Sun by appt; t 02 47 98 44 51, www.chateau-de-coulaine. com), on the way to Beaumont-en-Véron from Chinon. The Château de la Grille is a long-established wine-producing property; the Château de Coulaine is an up-and-coming one. Both châteaux have a fascinating history and at Coulaine they also produce *confiture de vin*, wine jam. In Chinon itself, the house of **Couly-Dutheil** *(Mon–Fri 9–5; 12 Rue Diderot, B.P. 234, t 02 47 97 20 20, www.coulydutheil-chinon.com; small fee)* has a high reputation for the quality of its wines, the Clos de l'Echo even mentioned in Rabelais. It has very modern winemaking equipment combined with ancient cellars.

East of Chinon, Cravant-les-Côteaux and Panzoult are highly-regarded Chinon wine parishes, and exceptionally picturesque. At Cravant, **Domaine Gouron** *(Mon–Sat 8–12 and 1.30–6, closed public hols; t 02 47 93 15 33, www.domaine-gouron.com)*, on the heights, with a modern-cut rock cellar, and **Domaine du Morilly** *(Mon–Fri 9–12.30 and 2–6, weekends by appt; t 02 47 93 38 25, www.chinon.com/vignoble/jacky-dumont)*, with an older troglodyte feel, including a tasting room with a troglodyte fireplace, are well used to receiving visitors. At Panzoult, the **Domaine de Beauséjour** *(t 02 47 58 64 64, www.chinon.com/vignoble/domaine-beausejour)* and the **Domaine du Roncée** *(Mon–Fri 9–12 and 2–6, Sat by appt; t 02 47 58 53 01, www.roncee.com)* make for extremely pleasant visits. When you're looking on wine lists in a restaurant, **Olga Raffault** and **Charles Joguet** are names of top-class Chinon producers that feature regularly.

Not actually in the Chinon *appellation*, but nearby at St-Germain-sur-Vienne, down river towards Candes-St-Martin, the **Château du Petit Thouars** *(closed Sun and Mon; t 02 47 95 96 40, www.stephane-filliatreau.com)* is another estate that combines good winemaking – here of AOC Touraine red and rosé – with a spectacular house and cave cellars. The family has been making wine here for 350 years.

obviously once a very fine piece of Romanesque architecture, however, with what must once have been an awe-inspiring front full of sculptured stone panels, hacked off in turbulent times. Mexme founded a monastery here in the 5th century. Archaeological evidence has shown seven periods of building on the site, from early Christian times through to the 15th century, but the bulk of the work left standing was carried out in the 11th and 12th centuries. The church will never recover from the neglect it suffered after the Revolution. Briefly serving as an arms depot, its crossing tower fell in 1817, destroying most of the choir. The town authorities bought the remnants to open a school in the nave! One side of the north aisle was simply done away with to extend the school buildings. The last pupils only left in 1983. It's worth joining a guided tour of the town if you're interested in seeing the now bare but atmospheric interior, with a few evocative traces of stone carving and wall paintings left in the impressive entrance tower.

South of St-Mexme lies the big **Place Jeanne d'Arc**, with its bellicose statue of Joan of Arc on horseback pelting over bodies, sword and flag triumphantly outstretched. It's a rather frightening vision of the maid who isn't supposed to have killed a single soul in battle. It was made in the late 19th century by Jules Roulleau.

The path up the hillside east of St-Mexme takes you to the very curious **Chapelle Ste-Radegonde** (*contact the tourist office to join a guided tour inside*), built partly into the rock. Walking along the Vienne cliffside to the chapel you get rather too good a view down on to the modern quarters of Chinon. The chapel itself is a curious ruin standing in front of a warren of caves, some of which were inhabited by very poor families up until the 1950s. The religious origins of the site go back to the early Christian era. This is the place to which Queen Radegonde fled from her violent husband Clotaire to find sanctuary with the hermit Jean le Reclus around 550. She went on to found the nunnery of Ste-Croix at Poitiers, while the hermit was buried in his cave. The hermitage became a place of pilgrimage, and to accommodate the Christian visitors a larger chapel was excavated and decorated. The semi-ruined place contains a significant little segment of wall paintings from around 1200. The courtly figures seen riding along on horseback are thought to be members of the royal Plantagenet family. One of the figures is thought to be a rare representation of Eleanor of Aquitaine, Henri's extraordinarily powerful wife. If the figures are unclear, the horses on which they ride look splendid with their flowing manes.

The set of caves around the chapel contains an atmospherically neglected museum of local traditions. After negotiating the narrow labyrinth of this troglodyte collection, you come to the most startling surprise in Chinon, an **underground well**, possibly dug in the 6th century. You peer down into it through a triangle of a hole in the rock, dug at a strange angle that somehow draws you in and makes you lose your sense of orientation. You can imagine pilgrims feeling awed by the sight. The waters were supposed to cure eye ailments. The place still feels magical, one of the most mesmer- izing subterranean visions in the Loire Valley.

La Devinière and the Musée Rabelais

Open daily April–Sept 9.30–7; Oct–Mar 9.30–12.30 and 2–5, closed 25 Dec and 1 Jan; t 02 47 95 91 18; adm.

Southwest from Chinon, head via the troglodyte village of **Cinais** for La Devinière, commemorating the Chinonais' favourite, most intelligent and most frivolous son, François Rabelais. If Rabelais has become even more of a popular marketing tool than Henri Plantagenêt or Joan of Arc in the Chinonais, let's face it, he was funnier than either of those two great historical figures. But the museum paying homage to him is a relatively sober affair.

What a quiet spot for the big mouth of French letters to have been born (around 1494). François Rabelais' mother was specially driven to this family farmhouse to give birth; such was often the custom for well-to-do women in that period, to be sent packing to the fresh air of the country. But her baby may well have come into the world in a field, rather than in the house itself. Readers of *Gargantua* may remember the way that Rabelais' fictional hero's mother, Gargamelle, gives birth to her giant of a son, first eating too much tripe, then vilely cursing her husband (wishing in particular that he had had his male member cut off) before the vast baby Gargantua squeezes out through her left ear. Rabelais, for most of the first six years of his life, was left in the hands of country tenants who brought him up, again a traditional practice. From

Rabelais and His Raunchy Romps through French Renaissance Ideas

Beuveurs tres illustres, et vous, Verolez, tres precieux... à vous, non à aultres, sont dediez mes escriptz... (Very illustrious drinkers, and you most precious people poxed with venereal disease, it's to you, not to others, that my writings are dedicated...)

Rabelais, prologue to *Gargantua*, 1530s

Rabelais' writing isn't all fornicating friars, gross feasting, belching and farting, endless inebriation and smutty word play worthy of today's sleaziest tabloids – although it does contain plenty of all that. His books are also crammed with classical, theological, medical and legal allusions and comment. Beneath the absurd bullshit lies serious philosophical enquiry.

The telling of bawdy tales of giants who might, for example, accidentally eat pilgrims in their salad or discover with delight that a live goose is the softest way to wipe their bum, Rabelais took from a well-established popular medieval tradition. It sounds very drily academic to interpret his uproarious fictional giant cycle as an intellectual investigation into forms of contemporary education and learning and the way to make sense of life more generally. But Rabelais mixes low culture with high culture in an increasingly masterful manner through his books. He has a go at all the serious professions of his time, subjecting them to debasing ridicule. He was extremely well placed to comment; the son of a lawyer, in his lifetime he tried his hand at being a monk, a doctor and a teacher. He also had to be careful of the powerful censors and of being too blatantly critical of the established Church at a time when the spread of Protestantism and the questioning of the grip of Catholicism were beginning to split French society apart. Rabelais was daring, but he also used his comedy as a clever defence.

Rabelais wrote four, possibly five, books in his cycle on giants. *Pantagruel* was the first, *Gargantua* the second, although it tells the tale of the upbringing of Pantagruel's father. Many of the scenes in these two works are set in the Chinonais, the little place names referred to still existing, but blown out of all proportion into mock-epic sites. The other books in the giant cycle – known by the really unimaginative titles of the *Tiers Livre*, the *Quart Livre* and the *Cinquiesme Livre* – take the adventures further afield into more obscure realms of the imagination and of language. They become increasingly experimental and philosophical. The protagonists travelling from isolated island to isolated island encounter one potty lot after another, rendered barmy by their fanatically blinkered views.

Nowadays, Rabelais' endless word play, absurdism and intellectual stabs can be a struggle to fathom out, and his contemporary love of puns a big pain, but reading his books in an edition with serious explanatory notes can be an engrossing pleasure.

the age of six to eleven he was educated at the nearby village of Seuilly, by Benedictine monks. The pretty late-medieval farmhouse of La Devinière is fronted by a fine *fuye*, or dovecote, from the 17th century, with numerous pigeon holes on its low gable. The Rabelais-related collections in the house concentrate on depictions of the man and his characters, as well as touching on legends more widely in France. Jean du Bellay left a contemporary description of Rabelais; he apparently had a wide forehead, a beard along the line of his jaw, a short-sighted gaze and, not surprisingly, a sarcastic smile. Matisse made a famous sketch of the writer for La Devinière in 1951, which appears an accurate rendering of the description. The other best-known drawings associated with Rabelais are Daumier's cluttered grotesque interpretations of Gargantuan episodes. The museum has also pursued country and medicinal themes, with displays on the great variety of plants Rabelais mentions in his writing.

The Battlegrounds of the Picrocholine Wars

A terrible war ravaged the area immediately around La Devinière, referred to in the tourist jargon as **La Rabelaisie**. It's scarcely believable that this quiet corner witnessed the megalomaniac ambitions of a terrible general. We are of course referring to Picrochole of the Picrocholine wars in Rabelais' *Gargantua*.

The shepherds of Gargantua's country were out at harvest time chasing the starlings from the vines when they saw the *fouaciers* (makers of a kind of unleavened bread) of Lerné passing by. The shepherds asked if they could buy some *fouaces*, but their request wasn't just turned down by the men of Lerné; the latter also threw a torrent of unrepeatable abuse on the shepherds. These responded, with their nut-picking allies nearby, in the only way they saw fit, beating the men of Lerné with their sticks '*comme sus seigle verd* (as on green rye)' and took some of the *fouaces*. Thus are wars started. Picrochole, irascible leader of the men of Lerné, wanted vengeance, refused reconciliation, and his bellicose ambitions took on proportions foreshadowing Napoleon's as he decided he could take on and conquer the world. At La Devinière you can buy a card which marks the various locations of the campaigns in this major European non-war.

Rabelais' birthplace is overseen in the distance by the magnificent silhouette of the **Château de Coudray-Montpensier**, the archetypal late-Gothic Loire castle, now housing a school for children with learning difficulties. The little village of **Seuilly** is charming, with a few 16th-century houses remaining between the church and the abbey, just like the one from which Rabelais' fictional hero of a monk, Frère Jean, emerged to defend his beloved vines against the louts of Lerné, making a particularly rousing speech to his fellow monks on the importance of wine. **La Roche Clermault** to the east of Seuilly and **Lerné** to the west continue the war trail, the latter entering troglodyte country.

The Loire from Saumur to Angers

18

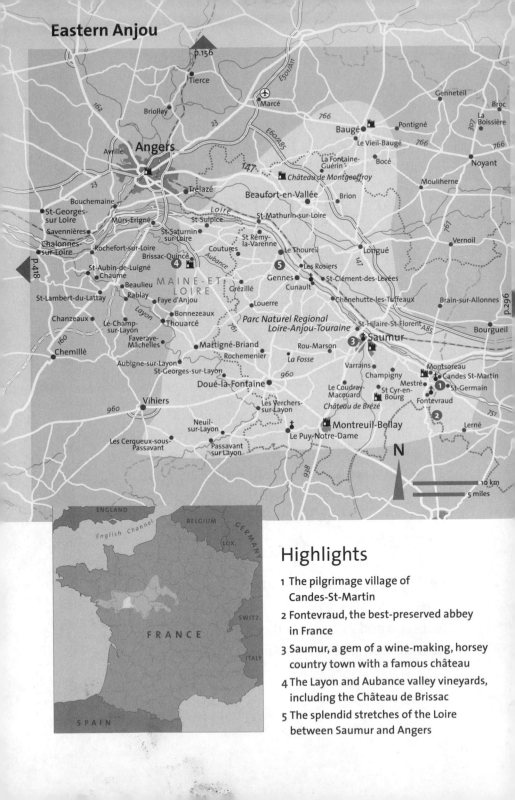

Eastern Anjou

Highlights

1 The pilgrimage village of Candes-St-Martin
2 Fontevraud, the best-preserved abbey in France
3 Saumur, a gem of a wine-making, horsey country town with a famous château
4 The Layon and Aubance valley vineyards, including the Château de Brissac
5 The splendid stretches of the Loire between Saumur and Angers

Plus me plaist le sejour qu'ont basty mes ayeux
Que des palais romains le front audacieux,
Plus que le marbre dur me plaist l'ardoise fine,
Plus mon Loyre gaulois, que le Tybre latin,
Plus mon petit Lyré que le mont Palatin:
Et plus que l'air marin la douceur angevine.

(The house which my ancestors built delights me more / Than Roman palaces putting pride to the fore / I find fine slate more pleasing than a marble frieze / More pleasing my Gallic Loire than the Latin Tiber / More pleasing than the Palatine my little Lyré / And more pleasing than the seas my Angevin peace.)

Joachim du Bellay, 16th-century Angevin and Pléiade poet

No wonder poor du Bellay yearned for his Angevin Loire when stuck in Rome – the Loire is at its most splendid and seductive in Anjou. East of the region's capital, Angers, the great sweeps of the river and its wide strands could mislead you into feeling that you're approaching the sea via a great estuary, while in fact the Loire still has a reasonably long course to run. But it certainly has a mesmerizing, exotic beauty here.

The stunning Loire-side town of Saumur is the main cultural centre of eastern Anjou. Known as the *perle de l'Anjou* because of its whiteness, and the *ville du cheval* because of its cavalry school and horse-riding traditions, it can claim to be one of the most interesting small provincial towns in France. It has a fairytale château, churches hung with extravagant tapestries and streets through which you can still easily imagine the carriages trundling by.

In the Saumurois, the area around and south of Saumur, the riches continue. The abbey of Fontevraud is one of the best-preserved medieval abbeys in Europe, where the famed Angevin kings of England, Henry II and Richard the Lionheart, lie buried, along with Eleanor of Aquitaine. The Loire cliff face between Saumur and Montsoreau to the east consists of an almost unbroken succession of extraordinary villages, not just built against the rock but actually into it. On the plateau above grow the vines of Saumur, producing excellent reds and sparkling whites.

The locals make the distinction between *troglodytisme de coteau*, hillside cave dwellings, and *troglodytisme de plaine*, where the caves have been dug down into the ground, as they have in and around Doué-la-Fontaine, west of Saumur. Here you'll find underground farms, underground houses, even an underground zoo. In a couple of spots artists have gone underground to create startling galleries.

Beyond these unusual and fascinating subterranean attractions, back above ground the Saumurois has more than its fair share of traditional Loire draws. Fine churches abound, from major ones like Cunault, to delightful little rural ones. And along with the château at Saumur, there are other splendid white-stoned castles to visit, notably those of Brézé, Montreuil-Bellay and Montsoreau, the latter by the headquarters of the Parc Régional Naturel Loire-Anjou-Touraine, which incorporates the vast majority of eastern Anjou, both sides of the Loire.

Eastern Anjou to the north of the Loire presents a very different picture. The river's broad flat flood plain stretches into the distance, wide enough for the Authion river to steal a strip of land from the Loire. The sandy plain, sometimes termed the Vallée d'Anjou, is ideal for the intensive growing of fruit, flowers and vegetables. It was also susceptible to massive floods until Henri Plantagenêt (King Henry II of England) decided to control the waters by ordering a long artificial bank to be built right to the outskirts of Angers. This *grande levée*, as well as serving a crucial practical purpose, makes one of the most picturesque of all Loire-side roads. Romanesque churches are one cultural feature northeastern Anjou shares with the richer southeast, several standing out because of their alarming twisted spires. And one convent in these parts claims still to possess a piece of Christ's cross, sumptuously mounted. Almost as extravagant, seek out the exceptionally well-preserved Ancien Régime Château de Montgeoffroy on the north bank of the Authion. But the star of this chapter remains the Loire, absolutely magnificent seen from both banks between Saumur and Angers.

The Loire East of Saumur

Along the Loire, the change from Touraine to Anjou is seamless. You also move from the modern region of Centre-Val de Loire to that of the Pays de la Loire. Candes-St-Martin and Montsoreau, two stunningly beautiful villages by the Loire, may be in separate regions, but they're stuck together like Siamese twins – we've kept the two together in this chapter. From Montsoreau westwards to Saumur, some of the Loire Valley's most spectacular troglodyte houses have been dug into the sharp limestone cliff. The abbey of Fontevraud, one of the finest abbeys left standing in the West, is the major cultural sight.

Candes-St-Martin

This riverside village steeped in the memory of the great 4th-century missionary and monastic St Martin (*see* Tours) has one of the prettiest locations along the whole of the Loire. It's particularly lovely viewed from the north, across the Loire or the Vienne, as it lies at the point where the last great Touraine tributary pours into the Loire, forming a wide mass of water and announcing the start of the splendid Angevin Loire. The name Candes derives from the Latin for confluence, and Gallo-Romans settled here. If you climb the steep path to the top of the village, you can get spectacular views of the two rivers forking away from each other into the distance. The village below is only slightly troubled nowadays by the busy road to Saumur which tries to squeeze through its narrow main street.

Church of St-Martin

St Martin had a particular affection for this spot. He had a church built here, dedicated to the memory of St Maurice, another converted Roman soldier, who refused to fight a band of Gaulish Christians and was punished for his insubordination with death. At the beginning of November 397, St Martin came to sort out a quarrel between religious men here, but fell ill and died. The story of the undignified

Getting Around

Reasonably regular **buses** link Fontevraud, Montsoreau, Turquant, Parnay, Souzay-Champigny and Dampierre with Saumur, except on Sundays.

Tourist Information

Montsoreau: Av de la Loire, 49730 Montsoreau, t 02 41 51 70 22, *www.ville-montsoreau.fr.*
Fontevraud-l'Abbaye: Allée Ste-Catherine, 49590 Fontevraud-l'Abbaye, t 02 41 51 79 45, *officetourisme-fontevraud@libertysurf.fr.*

Market Days

Montsoreau: Flea market; every second Sunday in the month.
Fontevraud l'Abbaye: Wednesday.

Where to Stay and Eat

Candes-St-Martin ✉ 37500
Auberge de la Route d'Or, 2 Place de l'Eglise, t 02 47 95 81 10 (*menus €20–32; closed Tues eve and Wed exc July–Aug*). Definitely worth a pilgrimage; a tiny restaurant tucked into the lovely square by the the great village church. The dining room is almost a grotto, with a comfortable feel. Gentle service and

interesting dishes such as eel in Roquefort sauce. *Closed mid-Nov–mid-Feb and Mar.*

Montsoreau ✉ 49730
★★**Hostellerie Le Bussy,** 4 Rue Jehanne d'Arc, t 02 41 38 11 11, *hotel.lebussy@wanadoo.fr* (*inexpensive; closed Tues mid-Jan–Mar and Oct–Dec*). Utterly charming hotel in a wonderful old house in the village street just above the château. Many of the rooms have been done up to three-star standard, so they're a real bargain. *Closed mid-Dec–mid-Jan; no restaurant.*
Diane de Méridor, 12 Quai Philippe de Commines, t 02 41 51 71 76 (*menus €17.05–35.50*). Standing close to the château, a warm place to eat.
Le Saut aux Loups, Route de Saumur, t 02 41 51 70 30 (*menu €8–23; closed Mon July–Aug*). In its sensational troglodyte setting above the Loire, a simple restaurant specializing in *galipettes*, monster mushrooms filled with goat's cheese, and *rillettes*, among other choices. *Closed mid-Dec–mid-Jan.*

Fontevraud-l'Abbaye ✉ 49590
★★**Prieuré Saint-Lazare,** Rue St-Jean-de-l'Habit, t 02 41 51 73 16, *www.hotelfp-fontevraud.com* (*moderate*). Actually part of the old abbey, a slick adaptation of the lepers' monastery, the cells turned into comfortable rooms, although a friend claimed she smelt a

argument over possession of his body is memorably told by Gregory of Tours, graphically revealing the importance attached to the securing of relics of holy men in early Christian times:

As soon as the holy man was taken ill in the village of Candes, as I have said already, the people of Poitiers and Tours began to assemble at his death-bed. When he was dead, a great altercation arose between the two groups. The men of Poitiers said: 'As a monk he is ours. He became an abbot in our town. We entrusted him to you, but we demand him back. It is sufficient for you that, while he was a Bishop on this earth, you enjoyed his company, you shared his table, you were strengthened by his blessing and above all you were cheered by his miracles. Let all these things suffice for you, and permit us at least to carry away his dead body.' To this the men of Tours replied: 'If you say that we should be satisfied with the miracles which he performed for us, then admit that while he was with you he did more than in our town. If all his other miracles are left out of the count, he raised two dead men for you and only one for us; and, as he himself used often to say, his miraculous power was greater before he was

lingering odour of nuns in her room. The cloister and church have been transformed into delightful dining areas. The tranquillity can often be broken, however, as the place is large enough to act as a conference centre (*menus €28–55*). *Closed early Nov–mid-April.*

**La Croix Blanche, 7 Place des Plantagenêts, t 02 41 51 71 11, *www.fontevraud.net* or *www. croix-blanche.com* (*inexpensive–moderate*). Well-established hotel in the village, almost at the entrance to the abbey. It's built around a very pleasant old-fashioned looking courtyard with gallery. The rooms are in old-fashioned style too, but well maintained. The restaurant looks rather functional, but the food is fine (*menus €19–40; closed Sun pm and Mon Nov–Mar*). *Closed early-Jan–early-Feb and mid–late Nov.*

La Licorne, Allée Ste-Catherine, t 02 41 51 72 49 (*menus €27–70; closed Wed pm out of season, Sun pm and Mon*). Set in an 18th-century house close to the church, with a private garden, this restaurant is highly reputed for its cuisine. Try such celebrated dishes as guinea fowl in Layon wine sauce. *Closed mid-Dec–Jan.*

Le Domaine de Mestré B&B, at Mestré between Fontevraud and Montsoreau, t 02 41 51 75 87 or t 02 41 51 72 32, *www. dauge-fontevraud.com* (*inexpensive– moderate*). Once part of the abbey's estates, a fine stone property where pilgrims were put up (*table d'hôte €23; no dinner Thurs or Sat*). *Closed 20 Dec–1 April.*

Turquant ✉ 49730

***Demeure de la Vignole, 3 Impasse Marguerite d'Anjou, t 02 41 53 67 00, *www. demeure-vignole.com* (*expensive*). Exquisite little new hotel between the cliffside and vines. The rooms and sitting rooms in the 15th- and 17th-century lodgings are beautifully decorated with tiles. There's a big troglodyte cave in which meals can be served on request. Just one or two jarring notes which the owners can't do much about: the nearby electricity pylons and the occasional gassy smell from the mushrooming caves nearby. But this place is utterly gorgeous. *Closed Jan–Mar.*

Saumur (western outskirts) ✉ 49400

Château de Beaulieu B&B, 98 Route de Montsoreau, t 02 41 67 69 51, *monsite. wanadoo.fr/chateaubeaulieu* (*expensive*). A charming young couple have taken over this delightful 17th-century manor neighbouring the large Gratien et Meyer sparkling wine centre. They've redone most of the rooms, but also invite their guests to make the most of the *enfilade* of salons down below, decorated with wood panelling. The place is a listed building, but there is a swimming pool in the garden (*table d'hôtes c.€39*).

made Bishop than it was afterwards. It is therefore necessary that what he did not achieve with us when he was alive he should complete now that he is dead...'

Ruse rather than reason settled this unseemly squabble:

When the men of Tours saw that all the Poitevins had fallen asleep, they took the mortal clay of that most holy body and some passed it out through the window while others stood outside to receive it. They placed it in a boat and all those present rowed down the River Vienne. As soon as they reached the River Loire, they set their course for the city of Tours, praising God and chanting psalms.

So much for high spiritual ideals. During the journey carrying St Martin's body back up the Loire to Tours, a further is miracle supposed to have occurred, the trees and shrubs on the banks coming into leaf or flower. A mild late autumn is known in French as an *été de la St-Martin*. Many of the most famous early French saints made it here to pay their respects to St Martin, including St Geneviève, who helped protect Paris from the Huns; Clotilde, Clovis' wife, who persuaded the Frankish leader to become the first French Christian king; and St Radegonde, the put-upon wife of the violent Clotaire.

Construction began in 1175 on the present solid church. It looks, from a distance, rather like a great hall topped by a small helmet of a Romanesque tower. The defensive appearance becomes still more apparent when you see the west front, which has crenellations and two square towers stuck to the front. There are also crenellations above the north porch. These 15th-century additions were deliberately made to impress and put off potential attackers.

The church was an important place of medieval pilgrimage. Many French kings stopped here. Pilgrims would arrive from the river bank, which may explain why the north porch was given such prominence, facing the river. A little sloping square leads up to it, the eye attracted by the wealth of sculpture decorating it and by a single, improbably slender column which stands in the centre of it like a fragile finger of stone supporting the weight of the Angevin vaults above. The outer statues are full-size figures, a mixture of the apostles and later saints. The tympanum represents the intercession of the Virgin and St John. Human faces and fabulous monsters congregate at the door, making the most remarkable lot of sculptures. The statuary dates from the first half of the 13th century, some in a reasonable state of repair, some mutilated in religious wars.

Inside, the church appears somewhat unstable, with sloping floor and irregular bays. The feeling of a spacious hall comes from the fact that the aisles are the same height as the nave. This plan was adopted from 1215, after a pause in the building programme due to warring between the French and the English. The choir end is the earliest part of the building. Before you reach it, peer up at the extraordinary painted sculptures at the tops of the columns. Among them, armoured knights and angels fight it out with monkeyish devils (the distance up makes it hard to make out these details clearly). The ceiling is covered by Angevin vaults. The northern side chapel commemorating St Martin probably occupies the site of the original chapel to St Maurice. A 19th-century stained-glass window here depicts St Martin's body being taken upriver by boat.

Montsoreau

Entre Candes et Montsoreau, il n'y paît ni vaches, ni veaux.
(Between Candes and Montsoreau neither cows nor calves can graze.)

As the old saying so poetically puts it, it's hard to see where the buildings of Candes-St-Martin stop and those of Montsoreau begin. Montsoreau has, like its neighbour, become a member of the association of Les Plus Beaux Villages de France. Passing into it from Candes, it's said that you cross a very ancient frontier between Touraine and Anjou, the point apparently once marking the division between the Gaulish tribes of the Turoni and the Andes.

A first medieval fort went up in the 9th century. The medieval lords of Montsoreau built their castle to oversee a thriving Loire port; they could make a good living exacting tolls from those crossing the regional border by river. Jean II de Chambes was the local lord in the middle of the 15th century and became an important adviser to King Charles VII, given numerous titles, including Master of the Royal Hunt. He had a new château built right by the Loire. The walls of this castle virtually bathed in the river itself, the Loire supplying the moat. Now his castle is separated from the river by the main road, the D947 to Saumur, which virtually touches its tufa walls.

Château de Montsoreau

Open May–Sept 9.30–7, Oct–Nov and Feb–April 2–6; t 02 41 67 12 60, www.chateau-montsoreau.com; adm.

Just one wing is left of Jean de Chambes' castle, but it's still a beautiful piece. The exterior looks sober and simple for the period, with big square end towers and a lack of decoration on the outside, even in the curious split-level dormer windows. But there is an openness to the building which shows the period's changing approach to lordly architecture, increasingly taking into consideration good living as well as strategic location and defence. Entering the courtyard with its courtyard on the cliff side, you'll see how the Renaissance has been tacked on here in the form of an ornate

La Dame de Montsoreau

The de Chambes family produced a number of dramatic characters in the 15th and 16th centuries. One of Jean II's daughters married the famous 15th-century French chronicler, Philippe de Commines, in 1472. Another became the mistress of Louis XI's brother, Charles de Berry, but just missed her sister's wedding when she apparently died from poisoning. More sinister still was the case of the great-grandson of Jean de Chambes who, in the course of the civil war of the Wars of Religion, led the slaughter of Protestants in Anjou during the St Bartholomew's Day massacres. Elevated to the rank of count for his services, he was in turn assassinated. His brother Charles took on the family title and married Françoise de Maridor.

She is the famed Dame de Montsoreau, as fictionalized by Alexandre Dumas in his typically heavy-handed manner in the novel of the same name, in a sequel to the book which produced the extremely popular and utterly historically misleading recent film, *La Reine Margot*. Françoise de Maridor was subtly rechristened as Diane de Maridor in Dumas' book. His story has it that Diane was forced to marry Count Charles de Chambes. The young Bussy d'Amboise tries to come to her rescue and falls madly for her. The two become lovers in the tale, but eventually Bussy is killed in cowardly manner.

In reality it seems that Bussy was a terrible scoundrel, a violent participant in the murder of Protestants in the St Bartholomew's Day massacre too, a ruthless ruler as governor of Anjou, and a major womanizer. He did seemingly attempt to seduce Françoise de Maridor, even writing to a friend at court that he 'had captured the grand huntsman's doe in his net'. A tender trap was set for him, though, in Anjou, and he fell into it. He went to meet Françoise, only to be assassinated. Dumas once again altered the facts and had his murder take place in the Château de Montsoreau, while the event actually took place at the family Château de la Coutancière, across from here on the north bank of the Loire.

stair tower of the 1520s, given typical Renaissance motifs. The stonemasons kept a medieval sense of humour, though – one scene depicts two monkeys at work, with the motto 'Je le feray (I'll do it)'. This extravagant stair tower was built to celebrate a family wedding.

Although some of the contemporary exhibition spaces prove slightly vacuous, others help you focus on the Loire and its many facets in presentations that are part museological, part show. With its light and visual effects, the place has been organized by past-masters in the art of entertainment, the Grévin company. Nature along the Loire, the history and economy of the river, the château's past and the legendary Dame de Montsoreau (see box opposite) are all covered. From inside the castle you can enjoy splendid views onto the Loire, with little boats and an island visible below.

To get an even better view onto both château and Loire, take some of the steep streets up through the enchanting village. Montsoreau has become the headquarters of the Parc Naturel Régional Loire-Anjou-Touraine, its headquarters beside the château, panels dotted around it explaining its mission.

Parc Naturel Régional Loire-Anjou-Touraine

Address for correspondence: Maison du Parc, 7 Jeanne d'Arc, 49730 Montsoreau, t 02 41 53 66 00, www.parc-loire-anjou-touraine.fr.

This specially protected area covers the lands between Tours and Angers, surely the richest culturally along the Loire, and certainly among the most beautiful. This area was almost turned into a separate *département* at the Revolution, and would have incorporated the wonderful towns of Saumur, Chinon, Richelieu and Bourgueil. This didn't come about, but in 1996 the Parc Naturel Régional Loire-Anjou-Touraine was established, also covering the areas around Azay-le-Rideau, L'Ile-Bouchard, Montreuil-Bellay, Doué-la-Fontaine and Beaufort-en-Vallée.

The park authorities' aim isn't to try to preserve the area in aspic; indeed the new A85 motorway linking Tours and Angers is still being built through it, despite protests. But their mission does include protecting the area's heritage and traditions and bringing them to the fore, encouraging the continuation of traditional life and ways as far as possible.

While navigation along the Loire died out long ago, the park's staff maintains its stretch of the river and is working to make people appreciate it more. For example, the atmospheric quays at Candes-St-Martin and Chouzé-sur-Loire have already been restored and are now illuminated at night. At Candes-St-Martin, one of the finest viewing points along the Loire, the park authorities have put up a big orientation table, while at St-Michel-sur-Loire they have erected a belvedere from which to appreciate the river better. Also, a Circuit de la Confluence has been prepared by the artist Denis Clavreuil to guide you round to particularly picturesque spots.

Another aim of the park is to make not just the local people, but also visitors, take note of more discreet pleasures locally. Already, some five **Sentiers d'Interprétation** have been laid out, walks of between 3 and 7km with panels along the way to get you to look more closely at the typical elements of the countryside. You can follow such Sentiers at **Gizeux** (near the château), **St-Rémy-la-Varenne** (passing by a Loire island), **Le Puy-Notre-Dame** (going through Loire vineyards), **Brain-sur-Allonnes** (concentrating on the forest) and **Andard** (leading you through the fertile flat plain north of the Loire). The brochures and panels take English-speaking visitors into consideration. A programme of special nature walks and events is also organized from May to October – look out for Les Carnet de Sorties for details, but to appreciate these you really need good French. Keep an eye out too for the Escapades, events organized around one specific place in the park each year. In addition, you can stay at special environmentally friendly *gîtes* chosen by the park authorities, the Gîtes Panda.

Plans for the future include the opening of a Maison du Parc for the public, as an introductory centre; Maisons à Thèmes, little museums each featuring a particular tradition; and a Circuit Patrimoine, a more substantial cultural trail. The one tradition which the park authorities have already tried to bring to the fore is the surprisingly inventive basket-weaving at Villaines-les-Rochers (*see* p.312).

The Abbey of Fontevraud

Open daily June–Sept 9–6.30, rest of year roughly 10–5.30; t 02 41 51 71 41, or for the abbey's cultural and concert programme contact the Centre Culturel de Rencontre de l'Abbaye Royale de Fontevraud, t 02 41 51 73 52, www.abbaye-fontevraud.com; adm.

The burial place of the Angevin Plantagenet kings of England; the greatest vestiges of a monastic establishment left standing in France; the first in a special order of monasteries founded from the early 12th century; originally set up as an ascetic community but to become one of the richest royal religious retreats in the realm; under Napoleon demoted to serve as a prison which saw one of the worst of France's literary *enfants terribles* locked up here... the abbey of Fontevraud has many claims to fame. Most surprisingly and exceptionally for the Middle Ages, women ruled the mixed male and female order of Fontevraud for virtually all of its history.

Only in 1963 was the abbey acquired by France's State Heritage Department. It then became the largest site of restoration of an historic monument in the country, and the prisoners were replaced by tourists. Today, the emptiness of most of Fontevraud's great spaces gives little notion of the busy communities which once brought life to it, but the architecture will impress you with its grandeur, including the largest cloister in France and a unique 12th-century fish-scale-roofed kitchen.

The History of Fontevraud

Robert d'Arbrissel, the Abbey's Charismatic Founder

The name of Fontevraud derives from the fountain of Evraud. Evraud wasn't the founder of the abbey; in fact nothing is known of him, although a story says that he was a local bandit who changed his ways under the influence of the great founding figure of the abbey at the end of the 11th century, Robert d'Arbrissel. Monasticism was in a state of crisis at that time. The best-known reforming influence of the period was Bernard de Clairvaux, the enormously influential early Cistercian monk who adopted a very strict form of the Benedictine order. At the same time Robert d'Arbrissel set up his own branch of this order.

Brought up in Arbrissel in Brittany, Robert was the son of a priest who lived unmarried with a woman. Well educated, Robert followed in his father's footsteps as a priest and helped Sylvestre de la Guerche, a soldier who hadn't received any training in the priesthood, to become bishop of Rennes. It seems Robert left Brittany because of complications caused by Sylvestre's dubious promotion. Continuing his studies in Paris at a time when the Church was undergoing major moral changes, Robert learnt that in the eyes of the reformers he came from a doubly sinful situation, as the son of a priest who lived in sin with a woman, and as someone benefiting from corrupt Church practices.

Both Robert and Sylvestre underwent a conversion to the reformers' ways. Robert was called upon by Sylvestre to help reform the Breton clergy in about 1085 'in order to liberate the Church from its shameful servitude to the secular and to stamp out the incestuous copulation between priests and lay people'. This heady conversion, Robert given the title of 'archipriest', didn't go down well with other Breton clergy. Such was the opposition to him that on Sylvestre's death, Robert had again to leave the region. He went to teach theology in Angers, but then decided to become a hermit in the region of Maine. By this time, however, he had won many supporters, and his reputation as a charismatic preacher had spread far and wide. He apparently attracted women in particularly large numbers. Followers quickly forced him out of his solitude and Robert founded a first community at Notre-Dame de la Roë, in Maine.

Pope Urban II travelled to western France in 1096, drumming up support for the First Crusade. He used the opportunity of his visit to put Robert's preaching to the test and was so impressed by what he heard that he declared d'Arbrissel 'sower of the divine word', ordering him to extend his work. While the pope continued madly recruiting knights to go off fighting abroad, Robert was left to spread Christian fervour at home. He attracted further followers in droves. More and more women were mesmerized by his preaching and their presence around Robert would lead to numerous rumours. Accusations were flung at d'Arbrissel, wild-haired and wildly popular ascetic that the sources make him out to have been, most notably that he slept with many of his women followers. He reportedly retorted in bold terms that if the women among his followers excited his sexual desires, it was all the better for him to reject these.

His ragbag of followers lived in hovels at first. Lepers counted among their number. Some order would soon be established with the founding of the abbey of Fontevraud in 1101; the land was offered by the lord of Montsoreau and placed under the protection of the bishop of Poitiers. From almost the beginning, it seems, Robert insisted that women should be given an important position in the mixed establishment, and very soon this would become a predominant one. Mixed orders had existed since the 5th century, although they were unusual, but the more exceptional aspect of Fontevraud was that overall control should have been given to women.

At first, however, Robert d'Arbrissel kept charge of the new community at Fontevraud. But he was intent on converting others and setting up new priories. It also seems that some of the women of noble birth who joined the order exerted their influence from a very early stage, for example objecting to some of the ambiguities of Robert's rule. They certainly contacted Geoffroy de Vendôme, a powerful Benedictine abbot and relative of one nun, Pétronille de Chemillé. Geoffroy wrote a stinging letter to Robert, euphemistically accusing him of wanting to crucify himself in a new form of martyrdom... in some of the women's beds. For whatever reasons, Robert went off to found further priories, leaving the abbey of Fontevraud in the hands of a woman, Hersende de Montsoreau, assisted by Pétronille de Chemillé. He had set up a whole separate Fontevrist order of monasteries before he died in 1116.

From as early as 1106, the community at the mother establishement was divided into four groups, a separation which then dictated the architecture of the abbey. The principal section, the Grand Moûtier, was the convent for young women of noble birth and widows of good virtue, dedicated to a contemplative life. Repentant women and women who had been married several times, as well as lay sisters, were settled in the convent of La Madeleine, devoting their attentions to manual labour. Lepers, meanwhile, were tended by sisters in the Prieuré St-Lazare, set a little distance away from the other buildings. The men were given the monastery of St-Jean-de-l'Habit (short for *habitation*).

Women Less Sinful Than Elsewhere in the Christian World?

After Hersende de Montsoreau's death in 1115, d'Arbrissel appointed Pétronille de Chemillé abbess of Fontevraud. At the same time, the statutes confirmed in writing that women should be placed before men in the establishment. This female leadership caused some tensions. It has been suggested that d'Arbrissel may have been particularly exceptional for his times in arguing against the deeply rooted Christian notion that women were to be regarded as more sinful than men, because one of their number had led Adam, and hence mankind, astray. D'Arbrissel may also have given women authority by way of thanks to the noble women who had joined his order and through whose wealthy connections the establishment had received generous donations of land. The cult of the Virgin had also grown strong in this period. D'Arbrissel advised that it might be best to appoint widows as abbesses, with their knowledge of the world, although for a long period the power of the cult of the Virgin meant that it was virgins who were selected to rule the abbey. Apparently d'Arbrissel placated many of the men in his order by pointing out that subservience to women was an act of humility and therefore could help them to attain paradise!

When d'Arbrissel died at his priory of Orsan in the Berry, Pétronille went to fight over his body with the monks there and won, transporting his remains back to Fontevraud. He was buried in the church choir, but unusually for medieval times, after his death no cult grew up around his relics. It may be that he had been too controversial a figure – certainly he was never canonized. Pétronille de Chemillé continued overseeing his wider work, ruling over all the Fontevrist establishments, with 50 priories set up by the time she passed away in 1150.

It was with the next abbess, Mathilde d'Anjou, sister of Geoffroy Plantagenêt, that a strong link was established between the famous Angevin dynasty and Fontevraud. Henri Plantagenêt even stayed at Fontevraud before he set off for England to be crowned King Henry II in Westminster Abbey in 1154. Two of his children, Joan and John, were educated for several years at the Angevin abbey. And, most famously, Henri was buried at Fontevraud in 1189. This wasn't as he had wished, but as his son Richard the Lionheart dictated. Such was the displeasure that this difficult son of his had caused Henri through his lifetime that one chronicler claimed that at the funeral, blood began to flow from the dead king's corpse in protest at this final act of insubordination.

Henri's powerful widow, Eleanor of Aquitaine, chose to live at Fontevraud from 1194 until her death in 1204. She even took the veil just before she passed away. She it was who deliberately decided to maintain Fontevraud as the royal Plantagenet resting place. Her children Richard the Lionheart and Joan died in 1199 and she ordered a necropolis for them. She in turn was buried here. Isabelle d'Angoulême, wife of King John, was also interred on the site, as was Raymond VII, son of Joan and a member of the powerful dynasty of Toulouse counts.

By 1189, 129 Fontevrist monasteries had been created. In all, 149 would come into existence, four in England, the best known at Amesbury in Wiltshire. After an initial illustrious period, however, the abbey of Fontevraud and the Fontevrist order declined in importance for a long time. Financial crises followed one after another, while the rules were flouted. The moral order changed completely, with the different sexes even said to have shared parts of the abbey.

A strict religious hand came to take back the reins in the mid-15th century. Mind you, the new abbess, Marie de Bretagne, had her position bought for her by her uncle, Duke Arthur III of Brittany. She spearheaded a thorough reform of the order. Then in 1491 the reign of Bourbon abbesses of royal blood began at Fontevraud. The job would be handed down from aunt to niece. Money poured in to maintain and add to the buildings. So the 16th century saw the second great period of building work at Fontevraud, with many of the earlier constructions, including the vast Grand Moûtier cloister, being replaced. Even with the powerful Bourbon abbesses, protests by the brothers arose periodically.

Medieval Men Getting a Taste of Their Own Medicine

Throughout the abbey's history, monks periodically protested against the rule of the abbesses. In the 17th century there are some particularly interesting examples of actions taken by the male inmates. Memorable struggles occurred with Jeanne-Baptiste de Bourbon after she imposed her strict leadership as abbess from 1639. One group of monks, sent away for a time to a Parisian priory, took the opportunity to run off to a different abbey in another order. The abbess was swift to take legal action, going straight to the king's Grand Council – she did have the slight advantage that the king happened to be her brother. The argument centred on who held superiority of spiritual jurisdiction, and many subtle arguments were constructed around questions of biblical interpretation. The abbess, needless to say, won the case. During the same troubled period, other monks at Fontevraud drew up a text with the unhappy title 'Reasons for which the brothers of St-Jean-de-l'Habit argue that they should not be forced to leave their problems in the hands of Madame'. Among their demands were that they should be treated as priests 'ordained by the Church and not as slaves'! For once, here we have historical examples of power politics between the sexes working the other way.

The noble Rochechouarts took on the title of abbess from the late 17th century. Mademoiselle de Montespan, a close family relation who was to become famous as Louis XIV's mistress, came to visit the abbey on several occasions. The naivety of the nuns amused her, but she was apparently most interested in being allowed to see some of their number who had gone mad in the institution. The ideals of convent life didn't suit all. Later, Mademoiselle de Montespan came to stay for a year. She brought her interest in culture to Fontevraud. Although the abbess of the time had reinstigated strict rules for the nuns and monks, the Racine play *Esther* was put on at the abbey. A new abbess's palace was built during this period and the gardens were well tended.

In 1738, Louis XV entrusted the education of his four daughters to Louise de Rochechouart. The royal princesses remained at Fontevraud until 1750. Louis XV was distressed to have so many daughters. That Fontevraud was chosen for them shows the importance of the abbey, but also how distanced the girls were from their royal parents. They took to calling the abbess '*maman*', as distinct from their mother whom they referred to more formally as '*maman reine*'.

Come the Revolution, the nuns and monks were expelled and the abbey was put up for sale in lots. St-Jean-de-l'Habit and La Madeleine found buyers, who dismantled many of the buildings for their stone. The furniture of the whole abbey disappeared. But the larger buildings were simply neglected. Napoleon's administration had the utilitarian idea of transforming the place into a vast penitentiary, the architect in charge of this unedifying conversion, Charles-Marie Normand, destroying old elements which interfered with his greater plans.

Fontevraud continued to serve as a prison even well after the Second World War. The outcast criminal and homosexual author Jean Genet spent time imprisoned here and revealed the chilling side to Fontevraud during that period in *Le Miracle de la Rose*: 'Of all the prisons in France, Fontevraud is the most disturbing. It is the one which gave me the strongest impression of distress and desolation, and I know that the inmates who were familiar with other prisons experienced comparable feelings of emotion and suffering as I did, just in hearing the mention of its name.' This part of the abbey's history is all too often forgotten. It's a shock to consider that the last inmates only left in 1985, although the Grand Moûtier began to be cleared from 1963. Meanwhile, Fontevraud had already been selected as the site for a more edifying project, the Centre Culturel de l'Ouest, a cultural centre serving several *départements*, as Fontevraud is well positioned close to Anjou's borders with Touraine and Poitou.

Visiting Fontevraud

You enter the abbey grounds via an impressive neoclassical gateway. The first big courtyard, cobbled and of curious shape, is lined with the Bourbon abbesses' house and stables, noble Ancien Régime architecture. This makes rather a wordly introduction to an ancient abbey. Only once through the ticket office and extensive shop does the more contemplative side of the place emerge.

Of the sections into which medieval Fontevraud abbey was divided, you principally see the Grand Moûtier – the Prieuré St-Lazare has been converted into a hotel-cum-conference centre. The other two priories practically disappeared, but the St-Benoît infirmary has survived. The **abbey church** is huge and plain, dating back to close to the abbey's founding. Inside, it presents one of those staggering church spaces which seems to gain in grandeur for being stripped of virtually all decoration now. The church was a massive project for its time, proof of what the Romanesque architects were capable. The apse, choir and transepts were built first, Pope Calixtus II coming to consecrate the high altar in 1119. The choir rises jubilantly skywards. The nave, from later in the 12th century, is less restrained in detail. Its bulk is held up by massive pillars with carved capitals, its ceiling by a row of beautifully shaped domes in the Angoulême style. When the church was turned to prison uses in the 19th century, the nave was divided into four floors, traces of which can be made out up the walls.

Dwarfed by the size of the great edifice, the four **Plantagenet tombs** lie on the church's floor like carefully arranged matchsticks. They haven't stayed here through history, but have been moved from cloisters to kitchen to a hiding place during the Revolution. With the entente cordiale, the idea was even advanced to dispatch them to England. They got as far as Versailles to be painted; the pale polychrome colours of blues, reds and pinks date from that time. All four royal figures have great nobility. Each lies on a bed, three in stone, Isabelle's of wood, with false drapery carved below the body. Henri's fine-featured head rests, crowned, on a plump pillow. One hand holds tightly onto his sceptre. Eleanor of Aquitaine is portrayed rather primly reading a book, a less restful figure, her raised hands giving her effigy more life. She had already seen her son Richard the Lionheart die. His effigy lies next to hers, a tough young bearded man asleep. Isabelle's tomb is of slighter proportions. She lies on her narrower bed, her hands rather anxiously clasped on her chest. Visitors sometimes leave roses at the feet of these tombs.

The **cloisters** off the abbey church are monumental. They reflect the scale on which they were planned in the 12th century, but were rebuilt in the mid-16th century, as were the surrounding buildings. The style is therefore French Renaissance. The double columns around the galleries have been said to symbolize the two sexes of the mixed order. While most of the buildings were relatively soberly decorated, the **chapterhouse** stands apart, held up by exquisite vaulting. Reforming the Bourbon abbesses may have been, shy and retiring they certainly weren't – humility doesn't seem to have be a strong point, to go by the initials left marked in the stone carving, referring to Renée de Bourbon and Louise de Bourbon. These initials are complemented by symbols of vanity, memento mori. Even more surprisingly, the semicircles beneath the arches have been painted with sumptuous New Testament scenes, concentrating in particular on stories of the Virgin – only Mary's glory has been added to by that of the abbesses; they pop up in the corners of the paintings, praying. Actually, most of their portraits were added after the artist Thomas Pot had completed his work, around

1560, although Louise and Renée de Bourbon were placed at the foot of Christ's deposition from the cross at the start.

Off the cloisters, you can wander through further empty chambers which sometimes serve for exhibitions. The *chauffoir* with fireplace was where nuns executed embroidery rather than manuscript copying. The interminably long dormitories are reached by a coffered Renaissance staircase. The cellar is given over to exhibitions on monastic life. A doorway takes you out into the massive courtyard of the **St-Benoît infirmary**, its architecture dating mainly from the end of the 16th century to the beginning of the 17th. It has a secular, almost château-like look, no symbols of religion clearly visible, except in the little Chapelle St-Benoît to one side, dating back to the abbey's early days. This chapel's architecture was terribly mangled when half of it was annexed off to create apartments for the abbesses, but it retains part of its Angevin vaulting. With over 600 people living at the abbey at one period, St-Benoît didn't just accommodate the sick but also the aged who needed care.

Next comes the massive **refectory**. Strict refectory rules were that the nuns should eat facing away from others. A sister would read in monotone through the meal. Silence was imposed, noise punished. The splendid, bizarrely byzantine octagonal roofed building at the end of refectory remained a mystery for a long time, its original purpose forgotten. Some reckoned it to be a mortuary chapel, others a baptismal parlour; one story even claimed it to be the tower where the legendary bandit Evraud had lived. Those stone fish-scales and mushroom chimneypots on the roof might provide you with some clues as to the building's real medieval use, as a **kitchen**. This characterful and rather comical building was possibly built around the time of the abbey's founding. The roofing was in fact redone at the start of the 20th century and the recreation of the chimneypots may be somewhat contrived. Inside, Fontevraud's kitchen is quite staggering with its eight hearths. The play of octagons and squares in the architecture makes for a lesson in the joys of geometry. Amusing little sculptural details add to the pleasure of the place. Probably different fireplaces were used according to the direction of the changing wind. Beyond the Romanesque kitchen, pleasant gardens have been recreated. The way through them leads to the separate **Prieuré St-Lazare**, once for lepers and those who tended them, now reserved for hotel and conference guests. The abbey runs an excellent **musical programme** from September to June, and sells recordings made here.

In the **village of Fontevraud** that spreads star-shaped down the valley roads surrounding the abbey, take a look inside the **Eglise St-Michel**, founded by Henri Plantagenêt no less, around 1180. He and Eleanor of Aquitaine may even be represented on two of the vaults' bosses. Several later artistic treasures adorn the Angevin Gothic space, including riches from the abbey and a Crucifixion by Etienne Dumontier, painted in the 1560s, and which has been interpreted as an allegory on the Wars of Religion, featuring many royal figures of the day. The abbess in the picture is probably the less than tolerant Louise de Bourbon, who received a visit from King Charles IX in 1565, during which she apparently exhorted him to massacre the Protestant 'heretics'.

From Montsoreau to Saumur

A line of amazing villages built into the Loire's limestone cliff runs west from Montsoreau to Saumur. Nowhere in the region will you see finer troglodyte dwellings. Some of the houses have several levels of rocky rooms. In certain parts, the neatly cut stone blocks of the windows and doors look almost as though they've become overgrown with a kind of rock ivy. Look out for the particularly elegant troglodyte houses at La Maumenière, La Vignole, Turquant and Le Val-Hulin.

Champignonnière du Saut aux Loups

Open daily July–Aug 10–6.30, Mar–mid-Nov 10–12 and 2.15–4;
t 02 41 51 70 30, www.sautauxloups.com; adm.

Climb the cliffside of **La Maumenière** to reach the impressive network of former quarrying caves at what is now a mushroom farm-cum-restaurant and tourist sight. The quarries around here were principally exploited between the 14th and 17th centuries, but stone extraction continued, by hand, right up until the 1950s. Among the places to be built from the local stone was the grand church of Les Ardilliers in Saumur. The troglodyte dwellings at the front of Le Saut aux Loups were lived in up until just after the war. In the hillside beyond lie kilometres of galleries, many of the corridors and chambers now devoted to mushroom growing. On the guided tour, you're shown around 700 metres of them.

You're first treated to an explanation of the quarrying work which lasted for so many centuries. Mushroom-growing began at the start of the 20th century, and the various methods of their cultivation are also presented. The many abandoned quarries across the Saumurois provide lots of cool, dark, humid spaces, essential elements in good mushroom-growing. With such advantages, the area produces the edible fungi on an enormous scale. It also has a couple of working museums on the subject,

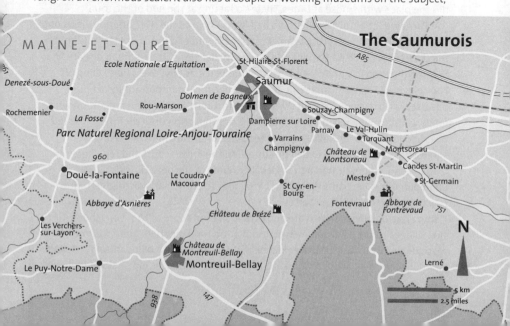

not just this one, but also one in St-Hilaire-St-Florent, west of Saumur. The horse manure produced in vast quantities by that horsey town, mixed with straw and pasteurized before use, makes the compost on which the mushrooms grow, once the mushroom spores have been sewn in sterilized rye and millet grain.

The main production in the Saumurois is of button mushrooms, known in French as *champignons de Paris*. But given that some three-quarters of the national production come from the Saumurois, you'd have thought that the locals might press for a change in name! Other mushrooms are also cultivated in the Saumurois caves. *Pleurotes*, oyster mushrooms, grow yellow, blue and pink. *Pieds-bleus*, or bluets, and *shitake* are further exotic-looking, tasty specialities. *Galipettes* are the big open mushrooms which are often served in Saumurois restaurants, stuffed with extra ingredients. Le Saut aux Loups also displays a selection of very wacky mushrooms from around the world.

At **La Vignole**, you can climb up to an extraordinary manor with a pretty little pepper-pot tower, its openings embellished with classical ornamentations. La Vignole is one of three sites along this stretch of river which lays claim to being the place where Marguerite d'Anjou, the ill-fortuned wife of King Henry VI of England, died. **Turquant**, too, has some very fine houses that emerge from the rockface, notably La Grande Vignolle (*open Easter–Oct 10–6*).

At **Le Val Hulin** next door, the main attraction is the **Troglo des Pommes Tapées** (*open July–Aug Tues–Sun 2.30–6, weekends and public hols May–June and Sept 10–12 and 2.30–6; t 02 41 51 48 30; adm*). The First World War tiger of a French prime minister Georges Clemenceau apparently liked to eat these carefully squashed apples with his gloves on during his frequent visits to the area; the British Royal Navy was the locals' best customer. American production put an end to the Saumur trade, but Alain Ludin revived the tradition recently. He shows you how the *pommes tapées* are delicately hammered into shape in a splendid cave with a special oven which atmospherically fills the place with smoke at times. There's a tasting at the end of the tour.

At **Parnay**, a little track by the town hall leads down to the river, offering views onto a Loire sandbank which attracts an exceptional number of birds in season. Climb to the charming church on the cliff and you get wider views. The Château de Parnay became the property of Antoine Cristal in the 1880s as phylloxera was killing off France's vines. This Parisian textile merchant became an important local figure, obsessed with reviving Saumur's viticultural fortunes. Rather than replanting white grape varieties, which had dominated Saumur production until then, he chose red ones and so helped radically change the course of the area's winemaking. So successful was he that he ended up supplying the British court and regaling Clemenceau, whom he had befriended. The name of the next cliffside village, **Champigny**, has been affixed to that of Saumur to particularly distinguish wine production in this area (*see box opposite*).

Souzay's troglodyte charms are better hidden than those of the more showy cliffside villages to the east, but are worth exploring too. From here on to Saumur, the roadside unfortunately becomes increasingly cluttered with billboards advertising Saumur's commercial attractions, but many beautiful houses hide behind high walls.

The Wines of Saumur-Champigny

Generally recognized as the best of the reds produced across the Saumurois, and probably Anjou, Saumur-Champigny wines come from nine parishes on the limestone plateau in the triangle of land between the Loire and the Thouet south of Saumur town. The vines extend over roughly 1,000 hectares, heading south from the cliff-face by the Loire.

To go with its cranberry, or even ruby, richness of colour, Saumur-Champigny often smells of cherries. It has the sweet bouquet of Cabernet Franc, by far the most important grape here, although winemakers may use some Cabernet Sauvignon or Pineau d'Aunis. It's a fruity wine which sometimes has a slightly dry aftertaste with hints of sloes. It generally has more complexity than the ordinary Saumur red, developing spicy aromas.

The wine cooperative or **Cave des Vignerons de Saumur St-Cyr-en-Bourg** (*open May–Sept 10–12.30 and 2–7, rest of year Mon–Sat 9.30–12.30 and 2–6; t 02 41 53 06 06 or t 02 41 53 06 18, www.vignerons-de-saumur.com; adm*) produces a healthy percentage of the *appellation*'s wine, up to as much as 40 per cent. A good individual property to visit would be the **Château de Villeneuve** at Souzay-Champigny. It's an estate around a 19th-century château that benefits from an attractive setting as well as making good wine. It sells both Saumur-Champigny and Saumur Blanc.

Some of the best Saumur-Champigny wines come from producers at **Varrains**, almost due south of Saumur. The **Domaine des Varinelles** again has more than its vinous attractions, with splendid troglodyte cellars resembling a Romanesque chapel. The winery is equipped with modern vats which help produce wines which regularly win medals. This well-known Saumur estate sells both Saumur reds and white, as well as sparkling. The **Domaine des Roches Neuves**, also at Varrains, has the highest of reputations, one of the very finest of producers of Saumur-Champigny.

And up on the hillside, **Gratien et Meyer's** (*open mid-June–mid-Sept 10–6, rest of year weekends and public hols Nov–Mar 10–12.30 and 3–6; t 02 41 83 13 32, www. gratienmeyer.com; adm*) Art Deco façade stands out before you arrive in town. This is one of the handful of very large Saumur sparkling wine-producing houses, with cliff-side caves for cellars. The others are clustered together in St-Hilaire-St-Florent, on the western side of Saumur, so you'll find a fuller description of Saumur sparkling wine on p.371. The collection of thousands of miniature model figures once held in the Château de Saumur has recently moved to Gratien et Meyer as a further tourist attraction of the house.

Château de Brézé

Open Mar–mid-Nov 10–6.30; t 02 41 51 60 15, www.chateaudebreze.com; adm.

The Château de Brézé is a staggering place, an enormous castle on a wood-topped hillock above the vineyards south of Champigny and some 10km from Saumur along the D93. The place isn't just immense overground, but also underground. In fact the first fortified dwelling, the Roche de Brézé, was totally hidden in the rock. It developed into quite a sophisticated subterranean maze in the 10th and 11th centuries. Wells were dug to bring light and air into the underground chambers, built in the shape of clover leaves around the wells. Such Roches were common in Anjou, maybe as many as 300 being dug in the region, but this one was clearly a particularly important, lordly one. For example, it was provided with four large silos to receive grain. The corridors into and out of the underground network were generally narrow, built with chicanes and other devices to help in the defence of the place should it be attacked.

A first overground fort went up from 1063. But the one you see now is a major 16th-century Renaissance castle. Exceptionally, Brézé has only known two lordly families in almost 1,000 years. For the first six centuries the proprietors were the Maillé-Brézés. Then the Dreux-Brézés took over. They still own the château, the present proprietors bearing the title of the Comte et Comtesse de Colbert.

Visiting the place, you'll first be overwhelmed by the size of the castle above ground, approached past a dovecote, built to fit the scale of the property, and the 17th-century outbuildings where wine tastings take place. The huge Renaissance pile beyond was much restored in the 19th century by Hodé. The impressive three wings around their courtyard are decorated with classical features. A few of the rooms inside are open to the public, but the main interest of a visit to the Château de Brézé is to see its underground chambers. These are reached via the largest dry moat in Europe, isolating the castle on its square platform. This moat was dug between the 13th and 15th centuries. Actually it looks more like a gorge than a moat, it's so deep. On the guided tour you learn about the uses to which the different subterranean chambers were put. There was basically a whole underground village operating here, with underground bakery of course. You can also look inside what are thought to have been a forge and a silk-making room. Wine-making has been important here for centuries, so it's no surprise to find viticultural equipment down here too, including massive 15th-century presses said to have been used up to the 1970s. The Château de Brézé still has some 30 hectares under vine. In the mid-17th century these troglodyte quarters were briefly occupied by 500 soldiers, troops of Louis II de Bourbon, better known as Le Grand Condé, one of the leaders of the Fronde, the aristocrats' uprising against the young King Louis XIV. The Grand Condé had married into the family which owned Brézé.

The tour ends in the so-called Cathédrales d'Images. Three of the largest underground galleries have been transformed into the setting for an outsized slide show of famous and extraordinary subterranean sights from around the world. Striking images are cleverly projected not just on to the walls, but also on to the ceilings and floors of the chambers.

Saumur

Two famous French works of art depict Saumur. The first is a page from one of the most famous illuminated manuscripts ever produced, the supremely beautiful medieval Book of Hours, the *Très Riches Heures du Duc de Berry*. Painted by the Flemish Limbourg brothers for Jean Duc de Berry (*see* Bourges) in the early 15th century, it shows a fantastic fairytale fortress with a dreamscape of towers and pinnacles. The other famous depiction of Saumur in French art appears in Balzac's great novel, *Eugénie Grandet*, set in the heart of old Saumur in the period after the Revolution. The fictional inhabitants don't come out as white and clean in Balzac's description as their château does in the medieval manuscript; provincial avarice and greed characterize the pinnacles of Balzac's caricatural society, although Eugénie's noble sentiments stand apart, along with those of her faithful servant Nanon.

Modern Saumur has had a reputation for being a rather posh, conservative town. It has deep-rooted links with the military, long home to a nationally famous cavalry regiment, along with the associated Cadre Noir riding school, France's answer to Austria's Spanish Riding School. The Ecole Nationale d'Equitation, which now incorporates the Cadre Noir has moved a few kilometres outside town, on to the hillside above St-Hilaire-St-Florent, a parish closely attached to Saumur. With advances in warfare, Saumur military training switched from horses to armoured mounts in the 20th century, and the place has a surprisingly fascinating tank museum. Given its military and horsey traditions, it's no surprise to find large numbers of men in stiff military garb wandering round Saumur, and numerous women in Sloane Ranger-type gear. But to national surprise, in the March 2001 elections, the Saumurois voted in a Green candidate as mayor!

For tourists, Saumur is utterly enchanting, one of the very finest towns on the Loire. It presents a very cheerful, well-scrubbed face to visitors, and boasts a magnificent architectural heritage for such a small place. The château is the obvious sight to make for first, but there are several grandiose churches to visit among the rich town houses. A couple of these churches are topped by viciously sharp-pointed steeples that look like great upturned tacks, puncturing the skyline almost as dramatically as the château's towers; another boasts a big breast of a dome, built in the Counter-Reformation to seduce the locals back to Catholicism after many had espoused Protestantism in the 16th century.

St-Hilaire-St-Florent has a clutch of attractions of its own beyond the Ecole Nationale d'Equitation, including a mushroom museum, a traditional Angevin bowling centre, and, above all, a handful of big producers of Saumur sparkling wine, who, in their attempts to woo tourists, vie with each other almost as competitively as the horseriders in the local show-jumping contests.

History

In the less inspiring southern outskirts of Saumur, the Dolmen de Bagneux provides a fine example of the Neolithic constructions of Anjou, with the largest dolmen chamber in France. You have to wait a long time to find further evidence of Saumur civilization, so let's jump to the 9th century. The monks of St-Florent, west of the town, were given a villa here after their monastery had been wrecked by the Breton leader Nomenoë. Scarcely had they settled than they had to flee from the Vikings coming up the Loire, taking St Florent's bones with them. A castle was built on Saumur's site around this time, known by the charming name of *le vieux tronc* (the old trunk).

Getting There and Around

Saumur's **train** station lies on the north side of the Loire, on the line from Angers to Tours. Saumur has direct TGV links with Paris, the journey taking 1 hour 50mins. There are **bus** links with the surrounding area going out in all directions, but the services, run by Anjou Bus, are very limited, and there are no buses on Sundays. The tourist office keeps bus timetables which you can consult. There is no bus station in town, but buses leave from close to the church of St-Nicolas.

To tour the town with children or to save on walking Saumur's slopes, you could hire a **horse and carriage** in summer – book via the tourist office. You can go out on *Le Saumur-Loire*, a **boat** on the Loire, mid-June–mid-Sept (except Mon) from Quai Gautier; make reservations via Le Service des Sports, t 02 41 53 65 37. To go **canoeing**, contact Saumur Canoë, Base de Loisirs de Millocheau (on the western tip of the Ile Offard), t 02 41 50 62 72.

Tourist Information

Saumur: Office de Tourisme de Saumur, Place de la Bilange, B.P.241, 49418 Saumur Cedex, t 02 41 40 20 60, www.saumur-tourisme.com.

Market Days

Saturday is major market day in Saumur, with the food market on Place St-Pierre (am only), the flower market on Place de la Bilange (am only), and the clothes market on Place de la République (all day).

Where to Stay and Eat

Saumur ✉ 49400

★★★**Hôtel Anne d'Anjou**, 32–33 Quai Mayaud, t 02 41 67 30 30, www.hotel-anneanjou.com (*moderate–expensive*). Absolutely splendid three-star hotel in very elegant 18th-century premises on the Loire's southern bank. The rooms are reached via a staircase so fine that it's been listed as a *monument historique*, as has the hotel's façade. Several of the first-floor rooms have amazing features, the most extravagant covered with moulded figures. The second-floor rooms are very comfortable but much more conventional. The rooms at the front look out onto the Loire, but the views from the rooms at the back are almost better, onto the château, which is stunningly illuminated at night. The very elegant restaurant, **Les Ménestrels**, lies at the bottom of the garden. It's reckoned by many to have the best cuisine in town (*menus €19–48; closed Sun*). *Restaurant closed late Dec.*

★★★**Hôtel Saint Pierre**, Rue Haute-Saint-Pierre, t 02 41 50 33 00, www.saintpierresaumur.com (*expensive*). This is the other stylish hotel in the delightful historic quarter of Saumur, although the 15th–17th-century house itself had to be restored from a ruin at the start of the 1990s. The rooms have been very nicely designed, with excellent facilities, such as air conditioning and well-kitted-out bathrooms. Some rooms are on the small side, if cute, and one side of the hotel stands opposite a less inspiring tall, modern apartment

By the middle of the 10th century some monks had returned, with a few relics in hand. Thibaud le Tricheur, count of Blois, was the lord of the land; his presence this far west shows how extensive the lands of the counts of Blois were at one stage. Thibaud offered the monks protection behind the castle walls. The name of the settlement is first recorded around this time as Salmurus, from the Latin for 'safe' rather than 'dirty' wall. It wasn't safe enough to protect the Blois counts' stronghold from that Angevin hothead Count Foulques Nerra; he destroyed the place in 1026.

Under Geoffroy Martel, next count of Anjou, the settlement grew up again, only to be devastated by Guy Comte de Poitiers in 1067. Geoffroy Plantagenêt then set up a new castle, while the monks opted for a retreat in what is now St-Hilaire-St-Florent, and the district of Nantilly was blessed with a parish church. The Plantagenet dynasty lost Anjou to the Capetians at the start of the 13th century. Charles d'Anjou, brother of King Louis IX (alias St Louis), had a much larger castle and city wall erected around

block. It doesn't have a restaurant, but does have a lovely bar, sitting room and breakfast room.

***Loire Hôtel/Restaurant les Mariniers**, Rue du Vieux Pont, t 02 41 67 22 42, *www. loire-hotel.fr (moderate–expensive)*. This modern hotel has bright, well-furnished rooms. Located on the Ile Offard, it benefits from views onto the old town and the château from its excellent riverside position. You can try tasty experimental cooking in the dining room with a view *(menus €15–34; closed Fri pm and Sat mid-Nov–Mar)*.

****Kyriad**, 23 Rue Daillé, t 02 41 51 05 78, *www.multi-micro.com/kyriad.saumur (inexpensive–moderate)*. It's in the middle of the town, only a short distance from the tourist office. The rooms are neat, quiet, well equipped and good value. *No restaurant*.

****Le Volney**, 1 Rue Volney, t 02 41 51 25 41, *www.le-volney.com (inexpensive)*. Also centrally located, a smaller family hotel where you should get a warm welcome. The place has an array of attractive personal touches, including home-sewn embroideries. *Closed 15 Dec–2 Jan*.

Les Délices du Château, Les Feuquières, in the château's courtyard, t 02 41 67 65 60 *(menus €30.50–58; closed Sun pm, Mon, and Tues pm Oct–mid-April)*. Has the privilege of being located in the outhouses of the castle, high on the hill. The furnishings are Louis XVI style in a 14th-century frame. The cook prepares extravagant dishes, such as *sandre* in potato 'scales' with a Champigny wine sauce. *Closed mid-Dec–mid-Jan*.

L'Orangeraie, same address as Les Délices, t 02 41 67 12 88. Attached to Les Délices but less expensive, offering an equally excellent setting with views on to the château, but simpler cuisine *(menus €14.50–20)*. Same closure as Les Délices.

Auberge St-Pierre, 6 Place St-Pierre and 33 Rue de la Tonnelle, t 02 41 51 26 25 *(menus €9–24)*. Best option among many on the wonderful square in front of the church of St-Pierre. This restaurant occupies part of a dramatic house. The place has plenty of atmosphere, waiters rushing round. The food is fairly ordinary, competent Loire Valley cooking. *Closed 24, 25 and 31 Dec and 1 Jan*.

St-Hilaire-St-Florent ✉ 49400

****Le Clos des Bénédictins**, 4 Rue des Lilas, t 02 41 67 28 48, *www.clos-des-benedictins.fr (inexpensive–expensive)*. The name of the hotel is misleading as the house is modern, set in a pleasant housing estate up the hill from St-Hilaire-St-Florent. It has comfortable, well-kept rooms with a modern French homely feel and fine views across to Saumur's major monuments in the distance. The swimming pool in the centre of the buildings also benefits from the views. In the restaurant, you may well find yourselves eating next to show-jumpers discussing their latest equestrian triumphs, and many of the tables are decorated with little sculptures of horse-riders. The cuisine is extremely refined, the chef paying great attention to detail *(menus €20–70; closed lunchtimes Mon–Thurs)*. *Closed 20–28 Dec*.

Saumur in 1230, extending the town's fortifications down to the river. Later, when King Jean le Bon distributed generous appanages to his competitive sons, Louis was given Anjou and developed Saumur's château according to his extravagant tastes (Jean Duc de Berry, who ordered the ravishing illuminated depiction of Saumur castle, was one of Louis' brothers). Louis' interest in the town encouraged traders to settle here.

Louis' successor, Louis II d'Anjou, married Yolande d'Aragon, who proved to be an extremely influential court figure and patron. In art history, she's known for commissioning the magnificent *Rohan Book of Hours*. The guardian of the future French King Charles VII for a time, she became his mother-in-law. Although relatively overlooked because of history's obsession with Joan of Arc, she played a significant role encouraging Charles VII to continue taking on the English invaders after Joan had been burnt at the stake; she had in fact earlier lent her support to Joan, who came to visit her in her early 15th-century Saumur house (one of the few historic houses to have survived the Second World War bombings of the town's main island on the Loire) – Yolande even defended Joan's adoption of male dress against the fanatical Bible-bashers of the time. René d'Anjou, the chivalric count who became known as Le Bon Roi René, was a son of Louis II and Yolande. He scarcely visited the castle at Saumur, but did order building work on it between 1454 and 1472. His properties eventually reverted to the French Crown and a royal garrison was posted to Saumur.

The merchants of Saumur continued to trade successfully, even if they seem to have felt some tensions with the mighty and privileged abbeys in the area, St-Florent and Fontevraud lying so close by. This may help explain in part why Protestantism caught on so readily among the town's merchants in the 16th century. In the Wars of Religion, Saumur's Huguenot contingent was so strong that in 1589 King Henri III granted the town the status of a Protestant safe haven, the theologian Philippe Duplessis-Mornay becoming its leader. A friend of Henri de Navarre, the future King Henri IV, Duplessis-Mornay founded an Académie Protestante in the town. Its main task was to train Protestant preachers before they set off around Europe, although it was considered much more moderate than certain other notorious Reformation schools. Among the scholars and teachers who came to Saumur was the admired Scottish polymath Mark Duncan. He didn't only lecture here; curiously, he also looked after one of the Bourbon abbesses of the abbey of Fontevraud. Such was the academy's reputation that it was at this time that Saumur became spoken of as a second Geneva, with Protestants making up around a fifth of the population and printing houses flourishing.

The Catholic faction in Anjou was deeply disturbed and fought back strongly through the 17th century, encouraged by the extreme Jansenist bishop of Angers, Henri Arnauld – with the support of the Virgin Mary, whose cult was vigorously promoted. Seven different religious institutions were set up around Saumur at the start of the 17th century. In 1615 one Catholic group, the Oratorians, was given the task of promoting the pilgrimage to the Virgin based around the miraculous fountain at Ardilliers, just west of town. Duplessis-Mornay, nicknamed the 'Huguenot pope', was deposed from his Saumur throne by Louis XIII in 1621. To combat the Protestant learning that was still thriving, a Catholic theology school was established in Saumur in 1649. For a brief period, the heads of the rival factions got on civilly, but the Catholic campaign was gaining greater strength and the pilgrimage to the sumptuous Notre-Dame des Ardilliers was acquiring more importance across France. In 1685, even before Louis XIV's Revocation of the Edict of Nantes of that year, which would suppress Protestantism in the country, Saumur's Protestant Academy was forced to close and the Protestant church (or *temple* in French) was destroyed. Many Protestants traders had to leave.

The château became by turns a barracks, a prison and an arsenal as Saumur became an increasingly important military town. In 1763 a cavalry training school was set up and by 1771 Saumur had become the centre for training cavalry officers from across France. At the start of the Revolution, in 1790, the Saumur authorities pressed unsuccessfully for the town to be made the head of a separate *département*. Anti-Revolutionary, pro-royalist troops from the Vendée uprising briefly occupied Saumur over the month of June 1793, and in 1822, General Berton tried to mount an abortive

Bonapartist conspiracy from here. After a rocky period through the Revolution and the First Empire, in 1825 the cavalry training school was properly re-established as the French Ecole de Cavalerie.

After the First World War, horses were replaced by tanks in the military training here and the town is still where the French mobile armoured divisions are instructed in the art of war – on maps you can see how far a big military camp stretches below Fontevraud. When the Germans reached Saumur in 1940, the school mounted a defence of the town. Despite the bravery of the act, it proved to no avail and much of Saumur's riverfront was devastated. Further bombing in 1944 caused more destruction; the buildings on the islands in the middle of the Loire, L'Ile Offard and L'Ile Millocheau, and the suburb on the north bank where the station is were worst affected. After the war Saumur regained its prestige through tourism. A wealth of architecture had survived the bombings and was gradually restored. Despite a dramatic shock during the rainy spring of 2001, when part of the outer fortifcations of the château collapsed on houses below, the town looks lovingly maintained now.

Château de Saumur

Open July–Aug 9.30–6 with night-time visits 8.30–10.30 Wed and Sat; otherwise 10–1 and 2–5.30: April–June daily; Nov–Dec and Feb–Mar Wed–Mon; Jan Wed–Sun; closed 25 Dec and 1 Jan; t 02 41 40 24 40; adm.

The Château de Saumur still dominates the town's skyline today, but it looks rather simple in comparison with the ornately roofed version in the Duc de Berry's medieval manuscript. From afar, it's still a joy to spot its silhouette on the horizon, its corner towers stretching into the sky like thick upturned pencils. These octagonal towers and many of the walls date in great part as far back as the 1360s, built for Louis Duc d'Anjou on the remnants of Charles d'Anjou's castle. A vineyard has recently been planted on the plateau outside it to help copy the image in the manuscript.

Up close to the château, it appears much sterner than from a distance. This impression comes in part from the fact that an outer range of fortifications was added for Duplessis-Mornay in the 1590s, at a time when the whole realm was on the defensive due to the upheaval of civil war. These carefully calculated, sharp-angled defences foreshadow the characteristic work of Vauban but were designed by an Italian, Bartolomeo. After the Protestant governor's enforced departure from Saumur, the castle was neglected. The place was originally enclosed on all four sides, but the western side fell down. The château went on to serve first as a barracks, then as a prison from Louis XIV's reign onwards; the Marquis de Sade was even held captive here for a time. During the 19th century the army took over the place, once again turning it into barracks. The town managed to buy it in 1906. Much restoration work has been carried out since then, Saumur's specialized museums installed within.

The inner courtyard still looks quite a mess. From the west side which collapsed, you get excellent views down on to the town. The **Musée des Arts Décoratifs** occupies the first floor. This museum includes hundreds of fine ceramic pieces, donated by Charles Lair in 1919, and making up one of the most important collections in the country. The first room contains some beautiful early medieval Limoges enamel pieces. Then the displays trace the development of French ceramics, concentrating on the work of Bernard Palissy in developing glazes, the evolution of regional variations, and the frustratingly long search to reproduce Chinese porcelain. Chests, religious statues and tapestries are among the other works on display, roughly ordered by period.

The **Musée du Cheval**, a fitting museum for this horse-crazy town, occupies the floor above, with its timberframe roof in the shape of an upturned hull. As you follow the history of the horse through different periods, a mass of saddles, stirrups, bits and boots add detail. The elaborate metalwork decoration is staggering at times, especially, for instance, on the knights' chamfers. The collections range across the continents; one of the main pieces on display is an extravagant sled from Eastern Europe decorated with mermaids and putti.

A Tour of Central Saumur

Start by Saumur's main bridge over the Loire, the **Pont Cessart**, which connects the main part of Saumur to the Ile d'Offard and gives you a fine view of the château. From the bridge you can also admire the substantial riverside quays which saw so much trade in centuries past. Now in summer you can take a river trip in an old-fashioned Loire boat (*see* p.362) from in front of the tourist office. This occupies part of the plush 19th-century Italianate **theatre** at the southern end of the Pont Cessart. So too does the **Maison du Vin de Saumur** (*open April–Sept Mon 2–7, Tues–Sat 9.30–1 and 2–7, Sun 9.30–1; Oct–Mar Tues–Sat 10–1 and 2–6.30; t/f 02 41 38 45 83, www.interloire. com; free*), a good place to get an introduction to the wines of the area. Lively **Place de la Bilange** beyond, the busy heart of Saumur, is full of shops and cafés. A *bilange*, by the way, was a kind of scales on which taxes in kind were once publicly measured.

Historic Saumur lies both sides of Place de la Bilange and the long straight line of shopping streets heading south. To the west of this axis, the atmosphere is dominated by military and cavalry Saumur. To the east, grand old churches and houses stand out below the castle. We start on the eastern side. Go along the river bank to **Place de la République** just beyond the theatre. The restored **Hôtel de Ville** (town hall) in bright white stone looks over the large car park taking up this square. The remarkable old building itself, with its machicolations and little towers, dates back to 1508. It was once incorporated into the city walls, hence its defensive elements. The façade holds a *pierre de la Bastille*, a stone from the famous Parisian prison whose storming signalled the start of the French Revolution in 1789. This stone was donated by Paris to the Saumurois Aubin Bonnemère, described as one of the four 'heroes of the Bastille'. Within the building, at the back of the courtyard, two sorry arches constitute the sad remnants of the Protestant Academy of Saumur.

Behind the town hall lie some of Saumur's most stylish shopping streets. Take the road on the east side of the town hall or the curving Rue de la Tonnelle off Place de la République to reach **Place St-Pierre**, a delightful sloping square with delicate trees providing shade. The **church of St-Pierre** at the end has a misleading classical façade, added on to a late 12th- and early 13th-century church after the front was struck by lightning. Within, the church is built on surprisingly wide arches, Gothic to the right,

Renaissance to the left. The choir stalls are decorated with splendid late-Gothic angels, dragons and fighters, while the 17th-century organ also boasts superb carving. You may be tempted to linger a while on Place St-Pierre, with its half-timbered houses, its café terraces shaded by tall branches, and a choice of restaurants.

Off the square, the **Montée du Fort** leads up to the château, fine old houses clambering up the hillside. This quarter was the setting for the Grandet house, the building almost a character in itself in Balzac's Saumur-based book (*see* box). Some modern apartments have been built along the way, slightly spoiling the effect. At the top of the Grandets' road you come out in front of a splendid 15th–16th-century house, beautifully restored by the Compagnons du Devoir du Tour de France, a kind of national crafts guild. Head back down the hillside via the **Chemin de l'Echelle**, past grandiose old town houses to the **Rue Dacier**. Walking along this street and those heading south from it, admire the grand *portes cochères*, the gateways into the Saumur mansions made for carriages to pass through.

Eugénie Grandet, The Saumur Tale the Saumurois May Not Tell You

Which jaundiced writer could attack the greed and pettiness of the French provinces and set his tale in such a pretty blonde bourgeois town as Saumur? Balzac of course. The author was himself obsessed with money throughout his career, or rather the shortage of it to pay for his failed enterprises and profligacy (*see* Château de Saché). But in Monsieur Grandet he created a monster of meanness, a man literally in love with gold. A barrel-maker and vineyard owner who jumps at the unexpected financial opportunities created by the upheaval of the Revolution and the Empire, this miser amasses a huge fortune, until it seems to some in Saumur that he might be able to buy up the whole town.

Eugénie Grandet is a story about inheritance as well as greed. Not just business rivals suffer at Grandet's hands. His family is shown enduring the most because of his heartless behaviour, his lone daughter Eugénie the principal victim. As her father's millions grow, she is hunted by the pack seeking the best marriage in town. The main battle for her hand and inheritance draws the Cruchotins against the Grassinistes, described with masterly comedy pitting their petty wits against each other.

The female characters in *Eugénie Grandet* merit separate study. The particular vulnerability of many of their number, especially because of their tendency to kindheartedness and love, is a recurring theme in Balzac. Men's lives, by contrast, are shown to be dominated by economic obsessions here, with no room for love. The arrival of Eugénie's cousin Charles comes like a thunderbolt to disrupt her life. The naive girl falls utterly in love with her foppish cousin, bringing the latest fashions from Paris. He finds what he considers to be a dismal town and a very drab house when he's sent to the Grandets by his bankrupt father. Ambitious young Charles decides his only option is to go and try to make his fortune in the Indies. Eugénie, to start him off, lends him the precious gold coins that her father has given her for each of her birthdays, expecting to marry him once he has proved himself. It's then all sharply downhill, almost 90 degrees, as so often in Balzac, as the battle between avarice and amour plays itself out.

Saumur's Two Churches to Our Lady

The churches of Notre-Dame de Nantilly and Notre-Dame des Ardilliers, two splendid religious buildings on the edges of central Saumur, reflect two different periods of strong campaigning and building by the Catholic Church. It's a fair walk in different directions from the centre to reach either of them.

Notre-Dame de Nantilly, south of the château, is a basic Romanesque block with a late-Gothic south aisle tacked on. As you arrive, a solid rectangle of defensive wall greets you by way of a façade. Within, the carved Romanesque capitals are hard to discern way up columns supporting the barrel vault. After the size comes the surprise of the church's **tapestry collection**, from the 16th and 17th centuries. In fact, the place looks like a tapestry museum. Some came from Flanders, others from Aubusson, while a few are even attributed to the Ateliers des Bords de Loire, regional craftsmen. The trouble with tapesteries is that they can look crudely unrefined, but many of the pieces here, although in various styles, are of superb quality. In the Capture of Jericho the triumphant Israelite army has been transformed into a big Flemish country dance party. The Crowning of the Virgin shows her surrounded by flowers and flames. A huge Tree of Jesse dresses up the only transept, Jesse his hand on his head in seeming horror at the inheritance he's created. In 1619 the church commissioned a series of eight Aubussons depicting scenes in the Virgin's life; they present the stories in dignified pastoral scenes, the characters ennobled by rich draperies.

Other notable features to look out for in this highly decorated church interior include the **statue of Notre-Dame-de-Nantilly**, a 12th-century painted Virgin with child. Pilgrims flocked to pay homage to her in medieval times, including King Louis XI, who payed for the addition of the south aisle of the church. The keystones there display the arms of the king, his second wife Charlotte de Savoie, and his son, the future Charles VIII. While in this quarter, consider visiting **Les Caves Louis de Grenelle** (*t 02 41 50 17 63, www.caves-de-grenelle.fr*) on Rue Marceau, one of the major producers of Saumur sparkling wines, with magnificent cellars.

To get to **Notre-Dame-des-Ardilliers**, east of the château, you pass through the Quartier de Fenet, wedged in between the Loire cliffside and the river. The pilgrimage to this church was greatly encouraged in the 17th century by the Catholic Church to combat the deep-rooted Protestantism of the town, and the whole quarter became devoted to the manufacture of rosaries and other religious objects to sell to the pilgrims. The 17th-century church itself shows Catholicism stamping its mark through outrageously seductive architecture – in the form of a propagandist breast-shaped dome. In fact, Notre-Dame-des-Ardilliers looks like a Venetian temptress imported into the Loire. The building is certainly stunning.

The origins of the church were slightly humbler than this. A small stone Pietà was supposedly unearthed in the clayey (*argilleux* in French, hence *ardilliers*, apparently) ground here in the mid-15th century. A century later, a first chapel was built on the spot. The fame of this Virgin spread far and wide and the royal authorities then exploited her popularity in the fight with Saumur's Protestantism. In 1614 the sanctuary was designated a royal chapel and the Oratorians in charge built their church and a convent. The church was subsequently added to under Cardinal Richelieu, who himself believed that the Virgin of Notre-Dame-des-Ardillers helped cure him of an illness once. The dome was planned in the 1650s, but it took until the end of the century to finish it. You enter an awe-inspiring circular space, a kind of Pantheon to the Counter-Reformation. The geometric black-and-white patterning of the floor and the coffered ceiling add to the thrill. Double columns lead up to medallions between the windows depicting the four Evangelists and the four Doctors of the Church. Four corner chapels lie at the square corners. The miraculous Pietà stands on the altar in the north aisle, which also contains a notable retable and two sculptures of Christ on the cross. But the most dramatic and anachronistic sculpture decorates the choir, with putti and God popping their heads out of garlands and clouds.

Military and Equestrian Saumur

Saumur is still horse- and military-mad. West of Place de la Bilange stand the town's formal cavalry buildings. On the western side of the square itself, the neoclassical **Hôtel Blancler**, built just before the Revolution, became by turns the brief headquarters for the Vendéen army and then the Republican one. A little later, Napoleon stayed here when he came to Saumur in 1808. Before concentrating on the cavalry, **Rue Beaurepaire** has an alcoholic distraction worth mentioning, the **Distillerie Combier** (*open 10–12 and 2–6: July–Aug daily, tours at 10.30, 12, 2.30, 4 and 5.30; June and Sept Wed–Mon, tours 10.30, 2.30, 4 and 5.30; May and Oct Fri–Mon, tours 10.30, 2.30 and 4.30; t 02 41 40 23 00, www.combier.fr; adm*), which makes a heady orange liqueur similar to Cointreau (the latter made in Angers, west along the Loire).

The quarter around **Rue St-Nicolas** was once home to Loire fishermen as well as merchants. It leads to a series of squares, including the vast **Place du Chardonnet**. This area is still packed with cavalry buildings, mainly from the 18th century, although several were added later. The Manège des Ecuyers, an 18th-century ring, was where the celebrated Cadre Noir used to perform its equestrian gymnastics; the showmen have now moved to the Ecole Nationale d'Equitation (*see* p.370). The stables from the early half of the 19th century house the Ecole d'Application de l'Armée Blindée et de la Cavalerie – the long-winded title of the school since cavalry practice was superseded by tank training. Exhibitions are regularly held here on specialist themes.

Stands line the sides of the monumental Place du Chardonnet for much of the summer in readiness for important equestrian events staged here. The most elegant building giving onto the square is the 18th-century neoclassical **Ecole de Cavalerie** itself. This school came into existence in 1763, when Louis XV asked his minister the Duc de Choiseul to reorganize the French cavalry. West from here, busy main roads lead you quickly into St-Hilaire-St-Florent, but as we're on military matters, we focus in first on the tank museum, just southeast of central Saumur.

With an extensive international collection of over 150 tanks, the **Musée des Blindés** (*open May–Sept 9.30–6.30, Oct–April 10–5; 1043 Route de Fontevraud, t 02 41 83 69 99, www.musee-des-blindes.asso.fr; adm*) outside the centre presents something of a history of the major European wars of the 20th century. Tanks came into existence to replace the horse-drawn gun in the First World War, and in an attempt to combat the effectiveness of increasingly sophisticated artillery against defenceless footsoldiers.

In that war of technological advances, with planes taking to the air and submarines to the seas, Churchill described the tank as 'the land battleship'. One of the few light moments in this pretty horrifying museum comes from seeing the early St-Chaumont, basically little more than a gun put on a tractor. Little Willy, the proto-type of all modern tanks, came into existence in Lincoln in Britain in 1915, introducing the caterpillar track. As technology developed at lightning speed, tanks became increasingly feared weapons of war. The details on the terse explanatory panels make for grim reading.

One reason for crossing north of the river from central Saumur is to visit the new culinary attraction of **A La Découverte de l'Huile** (*open June–Sept daily exc Sat pm, Sun, and Mon am 9–12 and 2-6; rest of year daily exc weekends 9–12 and 2–6; t 02 41 50 97 31, www.huileries-croixverte.fr; adm*), towards St-Lambert-des-Levées, where they make walnut oil the old-fashioned way. A rather older curiosity south of the centre is the **Dolmen de Bagneux** (*open April–mid-Sept daily 9–7, rest of year Thurs–Tues 9–7; 56 Rue du Dolmen, t 02 41 50 23 02, www.saumur-dolmen.com; adm*). This impressively sized prehistoric burial chamber, probably erected around 3000 BC, now sits in a café garden way down the long string of boulevards leading towards Cholet. The chamber, made up of 15 monumental pieces of stone, once served as a barn, it's so spacious.

St-Hilaire-St-Florent

St-Hilaire-St-Florent, now effectively a western suburb of Saumur, has a batch of tourist attractions. These include a cluster of sparkling wine houses, the Cadre Noir riding school, a mushroom museum and a newly carved cavern.

Saumur's prestigious national riding school, the **Ecole Nationale d'Equitation** (*open April–Sept Tues–Sat 9.30–11 and 2–4; rest of year groups by appt – note that you can only see the Cadre Noir training in the morning and that they are often away on tour; t 02 41 53 50 60, www.cadrenoir.fr; adm*), was built in the 1970s on the heights above St-Hilaire-St-Florent. It is home to the **Cadre Noir**, France's most glamorous horse-riding circle, an extremely exclusive band, with just 24 members drawn from the 50 trainers working at the school. Its origins lie in the development of a team of elite horse-riding officers to instruct the French cavalry. The Cadre Bleu was formed to instruct how to ride into battle, the Cadre Noir the more peaceable arts of riding. The trademark of the Cadre Noir's displays is three spectacular jumps of horsey aerobics, the *courbette*, the *croupade* and the *cabriole*, explained on the tour. On a visit on an ordinary morning you may not see these highly elaborate jumps being executed, but at least you can watch the trainers executing the perfect *piaffe* in what is described as the largest specialist horse-training ring in Europe. You will also be shown round the stables, which have room for some 400 horses in quite luxurious individual boxes.

If you prefer more relaxing sports, consider going to watch a game of ***boules de fort*** on Thursday evenings in the special long, low shed in the centre of St-Hilaire-St-Florent. *Boules de fort*, Anjou's answer to bowls, is played on a curved track with curved wooden balls which wander somewhat drunkenly in search of the jack.

The Sparkling Wines of Saumur

The parish of St-Hilaire-St-Florent boasts four out of the half-dozen big producers of sparkling Saumur. This is the Loire's best-known bubbly, much better recognized than the still relatively obscure Crémant de Loire. Saumur *mousseux* offers a much cheaper celebratory alternative to Champagne, but tastes much simpler too, with a fruity, fresh openness, rather than any biscuity dryness. It has a fair amount of fizz, although the bubbles don't seem to be nearly as well behaved as in Champagne.

Any of the big houses around Saumur makes for an interesting visit, such is the lively competition between them. **Gratien et Meyer** has already been mentioned on p.359, and **Les Caves de Grenelle** under Saumur. **Bouvet-Ladubay** (*open June–Sept 9–7, rest of year 9–12 and 2–6; closed 25 Dec and 1 Jan; Rue de l'Abbaye, t 02 41 83 83 83, www.bouvet-ladubay.fr; adm*) possibly comes out best of all through the number and diversity of its attractions. Not only does it have its fine cellars; in the 1990s it also opened a beautiful Galerie d'Art Contemporain, with four shows a year, some of a high quality. For children there's the distraction of a separate museum of masks. There's also the 19th-century theatre built for Etienne Bouvet and his employees, crossed wine glasses standing out among the elaborate period decorations.

Ackerman-Laurance (*open May–Sept 9.30–6.30, rest of year Tues–Sat and Sun pm 9.30–12.30 and 2–6.30; closed 25 Dec and first week of Jan; 19 Rue Léopold Palustre; t 02 41 53 03 21, www.ackerman.fr; adm*) is the oldest of Saumur's sparkling wine houses, dating back to 1811, and has enormous underground cellars. The other two major houses are **Veuve-Amiot** (*open July–Aug 10–7, April–June and Sept–Oct 10–6, Nov–Mar Mon–Fri am 9–12 and 2–5.30; 19–21 Rue Jean Ackerman; t 02 41 83 14 14, www.veuve-amiot.com; free*) and **Langlois-Château** (*open April–Oct 10–12.30 and 2–6.30, rest of year by appt; 3 Rue Léopold Palustre, t 02 41 40 21 40, www.langlois-chateau.fr; adm*), the last associated to Bollinger in Champagne. Several of these houses produce special *cuvées* which are more selectively made, some aged in oak barrels. The St-Cyr wine cooperative (*see p.359*) and other smaller producers sell Saumur *mousseux*.

The horses of the riding school provide a lot of manure and the quarries dug into the Loire cliffside lots of dark cool corridors, both essential elements in good mushroom growing, which you can learn about in the **Musée du Champignon** (*open early Feb–mid-Nov 10–7; t 02 41 50 31 55, www.musee-du-champignon.com; adm*), west out of St-Hilaire-St-Florent along the Loire. At the end of the tour, which is similar to that at Le Saut aux Loups west of Saumur (*see p.357*), separate rooms house a display of hundreds of types of wild mushroom, including the poisonous ones.

A cave or two west you'll find a new visitor attraction, a specially carved cavern, the **Parc Miniature Pierre et Lumière de Loire** (*open early Feb–mid-Nov and Christmas hols 10–7; t 02 41 50 70 04, www.pierre-et-lumiere.com; adm*). Using a chainsaw and a dentist's drill, among other tools, a contemporary sculptor by the name of Philippe Cormand has transformed the walls of a disused stone quarry into a quite engrossing and amusing new troglodyte sight. He worked inside the place for over two years before it opened in 2000. A Breton used to working with Brittany's tough granite, he says that carving the Loire limestone was like working with butter!

Strolling round the underground galleries, you can go and admire the twenty or so works Cormand has carved out, which recreate beautiful tourist sights along the Loire Valley. All the places featured lie between Amboise and Angers and are clearly labelled. The most spectacular carved scenes are the townscapes of Amboise, Chinon, Saumur and Angers, remarkably detailed, and reflected in pools of water in which Cormand had to work. If your children are inspired by his craftsmanship, the shop in front of the sight sells stone-sculpting kits for children.

The Troglodyte Territory South of Saumur

To discover a land where chimneys sprout out of the ground, where the houses consist of caves dug around sunken craters, where people once lived protected and comfortably underground – or hid there – and where a hardy handful still do, head southwest out of Saumur. This is the area where *troglodytisme de plaine* comes into its own. Beyond the caverns, other attractions include the splendid-towered Château de Montreuil-Bellay and the formidable pilgrimage church of Le Puy-Notre-Dame.

Le Coudray-Macouard and La Magnanerie

Le Coudray-Macouard is a rather frustratingly secretive troglodyte place, as so many of its attractive properties are hidden behind high stone walls. You can get a glimpse of the underground village by visiting **La Magnanerie du Coudray** (*open 15 June–15 Sept Sun pm–Fri, tours at 11, 2.30, 4 and 5.30; groups by appt Easter–Oct; 3 Impasse Bel Air, t 02 41 67 91 24 or t/f 02 41 52 29 16; adm*), where you can learn about the history of silk. For centuries, silk-making was a thriving industry in the region. A mulberry tree or two grows on the flowered path down to the pretty cave; the tree's leaves provide the food for the silkworms. The silkworms' cocoons, when unwound, provide the threads of silk. While the Chinese had discovered the secret of making silk thousands of years before, the French only worked it out in medieval times, first in the south of France. The word *magnanerie* derives from a Provençal word for a worm. King Louis XI made Tours the predominant silk-producing area and mulberries were widely planted in the region under Henri IV. The major period for Anjou silk production was from the mid-18th to the mid-19th century. The silk was spun in Saumur or Angers and then taken to the weavers of Tours. An epidemic in 1855 brought a sudden end to the silkworms. Since the 1980s a small-scale programme has begun to redevelop production, of which La Magnanerie forms a part.

Château de Montreuil-Bellay

Open April–Oct Wed–Mon 10–12 and 2–5.30; t 02 41 52 33 06, www.chateaux-france.com/montreuilbellay; adm.

Go to Montreuil-Bellay for the satisfaction of a dreamy Disney-like many-turreted castle. But this is the real thing, dominating the fortified medieval town below it. The château boasts 13 towers in all, making a splendid sight glimpsed from afar. A deep ditch separates the castle from the town on one side, adding to the drama of its

Getting Around

There's a regular **bus** service from Angers to Doué and rarer buses as far as Le Puy-Notre-Dame and Montreuil-Bellay. From Saumur, there are occasional buses to Doué and Montreuil-Bellay as well.

Tourist Information

Montreuil-Bellay: Place du Concorde, 49260 Montreuil-Bellay, **t** 02 41 52 32 39, *www.ville-montreuil-bellay.fr*.

Le Puy-Notre-Dame: 16 Rue des Hôtels, 49260 Le Puy-Notre-Dame, **t** 02 41 38 87 30, *www.ville-lepuynotredame.fr*.

Doué-la-Fontaine: 30 Place des Fontaines, 49700 Doué-la-Fontaine, **t** 02 41 59 20 49, *tourisme.doue.la.fontaine@wanadoo.fr*.

Market Days

Montreuil-Bellay: Tuesday and Sunday in summer.
Doué-la-Fontaine: Monday.

Where to Stay and Eat

Montreuil-Bellay ✉ 49260

Splendid' Hôtel et Relais du Bellay, 139 Rue du Dr Gaudrez, **t 02 41 53 10 00, *www.splendid-hotel.fr* (*inexpensive–moderate*). A stone's throw away from the château in elegant Loire buildings, with a variety of styles of rooms and a swimming pool in the large back garden. There's plenty of room for diners in the brashly wall-papered dining rooms serving traditional cuisine (*menus €12–35; closed Sun pm mid-Oct–mid-April*).

Auberge des Isles, 312 Rue du Boëlle, **t** 02 41 50 37 37. Down by the river, offers a tranquil setting and a delightful terrace where you can sample fish of all sorts (*menus €11–26*). *Closed Wed in winter, and Jan*.

Le Puy-Notre-Dame ✉ 49260

La Tour Grise B&B, **t** 02 41 38 82 42, **f** 02 41 52 39 96 (*inexpensive*). Delightful winemakers' property set around a charming courtyard in the village. *Table d'hôte (€19) possible*.

Rou-Marson ✉ 49400

Les Caves de Marson, 1 Rue Henri Fricotelle, **t** 02 41 50 50 05 (*menus €19.50–27; closed Mon exc reservation*). You couldn't get a much more atmospheric troglodyte setting than here. A pretty garden leads to the three main candlelit caves where you can taste the old-fashioned Angevin *fouaces*, dough balls which you can see being cooked in the troglodyte oven before being stuffed with various fillings. *Closed Christmas–Jan*.

Doué-la-Fontaine ✉ 49700

Hôtel de France, 19 Place du Champ de Foire, **t 02 41 59 12 27, *www.hoteldefrance-doue.com* (*inexpensive*). A typical unpretentious French provincial hotel in the centre of town (*menus €15–37; closed Sun pm–Mon exc July–Aug*). *Closed 24 June–4 July and 23 Dec–20 Jan*.

Le Dagobert, 14 Place du Champ de Foire, **t** 02 41 83 25 25, **f** 02 41 59 76 51 (*inexpensive*). The proprietors have made a big effort to redo their rooms to an excellent standard in this hotel on a slightly dull square. The big dining room is a bit vacuous, but the proprietor-chef is so full of enthusiasm that it can be fun to come here to try his old-fashioned recipes and fine cuisine (*menus €12–38*).

Auberge Bienvenue, 104 Route de Cholet, **t** 02 41 59 22 44, *www.aubergebienvenue.com* (*inexpensive*). Located opposite the zoo, and offers good cuisine and a warm welcome (*menus €15–48; closed Sun pm and Mon*). *Closed late Feb–mid-Mar*.

Rochemenier ✉ 49700

Les Caves de la Genevraie, **t** 02 41 59 34 22 (*menu €19; open July–Aug Tues–Sun, lunch and pm; rest of year Fri pm–Sun lunch and hols, otherwise by appt*). Another good troglodyte address offering *fouaces*.

complicated defences, while on the other side a steep embankment slides down to the Thouet river. The ubiquitous Foulques Nerra had of course already spotted the defensive potential of the hilltop setting in the 11th century, and built a keep here to protect his territories from the county of Poitou to the south. He put his vassal Berlay in charge, whose name was corrupted to Bellay through time. The word 'montreuil' signalled the presence of a little monastery, established in the same century. The Berlay family are described as a difficult line, rebelling against their overlords on several occasions. The Plantagenets laid siege to the place a few times to bring them into line, and once, so the story goes, to rescue a woman who had been raped by a Berlay. The château was greatly damaged by the consequences of these feudal mis-demeanours. At the end of the 12th century, the local lord allied himself to the English. This time troops of the French Capetian King Philippe Auguste came to destroy the château. The Melun-Tancarville family later resurrected the place and ruled it for two centuries, to be replaced by the Harcourts. It's in this family's time that the château took on its current appearance, expanding through the 15th century. The Duchesse de Longueville, sister of the Grand Condé, the prince who organized the mid-17th-century Fronde rebellion against royal power (*see* Brézé), stayed here when she was sent into exile for her part in the uprising. The grandson of Louis-Philippe also stopped here briefly when the Loire army retreated before the Prussian invasion of France in 1870.

The visit starts with the barbican, one of the few remnants from the 13th century, an impressive piece of defensive architecture. Then, passing under the splendid pepper-pot gateway towers, you enter the inner courtyard. Several buildings vie for your attention with their variety of roofscapes. The first part as you enter is the **Château-Vieux**, the first Harcourt edifice, built from 1420 on, with two octagonal towers and big dormer windows. The small freestanding building with the curious roof, a throw-back to Fontevraud, is the 15th-century kitchen. Behind it lies the **Petit-Château**, which was probably built for canons to serve the collegiate church within the fortifications. You don't visit this building but you do see inside the kitchen, provided with three impressive fireplaces.

The visit inside the **Château-Neuf** starts underground, as befits the region, with some splendid vaulted cellars. Apparently this became one of the largest arsenals in France before the 16th-century Wars of Religion. In the 20th century it found more amicable use, as the meeting place of Montreuil-Bellay's wine fraternity, with its comically rueful motto:

Lorsque le verre est plein je le vide,
Lorsqu'il est vide, je le plains.
(When the glass is full I empty it / When it's empty I regret it.)

The rooms above are fully furnished, in the main with works from the 16th–18th centuries. The most moving part of the visit is to the painted **oratory**. The art here dates from the end of the 15th century. On the ceiling, the vault is covered with delightful angels singing a musical score – composed, apparently, by a Scottish monk, Walter Fry. Below, some of the pictures, though faded, have kept their power, in partic-ular Christ suffering on the cross.

Among an overwhelming catalogue of interesting objects pointed out to you on the rest of the tour, look out for Queen Marie de' Medici's wedding chest; some fine tapestries; a superb Boulle bureau, made of copper encrusted with tinted turtleshell;

and a *bourdaloue*, a chamber pot which, it is claimed, was passed around the congregation during unbearably long sermons! After you've visited the interiors, you can wander round the lovely *chemin de ronde* and garden and then go and cast an eye into the collegiate church with its extraordinary spiky silhouette.

The **town** around the castle has retained great sections of its medieval walls, erected between the 13th and the 15th centuries and curiously pimpled with protruding stones. Anjou used to have 32 walled cities in medieval times, but Montreuil-Bellay is the only one to have retained such substantial ramparts. Although the place can seem somewhat lifeless nowadays, relegated to a southern outpost of modern Anjou, after medieval times it remained an important town, an administrative centre for a large area, until decline set in from the mid-18th century. With the Revolution, Saumur took over its administrative responsibilities.

Le Puy-Notre-Dame

The magnificent **collegiate church** of Le Puy-Notre-Dame, a short way west of Montreuil-Bellay, has towers which could be mistaken for giant rabbit ears from a hazy distance. As you come up close to the west front, the building becomes extremely daunting, a sheer wall of a façade rising above the five arches. The massive church seems way oversized for this quiet village set among its vineyards. The reason for its grandeur lies in the Girdle of the Virgin Mary, of which it still claims to hold a sizable piece. This immeasurably precious object was brought back from the Crusades by Guillaume, Comte de Poitiers, a grandfather of Eleanor of Aquitaine, in the 12th century. The church you see only dates from the first half of the 13th century, and the first recorded mention of the girdle here only from the end of the 14th, but it's assumed that the vast religious edifice was spawned from this miraculous fragment of garment. Pilgrims flocked to the place, women in particular coming to pray for fertility and safe childbirth.

The Angevin vaulting inside creates a brilliant effect. Beautiful little statues stand at the base of the ribs in the nave, while the keystones of the aisles also attract the attention. The choir, with its ceiling of wonderful fan vaulting, contains some hilarious and finely carved choir stalls of the 16th century, with many depictions of sinful behaviour, reminding visitors of the old French saying that monks '*s'assoient sur leurs péchés* (sit on their sins)'! Unfortunately the vast majority of the treasures that the church once held, in particular gifts from wealthy pilgrims, were lost through time. The supposed girdle remains, heavily protected in the south transept. Even royals had to write for permission to get hold of the thing, as a letter on display from Queen Anne, wife of Louis XIII, demonstrates. Taking the steps up to the top of the west front, you can get fine views onto the tops of the Angevin vaults and then wander along the parapet connecting the two front towers to appreciate the lovely views over the picturesque vineyards around Le Puy-Notre-Dame. The tourist office has a *dégustation* bar for tasting local wines, and the guides can direct you to interesting properties open to visitors.

There's also a well-marked walking path through the vines set up with the Parc Naturel Régional Loire-Anjou-Touraine.

Further regional traditions are recalled in two sights open to visitors. At **La Soie Vivante** (*open July–Aug Mon pm–Sun 10–12 and 1–6, May–June and Sept–Oct Tues–Sun 10–12 and 2–6; La Paleine, Place Jules Raimbault, t 02 41 38 28 25 or t 02 41 38 42 38, phwadoux@wanadoo.fr; adm*) you can learn more about the local tradition of silk-making (*see* Le Coudray-Macouard). The **Cave Vivante du Champignon** of the **Champignonnière Saint-Maur** (*open March–Oct daily 10–6; t 02 41 52 26 84, troglo.champi.free.fr; adm*) takes you into underground caves where the geology, quarrying, cave-dwelling and mushroom-farming of these parts is presented.

Abbaye d'Asnières

The stump of the church of the **abbaye d'Asnières** (*open July–Aug Wed–Mon 2–6.30; t 02 41 67 04 92, www.jpylou.freesurf.fr; adm*) is a sad and charming ruin north of the D761 between Montreuil-Bellay and Doué-la-Fontaine. The establishment was devastated by Huguenots in 1566 and much of its stone sold off for other construction work in the 19th century. The substantial choir and transepts which remain show how grand the church must have been in its time. It was built at the end of the 12th century and beginning of the 13th for the Tironensian order (close to the Benedictines) which settled here in 1114. The choir contains particularly elegant Angevin vaulting with highly ornate keystones and ribs. Take a look at the medieval enamel tiles by the altar. Several tombstones and effigies add to the atmosphere.

Doué-la-Fontaine

Doué-la-Fontaine may look superficially uninspiring, but dig a little deeper and unusual riches reveal themselves. The town has a couple of spectacular troglodyte sites, Les Perrières and the zoo, plus a handful of smaller subterranean surprises.

The rock of Doué is not the Loire Valley's best known limestone, tufa, but *faluns*, a more friable type of limestone filled with organic debris and shells in particular, deposited when a warm shallow sea covered this area back in the mists of time. In Merovingian times sarcophagi made from *faluns* were highly prized. At **La Cave aux Sarcophages** (*open April–mid-Sept daily 10–12 and 2–7; night-time visits July–Aug Mon–Tue at 8.30 by appt; 1 Rue de la Croix Mordret, t 02 41 59 24 95 or t 06 07 30 95 87, http://perso.wanadoo.fr/la.cave.aux.sarcophages; adm*) you can see an extraordinary archaeological site from which monolithic sarcophagi were extracted between the 6th and the 9th centuries.

Some quite substantial if not exactly attractive ruins of a **Carolingian house**, dating from the start of the 10th century, still stand on the outskirts of Doué. By the turn of the next century, the unavoidable Foulques Nerra had built a fortification here. Some *faluns* are strong enough to be used in building, as the centre of old Doué shows, the stone also known as *grison*, giving an idea of its greyish colour.

The local *faluns* were also quarried for road-building and for extracting lime, and the numerous disused quarries were later put to practical housing purposes. Craters form the courtyards for a good number of the startling underground houses in town. As to the **Arènes**, with their roughly elliptical ranks of seats, for a long time the story circulated that these were the vestiges of a Gallo-Roman arena, hence the name. Now it's known that this was in fact a medieval quarry, converted for entertainment in the 15th century. Rabelais set the mock Doué Games in *Pantagruel* here.

The Inverse Architecture of Les Caves Cathédrales

Rue d'Anjou and **Rue des Perrières** half-conceal an array of curious craters that form the core of rather poor-looking homes. You may feel a little uncomfortable peering down into these often rather tatty-looking yards, but it's fascinating all the same.

Do go and visit the **Caves Cathédrales** of **Les Perrières** (*open May–late Sept Tues–Sun 10–12.30 and 1.30–7, night visits July–Aug Mon 8.30; t 02 41 59 71 29; adm*), a phenomenal series of interconnecting underground quarries. The comparison to underground cathedrals may sound exaggerated, but even if the place has no spiritual history, and no windows whatsoever, architecturally it feels very grand and church-like. The reason for the extraordinary shapes of Les Perrières stems from the way these quarries were excavated. The land had a double use here. The topsoil could be used for agriculture, the stone beneath exploited. So that the agricultural land should be left relatively unspoilt once a quarry had been opened up, the quarrying cultivators here developed an ingenious system of excavation. They dug narrow trenches in the soil. Then they extracted the stone to form an underground arch. This inverse architecture resulted in bottle-shaped spaces underground. Once the *faluns* had been extracted, the chambers could be put to practical uses while the thin trench in the roof was covered up by blocks of stone, earth placed on top and the land was once again ready for cultivation.

Quarrying at Les Perrières started in the 18th century, and continued until 1930. The chambers served as homes and storage spaces. For 50 years, from 1930 to 1980, mushroom-growing went on here. Left impressively empty, the interconnecting series of chambers now offers the most superb architectural perspective. The shapes of the arches and bays certainly aren't regular as in a cathedral, but they are awe-inspiring. Great rather phallic-shaped openings lead from one bay to the next, the dim lighting casting fantastic shadows. You can imagine that the ingenious Spanish architect Antonio Gaudí might have appreciated the eccentricity of the forms and structure.

Two other small troglodyte sights to be recommended in the centre of Doué are **La Rose Bleue**, a small-scale craft pottery recently installed in its lovely cave setting, and **La Sablière**, which contains a rose-water distillery – which brings us to Doué's other claim to fame.

The Roses of Doué

The soil in the area has also proved particularly suited to growing roses and Doué is now the capital of rose cultivation in France. Millions of them thrive on the land around the town. The man who really made rose cultivation bloom in Doué was Joseph-François Foulon, in the second half of the 18th century. He also had a grand château built for himself in town. Foulon was deadheaded at the Revolution, and most of his château disappeared. But the grounds have been converted into the town's permanent, democratic **Roseraie**, or rose garden. Next to it, in the former stables of the town's vanished château, there's another rose-water distillery and the substantial **Musée des Commerces Anciens** (*open July–Aug 9–7; May–June and Sept 9.30–12 and 2–7; mid-Mar–April and Oct–mid-Nov Tues–Sun 9.30–12 and 2–6; t 02 41 59 28 23, f 02 41 59 72 39; adm*), another Doué sight that attracts large numbers. There's such a mass of objects displayed in these artificially recreated rows of olde shoppes that it does help to have to take the guided tour, even if that leaves you at the mercy of pre-packaged bad jokes.

A fantastic congregation of roses takes place each year in the Arènes. During the **Journées des Roses**, the town's festival of roses, thousands upon thousands of the plants adorn the town. Outside Doué you may pass whole fields of roses, cultivated in rows like vegetables. **Les Chemins de la Rose** (*open early May–mid-Sept 9.30–7; t 02 41 59 95 95, www.cheminsdelarose.com; adm*) is a rose garden planted in the mid-1990s off the road to Cholet, specializing in rare and botanical roses. Some 900 varieties are represented among the 8,000 rose bushes on the site.

Zoo de Doué

Open Easter–Sept 9–7.30, Feb–Easter and Oct–mid-Nov 10–6;
Route de Cholet, t 02 41 59 18 58, www.zoodoue.fr; adm.

Doué's other truly spectacular troglodyte sight apart from Les Perrières is its underground zoo, out to the southwest of town in the direction of Cholet. This again will amaze you. If you don't object to zoos, it's probably the most extraordinary, attractive one you'll ever see. The visitors' path first takes you through a trail of interconnecting craters devoted to different creatures. The first barren crater offers the bizarre sight of giraffes seemingly trying to stretch their necks far enough to see what might be going on up at ground level. In the next craters you enter a world of lush vegetation, planted with bamboo, acacias and wildflowers. Exotic birds greet you with their songs and squawks. You quite forget you're in the middle of a slightly dull plain by the time you reach the enclosures for the wild cats, again densely planted, with crooks and caverns in which the formidable creatures can lounge. Although the craters don't offer enough room for these animals to have a good run, they do make for unusually spacious cages. You can often get quite a close look at the big cats by using the hides, mimicking the effects of a safari. The zoo has a programme of breeding endangered species with the aim of reintroducing them to the wild, among which snow panthers and Sumatra tigers feature. There's also a hothouse for reptiles underground.

On the zoo's overground trail, once again the place is so densely planted that you feel in a different region. Raised observation posts allow you to see rare wolves and, on the well-landscaped islands, several types of lemurs, monkeys and a host of other animals. This dreamworld has been realized by the Gay family. Louis Gay started the zoo in 1961, his son Pierre continuing to add to it.

Troglodyte Sights North of Doué-la-Fontaine

Les Maisons Troglodytes de la Fosse à Forges (*open June–Sept 9.30–7, Mar–May and Oct 9.30–12.30 and 2–6.30, Nov weekends only 10–12.30 and 2–6; t 02 41 59 00 32 or* *t 02 41 52 27 60, f 02 41 59 94 68; adm*) is an underground complex which is different from virtually all the other troglodyte sites in the region in that it didn't serve as a quarry first, but was purpose-built in the 17th century. Chimneys and garden walls stick out above the ground, but otherwise the hamlet is totally hidden underground. You can visit the typical, cleverly conceived subterranean houses run by the extremely enthusiastic curator-cum-cave dweller. He came to live here with his family in 1979, bringing back to life this home around its sunken 'patio'. You also see the agricultural side, with grain silos, a hemp drying room and a well.

The visit round the **Village Troglodytique de Rochemenier** (*open April–Oct 9.30–7; Nov, Feb and Mar weekends and hols only 2–6; t 02 41 59 18 15, perso.club-internet.fr/ troglody; adm*), west of La Fosse, reveals a good deal about former life in such a troglodyte village. You can look into old barns, a wine cellar, bedrooms, a cowshed and stables, all decked out with old machinery, utensils and decoration, while Gélines de Touraine, the rare black hens of the region, cluck around. The subterranean community hall is one of the most atmospheric rooms, where people would gather for winter *veillées*, evenings spent in each other's company between All Saints's Day and Carnival. Although there was no fireplace, apparently the stable temperature of the cave was warmer than outside, and a good number of bodies would help to take the chill off the air as the small community wove baskets, span, or prepared their walnut oil together.

There aren't just the living rooms and farm outhouses down here, but also a secretive **underground chapel**. This is actually situated underneath the overground church. It was a quarry originally, but during the 16th-century Wars of Religion became the religious meeting place, the quarry's extraction-well transformed into the church dome. Niches dug into the rock may have been made to contain statues, while the three Gothic arches and cross carved into the wall make clear the purpose of the cave's transformation. The whole thing also has the shape of a cross. Above ground, the church of St-Emerance is from the 17th century and has a quaint old atmosphere.

The **Caverne Sculptée of Dénezé-sous-Doué** (*open Tues–Sun: June–Aug 10–7, Sept 10–6, April–May 2–6; open Mon public hols; t 02 41 59 15 40, f 02 41 59 21 72; adm*), a mysterious cave containing badly battered sculptures, lies below an uninspiring courtyard in a village just north of Rochemenier. Many of the crude carvings have had to be reconstituted as they've suffered through time and neglect, but the underground scenes still present an intriguing enigma.

The carvings were only rediscovered by local children in 1950, and no one's quite sure who executed them, when, or why. The preferred theory is that they were the work of a secret society, perhaps a Protestant group in the 16th century. The most famous scene depicts a Pietà, but the cross has been cleverly turned into an axe, while the woman, rather than looking the part of the Virgin, bears a noted resemblance to Catherine de' Medici. Such a cutting caricature brings to mind the Wars of Religion, which divided French Catholics and Protestants in the second half of the 16th century. Saumur in that troubled period became the centre of a strong Protestant community, while Angers remained staunchly Catholic. The whole area and its leaders were deeply divided.

Although the carving is naive, with a touch of medieval coarseness, the fashions on many of the figures look decidedly 16th century. An American Indian appears among the figures and interestingly the first native American settled in Anjou at the start of the 16th century. Certain motifs recur in the sculptures, such as figures astride heads, heads in others' hands, or three people standing intimately in a row. Some have seen signs of degenerate or even satanistic scenes down here. Was some kind of ritual tied up with these sculptures and this cavern? For the moment, it's been hard to assign any certain meaning to these sculptures, so wild speculation can run riot.

The Layon and Aubance Valleys

The landscape changes greatly just west of the flats around Doué-la-Fontaine as two delightful wine-producing valleys make their way north to the Loire. The Layon wines have made the name of this valley, its slopes worth discovering for their beauty, although there are only small tourist sights to visit along the route. Windmills mark the way. The Aubance wines remain relatively obscure, the valley best known for the enormous pile of the Château de Brissac.

The Layon

The Layon river rises just south of Anjou in the *département* of Deux-Sèvres. Having provided the waters for the lake of Beaurepaire, which runs along the regional border, it then heads off on an arc of some 75km to the Loire. First the Haut-Layon heads determinedly northeastwards towards Doué-la-Fontaine, but repelled by a geological barrier before reaching that town, it swings round to the northwest, into the so-called Bas-Layon, roughly paralleling the Aubance for its pretty run into the Loire.

The Layon valley is sometimes described as a dividing line between regions, not just geologically, with the change from limestone to schist (and from southern tiles to slate roofs), nor regionally, with the shift from Poitou to Anjou, but also politically – it was one of the frontiers of the 1793 anti-Republican Guerres de Vendée, the people to the southwest of here, Les Blancs, pro-Catholic and pro-royalist, rising against the Republican army, Les Bleus. Battles were fought here and much destruction wrought in 1793 and 1794 (see Les Mauges and Cholet). The Layon valley was particularly badly split by that conflict, as was the Aubance, while to the west, in Les Mauges, the populace was unified in its staunch anti-Republicanism. A large number of windmills once turned on the Layon heights, and the odd vestige of a château reminds of a certain importance this little region must have had in medieval times. The valley's name is nowadays familiar to wine connoisseurs because of the sweet white wines it produces (*see* p.384). The steep slopes on which the vines grow certainly make for splendid landscapes.

Les Cerqueux-sous-Passavant, southwest of Doué, pays homage to the Wild West with **Bisonland** (*open July–Aug daily exc Sun am 10–7; adm*), where you can see bison being reared and then eat some, while the children get a chance to play in tepees.

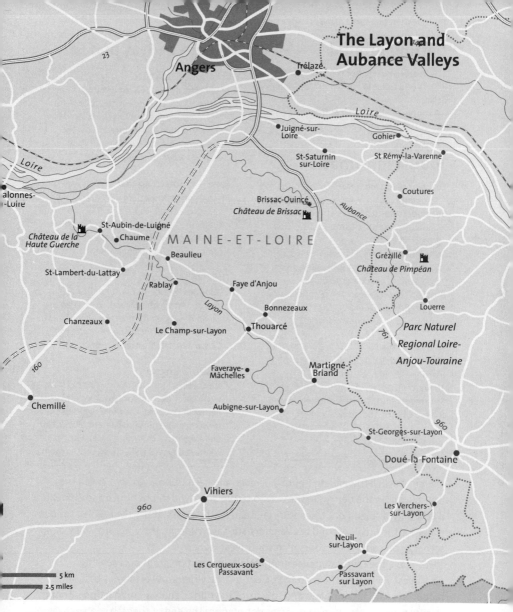

The Layon and Aubance Valleys

Angers

Trélazé

Loire

Juigné-sur-Loire

Gohier

St-Saturnin sur-Loire

St Rémy-la-Varenne

alonnes--Loire

Loire

Coutures

Brissac-Ouincé
Château de Brissac

Aubance

Château de la Haute Guerche

St-Aubin-de-Luigné

Chaume

MAINE-ET-LOIRE

Grézillé

Château de Pimpéan

Beaulieu

St-Lambert-du-Lattay

Rablay

Faye d'Anjou

Louerre

Layon

Bonnezeaux

Chanzeaux

Le Champ-sur-Layon

Thouarcé

Parc Naturel Regional Loire-Anjou-Touraine

761

Faveraye-Mâchelles

Martigné-Briand

Chemillé

Aubigne-sur-Layon

160

St-Georges-sur-Layon

960

Doué la Fontaine

Vihiers

Les Verchers-sur-Layon

960

Neuil-sur-Layon

Les Cerqueux-sous-Passavant

Passavant sur Layon

5 km

2.5 miles

This tourist attraction reveals the methods some French farmers are resorting to in order to make a living.

Passavant-sur-Layon's good position dominating the valley not surprisingly appealed to Foulques Nerra, who ordered a keep here. From the heights of the village you can look onto the remains of a 13th-century fortress that succeeded it. The vine-yards of the Coteaux du Layon have already begun to prettify the countryside by now. The next village, **Nueil**, has the rarity in the area of a monument to Republicans – a dozen villagers took refuge in the church bell tower when the Vendéen troops came to attack them in 1794 and rang the bells for help while the enemy set fire to the

Getting Around

By **bus**, Brissac-Quincé is on the line between Angers and Doué-la-Fontaine/Montreuil-Bellay.
A couple of other services from Angers serve stops along the Layon valley.

Tourist Information

Beaulieu-sur-Layon: 3 Rue St-Vincent, 49750 Beaulieu-sur-Layon, t/f 02 41 78 65 07.
St-Lambert-du-Lattay: Les Etangs de la Coudraye, 49750 St-Lambert-du-Lattay, t 02 41 78 44 26.
St-Aubin-de-Luigné: Place de l'Eglise, 49190 St-Aubin-de-Luigné, t 02 41 78 59 38 or t 02 41 78 52 98, f 02 41 78 66 34.
Brissac-Quincé: 8 Place de la République, 49320 Brissac-Quincé, t 02 41 91 21 50, www.brissac-tourisme.asso.fr.

Market Days

Vihiers: Wednesday.
Martigné-Briand: Saturday.
Thouarcé: Tuesday.
St-Lambert-du-Lattay: Wednesday.
Brissac-Quincé: Thursday.

Where to Stay and Eat

Thouarcé ✉ 49380
★★Le Relais de Bonnezeaux, Route d'Angers, t 02 41 54 08 33 (*menus €17–42; closed Sun pm, Mon, and Tues pm*). In the converted railway station, with panoramic views onto vineyards, this has a high reputation for its cuisine and vintage wines *Closed 2–20 Jan.*

Faye d'Anjou ✉ 49380
Au Logis de la Brunetière B&B, t/f 02 41 54 16 24 (*inexpensive*). These new B&B rooms are set in one wing of a lovely open farm courtyard, the buildings in typical local schist. The rooms are cosy and charming.

Grézillé ✉ 49320
Le Clos des Roches, Le Bourgneuf, t 02 41 45 59 36. Eat as many traditional *fouaces* as you can in this troglodyte setting (*book to eat here; menu €20, including wine and coffee*). *Closed Sun eve, Mon and Fri lunch.*

Brissac ✉ 49320
★★Le Castel, 1 Rue Louis Moron, t 02 41 91 24 74, www.hotel-lecastel.com (*inexpensive*). The owner of Le Castel has done wonders transforming a dull modern cement block of a building into a charming hotel with comfortably and stylishly presented rooms.

church. The bell tower didn't burn, however, and Revolutionary troops saved the Republicans in the belfry. On the way to Les Verchers you might notice the **Château d'Echeuilly**, a splendid 18th-century château on the banks of the river, which supplies water for the moat. Around **Les Verchers-sur-Layon** admire the vineyard valley scenery; you could think yourself in southwest France.

From here the Layon switches dramatically in direction, from northeast to northwest. Following the road to St-Georges, the vines grow on slopes that once produced coal. The chimneys and towers of the ruined château of **Martigné-Briand** strangely mark this place. This castle, dating from the end of the 15th century, was terribly scarred by fighting in 1793. Martigné produces a great deal of Cabernet d'Anjou rosé wine. On the opposite bank, the smart, walled properties show what a rich parish **Aubigné** was for many centuries. The 11th-century church of St-Denis has a surprising interior decoration of Italian grotesque paintings, done by Paolo Baronni in the 18th century. Just above these two villages, around **Faveraye**, the architecture changes with the geology, schist and slate taking over from limestone and tiles. The land around Thouarcé begins to undulate particularly sharply. Above Thouarcé lies **Bonnezeaux**, one of the Layon's two tiny specialized *appellations* which produce rare sweet white wines (*see* box p.384). From here north to the Loire you pass through the six wine villages allowed to add their names to distinguish themselves from run-of-the-mill Coteaux-du-Layon. Faye d'Anjou and Rablay are two of them. **Rablay-sur-Layon** has attracted a number of craftspeople to its **Village d'Artistes** (*open July–Aug and Dec daily exc Mon 2–6.30; April–June and Sept–Nov Thurs–Sun 2–6.30; free*).

Beaulieu-sur-Layon retains the choir end of a Romanesque church with a 12th-century wall painting of Christ in Majesty against a background of red stars. Around here, splendid views open up towards Les Mauges to the southwest. In that direction, **St-Lambert-du-Lattay** was devastated by Republican troops in the Vendée war. A chapel, statues and crosses stand in memory of this event, but for foreigners the main point of interest in the village nowadays is the **Musée de la Vigne et du Vin d'Anjou** (*open July–Aug 11–1 and 3–7, mid-Mar–June and Sept–mid-Nov weekends and hols 2.30–6.30; t 02 41 78 42 75, www.mvvanjou.com; adm*). This covers the history of the vine in Anjou from the Middle Ages to the 20th century with a well-set-out series of rooms and displays.

St-Aubin-de-Luigné, a pretty winemakers' village set in a vast amphitheatre of vines, has a good number of wealthy homes. People go boating on the Layon here in summer. Up above, you can take in the views from the belvedere at the Moulin Guérin. On the other side of the valley the ruined châteaux de Guerche look intriguing. The older **Château de la Haute-Guerche**, dating from the 13th and 15th centuries, was razed to the ground by Republican troops in 1794. This was the château whose lords claimed the right to a quarter of the production of the local vineyards, Chaume, which gave rise to the name of the *appellation* of that scarce sweet wine, Quarts-de-Chaume. The Layon runs into the Loire at Chalonnes (*see* p.427).

The Aubance

The Aubance runs north from above the troglodyte lands around Doué-la-Fontaine to the Loire below Angers, passing from the limestone lands into schist. Caves dug into the limestone rock line the road from Louerre to Grézillé. Up the gorgeous sloping valley here, the **Château de Pimpéan** (*open mid-June–mid-Sept daily 10–5; t 02 41 68 95 90 or t 02 41 68 95 95, www.pimpean.com; adm*) really looks like a big fortified farm. The original castle was built around 1440 for Bertrand de Beauvau, *sénéchal d'Anjou* and a friend of the Bon Roi René. It was much changed through time and had become terribly run-down in recent times, but a Paris impresario, Mme Tugendhat, has been bringing life back to the place. You get a little tour of some of the parts being renovated. The château's main attraction is the painted ceiling of the little chapel housed in one of the property's four corner towers. A very graceful Nativity scene stands out among the beautiful depictions, including angels and the animals representing the four Evangelists. This delightful room serves as the venue for a series of summer evening concerts by young musicians, preceded by a tour and a simple *foué* dinner.

The Wines of the Coteaux du Layon and the Coteaux de l'Aubance

In the **Coteaux du Layon**, Bonnezeaux and Quarts-de-Chaume are the crème de la crème, Anjou's answer to the sweet successes of Sauternes in the Bordelais. But these areas are minute. The Bonnezeaux *appellation* only covers 80 hectares, Quarts-de-Chaume still less, only 50 or so. Their wines are doubly rare then, as they're only produced from grapes painstakingly selected if and when so-called noble rot, *botrytis cinerea*, sets in late in the season. The resulting wines can be magnificent, only to be tasted after 10 years of ageing at the very least. The most famous address for Bonnezeaux is the **Château de Fesles** (*t 02 41 68 94 00, www.vgas.com*), dating back in part to the 11th century, but given the rarity of its sweet whites, you'll be tasting other Anjou wines if you visit it.

The more run-of-the mill Coteaux du Layon vineyards extend over quite some distance, covering around 1,500 hectares in all. They produce widely varying qualities of wines from the Chenin Blanc grape variety, dependent in good part on the lie of the land. To distinguish further particularly good territories, the Coteaux du Layon Villages denomination has been created to allow growers in six further parishes (Beaulieu, Faye, Rablay, Rochefort, St-Aubin and St-Lambert-du-Lattay) to stand out from the crowd. They have to achieve certain criteria, in particular making wines that attain an alcoholic strength of 12 per cent rather than the normal 11 per cent required. At Beaulieu, the **Château Soucherie** (*t 02 41 78 31 18, f 02 41 78 48 29*) is a good address to find good Layons, including Chaume, to be tasted in splendid cellars. Another property well used to receiving visitors is the **Domaine de Mihoudy** (*t 02 41 59 46 52, f 02 41 59 68 77*) at Aubigné-sur-Layon, the local produce giving good results.

The **Coteaux de l'Aubance** wines aren't widely known, unlike the neighbouring Coteaux du Layon. Mind you, production of this medium-sweet wine is minuscule, around 3,500 hectolitres a year. Peachy, with tastes of honey and hints of camomile or lime blossom, you could try it at the **Domaine de Montgilet** (*t 02 41 91 90 48, www.montgilet.com*), Juigné-sur-Loire, with its architecture which couldn't show better the shift in the region from limestone to schist. The Lebreton brothers are dynamic and enthusiastic and can offer a range of other Anjou *appellations* to taste.

Château de Brissac

Open daily July–mid-Sept 10–5.45, April–June and mid-Sept–Oct Wed–Mon 10–12 and 2.15–5.15; t 02 41 91 22 21; www.brissac.net; adm.

...un château neuf à moitié construit dans un château vieux à moitié détruit (a new château, half-built, in an old château, half-destroyed)
Description of Brissac attributed to the present duke

The Château de Brissac looks like a classical body trying to squeeze out of a medieval one. The clashing styles make Brissac a very peculiar hybrid but certainly give the architecture a dynamic feel. Built on a slope going down to the Aubance, the château is enormous, an unashamedly swaggering eccentric of a castle. It advertises itself as the tallest along the Loire Valley, reaching seven storeys in one part.

The two major medieval towers, what's left of the late-Gothic castle, date back to the mid-15th century. The schist stone mainly used in their building reminds you that at Brissac the so-called Parisian limestone plateau has given way to the Armorican *massif*. The openings, however, are surrounded by lighter limestone. In the left-hand tower the Gothic tracery of the chapel window stands out clearly.

The original Gothic château was built for Pierre de Brézé, a courtier who served both King Charles VII and, albeit very briefly, King Louis XI. He died in 1465, fighting to quash the Ligue du Bien Public rebellion against Louis. Pierre's nephew, who inherited the Gothic pile, sold it in 1502 to René de Cossé, a powerful minister under King Charles VIII. The same family (*see* box, overleaf), which has produced several illustrious members, has kept hold of the castle since then.

Charles II de Cossé wanted to mark his elevated rank on his château, and he and his architect, Jacques Corbineau, are, according to your taste, to blame or to be congratulated for the transformation of the family home. The main neoclassical wing and staircase are quite extraordinary in their detail. It seems as though no one was able to tell the architect where to stop. Just look at the windows of the stair tower above the main entrance, built like monumental gateways placed one on top of another. The Mannerist slate roof rises triumphantly above the medieval and adds further to the extravagant incompatibility of the effects. The architectural historian Marcus Binney very nicely described Corbineau's work as 'restless masonry'. Charles II's successor Louis then embarked on the new wing to the right of the main façade, a massive block rising to seven storeys.

Within, in the entrance hall, heavily decorated coats of arms press home the family honours. You then tour some of the splendid rooms, although you'll be relieved to hear you don't have to visit all 203 rooms the château is said to contain. The Grand Salon sets the tone with its 17th-century grandeur; it's highly decorated, with an ornate fireplace, coffered ceiling and Venetian glass candelabra. A Gobelin tapestry depicts Don Quixote, but most of the figures around the room are hard-headed family members who knew how to hold on to real power. The bust on the mantelpiece shows Charles II de Cossé. Several of the ceilings in the main rooms are painted, as in the Salle à Manger, the interlacing Cs referring immodestly to Charles de Cossé again. The wealth of decoration is too rich to take in on a guided tour, but you can't fail to miss the vast painting of the now vanished Château de Bercy, or the musicians' gallery.

Up the staircase, you enter the elongated Salle des Gardes, the ceiling beams all the way down painted with miniature pastoral scenes, decorative motifs and gilded putti. While gazing at bucolic views onto the Aubance from the windows, you'll note that even the shutters have been painted with further scenes. Splendid tapestries line the walls, some in lovely faded blues and greens. In the rich atmosphere of a crimson bedroom hung with gold and blue tapestries depicting the heroics of Alexander the Great in battle, the guide tells of King Louis XIII's little war on his mother, Marie de' Medici, and their connection with Brissac. Marie de' Medici was married to King Henri IV, and after his assassination served as regent from 1610 to 1617 while her son King Louis XIII was too young to rule. She surrounded herself with exploitative favourites, her Italian lover Concini the most notorious. She also advanced the young Armand du

A Model of a Courtly Family

The Cossé family offers a good example of pure *noblesse d'épée*, the military nobility of France's Ancien Régime, even if several members clearly also directed much attention to fighting battles with the fabric of their home. René's son Charles was conferred the title of count. The latter's son, Charles II de Cossé, went one stage better and became a duke, Brissac becoming the centre of his duchy. Charles II de Cossé turned out to be an impressive late 16th-century figure. A formidable fighter in the Wars of Religion, he was also reputed as an orator, and in the national crisis at the end of the 1580s represented the nobility in the meeting of the Estates General at the Château de Blois in 1588, not mincing his words with King Henri III.

Under King Henri IV, Charles II de Cossé would be rewarded with the highest honours in the land, as governor of Paris having opened the gates to the capital to the reconciling king. Charles became a *maréchal de France* as well as a duke, the two honours indicated by the symbols of the baton and the coronet respectively. Ian Dunlop, an historian of the Loire châteaux, even advances the speculative notion that he might have had higher ambitions still during the turmoil of the Wars of Religion – to become First Consul of a first French Republic. The time wasn't ripe. But in all, from his time, the family counts 13 dukes, four of whom became *maréchaux de France*.

Plessis, alias Cardinal Richelieu. When Louis XIII took power, he had Concini assassinated and banished his mother to the provinces, leaving her to govern Anjou. But her shenanigans here led the king to take action and he came to quell her rebelliousness, beating her troops at the Ponts-de-Cé, just south of Angers. Peace was sought, Richelieu acting as one of the mediators. The Duc de Brissac found himself caught between the two protagonists. He supported the king, but had already entertained the Queen Mother on several occasions at his château. It now served as the place where she and the king retired to make up properly after the public reconciliation at a nearby village. The best tapestries of all at Brissac remain protected from the light in the Chambre de Chasse. These 16th-century pieces were made in Flanders and show forest hunts after different wild animals, in minute detail. Rarely will you see tapestries of such refinement. Apparently they were once owned by royalty.

After the family picture gallery you get a chance for a quick sit-down in the theatre. Yes, without any hint of it on the outside, this château conceals a stage with auditorium for an audience of almost 200. This was incorporated into the castle on the whim of an absurdly rich 19th-century woman, Jeanne Say. Great-grandmother of the present duke, amateur opera singer, a friend of Gounod, Massenet, St-Saens, Debussy and Wagner, she had a floor removed from part of the château to indulge her passion. Abandoned with the First World War, the theatre was restored in the 1980s and its spacious, rich crimson setting serves once more. At the end of the tour you'll be taken down to the castle cellars for a wine-tasting, hardly much of an imposition.

In the picturesque **village of Brissac-Quincé** up the hill, you can see René de Cossé and his wife at the base of the stained-glass depiction of the Crucifixion in the church. You can then follow the broad meandering, wine-producing Aubance valley via St-Melanie and Mûrs-Erigné to the Loire.

The Loire from Saumur to Angers

Two utterly splendid stretches of Loire-side road compete for your attention between Saumur and Angers. You're strongly recommended not to miss either.

Saumur to Angers via the Loire's South Bank

After a scrappy exit from St-Hilaire-St-Florent, the D751 finds the wonderful, restful company of the Loire at Les Mimeroles. The road on to Gennes is delightfully wooded, offering tempting glimpses of the river through tree trunks and foliage. **Chênehutte-les-Tuffeaux**, the first in a string of utterly charming old Loire-side villages, has a 12th-century church much restored in the 19th. Joined to Chênehutte, **Trèves** is distinguished by the romantic ruin of a tufa tower, left over from a 15th-century fortress. Equally charming is the 12th-century Romanesque church of St-Aubin beside it.

Cunault

Neigbouring Cunault, like Trèves, once had a very active port on the Loire. It also had an important religious community. Christianity took root in the 5th century, when a follower of St Martin of Tours, one Maxenceul, who had set about converting the local populace, died here. His memory was later upstaged by the arrival in the 9th century of St Philibert's relics to escape the grasp of the destructive Vikings. The Vikings continued to advance further inland, however, so the monks ran off east again, carrying the saintly remains with them. By the start of the next century, some of the order were back. They had added to their substantial collection of relics, this time with a real whopper, a ring which had supposedly belonged to the Virgin Mary, plus a phial of her milk! It was enough to entice more than your fair share of medieval pilgrims, and a magnificent new church was built.

The belfry of the **priory church of Notre-Dame** dates from the mid-11th century. Some exceptionally imaginative stone carvings decorate its base, including a mermaid that looks rather like a nun with a fish's tail fighting a man in a Loire boat. A remarkable Annunciation also graces this belfry. But the bulk of the church you now see was built through the 12th century. The fortified elements on the west front were added in the troubled 15th century, although the Virgin and Child of the tympanum probably date from the end of the Romanesque campaign.

Descending the steps into the church, you peer into a vast tomb-like nave. On a sunny day, it's like a brief, dark vision of the underworld, the initial blackness within contrasting with the blinding whiteness of the stone outside. You enter one of the largest Romanesque edifices in western France. Once your eyes have adjusted to the dimness inside, the view towards the apse is elevating. The main church was constructed from the choir to the west end. The increasing richness of the carved capitals going westwards reflects the artistry that was developing in this period. A staggering number of scenes (more than 200, it's claimed) decorate the nave

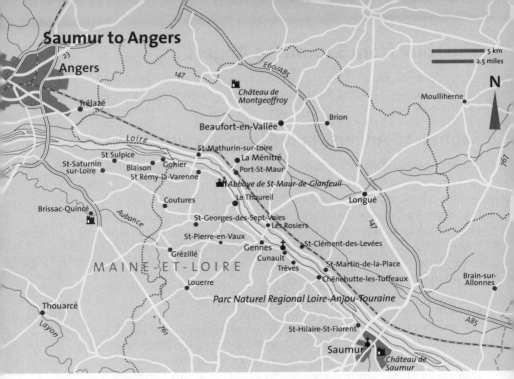

capitals. A bishop caught between two open-mouthed scaly dogs, dragon faces with gaping red mouths, men with legs splayed, vegetation covering their private parts, a choir of monks singing, combat scenes, armoured soldiers in preposterously precarious poses fighting a lance-carrying devil... these and many more show the medieval imagination fighting its monsters.

In the beautiful ambulatory, pretty plain leaves adorn the capitals. One of the apse's side-chapels contains St Maxenceul's reliquary chest, a beautiful polychrome piece with depictions of the Ascension, Pentecost and the apostles. To make a visit to Cunault's church even more uplifting, come during the *Heures Musicales* in July and August, when a concert takes place here every Sunday afternoon at 5pm.

From Gennes Towards Angers

Gennes, too, has its Romanesque legacy, with two early medieval churches, one either side of the Avort stream, but it also has a Gallo-Roman past. The remains of its **amphitheatre** (*open July–Aug Sun–Fri 10–6.30, April–June and Sept Sun and hols only 3–6.30; t 02 41 51 55 04; adm*) lie well hidden in woods south of town. The place was only officially rediscovered in 1847, excavated in 1985 and is still quite overgrown and wild. It may date from as early as the 1st century and could probably seat up to 5,000 spectators. The builders made good use of the hillside to install the seats overseeing the oval arena. Some parts of the chambers below the stage also remain. The theatre may have been destroyed by a devastating fire in the 3rd century, possibly caused by a revolt of Gaulish slaves.

From up by the **church of St-Eusèbe** you can enjoy a great view of the Loire. Also look out for a plaque recalling the vain but valiant resistance put up here by Saumur's cavalry trainees against the advancing Germans at the start of the Second World War.

Le Thoureil is a lovely village fully exposed to the beauty of the Loire. In summer, when the river dwindles in size, the children's swings planted in the firm sand banks make for a comical sight. There's even a Loire sailing school here. Prehistoric men liked the spot too; it's yielded many finds of tools, while menhirs and dolmens litter the hinterland. Now visitors from abroad seem to have colonized the Loire-side village, to go by the foreign car numberplates. That's nothing new; the 17th-century houses along the river bank were apparently built by Dutch merchants who came to trade along the Loire, exporting the local wines.

You can only appreciate the full extent of the grandeur of the **Abbaye de St-Maur-de-Glanfeuil**'s riverside façade from the Loire's north bank, and it can't be visited, but the late 17th-century building on the riverbank is superb. Continuing to **St-Rémy-la-Varenne**, the **Logis du Prieuré** may be run down, but it is very charmingly so. You can support the valiant efforts at restoration by having a look round at the carvings, including the monkeys at the entrance gate. Exhibitions are held here in summer.

The countryside around **Gohier**, **Blaison** and **St-Sulpice** is reassuringly peaceful. Various tracks lead down to shaded riverside spots opposite Loire islands on which birds fish. But here, the limestone gives way to schist, as you can't fail to notice in the architecture.

Artistic Treasures South of Gennes

Gennes has a hinterland of small delights. Seek out the enchanting Romanesque chapels at **St-Pierre-en-Vaux** and **St-Georges-des-Sept-Voies**. Contemporary artists have also created fascinating curiosities in caves in these parts.

L'Hélice Terrestre, L'Orbière (*open May–Sept 11–8, rest of year Wed–Sun 2.30–6.30, night visits in summer at 9pm; t 02 41 57 95 92; adm*), close to St-Georges-des-Sept-Voies, is a wacky troglodyte dwelling transformed into a work of art. Actually, there are several galleries of art here, created by the passionate Jacques Warminski, who died in the mid-1990s. One of his massive works in fact lies out of doors, a concretion of sculptures collected in a small amphitheatre. You can wander up around the science-fiction forms emerging from it. Underground, the sculpture takes on the warm light tones of the limestone. The entrance is like a spiral into the earth, hence the name of *l'hélice terrestre*. The caverns have walls covered with marvellous patternings. Whereas outside the shapes stand out, inside they indent the walls. Human forms have been set like shadows in the wall. Nothing is straight or clear down here. The narrow paths wind round in a head-spinning confusion. Shapes are turned upside down. Gymnastics seem a theme. The most fabulous experience awaits you in the Sphere, which emits a musical note when you stamp around in it.

The artist Richard Rak displays his intriguing works in his Etrange Galerie caves at the **Manoir de la Caillère** (*open May–Sept Tues–Sun 10–7, Oct–April weekends only 10–5; t 02 41 57 97 97; www.chez.com/artroglo; free*) in **Coutures**, just northwest of St-Georges-des-Sept-Voies. Rather than carving pieces into the rock, Richard Rak uses the

Getting Around

The **bus** service between Saumur and Angers offers you the choice between the south bank and the north bank routes, but there are only a few services a day. There are occasional **buses** to Beaufort-en-Vallée and Baugé from both Saumur and Angers.

Market Days

Gennes: Tuesday.
Les Rosiers: Monday.
La Menitré: Saturday.
St-Mathurin: Tuesday.
Baugé: Monday afternoon.
Le Vieil-Baugé: Thursday.
Beaufort-en-Vallée: Wednesday.

Tourist Information

Cunault: Mairie, Place V. Dialland, 49350 Cunault, t 02 41 67 92 55/t 02 41 67 92 70 (out of season).
Gennes: Square de l'Europe, 49350 Gennes, t 02 41 51 84 14, f 02 41 51 83 48.
St-Rémy-la-Varenne: Mairie, 49250 St-Rémy-la-Varenne, t/f 02 41 57 03 94.
Blaison-Gohier: Mairie, 49320 Blaison-Gohier, t 02 41 57 17 57.
St-Martin-de-la-Place: Mairie, 49160 St-Martin-de-la-Place, t 02 41 38 43 06, f 02 41 38 09 93.
Les Rosiers: Place du Mail, 49350 Les Rosiers-sur-Loire, t 02 41 51 90 22, www.les-rosiers-sur-loire.com.
La Ménitré: Espace André Pelé – Place Léon Faye, 49250 La Ménitré, t 02 41 45 67 51, t 02 41 45 63 63 (out of season).
St-Mathurin-sur-Loire: Place Charles Sigogne, 49250 St-Mathurin-sur-Loire, t 02 41 57 01 82, www.st-mathurin.org.
Brain-sur-Allonnes: 12 Place du Commerce, 49650 Brain-sur-Allonnes, t 02 41 52 87 40, perso.wanadoo.fr/tourisme.nord.saumurois.
Baugé: Place de l'Europe, 49150 Baugé, t 02 41 89 18 07, www.tourisme-bauge.fr.st.
Beaufort-en-Vallée: Place Joseph Denais, 49250 Beaufort-en-Vallée, t 02 41 57 42 30, www.beaufortenvallee.com.

Where to Stay and Eat

Chênehutte-les-Tuffeaux ⊠ **49350**
★★★★**L'Hostellerie du Prieuré**, t 02 41 67 90 14, www.prieure.com (expensive). The rooms in the converted priory hidden in woods just above the Loire are splendid, some with wonderful fireplaces. But be warned: there are also some hideous, if comfortable, maisonettes in the grounds. The views onto the Loire Valley are so spectacular from the luxurious terrace and dining room that the place makes a memorable stop for a special meal. Needless to say cuisine and Anjou wine list are top notch (menus €40–69). There's a swimming pool, tennis court and mini-golf in the grounds. Closed Jan–Feb.
Les Bateliers B&B, 28 Rue de Beauregard, t/f 02 41 67 94 49, bateliers.chez.tiscali.fr (inexpensive). Delightful atmospheric troglodyte suite as well as two rooms in the owner's typical limestone home by the Loire (table d'hôte €16; not available weekends).

Gennes ⊠ **49350**
★★**Aux Naulets d'Anjou**, 18 Rue Croix de Mission, t 02 41 51 81 88, f 02 41 38 00 78 (inexpensive). Peaceful modern hotel set back in grounds away from the road (menus €16–25; closed lunchtimes exc Sun, and Wed pm). Closed Feb–mid-Mar.

maze of corridors at his enchanting property as walls on which to hang his art works. Caves have often been places where remnants of older and different civilizations from our own have been discovered. Richard Rak's works seem to be constructed in good part from remnants and scraps he has culled from here, there and everywhere in modern society, but which he transforms to give a feel of a different culture. For example, he can make a battered old case look like the skin of a strange animal. The paintings, often involving collage, mix the playful elements of surreal and naive art into strangely intelligent, thought-provoking concoctions.

L'Aubergade, 7 Av des Cadets, **t** 02 41 51 81 07 (*menus €25.50–44; closed Sun pm out of season, Tues pm and Wed*). Distinguished Angevin cuisine served in a beamed setting. *Closed Feb hols.*

Le Thoureil ✉ 49350

Au Cabernet d'Anjou, 2 Place de l'Eglise, **t** 02 41 57 95 02, *remy-deretar@wanadoo.fr*. A former Loire mariners' bar, with a glorious terrace (*menus €17.50*). *Off season, only open lunchtimes Thurs–Sun.*

St-Rémy-la-Varenne ✉ 49250

La Riviera, **t** 02 41 57 02 19. A typical Loire-side *guinguette* (or mainly open-air restaurant with evening dances) right by the bridge to St-Mathurin, looking lazily onto the river and serving *fritures*, fried fish (*menus €23–28*). *July–Aug open every day, otherwise closed Wed, and all Nov–Mar.*

St-Saturnin-sur-Loire ✉ 49320

Auberge La Caillotte, 2 Rue de la Loire, **t** 02 41 54 63 74 (*menus €20.50–30*). Adorable inn up on the heights above the Loire. Splendid views over the valley to accompany good food and a good atmosphere.
Guinguette Chez Jojo, Chaloché, **t** 02 41 54 64 04. Go down to the Loire from St-Saturnin via increasingly small lanes and you finally end up on a rough track for this restaurant. The food may not be anything special, but this *guinguette* is all about the location, with hundreds of plastic seats set out under drooping branches in summer for diners to appreciate the Loire (*menu from around €19*).

Les Rosiers ✉ 49350

★★★Auberge Jeanne de Laval/Les Ducs d'Anjou, 54 Rue Nationale, **t** 02 41 51 80 17,

f 02 41 38 04 18 (*expensive*). The cuisine has made the name of this high-quality establishment. The comfortable rooms are in a grand building (*menus €30–70; closed Mon exc pm in season*). *Closed mid-Nov–Dec.*
★★Au Val de Loire, Place de l'Eglise, **t** 02 41 51 80 30, **f** 02 41 51 95 00 (*inexpensive*). Neat, smart little rooms and dining room with spacious round tables. The food is carefully prepared, using lots of fresh local produce (*menus €12.50–33.50; closed Sun pm and Mon out of season*). *Closed mid-Feb–mid-Mar.*

Brion ✉ 49250

Le Logis du Pressoir B&B, Villeneuve, **t/f** 02 41 57 27 33, *perso.wanadoo.fr/logisdupressoir* (*inexpensive*). Extremely stylishly modernized farm buildings, with very charming rooms, salons and garden. Located just east of Beaufort-en-Vallée (*table d'hôte €20*).

Bocé ✉ 49150

Le Chant d'Oiseau B&B, Les Rues, **t/f** 02 41 82 73 14 (*inexpensive*). Enchanting little place a short way south of Baugé, run by delightful hosts. This is a picture-book little farm with lovely blue shutters. The small rooms have been recently done up and are very cheerful, while the main part of the barn has been converted into a dining area (*table d'hôte €16*). You can also make the most of the hot tub in the garden.

Baugé ✉ 49150

Chez Elisabeth Forest, 2 Rue du Calvaire, **t** 02 41 89 80 85, *elisabeth.forest@wanadoo.fr*. Charming, newly done rooms in a white-stoned property tucked into a quiet street not far from the centre of town, and with charming little corners of garden.

Saumur to Angers Via the Loire's North Bank

While ancient cultural sites cram the southern Loire bank from Saumur to Angers, the northern one long lay uninhabited, vulnerable to flooding. It's still harshly exposed to the sun in summer, with few trees to offer any shade. The D952 along the north bank of the Loire is, however, probably the more ravishing of the two competing riverside routes, perhaps even deserving the prize for the prettiest of all stretches of road along the Loire. This is because it runs along the medieval *grande levée*, looking over to the gorgeous southern side of the river with its richer architectural heritage, limestone villages and churches peering out of the woods. The views of the romantic sweeps of the river itself are also unhindered by foliage. So you can appreciate the full glory of the river. With its islands and sandbanks, the Loire plays tricks on the imagination, making you think you're reaching the coast. In centuries past this was a busy shipping lane, many of the villages along this stretch developing thriving ports. Nowadays, in the middle of the river you may still spot the occasional reed-covered hut on the water, duck hunters' hides. The only marring aspect can be the weight of road traffic in summer; many cars slow to the pace of carthorses to take in the views.

North of the *levée*, the land looks flat as a pancake, the rich sandy earth producing excellent fruit, vegetables and flowers. This extensive river plain wasn't always so uncomplicatedly fertile. Henri Plantagenêt, in one of the most helpful decisions he took for the Loire, ordered the building of a very extensive bank – the *grande levée* – from Bourgueil to Angers in 1168 to hold in the river waters. Henri's plan wasn't totally disinterested of course. Any more cultivable land would also bring in tax revenues for him to spend on further adventures. The alluvial sands were certainly extremely well suited to agricultural exploitation. The Authion river runs along the flats north of the Loire, parallel to it, borrowing a bit of the wide valley. Before the *grande levée* was built, in flood periods, the Loire could spread out and join the Authion, converting this plain known as the Vallée d'Anjou into a massive stretch of water.

Stops Along the *Grande Levée*

The villages along the *grande levée* look splendidly sun-bleached in summer. The Loire dwindles in size in this season, exposing large sandbanks. Go down to admire the scene from the cobbled quays in the villages, reminders of how they used to thrive on river trade. They've now turned into popular Loire holiday resorts, with some delightfully situated camp sites.

Pass through **St-Martin-de-la-Place** and **St-Clément-des-Levées**, the latter with substantial quays, although the finest are probably at the next village, **Les Rosiers**, a thoroughly delightful place with a trellised iron bridge over the Loire and a church tower you can climb in summer for fine views. At the next village, **Port-St-Maur** by **La Ménitré**, you can go canoeing or boating on the Loire from the *base nautique*. Contact **Loire de Lumière** (*available daily May–mid-Oct; April weekends and hols; groups by reservation all year; t 02 41 45 24 24 or t 02 41 45 93 93 out of season, www.loiredelumiere.com*).

At **St-Mathurin-sur-Loire** you might stop at the **Observatoire de la Vallée d'Anjou** (*open July–Aug Tues–Sun 10–12 and 3–6; April–June and Sept–Oct weekends only 3–6; 1 Rue de l'Arcade, t 02 41 57 37 55, maisonloireanjou.free.fr; adm*) to find out more on the ecology and rich bird life of the area. Set in the disused railway station at the back of the village, the place doesn't look onto the Loire itself. But it does run organized ornithological trips from here; contact them well in advance if interested.

The D952 continues following the splendid stretch of river for several kilometres until it branches off towards Angers, the area then becoming rapidly more built-up.

From Beaufort-en-Vallée to Baugé

From the heights of **Beaufort-en-Vallée** north of La Ménitré, you can look down over the fertile plains back south to the Loire. This pleasing town has a fine church bristling with late-Gothic decoration. The **Musée Joseph Denais** (*open July–Aug 11–1 and 3–7, second half of June and first half of Sept Tues–Sun 2.30–6, April–mid-June and mid-Sept–Oct weekends only 2.30–6; t 02 41 57 40 50 or t 02 41 82 68 11 out of season; adm*) is crammed with the collections of a local journalist and writer from the end of the 19th century who, as well as compulsively amassing the kinds of treasures people store in their attics, also gathered old weapons and Egyptian artefacts.

Baugé can feel more than a little subdued outside its market day. It enjoyed its golden days many centuries ago, when Le Bon Roi René (*see* Angers) held the place in affection in the mid-15th-century. Foulques Nerra had left his mark here before him, mind, having one of his countless keeps built here, back in the 11th century. And earlier in the 15th century, in 1421, a significant battle in the second half of the Hundred Years' War saw the French carry off a much-needed victory after so many early setbacks, this a good few years before Joan of Arc came on the scene. Apart from the little château in the centre of town, Baugé's claim to fame is an exquisitely mounted supposed fragment of the cross on which Christ died.

The **Château de Baugé** (*open May–mid-Sept 10–6, mid-Sept–mid-Nov and Christmas hols 2–6; t 02 41 84 00 74, www.chateau-bauge.com; adm*) stands on the vast, vacuous market square at the centre of the town. Its rough, almost yellow façade gives it a pleasing look. It's essentially a 15th-century construction, built in part for Yolande d'Aragon, mother of René d'Anjou, in the 1430s and 40s, although René had much attention lavished on it through the 1450s and 60s – he loved to come out here on hunting expeditions.

Long the home to Baugé's town hall and gendarmerie, the interiors have recently been refashioned to introduce you to medieval Anjou, and Le Bon Roi René in particular. A smart tourist office-cum-boutique greets you in the big hall on the ground floor. Then you're led up a grand spiral staircase (only slightly marred by trite graffiti) to the attics, where Good King René (the commentary is available in English) introduces you in warm grandfatherly fashion to his period, and modestly presents his many achievements. Not only was he a major figure in French late-Gothic politics; he was also one of the finest of chivalric lords, sometimes nicknamed the 'Last of the Troubadours', his most famous work *Le Livre du coeur d'amour épris*. Down a flight of stairs, two further rooms pursue late-medieval themes cultural and political, recalling how important the counts and dukes of Anjou were even in the European context. Whilst it's good to be given really appealingly presented history lessons like this, René was not the paragon of virtue presented here (read on under Angers' history). Back on the ground floor, the Musée d'Art et d'Histoire offers a more classic array of local crafts, painting and pottery, plus some fine armour.

You can view what's said to be a tiny piece of Christ's cross at the **Chapelle de la Girouardière** (*open Wed–Mon exc major Christian festivals 2.30–4.15*). This extraordinary relic, with its two distinctive horizontal bars, is guarded in a room off an unremarkable modern chapel. A medieval crusader from Anjou, one Jean d'Alluye, was apparently given the fragment of the cross by the bishop of Crete by way of thanks for protecting the island. Jean d'Alluye returned home in 1241 with his invaluable relic and a parchment from the bishop of Constantinople vouching for its authenticity. But d'Alluye soon sold the piece to the monks of the Cistercian abbey of nearby La Boissière for 550 livres. Pilgrims flocked to see it and derive strength from it.

Some time later, because of the dangers of the Hundred Years' War, the monks took the relic to Angers for safekeeping under Duke Louis I d'Anjou. From 1359 it graced the castle chapel. Louis decided to embellish the cross on which it was mounted. The duke and his royal brothers adored gorgeous objects and King Charles V's Parisian jewellers were asked to beautify the object. Placing it on a gilded silver base, covering the top and arms with pure gold, they then went overboard, setting 17 rubies and 19 sapphires in it. The most exquisite parts are the two small statues of Christ on either side, his agony caught in solid gold.

Treasuring the cross in his chapel, Louis decided in the 1370s to make it the emblem of a new chivalric order, the Confrérie de la Vraie Croix. The form of the cross appears on the vast tapestry cycle of the Apocalypse he ordered, which hangs in Angers castle. His grandson René would adopt the cross as his symbol, placing it on his coat of arms and on his money. The cross stayed in Angers castle until the mid-15th century, when it was sent back to La Boissière. At the Battle of Nancy of 1477 between Lorraine and Burgundy in eastern France, the shape of the cross served as the banner under which the Lorraine troops fought, led by René's eponymous grandson, and after their victory, the cross became known as the Croix de Lorraine, the emblem of that eastern region of France. During the Revolution, the cross was taken from La Boissière and auctioned at Baugé. Anne de la Girouardière, founder of the hospice for the incurably sick of Baugé, bought it for 400 livres and it has stayed here ever since, although the community has changed to that of the Community of the Heart of Mary.

Why did a small Christian community spend so much money on what you might consider a vain piece like this, perhaps more appropriate for the posturing vanity and hypocrisy of princes? A document the sisters hand out offers another view of the relic: 'Christians venerate this vestige or tangible sign of the Passion of Christ of their Redemption. To all, this relic proposes reflection on the origins and permanence of our history and our civilization. Hail O Cross, unique hope, glorious cross of Jesus Christ. That in you all men may find grace and life!' In June 1940, at the start of the German occupation of France in the Second World War, the shape of the cross was adopted as the symbol of the French Resistance.

A series of churches with twisting spires marks the Baugeois countryside. The most obvious one stands out at **Le Vieil-Baugé**, a sweet old village next to Baugé, where the spire not only spirals, but also goes all crooked! **Pontigné**, a short way east of Baugé, has an equally startling church. Apart from the surprise of its twisted spire, the interior conceals splendid carved capitals and rich wall paintings of New Testament scenes by the wonderfully nicknamed Master of the Big Feet. Other of these delightfully eccentric churches can be seen at **Mouliherne** to the south and **Fontaine-Guérin** to the east. How or why these spires came about is not known for certain, although it may be that an accidental discovery of the technique led to its adoption.

Château de Montgeoffroy

Open daily 9.30–12 and 2.30–6.30; t 02 41 80 60 02; adm.

This is a rarity in the Loire Valley, an 18th-century château left pretty well intact. In fact the place has remained pretty well pickled in time. It was built on its gentle slope above the Authion west of Beaufort-en-Vallée for a very successful military man, the Maréchal de Contades, at a time when France was endlessly at war with Britain. The marshal only decided to rebuild the family property late in life, when he was already 67 and, as Commander-in-Chief of Alsace, not often at home. The architect, Jean Barré, was Parisian, but also worked on the Château du Lude (*see* p.167). While incorporating styles of the time, the plan also keeps some older elements to underline the ancestry of the family. The work was executed between 1773 and 1775, Louis XVI coming to the throne in 1774. The guide claims that some 4,000 workers were employed on the site. Two perpendicular wings run down from the main building. Each ends in a powerful, squat, conical-roofed tower, solid reminders of the 16th-century château. The chapel, too, dates from this earlier period. The exterior doesn't present a wealth of decoration. It's soberly symmetrical, the only sculpture on the outside the Contade arms in the pediment. But a wealth of detail lies within.

On entering the château you're greeted by the 18th-century marshal himself, beaming down at you, admittedly from a painting. This is still a proudly kept family home, full of refined period pieces and family portraits. The household inventory drawn up before the end of the 18th century has survived and, astonishingly for a French château, the rooms today still contain the furniture that was recorded at that time, most of it bought in Paris.

The Salle de Billard was deliberately designed to show two 17th-century Aubusson tapestries to good advantage. The Petit Salon Bleu served more as the games room. A portrait here shows the marshal's wife, whose father was president of the massively powerful Companie des Indes, France's equivalent to the British East India Company, which explains some of the exotic objects to be found later on the tour. The painting of Pompon, the couple's dog, a poodle of royal pedigree, rather curiously represented Anjou at the Seville Expo 92. Royal connections are emphasized by typical portraits of Louis XIV and chubby-cheeked Louis XVI.

The Grand Salon, set out with period chairs, the *bergères* broad enough to cope with the ballooning fashion of ladies' dresses, would have been the centre of social occasions. Apparently, seven different shades of grey were employed to decorate its walls. The quality of the original panelling and marquetry floors stands out. Plaster mouldings decorate this as well as the other ground floor ceilings. The Grand Salon contains more fine portraits, not only another picture of the marshal, but also one of his father, by Rigaud, in shining armour and fine periwig. The little boy of seven with a Boucher-like sweetness was the ill-fated Marie-Jean Héros de Seychelles, who briefly became a leading moderate in the French Revolution but was guillotined along with Danton in 1794, at the age of 35. Photos of contemporary family members and European royalty accompany these grand pictures.

The table remains permanently set in the most elegant oval dining room. The disproportionate size of the chairs was once again designed to accommodate the large dresses of the time. The plates bear the insignia of the Companie des Indes, while an exotic glazed earthenware stove takes the shape of a palm tree. Desportes executed the masterly still life, Van Loo the portrait of Louis XV, which has the place of honour here. It may surprise you to learn that formal dining rooms were most uncommon in the Ancien Régime – rather, *châtelains* would have movable tables set up in a room that pleased them. This dining room, therefore, was relatively innovative, but perhaps not surprising given the marshal's liking for food – he's credited with making foie gras the height of fashion in France. You then enter a series of private chambers with precious household objects displayed behind glass.

You see the very poshest rooms in the château, of course, but the inventory went into more basic detail, revealing even some of the differences in lifestyle between the staff. While a *valet de chambre* could sleep in a room adjoining the master's bedroom provided with, say, a canopied, upholstered bed, an ordinary manservant, for whom no bed is listed at all, would most likely sleep in the master's *garderobe* among the toiletries, on a straw mattress.

After the grand *salons*, you're taken out through the kitchen, supremely equipped with copper pans, to see the stables and saddle room. You finish in the chapel with its light vaulting, two bright rows of painted bosses and Renaissance stained-glass windows. It also contains a plaque commemorating the marshal's life. He died at the ripe old age of 91, surviving the Revolutionary Terror, just as his château would.

Angers

Angers

Hôpital St-Jean/ Musée Jean Lurçat 🏛 Ⓜ

Tour des Anglais ♟

PLACE DE LA PAIX

RUE DES CORDIERS-STEPHANS

RUE GAY-LUSSAC

BD D'AVIERS

PONT DE LA HAUTE-CHAINE

QUAI FELIX-FAURE

BOULEVARD ARAGO

QUAI MONGE

Abbaye du Ronceray/ La Trinité 🏛

RUE DE LA HARPE

RUE DE LA CENSERIE

AV DES ARTS-ET-MÉTIERS

BD DU RONCERAY

PLACE DE LA LAITERIE 🏛

PLACE GREGOIRE-BORDILLON

RUE BEAUREPAIRE

PONT DE VERDUN

RUE DE LA TANNERIE

BD HENRI ARNAULT

BD G. DUMESNIL

QUAI DES CARMES

QUAI LIGNY

PONT DE LA BASSE-CHAINE

BD DU GEN-DE-GAULLE

RUE QUATREBARBES

RUE DE L'ESVIERE

PLACE DE L'ACADÉMIE

Château d'Angers ♟

PLACE KENNEDY

Galerie David d'Angers ℹ️

RUE MARCEAU

RUE MAX-RICHARD

PLACE PIERRE SEMARD

Gare SNCF 🚂

PLACE DE LA VISITATION

RUE HOCHE

RUE DENIS PAPIN

BD DU ROI RENE

RUE DELAAGE

Maine

RUE DES GENEVIERS

RUE GAMBETTA

QUAI GAMBETTA

PLACE ST-SERGE

RUE THIERS

RUE MAILLE

RUE BOISNET

RUE MOLIERE

Gare Routière

RUE PARCHEMINERIE

RUE DE LA POISSONNERIE

PLACE DE LA RÉPUBLIQUE

RUE BAUDRIERE

RUE PLANTAGENET

RUE CLAVEAU

RUE BODINIER

RUE ROE

RUE ST-LAUD

PROM BOUT-DU MONDE

RUE ST-AIGNAN

RUE DU VOLLIER

RUE ST-EVROULT

RUE ST-TOUSSAINT

PLACE STE-CROIX

Cathédrale St-Maurice ⛪

Tour St-Aubin ⛪

Musée des Beaux-Arts 🏛

PLACE DE ROMAIN

RUE VOLTAIRE

RUE L. DE ROMAIN

Préfecture

RUE ST-AUBIN

RUE ST-MARTIN

RUE ST-JULIEN

RUE DELACROIX

RUE DE LA PREFECTURE

RUE DU HARAS

PLACE DE LA VISITATION

PLACE MARENGO

RUE DE BEL-AIR

Musée Pincé 🏛

PLACE DU RALLIEMENT

RUE CORDELLE

RUE DAVID D'ANGERS

RUE D'ALSACE

RUE GRANDET

PLACE LORRAINE

RUE PAUL-BERT

RUE DU COMMERCE

RUE DU CORNET

PLACE HERAULT

PLACE DU PILORI

RUE DU

PLACE IMBACH

RUE DES CORDELIERS

RUE DES URSULES

RUE CHEVREUL

RUE DAVID D'ANGERS

RUE LENEPVEU

MAIL

RUE J. GUITTON

PLACE DU GEN. LECLERC

Hôtel de Ville 🏛

BD DE LA RESISTANCE

AV DU 11 NOV. 1918

Jardin Du Mail

AV DU 8 MAI. 1945

RUE MARECHAL FOCH

BD DU MARECHAL FOCH

RUE HANNELOUP

RUE DES ARENES

RUE BRESSIGNY

RUE BECLARD

RUE DESJARDINS

St-Serge ✝

RUE DE BREST

RUE CHOUDIEU

BD AYRAULT

RUE BUFFON

AV MARIE TALET

RUE JUSSIEU

RUE BOREAU

RUE BARDOUL

BD CARNOT

Jardin Des Plantes

Centre des Congrès

Museum d'Histoire Naturelle Ⓜ

PLACE MENDES-FRANCE

BD DU MAL. JOFFRE

BD BESSONNEAU

RUE W. ROUSSEAU

Palais de Justice

RUE TARIN

St-Joseph ✝

N

250 metres
250 yards

Black Angers, Apocalypse Angers... the titles aren't reassuring to this city which saw the birth of the Plantagenet dynasty of western France and later, most famously, of England. The obvious English mispronunciation of the town's name makes the place sound unsettling too – but in French, the 'g' is soft, the word sounding closer to angels than angers. The town's nickname of 'black Angers' derives from its reputation for slate mining rather than a filthy character. The Apocalypse here comes in the form of two fabulous tapestry cycles, one from the 14th century, the other from the 20th, the first shown in Angers' heavyweight château, the second in surely the most elegant, as well as the oldest standing, hospital in France.

Angers doesn't quite lie along the Loire, but stretches across both banks of the Maine, a stocky tributary just north of it. Two chains used to be drawn across the river at night to stop boats trying to slip by and avoid paying taxes to the town. The river

Maine isn't always so easily controlled. Even in recent years, huge floods have swamped the lands north of the town. Most of Angers' historic sites were sensibly built on the slopes well above the river. The east bank rises particularly sharply, and it's here that you'll find the oldest part of the city, with the majority of the historic buildings, museums and shopping quarters. But even in the early medieval period, the town developed on the other side of the Maine, the mainly religious quarter on that side taking the name of La Doutre (a contraction of 'de l'autre côté', 'the other side'). The main draw on the outskirts of town is the Cointreau factory, but there's also a slate-mining museum and an early aviation museum, among further attractions.

History

As with Tours and Orléans, so with Angers – the centre of a Celtic tribe, the Andes or Andecaves, provided the site for the subsequent important Gallo-Roman centre. The town of Juliomagus oversaw a territory which became known as the Civitas Andecavorum. A good section of the fortifications of Gallo-Roman Juliomagus remain, built to protect the town from the advancing hordes from the east at the end of the 3rd century. A Christian community emerged maybe as early as the 3rd century too, but despite the known appointment of bishops who also held civic power in the 4th century, it was only in the 5th that a cathedral was built within the town walls. A number of religious institutions were set up in ensuing centuries: St-Aubin in the 6th, St-Serge and St-Martin in the 7th.

On the western border of the Angevin territory the Bretons would constitute a threat for many centuries to come, but it was the Vikings who wrought havoc in the mid-9th century. Pillaged in 853–4, occupied in 872, Angers was only liberated after a long siege by King Charles the Bald. After his death in 877, the Carolingian empire's central authority crumbled, and the regional counts set up under the Carolingian kings became much more independent. The Ingelgérien family took power in Angers and Anjou under Foulques le Roux in 898. He was the first in a string of Angevin counts to go by the name of Foulques, or Falcon. The most famous name in this line is Foulques Nerra, much blacker than the town from which he ruled. Angers expanded greatly under these galvanizing characters, the important new quarter of La Doutre growing on the west bank of the Maine. St-Nicolas was begun there around 1010, Notre-Dame de la Charité in 1028. The latter became known as La Ronceray.

The chroniclers of the period, ever so slightly prone to exaggeration, wrote of Foulques Nerra as 'another Caesar'. While his forebears had appropriated southern Maine and brought the counts of Nantes under their control, he took the Mauges, southwest of Angers, and then decided to expand to the east, clashing with the mighty counts of Blois, and taking over the Saumurois and most of Touraine by the time of his death. Towards the close of the 11th century, around 1089, Robert d'Arbrissel (see p.350), a charismatic preacher, came to Angers, where he taught theology for a time before founding his Fontevrist order, urged on by Pope Urban II, himself come to the city to rally support for the First Crusade. Foulques V, a formidable warrior who went on to become king of Jerusalem, also won the rather

Getting There and Around

By Air

The airport (t 02 41 33 50 00) is northeast of the centre, at Marcé. Regional Air Lines, t 02 41 33 50 20, runs internal flights to Angers-Marcé via the hub of Clermont-Ferrand.

For taxis to and from the airport, you can contact Taxi Marcé – Aéroport Angers-Marcé, t 02 41 33 50 00 or Accueil Taxi Radio – Aéroport Angers-Marcé, t 02 41 73 98 20.

By Train

The TGV between Angers and Paris takes 1½ hours. The train station, the Gare St-Laud, is just south of the centre.

By Bus

The gare routière (t 02 41 88 59 25) is beside the railway station. Anjou Bus, t 02 41 88 59 25, operates services in and around the city. Bus lines radiate out from Angers, serving Anjou quite well, except on Sundays, when there are very few services.

By Car

Angers lies on the A11 motorway, 'l'Océane', which comes down from Paris via Chartres and Le Mans. This continues on to Nantes. The non-paying alternative from Paris is to branch off at the N10 at Chartres and then take the N23.

A large amount of the A85 motorway between Angers and Tours has now been completed.

By Taxi

Beyond the airport taxi numbers above, you can try **Allo Anjou Taxi**, 5 Rue St-Martin, t 02 41 87 65 00, *www.alloanjoutaxi.com*.

Tourist Information

Angers: Office du Tourisme, 7 Place Kennedy, B.P. 15157, 49051 Angers Cedex 02, t 02 41 23 50 00, *www.angers-tourisme.com*.

Market Days

The main market takes place Saturday, from Place Leclerc to Place Imbach, with food, clothes and bric-a-brac on sale. The other most interesting markets for tourists are the Wednesday market in the Quartier Lafayette and the Thursday market in Place Bichon.

Festivals

The year starts with the **Premiers Plans** (*www.premiersplans.org*), the festival for first-time film-makers in Jan. Regional musicians come out to make music on platforms around town in **Tour de Scènes** for three or four days in May. June to July, Angers hosts one of the best French theatre festivals, the **Festival d'Anjou** (*www.festivaldanjou.com*). Throughout July and Aug the **Festival Angers l'Eté** offers a world music, classical music and dance programme, while **Les Accroche-Cœurs** presents street theatre and entertainment in mid-September.

Contemporary art can be seen at the **Salon d'Angers** in Oct–Nov, and there's a much-loved Christmas fair, **Soleils d'Hiver**, in Dec.

Where to Stay

Expensive

★★★**Hôtel d'Anjou**, 1 Bd M. Foch, t 02 41 21 12 11, *www.hoteldanjou.fr*. On a major, busy boulevard, a Best Western hotel with rooms renovated to quite a high standard. The **Salamandre** (t 02 41 88 99 55) restaurant

closer province of Maine (between the Loire Valley and Normandy) by marriage, and had a son called Geoffroy, nicknamed Plantagenêt because of his predilection for placing a piece of broom (*genêt* in French) in his helmet. Foulques V organized for his boy to be married in 1128 to Matilda, daughter of King Henry I of England, who also ruled Normandy at that time. Impatient upstart that he was, Geoffroy forced Normandy to accept his rule in 1144.

His son Henri Plantagenêt most famously married Eleanor of Aquitaine in 1152, after her divorce from the French King Louis VII. Eleanor's Aquitaine included not just the Périgord and Gascony, but also Toulouse, the Saintonge, the Angoumois, the Limousin

serves accomplished cuisine in a neo-Gothic setting (*menus €31–41; closed Sun*).

Moderate
***Hôtel Bleu Marine**, 18 Bd M. Foch, **t** 02 41 87 37 20, *www.destination-anjou.com/ bleumarine*. Slightly more basic than Hôtel d'Anjou, on the same boulevard (*menus €9–11.50*).
***Quality Hôtel de France**, 8 Place de la Gare, **t** 02 41 88 49 42, *www.destination-anjou. com/hoteldefrance*. Opposite the train station, which is an easy walk from the centre, a substantial hotel with a grand façade and rooms with decent facilities (*menus €17–51; closed Sat lunch, Sun pm and Mon pm*). *Restaurant closed 4 weeks July–Aug and over Christmas.*
***Mercure Angers Centre**, 1 Place Mendès-France, **t** 02 41 60 34 81, *www.mercure.com*. Reliable chain hotel (*menus €21*). *Restaurant closed late Dec–early Jan.*

Inexpensive
Hôtel du Mail, 8 Rue des Ursules, **t 02 41 25 05 25, *www.destination-anjou.com/mail*. The most characterful hotel in Angers, in a 17th-century town house set around a gravel courtyard. The place has a justifiably good reputation. Not only are the rooms atmospheric and good value, but the place is also well-run.
St-Julien, 9 Place du Ralliement, **t 02 41 88 41 62, *s-julien@wanadoo.fr*. Nicely located and central, with simple, pleasant rooms giving onto this lively square.
Continental, 12–14 Rue Louis de Romain, **t 02 41 86 94 94, *www.hotellecontinental. com*. Another friendly smallish hotel in the centre of town, this has recently been renovated.

Progrès, 26 Av Denis Papin, **t 02 41 88 10 14, *www.hotelleprogres.com*. Opposite the train station, a rather dull modern building but it's well looked after.

Cheap
Hôtel du Centre, 12 Rue St-Laud, **t** 02 41 87 45 07. An excellent central location for a cheap hotel, even if some of the rooms may be a bit run down. There's a brasserie attached.

Avrillé ✉ 49100
Le Cavier, Route de Laval, on the road north out of Angers to Laval, **t 02 41 42 30 45, *www.lacroixcadeau.fr* (*inexpensive*). Even if it stands just off a busy roundabout in the commercial belt, this unusual hotel built around a traditional Angevin windmill makes for a memorable stay. You can eat by the pool, but better still have dinner in one of the chambers in the heart of the windmill itself (*menus €17–32.50; closed Fri pm–Sun*). *Closed late Dec–early Jan.*

Eating Out

Moderate
La Rose d'Or, 21 Rue Delâge, **t** 02 41 88 38 38 (*menus from €25; closed Sun pm and Mon*). A diminutive restaurant which doesn't have a *menu*, but does offer a good choice of well-prepared dishes at reasonable prices.
La Ferme, 2 Place Freppel, **t** 02 41 87 09 90 (*menus €11.50–22.50; closed Wed and Sun pm*). Plenty of dishes incorporating Anjou wine at this popular restaurant with a terrace in the shadow of the cathedral.
Auberge Belle Rive, 32 Rue Basse de Reculée, **t** 02 41 48 18 70 (*menus from €15; closed Thurs

and Poitou! Henri suddenly found himself ruling an extensive Western European empire. A year later he forced Etienne de Blois, better known as King Stephen of England, to recognize him as the heir to the English throne and Henri Plantagenêt became King Henry II of England in 1154.

This expansion of power rather made Angers lose its position as centre stage for the Angevin counts. Geoffroy had already shown a preference for Le Mans in Maine anyway, while Henri preferred Chinon to Angers. He didn't neglect the family town, however, and had the superbly elegant Hôpital St-Jean built in the Doutre in 1175. Religious institutions would flourish in Angers under the Plantagenets, monks

pm, *Sat lunch and Sun*). By the Maine on La Doutre's side, chic cuisine and Cointreau-coloured materials at this bright, refined riverside restaurant.

Les Trois Rivières, 62 Promenade de Reculée, t 02 41 73 31 88 (*menus €14–26*). On the Doutre side again, with views of the Maine too and good fish on the menu. *Closed mid-Jan–mid-Feb.*

Le Lucullus, 5 Rue Hoche, t 02 41 87 00 44 (*menus €13.50–52; closed Sun and Mon*). Fish specialities in vaulted rooms. *Closed most of August.*

Cheap

L'Auberge Angevine, 9 Rue Cordelle, t 02 41 20 10 40 (*menus €6–24; closed Sun and Mon*). An amusing medieval-style restaurant, in a church with stained-glass windows. You can try *fouaces*, the local answer to pizza. Angevins come here for a laugh.

Le Petit Mâchon, 43 Rue Bressigny (a popular street for restaurants, east of Boulevard Foch), t 02 41 86 01 13 (*menu from €11; closed Sat lunch and Sun*). Simple, family-French restaurant.

Le Bouchon Angevin, 44 Rue Beaurepaire, t 02 41 24 77 97 (*menus from €10; closed Sun and Mon*). A pleasant option in a wine cellar in La Doutre.

For a range of cheap, ethnic restaurants look along the streets north of the cathedral: Rue St-Laud, Rue Baudrière, Rue Plantagenêt, Rue Parcheminerie and Rue Boisnet.

Entertainment

Cinema

Cinéma Les 400 Coups, 12 Rue Claveau, t 02 41 88 70 95 or t 08 92 68 00 72 (*€0.34/min*),

www.les400coups.org. For those who are passionate about cinema, classic films and foreign films in their original language.

Multiplexe St-Serge, 1 Av des Droits de l'Homme, t 08 92 69 66 96. New 12-screen complex in the central modern quarter of St-Serge, just north of the historic centre.

You'll find a clutch of further cinemas along Boulevard Foch.

Theatre

Grand Théâtre d'Angers, Place du Ralliement, t 02 41 96 12 80. Wonderfully over-the-top Italianate theatre with a diverse programme of cultural events. *Closed Mon.*

Nouveau Théâtre d'Angers Beaurepaire, 12 Bd G. Dumesnil, t 02 41 88 99 22. In La Doutre, another major theatre and cultural venue. *Closed Sun.*

Théâtre du Champ de Bataille, 10 Rue du Champ de Bataille, t 02 41 72 00 94. Lively new little theatre dating from the mid-1990s. Some jazz events too.

La Comédie, Rue Cordelle, t 02 41 87 24 24. Another successful little theatre set up in the mid-1990s. *Closed Sun.*

Music

Chapelle de l'Ancien Couvent des Ursulines, 175 Bd de Strasbourg, t 02 41 44 33 80. A Baroque music and Renaissance dance programme takes place in this Romanesque chapel.

Auditorium du Centre de Congrès, 33 Bd Carnot, t 02 41 96 32 32. The main venue for the Orchestre National des Pays de la Loire.

Le Chabada, 56 Bd du Doyenné, t 02 41 96 13 40, *www.lechabada.com*. Venue staging all manner of contemporary music concerts.

descending in great number on the town. Henri also ordered the building of a second bridge across the Maine. Tolls raised on river traffic provided substantial revenues and the bridge was covered with opulent shops.

The massive Angers cathedral was mostly constructed through the 12th century, with its fabulous new-style Angevin vaulting. Four Plantagenets would end up being buried not in Angers, but at the abbey of Fontevraud (*see* p.350). King John of England, Plantagenet heir after Richard the Lionheart, in fact came to besiege Angers when troops of his Breton nephew Arthur laid claim to the town. Much of the action in Shakespeare's play *King John*, pitting English king versus French, takes place under the 'flinty ribs of this contemptuous city' with its 'saucy walls'. Disastrously for the Plantagenet family fortunes, John would soon go on to lose his French territories to the French Capetian King Philippe Auguste at the start of the 13th century. In 1214, John returned to try to grasp back this land, but he failed at the Battle of La Roche-aux-Moines, just west of Angers at Savonnières.

Even after the Plantagenets, Angers remained an important strategic position, its protected promontory close to the Brittany and Poitou borders. Blanche de Castille, widow of King Louis VIII and regent for her son Louis IX, took a great interest in the town. She commissioned the building of a new castle in 1230 and had the city protected by a great wall on both sides of the Maine. Louis IX then made Anjou an appanage for his brother Charles in 1246. But this ambitious prince neglected Angers for his foreign forays. Spurred on by the pope, he concentrated his warring attentions on Naples and Sicily, he and his descendants laying claim to the royal title over these distant parts. Their main period of control over Sicily would be ended by the bloody Sicilian Vespers of 1282.

In the next century, King Jean le Bon of France offered Anjou as an appanage and dukedom to his son Louis. He vied with his brothers King Charles V, Jean Duc de Berry and Philippe le Hardi of Burgundy to see who could lead the life of the most sickening extravagance. Louis is the man who commissioned the 100m-plus Tapestry of the Apocalypse, among other little luxuries. But, under him, civic schemes were also encouraged in Angers, including the development of the town's government and of a university. The Hundred Years' War would distract attention eastwards along the Loire from Anjou, but the Battle of Baugé in 1421, not that far away, constituted an important early victory for the French in the second half of the terrible dispute before Joan of Arc hit the scene. Joan would be supported by Yolande d'Aragon, wife of Louis II d'Anjou, who extended the castle of Angers. Yolande and Louis produced a son called René, famously connected with the Angevin capital, where he was born in 1409.

René is commonly referred to as Le Bon Roi René (Good King René) in France, but he was never a king in reality. He simply inherited a claim to the kingdom of Naples and Sicily, which he tried, unsuccessfully, to make good. However, he did amass an amazing array of territories and titles, and became one of the best-connected figures in late-Gothic Europe. Through marriage to Isabelle de Lorraine at the beginning of the 1430s, he became Duke of Lorraine and Bar. On his brother Louis' death in 1434, he added the titles of Duke of Anjou and Count of Provence, as well as inheriting those claims to Italian kingdoms. As to René's sister Marie d'Anjou, she had been married to King Charles VII (see Loches) in 1422, and would produce the next king, Louis XI, the following year. This all left René with a finger in many a pie. His mother had supported Joan of Arc, and he continued to lend assistance to Charles VII in his battle to push the English out of France in the Hundred Years' War.

René is often portrayed as a model of 15th-century chivalric culture, encouraging artists, himself composing poetry and music, speaking a handful of languages, and showing enough sensitivity to introduce new flowers to northern France, in particular roses. He organized grand tournaments and created the courtly Ordre du Croissant (as in a crescent, not a pâtisserie). But while reorganizing the administration and taxation of his territories, in the general medieval lordly way he also bled his subjects dry with his extravagance and his grandiose dreams of kingship in Italy. After the death of his first wife, Isabelle de Lorraine, he married his popular mistress, Jeanne de Laval. He was often absent from Angers, but his administration saw to it that new plans for the city were executed, and significant changes were made to the château from 1435. He also encouraged the growth of the law faculty of the university. The dogged centralizing French monarch, Louis XI, however, challenged René's power, even confiscating Anjou for much of the 1470s, and managing to lay hold of Provence after Charles du Maine, the nephew to whom René left the province, died childless. But René's powerful daughter Marguerite d'Anjou would be married to King Henry VI of England, over whom she wielded great influence, playing a controversial part in the end of the Hundred Years' War and the Wars of the Roses.

Back by the Maine, Angers had been granted a new royal charter and acquired the first printing press in the Loire Valley in 1476. The city continued to grow commercially and academically. Many beautiful and grand late-Gothic and early Renaissance town houses were built by the wealthy in the region, such as the acrobatically carved Maison d'Adam, the more sober Logis Barrault and the ornamental Hôtel Pincé. Famous humanists studied here.

Trade prospered in the 17th century, as Anjou's wines and fruit were successfully exported to England and Holland. Naval sails and rope were produced in large quantities, using the hemp widely grown in the region. Slate, too, was being successfully quarried, both for local use and for export. The anti-Revolutionary tide which swept up in 1793 from the Vendée, southwest of Anjou, reached Angers, where fierce fighting occurred between the Republican army and the rebellious pro-Catholic, pro-royalist Vendéens (see Les Mauges and Cholet). A couple of thousand Vendéens were shot on Angers' Champs des Martyrs. The Revolutionaries wrought changes to the town's fabric. The Place du Ralliement, for example, replaced three churches. But much religious architecture survived. On a more edifying note, David d'Angers, the famous 19th-century sculptor born in the city, left a detailed record of the major French figures of the first half of the 19th century to his birthplace.

The 19th century wasn't particularly successful for Angers, but the city expanded beyond its medieval walls, destroyed to make way for the spacious boulevards. The railway reached Angers in 1849, leading to further urban development but also to the rapid decline of the port. Catholicism reasserted itself in a big way and a specialist Catholic university was set up by Monseigneur Freppel in 1875, its theology faculty becoming renowned in the country. Still today the Catholic university holds its own against the modern lay university.

During the Second World War, Angers was damaged by bombs, but in contrast to the big cities further east along the Loire, the historic centre remained relatively unscathed. Theatre bloomed with the creation of the Anjou festival, briefly managed by Albert Camus, then for much longer by Jean-Claude Brialy. With the installation of Jean Lurçat's tapestry of the Apocalypse, this art has also grown in importance in Angers since the late 1960s, while a young film-makers' festival encourages new talent. The town today is a curious mix between the progressive and the conservative. For visitors, it is underrated, full of interesting sights, and with an attractive centre.

Château d'Angers and the Medieval Tapestries of the Apocalypse

Open daily May–early Sept 9.30–6.30; early Sept–April 10–5.30; closed public hols; t 02 41 86 81 94 or t 02 41 87 43 47, www.monum.fr; adm.

This rough medieval pentagon is the most awesome of all the Loire Valley's military fortifications, better preserved and more intimidating than the enormous Château de Chinon even. The outer castle was built by order of Blanche de Castille between 1228 and 1238. The walls protect a high platform of land above the Maine. This corner lay within the Gallo-Roman ramparts and was the spot where the early Anjou counts had built a castle as early as 851, to defend themselves against Viking raids. This was also the site for Foulques Nerra's great hall, his headquarters of stone built in the early 11th century, but virtually nothing remains of them.

Seventeen massive towers stick out around the castle. They've been quite aptly compared to elephant's feet – only these measure between 40 and 60m in height, and are firmly planted in a wide dry moat. Most of the walls are made of local schist, repellent to invaders and not the most appealing of stone to the eye. To beautify the towers, bands of light limestone were added, imported from further east along the Loire. Originally, the towers would have been crowned with pepper-pot towers. They lost their heads as early as the Wars of Religion, to make way for artillery platforms. Peering down into the deep dry moat you can admire formal French parterres in one part, prancing deer in another. With the outer castle's dark penitentiary looks it is easy to imagine it playing the part of a prison from Louis XIV's reign on. Apparently, a good number of captured British sailors were banged up here. In 1856 the fortification came into the hands of the military, but by 1875 it had been listed a *monument historique*, protecting it for the future and handing it over to tourism.

Once across the drawbridge and through the formidably fortified gateway, you enter the extensive bailey, where you'll find a château within a château. Lightness prevails here. With its charming gardens and corners protected by the massive ramparts, you feel detached from the hoi polloi in this bailey. Unfortunately, signs of the cement age have left their ugly mark all too obviously in parts.

The inner castle goes back to Duc Louis I d'Anjou and the 14th century. Not a vast amount remains of the Logis Royal, which was mainly built by his successor, Louis II, and then extended for Le Bon Roi René with an elegant north gallery. René's gallery was completely devastated by bombing in 1944, so what you see is a postwar re-creation. On the guided tour, you only view a few rooms within the Logis Royal, and they contain virtually no furniture – the visit concentrates on the glorious tapestries. First, though, look into the Ste-Geneviève chapel, built for Louis II d'Anjou early in the 15th century. A light, airy room stripped of most of its religious features, it now contains a clear display of models of the château and explanations of how it changed through time. The rooms in the Logis Royal contain enchanting tapestries, giving a foretaste of the Apocalypse ones to come, although these ones are of later date. The guide describes the scenes being depicted, but also usefully explains the methods of making a tapestry, an art form that apparently arrived in Western Europe in the 12th century. A couple of the works illustrate miracles by St Maurice and St Martin. Texts in medieval script are included both on these and on the tapestries in the next room, flower-strewn *millefiori* made in Flanders around 1500 – it has been claimed that the little poems were the work of Good King René himself. Yet another tapestry cycle in a further room devotes its attention to Christ's Passion.

Tapestries of the Apocalypse

The major tapestry cycle at the Château d'Angers is housed in a separate underground bunker, a postwar monstrosity. But the massive medieval work, the most monumental decorative enterprise of northern European 14th-century art, is spectacular. To remind you a little of what this tapestry cycle is about, here's one telling piece from the *Apocalypse*, one of the nuttiest of the many raving biblical texts. Its great influence over the medieval imagination is reflected in the number of times it was interpreted in medieval art, although lords more traditionally commissioned tapestry cycles depicting courtly scenes or legendary tales.

In the *Apocalypse*, or *Book of Revelation* (well worth reading before any trip to see French medieval Church art), the evil dragon for a time overcomes the good. John narrates:

Then the dragon was enraged with the woman [delivered of a boy, the son who was to rule all the nations with an iron sceptre] and went away to make war on the rest of her children, who obey God's commandments and have in themselves the witness of Jesus.

And I took my stand on the seashore.

Then I saw a beast emerge from the sea: it had seven heads and ten horns, with a coronet on each of its ten horns, and its heads were marked with blasphemous titles. I saw that the beast was like a leopard, with paws like a bear and a mouth like a lion; the dragon had handed over to it his own power and his throne and his immense authority. I saw that one of its heads seemed to have had a fatal wound but that this deadly injury had healed and the whole world had marvelled and followed the beast. They prostrated themselves in front of the beast, saying, 'Who can compare with the beast? Who can fight against him?' The beast was allowed to mouth its boasts and blasphemies and to be active for forty-two months; and it mouthed its blasphemies against God, against his name, his heavenly Tent and all those who are sheltered there. It was allowed to make war against the saints and conquer them, and given power over every race, people, language and nation; and all the people of the world will worship it, that is, everybody whose name has not been written down since the foundation of the world in the sacrificial Lamb's book of life. Let anyone who can hear, listen; those for captivity to captivity; those for death by the sword to death. This is why the saints must have perseverance and faith.

Although the background reds and blues of the tapestries look jaded because they were exposed to the damaging effects of sun- and moonlight in the 1950s and 1960s, it's a miracle that this cycle survived at all, as its chequered history reveals. The work was commissioned by Duke Louis I d'Anjou in the mid-1370s. It should be recalled that tapestries were viewed as movable objects, transported from one place to another to be used for decoration, show and ceremony. This one, for example, is known to have been displayed in Arles, in the south of France, in 1400 for the splendid marriage of Louis' eponymous son to Yolande d'Aragon. When not on display or on tour, it was seemingly kept in a special *salle de la tapisserie*, where it was rolled up. René d'Anjou moved it to the castle of Baugé for a time to keep it out of Louis XI's reach, and left it in his will to the cathedral of Angers. Almost until the Revolution it was looked after by the canons there, and brought out for display in the church just four times a year.

However, the cathedral authorities became disenchanted with this difficult work, whose subject matter had become outmoded, not to say frowned upon, and they tried to sell it off in 1767. The trouble was that they couldn't find a buyer and the tapestry cycle was sadly neglected. After a brief period when it was confiscated during the Revolution, it was restored to the bishopric in 1806. But by 1825 the bishop found that it was too cumbersome and the work was cut into its individual panels. Various tales are told about the demeaning uses to which these were then subjected. The stories (some possibly apocryphal!) claim that certain sections served as horse blankets, others to protect melons and pumpkins from frost. The most decadent tale goes that some were used as bedside rugs. At any rate, many of the pieces were dispersed and maltreated, but the quality of the workmanship helped them to survive. One Canon Joubert came to the rescue in 1848 and undertook the monumental task of putting the tapestry cycle back together. Seventy-six out of the original 84 panels survived. The cartoons, or drawings, on which the tapestries were based were the work of King Charles V's court painter, or rather, his manuscript illuminator, Jean Bondol, otherwise known as Hennequin de Bruges, of the Flemish school. He apparently took as his inspiration illustrations of the Apocalypse from a 13th-century manuscript in Charles V's library. The tapestries were executed rapidly, in seven years, under the direction of Nicolas Bataille of Paris. The scale of the artistic enterprise may seem overwhelming at first. But there are sensible ways of viewing it in more digestible parts. The pattern of alternating background colouring stands out immediately, and certain recurring characters begin to emerge quite quickly.

The ensemble starts with a large vertical panel depicting Christ, John at his feet. Then the rest of the cycle is displayed, in the original sections of seven panels (as far as that's still possible), the number seven associated with divine will in the *Apocalypse*, with its references to the seven spirits of God, the seven seals and the seven angels who stand in the presence of God, trumpeting the punishments on wrongdoers. The narrator John stands by in all the panels, often under a kind of sentry box, and his reactions reflect the different tones of the scenes. The tale is essentially of the fight between Good and Evil. Originally, a Latin text in tapestry ran along the whole length, explaining the action. This has disappeared, but a little frieze decorated with comically innocent details from nature has survived, while the museum provides explanations on modern panels.

The panels can be divided into six main sections. In the **first section**, Christ comes, sword in mouth, to announce to John that he will receive the revelations of the Apocalypse. The 24 Elders who sit around God appear with the four Evangelists. The sacrificial lamb symbolizes Christ, while the horses and riders of the Apocalypse make their appearance. The monstrous creatures of the Apocalypse take on extreme attributes, such as a horse given a monster's tail and a dog's hanging tongue. In the **second section**, the seven trumpeting angels call out the plagues, John at one point hiding in horror in his sentry box. The angel with the book recording the names of those to be saved arrives, while St John literally gobbles up the messages from God to take them in properly. The **third section** tells the story of the witnesses come to spread the word of Christ. They are taunted and killed, but then resurrected. The angels under St Michael take on the dragon, St Michael depicted with the most beautiful of faces. The **fourth and fifth** sections concentrate in particular on the fall of Babylon, symbolized by the great vain prostitute – only two women feature in the *Apocalypse*, two extremes of good and evil, the one symbolizing the virtuous Church, the other vile decadence and irreligiousness, or Babylon and Rome. The just sleep, and the chosen are saved. The beast of the earth and the sea, the many-headed hybrid described in the quotation above, makes its extraordinary entrance, the devil's number six appearing on its tail, one of the many symbols with which this overloaded monster is charged. Finally, in the **sixth section**, Christ arrives dynamic and triumphant, long hair swept back, to push the evil into a lake of fire. The judges are put to work, while the devil makes a final terrible assault on the castle of the just. They resist and the New Jerusalem makes its magnificent apparition from the sky.

All the details in the Revelation to John had potential for many layers of symbolic interpretation, including the contemporary political reading of the persecution of Christians by the Romans, and the desire for the latters' comeuppance. Some recent commentators have detected what they believe to be pointed references in the tapestries to the early part of the Hundred Years' War with England. For example, in one or two spots, the guides can point to places where the evil knights appear to bear the helmets of English soldiers (look at panel 69 for instance). In panel 38, the sea monster might even be read as a symbol of the English crossing the Channel. Other enemies of France and Christianity may be evoked elsewhere, for example in panel 23, with its Saracen signs. The Revelation to John emphasizes rescue or salvation soon to come, and the overthrow of terrifying evil enemies who appear in so many guises. It is a text which carries a message of hope. Aspects of these tapestries could be interpreted then as both religious and political, emphasizing not just the eventual victory of Christianity, but also that of the supposedly divinely ordained French royal family, of which Louis was of course a part, against all manner of enemy forces: the English, the infidel, horrific plagues, and evil generally. The detail is absorbing, fantastical and fascinating, often distinctly weird, sometimes extraordinarily beautiful. You may notice the Cross of Anjou or Lorraine (*see* p.393) stamped on the series, symbol of the lord who commissioned the work. The tapestries were beautifully executed on both sides, so that both were worthy of display.

Before leaving the castle, take the time to wander through the bailey gardens or visit the delightful café at the eastern end, with tables beneath a weeping willow.

Cathédrale St-Maurice

Three towers soar up from the façade of St-Maurice, Angers' fearsome cathedral, a short way from the castle along Rue St-Evroult. It looks especially daunting when viewed from way down below on the Maine bank. A startlingly long stairway, cut through the old quarters in the 19th century, leads up from the river to the church front. The first cathedral on this spot was dedicated to a local bishop of the 4th century by the name of St Maurille. The change of name to honour the Egyptian Christian fighter Maurice (said to have been killed for rejecting pagan ritual at the start of the 4th century) only occurred at the end of the 12th century.

Most of the cathedral dates from that century, built on top of an 11th-century structure. The single west portal is filled with magnificent sculpture reminiscent of some of that at Chartres cathedral. Royal biblical figures count among the major sculptures, while lines of Elders of the Apocalypse and angels surround Christ and his apostles. Moving up the façade, you can't fail to be struck by the row of eight mighty statues below the towers. These formidable saints in battle gear are copies of the 1537 works by Jean Giffard and Antoine Desmarais, referred to collectively as the 'Galerie St Maurice'. They apparently represent St Maurice and some of the men who died with him. The Latin inscription below is translated as: 'Grant us peace in our time, Lord, and disperse those nations seeking war'. The three towers were added in the 1530s, but have been altered since.

Stepping inside, the cavernous church has a great aisle-less nave standing on just three broad bays. The place is admired in architectural circles for its domed ceiling, held up on graceful so-called **Angevin vaults** (sometimes known in French as Plantagenet vaults). Such was the success of their design that the fashion spread far and wide and quite affected the development of Gothic church building in the west of France from the end of the 12th century and through the 13th. A fine collection of **stained glass** dating from the 12th to the 15th centuries embellishes the bulky and sombre interior. On the north side of the nave look out for the three windows dedicated to St Vincent, St Catherine and the Virgin, with a deep intensity of colours and scenes. The most westerly north bay Virgin and Child from the early 13th century is another particularly imposing piece. The stained glass in the transept dates from the late medieval period; André Robin is the man credited with the glorious rose windows, made between 1434 and 1465. The south transept rose window shows Christ in Majesty, signs of the zodiac and music-making angels around him. That in the north transept depicts Christ's Passion, as well as symbols of the months and, it being Angers, the Apocalypse. The east window is also a reputed work of art, the Pietà added in 1499. Most of the remaining 13th-century stained glass of the cathedral has been gathered in the imposing choir. The depiction of St Martin originally adorned the west front. As well as a Tree of Jesse and scenes from Christ's and saints' lives, some of the glass tells the story of that great Plantagenet friend then foe, Thomas à Becket.

Several monumental furnishings embellish different parts of the vast interior. The altar of the 1570s, with its red marble columns and golden baldaquin, was the work of Denis Gervais, architect to Louis XV. The massive Gothic-revival pulpit, sculpted with symbols of the militant Church triumphant, was made in René Choyer's studios in Angers. The vast 18th-century organ is held up by colossal atlantes shown straining so much under the weight that they give the unnerving impression that the whole thing might collapse. Behind the altar, a sculpture of St Cecilia is a touching piece by the Angers sculptor David (*see* opposite). Caught behind the choir stalls are rare wall paintings of St Maurille, which can only be viewed on special tours.

Maison d'Adam

On picturesque **Place Ste-Croix**, just at the back of the cathedral, stands one of the most extraordinary and outrageous houses in the Loire Valley, the Maison d'Adam. You're unlikely ever to see a more splendidly carved building. It dates from around 1500. Half-men half-beasts, a mermaid and a three-balled man count among the weird wooden cast clambering over the beams of this remarkable half-timbered home. Biblical scenes also feature, Samson with his hand in a lion's mouth, and the Virgin Mary receiving her message from God. The house was known in the past as the Maison de l'Arbre de la Vie, and on the corner you can easily make out this Tree of Life, a superb work heavy with fruit. The statue in the middle of the square represents the late 19th-century Bishop Freppel, who looks nowhere near as amusing as the exuberant late-Gothic characters on the Maison d'Adam.

Musée des Beaux-Arts d'Angers

Open from summer 2004. For opening hours contact tourist office or consult www.angers.fr.

The Logis Barrault, one of the most splendid mansions in Angers, was built late in the 15th century for mayor Olivier Barrault. In the early 16th century, the house received Mary Stuart and Cesare Borgia, among other notable guests. The place was largely transformed in the 17th century. After the Revolution, it became home to the city's fine arts museum. It also received many religious items rescued from Angevin religious foundations. Long looking run-down, the museum was closed for many years to undergo a massive renovation programme, reopening in June 2004.

The religious collections include many highly decorated medieval pieces, crosses, croziers, chalices, dishes... Several items stand out for their splendid craftsmanship, including a crozier from the abbey of Fontevraud depicting St Michael and the dragon, and a mesmerizing tomb mask of a 13th-century noble woman, her beautiful horsey features captured in gilded bronze. Some splendid Limoges enamel work also draws the attention. The paintings include a small selection of *primitifs* (the name the French give to European artists pre-1500), most surprisingly not just Italian pieces, but also some made along the Loire. Among a few fine French courtly portraits, one supposedly shows Agnès Sorel, notorious mistress of King Charles VII, a beauty in pink holding a ratty dog, but the panel dates from the 16th century, well after her death. The refined likenesses of Queen Catherine de' Medici and her son the future Charles IX as a child are both thought to have been executed in François Clouet's 16th-century Loire studio.

But the period which gets the most exposure is the 18th century. This is explained by the fact the Marquis de Livois, whose acquisitions formed the core of the museum's original collection, was clearly titillated by the artistic tastes of his time. So you come upon an orgy of sugary *peintures galantes*, provided by the likes of Watteau, Boucher,

Van Loo, and de Troy, but all outdone by Fragonard's *Céphale et Procrie*, the raspberry nipples below the raspberry face hard to avoid. Chardin's still lifes offer some calming relief after all the flesh spilling over. But with Ingres' Dante-inspired *Paolo and Francesca* melodrama returns. After these excesses, the Angevin painters represented here come as a pleasant surprise, although Turpin de Crissé and J.E. Lenepveu tend to want to whisk you away to Italy. The beautiful *Vue du pont des Treilles à Angers* is apparently by an Englishman who went by the unlikely-sounding name of Jean de Fleury. A programme of major temporary exhibitions is put on each year at the museum, the wild exuberance of Niki de St-Phalle's work getting the reopening of the museum off with a bang in 2004.

Galerie David d'Angers

Open daily mid-June–mid-Sept 9.30–6.30, rest of year Tues–Sun 10–12 and 2–6; closed public hols; t 02 41 87 21 03; adm.

J'ai du marbre et du bronze pour le génie, la vertu, le courage héroïque. Je n'en ai point pour les tyrans (I have marble and bronze for genius, virtue and heroic courage. I have none for tyrants).

David d'Angers

Along **Rue Toussaint**, a pretty street lined on one side by the old city wall dating back in part to Gallo-Roman times, fine old houses look down from their protected platform above the wall. On the opposite side of the street you come to the **Eglise de Toussaint**, tucked away behind a walled entrance and a large portal. In part vandalized during the Revolution, this church lost its roof early in the 19th century and fell into a terrible state of disrepair. The town authorities restored it in the early 1980s, turning it into the Galerie David d'Angers, a museum to the glory of one of Anjou's most successful artistic sons, the sculptor after whom it is named. As so often in Angers, it's the architecture that first makes you gasp. However, no attempt was made to redo the lovely Angevin vaulting that the church was probably given in the 1230s, although the fine Gothic windows and some delightful biblical statues protected by stone canopies remain. The modern architect Pierre Prunet decided instead on a replacement roof of tinted glass and steel girders, allowing a beautiful light to fall onto the sculptures within.

The former church nave is cluttered with casts, the work of David d'Angers. Born in 1788, he was baptized Pierre-Jean David. Grateful to his home town for its early support of his endeavours, he referred to Angers as his mother and took its name in 1828. Going on to work in Paris, he sent back plaster casts of his output. The man who turned down the commission to sculpt Napoleon's tomb for the Invalides in Paris, David d'Angers was a man of strong principle, motivated by politics as well as art. In the mid-1830s he presented himself as a Democratic candidate in the Anjou elections. He played an active role in the 1848 revolution and was briefly mayor of a Paris *arrondissement* and MP for Anjou, but he was exiled with the coming of the Second Empire early in the 1850s. He once stated that: '*Avant d'être artiste, il faut être citoyen, voilà ma devise (Before being an artist you have to be a good citizen – that's my motto).*'

But it's his art for which he's remembered. David d'Angers won the prestigious French art prize, the Prix de Rome, in 1811, for the rather ungainly *Mort d'Epaminondas*, and went off to the Italian capital until 1816, where he fell under the spell of the classical influence and of Canova in particular. The original of the most famous of all his works, the funeral statue of Bonchamps, a hero of the anti-Revolutionary Guerres de Vendée, rises full of desperate hope from a tomb in the church of St-Florent-le-Vieil, west along the Loire (*see* p.427). But here you can view a copy of it along with the extensive collection of his plaster casts. D'Angers executed a great number of public monuments of major French historic personalities, and medallions of leading figures of the day. He was commissioned to portray many a famous native figure for individual French provincial towns: Johannes Gutenberg, the man regarded as the father of printing, holding a sheet freshly curling from the press, for the town of Strasbourg; Jean Bart, a slightly grotesque-sized corsair, for Dunkerque; Fénelon for Cambrai; Racine for La Ferté-Milon; and of course Le Bon Roi René for Angers.He also did many commissions in Paris, including, most famously, the pediment of the Panthéon (in this gallery reduced to one-third the real scale). Some of his early important commissions, for monuments to Bourcke and Foy, were made for the Père Lachaise cemetery in Paris, where he himself would be buried in 1856.

David d'Angers' medallions are displayed in the choir. Although generally much less dramatic, these works are finely executed and have the great historical value of illustrating many of the important figures of his times. Among them are the likes of Victor Hugo, Balzac, Lamartine, Chateaubriand, Goethe, Washington and Lafayette. D'Angers also executed, among others, a statue of Jefferson, while his rendering of Jeremy Bentham graces Senate House at the University of London. With or without visiting the museum, you can wander out into the pleasant **cloister gardens** by the church.

Hôpital St-Jean and the *Chant du Monde* Tapestries

Opening hours same as the Galerie David d'Angers; t 02 41 24 18 45; adm.

Across the river lies **La Doutre**. One sturdy tower, known as the **Tour des Anglais**, survives from Angers' medieval defences here. A great line of tall plane trees stretches down the Maine's bank, making this side of the river much more picturesque than the other, marred by a very busy road. Behind the towering curtain of trees you'll find one of the most beautiful of all early French medieval buildings, the **Hôpital St-Jean**.

This hospital is said to be the oldest one in France. The main **Salle des Malades** looks much more like a religious building than a secular one. It was built from 1175 for Etienne de Marsay, *seneschal* to King Henry II (Henri Plantagenêt), on the latter's orders, the charter stipulating that it should be governed by laymen. Some say this was one of the institutions Henry established in penance for Thomas à Becket's murder. The Salle des Malades is supremely graceful. Two rows of slender columns hold up the beautiful ceiling of Angevin vaults. The vaults look as though they've been filled with air to puff out like parachutes. The lightness of the architecture makes it hard to imagine the agony of the sick who were treated here. Copies of old engravings give some notion of this aspect of the building's past. The place did in fact serve as a hospital for seven centuries.

Although the hospital started out as a lay foundation, in the 13th century monks took over its management and a priory was built around it. The Augustinians may have been welcoming, the late 13th-century statutes promising a place for patients of whatever nation or religion, but they often had to cram in three or four people to a bed. The chances were that by staying here you would catch more diseases than you came in with. Apparently the medical treatment improved slightly when lay authorities regained control in the mid-16th century, but medicine in those days was still very much hit and miss.

The town built a large new hospital in the 1850s, and after that the Hôpital St-Jean served briefly as an archaeological museum. Nowadays, bits and pieces of the town's ancient fabric lie scattered in the garden at the front of the hospital, while within, the walls have been hung with the second stupendous cycle of Apocalypse tapestries in Angers, **Jean Lurçat's *Chant du Monde* cycle**. Lurçat came to Angers at the end of the 1930s and was profoundly moved by the Tapestries of the Apocalypse. He decided to embark on another vast series, this one interpreting man's potential for good and evil in the 20th century. Having looked closely at the medieval work, he revived some of the techniques used in that period's tapestry-making. These tapestries were woven at Aubusson in the Limousin region by the workshops of Tabard, Goubely and Picaud. The work commenced in 1957, but wasn't complete by the time the artist died in 1966. Of the 125m of tapestries planned, some 80m were executed. Rather than being inspired by a biblical text, the left-wing artist was moved by real things, such as the Hiroshima bomb and Champagne. You may find some of the imagery rather hackneyed and the colours garish, but the 10 panels certainly make a great impact. The violently bright colours almost shine out from their black backgrounds. The images are much more familiar and clear to us than those of the medieval Apocalypse. The positive gets the upper hand over the negative. The first four panels, however, are disturbing; the horrors scream out at you. In *La Grande Menace* (*The Great Threat*) an evil eagle flies overhead, while a bull ejaculates atomic poison over the globe. A man with an arc steers through this messy scene accompanied by his dog. *L'Homme d'Hiroshima* presents a terrible image of a man like a plucked bird, shredded by the atomic bomb. *Le Grand Charnier* (*The Great Charnel House*), a *danse macabre*, centres round a tank with skeletons. *La Fin de Tout* (*The End of Everything*) shows plant life dying under an ashen snow.

The tone then changes, with some of the images of the negative series recurring in a quite different context. *L'Homme en gloire avec la paix* (*Man in Glory and in Peace*), using the juxtaposed motifs of the globe and man again, also shows an owl of wisdom and feet bathing in the sun. *L'Eau et le feu* (*Water and Fire*) features the image of the salamander, surviving fire. The fish in pastel colours make for one of the most beautiful images in this cycle. *Champagne*, rather than being of subdued tastefulness, bursts out in unbridled colours, butterflies bubbling up the work. *La Conquête de l'espace* (*The Conquest of Space*) refers to Sputnik I, launched in 1956, the first artificial satellite to orbit the earth; the archer Sagittarius hits the bull's eye. *La Poésie* (*Poetry*) displays all the signs of the Zodiac. The series ends with *Ornamentos Sagrados* (*Sacred Ornaments*), a hymn to the sun and the planets, as well as to domestic life.

At the end of the Salle des Malades you can go through to see the **cloister**. The stern north and east sides date from the late 12th century, while the south side is 16th century. The **chapel** contains two differing types of Angevin vaulting, tomb effigies and stained glass of different periods cobbled together. Angers was chosen as the place to show Lurçat's cycle after the artist's death, and Lurçat's widow donated further works, to be found in a neighbouring building now housing the **Musée de la Tapisserie Contemporaine** (*same ticket and times as for the Lurçat museum; t 02 41 24 18 48*). This serves mainly as a setting for temporary tapestry exhibitions. It's worth wandering round to one last section of the foundation, the **Greniers St-Jean** on Place du Tertre, the 13th-century storerooms for the foundation. They have an extraordinary schist façade, while the sides are tufa.

While in La Doutre, explore its squares. **Place de la Paix** has several notable 17th-century houses. A short way south, **Place de la Laiterie** was the religious and commercial centre of the quarter in medieval times. The **abbaye du Ronceray**, or abbey of the Bramble Patch, dates back to Foulques Nerra's time, founded by his wife Hildegard in 1028 as a Benedictine establishment for women. Most of the buildings that have survived to this day are 17th century and house the Ecole des Arts et Métiers, a prestigious technical college. During special tapestry exhibitions, you can look inside the somewhat battered abbey church interior. The adjoining **church of La Trinité** has suffered from 19th-century over-restoration, but retains its pure Romanesque form on the outside, except for the addition by Jean de l'Espine of the 16th-century belfry. The most notable secular building on the square, the **Logis Simon Poisson**, boasts sculpted wooden beams which show off the wealth and generosity of the 17th-century pharmacist who commissioned it. The caryatids represent Science, Magnificence, Friendship and Generosity.

There are several possibilities for taking a boat trip on the Maine from the Cale de la Savatte in La Doutre. **Maine-Anjou-Rivières** (*t 02 41 95 10 83, www.maine-anjou-rivieres.com*) operates large boats from around March to October, with various cruises and meals on board possible. It also hires out small boats which don't require a permit to drive. **L'Union** (*t 02 41 42 12 12*) runs a sizable boat from May to September. For a smaller boat, try *La Doutre* (*t 06 82 86 89 27, www.e-angers.com/bateauladoutre*), plying the Maine's waters roughly between March and October.

A Walk Around Angers

The obvious point to start on a tour of Angers is in front of the castle and the tourist office on Place Kennedy. The statue clearly visible along the 19th-century Boulevard du Roi René off the square represents Good King René in chivalric dress which looks slightly comical today. Up on the north side of the castle, the **Maison du Vin de l'Anjou** (*open May–Sept Tues–Sun am 9–1 and 3–6.30, Oct–April Tues–Sat 9.30–1 and 3–6.30; 5 bis, Place Kennedy, t 02 41 88 81 13, www.interloire.com; free*) is a showcase shop for the wide selection of wines Anjou produces.

From the **Promenade du Bout du Monde** in front of the castle's entrance, head into the quietly atmospheric network of cobbled streets between castle and cathedral.

Walk down **Rue St-Aignan** and **Rue Donadieu de Puycharic** in particular to appreciate a fine array of late medieval and Renaissance houses. This little quarter also contains many buildings which once belonged to religious institutions settled close to the cathedral. After visiting the cathedral, pass round the back of it, through the delightful adjoining squares, **Place Freppel** and **Place Ste-Croix**, then go a short way along **Rue Toussaint**, which contains the Galerie David d'Angers. Branch off before the gallery on to Rue du Musée, where you can see the immense Logis Barrault.

Next you pass under the massive **Tour St-Aubin**, an isolated 12th-century tower which was never actually attached to other buildings; it was once part of Angers' most important Benedictine abbey. This institution, which claimed roots going back to the 6th century, was named after a bishop of Angers from that period. During the 12th century, the abbey expanded considerably to become one of the largest in western France. Most of the rest of the medieval abbey buildings haven't survived. They were replaced in the late 17th and early 18th century with sober architecture for the monks of the Congregation of St-Maur, who became very powerful in these parts. The abbey has long been used as the seat of local government – the Préfecture – for Anjou (or the *département* of Maine-et-Loire, as it's been officially known since the Revolution). During working hours, you can have a look inside at the cloister, which contains some wonderful little vestiges of Romanesque art in the form of carved capitals and fragments of faded wall paintings. In the vicinity lie the early medieval chapel and cloisters of St-Martin's (*not open to the public at the time of writing*).

From here, head up to the heart of Angers' central shopping district, **Place du Ralliement**, sparklingly clean following its mid-1990s renovation, several large 19th-century buildings surrounding the square, notably the extravagant late 19th-century **theatre**, with elaborate ceiling paintings by Jules Lenepveu, an Angevin artist also responsible for much of the excessive decoration inside the Paris Opéra. Shopping streets head out in all directions from the square. One of these streets, named after Lenepveu, contains the **Musée Pincé** (*open mid-June–mid-Sept 9.30–6.30, rest of year Tues–Sun 10–12 and 2–6; closed public hols; t 02 41 88 94 27; adm*). Behind the richly decorated Renaissance façade you can visit a surprising collection, with classical, Egyptian and Oriental works. Around this quarter, explore the lively network of streets, with their shops and restaurants. Rue Lenepveu leads up to **Place du Pilori**, where medieval public punishments were meted out. Parallel to Rue Lenepveu, **Rue St-Laud** has been turned into an appealing pedestrian street packed with shops and restaurants, tables spilling out onto the pavement in summer. Look up to admire medieval half-timbered façades along the way, as well as one Art Nouveau block.

East of Place du Ralliement, you hit the **19th-century boulevards**. Boulevard Foch, lined with modern cafés and restaurants, leads up to the **town hall**, which stands in front of the vast combined open spaces of the **Jardin du Mail** and **Place du Général Leclerc**, with the neoclassical law court (Palais du Justice) on the far side. Just off the square, down Rue Guitton, you'll find the **Muséum d'Histoire Naturelle** (*open Tues–Sun 2–6; t 02 41 05 48 50, www.ville-angers.fr/museum; adm*), with a large ornithological collection. Boulevard Bessoneau leads on up to Place Mendès-France, with Angers' conference centre straight ahead.

Behind the conference centre, the **Jardin des Plantes** is the botanical garden. The ruined church of St-Samson was attached to a Benedictine monastery, of which the **church of St-Serge**, opposite the gardens, has survived. It contains some of the most elegant of Angevin vaulting in the choir. Beyond it, you might explore the modern quarter of St-Serge, with some innovative architecture. West from here, the Pont de la Haute Chaîne crosses the Maine into La Doutre (*see* above).

The Outskirts of Angers

One of the most famous liqueurs in the world, Cointreau, is made in Angers. The **Cointreau factory and museum** (*open daily Feb–Dec; tours July–Aug at 10.30, 2.30, 3.30 and 4.30; May–June and Sept–Oct tours Mon–Sat 10.30 and 3, Sun 10.30, 3 and 4.30; Nov–April Mon–Sat tours at 3, Sun 3 and 4.30; t 02 41 31 50 50, www.cointreau.com; adm*) lies in the eastern suburb of St-Barthélemy-d'Angers. It's signposted off Angers' ring road, or *périphérique*. You come to a typical modern, uninspiring industrial estate, hardly a place to conjure up exotic Haiti, where the all-important green oranges for making Cointreau come from. Mind you, this former French colony is a difficult place to do business with, and is barely alluded to on the tour of the distillery and its museum, recently colourfully jazzed-up in bright oranges and yellows. Seville oranges are also used in vast quantities in Cointreau's preparation. Come on one of the 120 days of the year when distilling takes place and the factory is suffused with the most intense smell of the liqueur.

At the eastern edge of St-Barthélemy, the elegant 18th-century neoclassical **Château de Pignerolle**, set in beautiful grounds, contains a specialist **Musée de la Communication** (*open daily late Feb–mid-July, Sept–Oct, and weekends and school hols in Nov–Dec and Feb 10–12.30 and 2.30–6.30; mid-July–Aug until 7.30; special shows mid-July–late Aug Sat 8.30pm–midnight; t 02 41 93 38 38, www.musee-communication.com; adm*), where old radios, telephones and other means of communication have been collected together. Just south of St-Barthélemy, at **Trélazé**, you can visit Angers' **Musée de l'Ardoise** (*open July–mid-Sept Tues–Sun 2–6; mid-Sept–Nov and mid-Feb–June Sun and public hols 2–6; 32 Chemin de la Maraîchère, t 02 41 69 04 71, www.vousloire.com/museeardoise; adm*), or slate museum. You don't go underground, but you may be shown round by former slate miners and can often see an old-fashioned slate cutting expert, or *fendeur*, at work (*demonstrations at 3pm*), as well as looking round the museum, which covers the history of slate-mining in the region. Sculptural pieces made out of slate add an artistic touch. **Les Ponts-de-Cé**, southwest of Trélazé, has some pretty spots despite having been bombed in the war because of its important bridges across the broad Loire. It has a small museum dedicated to old *coiffes* from the region (*open July and Aug daily 10–12.30 and 2.30–6.30, April–June and Sept–Oct Sun and public hols 2.30–6.30; 4 Av Charles de Gaulle, t 02 41 79 75 75; adm*).

Northeast of Angers, at the airport at Marcé, the **Musée Régional de l'Air** (*open mid-April–mid-Oct Tues–Sat 2–6, Sun 3–7, rest of year weekends and school hols only 2–6; t 02 41 33 04 10, gppa.decollage.org; adm*) contains a substantial collection of early aircraft, including some pioneering pieces, all on display in a light, modern new hall.

The Loire from Angers to Nantes

20

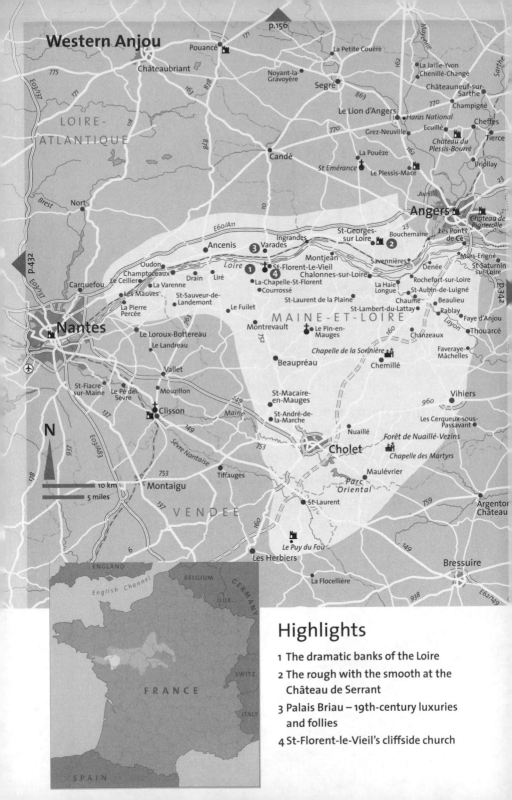

Western Anjou

p.156

Pouancé

Châteaubriant

La Petite Couère

Noyant-la-Gravoyère

Segré

La Jaille-Yvon
Chenillé-Changé

Châteauneuf-sur-Sarthe

Champigné

Le Lion d'Angers

Haras National

Cheffes

LOIRE-

Grez-Neuville

Ecuillé

Tierce

ATLANTIQUE

Château du
Plessis-Bourré

Candé

La Pouëze

St Emérance

Le Plessis-Macé

Briollay

Nort

Avrillé

Angers

Château de
Pignerolle

E60/A11

St-Georges-sur Loire

Bouchemaine

Les Ponts-de-Cé

Ingrandes

Ancenis

Varades

Montjean

Savennières

Denée

Mûrs-Érigné

St-Saturnin-sur-Loire

Loire

St-Florent-Le-Vieil

Chalonnes-sur-Loire

Oudon

Champtoceaux

Drain

Liré

La-Chapelle-St-Florent

La Haie
Longue

Rochefort-sur-Loire

Carquefou

Le Cellier

La Varenne

Courrossé

St-Aubin-de-Luigné

Les Mauves

St-Sauveur-de-Landemont

Chaume

Beaulieu

La Pierre
Percée

Le Fuilet

St-Laurent de la Plaine

St-Lambert-du-Lattay

Rablay

Faye d'Anjou

Nantes

MAINE-ET-LOIRE

Thouarcé

Le Loroux-Bottereau

Montrevault

Le Pin-en-Mauges

Chanzeaux

Le Landreau

Chapelle de la Sorinière

Faveraye-Mâchelles

Vallet

Beaupréau

Chemillé

St-Fiacre-sur-Maine

Le Pé de
Sèvre

Mouzillon

Vihiers

Clisson

Maine

St-Macaire-en-Mauges

St-André-de-la-Marche

Les Cerqueux-sous-Passavant

Nuaillé

Forêt de Nuaillé-Vezins

Montaigu

Tiffauges

Cholet

Chapelle des Martyrs

VENDÉE

Maulévrier

Parc
Oriental

Argenton
Château

St-Laurent

Le Puy du Fou

Les Herbiers

Bressuire

La Flocellière

England / English Channel / Belgium / Germany / (Lux.)

FRANCE

SWITZ.

ITALY

SPAIN

Highlights

1 The dramatic banks of the Loire

2 The rough with the smooth at the Château de Serrant

3 Palais Briau – 19th-century luxuries and follies

4 St-Florent-le-Vieil's cliffside church

The south bank route along the Loire from Angers to Nantes, with its dramatic roads high above the river, is more popular with tourists than the busy main roads of the north bank. But don't ignore the north side – it has its moments.

Before heading west along the Loire from Angers, we propose a detour into southwestern Anjou, an area deeply marked by its anti-Revolutionary past.

Southwestern Anjou

In southwestern Anjou, an area known as Les Mauges or the Choletais, when locals mention the 'Grande Guerre', the Great War, they may not be referring to the First World War but to the Guerre de Vendée. This bitter regional anti-Revolutionary uprising lasted from 1793 to 1795. Although the Vendée is a separate *département*, the southwest of Anjou was deeply involved in this painful civil war (*see* box overleaf). There certainly weren't celebrations here for the bicentennial of the French Revolution in 1989. Instead, Cholet, for example, organized a commemoration of the Vendéen War.

Cholet's history and art museum, a martyrs' chapel in the forest of Nuaillé-Vezins and the church of Le Pin-en-Mauges count among the sights most closely linked with this war in Anjou, along with St-Florent-le-Vieil. There are other, more light-hearted, things to see in the area, such as the surprising Oriental gardens at Maulévrier.

Angers to Cholet

Heading southwest from Angers, the N160 leads to Cholet. It passes close to **Chanzeaux**, which has a church containing stained-glass windows and frescoes recalling the Guerre de Vendée. In the vile war, the sacristan and friends hid up the tower as their village was being burned. **Chemillé** has a medicinal herb garden you can stop at, while the **Chapelle de la Sorinière** holds interesting 16th-century murals.

West of Chemillé, the stained glass in the church of **Le Pin-en-Mauges** tells the story of the Guerre de Vendée, notably the part played by Jacques Cathelineau, described as the *généralissime de la Grande Armée Catholique Royale qui fit trembler la Convention*. These partisan depictions of his fight against the irreligious evil of the Republic make him into a militant saviour figure. Where, you might ask, are God and Jesus in all this?

Cholet isn't an obvious stop, but it has unusual features, attractively presented. The **Musée d'Art et d'Histoire** (*open Wed–Mon 10–12 and 2–6; 27 Av de l'Abreuvoir, t 02 41 49 29 00; adm*) aims to recreate a feeling for Guerre de Vendée times, with weapons, maps, pamphlets, period objects and bold portraits of the main Vendéen leaders, commissioned by Louis XVIII. The town's fine arts collection is also housed in this building, the older works mainly 18th- and 19th-century French pieces. Cholet is associated across France with its chequered handkerchiefs, once produced here in vast numbers. At the **Musée du Textile Choletais** (*open June–Sept Wed–Mon 2–6.30, Oct–May Wed–Mon 2–6; Rue du Dr Roux, t 02 41 75 25 40; adm*), you can learn of the importance of textiles in Cholet's history. Cholet also serves as the dormitory town for the vast son-et-lumière of **Le Puy du Fou,** which lies just across the regional frontier, in

Getting Around

Buses from Angers to Cholet stop at Chanzeaux and Chemillé. There are also buses to Le Pin-en-Mauges.

Tourist Information

Chemillé: L'Albarel, Parc de l'Hôtel de Ville, 49120 Chemillé, **t** 02 41 46 14 64, *ot.chemille@wanadoo.fr.*

Cholet: Place Rougé, B.P. 636, 49306 Cholet Cedex, **t** 02 41 49 80 00, *www.ot-cholet.fr.*

Maulévrier: Parc Oriental, 49360 Maulévrier, **t** 02 41 55 50 14, **f** 02 41 55 48 89.

Beaupréau: Centre Culturel de la Loge, 49600 Beaupréau, **t** 02 41 75 38 31, *www.beaupreau-tourisme.com.*

Market Days

Chemillé: Thursday.
Cholet: Tuesday, Wednesday, Thursday and Saturday.
Beaupréau: Monday.

Where to Stay and Eat

Chemillé ✉ 49120

Auberge de l'Arrivée, 15 Rue de la Gare, **t** 02 41 30 60 31, *www.auberge-arrivee.com* (*inexpensive–moderate*). Cheap rooms and a pleasant restaurant set in a large town house (*menus €11–28; closed Sun pm out of season*).

Cholet ✉ 49300

★★★Château de la Tremblaye, Route des Sables, **t** 02 41 58 40 17, *www.chateauxhotels.com/tremblaye* (*expensive*). Stylish 19th-century pastiche of a Loire Valley château outside Cholet, on the site of the battle of Cholet in the Guerre de Vendée, with a decent restaurant (*menus €20–38; closed Mon lunch and Sun pm*). Hotel and restaurant closed 13–19 Jan and 3–9 Feb.

★★Grand Hôtel de la Poste, 26 Bd Gustave Richard, **t** 02 41 62 07 20, **f** 02 41 58 54 10 (*moderate*). Traditional-style, well-run French family hotel with restaurant (*menus €17.50–52.50; closed Fri pm, Sat lunch and Sun*). Hotel and restaurant closed late Dec–early Jan; restaurant closed 1–12 May.

La Flocellière ✉ 85700

Château de la Flocellière B&B, **t** 02 51 57 22 03, *www.flocellierecastle.com* (*expensive*). Just 7km south of the Le Puy du Fou, a dramatic amalgam of bits of castle from different periods, and surely the best choice near the big tourist sight (*table d'hôte €45*).

Maulévrier ✉ 49360

★★Château Colbert, Place du Château, **t** 02 41 55 51 33, *www.chateauxhotels.com/colbert* (*moderate*). A big, jolly, slightly tackily decorated but very good-value castle above the wonderful Oriental garden. Boasts a series of splendidly over-the-top *salons* to go with its very loud owner, who sometimes puts on his own shows with *dîners-spectacles*. There's some amazing wood panelling to admire along the main corridor outside the posher bedrooms (*menus €22–77*). Closed mid-Feb–early Mar and 3–10 Aug.

Nuaillé ✉ 49340

★★Le Relais des Biches, Place de l'Eglise, **t** 02 41 62 38 99, **f** 02 41 26 96 24 (*inexpensive*). Once a hunting lodge, this has been neatly done up, with a swimming pool in the garden. *Closed 30 Sept–4 May and over Christmas.*

Poitou. This is a major tourist draw. The artificial medieval village and attractions in the Grand Parcours are open during the day (*open June–mid-Sept daily 10–7, May weekends only; 30 Rue Georges Clemenceau, **t** 02 51 64 11 11, www.puydufou.com; adm*), with craftspeople in period costume. But the main performance, the Cinéscénie, takes place after dark on summer evenings (*early-June–mid-Sept Fri and Sat only at around 10–10.30pm*). The story once again revives the memories of the Guerre de Vendée. It was written by Philippe Devilliers, a highly popular right-wing politician in these parts, who rather disastrously stood for election as president in the 1990s. The evening ends with an impressive fireworks show.

The Guerre de Vendée

What sparked off the so-called Guerre de Vendée? First and foremost, the defence of the Catholic faith and the popular local priests, persecuted by the new Republic. Second, the execution of the king early in 1793 led to more protest. Third, the Republican authorities' attempt to enforce conscription by lottery of 300,000 bachelors across France aged between 18 and 40, what with the European powers menacing the French borders. This last act not only created deep and widespread resentment, but also caused large bands of rebellious young men to be gathered together. Riots broke out in many parts of France. While they were quickly stamped out elsewhere, incompetent Revolutionary forces in this part of western France failed to suppress the disorder. Resistance leaders had appeared from among the ordinary people, notably Cathelineau and Stofflet. Independently, certain aristocrats had led actions against the Revolutionary guards. In the course of the uprising, a few army officers would even join the Vendéen side, notably d'Elbée and Bonchamps. Republican troops came to quell the uprisings, but the Vendéen protesters enjoyed early victories, briefly taking control of Cholet, Saumur and Angers. Towards the end of June 1793 they attacked Nantes. But the old Breton capital resisted. With the death of Cathelineau – virtual leader of the chaotically ordered Vendéens by this stage – in Nantes on 29 June, fortunes were reversed. At the battle of Cholet in October, the Vendéens suffered a bruising defeat. Tens of thousands retreated northwards, crossing the Loire at St-Florent-le-Vieil. Bonchamp, their leader by this time, had been mortally wounded in action, but in a memorable act of mercy asked for the lives of 5,000 captive Republican soldiers to be spared. This act of forgiveness is interpreted in David d'Angers most famous and moving sculpture, at St-Florent-le-Vieil.

Southeast of Cholet, beyond reservoirs popular for swimming, water sports and ornithology, **Maulévrier** boasts a surprisingly luxuriant **Parc Oriental** (*open July–Aug 10.30–7.30, Mar–June and Sept–mid-Nov Tues–Sat 2–6, Sun and hols 2–7; night visits May–Nov; t 02 41 55 50 14, www.parc-oriental.com; adm*) below the Château Colbert (now a hotel), laid out with all sorts of Asiatic touches at the start of the 20th century in the steep Moine valley.

The Chapelle des Martyrs in the Forest of Nuaillé-Vezins

Si l'on pressait le sol comme une éponge, il en jaillirait le sang des martyrs (If you squeezed the ground like a sponge, the blood of the martyrs would gush out).
words of Pierre l'Ermite on the massacres in the Forêt de Nuaillé-Vezins

Take the D25 northeast from Maulévrier and then turn left onto the D196 to reach the **Chapelle des Martyrs** in the **Forêt de Nuaillé-Vezins**. This is a moving place for the descendants of the supporters of the Vendée uprising, deadly quiet. At the beginning of 1794, Stofflet had set up a well-hidden camp next to his headquarters to take in refugees running from the Republican *colonnes infernales* and to treat the sick. On 25 March the enemy, led by Grignon and Crouzat, two villains in local history,

The action then moved north of the Loire, in a campaign known as the Virée de Galerne. The Vendéens, under a young hotheaded would-be hero, Henri de La Rochejaquelin, general at the tender age of 21, swept into the province of Maine. The civil war entered a bloodier phase in the winter of 1793–4. Some 15,000 men were killed in the terrible defeat of the Vendéens at Le Mans in December 1793, and they suffered a further massive loss at Savenay, near Nantes.

Early 1794 saw the most awful devastation of the Vendéens' territories. The Republican leader Turreau was put in command of vicious troops, who tore through the rebellious lands into Vendée. These men were so destructive that they became known as the *colonnes infernales*. They tortured, killed, pillaged and burned as they went along, and many towns and villages across the Mauges were completely destroyed. Among the dispersed Vendéen leaders, Stofflet was the main figure in Les Mauges. He had established a refugee camp and hospital in the forest of Nuaillé-Vezins at the start of the year. A traitor gave away its whereabouts and the people there were massacred. In Nantes, Carrier organized ritual drownings of anti-Revolutionary protesters in the Loire. The mass anti-Revolutionary fighting would die down, to be replaced by the actions of small bands known as Chouans. In 1795 peace was negotiated between the Vendéens and the Republic and several treaties were signed, for example by Stofflet in May in St-Florent-le-Vieil, bringing an end to the major part of the war, although the Chouannerie would go on longer, particularly in Brittany. Some of the Vendéen leaders continued guerilla actions, but Stofflet and Charette were captured and shot in early 1796. Finally, in 1801, the Concordat passed laws guaranteeing Catholic freedoms. But the brutal repression of the Vendéen pro-Catholic Blancs (the Whites) by the Revolutionary or Republican *colonnes infernales* of the Bleus (the Blues) had left a terrible scar down this part of western France.

unearthed the population in hiding, given away by a traitor. The defenceless families were massacred. Behind the chapel (originally made for the Maulévrier Colbert family) you'll find a further modest chapel listing the martyrs' names, a touching reminder of the victims of a war too easily dismissed in France. The people of Les Mauges have certainly not let the atrocities be forgotten. Statues of the Vendéen leaders Stofflet and Cathelineau stand on the façade of the main chapel.

The Loire's North Bank from Angers to Nantes

Although the high-perched villages of the Corniche Angevine on the south bank of the stretch of the Loire between Angers and Nantes get more tourist attention than the north bank, there are some wonderful things to see along this route, from Bouchemaine to Le Cellier via the splendid Château de Serrant.

From Bouchemaine to Béhuard

Bouchemaine, or 'Mouth Maine', signals where the short Maine meets the Loire. You can easily reach the confluence from Angers; follow the signs to Bouchemaine and then the **Pointe de Bouchemaine**. Here you get expansive views onto the merging rivers, and can wander down to the very pleasant old cobbled quayside which recalls busier trading days. In winter and spring the expanse of water can seem almost Amazonian; in summer it dwindles considerably as the riverbank bursts into flower and the *épis*, or dykes, emerge. Fishermen colonize these *épis* or take to the water in little boats in the warm season.

Following the winding narrow rocky road along the Loire, you pass through **Epiré**, a charming village with a couple of churches and narrow walled streets. You're entering the very prosperous vineyards of **Savennières**, which produce a superlative dry white wine, one of the very greatest from the Loire, extremely exclusive. Many of the vineyards are enclosed behind high stone walls. The centre of the village has a sweet old Romanesque church. The TGV rushes by down by the river. Go down to the Loire to cross onto the **Ile Béhuard**, a delightful island named after a companion of one of the early counts of Anjou. The place is regularly submerged in winter, the houses finding themselves *les pieds dans l'eau*, their feet in the water. You can understand why the adorable little church here was perched on top of a rock. Pilgrims gathered here in centuries past to pay their respects to the local Virgin, who was supposed to look after the wellbeing of Loire mariners and travellers. The story goes that King Louis XI

Getting Around

A **bus** service covers the villages strung along the north bank. Ancenis is on the Angers–Nantes **train** line.

Tourist Information

Bouchemaine: Hotel de Ville, t 02 41 22 20 00, *www.ville-bouchemaine.fr.*
Savennières: 1 Rue de la Mairie, 49170 Savennières, t 02 41 72 84 46 or t 02 41 72 85 00 (out of season), *www.savennieres.com.*
Béhuard: Mairie, t 02 41 72 84 11.
Ingrandes-sur-Loire: Rue Michel, B.P.14 (in season) or Mairie, 49123 Ingrandes-sur-Loire, t 02 41 39 29 06 or t 02 41 39 20 21 (out of season).
Ancenis: 27 Rue du Château, 44150 Ancenis, t/f 02 40 83 07 44, *www.pays-ancenis.com.*
Oudon: Rue du Pont-Levis, 44521 Oudon t 02 40 83 80 04, *oudon.otsi@libertysurf.fr, www.ville-oudon.fr.*

Market Days

St-Georges-sur-Loire: Thursday.
Ingrandes-sur-Loire: Friday.
Varades: Saturday morning.
Ancenis: Thursday morning.

Where to Stay and Eat

Bouchemaine ✉ 49080
★ **L'Ancre de Marine**, 2 Place Ruzebouc, La Pointe de Bouchemaine, t 02 41 77 14 46, *www.la-terrasse.com (inexpensive)*. Hotel run by the same proprietor as La Terrasse, quite basic by comparison, with a bar below. But it's still well located, and serves food from the same kitchens as at La Terrasse.
La Terrasse, Place Ruzebouc, La Pointe de Bouchemaine, t 02 41 77 11 96 *(menus c.€16–53; closed Sun pm)*. The wide windows of this restaurant's bright dining room have a great view out over the confluence of the Maine and the Loire. It's a very good stop at which to try Loire fish and Angevin wines.

Béhuard ✉ 49170
Les Tonnelles, 12 Rue du Chevalier Béhuard, t 02 41 72 21 50 *(menus €20–91; closed Wed pm out of season, Sun pm and Mon)*. An enchanting stop on this secretive Loire island, with a deeply shaded terrace for summer dining. Fine fish dishes with wine sauces. *Closed 20–30 Dec and Feb hols.*
Notre-Dame, 12 Place de l'Eglise, t 02 41 72 20 17 *(menus from c.€14.50; closed Wed)*. May be much simpler, but its terrace also offers a delightful spot at which to sample Loire fish.

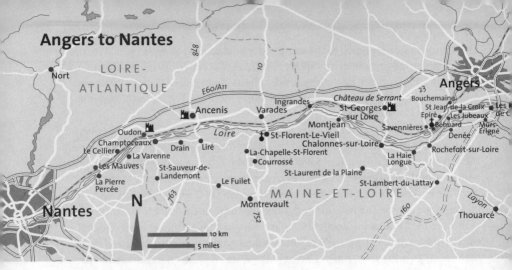

ordered the church after he narrowly escaped drowning around here. One section of the nave was quarried out of the rock. A couple of Virgins star within, while the chains of a galley slave are said to be an *ex voto* left in thanks by a prisoner of the Moors who escaped from captivity on the high seas. Back on the north bank of the Loire, from Béhuard you can follow a small but pretty route westwards, continuing along right by the river up to the bridge almost as far as Ingrandes. The more obvious but less attractive way from Angers to Ingrandes is the busy N23. This takes you right past the aristocratic gates of the Château de Serrant, just east of St-Georges-sur-Loire.

Château de Serrant

Open July–Aug daily 10–5.15, April–June and Sept–Oct Wed–Sun 10–12 and 2.15–5.15; t 02 41 39 13 01, www.serrant.net; adm.

Mixing the rough with the smooth (as is so often in the architecture of western Anjou) the outer sides of the Château de Serrant are built principally of irregular pieces of schist, with just the windows solidly surrounded by finely cut limestone. But within the courtyard, the walls are of pure tufa, blinding in the summer sunshine. This is a magnificent château, which really deserves to be better known. Though begun in the 16th century, work on it lasted more than 150 years, being completed in the 18th century, but the harmony of the Renaissance design was maintained. One Pontus de Brie, a chamberlain to Louis XI, had already built a castle on the site of an earlier one here around the 1480s. His grandson Charles decided on a remodelling of the family home. The name of the great architect Philibert de l'Orme has been linked to the plans, although there's no evidence of his involvement. The detail of the design looks rather sober and serious, Ionic pilasters on the ground floor giving way to Corinthian ones on the first. Further changes were made to the roof in the 19th century by the architect Lucien Magre. He added the dormer windows and the balustrade with decorative stone urns which runs round to the two southern towers. Topped by elegant, round, helmet-like slate roofs, each is crowned with a little domed observation tower.

One of the elements that points most strongly to de l'Orme's involvement is the splendid central staircase by which you enter the château, with its layers of openings, the last divided up caryatids. But first you're taken to see the **chapel** incorporated into the end of one wing. This grandiose room is associated with another of the most famous names in French architecture, Hardoin Mansart, who worked on Versailles. Inside, superb effects set the tone, black pilasters framing the white walls. The chapel serves as a mausoleum for the Marquis de Vaubrun, son-in-law of the second member of the de Bautru family to own the château; Guillaume de Bautru bought the property in 1636. The Marquis de Vaubrun died at the Battle of Altenheim in 1675. He is memorably depicted in a laudatory sculpture by Antoine Coysevox. He reclines, periwigged, togaed, semi-naked, seemingly unaware of the laurel wreath Victory has destined for his head. This chapel is a place charged with family emotion, heightened by the panels recording the deaths of five children from tuberculosis.

An exiled Irish family, the Walshes, became the next proprietors of Serrant. The Walshes had moved to Nantes, faithful to the fleeing King James II of England. Antoine, an arms dealer, acquired the home for his brother François. The stone arch gateway to the château courtyard carries the family coat of arms, with three swans, one pierced by an arrow. They recall the romantic legend of an ancestor wounded in battle and left in the water to die, who was rescued by two swans. François' son, also named Antoine, continued to support the Stuarts, financing two ships for Bonnie Prince Charlie to sail across the Channel in the course of his 1745 rebellion.

As you enter the château by its monumental stairway, the barrenness of the outer courtyard gives way to some sumptuous rooms, full of the extravagance of Ancien Régime noble living. Fine tapestries, paintings and a diversity of *objets d'art* adorn the rooms. The number of writing cases and writing tables gives the impression that these aristocrats spent their days writing letters to each other. In the Prince de Tarente's room you're shown how discreetly modern comforts were later installed. One corridor displays a genealogy of the very ancient noble family of La Trémoille, who married into the Walsh family in 1830. The finest rooms are on the first floor. The Grand Salon contains a marvellous set of tapestries specially made for this room, rich with forest scenes and fabulous animals. The Emperor Napoleon visited the château in 1808. He only stayed a few hours, but the room specially prepared for him has stayed intact, shrine-like to this day. The countess of Serrant of the time had been a lady-in-waiting to Josephine, but it's a bust by Canova of Napoleon's second wife, Marie-Louise of Austria, which looks out over the room.

From Ingrandes to Le Cellier

Ingrandes is the pretty, exposed village that marks the end of present-day Anjou on the north bank of the Loire. The *département* to the west is the Loire Atlantique, formerly an important part of Brittany, but since the changes in regional boundaries in the 1960s, part of the Pays de la Loire region. Ingrandes' extraordinary communal swimming pool lies on the Loire bank, or more accurately, in the Loire bank, as you'll see. Seen from the south side of the river, Ingrandes has a typical Angevin silhouette – portside slate roofs, a mill, a 19th-century limestone church and big bourgeois houses. Only the ugly modern block of the Ingrandes cooperative and the *château d'eau* slightly mar the picture. One of the grand houses is the Hôtel de la Gabelle, a reminder of the much-resented compulsory salt tax of the Ancien Régime. In Brittany, a salt-producing region, the *gabelle* wasn't payable; in Anjou it was often extortionate, salt costing up to ten times more than in Brittany. A police force made up of *gabelous* patrolled the border territories looking to catch the *faux-sauniers*, as the smugglers were known. You are on the *frontière du sel*, the old salt frontier.

The pretty village of **Varades** stands on the slope above the Loire. Below it lies the Loire fishermen's village of **La Meilleraie**. A plaque commemorates the death here from his war wounds of the Marquis de Bonchamps, considered a hero of the anti-Revolutionary Guerres de Vendée. Close to Varades, the **Palais Briau** (*house open April–July and Sept–Oct weekends 2–6, Aug daily; the grounds daily May–Sept 2–6; t 02 40 83 45 00, www.palais-briau.com; adm*) is a sumptuous brick and limestone château of the 19th century, commissioned by François Briau, a 19th-century engineer. He made his fortune planning the regional railway lines from Tours to Nantes and from Nantes to Pornic. He also worked in Italy, overseeing the construction of the Bologna–Ancona track. When he returned to the Loire, he decided to build his own *palazzo* along Italianate lines. The architect Edouard Moll planned the stocky building in 1854, following Palladian models. Inside, money was lavished on the stucco decoration, the elaborate wall coverings, the odd fresco and such features as the monumental staircase. But on the tour of the beautifully proportioned interiors, you also get an excellent feel for life at the cutting edge of design in France's Second Empire. Many pieces of period furniture have been retained, but the walls are also hung with paintings by the present owner.

In medieval times, Ancenis was an important Breton frontier post. The castle grew to substantial proportions through time, although it has long lain in ruins. Now Ancenis is most appealing to visit for its huge traditional market, which brings a good deal of life to its renovated heart. Ancenis has a **Maison des Vins** where you can taste and buy the local wines. Vineyards slope down to the Loire, producing **Coteaux d'Ancenis** (Slopes of Ancenis) wines. The wide local range includes VDQS wines made from Cabernet, Gamay, Pinot or Gros Plant. The Coteaux d'Ancenis Malvoisie VDQS is a rare sweet white made from either Pinot Beurot or Pinot Gris. The one wine given the added distinction of its own *appellation* in this area is the Coteaux de la Loire Muscadet. A many-sided keep rises high above the village of **Oudon**, visible from afar. It formed part of a medieval castle built here for the Malestroit family under Duke Jean IV of Brittany. You can climb the tower at certain times of year for superb views. You can also enjoy dreamy glimpses of the Loire from around **Le Cellier**, near which the Château de Clermont boasts the finest views of all. This mid-17th-century castle was owned in recent times by one of France's best-loved comedians, Louis de Funès.

The Loire's South Bank from Angers to Nantes

The most spectacular piece of road south of the Loire between Angers and Nantes is known as the Corniche Angevine – strictly speaking the stretch between Rochefort and Chalonnes – but further west, Montjean, St-Florent-le-Vieil and Champtoceaux all stand in dramatic locations above the Loire.

From Mûrs-Erigné to Montjean

You'll cross a confusing number of river-branches south of Angers to reach **Mûrs-Erigné**. The cliff of schist at Mûrs-Erigné was where the anti-Revolutionary Vendéen troops pushed 600 Republican fighters to their deaths on 26 July 1793. Surprisingly for this anti-Revolutionary region, a monument to the Republicans, in the form of Marianne, symbol of the French Republic, was put up here in 1889. **Rochefort-sur-Loire** could just as well be called Rochefort-sur-Louet, while its vines produce wines sold under the Layon *appellation*. From the Louet's island here, three brothers called St-Offrange caused chaos in the late stages of the Wars of Religion. The royal troops failed to dislodge them, so in 1598 King Henri IV bought peace with them, giving them positions at court. Their fort, whose remnants you can see, was destroyed, as Rochefort had been. The road west leads up to **La Haie Longue**, with its spectacular views – a picturesque place for the aviation pioneer René Gasnier to have set off on his first flights in 1908. To the south, the Layon river draws closer to the Loire, which it reaches at **Chalonnes**, where the Louet is also united with the great river. Down at Chalonnes' atmospheric old quays, Loire *barques* rest in the shade. The church practically has its feet in the water. This was where the new bishops of Angers used to come after their ceremony of consecration – the episcopal palace long stood in Chalonnes. Gilles de Rais, companion to King Charles VII and Joan of Arc, notoriously executed in Nantes for hundreds of child murders, was married here in 1422. From the quayside near the church you can look up to see a typical Angevin view, a windmill on the vine-covered hill above a curve in the river. To the south, **St-Laurent de la Plaine** has a substantial, well-presented museum devoted to old crafts, the **Cité des Métiers de Tradition** (*open June–Aug Mon–Fri 10–12.30 and 2.30–7, weekends 2.30–7; April–May and Sept Tues–Sun 2–6; t 02 41 78 24 08; adm*). In the Guerre de Vendée, half the inhabitants of this village died at the hands of the Republicans.

Montjean

From the top of Montjean, with its landmark neo-Gothic church, you can enjoy a typical view from the Angevin Corniche, with a tufty Loire island far below. The village descends prettily to the extensive Loire **quays**, from which a traditional **Loire *gabare*** sets sail regularly for tourists in the summer. Loire river trade forms the main theme of the scruffy **Ecomusée de la Loire Angevine** (*open Easter–All Saints' Day Tues–Sun 2.30–6.30; La forge, Rue d'Anjou, t 02 41 39 08 48; adm*). The place looks rather like a school crammed with sixth-formers' projects. Limestone, salt, coal, hemp, sails, wine, flour and sugar... all manner of important materials were shipped up and down the Loire around here, as is explained. Montjean had an important boatbuilding community. When the time came for the boats to be split up after service, their timber was sometimes incorporated into the local houses.

St-Florent-le-Vieil

St-Florent-le-Vieil is another clifftop village offering spectacular views next to its church. Little St-Florent has a long and notable history. It was a Celtic site and an early Christian one. The evangelical story has it that the hermit Florent settled here in the

Getting Around

Local **buses** stop at the villages along the south bank of the Loire.

Tourist Information

Rochefort-sur-Loire: Mairie, 49190 Rochefort-sur-Loire, t 02 41 78 70 24, *otsi.rochefort. sur.loire@wanadoo.fr*.

Chalonnes-sur-Loire: Place de l'Hôtel de Ville, 49290 Chalonnes-sur-Loire, t 02 41 78 26 21, *www.chalonnes-sur-loire.fr*.

Montjean-sur-Loire: Rue d'Anjou, 49570 Montjean-sur-Loire, t 02 41 39 07 10, *www.montjean.net*.

St-Florent-le-Vieil: Rue de Rénéville B.P. 54, 49410 St-Florent-le-Vieil, t 02 41 72 62 32, *off.tour.florentlevieil49@wanadoo.fr*.

Champtoceaux: Le Champalud, 49270 Champtoceaux, t 02 40 83 57 49, *champtoceaux.ot@wanadoo.fr*.

La Varenne: Mairie, 49270 La Varenne, t 02 40 98 51 04.

Market Days

Chalonnes-sur-Loire: Tuesday and Saturday.
Montjean-sur-Loire: Thursday.
St-Florent-le-Vieil: Friday afternoon.

Where to Stay and Eat

Rochefort-sur-Loire ✉ 49190

★★Le Grand Hôtel, 30 Rue René Gasnier, t 02 41 78 80 46, f 02 41 78 83 25 (*inexpensive*). Signals its discreet presence by palm trees. The rooms may be basic, but the cuisine is delicate, in summer served in the very pretty back garden (*menus €17–38; closed Wed, Sun pm, and Tues pm out of season*). Closed Feb and school hols.

Montjean-sur-Loire ✉ 49570

Auberge de la Loire, 2 Quai des Mariniers, t/f 02 41 39 80 20 (*inexpensive*). Really likeable unpretentious Loire-side inn, with good-value very tasty cooking and four rooms recently freshened up (*menus €16–33; closed Wed*). Closed 20 Dec–10 Jan.

Les Cèdres B&B, 17 Rue du Prieuré, t 02 41 39 39 25, *www.les-cedres.net* (*inexpensive*). Up in the town, a walled property with a pretty garden in which one cedar is left standing. The three stylish rooms carry the names of composers, a sign of the owners' passion for music. This is a cultured stop.

St-Florent-le-Vieil ✉ 49140

★★Hostellerie de la Gabelle, 12 Quai de la Loire, t/f 02 41 72 50 19 (*inexpensive*). In a fine location by the Loire, a traditional French

4th century to spread the Christian message. An abbey venerating his relics was founded by the 7th century, but Breton and then Norman attacks in the mid-9th century caused the monks to flee east, taking the saint's bones with them. They would only return some one hundred years later. However, a new abbey in honour of the saint was established just outside Saumur and the site of St-Florent relegated to a priory, albeit a powerfully independent one. The grandiose neoclassical **church** you now see dates in the main from the early 18th century. It was a survivor of the Republican wrath at the anti-Revolutionary movement. The architecture within is a model of Loire brightness. Typically for this pro-Vendéen area, religious thoughts are eclipsed by memories of the Guerre de Vendée, and the church contains a moving statue of a local hero: with windblown hair, veins standing out, the beautiful young Marquis de Bonchamps props himself up on his own tomb. The lower part of his perfect body, paler than a sheet, is draped with a toga. Bonchamps looks like a combination of classical virtue and a Christ of the Resurrection. His head is raised, his right hand stretching up to the sky in a powerful peace-making gesture. Below him, on the slab on which his body lies, are his words of restraint: '*Grâce aux prisonniers*'.

The sculptor of this sublime work, one of the most famous French sculptors of the 19th century, was David d'Angers (*see* p.411). His father is said to have been among the

provincial hotel in bright stone. The interiors are a bit old fashioned. There are some delicious sauces on the menu (*menus €13–38; closed Fri pm, Sun pm and Mon lunch*).

La Chapelle-St-Florent ✉ 49410
Le Moulin d'Epinay, Rue de l'Evre, t/f 02 41 72 70 70 (*menus €18–34*). You can try the flour produced by this windmill in crêpes and *galettes* at the modern restaurant in front of it which enjoys spectacular views. There's also traditional cuisine on offer. *Closed Mon, plus Tues eve and Wed eve in winter.*

Drain ✉ 49530
Le Mésangeau B&B, t 02 40 98 21 57, f 02 40 98 28 62, *www.anjou-et-loire.com/mesangeau* (*moderate*). An enormous, long, 19th-century farm building on the scale of a castle, with big, square, beamed rooms and well-kitted-out bathrooms, run by an energetic couple who will look after you over dinner, too, if you reserve in advance (*table d'hôte €25*).

Champtoceaux ✉ 49270
★★★**Les Jardins de la Forge**, 1 Place des Piliers, t 02 40 83 56 23, *www.jardins-de-la-forge.com* (*expensive*). The most highly reputed restaurant in the area. People come from far and wide to sample Paul Pauvert's cuisine, some particularly delicate fish

sauces among the specialities (*menus €30–78; closed Sun pm–Tues*). All is beautifully prepared in the stylish contemporary dining rooms. A few superbly designed and air-conditioned rooms are now available in the dull-looking house opposite the restaurant. There's a pool too, by the cemetery! *Closed 1–15 Mar and 1–15 Oct.*

★★**Chez Claudie**, Le Cul du Moulin, t 02 40 83 52 38, f 02 40 83 59 72 (*inexpensive*). Some rooms with views of the Loire in this quite characterful, traditional French hotel down the slope below the town (*menus €11–34; closed Sun eve and Wed*).

★★**Le Champalud**, Promenade du Champalud, t 02 40 83 50 09, *www.lechampalud.fr.st*, *www.membres.lycos.fr/champalud* (*moderate*). Good restaurant with French country cooking in a rustic setting. The basic rooms are being redone (*menus €11–42; closed Sun pm Oct–Easter*).

St-Sauveur-de-Landemont ✉ 49270
★★★★**Château de la Colaissière**, t 02 40 98 75 04, *www.chateauxhotels.com/colaissiere* (*expensive*). Splendid medieval castle behind fortified farm walls. Very smart rooms and sumptuous cuisine. Heated pool and tennis court in the grounds (*menus €28–59; closed Sun and Mon out of season*). *Closed most of Jan.*

Republican prisoners saved by Bonchamps' clemency. Take the monumental internal staircase down into the blinding neo-Gothic **crypt**, which has been turned into something of a museum, attractively exhibiting old stones from St-Florent, religious finery, and some relics of the saint himself. The church and its gardens serve as the setting for a highly regarded programme of music concerts in July. The local museum, the **Musée d'Histoire Locale et des Guerres de Vendée** (*open July–mid-Sept 2.30–6.30, early April–June and mid-Sept–early Oct weekends only 2.30–6.30; Place Marie Sourice, t 02 41 72 62 32, or t 02 41 72 50 39 out of season; adm*), set in a former 17th-century chapel, pursues the themes of the war of Vendée and Loire trade.

Beyond St-Florent-le-Vieil towards Nantes

At **La Chapelle-St-Florent**, the **Moulin de l'Epinay** (*July–Aug Tues–Fri 10–12.30 and 2.30–6.30, Sat and Sun 2.30–6.30; then 2.30–6.30 in May Tues–Fri and Sun, in June and Sept Tues–Sun, in Mar–April and Oct Sun only; t 02 41 72 73 33, www.moulinepinay.com; adm*) stands out in a spot with fantastic views, 18 church towers visible from it on clear days. Built in the mid-19th century, this towering windmill was restored by enthusiasts in the parish and started producing flour again in 1989. A small museum recalls the huge number of windmills that turned in Anjou in the past. Nearby, at the **Cirque de Courrossé**, the Evre river has formed a dramatic amphitheatre of slopes which you can walk down; the Catholic Church turned the delightful path into something of a religious route. Just a short way further southwest, the village of **Le Fuilet** is devoted to pottery. Visit the **Maison du Potier** (*open July–Aug Tues–Fri 10.30–12.30 and 2.30–6.30, Sat–Mon 2.30–6.30; April–June and Sept Sun only 3–6.30; 2 Rue des Recoins, t 02 41 70 90 21, www.maisondupotier.com; adm*) to appreciate the local tradition.

Back close to the Loire, the sleepy village of **Liré** is proud of its connections with a great 16th-century French poet, a native of the area, and has seen the **Musée Joachim du Bellay** (*open July–Aug Wed–Sun 10.30–12.30 and 2.30–6, Tues 2.30–6; April–June and Sept–Oct Wed–Fri and Sun 10.30–12.30 and 2.30–6, Tues and Sat 2.30–6; 1 Rue Ronsard, t 02 40 09 04 13, www.musee-du-bellay.fr.st; adm*) devoted to him recently brought into the modern age. The poet was actually born at the Château de la Turmelière, now a picturesque ruin just west of Liré. But the substantial 16th-century village mansion holding his museum is a fitting place to remember him. From an illustrious Angevin family, with many members who became important military and religious figures in France, he was able to travel widely, notably to Italy, which features prominently in his poems. But he was disillusioned by what he discovered in the capital of the Catholic Church, finding Rome the capital of vanity and corruption; in contrast, he found his native Anjou a joy. However, his works are beautifully crafted classical pieces, following Petrarch's sonnet form. He enchantingly said that he considered poetry a sumptuous banquet. The displays incite you to read some of du Bellay's poems, as well as to learn something of the importance of his times.

Continuing west along the Loire, **Champtoceaux** looks dramatically down on the river and across to Oudon on the north bank, the latter standing out with its lone tall castle tower. The whole medieval town of Châteauceaux was laid to waste by Jean V, Duc de Bretagne, in warring over the Breton succession. Just some ruins of the fortifications remain. Still further back in time, in the Dark Ages, Pépin le Bref apparently received the ambassadors of the caliph of Baghdad here! There's a delightful walk, the Coulée de la Luce, which you can take down to the Loire via an amphitheatre of a public garden. **La Varenne** makes the last, most westerly stop in Anjou. You can climb its freckled square church tower for splendid views of the surrounding area. Vines slope gracefully down into the Loire Atlantique and the Muscadet wine-making area of the Pays Nantais. The valley broadens out again as it heads for Nantes and the sea. Seamlessly entering the Loire Atlantique following the Loire's southern bank, look out for the tiny Romanesque chapel at **St-Simon**, just past a striking metal-lattice bridge over the Loire. Opposite it lies **Les Mauves**, depicted in a couple of Turner's most magical watercolours of the Loire. **La Pierre Percée**, beyond St-Simon, presents a particularly beautiful Loire-side picture, a big cobbled slope running down to the old port. A miniature modern marina has been constructed on the island in the Loire opposite. You then pass through extremely fine sandy fields ideal for market gardening and through patches of vineyards before reaching the Nantes suburbs.

The Loire from Nantes to the Atlantic

21

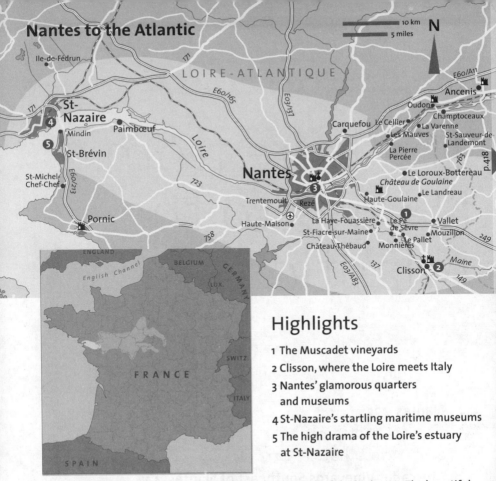

Highlights

1 The Muscadet vineyards
2 Clisson, where the Loire meets Italy
3 Nantes' glamorous quarters
   and museums
4 St-Nazaire's startling maritime museums
5 The high drama of the Loire's estuary
   at St-Nazaire

Along this final stretch of the Loire, you feel the pull of the high seas. The beautiful city of Nantes, once capital of an independent Brittany, then made its huge Ancien Régime fortune on the slave trade. Below Nantes, the best Muscadet vineyards stretch towards Clisson, an old Breton frontier town given an Italian makeover after it had been devastated during the Revolution. West of Nantes, the Loire quickly expands to impressive proportions as it reaches the Atlantic and St-Nazaire, a port renowned for making ocean liners, with a spectacular bridge spanning the estuary.

Nantes

We would go to the Pommeraye Arcade to buy Chinese shades, Turkish sandals or Nile baskets, to take our time examining all the knick-knacks brought back here from over-seas, to touch them with our own hands: the gods, the shoes, the parasols, the lanterns, the splendid, futile, colourful objects that make us dream of other worlds, useless frivolities which we take so seriously.

Gustave Flaubert

The cosmopolitan city that Flaubert conjured up still exists within the modern urban sprawl of Nantes. Nantes has an ocean feel to it – even if the Atlantic lies some 50km away, and even if most of the shipping trade that brought the place such riches in the Ancien Régime moved out towards the sea a long time ago. Despite the destruction of Second World War bombs, large portions of historic Nantes have survived, including the massive castle of the late medieval dukes of Brittany, the medieval cathedral where the last Breton duke was buried, and the grand streets and squares which the young Jules Verne would have known in his childhood.

The centre of Nantes shines brightly now. It's a delightful, vibrant, inspiring place, teeming with students in term time. However, a huge historical monster casts its shadow over the place. The vast 18th-century wealth of the city's merchants was built on the triangular slave trade. Clusters of ornate 18th-century town houses are the most obvious legacy. The finest are decorated with *mascarons*, appropriately grotesque stylized masks. To date, the slave-trading part of Nantes' past appears to have been almost totally ignored in the town museums, of which there are many. The best ones include the fine arts museum and the Musée Dobrée. It's somewhat ironic, given the city's forgetfulness about those slaving expeditions, that Nantes is best known in French history for a famous edict of tolerance, signed here by King Henri IV in 1598 at the end of the terrible French Wars of Religion.

History

The Gaulish tribe of the Namnetes had a port at the spot where the Erdre river joins the Loire. The Gaulish Pictones seem to have favoured the south bank. Few signs remain of Gallo-Roman Nantes that then grew up here. Christianity came early to the place, with its usual tales of cruel martyrdom. Donatien and Rogatien were the children of Aurlien, a Gallo-Roman governor of the town in the late Roman Empire, who converted to the new faith. Donatien had already been baptized, Rogatien had not, by the time the persecutors hounded them down at the start of the 4th century. The imprisoned Rogatien is said to have uttered the tender words: 'If my brother, who is baptized, will kiss me, his kiss will serve as a baptism for me.' The two were viciously tortured before having their heads cut off in 304. Christianity soon got the upper hand, however, the bishops of Nantes becoming powerful figures.

During much of the Dark Ages, the county of Nantes was fought over by Franks and Bretons; in Merovingian times, this county formed a part of the Frankish Marches. Nomenoë, appointed leader of Brittany by one Frankish king, made his successful bid for Breton independence under another. He conquered Nantes and its territories. But soon the Vikings sailed up the Loire to wreak havoc. Gohard, one bishop of Nantes of this time, had his throat cut at the cathedral altar.

In the Breton War of Succession in the mid-14th century, the city switched hands several times between the Penthièvres and the de Montforts. Nantes competed with Rennes as ducal capital through the later Middle Ages; under the de Montfort dukes, it got the upper hand. In the chaotic, war-torn, superstition-riddled first half of the 15th century, Gilles de Rais, or de Retz, became one of the most powerful and notorious Frenchmen of his age. He owned substantial estates south of Nantes and along

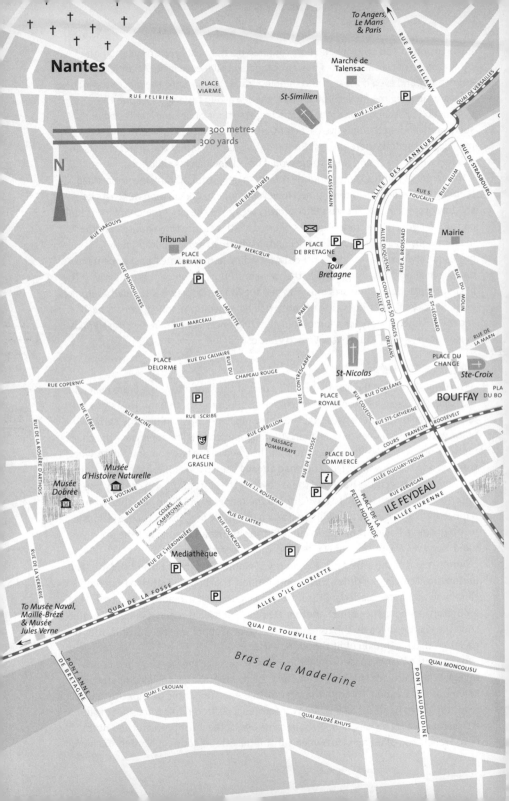

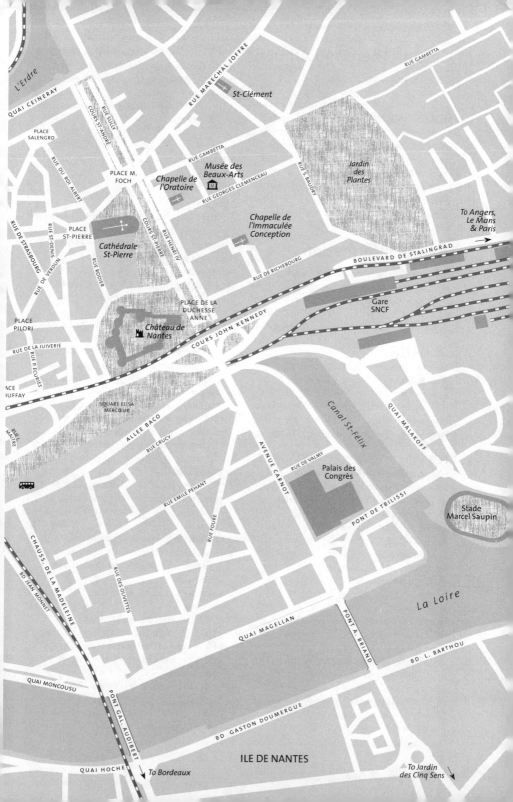

Getting There and Around

Nantes-Atlantique (t 02 40 84 80 00, www.nantes.aeroport.fr) is an international airport receiving flights from London Gatwick. You can also fly to Nantes from Paris, but the super-fast TGV **train** is really more convenient as it amazingly takes you from one centre of town to the other in a mere 2hrs.

Tramway lines crisscross the centre of town, complementing the **bus** service (call t 08 25 08 71 56 for bus info or t 08 10 44 44 44, www.tan.fr for tram information).

Tourist Information

Nantes: Office de Tourisme Nantes-Atlantique, B.P. 64106, 44041 Nantes Cedex 01, t 02 40 20 60 00, www.nantes-tourisme.com. The main tourist office is at 3 Cours Olivier de Clisson, plus there's an office at 2 Place St-Pierre.

Market Days

Talensac: Tuesday to Sunday mornings.
Place Bouffay: Food market; Tuesday to Sunday mornings.
Place du Commerce: Flower market; daily.
Place de la Petite Hollande: Saturday morning.
Place Viarme: Flea market; Saturday morning.

Festivals

Many of Nantes' festivals have a distinctly cosmopolitan flavour.

La Folle Journée, first weekend in February, concentrates on honouring a composer or school of composers. There is a big **carnival** every March. April sees the first of two major **Fêtes Foraines**, with all manner of rides on Cours St-Pierre and Cours St-André.

Le Printemps des Arts celebrates Baroque music and dance in venues across the area in April, May and June.

L'Eté Côté Ouest involves a programme of free cultural events, concerts and street entertainment throughout July and August.

All manner of boats and jazz musicians gather in Nantes for the **Rendez-Vous de l'Erdre**, the last weekend in August or first weekend in September.

The town's second major **Fête Foraine** takes place in September. In October, Celtic music gets a good airing with **Celtomania**. The **Festival des Trois Continents** focuses on films from Africa, Asia and South America every November.

Tissé et Métisse in December is yet another multicultural festival.

Where to Stay

Nantes ✉ 44000

Moderate

★★★La Pérouse, 3 Allée Duquesne, t 02 40 89 75 00, www.hotel-laperouse.fr. This is the most exciting hotel in Nantes, built in ultra-modern style by architects Barto & Barto, with walls at gravity-defying angles – the best of modern design. The hotel is well located, close to the main shopping and restaurant quarters.

★★★Hôtel de France, 24 Rue Crébillon, t 02 40 73 57 91, hoteldefrance-nantes@wanadoo.fr. The smartest of the old-style hotels in town, the rooms quite cosy (menus €13–25; closed weekends). Closed mid-July–mid-Aug, late Dec–early Jan.

★★★Le Jules Verne, 3 Rue de Couëdic, t 02 40 35 74 50, hoteljulesverne@wanadoo.fr. A member of the reliable Best Western chain of hotels, in the heart of Nantes.

Inexpensive

★★★L'Astoria, 11 Rue de Richebourg, t 02 40 74 39 90, hotel.astoria@wanadoo.fr. Large rooms reached by the fanciest of staircases behind its pre-war façade.

★★★L'Hôtel, 6 Rue Henri IV, t 02 40 29 30 31, www.nanteshotel.com. In a modern block right opposite the château, this has neat, good-value, comfortable if slightly characterless rooms. Closed late Dec–early Jan.

★★Cholet, 10 Rue Gresset, t 02 40 73 31 04, hotelcholet@wanadoo.fr. Well-positioned option close to the theatre, with pleasant recently renovated rooms which seem good value.

★★Les Colonies, 5 Rue du Chapeau Rouge, t 02 40 48 79 76, www.hoteldescolonies.fr. Quiet rooms conveniently located close to the central pedestrian area of Nantes.

Cheap

*St-Daniel, 4 Rue du Bouffay, off Place du Bouffay, t 02 40 47 41 25, *hotel.st.daniel@wanadoo.fr*. Extremely well located accommodation that is really quite good value for central Nantes.

*Fourcroy, 11 Rue Fourcroy, t 02 40 44 68 00, f 02 40 44 68 21. Basic option, but in a pleasantly posh part of town. *Closed late Dec–early Jan.*

Auberge de Jeunesse, Cité Universitaire Internationale, 2 Place Manu, t 02 40 29 29 20, *nanteslamanu@fuaj.org* (*you must present your youth hostelling card; beds €11.75*). North out of the centre.

Eating Out

Central Nantes has a much wider choice of restaurants than of hotels. In summer, specially constructed restaurant terraces are built out into the streets, many of them covered with green baize like fake lawn.

Moderate

L'Atlantide, 16 Quai Ernest-Renaud, t 02 40 73 23 23 (*menus €25–61; closed Sat lunch, Sun and public hols*). Michelin-star Nantes cuisine from a chef who has returned to his roots with the benefiting influence of his travels. Rooftop view over Nantes and the Erdre. *Closed 1–4 May, late July–late Aug and 24–28 Dec.*

La Cigale, 4 Place Graslin, t 02 51 84 94 94 (*menus c.€11.50–24*). Not just a classic French brasserie, but a tourist sight in itself for its outstanding and extravagant hundred-year-old Art Nouveau decor. It is set in one of Nantes' most elegant squares.

Auberge du Château, 5 Place de la Duchesse Anne, t 02 40 74 31 85 (*menus €20.50–35.50; closed Sun and Mon*). An intimate little restaurant opposite the massive castle. It has a warm atmosphere in which to try classic Nantes food. *Closed first three weeks of Aug.*

Le Chiwawa, 17 Rue Voltaire, t 02 40 69 01 65 (*menus c.€14–42; closed Sat lunch, Sun, and Mon lunch*). Excellent address for some innovative and inventive cuisine. *Closed spring hols.*

L'Esquinade, 7 Rue Saint Denis, t 02 40 48 17 22 (*menus €15–35; closed Sun and Mon*). Traditional Loire gastro cuisine with *menus du marché* and a speciality of sea bass cooked in potato skins. *Closed Aug and late Dec–early Jan.*

Le Galion – Les Boucaniers, 28 Rue Kervégan, t 02 40 47 68 83 (*menus €9.50–36.50; closed Sat lunch and Sun*). Good French food in an atmospheric 18th-century building. The set up here is a restaurant in one half and a more informal buffet in the other, serving *rapide* versions of the same food for a fraction of the price.

Lou Pescadou, 8 Allée Baco, t 02 40 35 29 50 (*menus €19–43; closed Sat lunch, Sun, and Mon pm*). Serves tasty fish dishes. *Closed most of Aug.*

La Poissonnerie, 4 Rue Léon Maître, t 02 49 47 79 50 (*menus €13–40; closed Sat lunch, Sun and Mon*). Another good fish restaurant which has a light, nautical look and aquarium inside. *Closed Easter hols, Christmas and in Aug.*

Le Carnivore, 7 Allée des Tanneurs, t 02 40 47 87 00 (*menus c.€9–39.50*). Traditional meat lovers might prefer this place, but might be surprised to see bison and ostrich meat on the menu.

Cheap

Chez l'Huître, 5 Rue des Petites Ecuries, t 02 51 82 02 02 (*oysters €5–12; closed Sun*). A tiny green-checked brasserie with fresh and fast seafood specialities served by an eccentric host. There's a little terrace and humorous blackboard drawings. *Closed late Dec–early Jan.*

Ile Verte, 3 Rue Siméon Foucault, t 02 40 48 01 26 (*menus €8.50–13; closed Wed, Sun and evenings*). A rarity – French vegetarian food. *Closed Aug.*

Pommier Laprugne, 3 Allée de l'Ile Gloriette, t 02 40 47 78 08 (*crêpes c.€13; closed Sat lunch, Sun, and Mon pm*). A crêperie that serves up some interesting fillings. *Closed late July–mid-Aug.*

La Baguett', 19 Rue Paul Bellamy, t 02 40 48 15 20. Almost a pastiche of the traditional Breton crêperie. *Closed mid–late Aug, Sun, and Mon pm.*

the Loire, and became a major figure at the French court under King Charles VII, where he is supposed to have sported a blue beard. Having fought alongside Joan of Arc, his profligacy and degeneracy then led him into deep waters, and he would end up accused of raping and murdering scores of young boys in his castles, using them in satanic rituals, including writing prayers to the devil in their blood. He may have been framed, but was certainly hanged and then burnt in Nantes, in 1440.

Under Duke François II, who was to be the last duke of Brittany, Nantes thrived as capital of that province. A prestigious university was inaugurated here in 1460, with the papacy's blessing. Duke François II's daughter, Duchess Anne de Bretagne, born at the Château de Nantes in 1477, would be viewed as a very fine catch for Europe's most powerful dynasties. She would end up married to two French kings in a row; the first, Charles VIII, she was wedded to at the Château de Langeais; the second, Louis XII, she married in the chapel of the Château de Nantes in 1499. Anne died at another château on the Loire, Blois, in 1514, but Nantes would remain a city close to her heart for all her life – and after it was over. While most of her mortal remains were taken to the French royal resting place of the abbey of St-Denis, outside Paris, she had specifically asked for her heart to be returned to Nantes to be buried in the most gorgeous of inscribed gold reliquaries. Anne's daughter Claude de France was married to King François I, who organised Brittany's official union with France in 1532, sealed at Nantes.

During the French Wars of Religion in the second half of the 16th century, Nantes fell under the control of the ultra-Catholic governor of Brittany, Philippe-Emmanuel de Lorraine, Duc de Mercœur, but at the end of the torments, the 1598 Edict of Nantes worked out by King Henri IV famously granted some limited toleration of worship for Protestants in France. At the close of the 17th century, King Louis XIV revoked the edict, rekindling the persecution of the Huguenots. In between times, Nantes was rapidly growing into one of the major French colonial ports.

Nantes and the Triangular Slave Trade

The most prosperous times for Nantes came with the acquisition of France's Caribbean colonies. By 1633, Guadeloupe and Martinique were in French hands. With the 1697 Treaty of Ryswick, France gained the western half of Saint-Domingue (present-day Haiti), which became the most lucrative of all of France's colonies. Before long, Nantes was possibly the largest centre in Europe for the triangular slave trade, outstripping all others in the 18th century. The first leg of the journey took the ships from Nantes to the east African coast. Goods such as guns, powder, alcohol, jewellery, trinkets and cloth were exchanged with the local slave traders for the human cargo that filled the vessels on the second leg of the journey. The slaves had to undergo the crossing of the Atlantic in the most appalling and degrading conditions. The horror of their treatment is painful to conceive. Many slaves died on these journeys; those who survived were sold to the colonial plantation owners of the Caribbean in exchange for the precious goods other slaves were already busily helping to produce, notably sugar, coffee, cotton and indigo. On the third and final leg of the triangular journey, these luxuries were brought back to Europe.

Between 1715 and 1775, the return to port of 787 slave ships was registered in Nantes, half the number recorded for the whole of France. However, the sailing ships grew too large to travel up to the city's quays. Much of the merchandise was loaded and unloaded at Paimbœuf, west along the Loire. New industries developed in and around Nantes on the back of the Caribbean imports. Sugar was refined here to be sold across Europe. Cotton was turned into printed calico, known in French as *indiennes*, much of which went back to Africa to be bartered for more slaves.

Hugh Thomas, in his fascinating book *The Slave Trade*, gives many telling insights into the activities of the Nantes shipping merchants. Apparently, the Montaudoins held the ignoble record in Nantes slave-trading. Between 1694 and 1791, they equipped 357 ships for the triangular journeys. Far behind in second place, the de Luynes prepared some 182, and in third place came the Boutelhiers with 171. One of the most significant players was Antoine Walsh, an Irish Catholic immigrant, who organized 57 slaving trips to Africa in the mid-18th century. With the backing of Parisian bankers, he set up the Société d'Angola, specializing in buying men from traders on the Loango coast. The company exported some 10,000 slaves in a mere seven years, but proved a financial failure as the Angolan slaves were considered inferior, less valuable workers to those bought from the Gold Coast. Black African slaves became a common sight in wealthy Nantes households. Hugh Thomas describes the casual attitude some of the rich merchants had towards their human chattels: 'Slave merchants, living in their fine town houses... would give such "négrillons" or "négrittes" to members of their household as tips. In 1754, an ordonnance provided that colonials could bring into France only one black apiece. But that rule was often forgotten.'

From the end of the 17th century to the end of the 18th, Nantes' population doubled, from 40,000 to 80,000. The successful merchants, putting their sickening wealth to aesthetic use, built their grand town houses (known as *hôtels* in French) in the Louis XV and Louis XVI styles. A concentration of particularly fine mansions went up on the Ile Feydeau, then still an island. Hugh Thomas notes how 'the one-time slave-trading residents of the mansions on the Ile Feydeau, in the 1780s, sent their dirty linen to be laundered in Saint-Domingue where the mountain streams were said to wash whiter than any in Brittany.' Before the Revolution, in the second half of the 18th century, new town planning was carried out on a large scale across the centre of Nantes by the architect Ceineray. Grand streets, squares and perspectives were added to the city. The architect Mathurin Crucy continued the work around the time of the Revolution.

The Revolution banned the slave trade for a time. This was a catastrophe for many Nantes merchants, poor things. When the slaves of Saint-Domingue rose up in revolt in 1791, the Nantes shipowners wrote in protest to the king. The terrifying Carrier was sent to Nantes by the Committee of Public Safety; his mission, to make some of the pig-headed royalists of Nantes wed the cause of the Revolution. The so-called 'republican marriages' were cruel mock ceremonies: the un-Revolutionary offenders were tied in pairs and bundled onto a boat with a hole in the bottom. The boat sank and the 'couples' drowned in the Loire. Charette, a nobleman from the Loire-Atlantique and one of the main leaders of the anti-Revolutionary, pro-Catholic and royalist

Vendée uprising, led a desperate attack on Nantes in 1793. But it failed. Cathelineau, another of the heroes of the anti-Revolutionary cause, was mortally wounded in the battle. Charette was eventually executed in Nantes in 1796.

The arrest a few decades later of the pro-royalist Duchesse de Berry at the foot of the château after she had tried unsuccessfully to spark off another Vendée uprising was much more farcical. But a sign of renewed royalism in Nantes stands atop a column close to the château. It's a figure of Louis XVI in Roman dress, the original statue inaugurated in 1823, 30 years after the king had been executed.

Nantes After Slavery

Turner came to paint here and along the Loire in 1828, the year that Jules Verne was born in Nantes. Somewhat less glamorously, but perhaps more significantly for everyday modern life, the techniques of tinning were developed in Nantes at this time, to preserve southern Breton fish catches. Canning became a big industry in Brittany as a consequence, and played an important part in employment as well as culinary culture. The slave trade, reinstated after the Revolution, petered out in the middle of the 19th century. Nantes' prosperity didn't entirely drain away after the Revolution, as you can see for example in the glamorous mid-19th-century shopping arcade of the Passage Pommeraye. Although the main Loire estuary shipping activity had moved still further west from Paimbœuf to St-Nazaire, the import and export of goods along the new train line to and from Nantes provided plenty of work. Trams started operating in town as early as 1874 and have recently been revived.

Aristide Briand, one of the major French political figures of the early 20th century, came from Nantes. He became general secretary of the French Socialist Party in 1901 and framed the important bill separating the Church from the French State in 1905. In the turbulent times at the start of the last century he served as prime minister no fewer than 11 times. After the First World War, as part of German war reparations, most of the seven channels of the Loire that had flowed through the city centre for so long were filled in by German workers. Aristide Briand continued to be a major figure in France after the war, when with Jean Jaurès he founded the left-wing newspaper L'Humanité. From 1925 to 1932, he served as French foreign minister and worked hard for reconciliation and disarmament, proposing a form of United States of Europe. In 1926 he and the German foreign minister Gustav Stresemann were awarded the Nobel Peace Prize. Unfortunately their efforts would prove fruitless, although Aristide Briand might be considered one of the forefathers of the European Union.

Occupied by the Nazis, Nantes inevitably became a target of major Allied bombing raids during the Second World War, which have left their scars. From 1941 to 1944, the city was targeted 25 times, with 2,000 bombs falling in a particularly destructive attack of September 1943. Before leaving, in August 1944, the Germans dynamited two kilometres of Loire-side quays. As to the wide modern road artery known as the Cour des 50 Otages cutting through the centre of Nantes, its name commemorates the execution of 50 hostages in 1942.

Since the war, several figures from the French art world have paid homage to Nantes, including the much-respected film-maker Jacques Demy, whose movie Lola was shot here, and the highly acclaimed writer Julien Gracq, whose work *La Forme d'une ville* is devoted to the city. The university, closed at the Revolution, was reinstated in 1962, giving youth to the streets. High-tech industries have settled here too. Nantes is close to the heart and stomach of many a French child, being a major centre of French biscuit-making; this industry originally grew up to cater for the shipping expeditions. Many of France's best-known biscuit brands are still made here, while sugar from the Caribbean still arrives in Nantes in large quantities.

A Tour of Nantes

Nantes does not have an obvious heart, but several quarters worth exploring. The most obvious place to start is with the massive Château de Nantes.

Château de Nantes (Château des Ducs de Bretagne)

Grounds open July–Aug daily 10–7, rest of year 10–6; exhibitions open Wed–Mon 10–6; t 02 40 41 56 56; adm.

This château is massive, forbidding and an architectural mess, to put it mildly. The thick dark outer walls enclose slightly more graceful, whiter wings. A deep broad dry **moat**, where many Nantais now take their dogs for a walk, separates the ramparts and their seven artillery towers from the surrounding boulevards, but originally the Loire lapped at the château's walls. The castle you see today, known as the Château des Ducs de Bretagne, was in fact built in the main for the last duke of Brittany and his daughter, although their forbears did have a fort on the spot.

This castle might be regarded as the most westerly of the châteaux of the Loire. It might also be considered the least harmonious of them all. On entering the enormous **inner courtyard** it's hard to know where to focus your attention, what with the irregular shape of the site, the diversity of buildings from down the centuries, and the miserable misleading alley of trees which goes nowhere in particular. The two main wings show reasonably well the change from French late-Gothic architecture to French Renaissance forms so characteristic of the Loire châteaux of the late 15th and early 16th centuries. The soaring vertical lines, the slight lack of symmetry in the windows, and the ornate *lucarnes*, or dormer windows, fit the bill. In the corner between the two main wings rises the **Tower of the Golden Crown**, lightened by Renaissance loggias high up. The name of the tower refers to the elaborate covering on top of the well in front of it. This crown in wrought iron was once gilded, and was meant to represent the crown of the kings of Brittany of the Dark Ages.

The **Petit Gouvernement** is the small 16th-century building added for King François I and covered with restored French Renaissance detail, such as the shells in the dormers and the slate inlaid in the chimneys. The large rectangular building stranded in the midst of the courtyard is the 18th-century **Bâtiment du Harnachement**, the architectural equivalent of a sore thumb, but it reminds you of the fact that the château served as an army camp from the beginning of the 18th century to the start of the 20th. Unfortunately, in 1800, the military managed to blow up a whole section of the castle by accident, including the chapel. You can climb some of the castle ramparts, but the views of the roads and modern town are disappointing.

The château used to house several museums. Now major work is under way to create one single, much grander museum, but this will not be ready until 2006. In the meantime, temporary **exhibitions** will be held each year in the swishly restored Harnachement building.

To the Cathédrale St-Pierre

From the château you might take the **Rue Rodier** (named after the man who planned the castle for Duke François II) straight up to the front of the cathedral on **Place St-Pierre**. Or if you prefer something a little grander, opt for the wide, mid-18th-century boulevard of the Cours St-Pierre, running up from the Place de la Duchesse Anne to the choir end of the cathedral. This Cours is of Parisian proportions and elegance. It takes you to the imposing **Place Maréchal Foch**, where the column commemorating King Louis XVI stands in the centre, traffic circling balletically round it. The big building on the north side was where Napoleon stayed on a visit to Nantes in 1808. The Hôtel Montaudoin, built for that infamously wealthy Nantes shipping family, stands out, the family arms proudly showing. The grand Cours St-André, the extension northwards of the **Cours St-Pierre**, leads to the Erdre boat station. Clashing with the careful classical planning of the rest of the square, the massive **Porte St-Pierre** is a remnant of Nantes' 15th-century town walls, built on much earlier Gallo-Roman vestiges.

While the exterior of the bulky, squat **Cathédrale St-Pierre** looks rather grey, the inside is superbly white. This is the cleanest cathedral you're ever likely to see, and one of the emptiest. The interior had in fact to be restored and cleaned after a terrible fire in 1972. Only a few patches of humidity marks remain on certain pillars holding up the white Gothic arches. Some of the uncluttered monuments down below appear even whiter than the Loire limestone used in the building of this cathedral. Work began on it in 1434, financed by Jean V Duc de Bretagne and Bishop Jean de Malestroit. It was constructed on the site of the previous Romanesque cathedral, and possibly of a Dark Ages one before that. Only the Romanesque crypt under the present choir was kept from the previous structures. The 15th-century architects were Guillaume de Dommartin-sur-Yèvre and Mathelin Rodier. The building work would prove laborious and lengthy, but the façade was completed before the end of the 15th century and the towers were added by 1508. The nave and the aisles slowly went up in the 16th century, worship in the building only starting in 1577.

The major artistic interest within lies in the **tomb of François II** Duc de Bretagne and his two wives. This moving work was commissioned by Anne de Bretagne and is said to have been executed in the Tours workshops of the sculptor Michel Colombe between 1502 and 1507, although an Italian artist of great ability may have carried out some of the work. The two main effigies represent the duke and his second wife, Marguerite de Foix, mother of Anne de Bretagne. The large corner statues show personifications of Justice (thought also to be a portrait of Anne), Fortitude, Temperance and Prudence, the last with its double-faced head, the one of a young woman, the other of an old man. Anne de Bretagne asked for her heart to be placed in the tomb after her death and her wish was granted.

Another remarkably fine tomb in the cathedral dates from the 19th century. It was made by Paul Dubois in 1879, in honour of the formidably moustached military commander General Lamoricière. A Nantais by birth, he was celebrated for his role in the French taking of Algeria, and in particular for his capturing of the Algerian leader Abd-el-Kader. Almost all of the cathedral's original stained-glass windows have been destroyed by explosions and fire. Some striking modern ones have replaced them, for instance that above Duc François II's tomb, the figures representing Nantes and Breton saints.

Rue du Roi Albert leads north from the cathedral square up to the **Préfecture**. This is Ceineray's classical masterpiece in the town, built from 1763. On the cathedral side, the arms of France have been sculpted in the pediment. On the side of the Erdre river, the arms of Brittany feature.

The best way to appreciate the beautiful **Erdre river** is on a **cruise**. The **Gare Fluviale** de l'Erdre from which the boats depart lies on the west bank of the river, near the Ile de Versailles. Contact **Bateaux Nantais**, t 02 40 14 51 14, *www.bateaux-nantais.fr*, for cruises on slick modern boats. They now operate a variety of different tours, including meals and cabaret performances, child-orientated cruises and floodlit tours of the Erdre's chateaux.

Musée des Beaux-Arts

Open Wed–Thurs and Sat–Mon 10–6, Fri 10–8; closed public hols;
10 Rue Georges Clémenceau, t 02 40 41 65 65 or t 02 51 17 45 00; adm.

The splendid Nantes fine arts museum lies on the other side of Cours St-Pierre from the cathedral. Allegorical statues on the façade represent the arts; architecture, with temple and measuring rod in hands is represented over the main entrance. The museum is a beautiful, cleanly planned work by the architect Josso, built in 1900 for the elevating educational purposes of the French Third Republic. The founding collection was actually donated to the town a century earlier, in 1801, or the Year IX as it was known under the Consulate; this was one of 15 major provincial museums set up around France after the Revolution. Some of the works came from war booty. Another large number arrived in 1810 from the collections of the Cacault brothers and their lovely Italianate villa in Clisson (*see* p.449). They had been on a wild art shopping spree in Italy in the late 18th century. Further generous 19th-century donations and the 20th-century legacy of Gildas Fardel added to the riches on display. If you want a crash course in the history of Western art from 13th-century religious works to present-day conceptual pieces, this would be as fine a place as any to come. The 19th- and 20th-century collections are exceptionally good. The galleries are very neatly set out on two levels around an arcaded courtyard. This courtyard is even whiter and brighter than the interior of the cathedral. Twentieth-century work is given pride of place on the ground floor. The patio at the centre is often put to good use for contemporary exhibitions. The upper storey takes you round from the Italian Early Masters to the end of the 19th century in France, the chronological sequence easy to follow.

There are so many masterpieces in this museum that it isn't possible to single them all out here. Among the highlights, of the three famous de la Tours, two show his archetypal candlelit effects cast on waxen figures. The best pieces from the 18th century include a typical Watteau inspired by commedia dell'arte – *Arlequin, Empereur de la Lune* – several Greuzes, and a whole series of portraits of rich families by Tournières. Gros' work *Le Combat de Nazareth* was an early 19th-century piece which had a profound effect on Delacroix and has been viewed as a precursor of the Romantic movement. The same room contains two exceptional sculptures, one by Canova of Pope Clement XIII; the other, by Ceracchi, of Washington. Ingres' *Madame de Senonnes* of 1814 is another of the major pieces.

Courbet's *Les Cribleuses de Blé* counts as one of the most famous works of the second half of the 19th century in the museum. There is a broad representation of wildly over-the-top, sickly French Romanticism too. You might view with some irony, given Nantes' history, *L'Esclave blanche* (The White Slave) by Lecomte du Nouy. *Le Sorcier Noir* by Herbert Ward shows a typical European vision of the black man as witch. On the ground floor, while Monet takes you off to Venice and the otherwordly visions of his *Nymphéas*, Emile Bernard's *Le Gaulage des pommes* depicts a Breton landscape in the style of the Pont-Aven school. Local artist Metzinger gives a Pointilliste interpretation of the Château de Clisson. A whole room is devoted to Kandinsky's abstract work, while Chagall's *Le Cheval Rouge* is a typical dream-world piece by that great artist. You can interpret the thought-provoking conceptual art on display as seriously or comically as the mood takes you. Raymond Hains, a well-known conceptual artist, pays homage to the Nantes biscuit industry via a barcode.

The Bouffay Quarter

Make your way back to the centre of historic Nantes and west of the castle lies the Bouffay quarter. The network of old streets makes this the liveliest and most charming part of old Nantes. The area is mainly pedestrian. Several street names recall the medieval activities along them, but only a few timberframe houses remain from the 15th and 16th centuries. In the Ancien Régime, grander town houses were built in what became the lawyers' quarter in particular. Nowadays, this is a neigh-bourhood of chic boutiques, restaurants and apartments. You will come across several little squares. **Place du Pilori** served for executions and other punishments until **Place Bouffay** took over that role. This square now plays host to a lively and smelly daily fish market. The former town belfry has been affixed to the **church of Ste-Croix** in **Place Ste-Croix** nearby. The church offers a quirky mix of architectural styles. North of **Rue de la Marne** and **Rue de la Barillerie** (the two forming one of the main shopping arteries), several further elegant-looking streets lead to the town hall, for instance those heading north from the **Place du Change**, once the hub of historic Nantes. The **Hôtel de Ville** (town hall) is a mix of 17th-century mansions and modernity.

Ile Feydeau

On the opposite side of the Allées from Place Bouffay, the Ile Feydeau was once an exclusive residential island on the Loire. It's now sadly isolated by wide roads. This is where some of the very grandest Nantes ship-owners had their houses and offices from the mid-18th century. You only really get a good impression of their wealth by wandering along the **Rue Kervégan**. The finest features on the façades are the grotesque Baroque masks carved above the windows, each one showing a different grimacing face. Look out, too, for the wrought-iron balconies and interior staircases.

Squares and Museums West of Cours des 50 Otages

To the west of the broad curving **Cours des 50 Otages** lie many elegant squares and streets from the late 18th and early 19th centuries. More chic shops line many of the streets. Rue d'Orléans leads to **Place Royale**. This sober-sided square was planned by the architect Crucy. Personifications of certain of the Loire's tributary rivers adorn the granite fountain. Just to the northeast of Place Royale lie the **Place Fournier** and the **Basilique St-Nicolas**. The latter is a neo-Gothic church from the mid-19th century, its soaring spire reaching 85m in height. A fair way further north rises the much taller **Tour de Bretagne**, Nantes' isolated central skyscraper, visible from afar as you approach the city. A modern shopping and business precinct surrounds it.

South of the Place Royale, a wonderful array of cafés lines up opposite the **Bourse** on **Place du Commerce**. The exchange building, with its impressive row of monumental Ionic columns, was again planned by Crucy and completed in 1812. A few of the original statues of famous Breton sailors (some notorious corsairs in fact) remain in place. The Loire used to flow by here and the quay was reserved for the Nantais wine trade. Now it's the domain of the beautiful, trendy student set.

Passage Pommeraye, Nantes' most elegant shopping arcade, heads up to Rue Crébillon from Rue de la Fosse. You won't find Passage Pommeraye as exotic as Flaubert did in his day, but the mid-19th-century sweeps of stairs have a kitsch romance to them. **Rue Crébillon** links **Place Royale** with the more serious **Place Graslin** to the west. This square was again planned by Crucy. It's dominated by the theatre, which saw its first performance in 1788. Statues of muses stand on top of the Corinthian columns. **Cours Cambronne**, off the southwest corner of Place Graslin, could hardly be more refined, crying out for you to bring your topiary poodle.

Musée Thomas Dobrée and Manoir de la Touche

Open Tues–Fri 9.45–5.30, Sat–Sun 2.30–5.30; closed public hols; 18 Rue Voltaire, t 02 40 71 03 50, www.culture.cg44.fr; adm. Currently undergoing refurbishment: times subject to change.

The golden reliquary for the heart of Anne de Bretagne stands on public display in this museum. Little can the last duchess of Brittany have imagined that it would one day be on view for all to see. It's the most striking piece of fine craftsmanship in a museum crammed with the stuff, including the finest stonework, woodwork and enamel work. Thomas Dobrée was a dedicated collector through the 19th century, the son of an extremely wealthy industrialist and shipowner. Among other objects, he amassed sculptures, paintings, furniture, art objects, manuscripts, and correspondence from royals, nobles and literary figures, all in an obsessive manner. He decided to build a grand house in which to install these collections, next to the Manoir de la

Touche. Dobrée even oversaw much of the construction work on this building, with its neo-Romanesque look. It was built in brown-bear coloured stone, with figures of carved bears added onto the corners. Dobrée also had the Manoir de la Touche restored. This manor had been constructed for Bishop Jean de Malestroit as his country retreat outside the city walls at the start of the 15th century. It later served as a Huguenot hospital in the Wars of Religion and from 1695 until the Revolution as a religious refuge for Irish priests who had been driven out of their country.

The museum contains many religious sculptures of great beauty. You can observe close up several huge statues originally made for Nantes' cathedral front, carved in Loire limestone, and a collection of Romanesque capitals with some weird grotesque faces. A magnificent length of wooden stringbeam shows a bizarre mix of particularly graceful faces and crudely gesturing figures. Among the exquisite medieval church ceremonial objects on display, the collection of enamel-decorated *pyxides* from the Limousin stand out, as do various encrusted altar crosses, the reliquary of St-Calminius and a staurothique, a reliquary for a fragment of the True Cross. As well as admiring some beautiful and significant old manuscripts, you can also see an extensive collection of ornate weapons.

The **Manoir de la Touche** contains a mixed bag of collections. The ground floor is devoted to Nantes at the time of the Revolution. Upstairs are archaeological finds from around the Loire-Atlantique, including some interesting Bronze Age, Celtic, Gallo-Roman and Merovingian pieces.

Jules Verne's Museum and Other Specialist Museums in Nantes

Nantes has at least another half-dozen smaller museums. The **Muséum** (*open Wed–Mon 10–6, closed public hols;* **t** *02 40 99 26 20, www.museum.nantes.fr; adm*), east of the Musée Dobrée on Rue Voltaire, is its respected natural history museum. Nearby, down on the quays with the modern Médiathèque, the **Musée de l'Imprimerie** (*open July–Aug Mon–Fri 10–12 and 2–5.30, rest of year Mon–Sat same times; closed public hols; 24 Quai de la Fosse,* **t** *02 40 73 26 55, musee.imprimerie.free.fr; adm*) covers the development of printing in the region, with an impressive collection of old presses. Looking further west along the Quai de la Fosse, it's hard to miss the **Maillé Brézé** (*open June–Sept daily 2–6; rest of year Wed, weekends, public hols and school hols 2–5; Mon, Tues, Thurs and Fri tours only at 2.30 and 4.30;* **t** *02 40 69 56 82, www.chez.com/maillebreze; adm*), a decommissioned naval squadron escort vessel which has been turned into a museum, with enthusiastic guides.

Head west for the Ste-Anne quarter on its hill, and there you'll find a further cluster of sights. The little **Musée Jules Verne** (*open Mon and Wed–Sat 10–12 and 2–6, Sun 2–6; 3 Rue de l'Hermitage,* **t** *02 40 69 72 52; adm*) pays its respects to the great French visionary 19th-century science fiction writer from Nantes with old editions, posters and topical displays, and has recently been redecorated to modern effect. Jules Verne was the author of such worldwide classics as *Le Tour du monde en quatre-vingt jours* (*Around the World in Eighty Days*), *Voyage au centre de la terre* (*Journey to the Centre of the Earth*) and *Vingt Mille Lieues sous les mers* (*Twenty Thousand Leagues Under the Sea*). You can easily imagine what an inspiration cosmopolitan Nantes must have been to him, even if it hardly features in his writing. Americans might also particu-larly enjoy his *De la Terre à la lune* (*From the Earth to the Moon Direct in 97 Hours 20 Minutes*), an hilarious story about Americans competing to becoming the first men on the moon – but in the 19th century! It seems appropriate that the **Planétarium** (*showings Mon–Fri at 10.30, 2.15 and 3.45, Sun at 3 and 4.30, closed Sat and public hols; 8 Rue des Acadiens, t 02 40 73 99 23; adm*) should stand close by.

The **Musée des Compagnons du Devoir**, in the Manoir de la Hautière in the same area (*open Sat 2–6; 14 Rue Guillon Verne, t 02 40 69 30 55; free*), presents masterpieces by French master craftsmen. Some distance north, the **Musée de la Poste** (*open Mon–Fri 9–7, Sat 9–12; 2 bis, Rue du Président Herriot; t 02 51 83 37 12; free*) is dedicated to the French postal services down the centuries. The **Parc de Procé** is another of what the French call an 'English garden', that is, not as formal as a French garden. This one has collections of rhododendrons, fuchsias, dahlias and magnolias.

South Across the Loire

On the **Ile de Nantes**, a hard-working island just south of the historic city, you might sniff out the **Jardin des Cinq Sens**, a garden which plays on the five senses with its different-textured paths and its musical fountain. Head right around the western tip of the island and you come to an astonishing industrial landscape of hills of scrap metal. Cross south from the Ile de Beaulieu for **Rezé**, which had a Gallo-Roman settle-ment like Nantes, but which is known today for modern architecture. The most famous piece in town is **Le Corbusier**'s cement experiment in new urban living, the *unité d'habitation de grandeur conforme*, or **Cité Radieuse**, built on stilts. It went up in the mid-1950s, providing a new concept in council housing. The striking curve of Rezé's modern town hall was conceived by the Romanian architect Anselmi.

Following the Loire bank west from the centre of Rezé, you hit upon the roughly charming old fishermen's village of **Trentemoult**, to which many Nantes captains used to retire, often planting exotic trees and shrubs in their little gardens.

Muscadet Vineyards Southeast of Nantes

The Loire-Atlantique makes one very well-known wine, Muscadet, confusingly produced from a grape variety called Melon de Bourgogne. Although much good Muscadet is produced, the region has received a bit of a bashing in the press over recent years for failing to maintain quality across the board.

A good place to start touring the Muscadet vineyards is the **Maison des Vins de Nantes** at **La Haye-Fouassière** (*open weekdays 8.30–12.30 and 2–5.45, July and Aug weekends also 10–12.30 and 2–6; t 02 40 36 90 10, www.muscadet.org*), overlooking hectare upon hectare of vines. You can taste a wide selection of Muscadets here and get general information on the wines of the Loire-Atlantique. If you wish to visit a winery, it's always wise to telephone in advance to see if you can fix a time. Near La Haye-Fouassière, the **Domaine Bonneteau-Guesselin** (*t 02 40 54 80 38*) has a welcoming ivy-covered courtyard. Here Olivier Bonneteau, young, eloquent and very pleasant, will give you a good introduction to Muscadet and his characterful wines, which he makes to have a strong impact and good aromas.

Among some recommendations of other good Muscadet vineyards, if you're looking for a spectacular property, try the **Château de Goulaine** (*open mid-June–mid-Sept Wed–Mon 2–6; Easter–Oct weekends and public hols 2–6; t 02 40 54 91 42, http://chateau.goulaine.online.fr; adm*), both a reputed Muscadet-producing estate and an historic castle you can visit just east of Haute-Goulaine, relatively close to the suburbs of Nantes. The history of the family goes back almost one thousand years. A beautiful new château arose in the last two decades of the 15th century. The present marquis, Robert de Goulaine, a crime and wine writer as well as a promoter of his beloved Muscadet, describes himself as the eleventh Marquis de Goulaine in a row. Inside the château you only see a small number of rooms, but they are sumptuously decorated.

Or try the **Château du Coing** (*t 02 40 54 85 24 for an appointment, www.chateau-du-coing.com*), by St-Fiacre-sur-Maine. The vineyards lie on some of the prettiest slopes in the region. The place, a true château, has impressive cellars where you can sample the wines. The winemaker is Véronique Günther Chéreau, a member of a well-known Muscadet-making family. She is willing to experiment with her wines, ageing some in barrel since 1986. Among other major producers, the **Château de la Galissonnière** (*t 02 40 80 42 03, www.chateaugalissonniere.com*), by Le Pallet, is well known and well used to receiving foreign visitors. With attractive cellars around a courtyard, this place has links with a French admiral and botanist who served as governor of Québec in the 18th century. De la Galissonnière supposedly planted the first magnolia in Europe here. The **Château du Cléray** (*Mon–Fri 8.30–12 and 2–4.30; t 02 40 36 22 55, www.sauvion.fr*), by Vallet, is less attractive to look at, but it is run by one of the families with the best reputations in Muscadet country, the Sauvions. (Just north of Vallet, you might like to visit the grounds of the 19th-century **Château de la Noé de Bel Air**, with its follies and English-style gardens as well as its vineyard. The place is still owned by the Malestroit family, descendants of the bishop of Nantes who started the cathedral and presided over the court which condemned Bluebeard to death.)

Among lesser-known addresses, you might try the **Domaine des Perrières** (*t 02 40 03 92 14*), at Mouzillon, south of Vallet or due east of Le Pallet. This is a small-scale winery set by a modern house. The grapes are still harvested by hand and brought to the vats set in the ground. Many of the wines have a good length to them, as well as being fruity. Mouzillon also has a charming Gallo-Roman bridge. **Christophe Maillard** (*t 02 40 80 44 92*) is an interesting *vigneron-récoltant* who makes very good Muscadet sur Lie, and Gros-Plant. He is based near Le Pallet at Le Pé-de-Sèvre. Sale and tasting are on site. Between Le Loroux-Bottereau and Vallet, at Le Landreau, the Couillauds at the **Domaine du Haut Planty** (*t 02 40 06 42 76, www.haut-planty.com*) produce good wine and one of the Madame Couillauds can greet you in English, being American.

There's an excellent book, *Découvertes en terroir du Muscadet*, published by Ouest-France for the wine and tourist authorities of the Loire-Atlantique, which introduces some 200 Muscadet vineyards you can visit, as well as providing much more historical and practical information on the region's wines.

Getting Around

Trains go down through the Muscadet area to Clisson, and there are bus services around this area from Nantes.

Tourist Information

Le Pallet: Mairie, 26 Rue St-Vincent, Le Pallet, t 02 40 80 40 24 or t 02 40 36 35 87, www.cc-vallet.fr.
Clisson: Place du Minage, B.P. 9124, Clisson Cedex 44190, t 02 40 54 02 95, www.clisson.com.

Where to Stay and Eat

St-Fiacre-sur-Maine ✉ 44690

Le Fiacre, 1 Rue des Echicheurs, t 02 40 54 83 92. Appealing, simple village bistrot-cum-bar (menus €10). The patron is passionate about Muscadet. Closed Sun, and 3 weeks in Aug.

Château-Thébaud ✉ 44690

Domaine de la Pénissière, t 02 40 06 51 22 (inexpensive). Offering smart B&B rooms in an atmospheric old house set on a wine estate on the opposite bank of the Maine, with good views of the vineyards.

Monnières ✉ 44690

Château de Plessis-Blézot, t 02 40 54 63 24, www.chateauplessisbrezot.com (moderate). Little 17th-century property set above the Sèvre Nantaise at Monnières. A reputed wine domain and a luxury B&B.

Clisson ✉ 44190

La Bonne Auberge, 1 Rue Olivier de Clisson, t 02 40 54 01 90 (menus €23–56.50; closed Sun pm, Mon, and Tues lunch). Stylish gastronomic restaurant.

Restaurant de la Vallée, 1 Rue de la Vallée, t 02 40 54 36 23 (menus c.€13–20; closed Mon pm and Tues exc public hols). Delightfully located over the river with a summer dining terrace. Under new ownership, the salle has been completely redone, and the cooking is fresh.

Clisson

Clisson is the town where Brittany and Italy meet, although the feudal **Château de Clisson** (open April–Sept Wed–Mon and Oct–Mar Wed–Sun 9.30–12 and 2–6; t 02 40 54 02 22, www.culture.cg44.fr) looks French enough. Its ruins dominate the slopes of the valley where the Maine joins the Sèvre Nantaise. The church and town, however, look as though they've been shipped straight from Italy. Clisson was devastated in the Vendée uprising, and what arose afterwards was the work of Pierre and François Cacault of Nantes and their friend, the sculptor Frédéric Lemot. All had travelled in Italy and they decided to rebuild in Roman style. The church of **Notre-Dame** is typical of Clisson's Italianate style, with a lovely campanile. From the Pont de la Vallée bridge you get beautiful views of the town. The wonderful Italianate villa of **La Garenne-Lemot** and its park (Villa and Maison du Jardinier open June–Sept Mon pm–Sun 10–12 and 2–7, Mar–May and Oct Tues–Sun 10–12 and 2–6, Nov–Feb Tues–Fri 10–12 and 2–5, weekends 2–5; park open April–Sept daily 9–8, Oct–Mar 9.30–6.30; t 02 40 54 75 85, www.culture.cg44.fr; park admission free) lie on the other bank of the Sèvre Nantaise. Frédéric Lemot, best known for his statue of Henri IV on the Pont-Neuf in Paris, bought La Garenne in 1805. The Maison du Jardinier is built in rustic Italian fashion and houses an exhibition that ranges widely over the Italian influence on French artistic circles in the 18th century. The villa is reached by a garden lined with statues, its front courtyard formed by a semicircle of granite columns. The house contains Lemot's prize-winning sculpture, the Judgement of Solomon, and serves as a venue for interesting temporary exhibitions, while the grounds offer a treasure hunt of follies.

The Loire from Nantes to St-Nazaire

The north bank of the Loire from Nantes to St-Nazaire is heavily industrial. The **south bank** offers a more appealing route, passing via the once-bustling riverside **Paimbœuf**. The scene here is very flat indeed. Small boats congregate in what was once a substantial port. Paimbœuf experienced lively times in slave-trading days. As ships grew in size through the 18th century, this became the stop where much merchandise was transferred onto smaller vessels to be taken upstream to Nantes. In the 19th century, Jules Verne came to Paimbœuf to dream of sailing to the Indies. Now the unhurried harbour streets can induce the most soporific daydreaming.

St-Nazaire

Hard hit by war bombs, hard hit by the recent decline of shipbuilding in Western Europe, traditionally hard hit by guidebooks, St-Nazaire in fact has plenty of character. And it has cleverly turned its attentions to tourism in recent years. The celebrated St-Nazaire shipbuilding yards were developed from the 1860s on, at first in association with the Scottish company of John Scott. Penhoët, in the east of town, was chosen as the site for the shipyards. The ship *L'Impératrice Eugénie* was the first to be built there, during the French Second Empire. St-Nazaire became one of the major European ports to build ocean liners and operate transatlantic services. Many sailed off from here to seek a new life in the Americas. During the First World War, thousands of North American soldiers arrived here before being sent out to the front. The major shipbuilding period came between the two world wars. The most famous of France's ocean liners were built here, the *Paris*, the *Ile-de-France*, the *Champlain* and, most impressive of the lot, the *Normandie*, launched in 1932. But this was also a time of world economic recession. The shipyard workers suffered terribly from the cyclical nature of their work, and in 1933 went on an important hunger march to Nantes.

Most notoriously, when the Nazis occupied France, they turned St-Nazaire into one of their most important submarine bases. St-Nazaire was also the only French Atlantic port large enough to take German battleships. The town became a crucial target for the British air force to wipe out; operation Chariot in 1942 wrought much damage. Several of the major St-Nazaire ocean liners were destroyed in the war. As for the *Normandie*, requisitioned by the US government during the conflict, it caught fire and sank in New York harbour in 1942. Intensive bombing of St-Nazaire continued, but the Germans hung on doggedly to this vital harbour. While most of France was liber- ated in the summer of 1944, St-Nazaire was one of the pockets of territory which the Nazis defended right through to May 1945 and the end of the Second World War in Europe. By then, St-Nazaire lay in ruins, 80 per cent destroyed. The town was rapidly rebuilt along a grid plan in the 1950s, and naval and aeronautical construction took off again. The ocean liner the *France* is the best-known vessel to have been built here since the war, although cruise ships are still made in the yards east of town. The stunning bridge across the mouth of the Loire to Mindin was inaugurated in 1975 and was

Getting There

St-Nazaire has a **train** station. For informa-tion about **buses** around the area, call **t** 02 40 11 53 00.

Tourist Information

St-Nazaire: Office de Tourisme, Boulevard de la Légion d'Honneur, Base sous-marine, Ville-Port B.P. 173, 44613 St-Nazaire Cedex, **t** 08 20 01 40 15, *www.saint-nazaire-tourisme.com*.

Market Days

St-Nazaire: Daily except Monday.

Eating Out

St-Nazaire ✉ 44600

*Le Touraine, 4 Av de la République, **t** 02 40 22 47 56, *hoteltouraine@free.fr* (*cheap*). In the centre, excellent value basic hotel, with garden. *Closed Christmas time–early Jan.*

St-Marc-sur-Mer 44600

***Hôtel de la Plage, 37 Rue du Commandant Charcot, **t** 02 40 91 99 01, *hotel.de.la.plage44 @wanadoo.fr* (*moderate*). For the *Vacances de Monsieur Hulot* experience, hotel where the famous film was shot, plus restaurant (*menus €15–32*). *Closed mid-Jan–early Feb.*

at the time the longest bridge in France. After a tragic gangplank accident just as construction was reaching completion, the massive *Queen Mary 2* left the St-Nazaire shipyards on its maiden voyage in 2003, the largest liner ever to sail the seas.

Escal' Atlantic

Open July–Aug 9.30–7.30, night visits mid-July–Aug Mon–Thurs from 10.15pm; April–June and Sept–Oct 9.30–12.30 and 1.30–6; Feb–Mar and Nov–Dec Wed–Sun 10–12.30 and 2–6; t 0810 888 444, www.escal-atlantic.com; adm.

The glamour of the *paquebot*, or ocean liner, inspired the gargantuan new enter-prise of Escal' Atlantic. Inside a massive hangar at the former German submarine base, this 'floating city' is quite unlike most sea museums. Dispensing with the tradi-tion of inhabiting a crabby old authentic vessel, here you enter an entirely recreated world of the ocean liner – all 3,500 sq m of it – made with the aid of top architects and theatre set designers. The project was 17 years in the planning, so the appearance of the hugely popular film *Titanic* a few years ago proved a happy coincidence.

Every conceivable part of a liner is supposedly represented, including the hair salon, the emigrants' quarters and the engine room, and everywhere are bits of comple-mentary movie footage (sometimes excerpts from the era's biggies that have only the vaguest connection to the ocean liner) on porthole screens. You get a fascinating idea of the cabins of each era, including the 1860s Jules Verne model, complete with *vomitoire*. The set design is at its most impressive inside the bar and dining room. Your tour should end inside the cinema, where more multimedia japes will have you swaying forcibly in your seats to archive film footage. If you're not feeling involved enough, the journey back to the real world requires the donning of a life jacket and a slightly hair-raising proximity to water, so you've been warned.

On coming out and regaining your senses, it's worth taking a moment to nip up to the roof of the submarine base. Apart from affording a great viewing point of the area, it's grimly fascinating to see how this last Nazi stronghold was designed to be bomb-proof, with its ugly great skin of concrete pimples.

The Ecomusée and the Espadon Submarine

Opening hours and contacts same as Escal' Atlantic;
www.sousmarin-espadon.com.

The town museum and submarine make for quite an engrossing visit, too. Outside, a moving sculptural group, *A l'Abolition de l'Esclavage*, put up in 1991 by the sculptor J-C. Mayo, recalls the slave trade that brought such wealth to the Loire estuary in the 18th century and the importance of the abolition of slavery. The Ecomusée retells the prehistory and history of St-Nazaire, while the guided tour around the submarine *Espadon* is engrossing. The submarine lies in the water in a heavily fortified concrete lock built by the Nazis in 1943. It was donated to the town in 1986, having served the French navy for 25 years. Built in Le Havre in 1957, this became the first French submarine to cross the North Pole under the ice fields, in 1964. Some 60 sailors lived down here for up to 45 days at a time; just a half-hour visit can make you feel claustrophobic. If you're lucky the guided tour will be given by a man who did his military service on board a submarine.

You might consider proceeding to one of the port's 'working' museums. The **Chantiers de l'Atlantique** (*open Wed and weekends and daily in school hols, reservation necessary; t 0810 888 444, www.chantiersatlantique.com; adm*) offers you the chance to explore the construction of the ocean liners. More industrial terrain is explored at **Airbus** (*open July–Aug Mon–Fri, rest of year exc Jan Wed 3.30, reservation necessary; t 0810 888 444, www.visite-airbus.com;adm*), where you can see sections of the Airbus A380, the largest passenger planes in the world, being built.

From the Centre to the Sea

In the **centre of town**, a slick shopping centre has been built to mimic some of the forms of an ocean liner. You could go in search of the **Place du Dolmen**, too, actually boasting a neolithic menhir and lech as well as the table of stone.

To the west of the centre, St-Nazaire has a long **sea front** which turns its back on the docks and looks out to the ocean. It is an interesting stretch of coast. Along Boulevard Président Wilson, some 19th-century villas survived the bombs. Further west you come to a string of beaches which are comfortably wide at low tide. Curious *carrelets*, square fishing nets left suspended in the air while not in action, add a picturesque note, as do the lighthouses. By **St-Marc** you reach a beach famous in world cinema, the setting for Jacques Tati's comedy classic, *Les Vacances de Monsieur Hulot*. The coast around St-Nazaire also featured in a brilliant recent French film. But in Sébastien Lifshitz's *Presque Rien*, the beaches served as backdrop for an amazingly sensitive portrayal of gay adolescent angst and romance, creating a modern-day masterpiece of cinema.

Some of the best beaches in Brittany lie just to the west, around La Baule, covered in the **Cadogan Guide to Brittany**. To the south of the Loire estuary, the flat beaches are more typical of the Vendéen coast. To reach them you have to cross St-Nazaire's splendid **serpent of a bridge**. When it was opened in 1975, it was the longest bridge in France. It provides a spectacular ending to the Loire.

Language

Everywhere in France the same level of politeness is expected: use *monsieur, madame* or *mademoiselle* when speaking to everyone (and never *garçon* in restaurants!), from your first *bonjour* to your last *au revoir*.
See p.55 for menu vocabulary.

General

hello *bonjour*
good evening/good night *bonsoir/bonne nuit*
goodbye *au revoir*
please *s'il vous plaît*
thank you (very much) *merci (beaucoup)*
yes/no *oui/non*
good/bad *bon (bonne)/mauvais*
excuse me *pardon, excusez-moi*
My name is... *Je m'appelle...*
What is your name? *Comment vous appelez-vous?*
How are you? *Comment allez-vous?*
Fine *Ça va bien*
I don't understand *Je ne comprend pas*
I don't know *Je ne sais pas*
Could you speak more slowly? *Pourriez-vous parler plus lentement?*
Can you help me? *Pourriez-vous m'aider?*
How do you say ... in French? *Comment dit-on ... en français?*
Help! *Au secours!*
WC *les toilettes*
men/ladies *hommes/dames* or *femmes*
doctor/hospital *le médecin/un hôpital*
A&E/emergency room *la salle des urgences*
police station *le commissariat de police*
tourist information office *l'office de tourisme*
No Smoking *Défense de fumer*
Monday *lundi*
Tuesday *mardi*
Wednesday *mercredi*
Thursday *jeudi*
Friday *vendredi*
Saturday *samedi*
Sunday *dimanche*

Shopping and Sightseeing

I would like... *J'aimerais...*
Where is/are...? *Où est/sont...*
How much is it? *C'est combien?*
It's too expensive *C'est trop cher*
entrance/exit *l'entrée/la sortie*
open/closed *ouvert/fermé*
push/pull *poussez/tirez*
bank *une banque*
money *l'argent*
traveller's cheque *un chèque de voyage*
post office *la poste*
stamp *un timbre*
phone card *la télécarte*
postcard *une carte postale*
Do you have change? *Avez-vous de la monnaie?*
shop *un magasin*
covered food market *les halles*
tobacconist *un tabac*
pharmacy *la pharmacie*
aspirin *l'aspirine*
condoms *les préservatifs*
insect repellent *crème anti-insecte*
sun cream *la crème solaire*
tampons *les tampons hygiéniques*
beach *la plage*
church *l'église*
museum *le musée*

Accommodation

Do you have a room? *Avez-vous une chambre?*
Can I look at the room? *Puis-je voir la chambre?*
How much is the room per day/week? *La chambre coûte combien par jour/semaine?*
single room *une chambre pour une personne*
twin room *une chambre à deux lits*
double room *une chambre pour deux personnes*
...with shower/bath *...avec douche/salle de bains*
...for one night/week *... pour une nuit/semaine*
bed/child's bed (cot) *un lit/un lit d'enfant*
blanket/pillow *une couverture/un oreiller*
soap/towel *du savon/une serviette*

Directions

Where is...? *Où se trouve...?*
left/right *à gauche/à droite*
straight on *tout droit*
here/there *ici/là*
close/far *proche* or *près/loin*
forwards/backwards *en avant/en arrière*
up/down *en haut/en bas*
street/square *la rue/la place*

Transport

I want to go to... *Je voudrais aller à...*
Do you stop at...? *Passez-vous par...?*
When is the next...? *Quel est le prochain...?*
What time does it leave (arrive)? *A quelle heure part-il (arrive-t-il)?*
From where does it leave? *D'où part-il?*
A (single/return) ticket to... *un (aller simple/ aller et retour) pour...*
airport/aeroplane *l'aéroport/l'avion*
flight *le vol*
customs *la douane*
train/railway station *le train/la gare*
ticket office *le guichet*
ticket *le billet*
sleeping berth *la couchette*
seat *la place*
timetable *l'horaire*
platform *le quai*
date-stamp machine *le composteur*
left-luggage locker *la consigne automatique*
bus/bus stop *l'autobus/l'arrêt d'autobus*
coach/coach station *l'autocar/la gare routière*
bicycle *la bicyclette/le vélo*
mountain bike *le vélo tout terrain (VTT)*
on foot *à pied*
underground system or subway *le métro*
delayed/on time *en retard/à l'heure*
car *la voiture*
petrol (unleaded) *l'essence (sans plomb)*
diesel *gazole/gasoil*
driving licence *un permis de conduire*
give way or yield *céder le passage*
road/roadworks *la route/les travaux*
entrance/exit *l'entrée/la sortie*
hire *louer*
motorbike/moped *la moto/le vélomoteur*
no parking *stationnement interdit*
breakdown *la panne*
This doesn't work *Ça ne marche pas*

Numbers

quarter *un quart*
half *une moitié* or *un demi*
1 *un*
2 *deux*
3 *trois*
4 *quatre*
5 *cinq*
6 *six*
7 *sept*
8 *huit*
9 *neuf*
10 *dix*
11 *onze*
12 *douze*
13 *treize*
14 *quatorze*
15 *quinze*
16 *seize*
17 *dix-sept*
18 *dix-huit*
19 *dix-neuf*
20 *vingt*
21 *vingt et un*
22 *vingt-deux*
30 *trente*
40 *quarante*
50 *cinquante*
60 *soixante*
70 *soixante-dix*
80 *quatre-vingts*
90 *quatre-vingt-dix*
100 *cent*
200 *deux cents*
1000 *mille*

Time

What time is it? *Quelle heure est-il?*
It's 2 o'clock *Il est deux heures*
2.15 *deux heures et quart*
2.30 *deux heures et demie*
2.45 *trois heures moins le quart*
it is early/late *il est tôt/tard*
fortnight/month *une quinzaine/un mois*
day/week *un jour* or *une journée/une semaine*
morning/afternoon *le matin/l'après-midi*
evening/night *le soir/la nuit*
today/soon *aujourd'hui/bientôt*
yesterday/day before yesterday *hier/avant-hier*
tomorrow/day after *demain/après-demain*

Index

Numbers in **bold** indicate main references. Numbers in *italic* indicate maps.

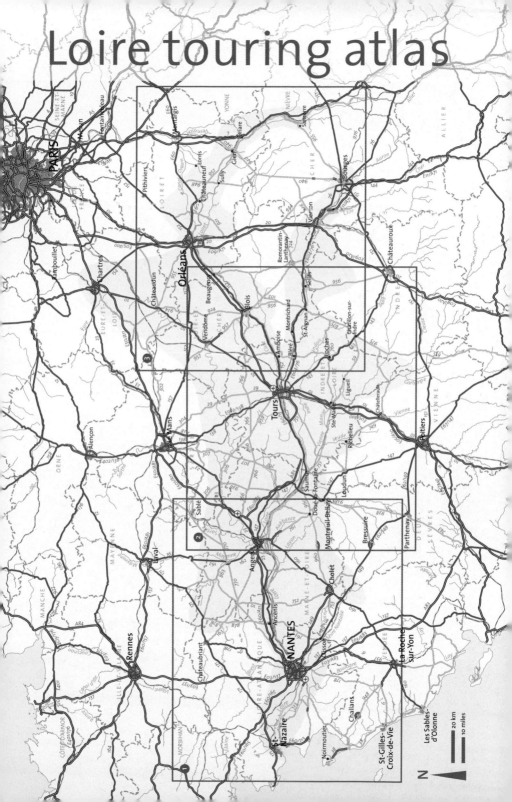

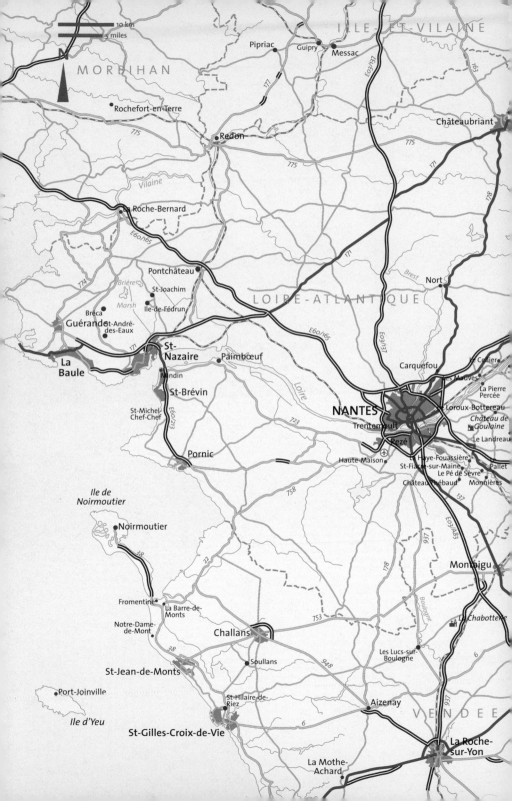

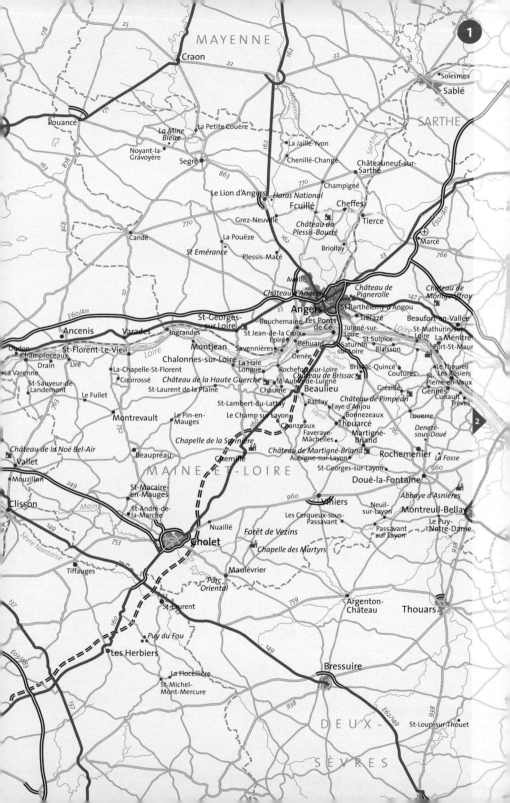

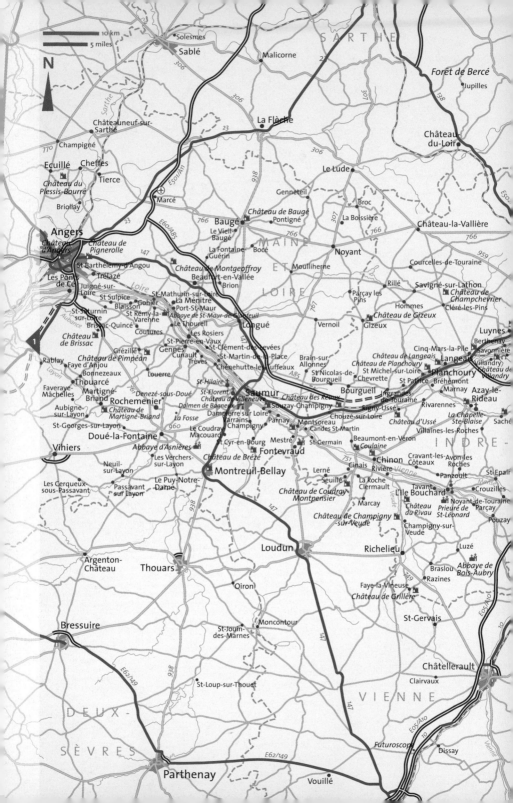

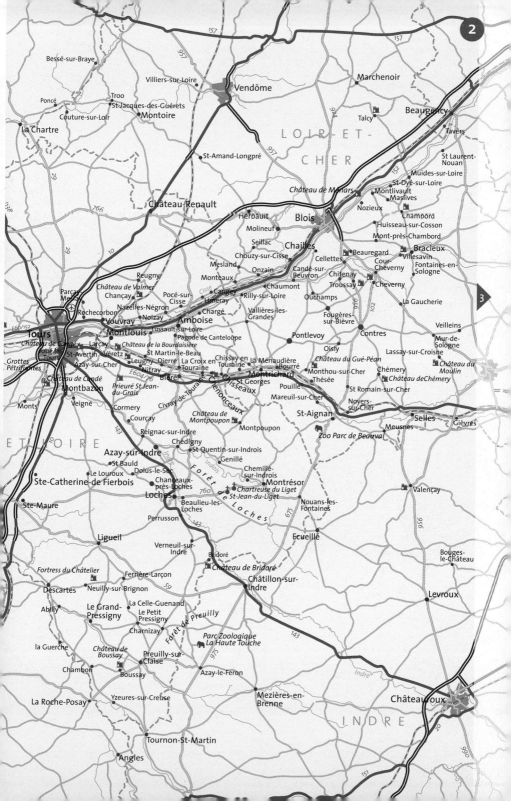

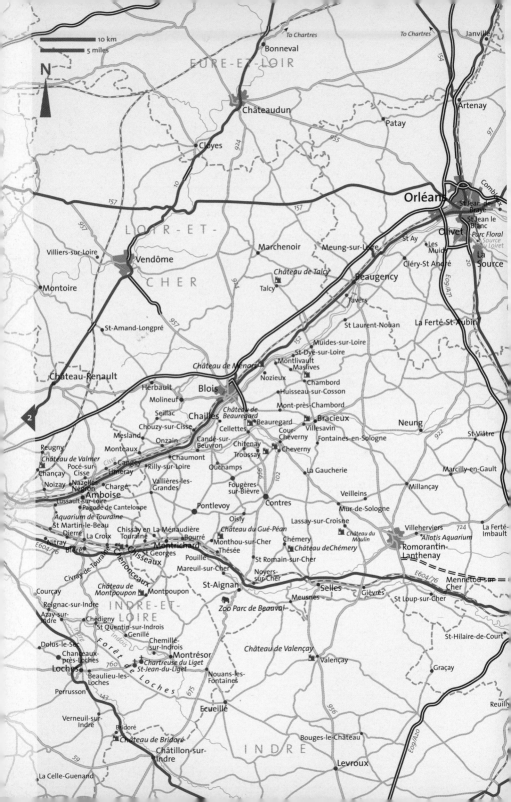

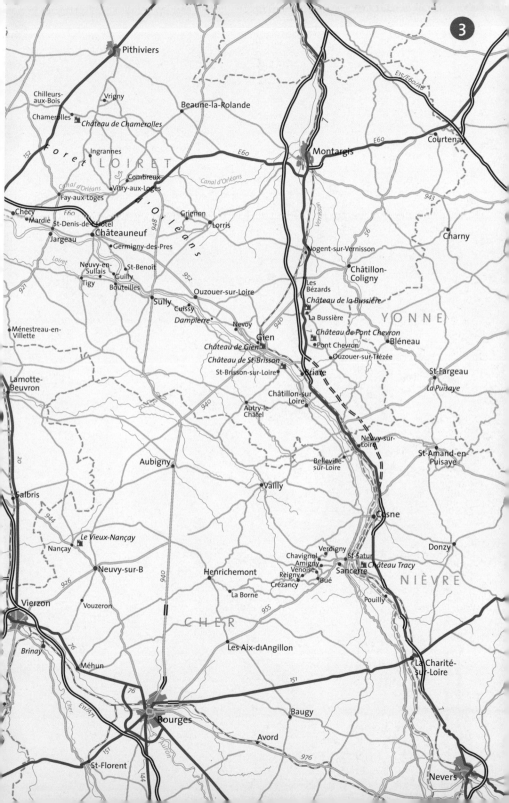

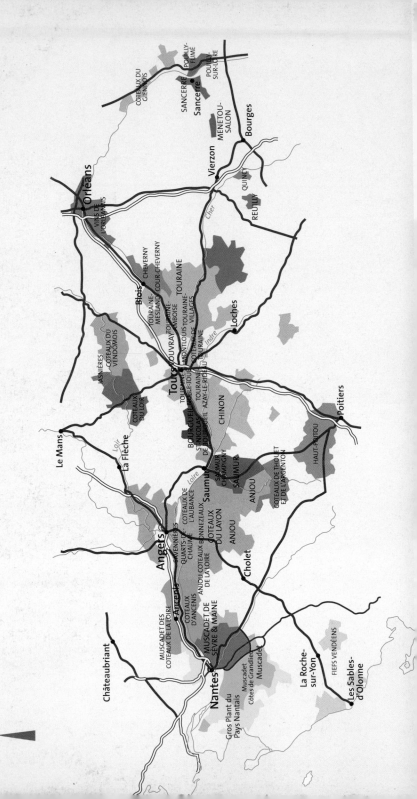

Loire Wines

50 kms
30 miles

N

Châteaubriant

Le Mans

La Flèche

Angers

Ancenis

Nantes

Cholet

La Roche-sur-Yon

Les Sables-d'Olonne

Orléans

Blois

Tours

Loches

Vierzon

Bourges

Poitiers

Sancerre

POUILLY-FUMÉ

POUILLY-SUR-LOIRE

COTEAUX DU GIENNOIS

MENETOU-SALON

QUINCY

REUILLY

VINS DE L'ORLÉANAIS

CHEVERNY

COUR-CHEVERNY

TOURAINE-MESLAND

TOURAINE-AMBOISE

TOURAINE

TOURAINE VILLAGES

VOUVRAY

MONTLOUIS

COTEAUX DU LOIR

JASNIÈRES

COTEAUX DU VENDÔMOIS

TOURAINE NOBLE-JOUÉ

TOURAINE AZAY-LE-RIDEAU

COTEAUX DU LOIR TOURAINE

BOURGUEIL

ST-NICOLAS DE BOURGUEIL

CHINON

SAUMUR

SAUMUR-CHAMPIGNY

SAUMUR

ANJOU

COTEAUX DE THOUET ET DE L'ARGENTON

HAUT-POITOU

COTEAUX DE SAUMUR

COTEAUX DE L'AUBANCE

SAVENNIÈRES

QUARTS-DE-CHAUME

COTEAUX BONNEZEAUX

COTEAUX DU LAYON

ANJOU COTEAUX DE LA LOIRE

ANJOU

COTEAUX D'ANCENIS

MUSCADET DES COTEAUX DE LA LOIRE

MUSCADET DE SÈVRE & MAINE

Muscadet Côtes de Grandlieu

Muscadet

Gros Plant du Pays Nantais

FIEFS VENDÉENS

Cher

Indre

Loir

Loire